MO
CH

Leeds Library and Information Service
24 hour renewals
http://www.leeds.gov.uk/librarycatalogue
or phone 0845 1207271
Overdue charges may apply

Stealth at Thorpe Park

Bob Sehl   erg

LD 5066672 X

1.

2.

3.

4.

5.

1. Highlands cattle at Hardy's Animal Farm
2. Knowsley Safari Park
3. A California sea lion at Blackpool Zoo
4. Jaguar at Chester Zoo
5. Hardy's Animal Farm
6. Knowsley Safari Park
7. Keep your luggage compartment locked as you drive through Knowsley.

1.

2.

Chessington World of Adventures
1. Vampire
2. Monkey Swinger
3. Dragon Falls
4. Hocus Pocus Hall
5. Rameses Revenge

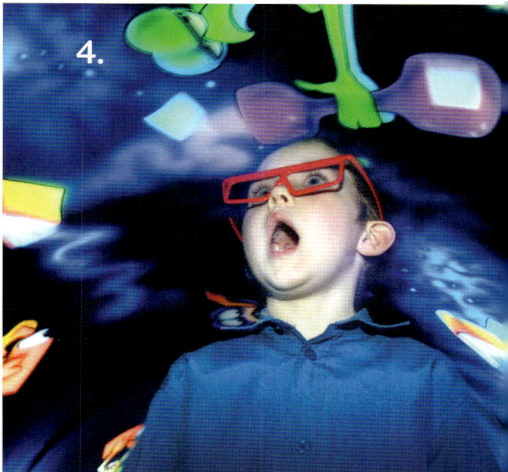

1.

2.

3.

1 & 2. Dinosaur Adventure Park
3. Neanderthal Walk at Dinosaur Adventure Park
4. Alton Towers
5. Congo River Rapids at Alton Towers
6. The Flume at Alton Towers

1.

2.

1. Miniland at LEGOLAND
2. Sonic Spinball at Alton Towers
3. Ultimate at Lightwater Valley
4. Pirate Falls Dynamite Drench at LEGOLAND
5. Wave Surfer at LEGOLAND
6. Vikings' River Splash at LEGOLAND

1.

3.

2.

4.

1 & 2. HMS *Victory* at Portsmouth Historic Dockyard
3. Stealth at Thorpe Park
4. Big Pit: National Coal Museum
5. Colossus at Thorpe Park
6. Tidal Wave at Thorpe Park
7. The Great Hall at Warwick Castle

Drayton Manor
1. Sir Topham Hatt and Thomas
2. G-Force
3. Troublesome Trucks Coaster in Thomas Land

4. Green sawfish at The Deep
5. The Tank Museum
6. The 1938 *Duchess of Hamilton* at the National Railway Museum
7. Morgan Motor Company

1.

4.

1 & 2. Fire jousting and fire breathing at Warwick Castle
3. Warwick Castle
4. Eden Project

Supermarine Spitfire at Imperial War Museum Duxford

Blackpool Beach

THE *unofficial* GUIDE®
TO Britain's Best Days Out

1ST EDITION

ALSO AVAILABLE FROM JOHN WILEY & SONS, INC., AND JOHN WILEY & SONS LTD:

Beyond Disney: The Unofficial Guide to Universal Orlando, SeaWorld, and the Best of Central Florida

Mini-Mickey: The Pocket-Sized Unofficial Guide to Walt Disney World

The Unofficial Guide Color Companion to Walt Disney World

The Unofficial Guide to California with Kids

The Unofficial Guide to Cruises

The Unofficial Guide to Disneyland

The Unofficial Guide to Disneyland Paris

The Unofficial Guide to Dubai

The Unofficial Guide to Hawaii

The Unofficial Guide to Las Vegas

The Unofficial Guide to Maui

The Unofficial Guide to Mexico's Best Beach Resorts

The Unofficial Guide to New York City

The Unofficial Guide to San Francisco

The Unofficial Guide to Walt Disney World

The Unofficial Guide to Walt Disney World for Grown-Ups

The Unofficial Guide to Walt Disney World with Kids

The Unofficial Guide to Washington, D.C.

THE *unofficial* GUIDE®
TO Britain's Best Days Out
Theme Parks & Attractions

1ST EDITION

BOB SEHLINGER,
LEN TESTA *and* LARRY BLEIBERG

Copyright © 2011 John Wiley & Sons Ltd
The Atrium, Southern Gate
Chichester, West Sussex PO19 8SQ, England
Telephone: +44 1243 779 777
Email (for orders and customer-service enquiries): cs-books@wiley.co.uk
Visit our website: wiley.com

All Rights Reserved. No part of this publication may be reproduced, stored in a retrieval system, or transmitted in any form or by any means – electronic, mechanical, photocopying, recording, scanning, or otherwise – except under the terms of the Copyright, Design and Patents Act of 1988 or under the terms of a licence issued by the Copyright Licensing Agency Ltd, 90 Tottenham Court Road, London W1T 4LP, UK, without the permission in writing of the Publisher. Requests to the Publisher should be directed to the Permissions Department, John Wiley & Sons Ltd, The Atrium, Southern Gate, Chichester, West Sussex PO19 8SQ, England; emailed to permreq@wiley.co.uk; or faxed to +44 1243 770620.

Designations used by companies to distinguish their products are often claimed as trademarks. All brand names and product names used in this book are trade names, service names, service marks, trademarks, or registered trademarks of their respective owners. The Publisher is not associated with any product or vendor mentioned in this book.

This publication is designed to provide accurate and authoritative information in regard to the subject matter covered. It is sold on the understanding that the Publisher is not engaged in rendering professional services. If advice or other expert assistance is required, the services of a competent professional should be sought.

UK Publisher: Sally Smith
Executive Project Editor: Daniel Mersey
Commissioning Editor: Mark Henshall
Project Editor (UK): Hannah Clement
Content Editor: Erica Peters
Editorial and Production Manager (US): Molly B. Merkle
Project Editor (US): Ritchey Halphen
Copy-editor: Lynn Edwards
Typesetter–Compositor: Annie Long
Cartographers: Steve Jones, Scott McGrew
Photo Researcher: Amber Kaye Henderson
Colour Insert Designer: Travis Bryant
Cover Designer: Paul Dinovo
Interior Designer: Vertigo Design
Indexer: Frances Lennie/Indexing Research
Pre-press Operations: Wiley Composition Services, Indianapolis, Indiana, USA
Printing and Binding: TJ International Ltd, Padstow, Cornwall, UK

John Wiley & Sons Ltd also publishes its books in a variety of electronic formats. Some content that appears in print may not be available electronically.

British Library Cataloguing in Publication Data
A catalogue record for this book is available from the British Library.

ISBN 978-0-470-68313-2

5 4 3 2 1

Photography credits: *Cover:* © Shutterstock. *Colour insert – Page 1:* Thorpe Park. *Page 2 (from top):* Blackpool Zoo, Knowsley Safari Park, Hardy's Animal Farm and Neil Birchall. *Page 3:* Hardy's Animal Farm (top left) and Knowsley Safari Park. *Pages 4 and 5:* Chessington World of Adventures. *Page 6:* © Martin Pearce (top and bottom right) and Spencer Wright (bottom left). *Page 7:* Alton Towers (center) and © Stefan Zwanzger/TheThemeParkGuy.com. *Page 8:* © Stefan Zwanzger/TheThemeParkGuy.com. *Page 9:* Lightwater Valley (top left), © Stefan Zwanzger/TheThemeParkGuy.com (center right) and LEGOLAND. LEGO, the LEGO logo and LEGOLAND are trademarks of the LEGO Group © 2010 The LEGO Group. *Page 10:* Portsmouth Historic Dockyard (top left and bottom left), Thorpe Park and Amgueddfa Cymru National Museum Wales. *Page 11:* Thorpe Park (top row) and Warwick Castle. *Page 12:* Drayton Manor. *Page 13 (clockwise from top):* The Deep, The Tank Museum, The National Railway Museum and Morgan Motor Company. *Page 14 (from top):* Warwick Castle and Ben Foster/Eden Project. *Page 15:* Warwick Castle (top left and top right). *Page 16 (from top):* Imperial War Museum Duxford and VisitBlackpool.com. *Interior – Page 20:* Lightwater Valley. *Page 21:* Alton Towers. *Page 22:* LEGOLAND. LEGO, the LEGO logo and LEGOLAND are trademarks of the LEGO Group © 2010 The LEGO Group. *Page 25:* Thorpe Park. *Page 26:* Stefan Zwanzger/TheThemeParkGuy.com. *Page 27:* Pleasure Beach Blackpool. *Page 28:* Chessington World of Adventures. *Page 32:* Stefan Zwanzger/TheThemeParkGuy.com. *Page 33:* Lightwater Valley.

CONTENTS

List of Maps x
About the Authors xi
Acknowledgements xii

Introduction 1
Why 'Unofficial'? 1
Best Days Out 1
How This Guide Was Researched and Written 2
What's in a Name? 2
The Sum of All Fears 3
The British Aristocracy and Tourist Attractions 3
What Makes British Theme Parks Special 4
Deciding Which Attractions and Theme Parks to Include 5
    Theme Parks (Leisure Parks) 6
    Zoological Attractions 8
    Aquariums and Marine-Life Attractions 10
    Museums 12
    Industry 13
    Farm Experiences 13
Letters and Comments from Readers 15

PART ONE The World of Theme-Park Rides 17
Wheels within Wheels: The Evolution of Non-Coaster Thrill Rides 17
    Other Non-Coaster Thrill Rides 21
Roller Coasters 24
    Types of Roller Coasters 25
    Coaster Problems: Whiplash and Nausea 29
    Losing Stuff 29
    How British Coasters Stack Up 30
Understanding Theme Park Rides 31
    Cutting Your Queuing Time by Understanding the Rides 32

CONTENTS

Shows 35
    Cutting Your Queuing Time by Understanding the Shows 36

PART TWO Organising Your Holiday before Leaving Home 37

Gathering Information 37
    Our Favourite Websites 38
Timing Your Holiday or Outing 39
Allocating Energy 41
    Building Rest and Relaxation in to Your Holiday 41
Destination versus Local Attractions and Parks 42
Admission Types 42
    Admissions: Where the Deals Are 43
Getting There 45
Practical Stuff 47
Accommodation 49
    National Quality Assessment Scheme 50
    Researching and Booking on the Web 52
Making the Most of Your Time 53
    The Cardinal Rules for Successful Touring 53
    Touring Plans: What They Are and How They Work 55

PART THREE British Theme Parks and Attractions with Kids 63

The Ecstasy and the Agony 63
    It's about Having Fun 64
About the *Unofficial Guide* Touring Plans 71
Stuff to Think About 71
Pushchairs 72
Lost Children 72
    How Kids Get Lost 73
Kids and Scary Stuff 74
    The Fright Factor 75
    A Bit of Preparation 76
    A Word about Height Requirements 76
Queue Strategies for Parents with Young Children 76

PART FOUR Greater London 79

Theme Parks and Attractions 82
    Chessington World of Adventures 82
    The London Dungeon 104
    Sea Life London Aquarium 107
    ZSL London Zoo 109

PART FIVE South East England 113

Theme Parks and Attractions 113
    Blue Reef Aquarium–Hastings 113
    Howletts Wild Animal Park 116
    Port Lympne Wild Animal Park 120

Sea Life Brighton 123
Thorpe Park 124
Farm Experiences 144

PART SIX **The South of England 147**

Theme Parks and Attractions 147

Blue Reef Aquarium–Southsea/Portsmouth 147
Cotswold Wildlife Park & Gardens 150
Legoland Windsor 152
Paultons Park 180
Portsmouth Historic Dockyard 183

Farm Experiences 187

PART SEVEN **South West England 189**

Theme Parks and Attractions 192

Blue Reef Aquarium–Bristol 192
Blue Reef Aquarium–Newquay 193
Brunel's SS *Great Britain* 194
Cornwall's Crealy Great Adventure Park 196
Devon's Crealy Great Adventure Park 198
Eden Project 200
Longleat House and Safari Park 204
National Marine Aquarium 207
Oceanarium 209
Paignton Zoo Environmental Park 210
Sea Life Weymouth 213
The Tank Museum 213
Weston-Super-Mare SeaQuarium 216

Farm Experiences 217

PART EIGHT **The East of England 219**

Theme Parks and Attractions 219

Adventure Island Sunken Gardens 219
Africa Alive 224
Banham Zoo 226
Dinosaur Adventure 229
Fantasy Island 231
Gulliver's Dinosaur and Farm Park 235
Gulliver's Land 236
Imperial War Museum Duxford 239
Pleasure Island Theme Park 242
Pleasurewood Hills 245
Sea Life Great Yarmouth 248
Thrigby Hall Wildlife Gardens 249
Woburn Safari Park 252
ZSL Whipsnade Zoo 255

Farm Experiences 258

CONTENTS

PART NINE East and West Midlands 261

Theme Parks and Attractions 261
- Alton Towers 261
- Bourton-on-the-Water 299
- Drayton Manor 303
- Gulliver's Kingdom 307
- Morgan Motor Company Factory Tour 310
- National Sea Life Centre Birmingham 312
- National Space Centre 313
- Twycross Zoo 317
- Warwick Castle 320
- West Midland Safari & Leisure Park 323
- Wicksteed Park 328

Farm Experiences 331

PART TEN Yorkshire 333

Theme Parks and Attractions 333
- The Deep 333
- Flamingo Land 338
- Jorvik Viking Centre 342
- Lightwater Valley 344
- National Coal Mining Museum 348
- National Railway Museum 350
- Sea Life Scarborough 353
- The York Dungeon 354

Farm Experiences 356

PART ELEVEN North West England 357

Theme Parks and Attractions 357
- The Beatles Story 357
- Blackpool Zoo 362
- Blue Planet Aquarium 365
- British Lawnmower Museum 367
- Camelot Theme Park 369
- Chester Zoo 371
- Gulliver's World 377
- Knowsley Safari Park 380
- Pleasure Beach Blackpool 384
- Sea Life Blackpool 408

Farm Experiences 408

PART TWELVE North East England 411

Attraction 411
- Blue Reef Aquarium–Tynemouth 411

Farm Experiences 413

CONTENTS ix

PART THIRTEEN Cumbria and the Lake District 415

Attractions 417
>Lakes Aquarium 417
>South Lakes Wild Animal Park 418

Farm Experiences 421

PART FOURTEEN Scotland 423

Theme Parks and Attractions 423
>Blair Drummond Safari and Adventure Park 423
>Deep Sea World 428
>The Edinburgh Dungeon 430
>M&D's, Scotland's Theme Park 432
>Sea Life Loch Lomond 434
>St Andrews Aquarium 436

Farm Experiences 437

PART FIFTEEN Wales 439

Theme Parks and Attractions 439
>Big Pit: National Coal Museum 439
>Oakwood Theme Park 444
>Rhyl SeaQuarium 447
>Twr-y-Felin Outdoor Centre 448
>Welsh Mountain Zoo 450

Farm Experiences 453

PART SIXTEEN In the Footsteps of Harry Potter 455

Attractions 455
>Alnwick Castle 455
>Durham Cathedral 457
>Gloucester Cathedral 459
>Lacock Alley 460
>University of Oxford 461
>West Coast Railway Jacobite Steam Train 462
>ZSL London Zoo 464

Appendixes 465

Index 465
***Unofficial Guide* Reader Survey 475**

LIST *of* MAPS

England Regions 16
Greater London 80–81
Chessington World of Adventures 84–85
South East England 114–115
Thorpe Park 126–127
The South of England 148–149
Legoland Windsor 154–155
South West England 190–191
The East of England 220–221
East and West Midlands 262–263
Alton Towers 266–267
Yorkshire 334–335
North West England 358–359
Pleasure Beach Blackpool 386–387
North East England 412
Cumbria and the Lake District 416
Scotland 424–425
North Wales 440
South Wales 441

ABOUT the AUTHORS

BOB SEHLINGER is executive publisher of the *Unofficial Guides* series. A winner of the Lowell Thomas Gold Award for travel journalism, he is the author of *The Unofficial Guide to Walt Disney World*, *The Unofficial Guide to Disneyland* and *The Unofficial Guide to Las Vegas*, each the number-one best-selling guidebook in the world on its respective subject, according to Amazon.

LEN TESTA has co-authored several books on theme parks, including *The Unofficial Guide to Walt Disney World* and *The Unofficial Guide to Disneyland*, over the past decade. He also wrote the computer software that produces most of the *Unofficial Guide* touring plans. Using nothing but public transportation for his research trips, Len ate far too much food in Victoria Station.

LARRY BLEIBERG served on a Pulitzer Prize–winning team and was honoured for producing the best newspaper travel section in North America for the *Dallas* (Texas) *Morning News*. He is a former senior editor at *Coastal Living* magazine, runs the website **civilrightstravel.com** and believes life's true meaning just may lie in the dizzying first drop of a wooden roller coaster.

ACKNOWLEDGEMENTS

MANY THANKS TO Jessica Smith, Mark Davis and Geoff Green for their support and hospitality, and to Kate, Bob's navigator, without whom he would still be trying to find Thorpe Park. Thanks also to Martin Sayers who assisted with park-visitation research, and to Darcie Vance, our liaison with the parks.

One of the great things about travel writing is the chance to meet readers when you're in their town. Thanks to Phillip Burton for the fish-and-chips. Thanks also to Nick and Natalie Sim of **themepark tourist.com** for graciously leading us around Thorpe Park. Liam Collerton met us for two days in Legoland Windsor, where it was not even a little weird to see grown men happily running between children's theme-park rides. (That's our story, anyway.) Mike Moody walked us through Chessington touring strategies and volunteered to try more theme-park food than we had the right to ask. Thanks to Alan Belmore for proofreading assistance and tips, and to Stephen Brewer for his help in composing the introductions to our regional chapters. Finally, a shout-out to Craig Duncan for being the barrister we were to call if put in jail. Maybe next time.

Our production and editorial crew is second to none and includes project editor Ritchey Halphen, copy-editor Lynn Edwards, photography researcher Amber Kaye Henderson, editorial and production manager Molly Merkle, cartographers Steve Jones and Scott McGrew, typesetter Annie Long, designer Travis Bryant and indexer Frances Lennie.

– *Bob Sehlinger, Len Testa and Larry Bleiberg*

INTRODUCTION

WHY 'UNOFFICIAL'?

THE AUTHORS AND RESEARCHERS OF THIS GUIDE specifically and categorically declare that they are and always have been totally independent. The material in this guide originated with the authors and has not been reviewed, edited or in any way approved by the enterprises whose travel products are discussed. The purpose of this guide is to provide you with the information necessary to sample the tourist attractions and theme parks of the United Kingdom with the greatest efficiency and economy, and with the least hassle and stress. In this guide we represent and serve you, the reader. If a restaurant serves bad food or a gift item is overpriced or a certain ride isn't worth the wait, we tell you so, and in the process we hope to make your visit more fun, efficient and affordable.

BEST DAYS OUT

AN OUTING CAN ASSUME MANY FORMS, from an afternoon picnic at a nearby park to a weekend splurge at Alton Towers. In this guide, with a couple of exceptions, we zero in on Britain's gated (that is, paid-admission) tourist attractions. You'll find zoos, theme parks, and aquariums, but not public parks, gardens, mellow walks, or special events like art shows or outdoor concerts. For the most part we exclude tourist haunts in London, focusing instead on the wealth of deserving parks and attractions peppered throughout the Kingdom.

HOW *This* GUIDE WAS RESEARCHED *and* WRITTEN

THIS GUIDEBOOK WAS RESEARCHED over a 2½-year period by authors Bob Sehlinger, Len Testa and Larry Bleiberg. With the exception of some preliminary work in the organisational stage, we visited attractions unannounced and paid for all of our own admissions, meals and hotels. None of the attractions in the guide were aware of our presence, and none influenced the contents of this guide.

Sometimes our independent methodology created problems. When we tried to purchase admission at Gulliver's Land at Milton Keynes, for instance, we were denied entry because we didn't have children in our party. In this situation – because we had travelled 4,000 mi from America, driven 2 hours that morning, and were on a very tight schedule – we presented our press credentials, but to no avail. We were told we could make an appointment to come back another day and be shown around by a minder, but that's exactly what we sought to avoid. Eventually we found a work-around and managed to see the park without management's knowledge. All three Gulliver's parks are described in this guide. What we can tell you now, however, is that if you go to a Gulliver's park, there are people working overtime to protect your children from independent journalists.

WHAT'S *in a* NAME?

FIRST OFF, WHEN WE SAY that this is a guide to days out and British theme parks, we use *British* inclusively, meaning England, Scotland and Wales.

The English, Scots and Welsh have more names for theme parks than any other population on earth. Traditionally such places have been called leisure parks, pleasure parks, pleasure piers, amusement parks and adventure parks, just to name the most prevalent appellations. Only within the last few decades has *theme park* been adopted, and, as we shall see, the term is often very loosely applied. In this guide we use *theme park*, *leisure park* and just plain *park* interchangeably, though many of the parks covered herein use one of the variations listed previously.

Along similar lines, the term *attraction* was used historically to describe an enterprise that offered something of interest to tourists, as in *tourist attraction*. According to this usage, the term was all-inclusive, referring to the collection of entertainment products available therein, be they rides, shows, displays, exhibits, animals or whatever. Then Disney came along and muddied the pond. For some probably deeply-pathological reason, Disney had an aversion to the easily-understood *ride* and *show,* and instead labelled individual elements of its parks – that is, rides and shows – as *attractions*. In the UK, people still know a ride or a show when they see one, though many British parks have adopted the Disney terminology. Thus Legoland might promote 'a new attraction', which usually means a new ride. In this guide we are comfortable with either usage, though more frequently than not we gravitate to *attraction* as an entire tourism enterprise that may include rides and shows amongst other elements.

The SUM *of* ALL FEARS

EVERY WRITER WHO EXPRESSES AN OPINION is accustomed to readers who strongly agree or disagree: it comes with the territory. Extremely troubling, however, is the possibility that our efforts to be objective might make some readers apprehensive or frighten others away from the parks and attractions we cover.

For the record, if you enjoy theme parks (or the other types of attractions reviewed), the UK has some of the best. For most parks, if you arrive without knowing a thing about the place and make every possible mistake, chances are about 90% that you'll have a wonderful time anyway. In the end, guidebooks don't make or break great destinations. Rather, they're simply tools to help you enhance your experience and get the most for your money.

As it happens, there are numerous ways to cut costs, minimise hassle and make the most of your time. That's what this guide is about: alerting you to possible opportunities and problems. Unfortunately, some *Unofficial Guide* readers add up the warnings and critical advice and conclude that this or that park is too intimidating, too expensive or too much work. They lose track of the park or attraction as a whole and focus instead on what might go wrong.

Our philosophy is that knowledge is power – and time and money, too. You're free to follow our advice or not at your discretion. But you can't exercise that discretion if we fail to present the issues.

With or without a guidebook, you'll have a great time. If you'll let us, we'll help you smooth the potential bumps. We're certain we can help you turn a great day into an absolutely-superb one. Either way, once there, you'll get the feel of the place and quickly reach a comfort level that will allay your apprehensions and allow you to have a great experience.

The BRITISH ARISTOCRACY *and* TOURIST ATTRACTIONS

WHEN DO ARISTOCRATS BECOME ENTREPRENEURS? When they can't afford the upkeep and taxes on their ancient castles and manors.

Many of Britain's most renowned theme parks, leisure parks, zoos and safari parks were once the ancestral homes of the British aristocracy. When the burden of maintaining these properties became prohibitive, many of the more-historically-significant estates found their way into the National Trust or into the hands of such charities as Historic Royal Palaces, which operates the Tower of London as a heritage site for the government.

Other lords and ladies, however, sold to or partnered with entertainment enterprises or saw their properties pass through developers to evolve into public leisure attractions. Alton Towers Theme Park, the UK's largest leisure park, occupies the grounds held by the Earls of Shrewsbury from 1412 until the 1920s. More recently, according to docents at Warwick Castle, the eighth Earl of Warwick, Fourth Creation, was reduced to using only the bedroom and kitchen of his rambling pile before his son David sold it to Madame Tussauds of wax-museum fame in 1978.

Blair Drummond House, which sits in the centre of the Blair Drummond Safari Park in Scotland, was once home to eighteenth-century Scottish philosopher Henry Home, Lord Kames. Thrigby Hall, built near Great Yarmouth in 1736 by Joshua Smith, Esquire, was turned into Thrigby Hall Wildlife Gardens in 1979 by Ken Sims, who had been a rubber-planter and poisonous-snake farmer in Malaya.

Several aristocrats, however, found the tourist industry a tough nut to crack. For example, the baronet Sir Charles Wolseley's foray into tourism ended badly. His ancestral home, said to have been given to the Wolseley family as a reward for clearing the area of wolves in the reign of King Edgar (who ruled Mercia, Wessex and Northumbria between AD 959 and 975), was sold by the Royal Bank of Scotland in 2008 after a failed attempt by Sir Charles to turn the estate into a tourist attraction.

WHAT MAKES BRITISH THEME PARKS SPECIAL

WHILE THE HISTORY OF MANY BRITISH THEME PARKS is intriguing, the real legacy of the receding gentry is the extraordinary gardens and grounds which surround the halls, manor houses and castles, and which now serve as backdrops to the roller coasters, carousels and grazing wildlife. These distinguish British theme parks and zoological parks as does no other single characteristic. To go, as we did, from the well-executed but ersatz environment of Disney theme parks to British and Scottish ones, laid out on a grand scale with formal gardens, broad manicured lawns, lakes, forests and even free-flowing streams, was an unimaginable delight. In many parks, the setting alone is worth the price of admission – the loveliness of the grounds and the welcome beauty of the natural world often standing in contrast to, but sometimes in unexpected harmony with, the park's bustle and nonstop activity.

Another characteristic of British theme parks and attractions relates to the rather relaxed way that visitors approach their day at the park.

Experiencing rides is a key component of a day at the theme park, but so are pleasures more commonly associated with local parks, such as picnicking and turning the children loose on playground equipment. Almost all British theme parks and attractions have elaborate picnic areas and playgrounds. Concerning the latter, some are so large and creative that it's hard to drag the kiddiewinks away from them.

In the United States and Europe, ride experiences are computer-programmed. This means roller coasters are dispatched at set intervals and that the flying-elephant ride, for example, is always 90 seconds in duration. In the UK, by way of contrast, ride operators are given a great deal of discretion and flexibility in running their ride. If the carousel queue is short, for instance, the operator may allow the ponies to revolve for 5 minutes. Conversely, if a large number of children are waiting to ride, he might cut the ride time down to 2 minutes or less. Sometimes ride operators will stop the ride for as long as it takes to fill every seat, even if the ride is at a standstill for 10 or 15 minutes. On other occasions the operator might crank up the ride for just five or six riders. Many parks encourage ride operators to interact with visitors, a practice that often compromises the efficient operation of the ride. At L-Riders at **Legoland Windsor,** a 'driving school' for the 3- to 5-year-old set, interaction with the kids before the ride, along with a driver's-licence ceremony after the ride, cuts the number of riders per hour roughly in half. Big fun if you're on the ride – not so much if you're in a queue.

DECIDING *Which* ATTRACTIONS *and* THEME PARKS *to* INCLUDE

THIS ASSIGNMENT WAS AWARDED because of our more than two decades of experience covering Disney theme parks around the world and American theme parks in particular. But Great Britain, of course, is neither Disney nor American. Where the theme-park-and-amusement industry in America is controlled or influenced by a relatively-small number of publicly-traded companies, in Britain it's very entrepreneurial. True, a few large UK entertainment conglomerates exist, such as Merlin Entertainments, but their product is anything but cookie-cutter and conformist. British attractions, then, are predicated upon their owners' particular vision rather than on a standard imposed by industry giants. Great Britain is a happy island of many more or less equal tourist attractions ... and we hope it stays that way.

As we ranged over England, Scotland and Wales, we were astonished by the number and variety of tourist attractions vying for the attention of British as well as international visitors on holiday. In addition to theme parks there were aquariums, various zoological attractions, industrial exhibits and tours, historical castles turned playgrounds, quirky museums, railroad excursions and even farms that invited you to spend a day feeding lambs and watching pigs race.

The features and offerings of Britain's myriad leisure attractions are singular, to say the least. **Wheelgate Adventure Park,** east of Mansfield, for example, offers the enigmatic 'Massive Senior Play Structure'. At **Hardy's Animal Farm** in Lincolnshire, you can 'watch the development of a happy porker through a special glazed viewing area', and at **Warwick Castle** witness the launching of 'fireballs' from a 59-ft-tall (18-m-tall) trebuchet. At the **Abbey Pumping Station** in Leicester, you can see the Gimson steam engines, housed in a glorious Victorian building that pumped the city's sewage from 1891 to 1964. (You wouldn't believe the gift shop at this place.) The **Lakeland Maize Maze** offered a huge and convoluted layout of the Battle of Britain. This is serious stuff, and maps are available in case 'you get stuck'. And though it's not really our thing, you're treated to 'Witches: Burned Alive' at **The York Dungeon** (that would be 'witches on the barbie' for you Aussies). The list goes on.

The ubiquitous brochure rack at each motorway-services area and hotel alerted us to dozens of local and regional offerings that had not up to this time been on our radar. So what to include? We began with an exhaustive Internet search, augmented by numerous discoveries while researching in the UK. Even then the list of possible inclusions was incomplete. We'll state up-front that there's undoubtedly some deserving leisure attraction that we missed, but that's what revised editions are for. If your personal favourite isn't included, tell us about it in an email to **unofficialguides@menasharidge.com.**

THEME PARKS (LEISURE PARKS)

WE KNEW WE WANTED TO INCLUDE theme parks – or leisure parks or adventure parks, as they are frequently called – but what exactly *is* a theme park? In Britain many leisure parks really don't have a theme. Instead, they derive their identity from the site on which they are built. The largest leisure park in the UK, **Alton Towers,** surrounds the ruins of a grand nineteenth-century hunting lodge built in the Gothic tradition. Once again, though the ruin dominates the landscape, it doesn't influence the park's themes. In fact, with a couple of exceptions, Britain's leisure parks are fairly theme-neutral. Even where there is theming, it is generally superficial, serving more to demarcate various sections of the park than to establish a particular setting or ambience.

DECIDING WHICH ATTRACTIONS AND THEME PARKS TO INCLUDE

Moreover, offerings within British theme parks are highly diversified. It's not uncommon to find some mix of rides, shows, zoological exhibits, elaborate children's play areas, gardens and even nature trails in a leisure park. The inland **Thorpe Park,** near London, even offers a beach! Ultimately, we accepted the reality that British leisure parks are too multi-faceted to be neatly pigeonholed, and that theming, though often compelling for specific rides, is largely irrelevant for sections of a park or for the park as a whole.

Included in this guide, then, are the larger leisure parks that draw visitors from all over the UK, along with some smaller regional parks, especially those that offer something unique. Most of the parks profiled are gated, meaning that you pay an admission charge to enter. Amongst the exceptions are parks where you either buy an admission good for all rides and attractions or alternatively buy tickets for individual rides. Not included are seaside amusement piers, leisure parks with a dozen or fewer rides and attractions, swimming parks and most parks offering rides only for younger children. Exclusion does not speak for the relative merit of these places, especially in terms of their importance in their local communities, but rather for their limited offerings compared with larger leisure attractions having regional or national appeal.

Many British theme parks operate in their own little time warp. Though they continually add new rides, the overall feel is mid-twentieth-century or older. This is especially true of parks next to or near the sea, where many of the rides are stunning antiques more notable for their history and beauty than for their amusement value. If you visit a number of parks, as we did, you'll see the evolution of the amusement-park ride unfold before your eyes. Other parks, though modern in concept, seem older because of their resident ruin. Most British parks are tidy affairs and maintain a high degree of cleanliness, but the island nation's weather makes upkeep a challenge. More than a few parks are badly in need of new paint.

We found food at the parks to be average to good, though the Brit habit of mummifying a hot dog in a roll the size of a sofa mystifies us Yanks. (I swear it's in there somewhere!) Another oddity: whereas salt is always available, black pepper is usually not. If you fancy fish-and-chips, you're in clover – chances are that you'll never be more than 30 yards from a chippy. Most parks also feature 'Southern fried chicken', but which particular South – in Britain or across the pond – is often unclear.

As in theme parks around the world, in the UK thrill rides and especially roller coasters are the big draw. Britain has some truly great coasters, ancient and modern, wooden and steel. While they are a varied lot, ranging from a diesel-powered specimen at **Camelot Theme Park** that can hardly make it over a 4-ft (1.2-m) hill to Saw – The Ride, at Thorpe Park, with a 'beyond-vertical drop of 100 degrees', most British-theme-park rides are variations on ones that have been around, sometimes evolving and sometimes not, for decades. We'll discuss the various ride genres later, but suffice it to say that most involve rotating around a central axis, floating along in a flume, riding on a track or being shot to the top of a tower and free-falling (sort of) back to earth.

With the exception of a couple of the largest parks, parking is complimentary. In terms of services, only a few parks offer pushchairs for hire, and fewer yet wheelchairs, though the surface of pedestrian walkways is usually fine for both. Queuing areas and most rides are exposed to the elements. If you'd like to avoid a wet bum, bring along a small towel to wipe down ride seats.

ZOOLOGICAL ATTRACTIONS

OKAY, SO THEME AND LEISURE PARKS ARE IN THE MIX... what else? Our next largest category is zoological attractions: aquariums, zoos, safari parks, wildlife gardens and falconry centres. Like leisure parks, these come in all sizes and shapes. Some offer rides in addition to the critters, others gardens, shows, scheduled feedings and/or educational lectures. 'Encounters' are also popular. Here children can accessorise their outfits with a live python or, as one 10-year-old put it, 'hold a middle-aged penguin'. As for shows, sea-lion performances and falconry exhibitions are most common. Almost all parks boast elaborate children's playgrounds and expansive picnic areas. Hot meals as well as vendor snacks and such are readily available. Most parks provide a handout park map, but others force you to buy a souvenir book (about £2.50–£4.50) to obtain a map. Parks that don't offer a free map will tell you that there are large maps of the park posted conveniently all over the place. *Hogwash.* The layouts of some of these parks are so convoluted that you'll be lost most of the time unless you spring for the souvenir book. If you're on a tight budget and you give the book a pass, pray that you don't need a toilet in a hurry.

*un*official **TIP**
We don't need to tell this to the sea-faring British, but for anyone else: be prepared for rain on any day at any time. Parks near the coast also experience gusty winds. In July at Southport we wore a jumper and a rain jacket.

One common model for zoological attractions is that of the traditional zoo, where visitors view animals in their enclosures, although the enclosures may be very expansive and a good replication of the animals' natural habitat. Some exhibits are so realistic, in fact, that it's possible for the tenants to hide completely from the view of frustrated onlookers. Most of the better zoos feature aviaries or other attractions in which visitors actually walk through the exhibit, with the resident animals or birds essentially roaming free around them. Lemurs, which are very popular and trendy in British zoos, are more often than not displayed this way. In most instances the animals become habituated to the presence of humans and go about their business as if you weren't

DECIDING WHICH ATTRACTIONS AND THEME PARKS TO INCLUDE

there . . . if you're lucky. Lemurs, monkeys and some birds visualise humans as targets or convenient things to sit or climb on.

Speaking of trends, British zoos have fallen in love with the Amazon River. During the past several years, dozens of zoological parks and aquariums have introduced elaborate exhibits showcasing the wildlife of the Amazon basin, including birds, lizards, snakes, fish, monkeys, turtles, spiders, crocodilians and even insects (leaf-cutting ants are all the rage).

Another popular model for zoological attractions is that of the 'safari park', where you drive through the various animals' habitats in your car. The lions are separated from the gazelles, of course, and so on. These parks require extensive acreage for the concept to work. The better parks are huge, with several miles of road winding amongst the species on display. It depends on the park, of course, but we were surprised to be able to drive amongst wolves, rhinos and lions, just to name a few. In one park we had six lions on the right, within 2 feet of the car, while we gingerly tried to navigate around another two sprawled in the road. Soft-top convertibles are usually not allowed, and it's prudent (to say the least) to keep your windows up in carnivore country.

What you really want to avoid are monkeys, baboons in particular. At one park we came to a fork in the safari road. A sign pointing to the left read SAFE WAY; a sign pointing right read TO THE BABOONS or some such. Most cars were turning right, so we thought, 'How bad can it be?' Well, first of all, there weren't a dozen or so baboons, as we had anticipated, but rather what looked like a family reunion of every baboon in Africa. Though some apes were at their leisure, most busied themselves dismantling the cars passing through their realm. Windscreen wipers, side mirrors and radio antennae were especially at risk. Whilst the occasional car was attended by a single baboon, most were serviced by an entire crew, often with so many on the hood that the driver couldn't see. Attempts to shoo them away were met with snarls and bared teeth. Horn-blowing invariably provoked jumping up and down on the bonnet and top. Because adult baboons weigh about 88 lb (40 kg), using your car as a trampoline can result in some serious craters.

As we entered this melee, all we could think about was explaining to Hertz why the hired car no longer had windscreen wipers. This prompted us to keep moving – at about triple the maximum speed allowed. While other cars were being attacked, the baboons were diving for cover when we barrelled past. We don't know how much a baboon costs compared with an Audi hired car, but we were legally liable for the car. As far as we were concerned, the baboons could look after themselves. In any case, we didn't maim any monkeys as far as we know, and we managed to extricate our car with no serious damage. We were still calming ourselves when at the end of the safari road we came upon a large car park full of visitors assessing baboon damage. Missing aerials and mangled windscreen wipers were the order of the day. We drove smugly past.

Some parks allow you to feed certain species (usually hoofed animals); others don't. If feeding is allowed, you won't have to worry about not seeing animals up close – they'll be in the middle of the road poking their heads through your open windows. Among other things, you'll discover that camels really do have bad breath and that giraffes have tongues long enough to wrap around your head. Feeding animals of any ilk creates terminal congestion on the safari roads. At one park, a single family feeding a llama managed to hold up traffic for more than 20 minutes. For this reason, we tend to prefer parks with a 'No Feeding' policy. Parks that allow feeding almost always sell appropriate, healthy munchies for the wildlife. Though it happens all the time, it's considered poor form to treat the beasts to biscuits and crisps.

Most parks segregate their animals according to their place of origin so, for example, all the African animals are in one area, Asian animals in another, and so on. Some parks, however, evidently believe in widening the social circle of their charges. Llamas, for example, must be convivial beasts, because we saw them tossed in with just about every creature. At **Blair Drummond Safari and Adventure Park,** the American buffalo (bison) roams with the camel instead of the antelope (contrary to the cowboy song 'Home on the Range'). At other parks and zoos, it's not beyond the pale for zookeepers to slip the fabled Madagascar hissing cockroach into their Amazon exhibits.

All safari parks operate a base area in addition to the drive-through. These vary but usually consist of additional wildlife exhibits, toilets, a café, a gift shop, a picnic area, a children's playground and sometimes rides or shows. Admission is paid at ticket kiosks on the entrance road. From there you can either take the driving safari or visit the base area. In our experience there's less traffic congestion in the drive-through safari after about 2 or 3 p.m., so we suggest arriving at the base area in the early afternoon and seeing it first. Save the drive-through safari for last. You're welcome to repeat the safari drive, but it's better to linger over it the first time through.

AQUARIUMS AND MARINE-LIFE ATTRACTIONS

IT MAKES SENSE THAT GREAT BRITAIN, an island nation, would have a fascination with the sea and the creatures that call it home. For millennia, inhabitants have drawn their sustenance from the ocean, and now they're drawing their entertainment from it too. Across the UK you can find more than two dozen aquariums and marine-life attractions. We cover the major ones in the book, but first a bit of context – and caution.

Two companies – **Sea Life,** with more than a dozen sites in the British Isles, and **Blue Reef,** with five branded aquariums – as well as two other attractions, **Blue Planet Aquarium** in Ellesmere Port and **Deep Sea World** in Fife, Scotland, dominate the aquarium scene with the most marine exhibits. While a few are stand-outs and each aquarium might trot out some small unique feature, in the main the aquariums are so many peas in a pod. The adage 'see one, you've seen them all' is more apt than we would like. Most can be visited in 30–40 minutes or so on a cursory tour, longer if you take in one or more of the feedings or educational talks. (By all means do catch these special programs: they are the key to getting the most from your visit and making it worthwhile.)

Nearly all aquariums have 'touch pools' where you can 'pet' rays and examine the kind of marine life you'd ordinarily find in a tide-pool. Larger sites have some sort of walk-through glass or acrylic tunnel, providing an engaging 'under the sea' experience. In many aquariums, you'll find a large central tank where sharks and other 'charismatic mega-fauna', as biologists call them, can be seen cruising around on perpetual hunt. At some, you can even sign up to dive in the tank – an expensive but memorable experience.

The better aquariums nod to the local sea life. Sure, clownfish and coral reefs are colourful, exotic and worth a look, but we feel it also makes sense to learn about the creatures that live off-shore here. Both Sea Life and Blue Reef make a good effort in this regard, with tanks or exhibits devoted to fish from the northern climes. Many aquariums are also set on the water, offering striking views and sometimes a chance to spot sea life in the wild. Often you'll find theatres and, at some locations, big screens showing films about the briny deep. Given the competition, the sites have been branching out from basic fish displays to include marine mammals such as seals, sea lions, and otters, along with reptiles, and even insects. While it's not exactly in theme, we say 'Bring it on.'

Touring, though, can be a challenge. While some aquariums provide an obvious route to proceed through the exhibits, others are a free-for-all of tanks, pools and films. This makes it harder to visit and easier to overlook worthwhile exhibits. Our advice: study the site map (if there is one), and make sure you're seeing it all.

Britain's premiere aquarium is **The Deep,** in Hull, East Yorkshire, where you can easily spend the better part of a day. Another excellent representative of the genre is Scotland's **Deep Sea World,** with the longest underwater-viewing tunnel in the UK. The **National Marine Aquarium** in Devon is the country's largest. You'll find detailed descriptions of all three in this guide.

Of all the Blue Reef properties, only one, Bristol, was designed by the company – the rest were acquired through buyouts and acquisitions. And the Bristol property, which opened in 2009, had to be retrofitted to the site of a failed science centre. Still, it's three times the size of other Blue Reef aquariums and includes an IMAX 3D theatre. As for Sea Life, it's the largest aquarium brand in the world, with tanks from Denmark to Dallas. Its UK flagship property is in London, near the London Eye, and is one of the largest aquariums in Europe. It's pricey but always seems to have queues.

In the regional chapters of this guide, because the aquariums are so similar, we limit our coverage of each 'chain' location. You'll find visitor information for the Sea Life– and Blue Reef–branded properties, along with the two owned by the Spanish company Parques Reunidos – **Oceanarium** in Bournemouth and **Lakes Aquarium** in Cumbria – and the two **SeaQuariums,** in Weston-Super-Mare and Rhyl, Wales. We include a basic overview, with address, contact information, hours and price, along with any special attractions or features that set them apart. For independent aquariums and those that stand out from the pack, we offer a more detailed look.

MUSEUMS

HERE WE TRIED TO AVOID the famous museums of London (which are in every guidebook) and instead home in on the quirky and often-overlooked speciality museums scattered throughout the UK. Entries range from large museums, such as the **National Railway Museum,** the **Imperial War Museum Duxford** and the **National Space Centre** to the tiny but well-done **British Lawnmower Museum** in Southport. Also included in this category are marine museums like the **Portsmouth Historic Dockyard,** where you can tour Nelson's *Victory,* and the Bristol Docks, where the **SS *Great Britain*** is berthed.

Let's be clear: museums require both energy and effort. There's lots of walking, in some cases as much as at theme parks, but what you really need to prepare for is the investment of time and effort in the learning experience. While it's true that there's something of value to be gleaned even from a speedy walk-through, it's necessary to read the written descriptions and explanations posted at each exhibit to really understand what you're seeing. Likewise, if you avail yourself of demonstrations, videos, interactive displays and short presentations by docents, your experience will be all the richer.

There's frequently a disconnect within families when it come to touring museums. It usually centres on each individual's interest in the subject, attention span and willingness to invest time. Younger children, for example, may have only enough attention in reserve for a hurried, superficial visit. This is often the case even when children have some intrinsic curiosity about the nature of the exposition. If a child or adult in your party doesn't have the interest or patience to explore the museum in depth, you can assume that he/she will pressure the entire party to expedite its visit. Similarly, there are people who study each exhibit in such detail that they bring the progress of the group to a crawl. The salient point is that museums are better suited to small parties of compatible individuals of similar age than to large, diverse groups composed of varying ages. If the latter more accurately describes your family or group, we recommend developing a plan before you go. Of necessity it will require a degree of compromise on the part of all. Decide how much time you wish to allot; once at the museum, break into small compatible pairs or threesomes and free each to tour at their own pace, meeting at an agreed time and place to exit the museum.

INDUSTRY

WE LOVE TO KNOW HOW THINGS WORK and how they're made, so we tried to include some industrial and factory tours. **Big Pit: National Coal Museum in Wales** is a good example, as is the factory tour of the **Morgan Motor Company** in Malvern. Because of their sheer numbers, we elected to exclude distillery and brewery tours. The former are a mainstay in Scotland (see **whisky.com/distilleries**), and brewery tours can be found throughout the UK (at **enjoyengland.com** go to 'Food and Drink', then click on 'Brewery Tours', or see **visitabrewery.co.uk**). As far as we know, there are no sausage-factory tours.

FARM EXPERIENCES

IT APPEARS THAT FARMERS have been feeling the same sort of squeeze that has affected aristocrats. Dozens of working farms all over the UK have added a tourist dimension to their operations or, in the case of a few, converted their entire farms into tourism enterprises. The farms are very similar, if not identical, in what they offer. All feature a barn or outdoor enclosure(s) where goats, sheep, pigs, cows and horses are on display. Most farms also have rabbits and guinea pigs, and some have ducks, swans, chickens or peacocks. A few have deer, llamas, American bison and even wallabies. Some animals can be petted, others not. Various events are scheduled throughout the course of the day, including lamb- or goat-feeding, cow-milking demonstrations, educational presentations concerning farming, pig or sheep races and, increasingly, birds-of-prey and falconry shows. Some farms will load you onto a tractor-pulled hay wagon and take you into the fields, while others use similar means to transport you from the car park. Because many activities are centred around the barns, farm experiences work well even on rainy days. Given that animals are more cuddly than crops, most farms pay scant attention to agriculture, but even here there are exceptions.

In terms of facilities, all of the farms we visited had both indoor and outdoor children's play areas, picnic areas, toilets and some sort of gift shop where produce from the farm was frequently available. A few farms feature walk-through maize mazes, some large enough to get seriously lost in – 'Dr Livingstone, I presume?' Several farms are centred around historic homes or manors, often with exceptional gardens, and a handful even offer children's funfair rides. All farms provide several sinks, both in and separate from the toilets, for washing your hands after contact with the animals. A number of farms provide 'nature trails', mostly short but very pleasant if the weather is dry. Farms with dairy cattle usually offer home-made ice-cream, and all farms provide a snack bar or a modest café.

Photos in most of the farms' brochures picture children cuddling bunnies or feeding lambs with a baby bottle. The reality is a little different. There is almost no one-on-one contact with the animals except in the petting areas, where guests are only loosely supervised. Instead of actually cuddling a bunny, most farms have a staff member hold the animal while the child pets it. The bunny (or whatever) is taken from child to child in a large gathering of children, and each child gets only a second or two to pat and stroke. Lamb and goat feeding works in much the same way: a staffer holds the baby bottle to the animal's mouth and moves both bottle and lamb or goat along the line of children. Each child is allowed to momentarily place her hand on the bottle for a moment, but the bottle is always under the control of the staffer. Though not quite comparable to the sweet images in the brochures, most children seem satisfied with the experience.

Because most Brits begin their outings in the morning, farms are busiest from just after opening until about 2 p.m. Consequently, we suggest arriving after lunch. The scheduled events are repeated throughout the day, so you'll still be able to easily see everything. What's more, owing to thinning numbers of visitors in the afternoon, your children will have less competition for the animals. Another advantage is that on farms with dairy cattle, the cows are usually milked at about 4 or 4.30 p.m. For reasons of hygiene, visitors are not allowed in the automated milking parlour but can observe the process from a gallery or platform through a picture window.

The farm calendar dictates what you'll see at various times of year. Though the aforementioned features and events are available year round, lambing and calving usually take place between Easter and the end of May. Similarly, sheep-shearing usually occurs in June and July. As mentioned earlier, the farm experiences tend to emphasise animal husbandry over agriculture, though some farms have demonstration vegetable gardens, while others schedule seasonal events related to planting and harvesting.

Finding the farms is often challenging, because farms rarely qualify for the brown-and-white PLACES OF INTEREST road signs. The most dependable strategy is to enter the farm's postcode into a satnav. We learned the hard way to always use the postcodes on the farm's website or brochure rather than the postcodes listed on Google Maps – there are sometimes several farms with almost identical names. As you would expect, it's almost always difficult to access the farms by way of public transport.

Admission usually is in the £4–£7 range for adults and the £4–£6 range for children. Most farms open between 10 and 11 a.m. and close about 5 or 5.30 p.m. Seasonal and daily opening times vary considerably from farm to farm, though as a rule most are open daily during the summer school holiday period and on weekends and bank holidays when school is in session. To be safe, confirm dates and operating hours on the farm's website or by phone.

LETTERS *and* COMMENTS *from* READERS

MANY OF THOSE WHO USE THE *UNOFFICIAL GUIDES* write to us to make comments or share their own strategies for holidays and days out. We appreciate all such input, both positive and critical, and we encourage our readers to continue writing. Readers' comments and observations are frequently incorporated into revised editions of the *Unofficial Guides* and have contributed immeasurably to their improvement. If you write to us, you can rest assured that we won't release your name and address to mailing lists, direct-mail advertisers or any other third party.

How to Write to the Authors

Bob, Len and Larry
The Unofficial Guide to Britain's Best Days Out
P.O. Box 43673
Birmingham, AL 35243
USA
unofficialguides@menasharidge.com

When you write by mail, put your postal address on both your letter and envelope, as sometimes the two get separated. It's also a good idea to include your phone number. And remember that as travel writers, we're often out of the office for long periods of time, so excuse us if our response is slow.

England Regions

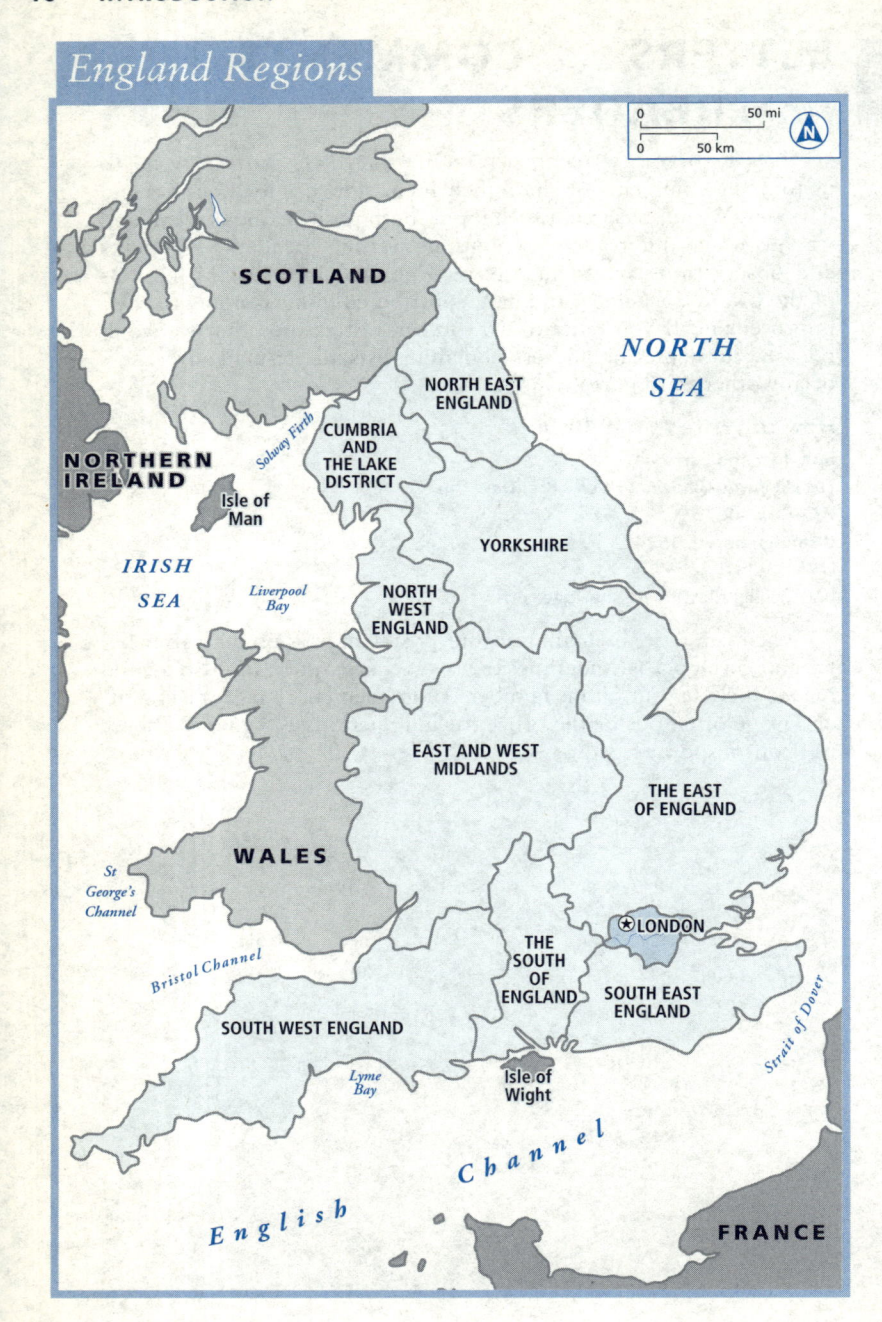

PART ONE
The WORLD of THEME-PARK RIDES

*There are more damn **wheels within wheels** here than you can possibly guess.*
– John le Carré,
Tinker, Tailor, Soldier, Spy

RIDES ARE THE HEART AND ESSENCE of every theme park, and knowing a little bit about them not only enhances your enjoyment and appreciation of them but can also help you avoid long waits in queues. Simple rides going in circles, dating back many hundreds of years, were the progenitors of just about every modern theme-park ride. Though we'll touch upon the evolution of all rides, our focus will be on those types of rides, usually thrill rides and roller coasters, that people travel miles to experience. And for most rides, it all started with the wheel.

WHEELS *within* WHEELS:
The Evolution of Non-Coaster Thrill Rides

THOUGH THE KNOWN HISTORY OF AMUSEMENT RIDES dates to ancient Byzantium, where children were spun around a post in woven baskets, the evolution of most rides we know today began with a sixteenth-century tournament game in which competitors on horseback tried to catch a small brass ring on the tip of each other's lances. The popularity of this endeavour occasioned the invention of a rotating platform on which a wooden version of a gymnast's vaulting horse was mounted. With this device and a ring suspended from a nearby tree, contestants could practise their aim. Observing this activity, craftsmen fashioned a facsimile for the amusement of their children. These became very popular at fairs, attracting the attention of skilled sculptors and artists who transformed the legless and headless horses into the magnificent, colourfully-painted and realistic ponies that have made the carousel a work of art.

As beloved as the carousel is, it wasn't the horses but rather the revolving round platform that was the ancestor of most theme-park rides which we enjoy today. It started with a wheel rotating around a central axis. What else can be done with that? If you move the wheel from shin-level to 20 ft (6 m) above the ground and suspend swings from it, you create a *flying carousel*, or a new ride genre simply called swings. Back on the ground, let's cut the platform into equal pie-shaped segments and hinge them together so they can go up and down over little humps as the platform revolves. Tack on independently-rotating teacup-shaped compartments to accommodate the riders, and you've just invented the classic Tilt-A-Whirl.

But why be satisfied with tacking various teacups, horses and boats to a platform? What if, instead, we ditch the platform altogether and attach whatever we want – rockets, flying elephants, little helicopters – to the end of spokes emanating from a central hub? The spokes free us from the limitations of the platform and also allow us to move our rockets up and down as well as round and round. A bigger motor lets us go faster and faster until we're screaming and holding on for dear life instead of lazily waving to Mum and Dad. Next we mount the whole contraption (ride vehicles at the end of spokes revolving around a central hub) onto a hydraulic lift-arm that rises off the ground like a guided-missile launcher lifting a weapon into launch position. Now we're cooking! With the addition of each element, we create a new axis of motion. In the process the ride moves from a horizontal plane to a vertical one and then back to the horizontal before stopping. Throw in speed, and the modern thrill ride is born.

Okay, let's go back to basics. The business end of most thrill rides is something rotating around a central axis. The rotating somethings are what you ride in. The generic name for them is *ride vehicle*, though on a particular ride they can be teacups, rockets, flying hippos, gondolas or most anything fashioned with seats. These are attached by spokes to a central hub, which in turn is attached to an axle. The spokes can radiate out from the hub directly to each ride vehicle, or they can extend outwards from the top of the ride like helicopter rotor blades. In the latter case the ride vehicle, or sometimes a pod (a cluster of two to four ride vehicles), is suspended from the overhead spokes or radial support arms.

You can create a surprising number of different rides by varying the position of the hub. If the hub is vertical, the spokes emanate horizontally, as in Disney's Dumbo ride. If the hub is horizontal, the spokes project vertically, as on a Ferris wheel. As discussed earlier, you can change the position of the hub mid-ride from horizontal to vertical by elevating the ride with a hydraulic lift-arm. If you want to make the ride more intense, add additional height and speed.

In the ride-manufacturing business, specific types of rides commonly take the name of the first or the most successful such ride introduced. Thus, the ride with the hydraulic lift-arm is known as an Enterprise, irrespective of what the ride might be called in a given park. (At Thorpe Park near London, for example, the Enterprise-type ride is called Zodiac.) This method of naming and defining rides is confusing and rarely consistent from country to country. To simplify, we've categorised rides based on their engineering design.

PLATFORM RIDES Carousels, Tilt-A-Whirls, teacup rides and any other ride in which the ride vehicles are mounted on a revolving platform, usually at or near ground level. Of course, as in the case of the carousel and many children's rides, not all platform rides are thrill rides.

Note: In the amusement industry, *platform rides* is also used to denote portable rides that can be transported from fair to fair. In this case *platform* refers to the ride's support base as opposed to a revolving platform that is part of the ride experience.

VERTICAL-HUB RADIAL RIDES Rides in which the hub and axle are vertical and ride vehicles are attached to spokes or steel arms radiating horizontally from the hub. Ride vehicles spin around the hub and, depending on the specific ride, may also go up and down. Examples include most revolving children's rides where the ride vehicles are not attached to a platform, as well as Disney's Dumbo ride.

VERTICAL-HUB SUSPENDED RIDES Rides in which the hub and axle are vertical and the spokes or support arms extend horizontally from the top of the ride. Ride vehicles (or vehicle pods) are suspended from the overhead supports. In the case of pods, each pod is attached to the horizontal support arm by a vertical arm that allows the pod additional freedom of rotation, thus maximising the effect of centrifugal force. These rides are variously called Twist, Sizzler, Scrambler, Cyclone, Merry Mixer and Grasscutter, among others. In many versions, the pods are spun in one direction while the ride as a whole revolves in the opposite direction. Vertical-hub suspended rides also include swing rides, in which individual swings or ride vehicles (such as rockets) are suspended from overhead supports by chains. The Flying Machines ride at Pleasure Beach Blackpool is representative of swing rides.

HYDRAULIC-LIFT-ARM RIDES Rides in which a hydraulic lift-arm can alter the position of the hub and axle from vertical to horizontal. The Enterprise ride described previously falls into this category.

HIGH-MOUNT HORIZONTAL-AXLE RIDES In the UK, more thrill rides fall into this category than any other save roller coasters. Within this classification there are two basic ride types: **wheel rides** and **pendulum rides**. A wheel ride for our purposes is a Ferris wheel or a close derivative. Pendulum rides are an evolutionary mutation of wheel rides. To

Lightwater Wheel at Lightwater Valley

understand both, let's start with the Ferris wheel, which consists of a support tower and a wheel. The wheel revolves around an axle-and-hub assembly positioned horizontally at the top of the support tower. Now, just as we'd change a car tyre, let's remove the wheel. What we have left are a tall support tower and a horizontal axle. This tower–axle combo serves as the essential cornerstone for dozens of pendulum ride designs.

PENDULUM RIDES Rides modelled on the motion of a fixed pendulum, defined as a weight suspended from a pivot so it can swing freely. In the case of pendulum thrill rides, the ride vehicle is attached the end of an arm (or arms) that in turn is attached to the axle. A motor powers the axle and lifts the vehicle, usually a gondola or boat-shaped carriage, from the loading platform up to a starting position. From here the brakes are released and the gondola or whatever swings to and fro. How high the gondola swings to either side isn't left to gravity, as with a true pendulum, but is controlled by the motor (actually a series of motors), so the gondola can swing much higher than gravity would allow. The oldest and most ubiquitous example of this type of pendulum ride is known universally as the Pirate Ship, which comes in mini-sizes for smaller kids and giant versions with 40-plus-person gondolas for older patrons. Sometimes a ride vehicle modelled on a 'flying carpet' is substituted for the ship-shaped carriage, as with Thorpe Park's Quantum ride.

With another variation on pendulum rides, the end of the arm is connected to a disc-shaped ride vehicle seating 30 or more riders. As the pendulum arm swings back and forth, the disc rotates independently. These rides are usually called Frisbees. Some models substitute pods or clusters of pods for the disc, and many models make complete revolutions around the axle, resulting in an inversion with each rotation. On one of the more-imaginative pendulum rides, the ride gondola makes complete inversions over a pool of spurting fountains, ultimately braking to an upside-down stop over the fountains, whereupon riders receive a free hair rinse (bring your own shampoo). At Chessington World of Adventures, this ride is called Rameses Revenge; at Alton Towers, it's Ripsaw. When it comes to rides as spectator sport, you can't top these.

Ripsaw at Alton Towers

On some pendulum rides the horizontal axle is positioned in the middle of the arm, similar to the way an aeroplane propeller is mounted. On one end of the arm is the ride vehicle, while the other is usually fitted with a heavy counterweight. Sometimes there are ride vehicles at both ends of the arm. Support towers for this design are quite tall, with the horizontal axle positioned as high as 60 ft (18 m) or more. At the top of the rotation, ride vehicles commonly reach heights of 120 ft (36 m). Bomber Mark 2 at M&D's in Scotland, for example, rises an astonishing 180 ft (55 m) and reaches speeds of 89 mph (143 km/h). The entire ride experience consists of steep dives and climbs, and of course the ride vehicle is designed to rotate at the end of the arm, so there are plenty of inversions.

With varied axle heights, multiple support-arm designs, dozens of ride-vehicle options, modern robotics and programmable operating systems, ride manufacturers stay busy cooking up new pendulum rides. Like the ones already in service, the new rides will look different and do different things, but each design will begin with a support tower and a horizontal axle.

OTHER NON-COASTER THRILL RIDES

THERE ARE MANY THRILL RIDES besides coasters and spinning-hub-and-axle rides. Most prevalent are the following:

TOWER RIDES Also known as drop towers, these rides are square towers measuring about 12 ft by 12 ft square (3.6 m by 3.6 m) at the base and rising as high as 390 ft (119 m) – though not in the UK. Riders are arrayed 4–8 persons to a side. Some towers are round, in which case a circular ride vehicle surrounds the tower. Most modern towers use pneumatic power to propel riders skyward to the top of the tower. From here they free-fall back to the base, with brakes governing their rate of descent and breaking the fall. Some models also use air blasts to propel the rides downward, momentarily surpassing the speed of a free-fall. Though the customary ride cycle is to ascend and descend once, with a bit of bouncing on the downward leg, some rides repeat the process or haul the riders aloft a second time with cables. Some towers are computer-controlled, while others are controlled manually. Much of the thrill of tower rides is in the anxious anticipation of being launched.

DARK RIDES Also called ghost trains, these rides operate indoors. Not all dark rides are thrill rides, and not all dark rides involve cars or trains running on tracks.

Space Tower at Legoland Windsor

Pleasure Beach Blackpool's premiere dark ride Valhalla, for example, is a boat ride. Early dark rides used absence of light to create a spooky environment punctuated with ghosts, ghouls, demons and monsters, hence 'ghost train'. Today, these darkly-themed rides are more often found at funfairs than at amusement parks. Many modern dark rides are based on adventure and fantasy themes and, though indoors, are not always dark. An excellent example of a traditional ghost train is Ghost Train (from which the genre took its name) at Pleasure Beach Blackpool, with its lurid facade and multi-level track. Dark rides with happier themes include Charlie and the Chocolate Factory at Alton Towers and Bubbleworks at Chessington World of Adventures.

The defining element of a dark ride is travelling through various artificially illuminated scenes relating to an overarching theme. Degrees of illumination vary, with scarier rides being very dark indeed, while happier rides are often brightly lit. Depending on their level of sophistication (which generally correlates with the age of the ride), they might contain elaborate and sometimes very realistic sets augmented by some combination of sound, music, animation, animatronics, interactive elements and special effects. Special effects are defined as better than regular effects. (No one knows what regular effects are.)

Typically called scenic railways, dark rides were introduced in the last decades of the nineteenth century. Early versions, which persist to this day, were technologically quite simple. The most common representative, known as a Tunnel of Love or an Old Mill, was a boat ride consisting of a lengthy flume running through a series of dark sheds. The rides were considered long enough for some heavy petting but too short for any attempt at conception.

Interactive versions have become popular over the past decade or so. These involve, amongst other things, shooting laser guns at menacing targets as your ride vehicle moves through the dark. You compete with the others in your car, and scores are automatically tabulated. Examples include Tomb Blaster at Chessington, Duel at Alton Towers and Laser Raiders at Legoland.

FLUME RIDES AND RAFT RIDES Also known as log rides, flume rides are water conveyances in which you float in boats or artificial hollowed logs through a half-pipe watercourse. Inspiration for the ride is drawn from the wooden flumes used by loggers to float their logs from a hillside down to the sawmill. Designed much like a roller coaster, boats are winched up a lift hill, whereupon gravity takes over. Most flume rides end with a long, steep plunge and a splashdown that showers the riders with water. Flume rides are ubiquitous in British theme parks, and it's a rare park that doesn't have at least one.

Raft rides involve a round raft travelling down an artificial stream. Often nicely landscaped and scenic, raft rides offer a taste of mild whitewater with small drops, reactionary and standing waves and narrow chutes. The raft careens off the sides of the stream and also off obstacles in the water. Where flume rides experience most of their descent in one climactic drop, the descent in raft rides follows a more uniform gradient, without the climax of an imposing drop at the end.

How wet you get on a flume or raft ride varies wildly from ride to ride. On some you can get away with a gentle spraying, while on others you'll get wetter than a cod. It was a startling revelation to us that the sea-faring Brits eagerly submit themselves for dousing on these rides, even on rainy, blustery days. Of course, you

> *unofficial* **TIP**
> If you're considering a wet ride, check out riders exiting the ride to get a feel for how wet you'll get.

can mitigate the soaking by wearing rain-gear, plastic bin-liners, ponchos, wellies or wetsuits. Some parks, like Pleasure Beach Blackpool, sell disposable rain outfits in the ride queue for about a pound. Skin dries faster than fabric, so expose as little clothing as possible. Most annoying are soaked bottoms and soaked feet. Carrying a small towel or cloth nappy to wipe down the seat when you board is a good idea. Wearing sandals also helps. Take off your socks no matter what footwear you have on. Most ride operators will not allow you to ride barefoot, but once your boat is launched you can snatch off your shoes and bundle them under whatever protective garment you're wearing. Failing that, stuff them in your armpits.

ROLLER COASTERS

COASTERS ARE THE DEFINING RIDES IN MOST THEME PARKS. Good roller coasters equal good theme park – it's as simple as that. Though non-coaster thrill rides often serve up a wilder ride experience, it's the coasters that draw us in and fire our imaginations. Show us the schoolboy who hasn't sketched his own fantasy roller coaster while the teacher drones on.

Roller coasters are certainly thrill rides, but their evolution followed a very different path. They sprung from a popular fad in fifteenth-century Russia to replicate the excitement of sledging. In places where the natural topography was not conducive to sledging, artificial hills were constructed by piling up snow and ice. In the eighteenth century, the sledge courses escaped the grip of winter by the substitution of a wooden trestle for the frozen hill and mounting wheels on the sledge. You hauled your sledge to the top of the trestle and, as they say, it was all downhill from there.

Interest in coasters, which western Europeans called 'Russian Mountains', waned after numerous injuries and fatalities. Though a small number of coasters, or 'centrifugal railways', were built in England and France in the 1800s, the genre was largely dormant until revived by LaMarcus Adna Thompson's Switchback Railway at Coney Island, near New York City, in 1884. Thompson's coaster, designed on the old Russian Mountain model, featured cars that rolled at 6 mph (9.6 km/h) down a 600-ft (183-m) undulating track from a starting elevation of 50 ft (15 m). In 1884 Charles Alcoke created the first coaster to make a complete circuit. The following year Phillip Hinkle introduced the concept of a 'lift hill', the initial hill on which the train was hauled to the highest elevation of the circuit on a cable and later by a chain-and-ratchet mechanism. The lift hill revolutionised coasters, allowing an expanded layout and the incorporation of an elliptical design into the course of the track.

Towards the middle of the nineteenth century, designers began to experiment with vertical loops. The first looping coaster was built in England and exported to Frascati Gardens in Paris, in 1846. Riders would descend a modest hill, from which their momentum would carry them through the loop and out the other side. The 1890s saw a renewed interest in loops, and several looping coasters were built. They were rough affairs, however, inflicting such serious whiplash on riders that most were taken out of service within a year.

The first half of the twentieth century witnessed the increased use of steel to replace wood in coaster superstructure, but steel didn't really come into its own in track design until 1959, when Disneyland, in California, opened the Matterhorn Bobsleds attraction. This was the first coaster to use a tubular-steel track. Tubular steel can be bent in any direction. This led to breakthroughs in coaster design that made possible such ride elements as loops, corkscrews, various kinds

Colossus at Thorpe Park

of rolls and inversions, overbanked turns and many other manoeuvres previously impossible. The Matterhorn was also the first coaster to use individual brake zones, sections of the layout where a train's speed could be adjusted. This innovation allowed for two or more trains to operate on the track simultaneously, thus increasing hourly capacity and cutting queuing times.

Coasters in UK parks figured prominently in the development and evolution of the roller coaster. Below are but a few of the more-recent firsts chalked up to British theme parks.

TYPES OF ROLLER COASTERS

COASTERS OPERATING TODAY are made either of steel or of wood. Among both types are 'adult' coasters, usually defined as coasters with a minimum height requirement of at least 40″ (1.01 m); and children's

1997	**First flying coaster:** Skytrak (roller coaster), Granada Studios (now closed), Manchester
1998	**First diving machine coaster and vertical drop:** Oblivion, Alton Towers, Alton, Staffordshire
2002	**First coaster with ten inversions:** Colossus, Thorpe Park, Surrey
2009	**First coaster with 100° free-fall drop:** Saw – The Ride, Thorpe Park, Surrey

coasters, smaller non-intimidating models designed to give younger children an introduction to the genre.

Most coasters are outdoors, but some are enclosed inside buildings. Disney's Space Mountain was the first major indoor coaster that made use of its enclosure to project a space-travel theme. Modern indoor coasters represent a combination of ghost train (dark ride) and roller coaster. Raptor Attack at Lightwater Valley in North Yorkshire is the UK's best indoor coaster, with Thorpe Park's X:\No Way Out a close second. Saw – The Ride, also at Thorpe Park, is a coaster with both indoor and outdoor segments.

While modern wooden coasters are capable of loops and other sophisticated manoeuvres, they are all essentially the same, consisting of a six- to eight-car train accommodating four persons per car, with the track beneath the train. In contrast, there are a number of different types of steel coasters:

TRADITIONAL COASTERS Exactly like wooden coasters, with multi-car trains sitting atop the tracks.

INVERTED COASTERS Here the train is suspended from an overhead track, leaving your feet to dangle in space as the coaster traces its circuit.

FLYING COASTERS Once again the track is overhead. This time, however, you are rotated from a sitting position to a prone one, with your

Air at Alton Towers

Avalanche at Pleasure Beach Blackpool

body parallel with the track, so you feel like you're flying. Air at Alton Towers is a flying coaster.

LAUNCHED (OR ACCELERATOR) COASTERS These coasters are launched up the first hill like jets off an aircraft carrier. Several technologies can be used, including linear-induction motors which power the launch using electromagnetic propulsion, catapults, and hydraulic pumps that compress nitrogen. Launch speeds vary but can range up to 0–60 mph (0–96 km/h) in 3 seconds.

BOBSLED COASTERS These are chain-pulled to the top of the lift hill and then released to roll down a half-pipe without tracks (think bobsled run). Avalanche at Pleasure Beach Blackpool is a bobsled coaster.

DIVING MACHINES The ride vehicle here has two rows of seats, with six or eight riders per row. After climbing the lift hill, the car rolls to the edge of a near-vertical first drop and then hangs momentarily over the edge before being released to dive down and complete the circuit. Oblivion at Alton Towers is a diving machine.

FLOORLESS COASTERS In this version, the train cars are mounted several feet above the track. After you board, the loading platform (the floor) drops away, leaving your feet dangling.

WILD MICE Small coasters with two- or four-person cars. The wild mouse is distinguished by tight, flat turns at low speeds; small dips; tight switchbacks; and a meandering layout. The name is inspired by the behaviour of mice running frantically through a maze. Because

Runaway Train at Chessington World of Adventures

many models are portable, the wild mouse can be found at many fairgrounds as well as at theme parks.

MINE TRAINS Usually, but not always, small coasters, frequently with both and indoor and outdoor segments, characterised by tight-banked turns and short, steep drops. Based on the concept of a runaway mine, the theming is occasionally very elaborate, as with Disney's Big Thunder Mountain Railroad. In the UK, theme execution for most mine-train rides is minimal. Such rides are found in almost every British theme park.

You're probably getting the drift that there's a whole vocabulary of roller-coaster jargon (for the record, we haven't even scratched the surface). If you want to impress your friends at dinner parties, you can bone up on coaster terminology at **themeparks.about.com/cs/coasterbooks/a/coasterspeak.htm** or **ultimaterollercoaster.com/coasters/glossary**.

COASTER PROBLEMS: WHIPLASH AND NAUSEA

AS A GENERALISATION, steel coasters offer a smoother ride than do wooden coasters, which are infamous for side-to-side jarring. The stress on the moving and structural parts of a roller coaster is immense. Consequently, the ride becomes rougher on both steel and wooden coasters as they age. It's very possible, sometimes even likely, to sustain neck, back and head injuries on a roller coaster (as well as on other thrill rides). To mitigate whiplash and other insults to the cervical vertebrae, the Los Angeles Decompression Therapy website (**la-spinal-decompression.blogspot.com**) recommends the following:

The way to lessen the likelihood of cervical trauma [on a roller coaster] is to look at where the next turn is and be ready for it. Being prepared means paying attention to what is going on. When going down a large slope look at what is next; if there is a turn to the left, get ready for it. The brain can communicate with the muscles to get ready for the turn. Some of the most damaging injuries to the ligaments and discs in the neck happen when a person is not ready for it. They are caught off-guard, the muscles are relaxed, and there is no defence to the trauma. Roller-coaster rides are fun and should be enjoyed; just pay attention while [riding] and keep your neck healthy.

As an addendum, you're likely to be more off-guard at the start or end of a ride than during the ride itself. We've experienced our most serious jarring when the coaster train violently lurched from the loading station and then again when it suddenly braked to a stop before re-entering the station. The severity of the movement in both cases was very much unexpected.

If you're prone to motion sickness, we can think of better places for you to be than on a roller coaster. But if, like many of us, nausea takes you by surprise while you ride, here are some do's and don'ts:

- Eat something before riding – riding on an empty stomach increases the probability of becoming nauseated.
- Don't ride with your eyes closed.
- Concentrate your gaze on a single fixed object if you begin to feel sick.

LOSING STUFF

IT'S VERY EASY TO LOSE PERSONAL ITEMS while riding a coaster. We always use an adjustable strap on our glasses and stow small items like pens in a pocket with a buttoned or Velcro flap. Many coasters have small lockers (usually free) where you can store things before getting in queue. Others have cubbyholes or other places to store personal items in the loading area. Among the items most frequently lost are hats, hair scrunchies, glasses and cameras.

HOW BRITISH COASTERS STACK UP

A WORLDWIDE ROLLER COASTER RANKING POLL is conducted each year. Following are the UK coasters that are ranked among the world's top 250:

British Roller-Coaster Rankings

STEEL COASTERS

WORLD RANKING	COASTER	PARK
7	Nemesis	Alton Towers
62	Stealth	Thorpe Park
73	Speed: No Limits	Oakwood
84	Oblivion	Alton Towers
88	Nemesis Inferno	Thorpe Park
96	Air	Alton Towers
117	Saw – The Ride	Thorpe Park
122	Knightmare	Camelot Theme Park
128	Rita	Alton Towers
146	Ultimate	Lightwater Valley
158	Mumbo Jumbo	Flamingo Land
172	Rage	Adventure Island
185	Kumali	Flamingo Land
189	Velocity	Flamingo Land
194	Vampire	Chessington World of Adventures
223	Pepsi Max Big One	Pleasure Beach Blackpool
224	Jubilee Odyssey	Fantasy Island
235	Avalanche	Pleasure Beach Blackpool
238	Cobra	Paultons Park
250	Millennium	Fantasy Island

WOODEN COASTERS

WORLD RANKING	COASTER	PARK
29	Megafobia	Oakwood
33	Grand National	Pleasure Beach Blackpool
49	Wild Mouse	Pleasure Beach Blackpool
64	Big Dipper	Pleasure Beach Blackpool
94	Rollercoaster	Pleasure Beach Blackpool
115	Roller Coaster	Pleasure Beach Great Yarmouth
147	Antelope	Gulliver's World
153	Zipper Dipper	Pleasure Beach Blackpool

Source: bestrollercoasterpoll.com

UNDERSTANDING THEME-PARK RIDES

UNDERSTANDING HOW RIDES ARE ENGINEERED to accommodate guests is interesting and invaluable to developing an efficient touring itinerary at any theme park.

All attractions, regardless of location, are affected by two elements: *capacity* and *popularity*. Capacity is how many guests the ride can serve at one time. Popularity is a measurement of how much visitors like a ride. Capacity can be adjusted at some attractions. It's possible, for example, to add rafts at Alton Towers' River Rapids or put extra cars on Legoland Windsor's Driving School ride. Longer coasters, for which more than one train can be running on the track simultaneously, can add additional trains. Generally, however, ride capacity remains relatively fixed.

Designers try to match capacity and popularity as closely as possible. A high-capacity ride that isn't popular is a failure: lots of money, space and equipment have been poured into the attraction, yet there are empty seats. It's extremely unusual for a new ride not to measure up, but it's fairly common for an older ride to lose appeal.

Some rides sustain great popularity years beyond their debut, while others decline in appeal after a few years. Most rides, however, work through the honeymoon and then settle down to handle the level of demand for which they were designed. When this happens, there are enough interested guests during peak hours to fill almost every seat, but not so many that long queues develop.

Sometimes a park correctly estimates an attraction's popularity but fouls the equation by mixing in a third variable such as location. Valhalla, at Pleasure Beach Blackpool, is a good example. Placing the combination ghost train–flume ride just inside the main entrance of the park assures that it will be extremely busy as soon as it opens. On the flip side, the Pirates Landing section of Legoland is so remotely located that many seats on its rides remain empty until early afternoon, when guests finally reach that part of the park.

If demand is high and capacity is low, long queues materialise. Several parks offer flying-elephant rides similar to Disney's Dumbo ride – for example, Flying Jumbos at Chessington and at M&D's in Scotland. All have a very limited carrying capacity, yet they are among the most popular children's rides. The result of this mismatch is that children and parents often suffer long, long waits for a 2-minute-or-less ride. The elephants are simple yet visually appealing funfair rides. Their capacity is limited by the very characteristics that make them popular.

Capacity design is predicated upon averages: the average number of people in the park, the normal distribution of traffic to specific areas and the average number of staff needed to operate the ride. On a holiday weekend, when all the averages are exceeded, all but a few rides operate at maximum capacity, and even then they're overwhelmed by the huge crowds. On days of low attendance, capacity is often not even approximated, and guests can ride without having to wait.

Most parks offer a number of low-capacity funfair rides and ghost train 'dark' rides. They range from state-of-the-art to antiquated. This diversity makes efficient touring of a park much more challenging. If guests don't understand the capacity–popularity relationship and don't plan accordingly, they might spend most of the day in a queue.

In many parks, crowd conditions are more a function of the popularity and engineering of individual rides. At other parks, traffic flow and crowding are more affected by park layout. Pleasure Beach Blackpool's Big One roller coaster, for instance, is as far from the entrance as possible. The location of the ride is designed to pull guests to the most far-flung reaches of the park.

To develop an efficient touring plan, it's necessary to understand how rides and shows are designed and function. We'll examine both.

CUTTING YOUR QUEUING TIME BY UNDERSTANDING THE RIDES

BRITISH THEME PARKS FEATURE MANY TYPES OF RIDES. Some, such as the Congo River Rapids raft ride at Alton Towers, can carry

Congo River Rapids at Alton Towers

almost 2,400 people an hour. At the other extreme, many children's rides can barely handle 150 riders an hour. Most rides fall somewhere in-between. Many factors figure into how long you'll wait to experience a ride: its popularity; how it loads and unloads; how many persons can ride at once; how many units/ride vehicles (cars, rockets, boats, flying elephants and the like) are in service at a time; and how many workers are available to operate the ride. Let's take the factors one by one.

1. How Popular Is the Ride?

Newer rides such as Saw – The Ride at Thorpe Park and TH13TEEN at Alton Towers attract a lot of people, as do such longtime favourites as Stormforce 10 at Drayton Manor and Lost River Ride at Flamingo Land. If a ride is popular, you need to know how it operates in order to determine the best time to ride. But a ride need not be especially popular to generate long lines; in some cases, such lines are due not to a ride's popularity but to poor engineering or under-staffing. This is the case at the Twirling Toadstool at Alton Towers and Whirlwind at Lightwater Valley. Both rides serve only a small percentage of any day's attendance, yet because they take so long to load and unload, long lines form regardless.

Whirlwind at Lightwater Valley

2. How Does the Ride Load and Unload?

Some rides never stop. They're like conveyor belts that go round and round. These are *continuous loaders*. The number of people that can be moved through in an hour depends on how many ride vehicles are on the conveyor. Continuous loaders using conveyors are very rare in the UK but are used in the US on such rides as Disney's Haunted Mansion (called Phantom Manor at Disneyland Paris).

Other rides are *interval loaders*. Cars are unloaded, loaded and dispatched at set intervals, sometimes controlled manually, sometimes by computer. X:\No Way Out at Thorpe Park is an interval loader. While cars are being unloaded and loaded on the loading platform, dozens of other cars are going through the ride. Loaded cars are advanced to a dispatch point, where they are launched according to whatever interval has been established. The greater the capacity and number of ride vehicles, and the shorter the dispatch interval, the more people who can ride in a given time period.

In one kind of interval loader, empty cars return to the loading platform, where they reload. In a second kind, one group of riders enters the vehicle while the previous group departs. Rides of the latter type are referred to as 'in and out' interval loaders. As a boat docks, those who have just completed their ride exit to the left; at almost the same time, those waiting to ride enter the boat from the right. The reloaded boat is released to the dispatch point a few yards down the line, where it's launched according to the interval being used.

Interval loaders of both types can be very efficient people-movers if (1) the dispatch (launch) interval is relatively short and (2) the ride can accommodate many vehicles at one time. Because many boats can float through Chessington's Bubbleworks at one time, and because the dispatch interval is short, hundreds of people can experience this attraction each hour.

The least-efficient rides, in terms of traffic engineering, are *cycle rides*, also called 'stop and go' rides. On cycle rides, those waiting to ride exchange places with those who have just ridden. Unlike in-and-out interval rides, cycle rides shut down during loading and unloading. While one boat is loading and unloading in Legoland's Pirate Falls flume ride, many other boats are advancing through the ride. But when Flamingo Land's Red Baron ride touches down, the whole ride is at a standstill until the next flight launches.

In cycle rides, the time in motion is *ride time*. The time the ride idles while loading and unloading is *load time*. Load time plus ride time equals *cycle time*, or the time from the start of one run of the ride until the start of the next. By our estimate, about 65% of all British theme park rides are cycle rides.

3. How Many Persons Can Ride at One Time?

This figure expresses *system capacity*, or the number of people who can ride at one time. The greater the carrying capacity of a ride (all other things being equal), the more visitors it can accommodate per hour. Some rides can add extra units (cars, boats and such) as crowds build, to increase capacity; others, such as carousels, have a fixed capacity (it's impossible to add more horses).

4. How Many Units Are in Service at a Given Time?

Unit is our term for the vehicle in which you ride. On a spinning-teacup ride, the unit is a teacup; on a flume ride, it's an artificial hollowed log. On some rides (mostly cycle rides), the number of units operating at one time is fixed. There's no way to increase the capacity of such rides by adding units. On a busy day, the only way to carry more people each hour on a fixed-unit cycle ride is to shorten the loading time or decrease the ride time. The bottom line: on a busy day for a cycle ride, you'll wait longer and possibly be rewarded with a shorter ride. This is why we steer you away from cycle rides unless you're willing to ride them early in the morning or late at night.

Many other rides can increase their capacity by adding units as crowds build. Roller coasters that operate multiple trains, for example, can start by running one train. If queues build, more trains are placed into operation. At capacity, most of the major British coasters can run three trains simultaneously. Likewise, flume rides can increase the number of logs on the course, and raft rides can add extra rafts. Sometimes a long queue will disappear almost instantly when new units are brought on-line. When an interval loader places more units into operation, the dispatch interval usually shortens, allowing more units to be dispatched more often.

5. How Many Staff Are Available to Operate the Ride?

Adding staff to a ride can allow more units to operate or additional loading platforms to open. Additional operators make a world of difference to some cycle rides. Often, Enterprise at Alton Towers has only one attendant. This person alone must clear visitors from the ride just completed, admit and seat visitors for the upcoming ride, check that each person is secured, return to the control panel, issue instructions to the riders and finally activate the ride (whew!). A second attendant divides these responsibilities and cuts loading time by 25–50%. At a time such as now, when economic uncertainty affects all tourism, minimum staffing is the rule rather the exception.

SHOWS

BELIEVE IT OR NOT, a lot of engineering goes into shows. Theatre productions, like rides, can be compared by their hourly capacity and the efficiency of their queuing schemes to deliver visitors to the theatre.

CUTTING YOUR QUEUING TIME BY UNDERSTANDING THE SHOWS

MANY FEATURED ATTRACTIONS AT BRITISH THEME PARKS are theatre presentations. While they aren't as complex as rides, understanding them from a traffic-engineering standpoint may save you touring time.

Most theatre attractions operate in three phases:
1. Guests are in the theatre viewing the presentation.
2. Guests who have passed through the turnstile wait in a holding area or lobby. They will be admitted to the theatre as soon as the show in progress concludes. Several attractions offer a pre-show to entertain guests until they're admitted to the main show. Examples include *Happy Feet 4D* at Drayton Manor and *Bob the Builder 4D* at Legoland.
3. A queue waits outside. Guests in the queue enter the lobby when there's room, and will ultimately move into the theatre.

Theatre capacity, the presentation's popularity and park attendance determine how long queues will be at a theatre attraction. Except for holidays and other days of heavy attendance, the longest wait for a show usually doesn't exceed the length of one performance if the theatre attraction runs continuously, stopping only long enough for the previous audience to leave and the waiting audience to enter.

Most indoor theatres are very strict about access. You can't enter during a performance, and that means you'll always have at least a short wait even if shows run back-to-back. Most theatres hold a lot of people. When a new audience is admitted, any outside queue will usually disappear. Amphitheatre productions, in which shows operate according to a daily entertainment schedule, are different. Here you are invited to arrive early and select a seat instead of being held in a lobby or a queue outside the theatre. Your reward for arriving early is a good seat, not to mention being able to get off your feet.

PART TWO

ORGANISING YOUR HOLIDAY *before* LEAVING HOME

GATHERING INFORMATION

THERE IS AN ABUNDANCE OF INFORMATION for some parks and attractions and little to none to be found for others. If you have Internet access and want to find info on a particular park or attraction, say, Howletts Wild Animal Park, just search for it by name. If you're interested in a particular region, such as Northern England, or a county, for example, Kent, and just want to know what's available, search for 'Northern England attractions' or 'Kent attractions'. Though there are oodles of attractions (Yorkshire alone claims 800), usually the most popular or important ones will be listed, along with links to their websites.

Not recommended is searching from the top down on most big national sites like **visitbritain.com**. You might end up where you want to be, but you'll prove the exception to the rule that 'getting there is half the fun'. Speaking of exceptions, a big national site we *do* recommend that you search is the one for the **National Trust**. You'll find a great interactive map of both natural and man-made Trust locations at **nationaltrust.org.uk/main/w-vh/w-visits/w-beta-map.htm**.

If you don't have Internet access, the process of collecting information via post and phone can be both time-consuming and expensive. Rather than make the effort to visit a tourist-information centre or the office of a travel-booking service, we recommend going to an Internet café, a library or a friend's office or home where you can go online and pursue your research. There is some value to visiting bricks-and-mortar information centres, where you can review dozens of promotional brochures and obtain maps and advice.

unofficial **TIP**
Unless you're just fishing, keep your Web searches as narrow and specific as possible. For example, if you're interested in attractions in York, search for 'York attractions' rather than 'Yorkshire attractions'. If you're looking for a particular type of attraction, specify it in your search, as in 'Oxford art museums' or 'London theme parks'.

This process is especially fruitful in terms of discovering places to visit that you weren't aware of. A fairly-comprehensive list of the hundreds of such centres can be found at **enjoyengland.com/find-tic**.

If you're a little foggy on your UK geography, there's a list of counties and their towns at **gbet.com/AtoZ_counties**. For a map that shows UK counties, see **printable-maps.blogspot.com/2008/09/uk-map-showing-counties.html** (there are several maps on this page – scroll down to find the largest, most detailed map).

OUR FAVOURITE WEBSITES

IN OUR HUMBLE OPINION, the Web is the best thing to happen to travel since the invention of the wheel. Use it properly and you'll enhance your visit, avoid pitfalls and even save money. But you can't just enter a search term and start clicking. There's too much junk out there, and too many advertisements masquerading as independent sources.

Here are some of the sites we find most helpful for planning a trip:

Individual Park Sites

It may be obvious, but these should really be your first stop. Not only can you usually buy admission online, providing a discount and often letting you bypass lines at the parks, but they're also the best source for directions and park hours, which change often. With a little poking around, you can work out the details of your visit, checking the times for zoo feedings and park shows. A few sites, like the Tank Museum, have audio tours you can download to your MP3 player. Also check to see if the park or attraction has a **Facebook** page. Often it will provide the latest news on developments, from park closings to extended hours, and sometimes links to deals.

YouTube

Yes, it's the place to go to watch videos of someone's cat playing with spaghetti, but **youtube.com** also lets you 'tour' a park before you touch your wallet. Nearly every theme-park ride and most attractions are featured here. So before terrifying your 3-year-old by hauling her onto a ghost train, take a sample ride from home at your computer. You'll quickly determine whether it's appropriate or will keep her (and the entire family) up with nightmares for weeks. Other park-goers can test-drive headliner attractions to see if they're worth the likely wait.

OFFICIAL TOURIST WEBSITES

visitbritain.com
(the overall site for all of Britain)

enjoyengland.com (for England)

visitwales.com (for Wales)

visitscotland.com (for Scotland)

Review Sites

You aren't the first person to ever visit a park, so why not see what others have said about their experiences? While it's by no means gospel, you can pick up on trends. If five different reviewers note a problem with wasps, or complain about the food, you can safely assume there's something to their concern. The most helpful sites include **tripadvisor.co.uk, dooyoo.co.uk, qype.co.uk** and **travel.ciao.co.uk**.

Park Fan Sites

The wonderful thing about the Internet is that everyone gets a voice. Most major parks seem to have a dedicated fan site, usually run by individuals or informal groups. While these are fun and can be a great source of inside information, they're often outdated, so double-check everything you read. The best way to find them is to enter the park name and 'fan site' into a search engine.

Zoos

There are a lot of animal-lovers out there. Like trainspotters, some zoo-spotters can tell you every attraction that has a red panda in the UK, and where the newest zebra births have taken place. That said, there's helpful info for travellers too. **Zoos-uk.com** offers a nice synopsis on the country's biggest zoos, while **zoochat.com** is opinionated and full of sometimes-obscure but often-helpful information. Just put the name of the zoo followed by 'review' in the search field, and you'll get a warts-and-all report on major and minor attractions.

Transport

If only Dr David Livingstone had had access to the Internet, he would have avoided all those years slogging through Africa. These sites are our favourites for rail and public-transport routes: **nationalrail.co.uk** offers rail options, including timetables, and **transportdirect.info** will give you door-to-door transportation routing, including rail, coach, ferry and even walking. And don't forget a site for driving directions – everyone seems to have a favourite. We find it's helpful to bring a set of directions along as backup even if you have a satnav. Too often the trusty machines will lead you into a farmer's field instead of the car park.

TIMING YOUR HOLIDAY *or* OUTING

THEME PARKS AND ATTRACTIONS ARE MOST CROWDED during the summer, bank holidays and other times of the year when school is not in session. Weekends see higher attendance than weekdays. The days of operation for parks and attractions vary immensely. Indoor attractions such as museums, aquariums, factory tours and the like are open all year. Many zoos and safari parks are likewise open all year, especially those that offer indoor viewing areas.

Most parks where outdoor rides are the main draw close during most of November and all of December and January. Some parks, such as Alton Towers, open for a week of school holidays in February, but others, like Pleasure Beach Blackpool, remain closed until late March.

For theme parks during the summer, we recommend arriving 20 minutes before the park opens. This is easily accomplished if you have a car but is often challenging if you use public transport, especially when transfers are involved. We include public-transport options in the coverage of each park, but understand that you'll need to get a very, very early start to be on hand at park opening. Bus shuttles are available from town centres or railway stations to some parks, but they may not commence service early enough to arrive when you prefer. If you take public transport it's often best to use a taxi for the last leg of your journey to the park – that way you're not subject to the vagaries of the shuttle services or local buses. If you drive, be sure to allot some extra time to park and make your way to the theme-park entrance.

> *unofficial* **TIP**
> The busiest season for all UK parks is from the last week in July to the last week in August. During this period especially, we advocate avoiding weekends for larger theme parks and for safari parks.

Many parks and attractions are grossly inefficient when it comes to selling admissions. Rarely are there enough ticket kiosks to handle opening crowds. To avoid long queues, try to purchase your admission online. Be aware, however, that some online tickets are merely admission vouchers that must be exchanged at park guest relations for a valid admission pass. Guest-relations windows are more mobbed than the ticket kiosks and are to be avoided at all costs. This means, among other things, that you don't want prepaid tickets held for pickup at guest relations.

At certain theme parks, some of the rides are on a delayed opening schedule. At Pleasure Beach Blackpool, for example, the park opens at 10 a.m. but several of the roller coasters and children's rides don't open until 11 or later. For these parks, the strategy is to ride the most popular rides available at opening and then position yourself in the queue for late-opening rides just before they come online.

For zoos, depending on the size, arriving about 90 minutes *after* the park opens works well. You'll miss the opening congestion and you can usually count on the animals being present in their viewing areas. As concerns safari parks, we suggest arriving about 1 p.m. and seeing the caged/enclosed exhibits first (think reptile house or aviary). Commence your safari drive about 2½ hours before park closing. By this time, congestion and traffic on the safari drive will have eased considerably.

With museums, the best time to arrive depends on the museum. If the museum is well known and popular, arrive 15 minutes before opening. This is especially important if the museum is relatively small. If the museum is especially large, like the National Railway Museum in York or the Imperial War Museum Duxford, plan to arrive by mid-morning.

Arriving early is advised for The Deep in Hull, East Yorkshire, and Deep Sea World in Scotland. We find that other aquariums are rarely crowded, so visit at your convenience anytime during operating hours. Factory and industrial tours, as well as railway excursions, usually operate on a fixed daily schedule, available on the Internet. For farm experiences, an early-afternoon arrival is suggested.

ALLOCATING ENERGY

WHEN'S THE LAST TIME YOU THOUGHT ABOUT this when organising a holiday? The reality is that many individuals and families pack so much into their holiday that they become too exhausted to enjoy it. This is all both foreseeable and avoidable. On a multi-day holiday, prepare physically by taking walks so that you build your and your family's endurance. Prepare mentally by researching how much effort you'll need to expend to get the most from your experience. This is especially important when preparing to visit an attraction that is educational and deals with complex subjects, as do the National Space Centre in Leicester or The Deep aquarium in northeast Yorkshire. For both, you need to be ready and willing to learn, to really spend time absorbing the exhibits. Be realistic too: if members of your party are too uninterested, leave them at home, and if your children are not old enough or too impatient to have a meaningful experience, postpone your visit until they mature a bit. If you have more than one attraction scheduled for the day, always schedule the most intellectually-demanding one for the morning, when you're fresh.

BUILDING REST AND RELAXATION IN TO YOUR HOLIDAY

YOU CAN GO FULL-TILT FOR A WEEKEND. For anything longer, incorporate some rest and relaxation into your schedule. Have a good lie-in one morning, or reserve an afternoon just to enjoy the beach. If your children are age 10 or younger, exit the park for a nap and a swim, returning refreshed later in the afternoon. If you plan to get up early, hit the sack early the night before. If you stay up late, allow yourself an extra hour or two of sleep in the morning. You get the idea.

DESTINATIONS *versus* LOCAL ATTRACTIONS *and* PARKS

UNLESS YOU CONSIDER THE LONDON ATTRACTIONS, parks and sites collectively, the UK doesn't have a major tourist destination centred around a theme park or other attractions. As close as it gets is Pleasure Beach Blackpool, but there are lots of folk on holiday in Blackpool who never visit the theme park. Alton Towers, the UK's largest theme park, has only two on-site hotels. Most British theme parks, even those in the countryside, have no lodging of their own at all. This indicates that even the larger parks are the focus of one-day outings as opposed to multi-day destination travel. Thus you could say that, like politics, all UK theme parks are local.

On multi-day holidays a theme park might be the top priority, but the itinerary will almost certainly include a number of other sites and attractions. Many park-and-ride visits are ancillary to a holiday at the beach or to a particular area such as the Lake District, where natural beauty combines with historical sites and various attractions to form the critical mass required of a true tourist destination.

Looking at the numbers, most people don't range very far from home on single day and weekend outings. Even for multi-day holidays, travelling more than 250 mi (400 km) from home (within the UK) is the exception. Most residents of the British Isles are well acquainted with, and patronise, the parks and attractions close to home.

Also, theme parks, aquariums, zoos and safari parks tend to be homogeneous within their genre. If you travel from theme park to theme park, you'll see many of the same rides offered in each park. Differentiation, as we noted in the introduction, is largely a matter of setting, gardens and architecture rather than (with a couple of exceptions) unique rides. The same holds true equally for zoos, safari parks and aquariums. For many, the incentive to bypass a park closer to home to visit a distant park with much the same features just isn't there. One consequence of this, with the exceptions of Greater London, is a relatively-even distribution of tourists throughout the UK, especially from Loch Lomond south. No doubt you'll encounter queues wherever you go, but they will be on a much smaller order of magnitude than those, say, at a Disney park which draws tourists from all over a continent.

ADMISSIONS TYPES

WE'VE HEARD *THEME PARK* defined as an amusement park unified by a governing theme, a place where all rides, shows and other features are included in the price of admission. While that definition might fly in America, it sometimes does and sometimes does not work in the UK. As it happens, there are more admission schemes and models in Britain than we could guess. The all-inclusive admission is alive and well, but so is the à la carte model, in which park admission is free or very modest and you pay for each ride separately. M&D's park in Scotland charges nothing to enter, for instance, but then charges for individual rides. Likewise, you'll get through the turnstiles at Pleasure Beach Blackpool for a modest £4, but you won't be able to ride anything unless you buy some ride tickets.

In some pay-as-you-go schemes you actually pay the ride operator (in British currency) prior to boarding. Variations include purchasing ride tokens from a machine or buying tickets from an attendant at a ticket window. When you buy tickets, there are usually volume discounts to encourage you to buy more. Most parks that sell tickets or tokens also offer an all-inclusive pass, often in the form of a wristband (you'll need garden shears to cut the thing off). A number of parks have a special bundled pass covering the top five or so thrill rides. Some of these also allow you to skip to the front of the queue. Where tokens or tickets are involved, rides will be priced differently, with kiddie rides costing the least and thrill rides, flumes and roller coasters costing the most.

ADMISSIONS: WHERE THE DEALS ARE

AS WE SEE IT, there are two basic strategies to cutting your park admission costs: high-tech and low-tech. The simplest way to save money is to pre-purchase your park ticket online. But quite often you can also snag a deal using an old-fashioned paper coupon. Kind of quaint, we know, but we've seen cases where a greasy half-ripped coupon from a newspaper can knock dozens of pounds off park admission. Wherever you look, your ultimate goal is the 'buy one, get one free' coupon, often abbreviated as BOGOF.

unofficial **TIP**
Unless you're at a park to people-watch or just take in the scene, you're almost always better off springing for the all-inclusive wristband.

Starting with the simplest approach, look at the **park or attraction's website** at least a day before your planned trip. Nearly all parks offer a discount for pre-purchasing your ticket online, and some will let you pre-purchase over the phone. Not only will you save money – usually at least 10% and sometimes more – but you also may save something just as valuable: time. Usually you print your tickets off at home and then can bypass the purchase line and head straight to the turnstiles. This is such a valuable perk that we'd suggest pre-purchasing tickets even if it didn't save money. Read the details carefully at each park website, though. Some will have pre-purchasers pick up tickets at special customer-service windows. In a few cases, the tickets or wristbands must be mailed to you. And some parks cut off pre-purchases at midnight for tickets for the next day. That's to keep you from printing out discounted tickets at an Internet café 5 minutes before you come to the park.

Even if you haven't pre-purchased a ticket, study the admission options carefully. Many parks offer a **family ticket,** usually for two adults and two children, but with many variations. These will always offer a price break. Sometimes it's even cheaper to buy the family ticket at the park than to purchase individual tickets online. Some parks also offer cheaper prices **off-season** or for afternoon or evening admission. We've seen cases in which you can save £10 a person by waiting another week to visit. Of course, that's not always easy since parks rarely discount on high-traffic days like school breaks and bank holidays.

When you're at the park, ask carefully about the prices, particularly at zoos and attractions run by charitable organisations. Quite often the price includes an **optional donation** to the charity. Now, we're not Scrooges, and we believe in helping others. But we don't think donations should be sneaked past unwary customers, particularly those hounded by children who are eager to enter the park. If you want to include the donation, good for you. But remember you're under no obligation.

With **paper coupons,** the challenge is finding them. Some likely spots are park brochures and local newspapers. Also, it's worth stopping by or at least ringing the local tourist office, which often has coupons.

There are other schemes for saving money too, like deals offered through **partners.** Sometimes you can get a free park ticket by purchasing a specific brand of cheese or other consumer product. Local fast-food restaurants are also likely sources for coupons. These deals come and go, and are often listed online. Although there may be a hassle factor, the savings can add up. The best source we've found for these is through **moneysavingexpert.com.** And don't forget your trusty **search engine.** Just enter the park name and the word *coupon,* and you'll be amazed at what you may find. Other helpful sites for discounts: **topdogdays.com** and **daysoutguide.co.uk.**

Finally, if your plans include five or more parks within a year, a **Merlin Annual Pass** may pay for itself. Merlin, the world's second-largest theme-park company, owns the UK's major parks, including Alton Towers, Chessington World of Adventures, Legoland Discovery Centre Manchester, Legoland Windsor, Thorpe Park, the London Eye, Madame Tussauds London, Sea Life Centres and Sanctuaries, The Dungeons and Warwick Castle. For details see **merlinannualpass.co.uk.** Make sure to use the price calculator, which will tell you if it's worth shelling out for the pass.

Tesco Clubcard

If you're like many Britons, you're already handing over much of your pay cheque to Tesco, the world's third-largest retailer. Why not get something back? The conglomerate's loyalty scheme will let you earn free or discounted admission to many of the parks and attractions in this book. By some estimates, Tesco spends more than £1 billion a year on programme rewards. Simply put, if you shop at Tesco and don't have a card, you're simply leaving money on the table. (Some consumers are concerned that they give up their privacy by letting a retailer track every penny they spend. If you fall into that camp, you may want to skip it. But personally we think the downside is small and worth the trade-off.)

You sign up for the free programme by picking up an application at any store. You'll get a card and key fob in the mail and can track your points online. Simply provide your Clubcard number every time you check out at a Tesco store or make a purchase from its website. In most cases, for every £1 you spend you get two Tesco Clubcard reward points, which can add up quickly and are available for everything from groceries to credit-card purchases to buying a car through a Tesco partner. Track your balance online at **tesco.com/clubcard.**

Once you've collected 150 points (which represent £75 of purchases), they're converted into a Clubcard voucher worth £1.50 which is sent to you in your Clubcard statement. The more pounds spent, the more points collected and the more vouchers earned. Vouchers can then be used at Tesco for their face value, but we suggest converting at least some of them into Clubcard Rewards, which in turn can be redeemed for up to three times their value with partners. In that case, every £100 you spend is worth 200 points, or £2, which is worth up to £6 in tokens towards park admission. Or to think of it another way, the scheme can provide a 6% rebate on your Tesco purchases when you apply the credit towards theme-park admission.

Because the park tokens are mailed to you, Clubcard Rewards don't work for last-minute trips, and it's imperative that you plan ahead. Also check each attraction's rules carefully: some won't allow use of Clubcard Rewards for special events or discounted family tickets. Also, you generally have to redeem them in person at the park, which means you'll have to wait in line and won't get to take advantage of web discounts. Still, as legions of bargain-hunting park-goers have discovered, it's usually worth the hassle. With admission covered, you may feel more willing to splurge on treats or souvenirs. See **tesco.com/clubcard/rewards** for the list of participating reward-partners and details on redeeming.

As with any complex programme, many strategies exist for earning extra points. We like **moneysavingexpert.com,** which stays on top of this lucrative shadow economy.

GETTING THERE

THOUGH THE NATIVES ENJOY GRUMBLING ABOUT IT, the UK is blessed with a pretty darn good public-transportation system. Even though some parks and attractions are in rural, sometimes isolated areas, it is almost always possible to access a park or travel by train or bus. It may be cumbersome, expensive and time-consuming, but you can do it. If, however, you plan on visiting more than one park in a single day, you may spend most of your day on public transport. In this situation it's by far preferable to drive, whether in your own car or in a hired one.

Folk in the public-transportation industry often refer to 'the last mile', this being the Achilles heel of most transportation systems. It means the distance from the closest public-transport access point to your destination. If there's no viable, hopefully-convenient way to cover this distance, public transport has essentially got you nowhere (and also possibly left you nowhere). If you take a bus or train, you need to have a plan for that last mile. The distance may be walkable, as at Chessington, or be served by dedicated shuttle buses, as at Legoland, but sometimes a taxi is the only option. In this event you don't want to alight from public transport someplace where it's all but impossible to get a taxi. Enough said. When you research how to get to the park, make sure you have the last mile sorted out.

Some parks and some hotels provide a shuttle service. Shuttles are great so long as they run frequently and carry enough passengers to meet demand. Most, however, are severely strained in the morning, when everyone wants to go to the park at the same time, and in the late afternoon and early evening, when everyone's ready to go home. During these times you might be bypassed by several full shuttles until one comes along with space available.

If you're driving to a park in an area that you don't know well, don't count on roadside signs to get you to your destination. Download and print numbered directions and detailed maps from **Google Maps** (**maps.google .com**) or a comparable site, and conscript your front-seat passenger as a navigator. We were confronted with an obscene number of turns and directions on every here-to-there route we charted. They come fast and furious, and there's no way a driver can safely reference his map and directions while on the move. Even with a navigator, it's easy to go off-course. And then there are the closed and diverted roads that Google Maps isn't aware of, so be sure to carry a good detailed road map so you can sort out alternate routes if necessary.

*un*official **TIP**
Not infrequently did we encounter downpours of such proportions that a great many visitors abandoned the park at once. Here, if you decide to pack it in, you might be trading such cover as is available in the park for an unprotected spot while you wait for your shuttle. Our advice: stay in the park until the first wave clears out, or forget the shuttle and take a taxi.

The very best way to get where you're headed with the least amount of stress is to use a TomTom or some other programmable satnav device. It you have neither a satnav nor a passenger–navigator, expect to pull over about every 5 minutes to study your maps.

PRACTICAL STUFF

CREDIT CARDS Visa, MasterCard and Eurocard are accepted at almost all parks and attractions. American Express and JBC, among others, are accepted at most of the major parks and attractions but often not at smaller venues. Many parks that accept credit cards for admission or shop purchases will not accept them for food and drink in the park.

North Americans and others without a chip-and-PIN credit card can expect to encounter park staff who do not know how to process a card with a magnetic strip on the back. Most card processors have a slot in the lower front of the device and a scanner slot on the side. Cards without a chip must be scanned using the side slot. Once the card is scanned, the sales person must manually enter the amount to be charged. When the charge is authorised, you'll be given a paper summary of the transaction to sign. If you use the card in a full-service restaurant, there will be nowhere on the signature form for you to add a gratuity. We had to use cash for tips most of the time, though some restaurants would process a second, separate credit-card transaction for the tip.

RAIN If the weather is wet, go to the park anyway – the rain will serve to diminish the crowds. Because most rides and queues are not under cover, bring a rain jacket and/or an umbrella. We also recommend a hat with a peak, even if your rain jacket has a hood, and a small towel or cloth nappy to wipe off wet seats on the rides. If you forgot your rain-gear, no worries; almost all outdoor parks and attractions sell inexpensive (read: disposable) hooded macs or ponchos. Some parks such as Pleasure Beach Blackpool even sell them in the queue.

CLOSED RIDES, SHOWS AND EXHIBITS Most tourists attractions are works in progress, so it's likely that you will encounter rides, shows

---

BLOWIN' IN THE WIND

The British are very ecologically-minded, so unlike in North America, public loos almost never provide paper towels for drying your hands after washing. Instead, electric hand-driers of varying levels of sophistication are the rule. Our observation while working in the UK is that many North Americans do not understand how to use these driers. So for the edification of our fellow colonists, here are some handy instructions.

After washing:
1. Vigorously shake excess water off hands.
2. Press the START button to activate the machine.
3. Hold your hands under the airflow.
4. Repeat Steps 2 and 3.
5. Wipe hands on pants. (That's *trousers* to the rest of you.)

or exhibits closed for maintenance or refurbishment. Several parks and attractions list closed rides on their websites, so check those first. If a particular ride or such is absolutely essential to your visit, phone the park to confirm that it's open and operating. We don't know of any park or attraction that will discount or refund your admission because certain rides are closed.

SAME-DAY RE-ENTRY TO THE PARKS AND ATTRACTIONS Almost all parks and attractions will allow you to leave and return on the same day. The most common practice is for the park to stamp your hand as you exit. The stamp is very durable and will (usually) not come off when swimming or washing your hands. When you return to the park, you must show your hand stamp along with your valid admission ticket or wristband.

CAR PARKS Some car parks have staff on hand, especially in the morning, to direct you to a parking place. If you arrive after noon, resist being directed either by an attendant or sign to the far-flung car parks. By this time of day, many of those who arrived early will have completed their visit and vacated some prime parking slots close to the entrance.

Most car parks do not have numbered or otherwise identified rows or parking spaces. To complicate matters, some parks have multiple, often non-contiguous car parks (Warwick Castle has ten!). This means that you must take note of objects and landmarks such as telephone poles, trees, and hedges to find your way back to your car. Though you'll be impatient to get to the park, slow down for a moment and identify at least one or two objects to help guide you back.

At most parks and attractions it's a 5- to 10-minute walk from the car park to the entrance. Be aware that many car parks are unpaved, and some are actually in fields. These can become very muddy after a good rain. There were many times when we wished we had our wellies. As you would expect, these car parks also pose problems for pushchairs.

The majority of car parks are free of charge; amongst the ones that charge a fee, there are three payment systems: At a few parks you pay at a kiosk before entering the car park. Other parks use the 'pay and display' scheme: you pay your parking fee at an automated machine and receive a receipt that you display on your dashboard as proof of payment. Lastly, there are car parks where barriers block the exit. Here you buy a parking token either from an automated machine or at an admission purchase window. When you depart you insert the token in a machine that raises the barrier.

CAR PROBLEMS In car parks with security patrols, these folk can usually help you with a dead battery, flat tyre or other minor problems. If there's no security patrol, or if the problem is more serious, you're on your own. The exception is when you get bogged down in one of the aforementioned soggy, unpaved car parks. In this case, report your problem to guest relations and they'll dispatch someone to haul you out.

VISITORS WITH SPECIAL NEEDS Though most parks and attractions make some effort to accommodate non-ambulatory visitors, many areas and rides remain inaccessible to those with disabilities. Ramps are the exception and steps the rule in 90% of British theme parks, zoos, safari parks, industrial tours and farm experiences. Museums tend to be the most accessible of all tourist attractions. Theme parks, zoos and safari parks sometime have walkways with deep gravel or uneven surfaces not at all friendly to wheelchairs. Some parks and attractions provide information regarding accessibility on their websites, but most you'll have to query by post, email or telephone.

If you have dietary restrictions, then you're basically on your own, though you'll find a wide variety of food selections at the major parks. Elsewhere you're better off bringing you own food.

> *unofficial* **TIP**
> Before you make contact, study the rides and park layout on the park's website and determine which areas are of greatest interest. Ask about these specifically when requesting information about access for persons with disabilities.

If you have a special need not discussed here that requires a special accommodation – for example, admission of service dogs, preferential treatment of autistic children in queues or telecommunications devices for the deaf (TDDs) – contact the park or attraction beforehand.

SMOKING Most parks and attractions are smoke-free, though some provide designated smoking areas. It's unusual these days to find tobacco products for sale at theme parks and attractions.

ACCOMMODATION

FEWER THAN 5% OF THE PARKS and attractions described in this guide offer on-site accommodation. Among those that do are Alton Towers, Chessington World of Adventures and Pleasure Beach Blackpool. By far the best on-site or adjacent hotel is the **Big Blue Hotel** at Pleasure Beach Blackpool. If your room is on the west side of the hotel, you have an ocean view; if on the east side, you get a view of the park's roller coasters, including the quirky, one-of-a-kind Steeplechase coaster, where you're strapped to a carousel horse and sent racing around a steel track. (We promise we're not making this up.)

For your sleeping pleasure you can choose from traditional hotels, inns, bed-and-breakfasts and guest houses, among others. Hotels are usually more expensive than the other options but provide amenities such as lifts, swimming pools, restaurants, lounges, phones, air-conditioning, Internet connections and ample parking. Inns cover everything from small hotels to pubs with a few available guest rooms.

We're very partial to inns for their intimacy, cozy atmosphere and the opportunity to meet and mix with local patrons. It's lovely after a long day at the park to simply walk downstairs for a pint and a meal. Also, inns almost always have ample parking, whereas parking is a problem for many B&Bs and guest houses – the majority have private parking for three to five cars, but it wasn't unusual in our experience to have to park on the street. Most inns, emulating B&Bs, include a full waddle-away-from-the-table English breakfast. B&Bs and guest houses generally don't serve meals other than breakfast, and some guest houses serve no food at all. Quite a few B&Bs and guest houses offer a sitting room where guests can congregate.

For all types of accommodation mentioned above, rooms tend towards the small side. Televisions in guest rooms are pretty standard in every category of accommodation, as are complementary toiletries and electric kettles, complete with tea. Though some inns, B&Bs and guest houses have shared baths, en suite bathrooms are the norm, with most of these providing a shower. Almost all hotel rooms and 60% of guest rooms in the other categories provide showers. Some also feature baths, sometimes in combination with the shower and sometimes separate. Room décor and furnishings run from spartan to ultra-luxurious. Duvets are the rule, sheets and blankets the exception.

DUVET DISMAY

Allow us to digress for a moment to express wonderment at how Europeans can sleep, apparently in any season, under something modelled on a bivouac sack for an Arctic expedition. Those of us from the States usually last less than 5 minutes before heaving the duvet off the bed and kicking it into the corridor. For any of our readers who also take exception to sleeping under something hot enough to cook a Christmas goose, we recommend removing the duvet from its cover and using the cover as a sheet, or alternatively bringing your own top-sheet.

NATIONAL QUALITY ASSESSMENT SCHEME

THE UK HAS AN ACCOMMODATION-RATINGS SCHEME that was supposed to standardise ratings throughout the Kingdom so that a four-star lodging rating in England would mean the same thing as a four-star rating in Wales or Scotland. The system was the brainchild of Visit Britain (the overall UK tourism-promotion organisation), in conjunction with similar groups promoting Wales, Scotland, and Ireland, along with the Automobile Association (see **qualityintourism .com/asp/letsgetassessed.asp**). Unfortunately, the whole system got bogged down in semantics concerning the sort of accommodation that could use the word *hotel* in its name and in its adverts. The idea of the scheme was to insure apples-to-apples comparisons by classifying and defining an outrageous number of different accommodation types. This classifying and defining is intended to help you understand that hotels are different from, say, B&Bs. *Duh*.

What you need to know is this: whatever the accommodation, the more stars the better. So if you know the difference between the Savoy and a guest house in Southport, you needn't trouble yourself with all the definitions. Just don't come round whining that your guest house didn't have room service and a revolving restaurant.

For those curious about the scheme's other categories, here's a *partial* list. *Scheme designators* have been developed to help consumers understand the different types of accommodation available:

HOTEL By general definition, a hotel has a minimum of 6 bedrooms but more likely in excess of 20. It must also be licensed, offer formal accommodation with full service and serve dinner (unless suitable for the **Metro Hotel** category, below). Also, all bedrooms must be en suite or have a private bathroom.

COUNTRY HOUSE HOTEL A hotel with ample grounds or gardens, in a rural or semi-rural situation, with an emphasis on peace and quiet.

SMALL HOTEL A hotel with a maximum of 20 bedrooms. It is personally run by the proprietor and is likely to have limited convention business.

TOWN HOUSE HOTEL A high-quality town- or city-centre property of individual and distinctive style, with a maximum of 50 rooms and a high staff-to-guest ratio. Public areas may be limited. Possibly no dinner is served, but room service is available instead. Where a dining room is not available, room-service breakfast is acceptable.

METRO HOTEL A town or city hotel providing full services with the exception of dinner. It is within easy walking distance of a range of places to eat.

B&B Accommodation provided in a private house, run by the owner and with no more than six paying guests.

GUEST HOUSE Accommodation provided for more than six paying guests and run on a more commercial basis than a B&B. Usually more services, for example dinner, provided by staff as well as the owner.

FARMHOUSE B&B or guest-house accommodation provided on a working farm or smallholding.

INN Accommodation provided in a fully-licensed establishment. The bar will be open to non-residents and provide food in the evenings.

RESTAURANT WITH ROOMS Destination restaurant offering overnight accommodation, with the restaurant being the main business and open to non-residents. The restaurant should offer a high standard of food and restaurant service at least five nights a week and have a liquor licence. The property may have no more than 12 bedrooms.

ROOM ONLY Accommodation which may or may not offer breakfast. Accommodation may be annexed and is likely to be fully en suite. If breakfast is offered, this may be in the form of a tray placed in the room in the refrigerator, a breakfast pack available for separate purchase or a Continental self-service option.

SELF-CATERING Accommodation with its own kitchen and bathroom facilities. Most self-catering establishments take bookings by the week, generally from a Friday or Saturday, but short breaks are increasingly common.

In addition to the foregoing, the scheme also has classifications for caravan parks, tent parks, holiday parks (accommodation plus camping), chalets, hostels, university accommodation and dormitory rooms, narrowboats, hotel boats, cruisers (yachts), serviced apartments and, finally, to leave no stone unturned, 'alternative accommodation', which includes the following:

- Wigwams and camping pods
- Nomadic structures (tepees, yurts, safari tents, ready-erected tents)
- Railway carriages
- Shepherd's trailers
- Tree houses
- Romani (Gypsy) caravans
- Camper vans
- Submarines
- Churches
- Abbeys and convents
- Cabanas

For the sake of being totally comprehensive, we recommend several new classifications:

- Pass Out at Pub, Discovered Next Morning (not eligible for breakfast)
- Sleepovers at Zoos
- Caves
- Haunted Homes (extra charge for a room with a ghost)

RESEARCHING AND BOOKING ON THE WEB

MOST PROPERTIES ACROSS ALL CATEGORIES have websites where you can find photos of guest rooms, baths, dining rooms, the hotel facade and more. Look at these images carefully and you can get a pretty good sense of the property. More photos are better, and very few or no photos should raise warning flags.

When you find a property you like, it's a good idea to check out its address on Google Maps and Google Earth. This will tell you whether the property is on a busy or quiet street, what kind of neighbourhood it's in and how far it is from the places you want to visit. The one time we failed to check, we wound up in an industrial area. The desk clerk said, 'You can either have a room in the front, where there's a lot of road noise, or one in the back where the railway is.' We took the railway.

For our research trips we used two excellent search engines. For conventional and chain hotels, we used **kayak.co.uk**. Search for the town or city where you want to stay, and Kayak will present a host of options with links to the Internet sellers offering the best rates. B&Bs, inns and guest houses are not well represented on Kayak, so for these we used **bookingangels.com** and had a very good experience. Hotels often require advance payment of one night's accommodation to hold the reservation. Some B&Bs, inns and guest houses do this as well, while others will charge for the entire stay.

MAKING *the* MOST *of* YOUR TIME

HAVING ENOUGH TIME TO SEE EVERYTHING at a museum, zoo, safari park, aquarium or farm is usually not an issue. At theme parks, however, seeing and doing all that you'd like is often challenging. In several studies, theme-park patrons have stated that their level of satisfaction correlates directly with the number of shows and rides they are able to experience during their visit. Our mission, then, is to help you make the most of your time.

> *unofficial* **TIP**
> Read the payment and cancellation policies before booking any kind of accommodation. Also make sure you print your confirmation and have it with you when you check in. If you reserve using the phone, have the hotel fax, email or mail a written confirmation to you.

We've discussed previously the optimal time of day to arrive at various types of parks and tourist attractions; now we'll look at what to do once there.

THE CARDINAL RULES FOR SUCCESSFUL TOURING

MOST VISITORS DON'T HAVE MORE THAN TWO DAYS to devote to a given theme park. Some are en route to other destinations or may wish to sample additional nearby parks and attractions. For these visitors, efficient touring is a must. Even the most time-effective touring plan won't allow you to comprehensively cover two or more major theme parks in one day. Plan to allocate an entire day to each park.

One-Day Touring

A comprehensive one-day tour of any of Britain's major theme parks is possible, but it requires knowledge of the park, good planning, good navigation and plenty of energy and endurance. It leaves little time for sit-down meals, prolonged browsing in shops or lengthy breaks. One-day touring can be fun and rewarding, but allocating two days per park, especially for Thorpe Park, Chessington World of Adventures, Legoland, Alton Towers and Pleasure Beach Blackpool, is preferable. Especially if you have preschoolers in your party and plan to enjoy the children's rides, Oakwood Theme Park in Wales and Drayton Manor in Staffordshire could easily be added to the list.

Successfully touring of any large park hinges on three rules:

1. Determine in Advance What You Really Want to See

Which rides appeal to you most? Which ones would you like to experience if you have time left? What are you willing to forgo?

To help you set your touring priorities, we describe the theme parks and their rides and shows in detail in this book. We include the authors' evaluation of each ride and the opinions of the park's guests, both expressed as star ratings. Five stars is the highest rating.

Finally, because rides range from funfair-type rides and horse-drawn wagons to high-tech extravaganzas, we've developed a hierarchy of categories to pinpoint a ride's magnitude:

SUPER-HEADLINERS The best rides the theme park has to offer. Mind-boggling in size, scope and imagination. Represent the cutting edge of ride technology and design.

HEADLINERS Expensive, full-scale themed rides and theatre presentations. Modern in technology and design and employing a full range of special effects.

MAJOR RIDES More-modestly-themed rides, but ones that incorporate state-of-the-art technologies, or larger-scale rides of older design.

MINOR RIDES Funfair-type rides, small 'dark' rides (cars on a track, zigzagging through the dark), small theatre presentations, transportation rides and elaborate walk-through rides.

DIVERSIONS Exhibits, both passive and interactive. Includes playgrounds, video arcades and street entertainment.

Though not every ride, show or exhibit fits neatly into these descriptions, the categories provide a comparison of ride size and scope. Remember that bigger and more elaborate doesn't always mean better. Steeplechase, a minor ride at Pleasure Beach Blackpool, continues to be one of the park's most beloved. Likewise, for many young children, no ride, regardless of size, surpasses the Flying Jumbos (a Dumbo-like ride).

2. Arrive Early! Arrive Early! Arrive Early!

This is the single most important key to efficient touring and avoiding long queues at theme parks. First thing in the morning, there are no queues and fewer people. The same four rides you experience in an hour in early morning can take two to three times as long after 10.30 a.m. Eat breakfast before you arrive; don't waste prime touring time sitting in a restaurant.

The earlier a park opens, the greater your advantage. This is because most holiday-makers won't rise early and get to a park before it opens. Fewer people are willing to make an 8 a.m. opening than a 9 a.m.

opening. When a park opens at 10 a.m. or later, almost everyone arrives at the same time, so it's almost impossible to beat the crowd. If you visit during mid-summer, arrive at the turnstile 15–30 minutes before opening. During holiday periods, arrive 30–40 minutes early.

If getting the kids up earlier than usual makes for rough sailing, don't despair: you'll have a great time no matter when you get to the park. Many families with young children have found that it's better to accept the relative inefficiencies of arriving at the park a bit late than to jar the children out of their routine.

3. Avoid Bottlenecks

Helping you avoid bottlenecks is what the *Unofficial Guide* is about. This involves being able to predict where, when and why they occur. Concentrations of hungry people create bottlenecks at restaurants during lunch and dinner; concentrations of people moving towards the exit near closing time cause gift shops en route to clog; concentrations of visitors at new and popular rides, and at rides slow to load and unload, create logjams and long queues.

Our solution for avoiding bottlenecks: touring plans for theme parks where long queues can drastically limit what you're able to experience in a day. For the larger parks we also provide detailed information on rides and performances, enabling you to estimate how long you may have to wait in the queue and allowing you to compare rides for their crowd capacity. Touring plans are included in our coverage of the parks that merit them.

TOURING PLANS: WHAT THEY ARE AND HOW THEY WORK

See More, Do More, Wait Less

From the first *Unofficial Guide* in 1985, minimising our readers' wait in queues has been a top priority. Thus, we develop and offer our readers field-tested touring plans that allow them to experience as many rides as possible with the least amount of waiting in line.

Our touring plans have always been based on theme-park-traffic flow, ride capacity, the maximum time a guest is willing to wait (called a 'balking constraint'), walking distance between rides and waiting-time data collected at specific intervals throughout the day and at various times of year. The plans created for the California and Florida Disney parks originally derived from a combinatorial model (for anyone who cares) that married the well-known assignment problem of linear programming with queuing theory. The model approximated the most time-efficient sequence in which to visit the rides and shows of a specific park. After we created a preliminary touring plan from the model, we field-tested it in the park, using a test group, who followed our plan, and a control group, who didn't have our plan and who toured according to their own best judgement.

The two groups were compared, and the results were amazing. On days of heavy attendance, the groups touring without our plans spent an average of 3 hours more in queues and experienced 37% fewer rides than did those who did use the plans.

Over the years, this research has been recognised by both the travel industry and academe, having been cited by such diverse sources as the *New York Times, USA Today, Travel Weekly, Bottom Line, Money, Operations Research Forum,* CBS News, Fox News, the BBC, the Travel Channel, and the *Dallas Morning News,* among others.

John Henry and the Nail-driving Machine

As sophisticated as our model may sound, we recognised that it was cumbersome and slow, and that it didn't approximate the 'perfect' touring plan as closely as we desired. Moreover, advances in computer technology and science, specifically in the field of genetic algorithms, demonstrated that it wouldn't be long before a model, or programme, was created that would leave ours in the dust.

Have you ever heard the story of American folk hero John Henry, the fastest nail-driver on the railroad? One day a man appeared with a machine he claimed could drive spikes faster than any human. John Henry challenged the machine to a race, which he won but which killed him in the process. We felt a bit like John Henry: we were still very good at what we were doing, but we knew with absolute certainty that sooner or later we'd have to confront someone else's touring-plan version of a nail-driving machine.

Our response was to build our own nail-driving machine. We teamed up during the mid-1990s with Len Testa, a scientist and computer programmer who was working in the field of evolutionary algorithms and who, coincidentally, is a theme-park junkie. Marrying our many years of collecting observations and data to Len's vision and programming expertise, we developed a state-of-the-art programme for creating nearly-perfect touring plans.

Several university professors, many of them leaders in their fields, have contributed research or ideas to the software programme. Findings from early versions of the software have been published in peer-reviewed academic journals. The most recent versions of the programme are protected through pending patent applications. Special thanks go to Albert C. Esterline, PhD, of North Carolina A&T State University and Gerry V. Dozier, PhD, of Auburn University. Credit is also due to Nikolaos Sahinidis, PhD, as well as to his graduate students at the University of Illinois at Urbana-Champaign, who have contributed a number of exceptionally-helpful studies. Chryssi Malandraki, PhD, of United Parcel Service and Robert Dial, PhD, of the Volpe National Transportation System Center have likewise provided assistance and encouragement over the years.

It has been a process of evolution and refinement, but in each year of its development the new programme came closer to beating the results of our long-lived model. In 2002, at field trials during the busy spring school holiday, the new programme beat the best touring plan generated by the traditional *Unofficial* model by 90 minutes at the Magic Kingdom in Walt Disney World. This was in addition to the 3 hours saved by the earlier model. Getting there, however, wasn't easy.

The Challenge

One thing that makes creating good touring plans difficult is that there are many ways to see the same rides. For example at Thorpe Park, if we want to experience Saw – The Ride, Tidal Wave and Colossus as soon as the park opens, there are six ways to do so:

1. First ride Saw – The Ride, then Tidal Wave, then Colossus.
2. First ride Saw – The Ride, then Colossus, then Tidal Wave.
3. First ride Colossus, then Saw – The Ride, then Tidal Wave.
4. First ride Colossus, then Tidal Wave, then Saw – The Ride.
5. First ride Tidal Wave, then Colossus, then Saw – The Ride.
6. First ride Tidal Wave, then Saw – The Ride, then Colossus.

Some of these combinations make better touring plans than others. Because the queue for Saw – The Ride increases rapidly, it's best to ride this particular ride first thing in the morning. For similar reasons, it would be better to ride Colossus before Tidal Wave. In this example, Touring Plan 2 would probably save us the most time standing in queues. Touring Plan 5 would probably result in the most queuing.

As we add rides to our list, the number of possible touring plans grows rapidly. Adding a fourth ride would result in 24 possible touring plans, because there are four possible variations for each of the 6 plans listed previously. In general, the number of possible touring plans for n rides is $n \cdot (n-1) \cdot (n-2) \ldots \cdot 1$. (Don't let the mathematical notation throw you; if we plug in real numbers, it's quite simple.) For five rides, as an example, there are $5 \times 4 \times 3 \times 2 \times 1$ possible touring plans. If you don't have a calculator handy, that adds up to 120 potential plans. For 6 rides, there are $6 \times 5 \times 4 \times 3 \times 2 \times 1$, or 720 possible plans. A list of 10 rides has more than 3 million possible plans. The 21 rides in the Thorpe Park One-Day Touring Plan for Adults (excludes children's rides) have a staggering 51,090,942,171,709,440,000 possible touring plans. That's more than 51 billion billion combinations, or roughly six times as many as the estimated number of grains of sand on Earth. Adding in complexities such as live entertainment, parades, meals and breaks further increases the combinations.

Scientists have been working on similar problems for years. Companies that deliver packages, for example, plan each driver's route to minimise the distance driven, saving time and fuel. In fact, finding ways to visit many places with minimal effort is such a common problem that it has its own nickname: the travelling-salesman problem.

For more than a small number of rides, the number of possible touring plans is so large it would take a very long time for even a powerful computer to find the single best plan. A number of proposed techniques give very good, but not necessarily-exact, solutions to the travelling-salesman problem in a reasonable amount of time.

The *Unofficial Guide* Touring Plan programme contains two algorithms that allow it to quickly analyse tens of millions of possible plans in a very short time. (An algorithm is to a computer what a recipe is to a chef. Just as a chef takes specific steps to make a cake, a computer takes specific steps to process information. Those steps, when grouped, form an algorithm.) The programme can analyse crowd conditions at all rides, for example, and suggest the best times of day to visit. The software can also schedule rest breaks throughout the day. If you're going to eat lunch in the park, the software can suggest restaurants near where you'll be at lunchtime that will minimise the time you spend looking for food. Numerous other features are available, many of which we'll discuss in the next section.

The programme, however, is only part of what's needed to create a good touring plan. Good data is also important. We collect data in the theme parks at every conceivable time of year. At each park, researchers record the estimated wait at every ride, show and restaurant every 30 minutes, from park opening to closing. On a typical day at Alton Towers, for example, each researcher walks about 16 mi (25 km) and collects around 450 pieces of data. One of several research routes would start researchers at the Rita roller coaster in the Dark Forest section of the park. After collecting data on all of the rides in Dark Forest, they would continue to the rides and restaurants in adjacent Cloud Cuckoo Land. After that would come the Towers section of the park, then finally X-Sector, before they returned to Dark Forest for a 10-minute break before starting the next round of data collection. At the same time, additional volunteers collect data in the other sections of the park.

So how good are the touring plans in the *Unofficial Guide*? Our computer programme typically gets within about 2% of the optimal touring plan and finds an optimal plan for most straightforward situations around 70% of the time. To put this in perspective, if the hypothetical 'perfect' Adult One-Day Touring Plan took about 10 hours for the computer to calculate, the *Unofficial* touring plan would take around 10 hours and 12 minutes. Since it would take about 30 years for a really-powerful computer to find that 'perfect' plan, the extra 12 minutes is a reasonable trade-off.

Overview of the Touring Plans

Our touring plans are step-by-step guides for seeing as much as possible with minimum queuing. They're designed to help you avoid crowds and bottlenecks on days of moderate-to-heavy attendance. On days when attendance is lighter, the plans will save time and help organise your visit, but they won't be as critical to successful touring.

Variables That Affect the Success of the Touring Plans

The plans' success will be affected by how quickly you move from ride to ride; when and how many refreshment and toilet breaks you take; when, where and how you eat meals; and your ability (or lack thereof) to find your way around. Smaller groups almost always move faster than larger groups, and parties of adults generally cover more ground than families with young children. Switching off (page 77), also known as 'The Baby Swap' or child swapping, among other things, inhibits families with little ones from moving expeditiously among rides. Plus, some folk simply cannot conform to the plans' 'early to rise' conditions.

While we realise that following the plans isn't always easy, we nevertheless recommend continuous, expeditious touring until around noon. After noon, breaks and diversions won't affect the plans significantly.

Some variables that can profoundly affect the plans are beyond your control. Chief amongst these are the manner and timing of bringing a particular ride to capacity. If the queue builds rapidly before operators go to full capacity, you could have a long wait, even in early morning.

Another variable relates to the time you arrive for a theatre performance. You'll wait from the time you arrive until the end of the presentation in progress. Thus, if a show is 15 minutes long and you arrive 1 minute after it has begun, your wait will be 14 minutes. Conversely, if you arrive as the show is wrapping up, your wait will be only a minute or two.

Flexibility

The rides included in the touring plans are the most popular ones as determined by visitor surveys and crowd data. Even so, your favourite rides might be different. Fortunately, the touring plans are flexible. If a plan calls for a ride you don't wish to experience, simply skip it and move on to the next one. You can also substitute similar rides in the same area of the park. If a plan calls for, say, riding Dino Dipper at Legoland and you're not interested but you'd enjoy the Dino Safari (which is not on the plan), then go ahead and substitute it for the Dino Dipper. As long as the substitution is a similar ride – substituting a show for a ride won't work – and is pretty close to the ride called for in the touring plan, you won't compromise the plan's overall effectiveness.

What to Do if You Lose the Thread

Anything from a blister to a broken ride can throw off a touring plan. If unforeseen events interrupt a plan:

1. Skip 1 step on the plan for every 20 minutes' delay. If, for example, you lose your wallet and spend an hour finding it, skip three steps and pick up from there.
2. Forget the plan and organise the remainder of your day using the Recommended Attraction Visitation Times charts in the profiles for

the 'Big Five' theme parks. These timetables summarise the best times to visit each ride.

A multi-generational family wonders how to know if you're on track or not, writing:

> It seemed like the touring plans were very time-dependent, yet there were no specific times attached to the plan outside of the early morning. On more than one day, I often had to guess as to whether we were 'on track'.

Honestly, there *is* no objective measurement for being on track. Each family's or touring group's experience will differ to some degree. Whether your group is large or small, fast or slow, the sequence of rides in the touring plans will allow you to enjoy the greatest number of rides in the least possible time. Two quickly-moving adults will probably take in more rides in a specific time period than will a large group consisting of children, parents and grandparents. However, given the characteristics of the respective groups, each will maximise its touring time and experience as many rides as possible.

Will the Plans Continue to Work Once the Secret Is Out?

Yes! First, all the plans require that a patron be present when a park opens. Many people simply won't get up early while on vacation. Second, less than 1% of any day's attendance has been exposed to the plans – too few to affect results. Last, most groups tailor the plans, skipping rides or shows according to taste.

'Bouncing Around'

Many readers may object to crisscrossing a theme park, as our touring plans sometimes require. In most parks, the most popular rides are positioned across the park from one another. This is no accident. It's a method of more equally distributing guests throughout the park. If you want to experience the most popular rides in one day without long waits, you can arrive before the park fills and see those popular rides first (which requires crisscrossing the park), or you can enjoy the main rides on one side of the park first, then try the most popular rides on the other side during the hour or so before closing, when crowds presumably have thinned.

How Rigorously Should You Stick to the Plans?

We suggest following them religiously, especially in the mornings, if you're visiting during busy times. The consequence of touring spontaneity in peak season is hours of queuing. During quieter times, there's no need to be compulsive about following the plans.

Here are some comments from readers who have used our touring plans:

> *Emphasise perhaps not following the touring plans in low season. There's no reason to crisscross the park when there are no queues.*

> *Please let your readers know to stop along the way to various rides to appreciate what else may be going on around them. We encountered many families using the* Unofficial Guide *who became too serious about getting from one place to the next.*

What can we say? It's a lesser-of-two-evils situation. If you visit at a busy time, you can either rise early and hustle around, or you can sleep in and see less. When using the plans, however, relax and always be prepared for surprises and setbacks.

Touring-Plan Rejection

Some people don't respond well to the regimentation of a touring plan. If you encounter this problem with someone in your party, roll with the punches, as this couple did:

> *The rest of the group was not receptive to the use of the touring plans. I think they all thought I was being a little too regimented about planning this holiday. Rather than argue, I left the touring plans behind as we ventured off for the parks. You can guess the outcome. We took our camcorder with us and watched the movies when we returned home. About every 5 minutes or so, there's a shot of us all gathered around a park map trying to decide what to do next.*

PART THREE
BRITISH THEME PARKS *and* ATTRACTIONS *with* KIDS

UNLIKE IN AMERICA, where the better theme parks are designed for the whole family to enjoy together, British theme parks target specific age groups. Some, like the Gulliver's parks, tailor their rides and shows to the 12-and-under crowd. Parks concentrating on the teen and young-adult markets specialise in roller coasters and other thrill rides. With a couple of exceptions, most parks have a little something for everyone, with emphasis on 'a little'. The most diversified parks are Britain's largest: Chessington World of Adventures, Alton Towers, Pleasure Beach Blackpool, Thorpe Park and Legoland. Thorpe has only a few rides for younger children, while Legoland has but three or four rides that appeal to the teens-and-older population. The other three parks offer the most variety, with plenty of rides for every age group. Several medium-sized parks, like Flamingo Land and Drayton Manor, are likewise very balanced in their ride assortments. Zoos and safari parks, if they have rides at all, are skewed towards rides for younger children. Farm experiences are definitely designed for little ones. Almost all theme parks, zoos, safari parks and farm experiences provide elaborate playgrounds as well as picnic grounds. Aquariums are pretty age-neutral, while museums can run the gamut and come the closest in the UK to attractions that families can tour together.

The **ECSTASY** *and the* **AGONY**

ALMOST ALL PARENTS BRIGHTEN at the prospect of guiding their children through a special day at a theme park. But the reality of taking a young child can be closer to agony than to ecstasy. Most young children are as picky about rides as they are about what they eat. And would you be surprised to learn that almost 60% of preschoolers said the thing they liked best about their holiday was the hotel swimming pool or the beach? You can get a sense of whether the park you're considering is age-appropriate for your children by checking out the rides on the park's website. Are there enough features that your children would enjoy to warrant the expense? This question is especially important if the park charges for an all-inclusive admission, less so for parks where you pay for rides individually. In the latter case, you pay only for the rides your children enjoy. Another question is whether you'd increase the probability of a successful visit by waiting a year or two. Is your child adventuresome enough to sample the variety of rides and shows offered? Does your child meet the rides' minimum height and age requirements? Finally, will your child have sufficient endurance and patience to cope with queues and large crowds?

IT'S ABOUT HAVING FUN

GETTING IN TOUCH WITH YOUR FEELINGS When you or your children get tired and irritable, take a break. Trust your instincts. What would feel best? Another ride? An ice-cream? Or going back to the hotel for a nap?

Levels of stamina can vary significantly within a family. Think in terms of least common denominators. Somebody is going to run out of steam first, and when he or she does the whole family will be affected. Sometimes a snack break will revive the tired trooper. Sometimes, however, it's better to leave the park. Pushing the weary or discontented beyond their capacity will spoil the day for them – and you. Be prepared to respond to members of your group who flag. *Hint:* 'We've driven 200 mi to take you to Alton Towers and now you're ruining everything!' is *not* an appropriate response.

> *unofficial* **TIP**
> No one is forcing you to experience every single ride and show. Focus on having fun and enjoying a great day, not on 'getting your money's worth'.

BUILDING ENDURANCE Though most children are active, their normal play usually doesn't condition them for the exertion required to tour a theme park or large zoo or museum. Start family walks four to six weeks before your trip to get in shape.

SETTING LIMITS AND MAKING PLANS In order to avoid arguments and disappointment, establish guidelines for each day that everybody will commit to. Include the following:

1. Wake-up time and breakfast plans
2. When to depart for the park
3. What to take with you
4. A policy for splitting the group or for staying together
5. What to do if the group gets separated or someone is lost
6. How long you intend to tour in the morning and what you want to see, including plans in the event a ride is closed or too crowded
7. A policy on what you can afford for snacks
8. How late you'll stay at the park
9. Dinner plans

10. A policy for buying souvenirs, including who pays: Mum and Dad or the kids
11. Bedtimes

BE FLEXIBLE Any day includes surprises; be prepared to adjust your plan. Listen to your intuition.

WHAT KIDS WANT According to research by Yesawich, Pepperdine, Brown, and Russell, 71% of children between the ages of 6 and 17 say they need a holiday because school and homework get them down. The chart following shows what kids want and don't want when taking a holiday. Kids surveyed have a lot in common about what they do want, less so concerning what they don't.

WHAT DO KIDS WANT?	WHAT DO KIDS NOT WANT?
To go swimming/have pool time 80%	To get up early 52%
To eat in restaurants 78%	To ride in a car 36%
To stay at a hotel or resort 76%	To play golf 34%
To visit a theme park 76%	To go to a museum 31%
To stay up late 73%	

Concerning what kids don't want, these are relatively-high percentages; but consider that if 31% of children don't want to go to a museum, 69% are at least neutral about going. It's the old glass-half-full, half-empty thing.

MAINTAINING SOME SEMBLANCE OF ORDER AND DISCIPLINE Okay, okay, wipe that smirk off your face. Order and discipline when travelling may seem like an oxymoron to you, but you won't be hooting when your 5-year-old launches a tantrum in the middle of the theme park. Your willingness to give this subject serious consideration before you leave home may well be the most important element of your pre-trip preparation.

Discipline and maintaining order are more difficult when travelling than at home because everyone is, as one mum puts it, 'in and out' – in strange surroundings and out of the normal routine. For children, it's hard to contain excitement and anticipation, which pop to the surface in the form of fidgety hyperactivity, nervous energy and, sometimes, acting up. Confinement in a car, plane or hotel room only exacerbates the situation, and kids often tend to be louder than normal, more aggressive with siblings and much more inclined to push the envelope of parental patience. Once you're in the theme parks, it doesn't get much better. There's more elbow room, but with it come over-stimulation, crowds, the vagaries of weather, and miles of walking. All this, coupled with marginal or inadequate rest, can lead to a meltdown in the most harmonious of families.

Sound parenting and standards of discipline practised at home, applied consistently, will suffice to handle most situations on holiday. Still, it's instructive to study the hand you're dealt when travelling. For starters, aside from being jazzed and ablaze with adrenaline, your kids may believe that rules followed at home are somehow suspended when travelling. Parents reinforce this misguided intuition by being inordinately lenient in the interest of maintaining peace in the family. While some of your home protocols (like kids cleaning their plates and going to bed at a set time) might be relaxed to good effect on holiday, differing from your normal approach to discipline can precipitate major misunderstanding and possibly disaster.

Children, not unexpectedly, are likely to believe that a holiday is intended expressly for them. This reinforces their focus on their own needs and largely erases any consideration of yours. Such a mind-set dramatically increases their sense of hurt and disappointment when you correct them or deny them something they want. An incident that would hardly elicit a pouty lip at home could well escalate to tears or defiance when travelling.

The stakes are high for everyone on a holiday – for you because of the cost in time and money, but also because your holiday represents a rare opportunity for rejuvenation and renewal. The stakes are high for your children too. Children tend to romanticise travel, building anticipation to an almost unbearable level. Discussing the trip in advance can ground expectations to a certain extent, but a child's imagination will, in the end, trump reality every time. The good news is that you can take advantage of your children's emotional state to establish pre-set rules and conditions for their conduct while on holiday. Because your children want what's being offered *sooooo* badly, they will be unusually accepting and conscientious regarding whatever rules are agreed upon.

> **unofficial TIP**
> It's important before you depart on your trip to discuss your holiday needs with your children, and to explore their wants and expectations as well.

According to *Unofficial Guide* child psychologist Karen Turnbow, PhD, successful response to (or avoidance of) behavioural problems on the road begins with a clear-cut disciplinary policy at home. Both at home and on holiday the approach should be the same, and should be based on the following key concepts:

1. LET EXPECTATIONS BE KNOWN Discuss what you expect from your children, but don't try to cover every imaginable situation. Cover expectations regarding compliance with parental directives, treatment of siblings, resolution of disputes, schedules (including morning wake-up and bedtimes), courtesy and manners, staying together and who pays for what.

2. EXPLAIN THE CONSEQUENCES OF NONCOMPLIANCE Detail very clearly and firmly the consequence of not meeting expectations. This should be very straightforward and unambiguous: 'If you do (or don't do) X, this is what will happen.'

3. WARNING You are dealing with excited, expectant children, not machines, so it's important to issue a warning before meting out discipline. It's critical to understand that we're talking about one unequivocal warning rather than multiple warnings or nagging. These last undermine your credibility and make your expectations appear relative or less than serious. Failing to deliver on a warning also effectively passes control of the situation from you to your child (who sometimes may continue acting up as an attention-getting strategy).

4. FOLLOW THROUGH If you say you're going to do something, do it. Full stop. Children must understand that you mean business.

5. CONSISTENCY Inconsistency makes discipline a random event in the eyes of your children. Random discipline encourages random behaviour, which translates to a nearly-total loss of parental control. Long-term, both at home and on the road, your response to a given situation or transgression must be perfectly predictable. Structure and repetition, essential for a child to learn, cannot be achieved in the absence of consistency.

Although the previous methods are the five biggies, several corollary concepts and techniques are worthy of consideration:

Understand that whining, tantrums, defiance, sibling friction and even holding up the group are ways in which children communicate with parents. Frequently the object or precipitant of a situation has little or no relation to the unacceptable behaviour. A fit may on the surface appear to be about the ice-cream you refused to buy little Robby, but there's almost always something deeper, a subtext that is closer to the truth (this is why ill behaviour often persists after you give in to a child's demands). As often as not, the real cause is a need for attention. This need is so powerful in some children that they will subject themselves to certain punishment and parental displeasure to garner the attention they crave, even if it's negative.

To get at the root cause of the behaviour in question requires both active listening and empowering your child with a 'feeling vocabulary'. Active listening is a concept that's been around a long time – it involves being alert not only to what a child says but also to the context in which it's said, to the words used and possible subtext, to the child's emotional state and body language and even to what's not said. This sounds complicated, but it's basically being attentive to the larger picture and, more to the point, being aware that there *is* a larger picture.

It all begins with convincing your child that you're willing to listen attentively and take what he's saying seriously. By listening to your child, you help him transcend the topical by re-framing the conversation to address the underlying emotional state(s). That Nigel's brother hit him may have precipitated the mood-state, but the act is topical and of secondary importance. What you want is for your child to be able to communicate how that makes him feel, and to get in touch with those emotions. When you reduce an incident (hitting) to the emotions triggered – anger, hurt, rejection – you have the foundation for helping him develop constructive coping strategies. Being in touch with one's feelings and developing constructive coping strategies are essential to emotional well-being, and they also have a positive effect on behaviour. A child who can tell his mother why he is distressed is a child who has discovered a coping strategy far more effective, not to mention easier for all concerned, than a tantrum.

Children are almost never too young to begin learning a feeling vocabulary. And helping your child to be in touch with – and to communicate – his or her emotions will stimulate you to focus on your feelings and mood states in a similar way. In the end, with persistence and effort, the whole family will achieve a vastly-improved ability to communicate.

> *unofficial* **TIP**
> Helping your child develop a feeling vocabulary consists of teaching your child to use words to describe what's going on. The idea is to teach the child to articulate what's really troubling him, to be able to identify and express emotions and mood-states in language.

Until you get the active listening and feeling vocabulary going, be careful not to become part of the problem. There's a whole laundry-list of adult responses to bad behaviour that only make things worse. Hitting, swatting, yelling, name-calling, insulting, belittling, using sarcasm, pleading, nagging and inducing guilt (as in 'We've spent hundreds of pounds on this holiday, and now you're spoiling it for everyone!') figure prominently on the list.

Responding to a child appropriately in a disciplinary situation requires thought and preparation. Following are things to keep in mind and techniques to try when your world blows up while waiting in the queue for the carousel.

1. BE THE ADULT It's well understood that children can push their parents' buttons faster and more skillfully than just about anyone or anything else. They've got your number, know precisely how to elicit a response and are not reluctant to go for the jugular. Fortunately (or unfortunately), you're the adult, and to deal with a situation effectively, you've got to act like one. If your kids get you ranting and caterwauling, you effectively abdicate your adult status. Worse, you suggest by way of example that being out of control is an acceptable expression of hurt or anger. No matter what happens, repeat the mantra 'I am the adult in this relationship.'

2. FREEZE THE ACTION Being the adult and maintaining control almost always translates to freezing the action (to borrow a sports term). Instead of responding in knee-jerk fashion – that is, at a maturity level closer to your child's than yours – freeze the action by disengaging. Wherever you are or whatever the family is doing, stop in place and concentrate on one thing, and one thing only: getting all involved calmed down. Practically speaking, this usually means initiating a time-out. It's essential that you take this action immediately. Grabbing your child by the arm or collar and dragging him towards the car or hotel room only escalates the turmoil by prolonging the confrontation and by adding a coercive physical dimension to an already-volatile emotional event. For the sake of everyone involved, including the people around you (as when a toddler throws a tantrum in church), it's essential to retreat to a more private place. Choose the first place available. Firmly sit the child down and refrain from talking to him until you've both cooled off. This might take a little time, but the investment is worthwhile. Truncating the process is like trying to get on your feet too soon after surgery.

3. ISOLATE THE CHILD You'll be able to deal with the situation more effectively and expeditiously if the child is isolated with one parent. Dispatch the uninvolved members of your party for a snack break or have them go on with the activity or itinerary without you (if possible), and arrange for a rendezvous later at an agreed time and place. In addition to letting the others get on with their day, isolating the offending child with one parent relieves him of the pressure of being the group's focus of attention and object of anger. Equally important, isolation frees you from the scrutiny and expectations of the others in regard to how to handle the situation.

4. REVIEW THE SITUATION WITH THE CHILD If, as discussed a while back, you've made your expectations clear, stated the consequences of failing to meet those expectations and administered a warning, review the situation with the child and follow through with the discipline warranted. If, as often occurs, things are not so black-and-white, encourage the child to communicate his feelings. Try to uncover what occasioned the acting up. Lectures and accusatory language don't work well here, nor do threats. Dr Turnbow suggests that a better approach (after the child is calm) is to ask, 'What can we do to make this a better day for you?'

5. FREQUENT TANTRUMS The preceding four points relate to dealing with an incident as opposed to a chronic condition. If a child frequently acts up or throws tantrums, you'll need to employ a somewhat different strategy.

Tantrums are cyclical events evolved from learned behaviour. A child learns that he or she can get your undivided attention by acting up. When you respond, whether by scolding, admonishing, threatening or negotiating, your response draws you further into the cycle and prolongs the behaviour. When you accede to the child's demands, you reinforce the effectiveness of the tantrum and raise the cost of capitulation next time around. When a child thus succeeds in monopolising your attention, he effectively becomes the person in charge.

To break this cycle, you must disengage from the child. The object is to demonstrate that the cause-and-effect relationship (that is, tantrum elicits parental attention) is no longer operative. This can be accomplished by refusing to interact with the child as long as the untoward behaviour continues. Tell the child that you're unwilling to discuss his problem until he calms down. You can ignore the behaviour, remove yourself from the child's presence (or vice versa) or isolate the child with a time-out. It's important to disengage quickly and decisively, with no discussion or negotiation.

Most children don't pick the family holiday as the time to start throwing tantrums. The behaviour will be evident before you leave home, and home is the best place to deal with it. Be forewarned, however, that bad habits die hard, and that a child accustomed to getting attention by throwing tantrums will not simply give up after a single instance of disengagement. More likely, the child will at first escalate the intensity and length of his tantrums. With your consistent refusal over several weeks or even months to respond to his behaviour, however, he will finally adjust to the new paradigm.

Children are cunning as well as observant. Many understand that a tantrum in public is embarrassing to you and that you're more likely to cave in than you would at home. Once again, consistency is the key, along with a bit of anticipation. When travelling, it's not necessary to retreat to the privacy of a hotel room to isolate your child. You can carve out space for a time-out almost anywhere: on a theme-park bench, in your car, in a loo, even on the pavement.

You can often spot the warning signs of an impending tantrum and head it off by talking to the child before he reaches an explosive emotional pitch. And don't forget that tantrums are about getting attention. Giving your child attention when things are on an even keel often pre-empts acting up.

6. SALVAGE OPERATIONS Who knows what evil lurks in the hearts of children? What's for sure is that they're full of surprises, and sometimes the surprises are not good. If your sweet child manages to pull a stunt of mammoth proportions, what do you do? This happened to an Ohio couple, resulting in the offending kid pretty much being grounded for life. Fortunately there were no injuries or lives lost, but the parents had to determine what to do for the remainder of the holiday. For starters, they split up the group. One parent escorted the offending child back to the hotel, where he was effectively confined to his guest room for the duration. That evening, the parents arranged for in-room sitters for the rest of the stay. Expensive? You bet. But better than watching your whole holiday go down the tube.

Another family at a theme park had a similar experience, although the offence was of a more modest order of magnitude. Because it was the last day of their holiday, they elected to place the misbehaver in a time-out, in the theme park, for the rest of the day. One parent monitored the culprit while the other parent and the siblings enjoyed the rides. At agreed times the parents would switch places. Once again, not ideal, but preferable to stopping the holiday.

ABOUT *the* UNOFFICIAL GUIDE TOURING PLANS

PARENTS WHO USE OUR TOURING PLANS are often frustrated by interruptions and delays caused by their young children. Here's what to expect:

1. **Our touring plans call for visiting rides in a sequence, often skipping rides along the way.** Children don't like to skip *anything*! If something catches their eye, they want to see it that moment. Some can be persuaded to skip rides if parents explain their plans in advance. Other kids flip out at skipping something.
2. **Children have an instinct for finding the WC.** We have seen adults with maps search interminably for a toilet. Young children, however, including those who can't read, will head for the nearest WC with the certainty of a homing pigeon. You can be sure your children will ferret out (and want to use) every loo in the park.
3. **If you're using a pushchair, you won't be able to take it into theatres or onto rides.** This usually also includes in-park transport.
4. **You might not finish the touring plan.** Varying hours of operation, crowds, your group's size, your children's ages and your stamina will all affect how much of the plan you'll complete. Tailor your expectations to this reality or you'll be frustrated, as was this mum of two:

    We don't understand how anyone could fit everything you have on your plans into the time allotted while attending to small children. We found that long queues, potty stops and nappy changes, pushchair searches and breaks ate huge chunks of time.

While our touring plans allow you to make the most of your time at the parks, it's impossible to define what *most* will be. It differs from family to family. If you have two young children, you probably won't see as much as two adults will. If you have four children, you probably won't see as much as a couple with only two children.

STUFF *to* THINK ABOUT

BLISTERS AND SORE FEET All guests should wear comfortable, broken-in shoes, and socks that wick away perspiration. If you or your children are susceptible to blisters, bring along some pre-cut moleskin and blister plasters. They offer excellent protection, stick well and won't sweat off. When you feel a 'hot spot', stop, air out your foot and place a moleskin plaster over the area before a blister forms. Moleskin is available at chemists. Preschoolers or toddlers may not say they're developing a blister until it's too late, so inspect their feet two or more times a day.

FIRST AID Almost all theme parks and attractions have a first-aid centre. If you or your children have a medical problem, seek it out at once.

These centres are friendlier than most doctor's clinics and are accustomed to treating everything from paper cuts to allergic reactions.

CHILDREN ON MEDICATION Some parents of hyperactive children on medication discontinue or decrease the child's dosage at the end of the school year. If you have such a child, be aware that theme parks and attractions might overstimulate him or her. Consult your physician before altering your child's medication regimen.

SUNGLASSES If your younger children wear sunglasses, put a strap or string on the frames so the glasses will stay on during rides and can hang from the child's neck while indoors. This also works for adults.

INFANTS AND TODDLERS AT THE THEME PARKS Some larger parks have centralised facilities for infant and toddler care. Everything necessary for changing nappies, preparing formulas and warming bottles, along with food, is available. Supplies are for sale, and rockers and special chairs for nursing mothers are often provided. In addition, both gents' and ladies' WCs in many parks have changing tables. Unless otherwise stated, infants and toddlers are allowed on any ride that doesn't have minimum height or age restrictions. Some rides have a lap-bar that descends when the ride begins. Because it's possible for toddlers to slip under the lap-bar, hold on to your child throughout the ride.

PUSHCHAIRS

ONLY ABOUT 12% OF BRITAIN'S THEME PARKS and attractions have pushchairs for hire. Hire rates vary, but it is almost always necessary to make a refundable cash deposit. Hired pushchairs are too large for all infants and many toddlers. If you plan to hire a pushchair for your infant or toddler, bring pillows, cushions or rolled towels to buttress him in. Bringing your own pushchair is permitted. Your pushchair is unlikely to be stolen, but mark it with your name and something distinctive like a bright scarf. Walkways in theme parks and most attractions are usually fine, though you might encounter loose gravel or soft sand and, in unpaved car parks, mud. Zoos and farm experiences are the most challenging.

LOST CHILDREN

ALTHOUGH IT'S AMAZINGLY EASY to lose a child (or two) in the theme parks and attractions, it usually isn't a serious problem – employees are schooled in handling the situation. If you lose a child, report it to an employee. Paging is almost never used, but in an emergency many parks will make an exception. In most parks, if an employee encounters a lost child, he or she will take the child immediately to the park's child/baby centre or some other designated place.

Sew a label into each child's shirt that states his or her name, your name, the name of your hotel (if applicable) and, if you have one, your mobile-phone number. Accomplish the same thing by writing the information on a strip of masking tape. Security professionals suggest the information be printed in small letters and the tape be affixed to the outside of the child's shirt, 5″ (12 cm) below the armpit. Also, name tags can be obtained at the major theme parks.

One mum recommends recording vital info for each child on a plastic key tag or luggage tag and affixing it to the child's shoe. She also snaps a photo of the kids each morning to document what they're wearing. One way to better keep track of your family is to buy each person a 'holiday uniform' – for example, a brightly- and distinctively-coloured T-shirt. A Swindon, Wiltshire, mum offers this advice:

> *In case they got lost, I photo'd my 7-year-old twins every morning so we had a picture of what they were wearing. They wore wristbands with our mobile-phone numbers on them. I made one adult responsible for each twin for the morning so that no one assumed someone else was holding their hand; then we switched after lunch. We also taught them if they got lost to shout our first names, not just 'Mum' or 'Dad.'*

HOW KIDS GET LOST

CHILDREN GET SEPARATED FROM THEIR PARENTS every day at theme parks and attractions under remarkably similar (and predictable) circumstances:

1. PREOCCUPIED SOLO PARENT The party's only adult is preoccupied with something like buying refreshments, loading the camera or using the WC. Junior is there one second and gone the next.

2. THE HIDDEN EXIT Sometimes parents wait on the sidelines while two or more young children experience a ride together. Parents expect the kids to exit in one place and the youngsters pop out elsewhere. Exits from some rides are distant from entrances. Know exactly where your children will emerge before letting them ride by themselves.

3. AFTER THE SHOW At the end of many shows and rides, a theme-park staffer says something like 'Check for personal belongings and take small children by the hand.' When dozens of people leave a ride simultaneously, it's easy for parents to lose their children unless they have direct contact.

4. WC PROBLEMS Mum tells 6-year-old Tommy, 'I'll be sitting on this bench when you come out of the toilet.' Three possibilities: (1) Tommy exits through a different door and becomes disorientated (Mum may not know there's another door). (2) Mum decides she also will use the loo and Tommy emerges to find her gone. (3) Mum pokes around in a shop while keeping an eye on the bench but misses Tommy when he comes out.

If you can't accompany with your child to the toilet, make sure there's only one exit. Designate a distinctive meeting-spot and give clear instructions: 'I'll meet you by this flagpole. If you get out first, stay right here.' Have your child repeat the directions back to you. When children are too young to leave alone, sometimes you have to think outside the box. Pushchairs won't fit in a regular WC stall, for example, but will in a stall for disabled persons.

5. SHOWS AND STREET ENTERTAINMENT There are many shows and street performances during which the audience stands. Children tend to jockey for a better view. By moving a little this way and that, the child quickly puts distance between you and him before either of you notices.

6. AQUARIUMS AND MUSEUMS Many museums and aquariums have very convoluted, and sometimes multi-storey, layouts. You're looking at the rays while Teddy, 8 feet away, is looking at an alligator. After a minute you turn around and he's gone. Especially when the museum or aquarium is congested and/or dimly lit, children can vanish in a heartbeat. As before, establish a meeting-place in case the group becomes separated, and in the case of a younger child, report him missing to a staff member.

KIDS *and* SCARY STUFF

FOR ANY CHILD, THEME-PARK RIDES and shows are adventures, some of them scary. There are rides with menacing witches and ghouls popping out of their graves, all done with humour – provided you're old enough to understand the joke. You can reliably predict that such rides will, at one time or another, send a young child into system overload. Be sensitive, alert and prepared for almost anything, even behaviour that is out of character for your child. Most children take the scary stuff in stride, and others are easily comforted by an arm around the shoulder or a squeeze of the hand. Parents who know that their kids tend to become upset should take it slow and easy, sampling more-benign rides, gauging reactions and discussing with the children how they felt about what they saw.

Sometimes young children will rise above their anxiety in an effort to please their parents or siblings. This doesn't necessarily indicate a mastery of fear, much less enjoyment. If children leave a ride in apparently good shape, ask if they would like to go on it again – not necessarily now, but sometime. The response usually will indicate how much they actually enjoyed the experience.

Evaluating a child's capacity to handle the visual and tactile effects of a theme park requires patience, understanding and experimentation. Each of us has our own demons. Help your children understand that it's okay if they get frightened and that their fear doesn't lessen your love or respect. Take pains not to compound the discomfort by making a child feel inadequate; try not to undermine self-esteem, impugn courage or ridicule. Most of all, don't induce guilt by suggesting that the child's trepidation might be ruining the family's fun. It's also sometimes necessary to restrain older siblings' taunting.

A visit to a major theme park is more than an outing or an adventure for a young child. It's a testing experience, a sort of controlled rite of passage. If you help your little one work through the challenges, the time can be immeasurably rewarding and a bonding experience for you both.

> *unofficial* **TIP**
> If a child balks at or is frightened by a ride, respond constructively. Let your children know that lots of people – adults and children – are scared by what they see and feel.

THE FRIGHT FACTOR

WHILE EACH YOUNGSTER IS DIFFERENT, following are seven ride elements that alone or combined could push a child's buttons and indicate that a certain ride isn't age-appropriate for that child:

1. NAME OF THE RIDE Young children will naturally be apprehensive about something called Ghost Train (Blackpool) or Tomb Blaster (Chessington).

2. VISUAL IMPACT OF THE RIDE FROM OUTSIDE Many roller coasters and thrill rides look scary enough to give adults second thoughts, and they terrify many young children.

3. VISUAL IMPACT OF THE INDOOR QUEUING AREA The dark, wet tunnels of Raptor Attack at Lightwater Valley or the menacing swamp of Pirate Adventure at Drayton Manor can frighten children before they even approach the boarding platform.

4. INTENSITY OF THE RIDE OR SHOW Some rides inundate the senses with sights, sounds, movement and even smells. Duel at Alton Towers, for example, combines loud sounds, lasers, lights and animatronics to create a total sensory experience. For some children, this is two or three senses too many.

5. VISUAL IMPACT OF THE RIDE Sights in various rides range from falling boulders to revolving chambers, from torture chambers to menacing demons. What one child calmly absorbs may scare the socks off another the same age.

6. DARK Many rides operate indoors in the dark. For some children, this triggers fear. A child who gets frightened on one dark ride – Laser Raiders at Legoland, for example – may be unwilling to try other indoor rides.

7. THE TACTILE EXPERIENCE OF THE RIDE Some rides are wild enough to cause motion sickness, wrench backs and discombobulate guests of any age.

A BIT OF PREPARATION

WE RECEIVE MANY TIPS FROM PARENTS telling how they prepared their young children for their theme-park experience. A common strategy is to acquaint children with the characters and stories behind the rides by reading books or watching associated movies. Today, almost every ride in every theme park can be seen on **YouTube** (**youtube.com**). The quality of the video for dark indoor attractions is usually pretty dismal, but you can get an idea of what to expect. Videos of outdoor rides are plentiful and usually of acceptable quality.

A WORD ABOUT HEIGHT REQUIREMENTS

A NUMBER OF RIDES REQUIRE CHILDREN to meet minimum height and age requirements. If you have children who are too short or too young to ride, you have several options, including switching off (covered a bit later) and splitting the group. Although the alternatives may resolve some practical and logistical issues, your smaller children may nonetheless resent their older (or taller) siblings who qualify to ride the big coasters and thrill rides. If you have a child whom you know won't meet the minimum height requirement, split him from the group to do something fun with Mum or Dad *before* you come to the ride that he's not tall enough to experience. Reunite your group later. Understand, however, that you'll be doing this all day if you take a younger child to Thorpe Park or one of several other parks where extreme thrill rides are the name of the game.

> *unofficial* **TIP**
> In addition to using this guide, we recommend checking out minimum height requirements at the theme parks' websites before you leave home.

QUEUE STRATEGIES *for* PARENTS *with* YOUNG CHILDREN

CHILDREN HOLD UP BETTER THROUGH THE DAY if you limit the time they spend in queues. Arriving early and using our touring plans greatly reduce waiting. Here are other ways to lessen stress for children:

QUEUE GAMES Anticipate that children will get restless in a queue, and plan activities to reduce the stress and boredom. In the morning, have waiting children discuss what they want to see and do during the day. Later, play simple games such as Twenty Questions. Queues move continuously; games requiring pen and paper are impractical. Waiting in the holding area of a theatre attraction is a different story. Here, noughts and crosses, hangman, drawing and colouring make the time fly.

LAST-MINUTE ENTRY If a ride can accommodate many people at once, standing in a queue is often unnecessary. Instead of standing in a crowd, grab a snack and sit in the shade until loading is under way. When the queue is almost gone, join it. At large-capacity shows such as *Happy Feet 4-D* at Drayton Manor, ask the park staffer how long it will be until guests are admitted for the next show. If it's 15 minutes or more, take a toilet break or get a snack, returning a few minutes before show time. Food and drink aren't allowed in most shows; be sure you have time to finish your snack before entering.

SWITCHING OFF Many coasters and thrill rides employ a scheme known as switching off, child swapping, the Baby Swap, and the like. To switch off, there must be at least two adults. Adults and children wait in the queue together. When you reach a staff member, say you want to switch off. The staff member will allow everyone, including young children, to enter the ride. When you reach the loading area, one adult rides while the other stays with the kids. Then the riding adult disembarks and takes charge of the children while the other adult rides. Rides where switching off is practised are orientated to more-mature guests. Sometimes it takes a lot of courage for a child just to move through the queue holding Dad's hand. In the boarding area, many children suddenly fear abandonment when one parent leaves to ride. Prepare your children for switching off, or you might have an emotional crisis on your hands. During our research we encountered ride staff who weren't familiar with the concept, but once we explained it to them they were able to accommodate us.

LAST-MINUTE COLD FEET If your young child balks just before boarding a ride where there's no age or height requirement, you usually can arrange a switch-off with the loading attendant. No law says you have to ride. If you reach the boarding area and someone is unhappy, simply tell an attendant you've changed your mind and you'll be shown the way out.

PART FOUR

GREATER LONDON

BE PREPARED: YOU MAY NOT HEAR THIS NAME too often as you wander through this ancient and fascinating conglomeration on the Thames. London, you see, is still a collection of villages that sprawl across the Thames basin. Oh, London has a centre, all right, many of them – the **City** (centre of finance and old London), **Westminster** (centre of British government) and on and on it goes.

While the lack of an epicentre may confuse a visitor and mandate the purchase of a good map, the sheer number of thriving, bustling neighbourhoods in London accounts for much of the city's appeal. You will not, to invoke good old Dr Johnson, ever tire of London. Should you exhaust the sights of Westminster, you can simply stroll into another London stage set, like **Covent Garden** or **Belgravia** or the trendy **South Bank** across the river. Within this maze of neighbourhoods are the London attractions and institutions that seem to improve all the time – the museums, historic monuments, restaurants, shops and parks – reminders of the past and emblems of the future. Wherever you wander in London, you can't help but notice how this city embraces the new, welcomes people from all over the world and, despite some frustrating inconveniences like tube stoppages and high prices, is one of the most exhilarating places on earth in which to spend time.

We'll state up-front that we don't do London justice in this guide. London attractions are the central focus of every London guidebook and of most guides to England. Because London's attractions are covered so comprehensively elsewhere, and because the purpose of this guide is to encourage you to explore the whole of England, Scotland and Wales, we've limited our assortment of Greater London attractions to a select few.

PART 4 GREATER LONDON

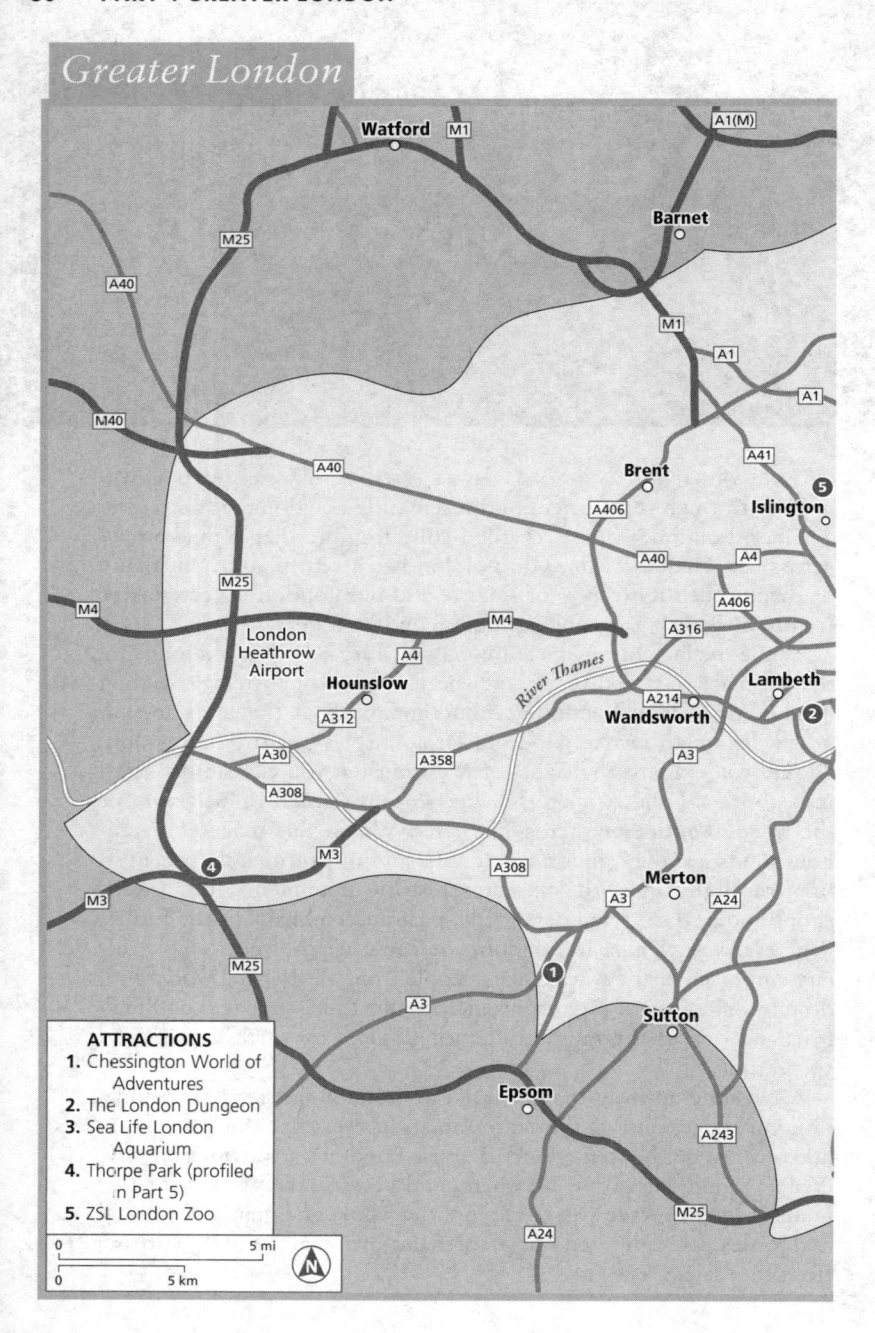

Greater London

ATTRACTIONS
1. Chessington World of Adventures
2. The London Dungeon
3. Sea Life London Aquarium
4. Thorpe Park (profiled in Part 5)
5. ZSL London Zoo

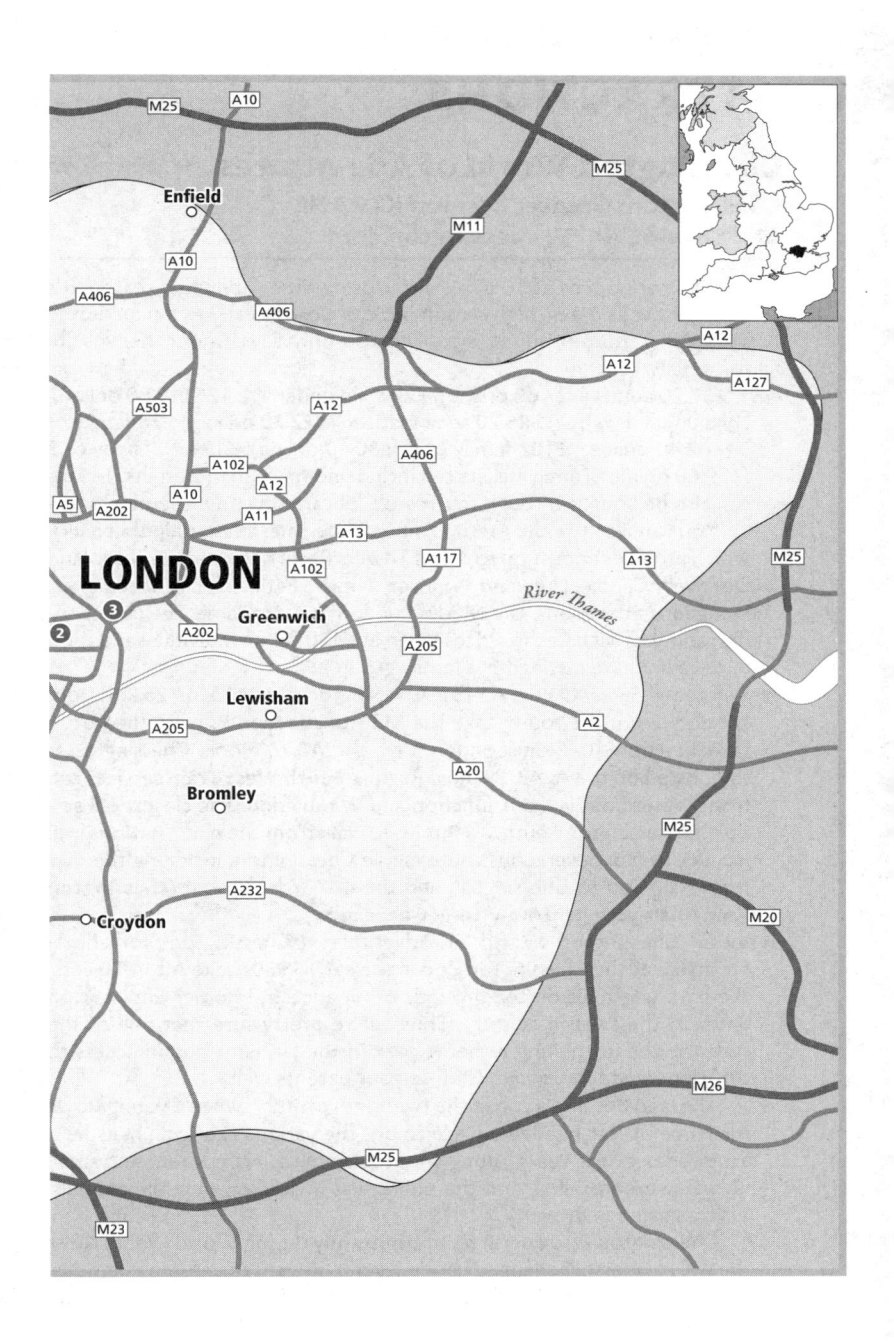

GREATER LONDON MAP 81

THEME PARKS and ATTRACTIONS

Chessington World of Adventures ★★★★★
Chessington, Greater London KT9 2NE
☎ **0871 663 4477; chessington.com**

HOURS The park opens at 10 a.m., with closing time varying by season. It's open as late as 8 p.m. high season but can close as early as 5 p.m. during spring and autumn, and at 3 p.m. on zoo-only days. Check the website for details.

COST £37.20 adults (£27.60 online); £27 child under age 12 (£19.80 online); child under 1 m free; £25.20 senior citizen (£22.20 online); £78 family of 3 (£62.40 online); £102 family of 4 (£80.40 online); £124.20 family of 5 (£99.60 online). Family tickets can include no more than 2 adults. Tickets can also be bought through the Tesco Clubcard rewards scheme.

You can also use the **Merlin Annual Pass** (**merlinannualpass.co.uk**), which provides admission to Alton Towers Resort Theme Park, Legoland Discovery Centre, Legoland Windsor, Thorpe Park, Sea Life sanctuaries, Dungeons attractions, the Merlin London Eye, Madame Tussauds London and Warwick Castle. Prices begin at £150 for an individual and drop in price if you're buying for a family group.

GETTING THERE *By car:* On the A243 in Chessington, about 16 mi (26 km) from London. From the south, take the M25 to Junction 9; from the north, take Junction 10. From London, take the A3 to Hook. Chessington is signposted on the A243. *By train:* Regular **South West Train** services run from Waterloo, Clapham Junction and Wimbledon. The closest rail station is Chessington South, a 10-minute walk from the park (**nationalrail.co.uk**). *By bus:* Several bus routes serve Chessington, including the **465** from Kingston to Chessington and the **467** from Epsom (**chessington.com/plan-your-trip/how-to-get-here.aspx**).

OVERVIEW Chessington World of Adventures ('Chessington' for short) began life as the Chessington Zoo in the early 1930s. Like Alton Towers, the park was built on the grounds of an ancestral home; Chessington dates to the twelfth century. Thus, we're pretty sure that one of the surest paths to running a theme park in the UK is to obtain access to sufficient aristocratic land. Choose your parents well.

The land became a zoo in the twentieth century, when a young Royal Air Force officer needed a place to put the various exotic animals he'd acquired over the years. Along with the animals, a circus tent and small railway were installed, and the public was invited to view the animals. Visitors came in droves.

Chessington Zoo operated intermittently during World War II. After the war, ownership changed hands several times in the ensuing decades. The zoo was sold to the Tussauds Group in 1981, which turned Chessington into an animal-orientated theme park in 1987.

THEME PARKS AND ATTRACTIONS

Today, Chessington is owned by Merlin Entertainments, which also controls Alton Towers, Legoland Windsor and Thorpe Park among their various holdings. Within a short drive of Legoland Windsor and Thorpe Park, Chessington promotes itself as a child-friendly park, with attractions more like Legoland Windsor's gentle coasters and themed attractions than Thorpe Park's teen-focused thrill rides.

ARRIVING If you're driving to Chessington, you'll have the option of two car parks on opposite ends of the complex. The **Lodge Gate** parking is closest to the Holiday Inn Chessington; more parking is available at the **Explorer Gate** entrance. While it's a short walk from one end to the other, it's still helpful to remember where you parked. The car parks' rows and spaces are poorly marked, so you'll need to find some landmark such as a tree, lamp post or fence to guide you back to your car. (It's also useful to text-message someone else in your group with this information, in case you forget.) Parking at Chessington is free. Gates usually open at 9.30 a.m., but everyone is held in the front section of the park until 10 a.m.

GETTING ORIENTATED As mentioned above, Chessington has two entrances at opposite ends of the park. Many park guests, including those travelling by bus or rail and those staying at the Chessington Holiday Inn, will enter the park through the Lodge Gate.

Chessington is a cluttered, non-linear and oddly-arranged park, with rides and zoological exhibits tucked into corners and various out-of-the-way places (behind the adjoining hotel, for example). There's no central landmark to help you get your bearings, though the **Burnt Stub Mansion,** dating from the English Civil War and now called **Hocus Pocus Hall,** is a good place to re-group if your party becomes separated. It's very easy to get disorientated and very difficult to chart any kind of logical route for touring the park. We missed whole sections during our research trips and had to go back to locate them – not always an easy task.

Like those of Alton Towers and Legoland Windsor, Chessington's attractions are organised into themed lands. Once admitted through the Lodge Gate you'll be standing in an open, spacious section of land fronting the Burnt Stub Mansion. The mansion houses **Hocus Pocus Hall,** a walk-through attraction. Behind the mansion is **Market Square,** with two attractions, shops and food service. It's also park headquarters for all guest services, including lockers, WCs, baby changing, information and cash machines. Proceeding roughly clockwise from Market Square is **Pirates Cove,** with a couple of obligatory pirate-themed attractions. **Transylvania** is next, which includes **Vampire,** perhaps the park's best ride, as well as one of the most efficient **Burger King** restaurants we've ever seen.

Toytown occupies the centre of the park, with many attractions devoted to small children. **Land of the Dragons** is above Toytown. At the end of the park, opposite the Lodge Gate, is **Wild Asia,** one of the largest of Chessington's 'lands'. Bordering Wild Asia is **Mystic East,** which is the best-themed area and which also includes the Explorer Gate entrance to the park. Next come **Forbidden Kingdom,** a small Egyptian-themed land, and **Mexicana,** a small area with two attractions

Chessington World of Adventures

Explorers Gate

Leatherhead Rd

A243

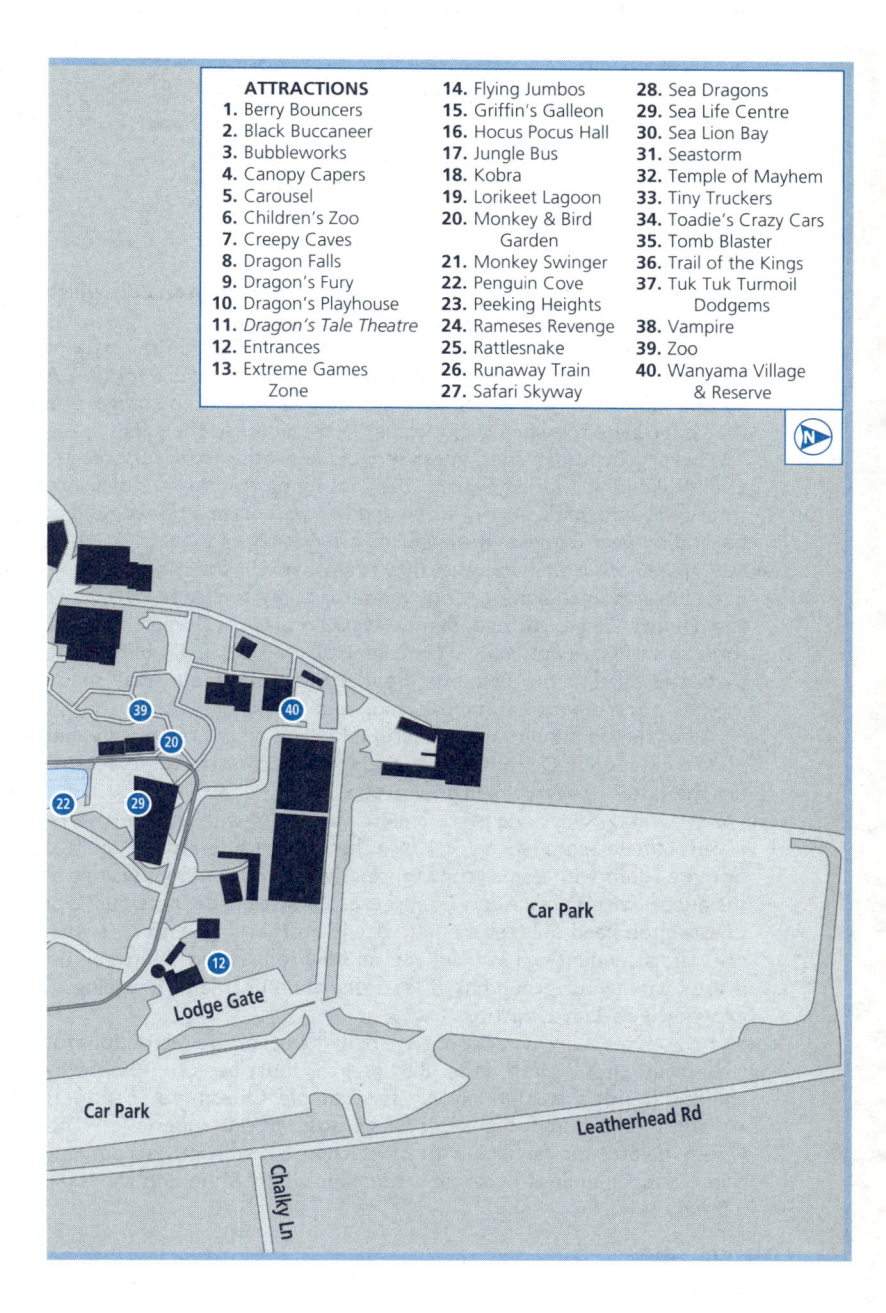

CHESSINGTON WORLD OF ADVENTURES MAP 85

ATTRACTIONS
1. Berry Bouncers
2. Black Buccaneer
3. Bubbleworks
4. Canopy Capers
5. Carousel
6. Children's Zoo
7. Creepy Caves
8. Dragon Falls
9. Dragon's Fury
10. Dragon's Playhouse
11. *Dragon's Tale Theatre*
12. Entrances
13. Extreme Games Zone
14. Flying Jumbos
15. Griffin's Galleon
16. Hocus Pocus Hall
17. Jungle Bus
18. Kobra
19. Lorikeet Lagoon
20. Monkey & Bird Garden
21. Monkey Swinger
22. Penguin Cove
23. Peeking Heights
24. Rameses Revenge
25. Rattlesnake
26. Runaway Train
27. Safari Skyway
28. Sea Dragons
29. Sea Life Centre
30. Sea Lion Bay
31. Seastorm
32. Temple of Mayhem
33. Tiny Truckers
34. Toadie's Crazy Cars
35. Tomb Blaster
36. Trail of the Kings
37. Tuk Tuk Turmoil Dodgems
38. Vampire
39. Zoo
40. Wanyama Village & Reserve

> **NOT TO BE MISSED AT CHESSINGTON WORLD OF ADVENTURES**
>
> **Forbidden Kingdom**
> Rameses Revenge
> Tomb Blaster
>
> **Land of the Dragons**
> Dragon's Fury
>
> **Market Square**
> Safari Skyway
>
> **Mexicana**
> Rattlesnake
> Runaway Train
>
> **Mystic East**
> Dragon Falls
>
> **Transylvania**
> Vampire
>
> **Wild Asia**
> Kobra

and a restaurant. Rounding out the lands is the **Chessington Zoo**, which includes more animal exhibits and a **Sea Life Centre**.

PARK SERVICES Most are found at the Lodge Gate and inside the park at Market Square. A limited number of pushchairs are available for hire. A limited number of wheelchairs are available as well, at no charge. Use the Lodge Gate for wheelchair-accessible entrances to the park.

Lockers, cash machines, guest services and other park services are also available at Market Square. Baby-changing stations are available throughout the park. Lost children and lost parents can be reunited at the station near Rameses Revenge, in Forbidden Kingdom.

DINING We're not sure if it's because they're all owned by the same company, but Chessington's dining options are remarkably similar to Legoland's and Thorpe Park's. Each contains a Mexican place, a Burger King and some sort of pizza option. The pizza joint, an all-you-can-eat buffet with pasta and salad, is our favourite. Besides these, there are small snack, ice-cream and other treat stands throughout the park.

All of the dining options are acceptable and priced reasonably, but none is a standout. Our advice is to find the closest restaurant that satisfies the tastes of everyone in your group.

PARENT SWAP (AKA 'SWITCHING OFF' OR 'CHILD SWAP') As with Alton Towers' Parent Queue Share (see page 271), Chessington offers a way for two or more adults with a small child to experience a ride without waiting in the queue twice. While Alton Towers uses a printed paper pass, guests at Chessington need only tell a queue attendant that they wish to 'switch off'. The attendant will instruct you on how to proceed. Switching off is used when your group has at least one child unable or unwilling to experience certain attractions.

WHO'S THE ADULT? Many attractions have height and/or age restrictions for small children. Children under 3'5" (1.1 m) must be accompanied by an adult to ride the Safari Skyway, for example. Chessington considers anyone age 16 or above an adult for purposes of ride supervision. This is very helpful for families with older children, who can accompany their younger siblings on some attractions whilst Mum and Dad take a break.

Market Square

The central area for park services and entry into the park from the

Lodge Gate, Market Square contains two attractions, two restaurants and many of the park's guest services.

Of the restaurants, **Market Square Pizza Pasta** is one of the most popular in the park. Featuring an all-you-can-eat buffet of (you could have guessed this) pizza, pasta and salad, this is one of the best dining values in the park. The other restaurant, **Greedy Goblin Family Inn,** serves burgers, pasta, salads and chicken. Alcoholic drinks and vegetarian options are also available.

Safari Skyway ★★½

What it is Elevated train ride. **Scope and scale** Minor attraction. **Height requirement** Under 3'5" (1.1 m) must be accompanied by an adult; maximum height of 6'5" (1.96 m). **Fright potential** None. **When to go** Anytime. **Authors' rating** Nice view of the front third of the park; ★★½. **Duration of ride** About 6 minutes. **Average wait in line per 100 people ahead of you** About 7 minutes. **Loading speed** Moderate.

DESCRIPTION AND COMMENTS A leisurely elevated train ride around the perimeter of Market Square and several animal habitats, including over Sealion Bay, Penguin Cove, Trail of the Kings and Sea Life, plus part of Chessington Zoo.

TOURING TIPS Not usually crowded. If you happen to arrive and see a queue, try back in 30 minutes. A nice way to take a midday break.

Hocus Pocus Hall ★★½

What it is Walk-through 3D fun house. **Scope and scale** Minor attraction. **Height requirement** Maximum height of 4'7" (1.4 m) unless accompanied by someone under 4'7" (1.4 m). The rule is to prohibit adults without children. **Fright potential** None. **When to go** Before 11 a.m. or after 3 p.m. **Authors' rating** Detailed and colourful; ★★½. Duration of walk-through About 3–8 minutes. **Average wait in line per 100 people ahead of you** About 25 minutes.

DESCRIPTION AND COMMENTS An updated variation on a traditional walk-through fun house, Hocus Pocus Hall is an ivy-covered 2-storey building looking every bit like a traditional English mansion. A short pre-walk film explains the background story – that the home, owned by a kindly magician, has been infested by goblins. Guests don 3D glasses to walk through the house, and these glasses enable you to see goblins hidden in various room corners and behind every nook and cranny in the house.

The effects throughout the house are quite good, and we don't think there's anything in the house that would be obviously frightening to small children.

TOURING TIPS Because it's a walk-through attraction, different groups will tour at different paces. For this reason we recommend touring in late afternoon, when many families have completed their visit and are heading home. The 3D glasses are washed after each use but not dried, so it's helpful to have a handkerchief or a clean cloth nappy to dry the glasses.

Pirates Cove

We noted earlier that every theme park must have a pirate-themed attraction or land, and Chessington is no exception. Pirates Cove is about the size of a postage stamp. It contains two attractions and **Chips Ahoy,** a fish-and-chips stand that operates seasonally.

Black Buccaneer ★★★

What it is Funfair-type swinging-boat ride. **Scope and scale** Minor attraction. **Height requirement** 3' (0.9 m) to ride; under 3'5" (1.1 m) must be accompanied by an adult. **Fright potential** Frightens some young children and those prone to motion sickness or afraid of heights. **When to go** Before noon or after 3 p.m. **Authors' rating** Surprisingly fun; ★★★. **Duration of ride** About 2 minutes. **Average wait in line per 100 people ahead of you** About 11 minutes. **Loading speed** Moderate.

DESCRIPTION AND COMMENTS A swinging-boat ride of the pirate-ship genre, a staple of funfairs and sideshows across the country, Black Buccaneer is well done in that the attraction is set above a small pond, with lush green foliage all around. Because it's visually isolated, there's little to distract you from the swinging sensation while riding.

At either apex, riders on one end of the boat will be slightly more than 90° from vertical – essentially parallel to the ground – and suspended for a good few tenths of a second before whooshing down and back up the other side. It's a great sensation, and 2 minutes is more than enough for most people to get their fill. If you're unsure about whether you like this kind of attraction, sit in the middle rows to swing less.

TOURING TIPS Not a headliner attraction but can move through more than 500 people per hour. If you find a queue of more than 10 minutes, try back later in the day.

Seastorm ★★★

What it is Spinning funfair ride. **Scope and scale** Minor attraction. **Height requirement** 3' (0.9 m) to ride; under 3'5" (1.1 m) must be accompanied by an adult. **Fright potential** None. **When to go** Before noon or after 3 p.m. **Authors' rating** Not very original, but more efficient than most; ★★★. **Duration of ride** About 1¼ minutes. **Average wait in line per 100 people ahead of you** About 8 minutes. **Loading speed** Moderate.

DESCRIPTION AND COMMENTS Another typical funfair-type attraction in which ride vehicles spin slowly around a central axis. In this case, the vehicles are miniature sail-rigged pirate ships, and their circular path includes a couple of hills and dips to simulate ocean waves.

While there's nothing special about the technology or the theme, Seastorm is more efficient than most rides of its kind in the number of guests it can accommodate in an hour.

TOURING TIPS Not a headliner attraction but has a higher-than-usual hourly capacity – more than 800. Try back after 4 p.m. if you happen to catch it on a particularly busy day.

Transylvania

Another small land, Transylvania is in the back left of the park. Like Pirates Cove, it contains two attractions and a restaurant, plus a gift shop. Toilets are also located in Transylvania, answering the question of what vampires do if they have to pee during daylight hours.

The restaurant, a **Burger King**, is large enough to handle big groups well. Although it's near **Vampire**, the park's best ride, the whole area is remote enough that long queues don't tend to develop at the Burger King until 12.30 or 1.00 p.m.

Vampire ★★★★

What it is Suspended-car roller coaster. **Scope and scale** Headliner. **Height requirement** 3'5" (1.1 m) to ride; under 4'3" (1.3 m) must be accompanied by an adult. **Fright potential** Frightens some young children and those prone to motion sickness or afraid of heights. **When to go** As soon as the park opens or the last hour the park is open. **Authors' rating** The best ride at Chessington, it would hold its own in any theme park anywhere; ★★★★. **Duration of ride** About 2 minutes. **Average wait in line per 100 people ahead of you** About 7 minutes. **Loading speed** Moderate.

DESCRIPTION AND COMMENTS A suspended-car roller coaster with tight turns, dips and hills but no inversions or loops, Vampire is the perfect introduction to roller coasters for older children who are ready to try bigger rides.

Riders for Vampire sit in seats suspended from a track above their heads. The benefit of this configuration is that it allows you to see oncoming trees and obstacles, as well as the ground rushing by you, as you weave your way around the track's turns and dips.

The Chessington park-maintenance team has done an excellent job of letting the trees and foliage grow just close enough to the ride's safety clearances that you feel as though you're flying through the forest like a speeding bat. This effect is particularly gripping at night. If your schedule permits you to ride after dark, do so.

The exit for Vampire is like a national secret. Many families have no idea where riding members of their party will pop out. Look for them to exit through the gift shop near Bubbleworks.

TOURING TIPS One of the first attractions that people head for when the park opens. If you can get in the queue early enough, ask to sit up front; the sensation of flight is much more pronounced there.

If you arrive at the park more than 30 minutes after opening, send one member of your party to check the waiting times for Vampire. We'd recommend getting in the queue if the wait is 20 minutes or less. Try back during lunch or dinner or in the last hour the park is open.

Bubbleworks ★★★½

What it is Indoor raft ride through a bubble-making factory. **Scope and scale** Major attraction. **Height requirement** Under 3'5" (1.1 m) must be accompanied by an adult. **Fright potential** None. **When to go** Anytime. **Authors' rating** Detailed and done on a large scale; ★★★½. **Duration of ride** About 6½ minutes. **Average wait in line per 100 people ahead of you** About 3 minutes. **Loading speed** Fast.

DESCRIPTION AND COMMENTS Bubbleworks is a whimsical raft, er, tub ride through the inner workings of a soap-bubble-making factory. We have no idea what this attraction is doing in Transylvania, although we admit that there has been a lot of off-shoring of domestic soap production in the UK over the last few years. We would have guessed Asia, not Romania, but what do we know about global outsourcing?

The ride is impressive for its imagination, scope and detail. A few of the scenes and several effects are remarkably clever and would be at home in similar rides in Disney theme parks. While the attraction has been criticised for over-promoting its corporate sponsor (Imperial Leather soap), we didn't get that impression.

If you're not sure what Bubbleworks is all about, the drain on the floor of your ride vehicle will give you a clue. For the next 6 minutes you'll dodge water spouts arching over you and raining down on you. You won't get soaked, however, unless you're unlucky enough to have the ride stopped unexpectedly in a particularly-soggy spot.

TOURING TIPS Possibly the most efficient attraction in the park, Bubbleworks is the one to head for when the park is packed and everyone needs a break from the sun. Tour anytime. If this attraction is crowded, everything else will be completely mobbed.

Toytown

In the middle of the park, Toytown features five attractions designed specifically for smaller children. This area has no restaurants but is small enough and close enough to other lands (such as Mexicana and Market Square) that dining and snacks are only a few minutes' walk away.

Flying Jumbos ★★★

What it is Spinning funfair-type ride. **Scope and scale** Minor attraction. **Height requirement** Under 3'5" (1.1 m) must be accompanied by an adult. **Fright potential** Frightens some young children who are afraid of heights. **When to go** Before 11 a.m. or in the last 2 hours the park is open. **Authors' rating** An attractive child's ride; ★★★. **Duration of ride** About 3 minutes. **Average wait in line per 100 people ahead of you** About 26 minutes. **Loading speed** Slow.

DESCRIPTION AND COMMENTS A virtual clone of Disney's Dumbo ride, Flying Jumbos is a funfair-type ride with ride vehicles mounted on long metal arms connected at a central spinning axis. The ride vehicles are pink elephants (so don't drink excessively before riding), and riders can control a hydraulic valve that determines how high the elephant is lifted while it spins in its circle.

TOURING TIPS Has about the same capacity as the other attractions in Toytown. Our advice is to see Berry Bouncers and Tiny Truckers first, then Flying Jumbos.

Tiny Truckers ★★

What it is Miniature lorries driving around a small guided track. **Scope and scale** Minor attraction. **Height requirement** Under 3'5" (1.1 m) must be accompanied by an adult. **Fright potential** None. **When to go** Before 11 a.m. or in the last 2 hours the park is open. **Authors' rating** Prepares children for mutton-chop sideburns; ★★. **Duration of ride** About 2 minutes. **Average wait in line per 100 people ahead of you** About 28 minutes. **Loading speed** Slow.

DESCRIPTION AND COMMENTS Children drive colourful miniature trucks around a small guided track. About as simple an attraction as can be.

TOURING TIPS Kids sit in the cab up front, while adults ride in the back.

Toadie's Crazy Cars ★★★

What it is Antique-car ride on a guided track. **Scope and scale** Minor attraction. **Height requirement** Under 3'5" (1.1 m) must be accompanied by an adult. **Fright potential** None. **When to go** Before 11 a.m. or in the last 2 hours the park is open. **Authors' rating** Whimsical and fun; ★★★. **Duration of ride** About 4 minutes. **Average wait in line per 100 people ahead of you** About 23 minutes. **Loading speed** Slow.

DESCRIPTION AND COMMENTS If the Flying Jumbos copy Disney's Dumbo attraction, Toadie's Crazy Cars is Chessington's version of Disney's Mr Toad's Wild Ride. Guests board an open car and drive around an eccentric amphibian's country estate. The major difference between the two attractions is that Disney's version takes place inside Mr Toad's home, and Chessington's is outdoors. There's plenty to see in this small attraction, however, and children love it.

TOURING TIPS May open an hour after the rest of the park on days of lighter attendance.

Berry Bouncers ★½

What it is Bouncing funfair-type ride. **Scope and scale** Minor attraction. **Height requirement** 3' (0.9 m) to ride; under 3'5" (1.1 m) must be accompanied by an adult. **Fright potential** None. **When to go** First or last hour the park is open. **Authors' rating** Not worth the queuing time; ★½. **Duration of ride** About 2 minutes. **Average wait in line per 100 people ahead of you** About 29 minutes. **Loading speed** Slow.

DESCRIPTION AND COMMENTS Berry Bouncers is a relatively-simple attraction: Six riders sit in a row of seats, which is then lifted about 10 feet off the ground. Once suspended, the row begins to bounce its way back to the ground. Most variations, including this one, include a couple of quick trips back to the top before a final hop to the ground.

Berry Bouncers is visually appealing to small children because all the activity takes place outdoors. The display of bouncing legs, laughing and shrieking adds to the excitement of riding.

TOURING TIPS Berry Bouncers has one of the smallest capacities of any Chessington attraction. If this is on your child's must-see list, make it the first thing you see in Toytown, early in the morning.

Carousel ★★½

What it is Traditional funfair carousel horses. **Scope and scale** Minor attraction. **Height requirement** Under 4'3" (1.3 m) must be accompanied by an adult. **Fright potential** None. **When to go** Before noon or after 4 p.m. **Authors' rating** Attractive; ★★½. **Duration of ride** About 2 minutes. **Average wait in line per 100 people ahead of you** About 9 minutes. **Loading speed** Slow.

DESCRIPTION AND COMMENTS Another funfair staple, Carousel is a typical horse-themed merry-go-round.

TOURING TIPS More efficient than any other attraction in Toytown. If you're visiting first thing in the morning, see everything else in Toytown first before riding the Carousel.

Land of the Dragons

Between Toytown and Wild Asia in the middle of the park is Land of the Dragons, a small land where every bit is packed with attractions. As with Toytown, there are no restaurants or snacks here, but there is enough within a short walk to satisfy anyone.

Dragon's Fury ★★★½

What it is Spinning roller coaster. **Scope and scale** Major attraction. **Height requirement** 3'11" (1.2 m) to ride; maximum height of 6'5" (1.96 m). **Fright potential** Frightens some small children and those prone to motion sickness. **When to go** Before noon or in the last 2 hours the park is open. **Authors' rating** Spinning, twisting, diving fun; ★★★½. **Duration of ride** About 1¼ minutes. **Average wait in line per 100 people ahead of you** About 8 minutes. **Loading speed** Moderate.

DESCRIPTION AND COMMENTS Similar to Sonic Spinball at Alton Towers, Dragon's Fury is a small roller coaster whose novel feature is that your ride vehicle can rotate in a complete circle while riding atop the track. The track features short drops, big curves and tight spins. You've got no control over the spin; it depends on how the ride was programmed. Thus, some really tight turns become gentle glides because you spin with the turn; others become bone-jarring endurance experiments if you happen to spin against the force of the turn.

This might not sound like fun, but it is. Because Dragon's Fury is designed for smaller children, the ride experience is smooth and gentle, and very, very pleasant even for adults.

TOURING TIPS The attraction with the highest capacity in Land of the Dragons. Experience it as the last attraction in this land and before any shows.

Dragon's Playhouse ★★½

What it is Indoor play area with slides and inflatable bouncing rooms. **Scope and scale** Diversion. **Height requirement** Maximum height of 4'7" (1.4 m). **Fright potential** None. **When to go** Anytime. **Authors' rating** Some welcomed unstructured play time; ★★½. **Duration of play** Varies. **Average wait in line per 100 people ahead of you** Varies.

DESCRIPTION AND COMMENTS A small indoor play area with slides and inflatable air mattresses for bouncing. A good way for kids to let off some steam after a morning of standing in queues. Staff members are on hand to assist in supervision.

TOURING TIPS Expendable if necessary, but might be welcomed by the kids. Grab yourself a snack and a drink before turning the kids loose inside.

Sea Dragons ★½

What it is Funfair-type spinning ride. **Scope and scale** Minor attraction. **Height requirement** Under 3'5" (1.1 m) must be accompanied by an adult. **Fright potential** None. **When to go** Before noon or after 3 p.m. **Authors' rating** Nothing special; ★½. **Duration of ride** About 1½ minutes. **Average wait in line per 100 people ahead of you** About 10 minutes. **Loading speed** Slow.

DESCRIPTION AND COMMENTS Small boats spin around a central axis. A typical funfair ride with minimal theming.

TOURING TIPS If visiting in the morning, see Griffin's Galleon and Dragon's Fury first, then Sea Dragons.

Canopy Capers ★★★

What it is Two-storey play area and tree house. **Scope and scale** Minor attraction. **Height requirement** Maximum height of 4'7" (1.4 m). **Fright potential** None. **When to go** Anytime. **Authors' rating** Well done and worth a visit; ★★★. **Duration of play** Varies. **Average wait in line per 100 people ahead of you** Varies.

DESCRIPTION AND COMMENTS An interactive play area with enough stairs, rope bridges and tree houses to keep any child occupied for a good long time. We like Canopy Capers quite a bit, from the oversized mushrooms dotting the landscape to the colourful paint on virtually every surface. We would have been happy to romp around here if we were short enough.

The one concern we'd have as parents would be keeping an eye on our brood while they're playing. If you've got more than one child, it's inevitable that they'll go in different directions at some point. Make sure you've identified a meeting-spot in case you get separated.

TOURING TIPS If you're looking for someplace to let the kids run about for a while, Canopy Capers is far superior to Dragon's Playhouse.

Dragon's Tale Theatre ★★½

What it is Live puppet show. **Scope and scale** Minor attraction. **Height requirement** None. **Fright potential** None. **When to go** As per the daily entertainment schedule. **Authors' rating** Well done for small children; ★★½. **Duration of show** About 20 minutes.

DESCRIPTION AND COMMENTS A live stage show featuring colourful animal puppets, *Dragon's Tale Theatre* is inspired by the recent trend of children's television programmes that ask kids to shout out the answers to questions asked by the characters. In this case, the show's plot concerns a set of magic words that provide clues to decoding an old map, which must be used to find one of the characters who has gone missing. It takes a couple of questions before the kids in the audience catch on that they're allowed to shout out the answers, but once they do, they embrace their roles with enthusiasm. Remind them when the show's over that they need to go back to their 'inside voice'.

TOURING TIPS Typically performed three times per day, usually with the first performance at 11 a.m. Extra performances are added when the park is open past 6 p.m.

Griffin's Galleon ★★½

What it is Side-to-side swinging-boat ride. **Scope and scale** Minor attraction. **Height requirement** 3' (0.9 m) to ride; under 3'5" (1.1 m) must ride with an adult. **Fright potential** None, but may induce motion sickness. **When to go** Before noon or after 3 p.m. **Authors' rating** More fun than it looks; ★★½. **Duration of ride** About 2 minutes. **Average wait in line per 100 people ahead of you** About 16 minutes. **Loading speed** Slow.

DESCRIPTION AND COMMENTS Riders board a miniature pirate ship that rolls back and forth on a track. The ship also spins in a small circle while it rolls. Griffin's Galleon is much like a smaller, less intense version of Black Buccaneer in Pirates Cove (which doesn't spin) and is appropriate for small children.

TOURING TIPS Not especially popular, but Griffin's Galleon has the smallest capacity of any attraction in Land of the Dragons. If you're visiting in the morning, see Griffin's Galleon before anything else in this land.

Wild Asia

Wild Asia is the first land you'll encounter if you enter Chessington through the Explorer Gate. Wild Asia contains five attractions, an animal exhibit, an Asian-noodle eatery and a gift store. We like **Noodle Noodle,** the Asian restaurant, quite a bit. The food is fresh and crowds aren't usually a problem.

Kobra ★★★

What it is Large-scale version of classic funfair spinning ride. **Scope and scale** Major attraction. **Height requirement** 3'11" (1.2 m) to ride. **Fright potential**

Frightens some small children and those prone to motion sickness. **When to go** Before 11 a.m. or in the last 2 hours the park is open. **Authors' rating** Loads of fun! ★★★. **Duration of ride** About 4 minutes. **Average wait in line per 100 people ahead of you** About 19 minutes. **Loading speed** Slow.

DESCRIPTION AND COMMENTS Kobra is a variation on back-and-forth sliding rides such as Griffin's Galleon, writ large. It consists of a large disc mounted on a long metal tracked shaped like a W. The disc moves back and forth along the track, alternately rising and falling. While doing this, the disc is also spinning around its centre. The best effects happen when the spinning coincides with hitting the top of the track, and you get the sensation of spinning in space. By the time the disc is headed back down, you're spinning in the same direction, and it seems like you're going faster than you really are. We liked it quite a bit.

TOURING TIPS Kobra has the second-smallest capacity of any attraction in Wild Asia. We suggest seeing it after Jungle Bus, if both are on your itinerary.

Jungle Bus ★★

What it is Funfair-type ride. **Scope and scale** Minor attraction. **Height requirement** 3' (0.9 m) to ride; under 3'5" (1.1 m) must be accompanied by an adult. **Fright potential** Frightens some small children. **When to go** First or last hour the park is open. **Authors' rating** Colourful and visually interesting from the outside; ★★. **Duration of ride** About 2¼ minutes. **Average wait in line per 100 people ahead of you** About 38 minutes. **Loading speed** Slow.

DESCRIPTION AND COMMENTS Jungle Bus is essentially a small funfair variation of a Ferris wheel. One ride vehicle, shaped like a small school bus and painted in festive tropical colours, is mounted on two metal arms that rotate around a central axis. This raises and lowers the bus just as a Ferris wheel spins its seats, only Jungle Bus has a much smaller circular orbit – perhaps 10–13 ft (3–4 m), tops. Kids seem to enjoy it, but this isn't anything you haven't seen before.

TOURING TIPS The slowest-loading attraction in Wild Asia. If this otherwise-expendable attraction is on your itinerary, see it first.

Monkey Swinger ★★

What it is Funfair-type swinging chair ride. **Scope and scale** Minor attraction. **Height requirement** 3'11" (1.2 m) to ride. **Fright potential** Frightens some small children. **When to go** Before noon or after 4 p.m. **Authors' rating** The water feature is a nice touch; ★★. **Duration of ride** About 2½ minutes. **Average wait in line per 100 people ahead of you** About 11 minutes. **Loading speed** Slow.

DESCRIPTION AND COMMENTS This recently-re-themed ride was formerly called 'Billy's Whizzer'. We can tell you with some certainty that there are no rides in America named after somebody's 'whizzer'.

Similar to Twirling Toadstool at Alton Towers, Monkey Swinger is a variation on the classic funfair swinging chair (aka flying carousel) ride.

Individual seats are suspended via long chains from the bottom of a circular roof. Once riders are seated, the roof raises a few feet off the ground and begins to spin, taking the riders with it.

Monkey Swinger's roof oscillates up and down, like a spun coin about to settle on a tabletop. Thus, during one complete spin around the base, riders go up and down while swinging around. An interesting variation at Monkey Swinger is that spurts of water periodically shoot upward from fountains in the ground, occasionally soaking the riders flying by (inside seats are the driest).

TOURING TIPS The most efficient attraction in Wild Asia; see after the other attractions here.

Tuk Tuk Turmoil Dodgems ★★

What it is Funfair-type dodgem cars. **Scope and scale** Minor attraction. **Height requirement** 3' (0.9 m) to ride; under 4'3" (1.3 m) must ride with an adult. **Fright potential** None. **When to go** Before noon or after 4 p.m. **Authors' rating** A good choice for the park; ★★. **Duration of ride** About 3 minutes. **Average wait in line per 100 people ahead of you** About 12 minutes. **Loading speed** Slow.

DESCRIPTION AND COMMENTS Funfair-type electric dodgem cars drive around a covered track. The cars can get up enough speed to make bouncing into your fellow riders a lot of fun.

TOURING TIPS About as efficient as Monkey Swingers; save until after you've experienced Jungle Bus and Kobra.

Temple of Mayhem ★★½

What it is Interactive play area with air-powered cannons shooting foam balls. **Scope and scale** Diversion. **Height requirement** 4'7" (1.4 m) maximum height. **Fright potential** None. **When to go** Anytime. **Authors' rating** Turn the kids loose, stand back and watch; ★★½. **Duration of play** About 15 minutes on average. **Average wait in line per 100 people ahead of you** About 80 minutes.

DESCRIPTION AND COMMENTS A 2-storey interactive play area that lets kids gather colourful, round foam 'balls' to shoot at their friends using low-pressure air cannons. Adults are allowed to accompany their children into the play area, but we didn't see many takers during our visit. That's all just as well – kids were running around like chickens, and the adults wouldn't stand a chance of keeping up. Similar to Berry Bish Bash at Alton Towers.

TOURING TIPS Grab some video if you can. See anytime.

Lorikeet Lagoon ★★

What it is Walk-through exhibit of live birds. **Scope and scale** Diversion. **Height requirement** None. **Fright potential** None. **When to go** Anytime. **Authors' rating** Well done; ★★.

DESCRIPTION AND COMMENTS Lorikeets are medium-sized birds related to parakeets. In Lorikeet Lagoon, visitors walk through a large enclosed habitat and hand-feed selected animals. The birds are quite used to humans and are very gentle.

TOURING TIPS The lorikeets are very colourful and make for some great photos. Have your camera ready as you walk in.

Mystic East

Another Asian-themed land, Mystic East contains two attractions, a restaurant and a gift shop. The restaurant, **Oriental Express,** serves a variety of snacks and rice dishes.

Dragon Falls ★★★★

What it is Log-flume ride. **Scope and scale** Headliner. **Height requirement** 3' (0.9 m) to ride; under 3'5" (1.1 m) must ride with an adult. **Fright potential** Some small children may be frightened by the falls. Most will take them in stride. **When to go** Anytime. **Authors' rating** One of the best-themed flume rides in the UK. Not to be missed; ★★★★. **Duration of ride** Around 4½ minutes. **Average wait in line per 100 people ahead of you** Around 6 minutes. **Loading speed** Fast.

DESCRIPTION AND COMMENTS A log-flume ride through and around the grounds of an ancient temple. Both the queuing area and ride itself have very good detail, including the use of bamboo for the queue guide-rails, red faux-paper lanterns as lighting, arched bridges and oriental-style buildings surrounding the attraction. The surroundings are immersive and well done.

The actual ride is quite pleasant. There are a couple of small dips and one medium-sized splashdown hill at the end. Riders are likely to get wet but not soaked. We think the attraction is suitable for any child who meets the height requirement. *Warning!* There is an eye-level squirter at the end of the ride.

TOURING TIPS Along with Peeking Heights, one of the most efficient attractions in the park. Save Dragon Falls until after you've seen the other major attractions in Transylvania and Mexicana.

Peeking Heights ★★½

What it is Ferris wheel. **Scope and scale** Minor attraction. **Height requirement** Under 3'5" (1.1 m) must ride with an adult. **Fright potential** Not for those afraid of heights. **When to go** Anytime. **Authors' rating** Nice views; ★★½. **Duration of ride** Around 3 minutes. **Average wait in line per 100 people ahead of you** Around 15 minutes to board, but all cars must load before ride begins. **Loading speed** Moderate.

DESCRIPTION AND COMMENTS An 82-ft (25-m) traditional observation wheel with gorgeous views of the surrounding city. On clear days you may be able to see London.

TOURING TIPS Three cars can load at once, but there are 18 cars, so it takes

13½ minutes to load the whole wheel. See after you've experienced the other major attractions in Transylvania and Mexicana.

Forbidden Kingdom

Decorated in an Egyptian theme, Forbidden Kingdom is wedged between Mexicana and Mystic East on the east side of the park. Forbidden Kingdom holds two attractions and a restaurant serving good fried chicken. First aid, a baby-care centre and the park's lost-children/lost-parents rendezvous point are also in Forbidden Kingdom.

Tomb Blaster ★★★★

What it is Ride-through shooting gallery. **Scope and scale** Headliner. **Height requirement** Under 3'5" (1.1 m) must ride with an adult. **Fright potential** Has skeletons, mummies and snakes, which can frighten small children. **When to go** Before noon or after 3 p.m. **Authors' rating** Worth riding a couple of times, and not to be missed; ★★★★. **Duration of ride** Around 6½ minutes. **Average wait in line per 100 people ahead of you** Around 9 minutes; assumes 3 trains operating. **Loading speed** Moderate.

DESCRIPTION AND COMMENTS An Egyptian-themed ride-through shooting gallery similar to Legoland Windsor's Laser Raiders (see page 169). Guests experiencing Chessington's Tomb Blaster use a hand-held plastic laser to shoot at light-sensitive targets placed on mummies, pyramids, sarcophagi and other relics as you zoom through this dark ride. There are plenty of targets to aim for, and the ride's high-tempo background music makes the journey seem more intense.

If you haven't played video games in a while and your fingers aren't used to the stress of repeatedly operating hand-held controllers, you may want to practise a bit before visiting Chessington. The ride's length, coupled with the number of targets, means you'll be giving your trigger fingers a good workout.

TOURING TIPS Tomb Blaster can develop long lines during the middle of busy days in the park. We recommend visiting after Rameses Revenge and as early in the morning or as late in the day as possible.

Rameses Revenge ★★★

What it is Like riding an oversized washing machine. **Scope and scale** Minor attraction. **Height requirement** Riders must be 4'7"–6'5" (1.4–1.96 m). **Fright potential** The height and spinning can frighten many children and adults. **When to go** Before 11 a.m. or after 4 p.m. **Authors' rating** Great on a warm day; ★★★★. **Duration of ride** About 1½ minutes. **Average wait in line per 100 people ahead of you** About 18 minutes. **Loading speed** Slow.

DESCRIPTION AND COMMENTS Similar to Alton Towers' Ripsaw (see page 278), Rameses Revenge consists of two rows of seats mounted between spinning mechanical arms. The arms move in circles, and the seats also rotate about their axis, meaning riders make small circles within a larger circular orbit. Over water. Which occasionally shoots up to soak unsuspecting riders. Getting wet is unavoidable, but end seats are drier than middle seats. Women with loose tops should worry about fall-out.

TOURING TIPS No seat is protected from getting wet. Wear a poncho.

Mexicana

Slightly up and to the right of Market Square and the Lodge Gate entrance of the park is Mexicana. Unlike Land of the Dragons, whose attractions are little more than funfair rides painted with scales and claws to match the land's theme, Mexicana's American desert theme extends to its attractions and restaurants. The **Runaway Train** ride takes place on a red-coloured mountain, and the entrance to **Rattlesnake** is an adobe structure with a wood bridge.

Note that Mexicana's restaurant, the **Mexican Cantina,** may operate only on days of peak attendance. We recommend the **Fried Chicken Co.** restaurant in Forbidden Kingdom as an alternative.

Runaway Train ★★★½

What it is Small roller coaster. **Scope and scale** Minor attraction. **Height requirement** 3' (0.9 m) to ride; under 3'5" (1.1 m) must ride with an adult. **Fright potential** None. **When to go** Before 11 a.m. or after 4 p.m. **Authors' rating** Charming and well themed; ★★★½. **Duration of ride** About 3 minutes. **Average wait in line per 100 people ahead of you** About 14 minutes; assumes 1 train running. **Loading speed** Moderate.

DESCRIPTION AND COMMENTS Runaway Train is a relatively-gentle introduction to roller coasters for young children. Decorated in the style of an abandoned mine, with lots of tied wood logs, fence posts and the like, it's one of the best-themed attractions in the park. Except for some differences in theme and track layout, it's essentially the same attraction as Alton Towers' Runaway Mine Train (see page 276).

The Runaway Train's track is short, and one lap takes a little less than a minute. Because of this, most rides consist of two or three laps around the track.

TOURING TIPS Riders sit in rows of two, so families with small children and an odd number of members should decide in advance who is sitting with whom.

Rattlesnake ★★★

What it is Small roller coaster. **Scope and scale** Major attraction. **Height requirement** 4'7" (1.4 m) to ride. **Fright potential** None. **When to go** Before noon or after 3 p.m. **Authors' rating** Good introduction for older kids; ★★★. **Duration of ride** Around 1½ minutes. **Average wait in line per 100 people ahead of you** Around 14 minutes. **Loading speed** Slow.

DESCRIPTION AND COMMENTS Similar in concept to Pleasure Beach Blackpool's Wild Mouse (see page 394) but longer, larger and better themed, Rattlesnake is a twisting, turning small roller coaster which emphasises lateral forces and small dips over extreme speed, loops and inversions.

It's a good choice for children who have mastered many of the smaller rides in the park and are interested in experiencing the kinds of attractions on which they see older siblings or friends.

A steel-track coaster, Rattlesnake is far more smooth and gentle than Pleasure Beach Blackpool's Wild Mouse.

TOURING TIPS Rattlesnake can handle crowds slightly better than can Runaway Train. Ride Runaway Train first, then Rattlesnake, in the morning. If visiting in the afternoon, see Rattlesnake first to let crowds thin a bit before riding Runaway Train.

Chessington Zoo

Separated into two parts on either side of Market Square, the Chessington Zoo exhibits offer a look at a wide range of animals, from tigers, lions, monkeys and gorillas to sea life including penguins, sea lions, otters and a complete aquarium.

Three exhibits stand out as not to be missed. The first is the **Trail of the Kings** walking path, which contains the tigers, lions and gorillas. Each set of habitats is lush and themed to fit in with the rest of the park. Most of these animals spend the majority of their day resting, but the park management was forward-thinking enough to put the best napping spots within view of the guests. We were able to see each of the animals on our walk-through, even in poor, cooler weather. There is a wonderfully-British sign posted on the Trail of the Kings that reads, TODAY WE ARE FEEDING DEAD RABBITS. *Hmmm*, we thought, *what's the point?*

The second must-see exhibit is the **Sea Life Centre,** a large, detailed walk-through exhibit of marine life, including sharks, rays and hundreds of colourful fish. Besides a large aquarium that surrounds (and sits on top of) much of the presentation area, there are dozens of smaller displays dedicated to various species. Among our favourites were the homely Arctic lumpsucker and the even uglier wolf fish, which is reportedly sold headless so as not to frighten the customers. All are presented with short educational descriptions of the creatures' habits and special adaptations to them. In addition, regular live presentations are held at some of the larger exhibits. Ask a member of staff for the schedule. Touring the aquarium takes 15–30 minutes, longer if you take in a feeding or presentation.

The third exhibit that should be on your schedule is the **Wanyama Village & Reserve**, on the east side of the park. A simulated tour of an African grassland, the reserve looks out over an expansive tract of land behind the park's hotel. Visitors walk along an elevated wooden walkway, past zebra and antelope. One of the antelope species on display, the scimitar-horned oryx, is thought to be extinct in the wild, with fewer than five thousand animals left in zoos and wildlife preserves. Because the area in which these animals can roam is so large, it's possible that you may not see some of them during your walk-through (just like on a real safari!). Try back again in a couple of hours, and you may have better luck.

THEME PARKS AND ATTRACTIONS

Chessington Touring Plans

We've included touring plans for parents with small children, as well as plans for adults and teens. Because Chessington is a relatively-small park, it's fairly straightforward for both groups to see most of the park in a single day.

One-Day Touring Plan for Parents with Children under 3' (0.9 m)

1. The night before your visit, check **chessington.com** for park hours and weather.
2. Arrive at the park entrance 30 minutes prior to official opening. If possible, have your admission in hand before you arrive. Otherwise, arrive 15 minutes earlier and send one member of your party to obtain admission.
3. As soon as the park opens, experience Tiny Truckers in Toytown.
4. Ride Flying Jumbos in Toytown.
5. Ride the Carousel in Toytown.
6. Take a spin on Toadie's Crazy Cars.
7. In Land of the Dragons, experience Sea Dragons.
8. Ride Dragon's Fury, also in Land of the Dragons.
9. Make your way to Forbidden Kingdom and experience Tomb Blaster.
10. In Mystic East, try the Peeking Heights observation wheel if the weather is nice.
11. Eat lunch. Good nearby choices include Burger King and the Fried Chicken Co. in Forbidden Kingdom.
12. Ride the Safari Skyway in Market Square.
13. Take a float through Bubbleworks in Transylvania.
14. Check the daily entertainment schedule for the next performance of *Dragon's Tale Theatre* in Land of the Dragons. Work in some unstructured playtime at Canopy Capers.
15. Try the Temple of Mayhem in Wild Asia.
16. Check out the birds at Lorikeet Lagoon.
17. Tour Hocus Pocus Hall in Market Square.
18. Tour the Trail of the Kings, Sea Life Centre and Wanyama Village & Reserve experiences in Chessington Zoo.
19. See any missed attractions or repeat any favourites.
20. Depart Chessington World of Adventures.

One-Day Touring Plan for Parents with Older and Younger Children

1. The night before your visit, check **chessington.com** for park hours and weather.
2. Arrive at the park entrance 30 minutes prior to official opening. If possible, have your admission in hand before you arrive. Otherwise, arrive 15 minutes earlier and send one member of your party to obtain admission.
3. As soon as the park opens, see Tomb Blaster in Forbidden Kingdom.

Chessington Recommended Attraction Visitation Times

AREA | ATTRACTION | BEST TIME TO VISIT

MARKET SQUARE
Safari Skyway | Anytime
Hocus Pocus Hall | Before 11 a.m. or after 3 p.m.

PIRATES' COVE
Black Buccaneer | Before noon or after 3 p.m.
Seastorm | Before noon or after 3 p.m.

TRANSYLVANIA
Vampire | As soon as the park opens or the last hour the park is open
Bubbleworks | Anytime

TOYTOWN
Flying Jumbos | Before 11 a.m. or in the last 2 hours the park is open
Tiny Truckers | Before 11 a.m. or in the last 2 hours the park is open
Toadie's Crazy Cars | Before 11 a.m. or in the last 2 hours the park is open
Berry Bouncers | First or last hour the park is open
Carousel | Before noon or after 4 p.m.

LAND OF THE DRAGONS
Dragon's Fury | Before noon or in the last 2 hours the park is open
Dragon's Playhouse | Anytime
Sea Dragons | Before noon or after 3 p.m.
Canopy Capers | Anytime
Dragon's Tale Theatre | As per the daily entertainment schedule
Griffin's Galleon | Before noon or after 3 p.m.

WILD ASIA
Kobra | Before 11 a.m. or in the last 2 hours the park is open
Jungle Bus | First or last hour the park is open
Monkey Swinger | Before noon or after 4 p.m.
Tuk Tuk Turmoil Dodgems | Before noon or after 4 p.m.
Temple of Mayhem | Anytime
Lorikeet Lagoon | Anytime

MYSTIC EAST
Dragon Falls | Anytime
Peeking Heights | Anytime

FORBIDDEN KINGDOM
Tomb Blaster | Before noon or after 3 p.m.
Rameses Revenge | Before 11 a.m. or after 4 p.m.
Runaway Train | Before 11 a.m. or after 4 p.m.
Rattlesnake | Before noon or after 3 p.m.

4. Ride Vampire in Transylvania.
5. Experience Toadie's Crazy Cars in Toytown.
6. Also ride the Carousel in Toytown.
7. In Land of the Dragons, ride Griffin's Galleon.
8. See Dragon's Fury in Land of the Dragons.
9. Try the Runaway Train in Mexicana.
10. Eat lunch. Good nearby choices include the Fried Chicken Co. in Forbidden Kingdom.
11. Try Tuk Tuk Turmoil in Wild Asia.
12. Float down Dragon Falls in Mystic East.
13. Ride the Peeking Heights observation wheel.
14. Experience Black Buccaneer in Pirates Cove.
15. Ride Seastorm in Pirates Cove.
16. Try Bubbleworks in Transylvania. (Let us know if you can think of why this attraction is located in Transylvania.)
17. Check the daily entertainment schedule for the next *Dragon's Tale Theatre* show and work in the next couple of steps around that performance.
18. Ride the Safari Skyway in Market Square.
19. Tour Hocus Pocus Hall in Market Square.
20. Tour the Trail of the Kings, Sea Life Centre and Wanyama Village & Reserve experiences in Chessington Zoo.
21. See any missed attractions or repeat any favourites.
22. Depart Chessington World of Adventures.

One-Day Touring Plan for Teens and Adults

1. The night before your visit, check **chessington.com** for park hours and weather.
2. Arrive at the park entrance 30 minutes prior to official opening. If possible, have your admission in hand before you arrive. Otherwise, arrive 15 minutes earlier and send one member of your party to obtain admission.
3. As soon as the park opens, ride Tomb Blaster in Forbidden Kingdom.
4. Take the Runaway Train in Mexicana.
5. Ride Rattlesnake, also in Mexicana.
6. In Transylvania, try Vampire.
7. Experience Kobra in Wild Asia.
8. Try your hand at Tuk Tuk Turmoil, also in Wild Asia.
9. Swing on Monkey Swinger in Wild Asia.
10. If the weather is warm enough, try Rameses Revenge in Forbidden Kingdom.
11. Eat lunch.
12. Try Dragon's Fury in Land of the Dragons.
13. In Mystic East, try Dragon Falls.

14. Ride the Peeking Heights observation wheel.
15. Tour the Lorikeet Lagoon in Wild Asia.
16. If time permits, try the Black Buccaneer in Pirates' Cove.
17. Float through Bubbleworks in Transylvania.
18. Ride the Safari Skyway in Market Square.
19. Tour Hocus Pocus Hall.
20. Tour the Trail of the Kings, Sea Life Centre and Wanyama Village & Reserve experiences in Chessington Zoo.
21. See any missed attractions or repeat any favourites.
22. Depart Chessington World of Adventures.

Legoland Windsor *See The South of England, page 152.*

The London Dungeon ★★★

APPEAL BY AGE	PRESCHOOL ★	PRIMARY SCHOOL ★★★	TEENS ★★★★
YOUNG ADULTS ★★★		OVER 30 ★★★	SENIORS ★★

28–34 Tooley St, London SE1 2SZ
☎ 0207 403 7221; the-dungeons.co.uk

HOURS 9.30 a.m.–7 p.m. during August; otherwise opening times vary from 9.30 to 11 a.m., and closing from 4 to 7 p.m. (check website for details).

COST £23 adults, (from £20.50 online peak; from £13 online off-peak); £17 children (4–15) (from £15.50 online peak; from £11 online off-peak); £21 senior citizens, students (from £17.50 online peak; from £11 online off-peak); £21 disabled adults (from £18 online peak; from £15.95 online off-peak); £15 disabled children (4–15) (from £13 online peak; from £12.95 online off-peak). Priority tickets generally run about £4 more per ticket. While there are no age limits, management does say 'the Dungeon is not suitable for people of a nervous disposition or very young children'.

Various package tickets are sold for combined entrance to other Merlin attractions in the area, including Madame Tussauds, Sea Life London Aquarium, the Merlin London Eye and the London Eye River Cruise. Two-for-one deals are available with train travel (**daysoutguide.co.uk**). Tickets can also be bought through the Tesco Clubcard rewards scheme.

You can also use the **Merlin Annual Pass** (**merlinannualpass.co.uk**), which provides admission to Alton Towers Resort Theme Park, Legoland Discovery Centre, Legoland Windsor, Thorpe Park, Sea Life aquariums and sanctuaries, Dungeons attractions, the Merlin London Eye, Madame Tussauds London and Warwick Castle. Prices begin at £150 for an individual and drop in price if you're buying for a family group.

GETTING THERE *By car:* The Dungeon is within the London congestion zone: £8 charge (☎ 0845 900 1234; **tfl.gov.uk/roadusers/congestioncharging**). Parking is at NCP at St Thomas and Upper Thames streets. *By rail:* About 330 ft (100 m) from London Bridge Station, served by **British Rail**

THEME PARKS AND ATTRACTIONS

(**nationalrail.co.uk**) and **London Underground** (Northern and Jubilee lines; **tfl.gov.uk/tube**), and about 1,300 ft (400 m) from Monument/Bank Station, served by **Docklands Light Railway** (**tfl.gov.uk/modal pages/2632.aspx**) and **London Underground** (District, Circle, Central and Northern lines). *By bus:* Served by **Routes 21, 35, 40, 43, 47, 48, 78, 133, 149,** and **381**. (Route information: **transportdirect.info.**)

DESCRIPTION AND COMMENTS London hasn't always been such a civilised place. Between plague, fire, serial killers, madhouses and bloodthirsty queens, the city has seen its share of gloom, doom and mayhem. Certainly all this has meant countless deaths and suffering over the centuries. But given a few hundred years' distance, it's also an excuse for a popular tourist attraction.

The Dungeon (you'll find them across the UK as well as in Amsterdam and Hamburg, Germany) operates on the principle that people have an unquenchable appetite for the ghoulish. (How else to explain zombie movies?) Although the attraction isn't over-the-top terrifying, it will give some in your party the shivers, particularly children in the 10–14 age group; but there are plenty of droll laughs too. While the experience is hardly the equivalent of spending an afternoon at the museum, you will learn something about London's less-than-savoury history.

You'll also get to see London's next generation of aspiring actors polish their technique. Many are quite good and add to the fun, but occasionally you'll get one just reciting the script. As you arrive, you are split into groups of about two dozen, and then spend some 90 minutes working your way through various rooms or scenes where actors dressed in full creep-out (corpses, killers, and the like) present tales based on history. Most 'scenes' involve a recruited audience member who becomes the butt of jokes and some mock torture. If you like this sort of thing, stand near the front and establish eye contact with your guide. If you don't, do your best to hide behind someone tall, because the guides have a sixth sense for finding the most reluctant in their group and dragging them straight into the scene.

The first thing you need to know, though, is that if you don't time it right, your visit will feel very much like torture. Queuing can be notorious here, lasting more than 2 hours – and that's just to get through the door. Once inside, you queue again for a photo – someone in your party poses in stocks while another party member readies an axe over their head (you'll be offered the photo for purchase at the end of the visit). And then there may be another wait before your group starts the tour, which leaves every 5–10 minutes. The Dungeon sells priority tickets that let you get inside the building more quickly, but you'll often still face a queue. You'll also find crowds inside, where it can get very warm. Our advice is to time your visit carefully to avoid the crush – and the extra cost of priority tickets. If possible, avoid weekends and school holidays, or arrive about 10 minutes before the Dungeon opens in the morning, or late in the afternoon.

Once you enter and pose for your picture, your next stop should be a visit to the loo. There's no convenient toilet along the 90-minute tour, and if you do need to make a stop, you'll have to leave your party and miss part of the show. Next, a staff member sends you off with 'Have a horrible time!' and your journey begins. You enter the crypt of **All Hallows Church** and are sent into the **Labyrinth of the Lost,** a dimly-lit mirror maze where actors occasionally jump out to give you a scare. From there, you're led to 1665 London and the **Great Plague.** As the story's told, you learn in grotesque detail how victims died and collectors gathered their bodies. Next comes the **Great Fire of London,** which includes a video presentation made much more dramatic with smoke that begins to fill the room.

That leads to **Surgery: Blood and Guts,** where a doctor shows the latest mediaeval medical techniques. He recruits an audience member as a patient, who is strapped to a chair. Then, as you're told how doctors sold body parts on the black market, the physician pulls out various organs from what appears to be a cadaver. Next he turns his attention to the volunteer, and as he raises an axe, the lights cut out and you're sprayed with what you imagine is blood.

You also visit a **Torture Chamber,** where a guide demonstrates some fiendish equipment on volunteers. Things lighten up just a bit in **Judgement**, where you may be found guilty of having an ugly jumper. Perhaps it's fitting you find yourself in **Bedlam,** London's historic insane asylum, and then you hop aboard **Traitor: Boat Ride to Hell,** a floating journey inspired by the Traitors' Gate, the water entrance to the Tower of London. Your journey through the darkness includes unexpected turns, drops and startling noises – and actors.

Now you're in the eighteenth century, and your first stop is **Sweeney Todd**'s barber shop. As you sit in one of his chairs, you face a likely throat-slitting, with the knowledge you'll be ground up for Mrs Lovett's meat pies like that corpse you saw when you entered. *Yum!* Now you'll meet an even more famous scoundrel, **Jack the Ripper.** You meet a prostitute he killed, witness an autopsy and watch a video about the possible identity of the serial killer. It ends with a surprise that may startle even the blasé in your group. There's also a chance to meet the man himself.

Now it's back in time to visit **Bloody Mary.** You'll get to see her in full rant as someone in your group is sentenced to death by burning. As the sentence is delivered, there's smoke and light, and the volunteer victim is replaced by a charred, ghoulish model. Finally comes **Extremis: Drop Ride to Doom** (3'11"/1.2 m to ride). This is a funfair drop tower that's been cleverly themed to make you think you're on a gallows at Newgate Prison. When the scaffolding drops, so do you, amid screams and laughter.

TOURING TIPS Plan your visit carefully to avoid daunting crowds and queues. Wear multiple layers. Even when it's cold outside, it can get quite warm inside. Enter with the right frame of mind. This isn't meant to be a history lesson, although you may learn something. Buy tickets online or look around for coupons – at more than £20 a person at the door, it can be an expensive experience, and a discount makes the price much more palatable.

Sea Life London Aquarium ★★★

APPEAL BY AGE	PRESCHOOL ★★★★	PRIMARY SCHOOL ★★★	TEENS ★★
YOUNG ADULTS ★★	OVER 30 ★★★		SENIORS ★★★

County Hall, Westminster Bridge Road, London SE1 2SZ
☎ 0871 663 1678; visitsealife.com/London

HOURS 10 a.m.–6 p.m. Monday–Thursday; 10 a.m.–7 p.m. Friday–Sunday. Last entry 1 hour before closing. Closed Christmas Day.

COST £18 adults (£16.20 online); £12.50 children 3–15 (£11.25 online); £16.50 senior citizens (£14.85 online); £55 family ticket (2 adults, 2 children) (£49.40 online). For an extra £3 per ticket (slightly less online), you get priority access, allowing you to jump the entrance queue. Tickets after 3 p.m.: £13 adults; £9.25 children 3–15. Various package tickets are sold for combined entrance to other Merlin attractions, including Madame Tussauds, The London Dungeon, the London Eye and the London Eye River Cruise.

You can also use the **Merlin Annual Pass** (**merlinannualpass.co.uk**), which provides admission to Alton Towers Resort Theme Park, Legoland Discovery Centre, Legoland Windsor, Thorpe Park, Sea Life aquariums and sanctuaries, Dungeons attractions, the Merlin London Eye, Madame Tussauds London and Warwick Castle. Prices begin at £150 for an individual and drop in price if you're buying for a family group.

GETTING THERE *By car:* The nearest car parking is a short walk away, along the South Bank at the Royal Festival Hall or at the underground parking facility at Waterloo Station. Note the central-London congestion charge of £8 (details: ☎ 0845 900 1234; **tfl.gov.uk/roadusers/congestion charging**). *By rail:* The nearest rail station is Waterloo East. Follow the exit signs for the South Bank (Exit 6) and walk towards the London Eye. The aquarium is in County Hall, next to the Eye. Charing Cross train station is also close to the site. From Charing Cross, take the exit next to Platform 1 for Hungerford Bridge; go over the bridge and follow signs for Jubilee Gardens. Follow the riverfront past the London Eye, and the aquarium is on your left (**journeyplanner.tfl.gov.uk**). *By bus:* Many bus services stop near Waterloo or Westminster Bridge Road, both near the aquarium. For Westminster Bridge Road, take the **12, 53, 59, 76, 148, 159, 211** or **341.** For Belvedere Road (just behind the aquarium, parallel to the South Bank), take the **77** or **RV1.** For York Road (next to Waterloo and behind the aquarium), take the **211, 77** or **381.** Many other buses stop on Waterloo Road, which is a few minutes' walk from the aquarium. These include **1, 4, 26, X68, 76, 168, 171, 172, 176, 188, 243, 507** and **638** (**journeyplanner.tfl.gov.uk**). All the London sightseeing buses also pick up and drop off at these points.

DESCRIPTION AND COMMENTS The flagship of the Sea Life chain's UK sites, the London Aquarium isn't remarkably different from the other Sea Life centres around the country, just bigger. Still, if you're a fish-lover, it's worth visiting this multi-level basement display, with 500 species and more than 440,000 gal (2 million litres) of water.

The attraction opened in 1997 in the old County Hall building on the south bank of the Thames. In 2008, it was acquired by Merlin Entertainments (which also owns several of the country's major theme parks and the neighbouring London Eye) and underwent an overdue £5 million refurbishment. Although hallways are dimly lit, the aquarium creates atmosphere with careful exhibit lighting and mood music.

The site's easily accessed by tube or bus – you really don't want to drive here. As you approach the aquarium, there's often a queue. You can bypass it by paying an extra £3 or so per ticket, but we suggest just trying to time your visit to avoid the crowd. Once you pay admission, descend to the **Atlantic Depths** exhibit, home to creatures found in the North Atlantic. Look for sand eels, lobsters, John Dory, starfish and cold-water anemones. The first few exhibits may seem crowded, but don't worry: the traffic will dissipate as you move along. If it's too much now, take a look at the jellyfish that hover hypnotically in a circular tank – it's an instant bit of calming therapy.

Next, you'll work your way to the **Ray Lagoon,** home to one of the largest collections of Californian cownose rays in the world, with several dozen of the creatures. The exhibit is designed like a touch tank, but although you'll be tempted to pet the residents, it's not allowed. Don't worry; you soon reach a bona fide touch pool with crabs, starfish and anemones. Now comes the **ocean tunnel** through the 165,000-gal (750,000-litre) reef tank. The path is covered with the cast of an 82-ft (25-m) blue-whale skeleton for effect, but you'll be drawn to the assortment of rays, tangs, clown triggerfish and blacktip reef sharks. Everyone's favourite resident, though, seems to be Boris, a huge green sea turtle named for London mayor Boris Johnson.

Next comes the **Pacific Wreck** area, a 220,000-gal (1-million-litre) tank decorated with Easter Island statues – mere window dressing for the nurse, brown and zebra sharks cruising through the scenery. You'll also see sand tigers and a southern stingray.

It's a good thing that Pixar Animation couldn't trademark the clownfish, because every aquarium in the world now seems to have its own *Finding Nemo* exhibit featuring the species that starred in the 2003 animated hit movie. You'll find Sea Life's version in **Nemo's Coral Cave,** where dozens of the fish congregate. Next head to **Seahorse Temple,** with a nice assortment of the aquatic oddities.

Every aquarium also seems to have a jungle-inspired exhibit too. Sea Life's **Tropical Rainforest** is well done. Starting with red-bellied piranhas, it leads to a mangrove area with mudskippers and the over-achieving archerfish, which shoots bugs out of the air with a stream of water. The final section has larger residents, like catfish and gourami, a huge version of the popular home aquarium fish. Another tank swirls with brightly-coloured fish from Lake Malawi in Africa.

Then head upstairs to something closer to home, **The River Thames Story.** Decorated with miniature versions of London's bridges, its freshwater tanks have stickleback, carp and a few other local residents.

After all that touring, it's time for a break. **Antarctic Antics** is a fancy name for a craft area, where kids can make a keepsake and anyone can buy a souvenir photo with their head superimposed on a sea creature. There are also pick-and-mix sweets for sale. Then you can take a load off while you watch a short film on sharks, which helps set the stage for the final exhibits.

A conservation area argues for making environmentally-friendly choices in your day-to-day life. Finally, you get another view at the huge Pacific tank, and then end your visit with the **Shark Walk.** It sounds like a pirate's death sentence, but it's actually a walkway with a few glass floor panels giving a from-the-top look at sharks. The attraction is decorated with shark jaws, and even if it's not the grandest of finales, it's not a bad way to end the visit.

TOURING TIPS The biggest drawback at Sea Life London is the price. Cut your costs by seeking coupons online or in tourist brochures, or come after 3 p.m. for reduced admission. If nothing else, make sure to buy a combination ticket if your London touring plans include the London Eye, The London Dungeon or Madame Tussauds.

Given that the aquarium attracts three-quarters of a million visitors a year, queues here are the norm. Minimise your waiting by carefully planning your visit – late afternoons or early mornings are generally the best.

With the dim lighting and the twisting layout, it's easy to lose some of your party. Stick together, but have a designated meeting-spot just in case.

(For more on aquariums, see page 10.)

Thorpe Park See South East England, page 124.

ZSL London Zoo ★★★½

| APPEAL BY AGE | PRESCHOOL ★★★ | PRIMARY SCHOOL ★★★ | TEENS ★★★ |
| YOUNG ADULTS ★★★ | | OVER 30 ★★★★ | SENIORS ★★★★ |

Regents Park, London NW1 4RY
☎ **020 7722 3333; zsl.org/london-zoo**

HOURS Opens at 10 a.m., with closing time varying by season, usually until 5.30 p.m. mid-March–early October; between 4.00 and 4.30 p.m. other times of year. Last admission 1 hour before closing time. Some animal houses may close 30 minutes before this time. Closed Christmas Day.

COST (High season) £19.80 adults; £16 children (3–15; not admitted without an adult); £18.30 senior citizens 60+, students, disabled; 10% discount for family of 4 if purchased online. Slight discounts during mid- and winter seasons. All prices include a £1.80 charitable donation per ticket, which is optional. Tickets can also be bought through the Tesco Clubcard rewards scheme.

GETTING THERE By car: The zoo has a sizeable car park and is outside the London congestion-charge zone. Parking costs £12.50. Pay-and-display parking is also available on the Outer Circle at £2.40 per hour, Monday–Saturday, and £1.40 per hour on Sundays, 9 a.m.–6.30 p.m. There is a 4-hour maximum stay Monday–Saturday, but no limit on Sundays. By *tube:* Camden Town is the nearest tube station, with its Northern Line connection. Exit the station on the right and walk along Parkway until you reach Prince Albert Road. Turn right into Prince Albert Road and continue for about 5 minutes until you reach the traffic-light-controlled pedestrian crossing. Cross left here and walk over the Regent's Canal footbridge. Turn right, and the zoo is up the road on the left. Alternatively, you can use Regent's Park Tube station (Bakerloo Line) or Baker Street Station (Jubilee, Bakerloo & Metropolitan lines). *By rail:* The nearest mainline station is Euston (**nationalrail.co.uk**). From Euston go to Bus Stop G and take Bus 253 towards the Narroway/Hackney Central to Camden High Street. At Camden High Street go to Stop T and take Bus 274 towards Victoria Gate to ZSL London Zoo. *By bus:* **Route 274** runs from Marble Arch and Baker Street to Ormonde Terrace. Or take **Route C2** from Victoria Station, Oxford Circus or Great Portland Street to Gloucester Gate. *By waterbus:* The **London Waterbus Company** (☎ 020 7482 2550; **londonwaterbus.com**) runs scheduled service along the Regent's Canal between Camden Lock or Little Venice and the zoo.

DESCRIPTION AND COMMENTS   If you love animals, you owe a debt of gratitude to the London Zoo. As the world's first scientific zoo, which opened to researchers in 1828, it's also the site of the world's first public reptile house and aquarium, and even the first children's zoo, in 1939. Its historic buildings in London's Regent Park were home to Winnie, an American bear that inspired A. A. Milne to write his Winnie-the-Pooh books. It also housed the first hippopotamus seen in Europe since Roman times, and kept the last quagga before the zebra subspecies became extinct in 1883. The Reptile House even had a cameo in the first Harry Potter film, when the young wizard learned he could talk to snakes. (Like other significant historical sites, it's dutifully marked with a plaque.)

All that said, you may not want to visit the London Zoo. It's expensive and cramped, and because of their historic importance, many of the enclosures can't be expanded, so some animals are kept in less-than-ideal conditions. While the property has made notable upgrades in recent years, there are better zoos in the country, starting with the London Zoo's sister site, Whipsnade, about 35 mi (56 km) away. The Chester, Twycross and Paignton zoos are excellent, as are many of the safari parks scattered around the country, which have turned manor house grounds into mini-Tanzanias, giving you the chance to drive through habitats teeming with baboons, giraffes and prides of lions.

That said, the zoo's rich history can't be overlooked, and it's convenient if you're in London and need a break from churches, museums and city crowds. Not that you'll have the zoo to yourself – hardly. On summer days and school holidays, the attraction can be packed. Buy your tickets online to avoid the crush, or at least look for two-for-one deals to take the sting off the admission price.

While the property may seem large, it's actually compact by zoo standards, covering just 36 ac (15 ha). It has more than 750 species, and over 15,000 separate animals, from leaf-cutter ants to Chapman's zebras. The zoo grounds aren't clearly laid out, and the map isn't a great help either. Expect to do some wandering and asking for directions. As you enter the turnstiles, you'll find the bulk of the exhibits in front of you, but don't forget to turn around. Underpasses lead beneath the main road to another section, with rainforest and African exhibits and a large walk-through aviary.

From the entrance, look ahead to the left for one of the newest exhibits, **Gorilla Kingdom,** opened by the Duke of Edinburgh in 2007. The 65,000-sq-ft (6,000-m²) exhibit includes western lowland gorillas, black and white colobus monkeys and several other primate species. The area is landscaped with plants which the gorillas eat in their native Central Africa. In nice weather, you can observe the animals on a moated island; at other times, you can watch them gambol about on an indoor gym through glass walls.

Continuing clockwise, you'll reach the new **Penguin Beach** exhibit, scheduled to open in 2011. The area, a vast improvement over the old penguin pool, re-creates a South American beach inhabited by Humboldt and Macaroni penguins. The area includes an sub-aquatic viewing area, allowing you to watch the birds 'fly' under water. The covered demonstration area provides a good view of the daily feedings, long a zoo highlight. There's a small playground across the path, but even young ones will be drawn to the caterpillar-shaped **Butterfly Paradise** tent, which looks a little like a Quonset hut with antennae. Inside, you'll see hundreds of swirling butterflies, caterpillars and moths as big as your face. Look in the pupae-holding room to see the next generation of fliers emerging to take wing.

Continuing on the main path, you'll find **anteaters,** a great rarity in UK zoos. If the mammals ever escape, they'll find an unforgettable feast across the path at **B.U.G.S.,** the zoo's flagship insect exhibit. The initials stand for Biodiversity Underpinning Global Survival, but as we see it, the display is primarily an excuse to overwhelm you with creepy-crawlies. Look for hissing cockroaches, leaf-cutter ants, maggots, locust swarms, giant spiders and Polynesian tree snails, some of which are extinct in the wild.

In the top-left corner of the zoo, you'll have a chance to **Meet the Monkeys** in a walk-through exhibit that lives up to its name. Here you're in the realm of squirrel monkeys, which play, swing and wander around, mostly oblivious to their visitors. Although they only weigh about 2 lb (less than 1 kg), signs warn the primates will bite if provoked. Our advice: Don't.

Next door, at the top of the zoo, you'll find **Blackburn Pavilion,** a walk-through tropical bird aviary with more than 50 avian species. Look for red-crested turacos, bleeding-heart doves (with a distinctive red colouring on the breast), hummingbirds, partridges and orioles. Even the clock outside the exhibit is bird-brained, marking every half-hour with a bird chime. It's just a short walk to **Animal Adventure,** a children's zoo, with aardvarks, red pandas, yellow mongooses, meerkats, prairie dogs and porcupines.

Continuing clockwise, you'll reach the **Outback,** with emus and wallabies. Follow the path to the **Reptile House** on your right. The historic building opened in 1927, and the front is covered with animal carvings. Inside, you'll see lizards, crocodiles, tortoises and snakes. But don't look for the Burmese python that chatted up Harry Potter in the 2001 film *Harry Potter and the Philosopher's Stone* (*Sorcerer's Stone* in the United States and India). That habitat is occupied by a black mamba that, as the longest venomous snake in Africa, is still an intimidating fellow. Next door you'll find **Komodo dragons,** man-eating lizards that also make an impression. The creatures can grow up to almost 10 ft (3 m) long and weigh 176 lb (80 kg). You're now just across from the **Giants of the Galápagos** exhibit, featuring Galápagos tortoises, the largest in the world, weighing in at more than 882 lb (400 kg).

Now backtrack towards the entrance and take the subway passage under the road, and you'll find the **Into Africa** exhibit on your left. Here you can get face-to-face with giraffes on a platform viewing area, and see zebras and African hunting dogs through periscopes and special observation windows that can put you literally in their face. Next door you'll find the **Snowdon Aviary,** with peafowl, sacred ibis, egrets, herons and African grey-headed gulls. Continuing clockwise you'll encounter **Rainforest Life** on your right, with red titi monkeys, sloths, tamarins and armadillos. There's also **Night Zone,** a nocturnal area with fruit bats, scorpions and Malagasy jumping rats, all of which make the dark their home – and will the scare the daylights out of most of us.

TOURING TIPS Although you're here for animals, make sure to admire the historic architecture and animal statues. Purchase your tickets ahead of time, as queues can get long. Check times for feeding times and zoo-keeper talks – they can make a visit. Food choices are expensive, but there aren't many picnic areas. In addition, the zoo doesn't offer in-and-out privileges. You may just have to bite the bullet and grab a hot dog or ice-cream from one of the vendors.

PART FIVE

SOUTH EAST ENGLAND

THE ROLLING FIELDS, ORCHARDS, PASTORAL VILLAGES and chalky downs of South East England have nurtured any number of great figures, from Charles Dickens to Henry James to Winston Churchill, to name just a few. Once you begin exploring the back roads of this small corner of England – the most remote bit of which is only 2 hours from London – it's easy to see why so many writers, kings, queens, statesmen and, especially in recent times, untold numbers of vacationers seeking a rural retreat have taken refuge in these landscapes. In these southern counties of **Kent, Surrey,** and **East and West Sussex,** you'll find beautiful countryside; miles of English Channel beaches; and the palaces, gardens, cathedrals and historical homes that past residents have left behind. You'll also find theme parks, zoos and safari parks, farm experiences and aquariums. As you manoeuvre the twisting lanes, you may want to remember a line from another great English writer, C. K. Chesterton: 'Before the Roman came to Rye or out to Severn strode, the rolling English drunkard made the rolling English road.'

THEME PARKS and ATTRACTIONS

Blue Reef Aquarium–Hastings ★★

APPEAL BY AGE	PRESCHOOL ★★★★	PRIMARY SCHOOL ★★★	TEENS ★★
YOUNG ADULTS ★★		OVER 30 ★★★	SENIORS ★★★

Rock-A-Nore Road, Hastings, East Sussex TN34 3DW
☎ 01424 718 776; bluereefaquarium.co.uk/hastings.htm

HOURS (March–October) 10 a.m.–5 p.m. (last admission). (November–February) 10 a.m.–5 p.m. (last admission). Closed Christmas Day.

114 PART 5 SOUTH EAST ENGLAND

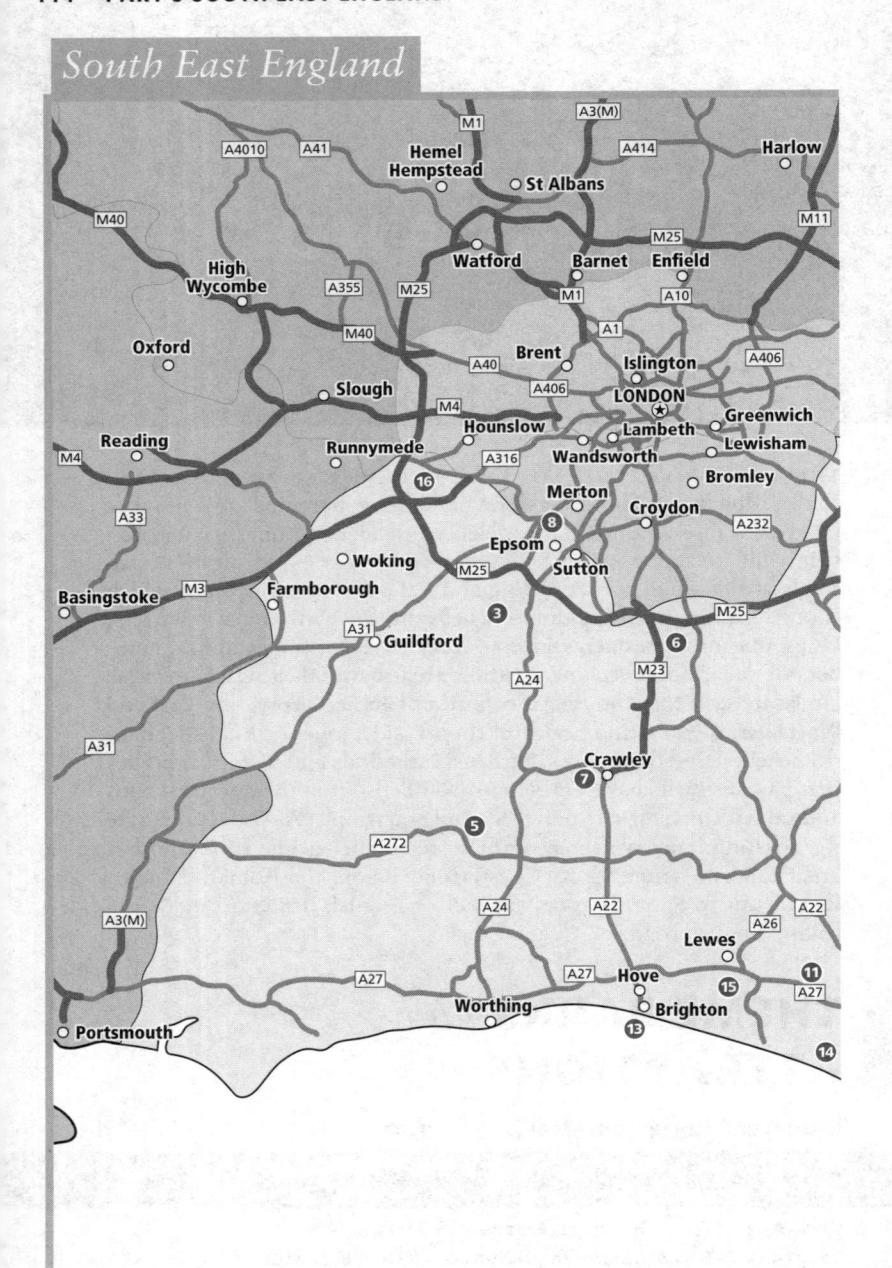

South East England

SOUTH EAST ENGLAND MAP 115

ATTRACTIONS
1. Blackberry Farm
2. Blue Reef Aquarium–Hastings
3. Bocketts Farm Park
4. Farming World
5. Fishers Farm Park
6. Godstone Farm
7. Holmbush Farm World
8. Horton Park Children's Farm
9. Howletts Wild Animal Park
10. Kent Life (farm experience)
11. Middle Farm Countryside Centre
12. Port Lympne Wild Animal Park
13. Sea Life Brighton
14. Seven Sisters Sheep Centre
15. Spring Barn Farm Park
16. Thorpe Park

COST £7.95 adults; £5.95 children 3–14 (must be accompanied by an adult); £6.95 senior citizens, students; £25.80 family ticket (2 adults, 2 children); £30.75 family ticket (2 adults, 3 children).

GETTING THERE *By car:* Hastings is about 65 mi (105 km) southeast of London on the A21, which can be reached from Junction 5 on the M25. There is a public car park beside the aquarium, and two more located farther along the seafront. *By rail:* Frequent trains serve Hastings from London Charing Cross and London Victoria (**nationalrail.co.uk**). From the rail station, it's .8 mi (1.25 km) to the aquarium. *By bus:* From Hastings rail station, take **Stagecoach Hastings/20A** bus to Old Town (**stagecoachbus.com/eastsussex**). There's also **National Express** bus service from London, Brighton and Kent (**nationalexpress.com**). (Route information: **transportdirect.info**.)

DESCRIPTION AND COMMENTS This smallish attraction in historic Hastings covers the aquarium basics with its 30 habitats. Standouts include jellyfish, a 50-ft (15-m) underwater walk-through tunnel providing views of pufferfish and blacktip reef sharks, and amphibians like the poison dart frog. You'll find dozens of sea horses here as well. Best of all, however, is the Chilton sea slug, with teeth that can bite through rock (or you). The aquarium chain has been successful in breeding the endangered species.

TOURING TIPS A bit pricey for what's available. To get full value, allot time for feedings and educational talks. The facility is quite small and does not handle crowds well, which makes viewing the exhibits a problem on busier days, especially for children.

Just a few doors down is the **Fishermen's Museum,** a modest affair that offers an interesting glimpse of the history of commercial fishing and the lives and equipment of fishermen past and present. Switching gears, the popular television series *Foyle's War* was partially filmed in Hastings, and **Foyle's house,** on Croft Street, is about a 10-minute walk from the aquarium.

(For more on aquariums, see page 10.)

Howletts Wild Animal Park ★★★

APPEAL BY AGE	PRESCHOOL ★★★	PRIMARY SCHOOL ★★★	TEENS ★★★
YOUNG ADULTS ★★★		OVER 30 ★★★★	SENIORS ★★★★

Bekesbourne, nr Canterbury, Kent CT4 5EL
☎ **0844 842 4647; aspinallfoundation.org/howletts**

HOURS 10 a.m.–6 p.m. summer; until 5 p.m. winter. Closed Christmas Day.

COST £16.95 adults; £12.95 children (3–15); £13.95 students; £10.95 senior citizens, disabled and carers, disabled children; £54 family of 4; £62 family of 5. Get a 20% discount for buying online. Tickets can also be bought through the Tesco Clubcard rewards scheme.

GETTING THERE *By car:* Under 2 hours from Cambridge, Brighton and central London. Parking is free. From London and Essex, follow the A2 out of the city or pick it up at the M25 intersection, and follow signs for Dover and Folkestone. Once you pass the exit for Canterbury, the route to Howletts is marked with brown tourist signs. From Surrey and

Sussex, join the M25 and travel to join the M26/M20 in the direction of Dover and Folkestone. Exit the M20 at Junction 7, and join the A249 and follow signposts to the A2 and Dover and Folkestone. Once you pass Canterbury, the route to Howletts is marked with brown tourist signs. *By rail:* It's a 90-minute journey from London's Victoria station to Bekesbourne station (**nationalrail.co.uk**). *By bus:* A minibus shuttle runs to the park from the train station at peak times, but at other times of year it runs weekends only (☎ 0122 772 1286). (Route information: **transportdirect.info.**)

DESCRIPTION AND COMMENTS Tucked away in the Kent countryside near the historic city of Canterbury, Howletts Wild Animal Park is one of a pair of zoos, along with nearby Port Lympne, founded by millionaire conservationist John Aspinall, with the aim of breeding rare and endangered species. Somewhat confusingly, Howletts makes the firm assertion that it is not a zoo, although we are confused as regards why, because all the animals are housed in secure enclosures and there is no drive-through safari park. For a comparison of Howletts and Port Lympne and advice concerning which might best suit your party, see the profile of Port Lympne on page 120.

And a very good zoo (sorry, wild-animal park) it is too – the 90-ac (36-ha) site is home to a total of 44 different species and boasts what the park describes as the largest breeding family group of western lowland gorillas in the world – more than 50 of them at the last count. There is a range of other endangered species on show, such as a python, tigers, elephants and a host of different primates. There are also some really rare animals that don't crop up in your average zoo, such as snow leopards and serval cats. All the animals look healthy and well cared for, and they enjoy spacious enclosures full of trees and ponds to keep the animals stimulated while still being open enough to enable good viewing.

The property was acquired by Aspinall in 1957, when it became clear the apartment building he shared with his wife in London was too small to house his capuchin monkey, tiger and two Himalayan bears. Aspinall was a legendary gambler – he is reported to have skipped his final examinations at Oxford because they conflicted with Royal Ascot – and he secured the down payment for the Howletts property with a large win on the famous Cesarewitch horse race. The park opened to the public in 1975, and although Aspinall died in 2000, his influence is still strongly felt. He had unorthodox approaches to zookeeping, advocating that keepers develop strong bonds with the animals in their care.

Today, although Howletts is a lovely place to visit, one of the main drawbacks is its location – it's a long drive from London and other big cities and, as it's quite small, is only likely to keep you occupied for 2 or so hours. It is also quite expensive for what it is. Whipsnade, on the other side of London, is similarly priced, but offers a better zoo experience and is less of a drive. But you can combine a Howletts visit with a trip to nearby Canterbury, a historic city offering plenty to see and do.

You'll find the park nicely laid out, following the rolling contours of the surrounding countryside, with lots of pleasant wooded areas and some beautiful views. None of the paths are particularly steep and all are in good condition, offering no problems for wheelchairs or pushchairs. Wheelchairs are available for a £20 refundable deposit (you are advised to book in advance, as availability is limited).

The park's shaped like a rectangle, and you enter from one of the shorter sides, on the right. You'll want to zigzag through the first third of the property to take in the animals at the front of the park, and then work your way to the large deer enclosure occupying the centre of the site, which you'll circle. Given Howletts' relatively-small size, it can get very busy on summer weekends.

As you enter the park, you'll see the distinctly-striped **bongos** to your right, and behind them a paddock with **black rhinos.** You'll next pass by cute but scary carnivores, the **African hunting dogs.** Now cross the main path past the open-topped monkey enclosure and make your way to the sizeable **gorilla exhibit.** There's no better place to see the western lowland, the largest of the great apes. The collection can be traced back to founder Aspinall. As he became interested in animals, he made frequent visits to the London Zoo and would always stop and see Guy, the zoo's silverback gorilla. Over time, the primate began to recognise his frequent visitor, and a friendship of sorts formed. That eventually led to Aspinall's interest in the primates. A male gorilla can weigh as much as 475 lb (215 kg), almost three times as much as an average human male of the same height. Numbers of the species are declining in the wild, and the park plays an important role in captive breeding.

Next pass by the wolves and the elegant **pudu deer.** Take a moment to study the **capybara,** the world's largest rodent. The park has more than a dozen members of this highly-social species, which communicates with whistles and barks. Now cut back across the main path, past the tigers, and continue back to the **African elephants,** the largest herd in the UK, presided over by a bull named Jums. These giants reach 11 ft (3.4 m) at the shoulder and weigh over 13,200 lb (6 t). If you have trouble seeing them here, you'll be able to catch up with them by the sand paddock near the pizzeria, which you'll reach shortly.

You'll have to backtrack past the majestic snow leopards and take a right at the main path, which will bring you to the requisite **walk-through lemur exhibit.** Although the primates are endangered in their native Madagascar, they're practically unavoidable in UK zoos. Given their popularity, we wouldn't be surprised to see them turn up at Tesco soon. Still, the black-and-white-ruffed lemurs are undeniably precocious, and you'll find a good selection here. Take some time to see if you can identify the dominant members of the group. Continue on the main path past the four **servals,** with their distinctive spotted coats, and follow the trail to the right, past the **red river hogs,** Africa's version of the Eurasian wild boar. With their red coats, they're the most attractive of the pig species, showing that it's not important what you are as long as you look good in your outfit.

Now you've reached the main deer and antelope park. We suggest circling it anti-clockwise, mainly because that's how you'll find the closest WC. On the way, you'll pass the elephant yard on your right. When you reach the pizzeria, duck behind it to see the African elephants if you didn't spot them earlier. Rounding the corner, you'll pass **dusky langurs.** These small Malaysian monkeys might look overweight, but there's a reason for their pot bellies. The species lives on a diet of toxic leaves and has developed a complex digestive system to get enough nutrition and neutralise the poison. In some cases, the stomach contents can account for more than a quarter of their total body weight. Because they have pot bellies no matter what, someone might suggest to the langurs that a diet of puddings might be more enjoyable than poisonous leaves. Their choice, of course . . . we're just saying.

As you move along, you'll want to take in another type of wild attraction: the chestnut tree on the left side of the path. The **Howletts chestnut** is one of the oldest in Britain. The park grounds have existed since the time of Henry VIII, and many of the great trees are believed to be his contemporaries. Continuing on the path, look for the **ocelots** on the right. Their varied coat markings offer camouflage but are also coveted by the fur trade, and the felines are almost extinct in North America. Now look for the **Moloch gibbons** – primates so rare that the park says it holds half of the world's captive population. They live in the rainforests of Java and spend much of their life in trees.

The path becomes wooded now and, like in a scene from Little Red Riding Hood, you'll soon encounter **Iberian wolves,** along with other predators like **leopards, jaguars** and the thick-furred **Pallas cats** from China. Working your way to the bottom corner of the park, look for the **bison, lynx** and **honey badger,** but don't turn back until you reach the **Burmese python** at the end of the path. The Asian reptile is one of the largest snake species in the world, reaching on average 12 ft (3.7 m) long. And although they're generally afraid of man, adult specimens have killed humans. With that knowledge, you'll want to quickly retreat to the main path and start circling towards the entrance. You'll pass a pair of **Heck's macaques.** If the primates' cheeks appear particularly puffy, it's because they're storing fruit there while they forage. Finally you'll pass **tapirs,** pig-like mammals considered 'living fossils' because the species has changed little in the last 20 million years.

Now you can work your way back to the entrance, spending time with any animals you might have missed.

TOURING TIPS Howletts would not be a good place to visit if the weather were bad, as the only animal exhibit under cover is the tank of blind cave fish in the gift shop near the Pavilion Restaurant. Interesting as they are, there's only so long you want to spend looking at blind cave fish. Check on keeper talks, which are given during high season. They'll greatly enhance your visit, particularly since Howletts' staff build strong bonds with the animals under their care.

Port Lympne Wild Animal Park ★★★

APPEAL BY AGE	PRESCHOOL ★★★	PRIMARY SCHOOL ★★★	TEENS ★★★★
YOUNG ADULTS ★★★		OVER 30 ★★★★	SENIORS ★★★★

Lympne, Nr Hythe, Kent CT21 4PD
☎ **0844 842 4647;** aspinallfoundation.org/portlympne

HOURS (Summer) 10 a.m.–6 p.m. (last entrance 4.30 p.m.). (Winter) 10 a.m.–5 p.m. (last entrance 3.30 p.m.). Closed Christmas Day.

COST £16.95 adults; £12.95 children (3–15); £14.95 senior citizens, disabled, carers; £13.95 students; £10.95 disabled children; £54 family of 4; £62 family of 5. Safari Experience: an additional £5 adults; £3 children (3–15). Discount of 20% for buying online. Tickets can also be bought through the Tesco Clubcard rewards scheme.

GETTING THERE *By car:* About 2 hours from Cambridge, Brighton and central London. Parking is free. From London, Essex and East Sussex, join the M25/M26; look for signposts to the M20 in the direction of Ashford. Follow the M20 to Junction 11 and then follow the brown tourist signs to Port Lympne. From Surrey and West Sussex, join the M25 and travel in the direction of the Dartford Tunnel. Then take the M26/M20 and leave the M20 at Junction 11, just past Ashford. Follow the signs to Port Lympne. *By rail:* The closest station is Ashford International, 7 mi (11.4 km) from the park. The journey takes about 40 minutes from London's St Pancras station on the high-speed service (**southeasternrailway.co.uk** or **nationalrail.co.uk**). *By bus:* The **Stagecoach East Kent No. 10 bus** runs between Ashford and Folkestone via the park (☎ 0870 243 3711; **stagecoachbus.com**). (Route information: **transportdirect.info**.)

DESCRIPTION AND COMMENTS Take a stunning country estate, mix in the world's biggest gorilla enclosure and the largest breeding herd of black rhinoceros outside of Africa, and you get a sense of Port Lympne Wild Animal Park. The 600-ac (243-ha) property is home to more than 50 species, including many little-seen and endangered ones.

But one of the most interesting figures at Lympne isn't even on display. The park reflects the vision of founder John Aspinall. Known to friends as Aspers, he was a gambler and bookmaker who rubbed shoulders with royalty. He also had a love for animals, and began collecting them even while living in an apartment in London. As his menagerie grew, he bought the property that would become nearby Howletts Animal Park to give his collection room to grow. When that property was filled, he purchased Port Lympne in 1973 and opened it to the public in 1976. Both animal attractions have been run by the John Aspinall Foundation since 1984.

Given their similarities, there is little point in visiting both Port Lympne and Howletts, so which one is best? That rather depends on what you're looking for. In our view, Howletts offers a better visitor experience, as it has a more customer-friendly set-up, the animals are easier to see and it's much easier to walk around, both in terms of navigation and the quality of the paths. If you have pushchairs or wheelchairs, then you should definitely opt for Howletts. However, there is more to do at Port Lympne if you are prepared to pay extra for the **Safari Experience,** which offers an added dimension to your day out; and if you have older children with you, then they are likely to enjoy this option more. Port Lympne also has much more space to accommodate visitors, so would probably be a better option on a bank holiday or a summer's weekend.

Port Lympne is set on the side of a hill, so if you are pushing anything you would be well advised to not venture too far down, as getting back up again could prove difficult. Although the main paths are in good order, some of the side paths are quite rough. However, wheelchairs are available for a £20 refundable deposit, and you are advised to book in advance, as availability is limited.

The park is also home to a mansion, which reflects the glamour of the Roaring '20s. It was built for politician and bon vivant Philip Sassoon by some of the world's leading craftsmen, and was planned by architect Sir Herbert Baker, famous for the design of New Delhi, India. Budget obviously wasn't a concern, as the project includes handmade French bricks, rafters built from Oregon pine, and a hallway floor made of black and white marble in concentric curves, which is almost hypnotising. Other highlights are the Art Deco murals painted by leading English artists of the era. Guests at the mansion included royalty and Winston Churchill, and paintings of them still hang on some of the walls. The sumptuous setting continues outdoors, in the 15-ac (6-ha) park and gardens, which include a vineyard, fig orchard, chessboard and stripe garden. Views extend as far as the **English Channel** and over **Romney Marsh.** The park offers worthwhile **Garden & Mansion Tours** from 10 a.m. to 4 p.m. (The mansion may be closed for special events, so if you're set on a visit, call ahead to make sure it's open the day of your visit.)

A sign at the park entrance makes it clear that the purpose of Port Lympne is first and foremost as a conservation centre, and its role as a visitor attraction is secondary. This is borne out by the fact that many of the enclosures are so thick with trees and undergrowth that it is difficult to spot anything, which is undoubtedly in the interest of the animals but is less than enthralling for the paying public. That said, the wooded setting lends a pleasingly jungle-like quality, which is accentuated by the screeching of monkeys and the occasional roar of a big cat.

Port Lympne is shaped like a large rectangle, with the car park and entrance at the bottom right-hand corner. The property is laid out in a haphazard fashion and is somewhat difficult to navigate, so the maps available at 95p are a worthwhile investment. If you want to take the safari, get tickets at the gift shop near the entrance. It's a fun 90-minute ride that includes a few animals you won't see in other parts of the park, including giraffe, zebra and wildebeest. But long queues with waiting times of more than 90 minutes can develop throughout the day, so if you're set on the safari, arrive early and do it first.

Otherwise, enter the property and cut to the right, and you'll pass a wooded enclosure with **wolves,** and then follow the path by the **tigers** before looping back to the mansion. If you're interested, you can tour the home now, as knowing the Aspinall history will enhance your visit. But if you're eager to see animals, continue down the path to the right of the mansion and take a right on the path to the **Monkey Walk.**

On the right you'll first pass the **greater bamboo lemur,** perhaps the most endangered species at the park, which is saying something. Only about 300 of the primates are believed to be left in the wild in their native Madagascar. This leads you directly to the **Palace of the Apes,** the world's largest gorillarium (try that word in your next game of Scrabble) and home to a complete family group of **western lowland gorillas.** The exhibit has a glass-fronted section in the indoor enclosure and a 1-ac (.4-ha) garden with climbing frame. The family group and the bachelor group are fed daily at noon and 3 p.m. Continuing down the walk, you'll encounter more lemurs, including the cream-coloured **sifaka.** Only about two dozen of the primates are in captivity in Europe and North America, and you'll find two here.

Round the corner, take a right at the **tapirs** and pass the **African hunting dogs,** two unusual species that are worth a look. Then cut to the left to **Fishing Cat Corner** to see these Asian felines that swim and skillfully pluck their meals from wetland waters. These unfamiliar cats, with their short legs and stocky bodies, look nothing like your kitty at home. Now cut back by the **Barbary lions,** which sadly are extinct in the wild, and the always-fascinating **hyenas.** You're at the top right-hand corner of the park now. As you cut across the top, you'll pass a **tiger house** and, thankfully, a WC.

Continue past a herd of **water buffalo** on your right, then stay on your right at the roundabout to see **deer** and **roan antelope.** On your left, look for the endangered **black rhinos,** which are hunted for their horns (only about 3,000 of the animals are left in the wild), and a **bush dog** group, a family of rare South American canines who communicate with whines when they're on the hunt. Now continue on your diagonal path across the park. When it ends, take a right to see the park's three **African elephants.** You'll find refreshments and a WC near the bull-elephant house. Kruger, the park's male elephant, was born in the wild in 1984.

Backtracking a bit will bring you to the always-curious **meerkats,** along with **cheetahs, snow leopards** and almost-regal **red river hogs.** Now you've got a long walk along the drive as you head back towards the mansion. Along the way, look for black rhinos in the pasture on your left and **dhole,** an Asian wild-dog species, on your right. As you approach the mansion, cut back to the left to see the park's pair of **agoutis,** who share quarters with **black howler monkeys.** Agoutis, South American rodents, often live near the primates in the wild, scavenging the fruit the howlers drop.

Now cut to the right to see the **red pandas,** and if you're ambitious, leg it up the path a little farther to see the **porcupines.** The park may have seemed like a maze, but you can see a real one now back behind the mansion, planted in 2009.

TOURING TIPS Come prepared for a day of hiking, with water bottles and appropriate footwear. Port Lympne wouldn't be much fun on a wet day

THEME PARKS AND ATTRACTIONS

(although at least you could look around the house). If you're enthralled by the setting, consider spending the night in the park's **Livingstone Safari Lodge tents,** from £119 per adult, including meals and park tours.

Sea Life Brighton ★★½

APPEAL BY AGE	PRESCHOOL ★★★★	PRIMARY SCHOOL ★★★	TEENS ★★
YOUNG ADULTS ★★		OVER 30 ★★★	SENIORS ★★★

Marine Parade, Brighton, East Sussex BN2 1TB
☎ **01273 604 234; visitsealife.com/brighton**

HOURS 10 a.m.–4 p.m. (last entry 3 p.m.). Closed Christmas Day.

COST £15.50 adults (£10.50 online); £10.50 children 3–14 (£5.50 online); £45 family ticket (2 adults, 2 children) (£33 online). Admission can also be bought through the Tesco Clubcard rewards scheme.

GETTING THERE *By car:* From the M25, exit at the M23 and follow it south until it becomes the A23. Then follow signs to Brighton town centre. The aquarium, which is adjacent to Brighton Pier, is signposted as well. Pay-and-display parking on nearby Madeira Drive. *By rail:* The nearest rail station is Brighton (**nationalrail.co.uk**). From the station walk down Queens Road to the sea, then turn left. The aquarium is adjacent to Brighton Pier. *By bus:* Take any bus into Brighton town centre and head for the seafront. (Route information: **transportdirect.info**.)

DESCRIPTION AND COMMENTS This seaside aquarium, with more than 150 species and 50 displays, sets itself apart with a glass-bottomed boat that floats atop the centre's huge ocean tank, putting you directly above and quite close to giant sea turtles and sharks. The boat, more of a floating platform, costs an extra £3 for adults and £1 for children, but does provide a unique view of the sea life. Keep in mind that your ticket is timed, and you may have to return later in the day for your ride.

As you pass the café, look for the special circular tank holding moon jellies. This habitat creates a slow, gentle water flow, protecting the delicate jellyfish. They look so enchanting, you might momentarily forget the nasty sting they can deliver. You'll also see a variety of turtles: loggerheads, pig-nosed and Lulu, a green turtle the centre likes to say is the oldest aquarium resident in the UK, having been born some 70 years ago.

TOURING TIPS Sea Life Brighton can be seen at a leisurely pace in about 30 minutes, or an hour or so if you want to catch a feeding or a staff presentation. Like most Sea Life aquariums, it's pricey if you don't take advantage of the scheduled offerings. Parking is on the left side of the aquarium.

Congestion along the Brighton waterfront is horrible. To avoid this mess use the Churchill Square–Debenhams car park, accessible from Russell Road on the south side of Churchill Square. From there it's a short walk to the waterfront and the aquarium.

(For more on aquariums, see page 10.)

Thorpe Park ★★★★★
Staines Road, Chertsey, Surrey KT16 8PN
☎ 0871 663 1673; thorpepark.com

HOURS The park opens at either 9.30 or 10 a.m., varying by date and season. Likewise, closing times vary. It's open as late as 8 p.m., high season, and until 10 p.m. around Halloween, but can close as early as 5 p.m. other days. Check the website for details.

COST £39 adults (£28 online); £25 children under 12 (£19.50 online); children under 1 m free; £26 senior citizens (£23 online); £21 disabled and carers (£19 online); £104 family of 4 (no more than 2 adults, £88 online). Tickets can also be bought through the Tesco Clubcard rewards scheme.

You can also use the **Merlin Annual Pass** (**merlinannualpass.co.uk**), which provides admission to Alton Towers Resort Theme Park, Legoland Discovery Centre, Legoland Windsor, Chessington World of Adventures, Sea Life Sanctuaries, Dungeons attractions, the Merlin London Eye, Madame Tussauds London and Warwick Castle. Prices begin at £150 for an individual and drop in price if you're buying for a family group.

GETTING THERE *By car:* The park is approximately 20 mi (32 km) from London. It's between Junctions 11 and 13 off the M25 but cannot be reached from Junction 12. Parking costs £5. *By rail:* The nearest rail station is Staines (**southwesttrains.co.uk; nationalrail.co.uk**), a short walk from the bus station, where you can catch the **950 express shuttle** to Thorpe. It leaves from Stand 2 every 15–20 minutes. Train-travel and park-admission packages offer a savings of up to £8 per person. *By bus:* Besides the shuttle, many other bus routes are available to get you to Thorpe. (See **thorpepark.com/plan-your-visit/how-to-get-here.aspx** for a complete list of options.)

OVERVIEW Before it became a theme park in the late 1970s, the land around Thorpe Park was used as a rock quarry. The lake, or more correctly the flooded quarry, that surrounds the park is evidence of its past life. Though the park's grounds are attractive, they can't compete in landscaping or natural beauty with parks such as Alton Towers, Chessington World of Adventures or Legoland, which were built around former estates with manor houses, historical ruins and formal gardens. Still, the park is clean, and the admission price is fair relative to the value. Our visits to Thorpe were a highlight of our two years of research.

Thorpe Park bills itself as 'England's thrill capital', and they're probably right. Thorpe has two of the three best thrill rides in England, with Stealth and Nemesis Inferno (the other is Pleasure Beach Blackpool's Big One). While Thorpe's attractions and 'lands' lag behind Alton Towers, Legoland and Chessington in theming and story, they serve up maximum thrills just as advertised.

Thorpe Park, like Alton Towers, Chessington and Legoland Windsor, is owned by Merlin Entertainments. Chessington and Legoland are within a short drive or rail ride of Thorpe, so it has been interesting to see how Merlin differentiates each park. In the case of Thorpe, Merlin has decided to move a number of child-themed attractions out (to Chessington, purportedly), to make way for a new water-themed thrill ride in 2011. This continues Merlin's positioning of Thorpe for tweens, teens and young adults. If your family consists mostly of younger children, you may be happier at Chessington or Legoland.

Tip: Apple iPhone and iPad users can download an official Thorpe Park app, which shows the park map and current waiting times at all of the attractions.

ARRIVING If you're driving to Thorpe Park, you'll be directed to one of the car parks. The car park is divided into three named areas: Lakeside, Beomands and Central, plus an overflow car park. The respective sections are large enough to make finding your car time-consuming if you haven't made careful note of where you parked. It's suggested that you text-message someone else in your group with this information, in case you forget after all those brain-rattling rides.

GETTING ORIENTATED You enter and exit Thorpe Park through **The Dome,** a flying-saucer-shaped building that contains restaurants, stores and Fastrack sales (described following). Indoors and air-conditioned, The Dome overlooks the park and is a popular spot for meals. Four paths emanate from The Dome.

With few exceptions, Thorpe Park's attractions are not organised into themed lands, making it difficult for first-time visitors to determine quickly which approximate area of the park they're in. (Thorpe may have tried names for different areas at one time, but current park maps show none.) Going roughly anti-clockwise, with The Dome as the six o'clock marker, you'll find water rides just past The Dome, flanked by a children's playground and a picnic area. This section of the park includes the New England–themed faux town of **Amity Cove,** where the **Tidal Wave** boat ride is located, along with several restaurants and smaller attractions.

Thrill rides are above Amity Cove, including **Stealth** and **Detonator.** In the back of the park, opposite The Dome, are **Nemesis Inferno** and **Slammer.** Another child-friendly area, this one with a Canadian-wilderness theme, is in the far-left corner of the park. Attractions here include **Logger's Leap, Rocky Express** and the **Canada Creek Railway.**

Colossus and the pyramid-shaped building of **X:\No Way Out** are in the centre-left part of the park. On an island in the middle of the man-made lake in the bottom left of the park are attractions inspired by the *Saw* horror-film franchise.

PARK SERVICES Most of these are available at The Dome. A limited number of pushchairs are available for hire at a cost of £9 per day, plus an additional £20 refundable deposit. A limited number of wheelchairs are available as well, for a deposit of £25 per day. You'll need to bring proof of disability, such as a Disability Living Allowance book, Attendance Allowance book or Invalidity Benefit book, or face an additional £5 charge per day. The Dome's Guest Services also include Lost and Found and a medical centre.

FASTRACK Available at several Merlin Entertainments–owned theme parks in England, Fastrack is a pay scheme that allows you to bypass the

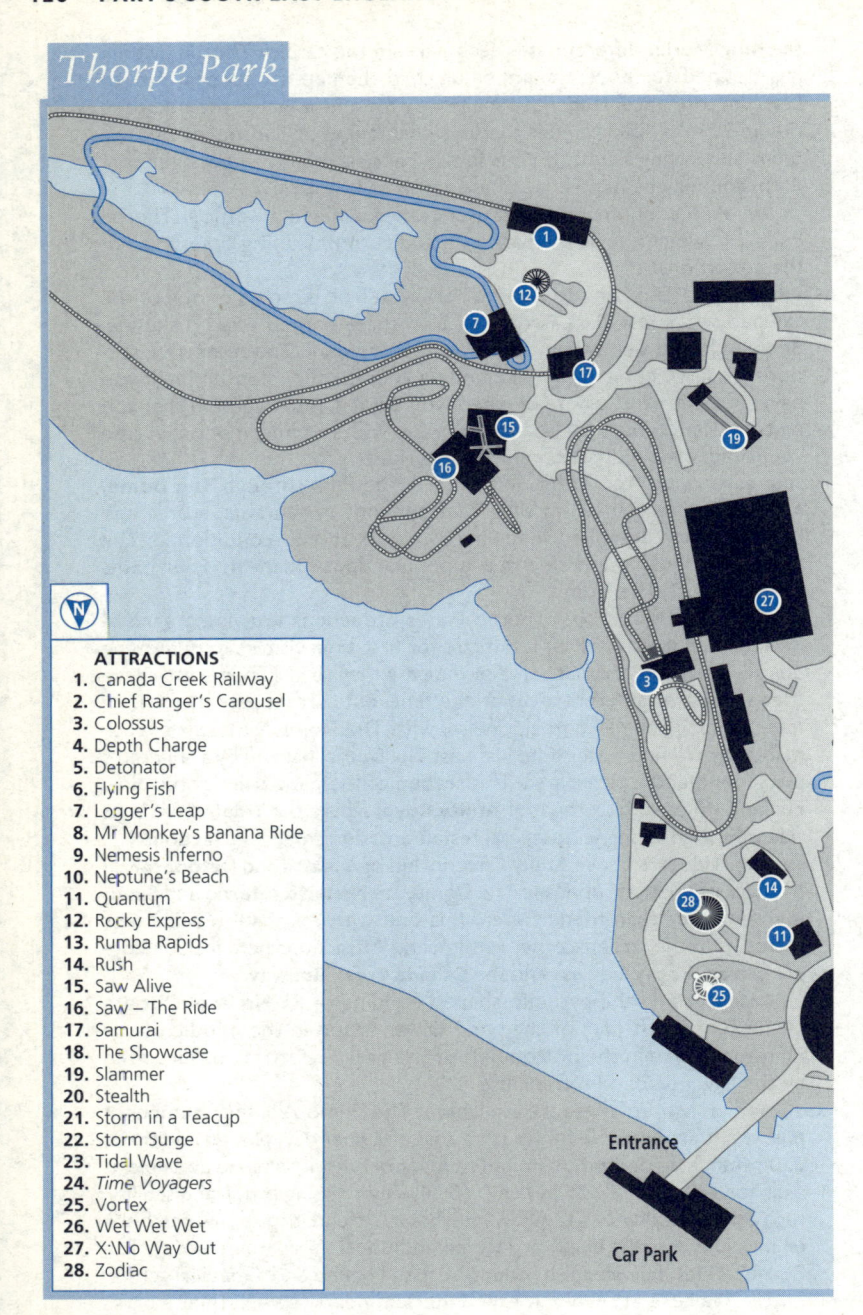

Thorpe Park

ATTRACTIONS
1. Canada Creek Railway
2. Chief Ranger's Carousel
3. Colossus
4. Depth Charge
5. Detonator
6. Flying Fish
7. Logger's Leap
8. Mr Monkey's Banana Ride
9. Nemesis Inferno
10. Neptune's Beach
11. Quantum
12. Rocky Express
13. Rumba Rapids
14. Rush
15. Saw Alive
16. Saw – The Ride
17. Samurai
18. The Showcase
19. Slammer
20. Stealth
21. Storm in a Teacup
22. Storm Surge
23. Tidal Wave
24. *Time Voyagers*
25. Vortex
26. Wet Wet Wet
27. X:\No Way Out
28. Zodiac

Entrance

Car Park

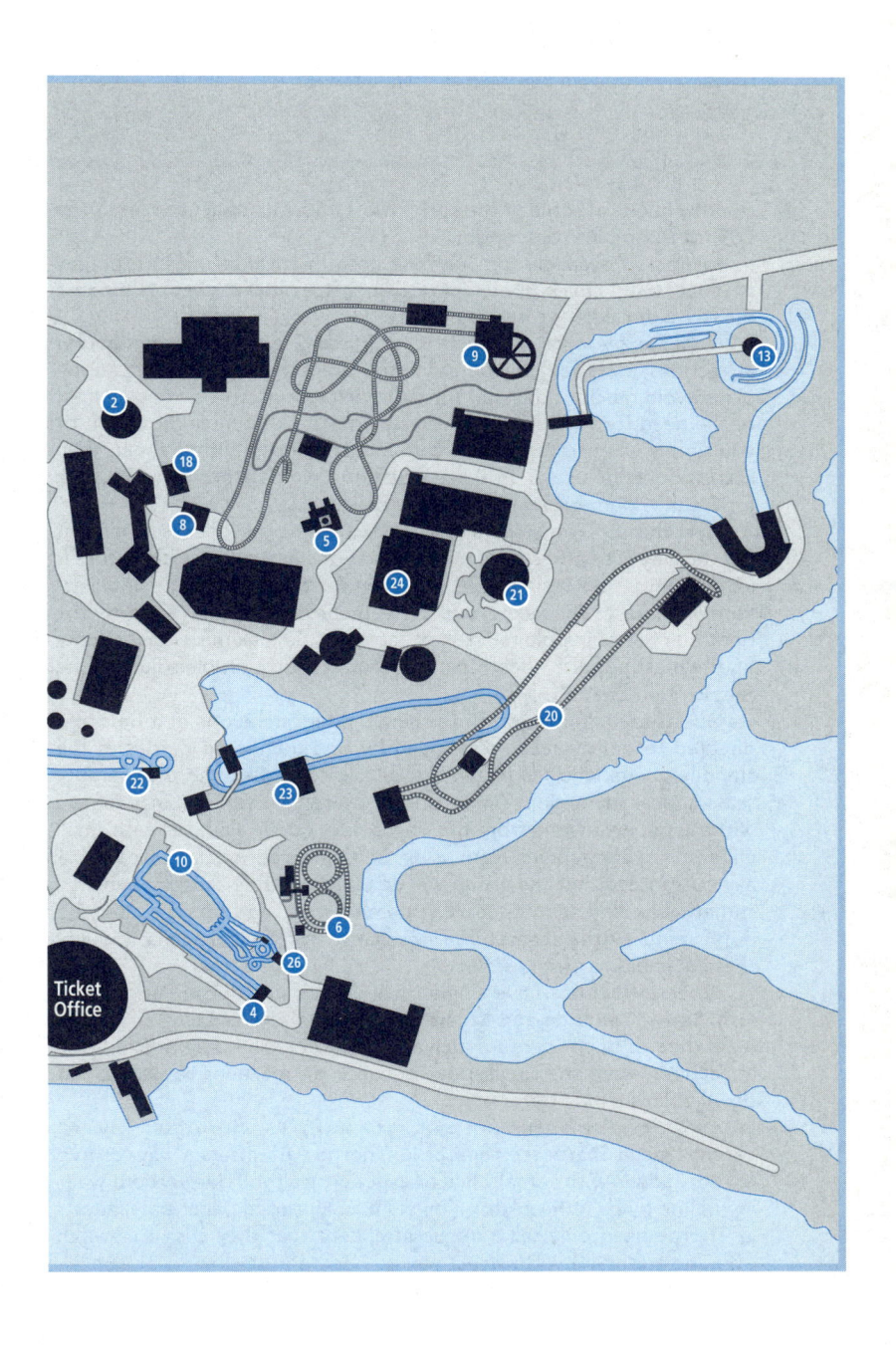

THORPE PARK MAP 127

NOT TO BE MISSED AT THORPE PARK			
Colossus	Nemesis Inferno	Samurai	Stealth
Logger's Leap	Rumba Rapids	Saw – The Ride	Tidal Wave
	Rush		

standby queue at some of the park's most popular attractions. See page 269 for a complete description.

Fastrack is available for purchase both in advance and on the day of your visit; check **thorpepark.com/prices/tickets.aspx?tabname=fastrack** for package details.

In our experience, Fastrack is useful only on a small number of attractions, and then only during busier times of the year. Our touring plans avoid much of the wait for these attractions, too, removing a lot of the need for Fastrack. If you arrive after park opening, however, or you simply want to experience certain attractions multiple times, then Fastrack may be useful. In those situations, we'd recommend Fastrack for Stealth, Nemesis and Tidal Wave.

SINGLE-RIDER QUEUES The best way to ensure a theme-park ride is running at full capacity is to put a guest in every seat of every ride vehicle before it leaves the station. It's possible, however, for there to be an empty seat here or there, as the next group in the queue may not have exactly the right number of people to fill all of the seats. To maximise ride capacity on the most popular rides, most theme parks use a simple solution: the 'single rider' queue.

Guests are admitted from the single-rider queue one at a time and directed to empty seats occasioned by odd-numbered parties in the standby queue who fail to fill all available seats. Because these empty seats appear at random times, one or more ride vehicles may depart without taking anyone from the single-rider queue. Families with small children are discouraged from using the single-rider queue, as it's virtually guaranteed that the group will be placed in different ride vehicles, sometimes many minutes apart. For teens, adults and small groups who don't mind a little separation in exchange for shorter waits, though, these queues are often useful.

Three attractions have single-rider queues at Thorpe Park: **Flying Fish, Saw – The Ride** and **Stealth**. If you don't mind being separated from the rest of your group, such as when you're re-riding one of these attractions, then the single-rider queue is an inexpensive way to cut down your queuing time.

PARENT SWAP (AKA 'SWITCHING OFF' OR 'CHILD SWAP') As with Alton Towers' Parent Queue Share (see page 271), Thorpe Park offers a way for two or more adults with a small child to experience a thrill ride without waiting in line twice. While Alton Towers uses a printed paper pass, guests at Thorpe need only tell a queue attendant that they wish to 'switch off'. The attendant will instruct you on how to proceed.

DINING Most dining facilities are in The Dome, which can get crowded during mealtimes. A **Mexican place, Burger King** and **Pizza Hut** are between

THEME PARKS AND ATTRACTIONS

FASTRACK ATTRACTIONS AT THORPE PARK		
Colossus	Samurai	Tidal Wave
Logger's Leap	Saw Alive	Vortex
Nemesis Inferno	Saw – The Ride	X:\No Way Out
Rush	Stealth	

Detonator and Stealth in the back-right side of the park. Of those, Pizza Hut is our favourite. Another Burger King is in the back-left side of the park near the Canada Creek Railway, along with a decent **barbecue joint**. Besides these, there are small snack, ice-cream and other treat stands throughout the park.

All of the dining options are acceptable and priced reasonably, but none is a standout. Our advice is to find the closest restaurant that satisfies the tastes of everyone in your group.

The Attractions

Going roughly anti-clockwise, here are our descriptions of Thorpe Park's attractions.

Depth Charge ★★

What it is Small water slide. **Scope and scale** Minor attraction. **Height requirement** Under 2'11" (0.9 m) must be accompanied by an adult. **Fright potential** None. **When to go** Anytime. **Authors' rating** A quick shower if the kids need one; ★★. **Duration of ride** About 10 seconds. **Average wait in queue per 100 people ahead of you** About 6 minutes. **Loading speed** Moderate.

DESCRIPTION AND COMMENTS A wet slide down a 3-storey water flume onboard a small rubber mat. There are a couple of small hills along the way, but the course is otherwise straight. Besides the height there's nothing that would be frightening to small children.

TOURING TIPS Along with Tidal Wave and Wet Wet Wet, Depth Charge is the attraction most likely to leave you soaked. Try to see these together so you can get most of your soaking done at once.

Wet Wet Wet ★★

What it is Small water slide. **Scope and scale** Minor attraction. **Height requirement** Varies; see the posted signs for details. **Fright potential** None. **When to go** Anytime. **Authors' rating** Yes, but do you get wet on this? ★★. **Duration of ride** About 20 seconds. **Average wait in queue per 100 people ahead of you** About 9 minutes. **Loading speed** Moderate.

DESCRIPTION AND COMMENTS For those children frightened by Depth Charge's height, Wet Wet Wet offers a similar experience, except Wet Wet Wet curves in small circles.

TOURING TIPS May be closed during off-peak times of the year. If your kids enjoy Depth Charge, there's really no need to visit this one.

Flying Fish ★★

What it is Small roller coaster. **Scope and scale** Minor attraction. **Height requirement** Under 2'11" (0.9 m) must ride with an adult. **Fright potential** None. **When to go** First 2 hours the park is open or in the hour before park closes. **Authors' rating** A good introduction to coasters; ★★. **Duration of ride** About 1½ minutes. **Average wait in queue per 100 people ahead of you** About 20 minutes. **Loading speed** Slow.

DESCRIPTION AND COMMENTS Flying Fish is a small, relatively-slow roller coaster designed for small children. The track consists of a couple of stacked figures of eight, with tight turns and a couple of minor hills. The entire track is visible from the queue, so kids can see that there are no surprises once the ride begins.

TOURING TIPS Tucked away in the lower right corner of the park, Flying Fish gets bypassed by crowds rushing to Stealth, Nemesis and Saw. If long queues develop, it's most likely due to Fish's relatively-low ride capacity (about 300 people per hour, according to our observations), not a sudden surge in popularity.

Tidal Wave (Fastrack) ★★

What it is Water-flume ride. **Scope and scale** Headliner attraction. **Height requirement** Under 3'11" (1.2 m) must ride with an adult. **Fright potential** May frighten some small children, but tame overall. **When to go** First 2 hours the park is open or in the hour before park closes. **Authors' rating** Bring soap and make it a bath; ★★. **Duration of ride** About 2½ minutes. **Average wait in queue per 100 people ahead of you** About 9 minutes; assumes 3 boats operating. **Loading speed** Moderate.

DESCRIPTION AND COMMENTS Let's face it – Tidal Wave is an excuse to get your family and friends absolutely soaked to the bone. In this simplest of water rides, you board a large boat, which is chain-hoisted up a steep hill. Your boat glides on rails in a half-circle to the drop point; you plummet to splashdown and then coast into the unload area. There's no theming or story to be told, and Tidal Wave doesn't even try.

Of the approximately-2½-minute ride time, a full minute is spent going up the lift hill. The big draw of Tidal Wave is its single drop, which sprays the largest gusher of water we've ever seen: 3 storeys high, topping the roof of the ride's unloading facility. It's entirely possible to stand a good 30 yd (27 m) from the splashdown point, with a building between you and the offending boat, and *still* get soaked.

TOURING TIPS Oddly popular even on chilly days, Tidal Wave should be experienced either early in the day when you have a chance to dry off or last thing before leaving. If you're taking the train or bus, expect stares from other passengers as you drip your way onto your transportation.

Storm Surge *(too new to rate)*

What it is Water-raft ride. **Scope and scale** Headliner. **Height requirement** Not yet available, but we've heard 3' (0.9) m to ride; under 3'6" (1.1 m) must ride with an adult. **When to go** First 2 hours the park is open or in the hour before closing.

DESCRIPTION AND COMMENTS Bought from a bankrupt US theme park – Florida's Cypress Gardens – and carted to the UK piece-by-piece, Storm Surge is a combined raft ride and water slide. As we went to press, no details were available regarding whether Thorpe Park will modify the ride during its reconstruction. We've heard, however, that no major changes are scheduled.

In Cypress Gardens' version, up to six people board a circular rubber raft which is carried by conveyor belt more than 60 feet up to the top of a long, spiralling water slide. The raft glides down the track, spinning at random spots along the way. The ride ends with the raft sliding down a small hill.

The promotional photos on Thorpe Park's website show the ride track passing through a series of water jets, meaning each raft (and its occupants) is likely to get wet, but probably not as much as on Tidal Wave.

TOURING TIPS As one of the park's newest rides, Storm Surge will almost certainly be popular from the moment it opens.

Storm in a Teacup ★★

What it is Funfair-type spinning ride. **Scope and scale** Minor attraction. **Height requirement** Under 2'11" (0.9 m) must ride with an adult. **Fright potential** None, but may cause motion sickness in those so prone. **When to go** First 2 hours the park is open or in the hour before park closes. **Authors' rating** Nothing you haven't seen before; ★★. **Duration of ride** About 2 minutes. **Average wait in queue per 100 people ahead of you** About 13 minutes; assumes 4 people per teacup. **Loading speed** Slow.

DESCRIPTION AND COMMENTS Similar to Marauder's Mayhem at Alton Towers. You sit in a small vehicle and turn a metal wheel to make the teacup spin in a circle; while you're turning that wheel, the teacup is spinning in a larger circle with two other cups, and the entire set of cups is spinning in yet another orbit.

TOURING TIPS A secondary attraction for most guests. The primary appeal of Storm in a Teacup is the potential for older kids to make one another sick. Ah, to be young again!

Time Voyagers ★★★½

What it is 3D film with in-theatre special effects. **Scope and scale** Major attraction. **Height requirement** None. **Fright potential** The film's special effects and the audience's screaming may scare young children. **When to go** Anytime. **Authors' rating** Nicely done; ★★★½. **Duration of presentation** About 9 minutes.

DESCRIPTION AND COMMENTS The park's only theatre presentation, *Time Voyagers* is a 3D film whose plot has you accompanying two time-travelling robots as they journey through the past, trying to rescue two stranded archaeologists. The plot takes a back seat to the 3D special effects, which include swooping bats, slithering snakes and fish. Besides the special effects, the theatre's chairs vibrate, and water sprays from the back of the seat in front of you.

TOURING TIPS While the film isn't great, it is a chance to sit in air-conditioned darkness on hot days. We never saw long queues develop for *Time Voyagers,* even on summer holiday weekends.

Stealth (Fastrack) ★★★★

What it is Fast-launching roller coaster. **Scope and scale** Headliner. **Height requirement** 4'7" (1.4 m). **Fright potential** Frightening to young and old alike. **When to go** First hour the park is open, the hour before park closing or use Fastrack. **Authors' rating** One of our favourite rides in any British theme park; ★★★★. **Duration of ride** About 2 minutes. **Average wait in queue per 100 people ahead of you** About 5 minutes; assumes 2 trains operating. **Loading speed** Moderate.

DESCRIPTION AND COMMENTS Similar to Rita at Alton Towers, Stealth is a high-speed roller coaster that launches you from a standing start to 80 mph (129 km/h) in just under 2 seconds. There's barely time to scream before you're heading into a vertical, twisting 180° turn.

The clever thing about the turn is that you're not leaning to the side, as in a traditional coaster's banked turn. Instead, Stealth's track rotates the ride vehicle a quarter-turn anti-clockwise, so that at the top part of the turn you're still riding flat on the top of the track.

To imagine this, take your right hand and place it parallel to the floor, palm down, and imagine this is your ride vehicle at launch. Next, bend your wrist so that your fingers are pointing straight up; this is your ride vehicle at the beginning of the turn. Now rotate your hand 90° so your thumb is facing you; this is how you enter the top of the curve in Stealth. Finally, make a *C*-shaped diving motion with your hand and let loose a string of foul oaths. That represents the last part of the ride, where you head straight down from the top of the curve, around one more 180° turn and back to the unloading area.

TOURING TIPS Immensely popular as soon as the park opens, so we recommend riding as soon in the morning as possible. If you'd like to ride multiple times, consider Fastrack or the single-rider queue.

Rumba Rapids ★★★

What it is River-raft ride. **Scope and scale** Major attraction. **Height requirement** Under 2'11" (0.9 m) must ride with an adult. **Fright potential** Not frightening. **When to go** Between 11 a.m. and 4 p.m. **Authors' rating** Would be better with more theming; ★★★. **Duration of ride** About 4½ minutes. **Average wait in queue per 100 people ahead of you** About 4 minutes; assumes at least 19 rafts operating. **Loading speed** Fast.

DESCRIPTION AND COMMENTS A mild raft ride around the back of the park property, Rumba Rapids is typical of the genre. There are a few bouncing, bobbing turns and some relatively-fast water, but not a whole lot to see along the route. The main feature, as always, seems to be the unpredictable nature of the water, which makes the ride experience different each time. The ride could be better if it had a cohesive theme or more show elements – not that anyone under the age of 18 will care one whit.

TOURING TIPS Obviously more popular on warm days, but not one of the park's main draws. Most guests find it on the park map around lunchtime, as it's directly behind one of the major dining locations on this side of the park. If you see long queues in the early afternoon, try the last hour before the park closes.

Detonator ★★★

What it is Vertical ascent and free-fall. **Scope and scale** Minor attraction. **Height requirement** 4'3" (1.3 m). **Fright potential** Frightens many small children and adults. **When to go** Before noon or after 4 p.m. **Authors' rating** We're thankful Thorpe doesn't design lifts; ★★★. **Duration of ride** About 40 seconds. **Average wait in queue per 100 people ahead of you** About 19 minutes; assumes all seats filled for each ride. **Loading speed** Slow.

DESCRIPTION AND COMMENTS If you've ever wondered what it's like to fall 100 ft (30.4 m) while sitting in the relative safety of your armchair, Detonator is the ride for you.

The ride mechanics are fairly simple: You and 11 others are strapped to seats at the base of a 115-ft (35-m) vertical tower. Once safely aboard, you're hoisted slowly to the top. You get a few seconds to enjoy the view before you're let go and you fall at speeds of more than 46 mph (74 km/h). It's just long enough for you to express a complete thought along the lines of 'This was a really bad idea.' Fortunately, technology is in place to slow your descent before you become pavement-pizza.

TOURING TIPS One of the lowest-capacity rides in the park; we recommend visiting Detonator either early in the morning or late in the afternoon.

Nemesis Inferno (Fastrack) ★★★★

What it is Inverted roller coaster. **Scope and scale** Headliner. **Height requirement** 4'7" (1.4 m). **Fright potential** Frightens many children and adults. **When to go** As soon as the park opens, in the last hour before park closes, or use Fastrack. **Authors' rating** One of the best theme-park rides in Britain; ★★★★. **Duration of ride** About 1½ minutes. **Average wait in queue per 100 people ahead of you** About 7 minutes; assumes 2 ride vehicles and all seats filled for each ride. **Loading speed** Moderate.

DESCRIPTION AND COMMENTS Possibly the best ride in Thorpe Park, and one of the best roller coasters in Europe, Nemesis Inferno includes four inversions at speeds of more than 50 mph (80 km/h). The amazing thing about the attraction, however, is how smooth the ride is. Unlike, say, on Blackpool's Big One or even Thorpe's Colossus, your body isn't jostled around in its restraints, your head bouncing around like it just took part in a corner kick. This leaves you able to focus on the ride sensations.

And what sensations they are! Your ride vehicle climbs, dives and swoops among treetops and steel columns and along the ground at breathtaking speeds. Even the loops are fun, something that isn't always true for extreme thrill rides.

We don't usually recommend spending extra time to sit up front on roller coasters, as the experience doesn't usually justify the wait. Nemesis Inferno is an exception. If you get to the ride early in the day, queue up for the front seats. It's a totally-different experience that makes a great ride even better.

TOURING TIPS Along with Saw – The Ride, Nemesis Inferno develops long queues almost as soon as the park opens. Our suggestion is to ride it right after Saw and Colossus. Finally, Nemesis Inferno is one of the few attractions for which we think paying extra for Fastrack is worth the cost.

Mr Monkey's Banana Ride ★★½

What it is Swinging-boat ride. **Scope and scale** Minor attraction. **Height requirement** Under 2'11" (0.9 m) must be accompanied by an adult. **Fright potential** May frighten some small children. **When to go** Before noon or after 4 p.m. **Authors' rating** Nice theme and setting; ★★½. **Duration of ride** About 2½ minutes. **Average wait in queue per 100 people ahead of you** About 19 minutes; assumes all seats filled for each ride. **Loading speed** Slow.

DESCRIPTION AND COMMENTS A typical swinging-boat ride found at many amusement parks – similar to The Blade at Alton Towers, on a much smaller scale. This one has a tropical theme, with bunches of bananas on either end of the boat. And by 'bunches of bananas' we don't mean your crazy brother-in-law and his family.

TOURING TIPS Mr Monkey's can handle only a few hundred guests per hour, making it a relatively-low-capacity attraction. It's also one of the few attractions in the park that's friendly to small children. We wouldn't be surprised to see Mr Monkey make his way to Chessington.

Chief Ranger's Carousel ★★

What it is Merry-go-round. **Scope and scale** Minor attraction. **Height requirement** Under 4'3" (1.3 m) must be accompanied by an adult. **Fright potential** None. **When to go** Before noon or after 4 p.m. **Authors' rating** Nice homage to past Thorpe attractions; ★★. **Duration of ride** About 2½ minutes. **Average wait in queue per 100 people ahead of you** About 12 minutes; assumes all seats filled for each ride. **Loading speed** Slow.

DESCRIPTION AND COMMENTS Another typical funfair merry-go-round for small children. The nice touch on this one is that some of the ride's vehicles represent current and past Thorpe Park attractions, such as Flying Fish. We're told some of the attractions shown here have been gone for years, and you can occasionally hear parents reminiscing about them.

Next to Mr Monkey's Banana Ride, Chief Ranger's would be better situated near the other child-friendly attractions at the front of the park, or nearer the Canada Creek area.

TOURING TIPS Our advice is to see Mr Monkey first, then ride the carousel.

Canada Creek Railway ★★★

What it is Scenic train ride. **Scope and scale** Minor attraction. **Height requirement** Under 4'7" (1.4 m) must be accompanied by an adult. **Fright potential** None. **When to go** Anytime. **Authors' rating** Relaxing and cool; ★★★. **Duration of ride** About 1½ minutes. **Average wait in queue per 100 people ahead of you** About 12 minutes; assumes all seats filled for each ride. **Loading speed** Slow.

DESCRIPTION AND COMMENTS A short train ride around the small wooded area in this section of the park. Along with trees and rocks, you get a brief look at the back of Logger's Leap.

TOURING TIPS The trip isn't long, so it almost always takes more time to load and unload the train than it does to complete the ride. See it in the middle of the day when it's hot and you can use a cool seat to rest.

Rocky Express ★★

What it is Funfair-style train-themed spinning ride. **Scope and scale** Minor attraction. **Height requirement** Under 2'11" (0.9 m) must be accompanied by an adult. **Fright potential** None. **When to go** Anytime. **Authors' rating** Colourful; ★★. **Duration of ride** About 1½ minutes. **Average wait in queue per 100 people ahead of you** About 15 minutes; assumes all seats filled for each ride. **Loading speed** Slow.

DESCRIPTION AND COMMENTS Riders board small, colourful locomotives that spin around in a small circle. There are a couple of very, very gentle hills, but nothing too fast or scary.

TOURING TIPS There's no shade or canopy for this attraction. During summer it might be best to try the Express either in the early morning or late afternoon.

Logger's Leap (Fastrack) ★★★

What it is Water-flume ride. **Scope and scale** Minor attraction. **Height requirement** 2'11" (0.9 m) to ride; under 3'7" (1.1 m) must ride with an adult. **Fright potential** None. **When to go** Before noon or after 3 p.m. **Authors' rating** More fun than you might expect; ★★★. **Duration of ride** About 4½ minutes. **Average wait in queue per 100 people ahead of you** About 7 minutes; assumes at least 15 boats operating. **Loading speed** Moderate.

DESCRIPTION AND COMMENTS A traditional water-flume ride around the Canada Creek section of the park, Logger's Leap features more scenery than most, including a couple of posing bears amidst lots of trees and boulders. There are a few hills, but nothing terrifying. Most riders will get wet, but not many get soaked.

TOURING TIPS Thorpe Park did something smart by putting its water-flume and raft rides on opposite ends of the park. We think Logger's Leap is the better-themed of the two, but Rumba Rapids can handle more guests.

Slammer ★★★

What it is Tall, swinging mechanical-arm ride. **Scope and scale** Major attraction. **Height requirement** 4'7" (1.4 m). **Fright potential** Frightens children and adults alike. **When to go** Before noon or after 4 p.m. **Authors' rating** A novel twist on the swinging-ride genre; ★★★. **Duration of ride** About 2 minutes. **Average wait in queue per 100 people ahead of you** About 10 minutes; assumes all seats filled for each ride. **Loading speed** Slow.

DESCRIPTION AND COMMENTS Thirty-two riders choose a seat on either end of a pair of long metal rods. Once everyone is strapped in, the rods are lifted and centred on a giant axle, which spins both rods – and their riders – in giant circles like bugs caught on an aeroplane propeller. Riders spend half of each circle in various stages of upside-downness (and if that's not yet a word, it should be, just to describe this ride).

Slammer's restraint system consists of a lap bar and shoulder harness, which provide a remarkable amount of freedom during the ride.

TOURING TIPS Slammer isn't one of the park's more popular rides, but it delivers enough thrills to warrant a visit. Not usually crowded before noon; try to see Slammer after Saw, Colossus, Nemesis and Stealth.

X:\No Way Out (Fastrack) ★½

What it is Indoor, backwards roller coaster. **Scope and scale** Major attraction. **Height requirement** 4'7" (1.4 m). **Fright potential** The darkness scares some small children. **When to go** Only if there's lightning in the immediate area, you've recently renounced God and you desperately need shelter. **Authors' rating** Somebody pull the plug on this thing; ★½. **Duration of ride** About 2 minutes. **Average wait in queue per 100 people ahead of you** About 13 minutes; assumes at least 2 trains running. **Loading speed** Moderate.

DESCRIPTION AND COMMENTS X:\No Way Out is (we're told) based on the idea that you're trapped inside a computer virus. Somehow this involves an indoor roller coaster that travels backwards, in the dark. We couldn't discern anything remotely like a theme or story inside the long, dark queue, which was devoid of anything save black hallways in need of fresh paint and air freshener. Nor could we figure out any sort of story whilst on the ride, which inexplicably and jarringly stops a couple of times as you're zipping about. All in all, 3 minutes of your life you'll never get back.

TOURING TIPS Don't go. Full stop. But if you must, try late afternoon.

Samurai (Fastrack) ★★★

What it is Spinning-arm ride. **Scope and scale** Major attraction. **Height requirement** 4'7" (1.4 m). **Fright potential** Frightens children and adults alike. **When to go** Before noon, after 4 p.m. or use Fastrack. **Authors' rating** Like riding an out-of-control Cuisinart; ★★★. **Duration of ride** About 3 minutes. **Average wait in queue per 100 people ahead of you** About 25 minutes; assumes all seats filled for each ride. **Loading speed** Slow.

DESCRIPTION AND COMMENTS If you've ever wondered what it's like for cake batter to get spun around on the end of an electric mixer, Samurai will give you an idea of the experience.

Five groups of five riders each sit in seats that extend from a large metal arm. Once riders are strapped in, each row of seats rotates you head-over-feet on its central axis, while all five rows of seats spin in a giant circle. And as that's going on, the metal arm spins around in a circle as well. It's sort of like a three-dimensional version of Storm in a Teacup.

Velocity builds up fairly fast, and you can go through a number of revolutions in a short amount of time. This isn't for the faint of heart or anyone who's just had lunch and wants to keep it (though it's better to ride with something in your stomach than with an empty stomach – remember Bob's Theorem: when in doubt, eat).

TOURING TIPS In our observations, Samurai was the lowest-capacity featured attraction in the park, struggling to get 300 riders per hour. For this reason, we suggest riding in the morning or just before park closing, or using Fastrack.

Colossus (Fastrack)   ★★★★

What it is Roller coaster with loops and rolls. **Scope and scale** Headliner. **Height requirement** 4'7" (1.4 m). **Fright potential** Frightens children and adults alike. **When to go** Before 11 a.m., after 4 p.m.or use Fastrack. **Authors' rating** Lots of fun; ★★★★. **Duration of ride** About 3 minutes. **Average wait in queue per 100 people ahead of you** About 9 minutes; assumes 2 trains operating. **Loading speed** Moderate.

DESCRIPTION AND COMMENTS Colossus is one of Thorpe Park's main draws. It generates excitement not from sheer speed, but in the total number of loops and rolls you get within its 3-minute ride.

By our count – and we were a little distracted, so forgive us if our maths is off – there are eight rolls and two complete loops in Colossus. Discounting the time it takes to climb up and around the first hill, that's roughly one feet-over-head moment every 7 or 8 seconds.

The best part of Colossus is towards the end, where you experience four consecutive rolls. Observers on the ground will note that the ride vehicle isn't going all that fast into any of the rolls, but on-board riders will have a completely-different opinion.

The one complaint we have about Colossus is that all the looping tends to bounce your head around inside the restraint harness. While that's padded, it's still somewhat of a jarring ride. We found that leaning your head forwards a bit helps considerably.

TOURING TIPS Plenty of people get sidetracked here on the way to Saw – The Ride. Our advice is to see Saw first and immediately get in the queue for Colossus.

Saw – The Ride (Fastrack) ★★★½

What it is Roller coaster. **Scope and scale** Headliner. **Height requirement** 4'7" (1.4 m). **Fright potential** Not appropriate for young children. **When to go** As soon as the park opens or use Fastrack. **Authors' rating** The ride's much better than the film; ★★★½. **Duration of ride** About 2 minutes. **Average wait in queue per 100 people ahead of you** About 12 minutes; assumes all seats filled for each ride. **Loading speed** Slow.

DESCRIPTION AND COMMENTS Based on the *Saw* torture/horror-film franchise, Saw – The Ride's claim to fame is that it's the steepest free-fall roller coaster in the world. At one point in the ride you ascend at 100° – that's 10° past straight – into a nearly-100-ft (30-m) free-fall straight down. Besides that, there are two rolls and one loop on the ride; the first roll happens while you're still inside the ride's load–unload building. Like the return of 'hot pants' and the popularity of David Hasselhoff's singing career, this takes a lot of people by surprise.

TOURING TIPS Ride Saw – The Ride first thing in the morning. Even with Fastrack, your waits can exceed 30 minutes on a moderately-busy day. Save the Saw Alive horror maze until later. Queues will still be long, but your time is better spent on the other attractions.

Saw Alive (Fastrack) ★★½

What it is Dark walk-through maze with actors jumping out to scare you. **Scope and scale** Major attraction. **Height requirement** None, but no one under 12 permitted. **Fright potential** Exceedingly frightening to children and adults. **When to go** After all of the roller coasters or use Fastrack. **Authors' rating** Boo! ★★½. **Duration of ride** About 5 minutes. **Average wait in queue per 100 people ahead of you** About 13 minutes; assumes 10 people per group and 4 groups in the maze at a time. **Loading speed** Slow.

DESCRIPTION AND COMMENTS Also based on the *Saw* film franchise, the horror maze takes groups of ten people into a dark industrial building filled with torture scenes from the half-dozen movies. Each group is arranged single-file and is unescorted; essentially you're left to find your way through the maze.

The scenes in each room are gory and disturbing to begin with. The addition of dark lighting, smoke, a loud soundtrack and strobe effects makes it that much worse. To cap this all off, actors hide in the dark recesses of some scenes and will jump out and grab members of the group as they walk by. (We're pretty sure this attraction gets a few American visitors per year, because there's a warning before you start not to hit the actors when they jump out at you. It's sort of a national impulse – at least when we're not toting a six-shooter. Sorry!)

We're not fans of the films, and experiencing this maze once was enough for us. That said, there are a couple of clever bits inside the maze. We'll tell you one of them: Just before you're let into the maze, your group is gathered together for a photo. Bright flashes go off and dilate everyone's pupils, after which you're immediately put into the maze. The effect of the flash is to make it much more difficult to see what's going on in the dark (you can purchase the photo on the way out).

TOURING TIPS Save the horror maze until later in the day and ride Saw – The Ride first thing in the morning; even with Fastrack your waits for the coaster can exceed 30 minutes on a moderately-busy day. Queues will still be long for the maze, but your time is better spent on the other attractions.

Zodiac ★★½

What it is Fast-spinning funfair ride. **Scope and scale** Minor attraction. **Height requirement** 2'11" (0.9 m) to ride; under 4'7" (1.4 m) must ride with an adult. **Fright potential** Frightening to many small children and those prone to motion sickness. **When to go** Anytime. **Authors' rating** We haven't been this dizzy since pound-a-pint night at uni; ★★½. **Duration of ride** About 2 minutes. **Average wait in queue per 100 people ahead of you** 16 minutes; assumes all 20 ride vehicles filled for each cycle. **Loading speed** Slow.

DESCRIPTION AND COMMENTS Identical to Enterprise at Alton Towers. In Zodiac, one or two riders sit in enclosed metal capsules, which spin around a central axis. Zodiac's twist is that the central axis is actually a movable metal arm, which pivots from flat on the ground to nearly vertical. Riders go from spinning parallel to the ground to looping up and down on a high-speed wheel before the metal arm pivots back down to the ground.

TOURING TIPS While Zodiac has a relatively-small capacity of around 500 riders per hour, most people bypass it for the headliner attractions. For this reason, it might be one of the better attractions to try during midday.

Rush (Fastrack) ★★★

What it is Swinging-arm ride. **Scope and scale** Minor attraction. **Height requirement** 4'3" (1.3 m) to ride. **Fright potential** Frightening to many small children and those prone to motion sickness. **When to go** Anytime. **Authors' rating** Way more fun than it looks, and it looks fun! ★★★. **Duration of ride** About 1 minute. **Average wait in queue per 100 people ahead of you** About 12 minutes; assumes both ride vehicles filled for each cycle. **Loading speed** Moderate.

DESCRIPTION AND COMMENTS A classic funfair-style swing ride in which your vehicle is suspended from a long metal rod, then swung back and forth as if on a swing set. The great thing about Rush is how fast your ride vehicle develops speed. After a couple of low, slow-speed oscillations, you're quickly being tossed back and forth at speeds of up to 50 mph (80 km/h). You also reach a maximum height of around 75 ft (23 m), so you're really covering a lot of distance very quickly. It's enough force for those outside the attraction to feel the breeze created by your ride vehicles as they swing by.

TOURING TIPS Rush can be seen on the way to Colossus, Saw – The Ride and Nemesis, so it gets its share of riders. That said, queues don't really develop until afternoon. Even then, the sheer intensity of the ride discourages many from trying it. It's a lot of fun, however, if you enjoy the falling sensation these kinds of attractions impart.

Vortex (Fastrack) ★★★

What it is Funfair-style spinning ride on a swinging arm. **Scope and scale** Minor attraction. **Height requirement** 4'7" (1.4 m) to ride. **Fright potential** Frightening to many small children and those prone to motion sickness. **When to go** Before 11 a.m. or after 4 p.m. **Authors' rating** If you didn't get enough from Samurai and Zodiac . . . ; ★★★. **Duration of ride** About 1 minute. **Average wait in queue per 100 people ahead of you** About 12 minutes; assumes both ride vehicles filled for each cycle. **Loading speed** Moderate.

DESCRIPTION AND COMMENTS Ride designers often like to combine elements of individual attractions together to form a new ride, and Vortex is an example. You've probably seen funfair-style rides where you're spun around in a tight circle while the whole contraption is tilted at various angles. Imagine putting than on a giant swinging arm, and you've got Vortex. It's a bit like putting the spinning Zodiac ride on the end of one of Rush's arms.

Together, Rush, Zodiac and Vortex form an unholy trinity of spinning, swinging rides. The easiest way to tell whether you've got some kind of inner-ear disorder is to try these in succession. It's also a great way to test whether you can keep your lunch down.

TOURING TIPS One of the lowest-capacity rides in the park, but not as popular as some of the others. Your morning time is better spent at the headliner attractions. Unfortunately, the best time to try Vortex may be right after lunch.

Quantum ★★★

What it is Swinging-boat ride. **Scope and scale** Minor attraction. **Height requirement** 3'11" (1.2 m) to ride. **Fright potential** Frightening to many small children and those prone to motion sickness. **When to go** Before 11 a.m. or after 4 p.m. **Authors' rating** Relatively mild, or maybe we're just used to worse now; ★★★. **Duration of ride** About 1½ minutes. **Average wait in queue per 100 people ahead of you** About 16 minutes; assumes all seats filled for each ride. **Loading speed** Slow.

DESCRIPTION AND COMMENTS A variation on the classic pirate-ship swinging-boat ride found in amusement parks worldwide (including Mr Monkey's Banana Ride at Thorpe). Quantum is different in that it makes a complete circle. You don't go upside-down, however, because the swinging arms that suspend the boat are mounted near the middle of the boat, not on the ends. Thus, you remain upright through the entire circle.

Because the ride doesn't go upside-down, it may be suitable for younger kids. Also, the entire attraction is outdoors, so it's possible to see exactly what the ride consists of.

THEME PARKS AND ATTRACTIONS

Thorpe Park Recommended Attraction Visitation Times

ATTRACTION | BEST TIME TO VISIT

Depth Charge | Anytime

Wet Wet Wet | Anytime

Flying Fish | First 2 hours the park is open or in the hour before park closes

Tidal Wave | First 2 hours the park is open or in the hour before park closes

Storm Surge | First 2 hours the park is open or in the hour before park closes

Storm in a Teacup | First 2 hours the park is open or in the hour before park closes

Time Voyagers | Anytime

Stealth | First hour the park is open, the hour before park closing or use Fastrack

Rumba Rapids | Between 11 a.m. and 4 p.m.

Detonator | Before noon or after 4 p.m.

Nemesis Inferno | As soon as the park opens, in the last hour before park closes, or use Fastrack

Mr Monkey's Banana Ride | Before noon or after 4 p.m.

Chief Ranger's Carousel | Before noon or after 4 p.m.

Canada Creek Railway | Anytime

Rocky Express | Anytime

Logger's Leap | Before noon or after 3 p.m.

Slammer | Before noon or after 4 p.m.

X:\No Way Out | Never – it's that bad

Samurai | Before noon, after 4 p.m. or use Fastrack.

Colossus | Before 11 a.m., after 4 p.m.or use Fastrack.

Saw – The Ride | As soon as the park opens or use Fastrack

Saw Alive | After all of the roller coasters or use Fastrack

Zodiac | Anytime

Rush | Anytime

Vortex | Before 11 a.m. or after 4 p.m.

Quantum | Before 11 a.m. or after 4 p.m.

TOURING TIPS Another of the lowest-capacity rides in the park, but not as popular as some of the others. Your morning time is better spent at the headliner attractions. Try Quantum in the afternoon.

Thorpe Park Touring Plans

We've included touring plans for parents with small children, as well as plans for adults and teens. Because Thorpe is a relatively-small park, it's fairly straightforward for both groups to see most of the park in a single day.

Thorpe Park targets tweens, teens and young adults. As such, there are extremely few attractions for children under 2′11″ (0.9 m). Our touring plan for parents with small children assumes the children are *at least* 2′11″ tall.

One-Day Touring Plan for Parents with Children (At Least 2'11"/0.9m)

1. The night before your visit, check **thorpepark.com** for park hours and weather.
2. Arrive at the park entrance 30 minutes prior to official opening. If possible, have your admission in hand before you arrive. Otherwise, arrive 15 minutes earlier and send one member of your party to obtain admission.
3. Thorpe Park is set to launch Storm Surge, a new family raft ride, in 2011. If the ride is open and your children meet the height requirement, see this attraction first. Otherwise, skip this step.
4. Ride Flying Fish, to your right as you exit The Dome.
5. See Mr Monkey's Banana Ride, near Slammer.
6. Ride Chief Ranger's Carousel, next to Mr Monkey's Banana Ride.
7. Float down Logger's Leap. While you probably won't get soaked, a poncho will help you avoid getting wet.
8. Take a spin on Storm in a Teacup, just past Detonator and before Stealth on the right-hand side of the park.
9. Stop for lunch. Mexican food, fish-and-chips, a Burger King and a Pizza Hut are all within a walk of a minute or two from here.
10. Check the performance schedule of *Time Voyagers* and work the show into the next few steps of the plan.
11. Experience Rumba Rapids, to the left of Stealth in the park. A poncho will help keep you dry.
12. Try Tidal Wave, near the front of the park.
13. Ride Wet Wet Wet, attached to Depth Charge at the front of the park.
14. Ride Zodiac if your kids are up for it; it's a great way to spin-dry your clothes.
15. Take a round-trip on the Canada Creek Railway.
16. Ride the Rocky Express.
17. See any missed attractions or repeat any favourites.
18. Depart Thorpe Park.

Combined One-Day Touring Plan for Families with Children Over and under 3' (0.9 m)

Note: See our descriptions of switching off on pages 77 and 128.

1. The night before your visit, check **thorpepark.com** for park hours and weather.
2. Arrive at the park entrance 30 minutes prior to official opening. If possible, have your admission in hand before you arrive. Otherwise, arrive 15 minutes earlier and send one member of your party to obtain admission.
3. As soon as the park opens, have at least one adult and the older children experience either Saw – The Ride or Colossus. One other adult should take the younger children to see Flying Fish, to your right as you exit The Dome. Have everyone rendezvous at Logger's Leap, then switch possession of the children so the other adults can experience a thrill ride.
4. If time permits after Flying Fish, the adults with the younger children should try Mr Monkey's Banana Ride and Chief Ranger's Carousel.
5. Have one adult take the younger children to experience the Canada Creek Railway and the Rocky Express, while the other adults experience Stealth. Have everyone meet back up at the exit to Stealth, then switch possession of the children.
6. Have everyone ride Logger's Leap.
7. Thorpe Park is set to launch Storm Surge, a new family raft ride, in 2011. If the ride is open and everyone meets the height requirement, see this attraction now. Otherwise, skip this step.
8. Stop for lunch. Mexican food, fish-and-chips, a Burger King and a Pizza Hut are all within a walk of a minute or two from here.
9. Take a spin on Storm in a Teacup, just past Detonator and before Stealth on the right-hand side of the park.
10. Check the performance schedule of *Time Voyagers* and work the show into the next few steps of the plan.
11. Experience Rumba Rapids, to the left of Stealth in the park. A poncho will help keep you dry.
12. Try Tidal Wave, near the front of the park.
13. Ride Zodiac if the kids are up for it, otherwise have one adult and the children try Wet Wet Wet near the front of the park. Meet back at the exit to Zodiac and switch possession of the children.
14. See any missed attractions or repeat any favourites.
15. Depart Thorpe Park.

One-Day Touring Plan for Teens and Adults

1. The night before your visit, check **thorpepark.com** for park hours and weather.
2. Arrive at the park entrance 30 minutes prior to official opening. If possible, have your admission in hand before you arrive. Otherwise, arrive 15 minutes earlier and send one member of your party to obtain admission.
3. As soon as the park opens, see Saw – The Ride.
4. Ride Colossus.

5. Experience Nemesis Inferno, near the back of the park.
6. Ride Stealth, near Rumba Rapids at the back right of the park.
7. Take a spin on Samurai.
8. Try Detonator next.
9. If your stomach can stand it, stop for lunch. Good nearby restaurants include Burger King, Pizza Hut and Amity Fish & Chips.
10. Ride Slammer, between Nemesis Inferno and Samurai.
11. Float down Logger's Leap. While you won't get soaked, use a poncho if you don't want to get wet.
12. Thorpe Park is set to launch Storm Surge, a new family raft ride, in 2011. If this ride is open, try it now.
13. And while you're wet, you may as well try Rumba Rapids, near Stealth at the back of the park.
14. Keep the theme going by riding Tidal Wave.
15. Take a swing on Rush.
16. Try Zodiac and Quantum, near Rush.
17. If time permits, ride Vortex.
18. If you're up for it, walk through the Saw Alive horror maze.
19. See any missed attractions or repeat any favourites.
20. Depart Thorpe Park.

FARM EXPERIENCES

BECAUSE THE VARIOUS FARM EXPERIENCES ARE SO SIMILAR (see page 13), we felt it unnecessary to provide individual profiles as we do with other types of attractions. Following is a selective list of South East England farm experiences.

EAST SUSSEX

BLACKBERRY FARM
Whitesmith, nr Lewes on A22
East Sussex BN8 6JD
☎ 01825 872 912
blackberry-farm.co.uk

MIDDLE FARM COUNTRYSIDE CENTRE
Middle Farm
Firle, Lewes
East Sussex BN8 6LJ
☎ 01323 811 411
middlefarm.com
info@middlefarm.com

SEVEN SISTERS SHEEP CENTRE
Gilberts Drive, East Dean
East Sussex BN20 0AA
☎ 01323 423 302
sheepcentre.co.uk
enquiry@sheepcentre.co.uk

SPRING BARN FARM PARK
Kingston Road, Lewes
East Sussex BN7 3ND
☎ 01273 488 450
springbarnfarmpark.co.uk
springbarn@gmail.com

WEST SUSSEX

FISHERS FARM PARK
Newpound Lane
Wisborough Green, Billinghurst
West Sussex RH14 0EG
☎ 01403 700 063
fishersfarmpark.co.uk
fishersfarmpark@aol.com

KENT

FARMING WORLD
Nash Court
Boughton, Faversham
Kent ME13 9HY
☎ 01227 751 144
farming-world.com
farmingworld@hotmail.com

SURREY

BOCKETTS FARM PARK
Young Street
Fetcham, Leatherhead
Surrey KT22 9BS
☎ 01372 363 764
bockettsfarm.co.uk
jane@bockettsfarm.co.uk

GODSTONE FARM
Tilburstow Hill Road
Godstone
Surrey RH9 8LX
☎ 01883 742 546
godstonefarm.co.uk
havefun@godstonefarm.co.uk

HOLMBUSH FARM WORLD
Crawley Road
Faygate, nr Horsham
West Sussex RH12 4SE
☎ 01293 851 110
holmbushfarm.co.uk
info@holmbushfarm.co.uk

KENT LIFE
Lock Lane
Sandling, Maidstone
Kent ME14 3AU
☎ 01622 763 936
kentlife.org.uk
tread@kentlife.org.uk

HORTON PARK CHILDREN'S FARM
Horton Lane
Epsom
Surrey KT19 8PT
☎ 01372 743 984
hortonpark.co.uk
**childrensfarm@horton
    park.co.uk**

PART SIX
The SOUTH of ENGLAND

THREE OF ENGLAND'S MOST REWARDING CITIES are in the South. **Portsmouth** will impress you with its relaxed seaside atmosphere. The cathedral city of **Winchester** is a bit more low-key, but also more soothing; in fact, many travellers find this quintessentially English city, along with **Oxford,** to be two of the most appealing places in the land.

Around these cities are meadow-covered downs and plains that invite easygoing exploration. Every bend in the lane hides pleasant inns and pubs where you'll feel comfortable plunking down in front of a fire and taking in a slice of British provincial life. You'll also come upon stately country houses – the homes of such luminaries as Jane Austen, at **Chawton** outside of Winchester, and the rural southerly retreats of Virginia Woolf and the Bloomsbury Group. In this guide we concentrate on selected tourist attractions in Berkshire, Hampshire, and Oxfordshire, from Nelson's **HMS Victory** at Portsmouth to **Legoland Windsor.**

THEME PARKS *and* ATTRACTIONS

Blue Reef Aquarium–Southsea/Portsmouth ★★½

APPEAL BY AGE	PRESCHOOL ★★★★	PRIMARY SCHOOL ★★★	TEENS ★★
YOUNG ADULTS ★★		OVER 30 ★★★	SENIORS ★★★

Clarence Esplanade, Southsea, Hampshire PO5 3PB
☎ 0239 287 5222; bluereefaquarium.co.uk/portsmouth.htm

HOURS (March–October) 10 a.m.–5 p.m. (last admission). (November–February) 10 a.m.–4 p.m. (last admission). Closed Christmas Day.
COST £9.40 adults; £7.40 children 3–14 (must be accompanied by an

148 PART 6 THE SOUTH OF ENGLAND

The South of England

ATTRACTIONS
1. Abbotsbury Children's Farm
2. Blue Reef Aquarium–Southsea/Portsmouth
3. Bucklebury Farm Park
4. Cotswold Wildlife Park & Gardens
5. Farmer Gow's
6. Farmer Palmer's Farm Park
7. Legoland Windsor
8. Longdown Activity Farm
9. Oxford University (Harry Potter site)
10. Paultons Park
11. Portsmouth Historic Dockyard

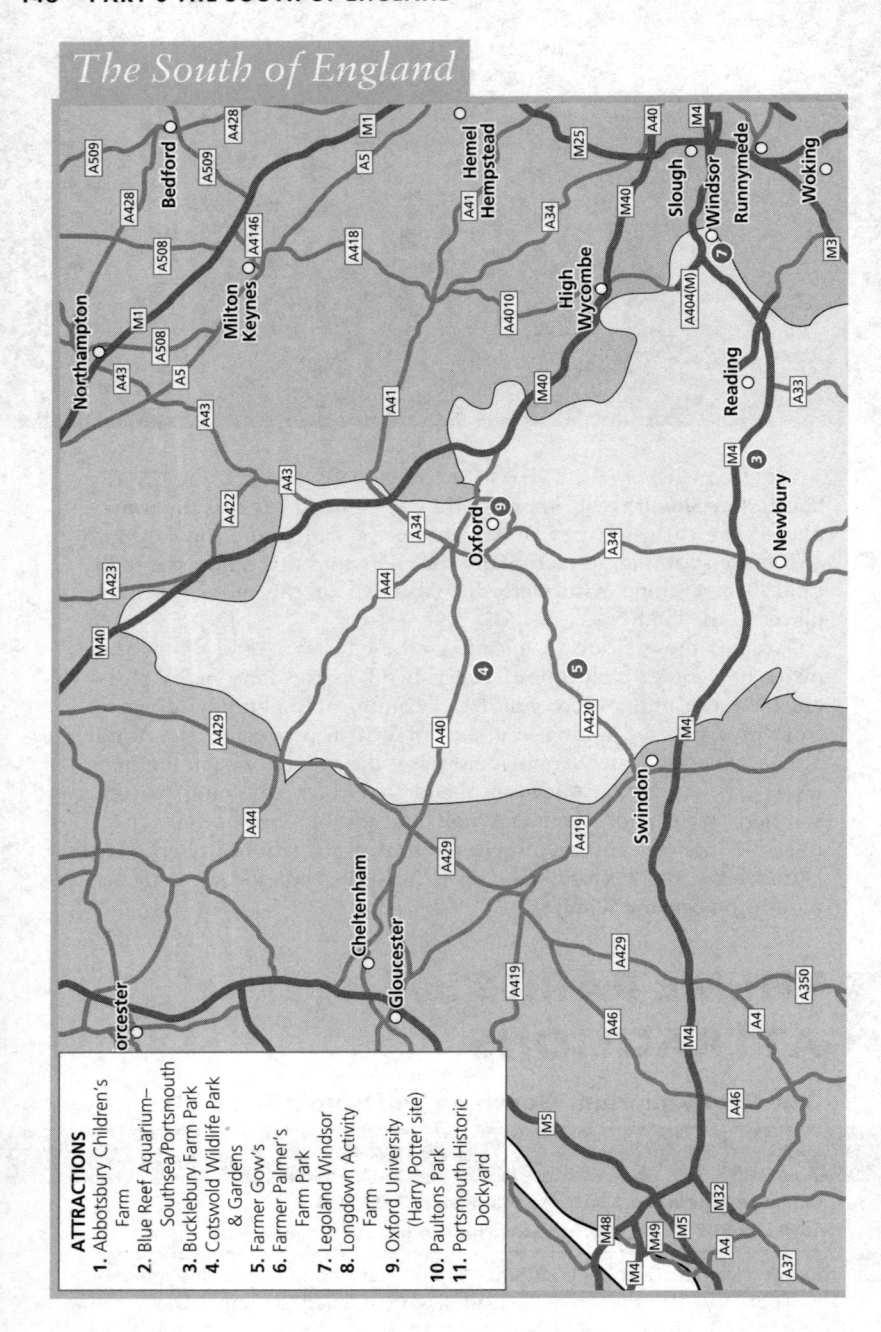

SOUTH OF ENGLAND MAP 149

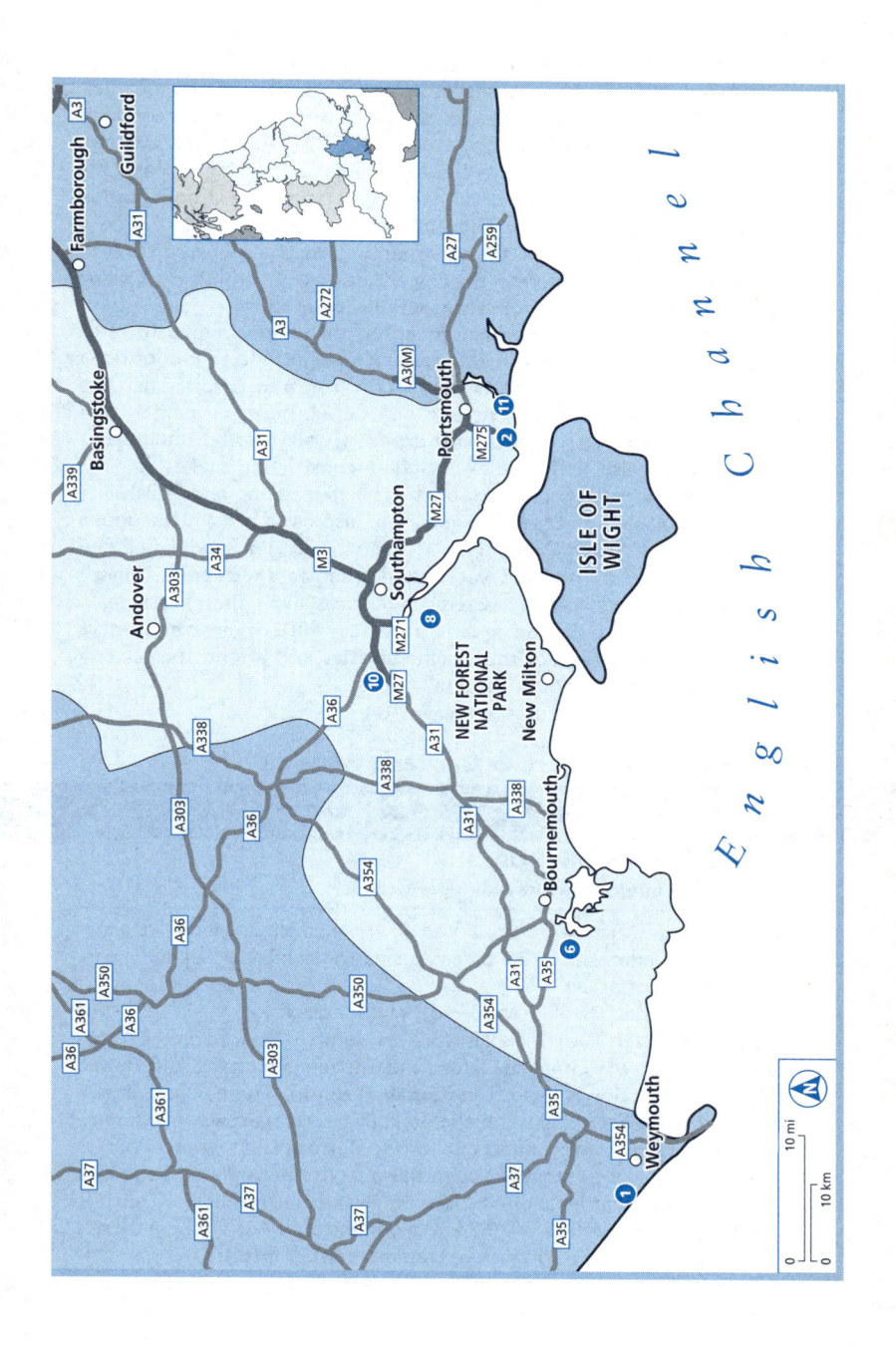

adult); £8.50 senior citizens, students; £30.80 family ticket (2 adults, 2 children); £38 family ticket (2 adults, 3 children).

GETTING THERE *By car:* In the Southsea resort area of Portsmouth, the aquarium is about 75 mi (120 km) southwest of London on the A3, which connects to the A27. Follow the brown signs from the M27/A27 to the seafront, where signs will direct you to the aquarium. Car parking is along the Esplanade. *By rail:* The nearest rail station is Portsmouth Harbour Station (**nationalrail.co.uk**). *By bus:* The **700 bus** from Portsmouth's Harbour Station will drop you off at the aquarium. Alternatively, buses to Southsea Centre from anywhere in the city will bring you within easy walking distance. (Route information: **transportdirect.info**.)

DESCRIPTION AND COMMENTS A chain aquarium that seems aimed towards the Southsea holiday crowd. Standout exhibits include an indoor otter enclosure that provides the critters lots of room to cavort. There's a reason, however, that most otter exhibits are outdoors – namely that otters have bad B.O. Along with the expected walk-through underwater tunnel, you'll also find reptiles, including constricting snakes, iguanas and snapping turtles, plus poison frogs, chameleons and Australia's notorious giant cane toad. The aquarium also has a retro attraction: a sandy outdoor beach. Along with 110,000 lb (50 t) of sand, you'll find a splash play area, with giant water nozzles, showers and sprays. There's also a covered picnic area, grassed sun terraces and a pirates' bridge.

TOURING TIPS It's more than an aquarium. You can kill 2 or more hours here if you take advantage of the beach activities and attend the feeding demonstrations and educational talks.

(For more on aquariums, see page 10.)

Cotswold Wildlife Park & Gardens ★★★

APPEAL BY AGE	PRESCHOOL ★★★	PRIMARY SCHOOL ★★★★	TEENS ★★
YOUNG ADULTS ★★★	OVER 30 ★★★		SENIORS ★★★

Burford, Oxfordshire OX18 4JP
☎ **01993 823 006; cotswoldwildlifepark.co.uk**

HOURS (Summer) 10 a.m.–6 p.m., last admission 4.30 p.m.; (winter) 10 a.m.–5 p.m., last admission 3.30 p.m. Madagascar exhibit closes at 3 p.m. Closed Christmas Day.

COST £10.50 adults; £8 children (3–16), senior citizens.

GETTING THERE *By car:* The park is 2 mi (3.2 km) south of Burford on the A361. Burford is mid-way between Oxford and Cheltenham on the A40. *By rail:* The nearest station is Oxford (**nationalrail.co.uk**), where you can get a bus that will take you close to the park. *By bus:* **Stagecoach** bus service (**stagecoachbus.com**) connects Oxford to Burford High Street, which is generally the closest stop, although there's extremely-limited service to the park from that location. It's best to get a taxi from Burford, as it is inadvisable to walk the 2 mi (3.2 km) along the busy A361, where there's no footpath. (Route information: **transportdirect.info**.)

DESCRIPTION AND COMMENTS It can look a little odd at first – a white rhinoceros grazing in front of a Victorian manor house – but that's part of the charm of this ambitious wildlife park 8 mi (13 km) outside of Oxford. Covering 160 ac (65 ha), it offers visitors much more than the typical lions, tigers and bears. With nearly 300 species of animals, the park, founded in 1970, has one of the largest collections in the UK, and certainly one of the most diverse. The newest interactive walk-through enclosure, **Madagascar,** features several species of lemurs, jumping rats, tree boas and more from the Indian Ocean island known for its biodiversity.

The park is divided into four sections – **Large Mammals, Reptiles and Invertebrates, Primates** and **Birds** – and each has something surprising on view, like the exhibit of wolverines acquired from Russia. Exhibits generally give animals room to roam, so you won't see cramped cages here. In addition, garden-lovers will delight in the horticultural collection. So while some in your party may be marvelling at the mongooses, others will be wondering how the staff have managed to get palm trees and bougainvillea to grow in the South of England. They'll also want to see the 50 varieties of bamboo, the Burmese giant honeysuckle and the extensive collection of specimen trees.

A visit can start with a trip around the premises on the narrow-gauge railway (running April–October; an additional £1), providing glimpses of camels, ostriches and zebras from the comfort of a train seat. But before you begin prowling, check the daily feeding schedules and keeper talks. One of the park's distinguishing factors is its dedicated, earnest staff, who really do want you to know why the Morelet's crocodiles are endangered and what you can do to help – like sponsor one of the park's animals for £20. But by and large, the pitch is low-key here, focused on education and not on extracting money from your wallet.

Popular exhibits include **Canadian timber wolves,** a breeding pair of **red pandas,** 100 **fruit bats, giant tortoises, meerkats** and the **Amur (Siberian) leopard,** the world's rarest cat. Also visit the Reptile House to see the huge 33-ft (10-m) reticulated python and the deadly gaboon viper, with the longest fangs in the snake world.

And don't miss the Humboldt penguin feedings: the fancy-dress birds put on a show twice daily at their new pool within the walled garden, with feedings at 11 a.m. and 4 p.m. (3 p.m. during winter). In addition, lemur talks and feedings are daily at noon in Madagascar.

Education is fun only for so long. Young children will want to visit the adventure playground, with a large slide from a tree house, swings and space net. But if you're truly inspired by the animals and the conservation message, consider the park's 'Keeper for the Day' programme, which for £200 provides behind-the-scenes access and experiences for those aged 18 and over.

TOURING TIPS Listen for the shrieks of the white-lipped peccaries, pig-like mammals from South America. This is the only place in the UK where the species can be found. If you get a hungry, a restaurant offers typical fare, but the park's acres of open grounds are perfect for a picnic.

Legoland Windsor ★★★★★
Winkfield Road, Windsor, Berkshire SL4 4AY
☎ 0871 222 2001; legoland.co.uk

HOURS The park opens as early as 9.30 a.m. during high season, and 10 a.m. other times. Closing varies from 8 p.m. high season to as early as 5 p.m. It's open daily mid-May–August, and on a more limited schedule April–early November.

COST £39 adults (£35.10 online); £30 senior citizens and children 3–12 (£27 online). If you're going to return a second day, you'll typically save more money buying a basic annual pass, which runs £55 adults (£49.50 online) and £39 children (£35.10 online), than buying a 2-day ticket. (The basic pass, though, has some exclusion dates.) If you have an annual pass and photo identification, or if you've purchased tickets online and printed them at home, you can proceed to the turnstiles, avoiding the ticket queue. Tickets can also be bought through the Tesco Clubcard rewards scheme.

You can also use the **Merlin Annual Pass** (**merlinannualpass.co.uk**), which also provides admission to Alton Towers Resort Theme Park, Legoland Discovery Centre, Thorpe Park, Chessington World of Adventures, Sea Life Sanctuaries, Dungeons attractions, the Merlin London Eye, Madame Tussauds London and Warwick Castle. Prices begin at £150 for an individual and drop in price if you're buying for a family group.

GETTING THERE *By car:* The park is on the **B3022 Windsor/Ascot road**, 2 mi (3 km) from Windsor town centre. It's easily reached via the M25 and signed from the M3 (Junction 3), M4 (Junction 6) and all approach roads. If you're using a satnav system, follow the brown tourist-information signs, as some systems incorrectly direct you into a residential street. Parking costs £2, and £6 for preferred parking closer to the entrance. Note that getting out of the Legoland car park at closing time can be a nightmare during busier seasons. It's best to leave a little early or save your shopping for when the park closes. By the time you're ready to leave after shopping, much of the traffic will be gone. *By rail:* It's 30 minutes from London Paddington to Windsor & Eton Central, via Slough on the **First Great Western,** or direct from London Waterloo to Windsor & Eton Riverside on **South West Trains** (**nationalrail.co.uk**). A shuttle-bus service to the park stops close to both rail stations, although it is not operated by the park and carries an additional charge. You can buy a package covering rail, shuttle and park admission from most major **British Rail** stations. Otherwise, the shuttle runs £4.40 for adults and £2.20 for children (one-way £3.40, £1.70 respectively). The first bus leaves Windsor at 10 a.m., and the last bus leaves 30 minutes after the park has closed. Alternatively, you can get a taxi from **Windsor Radio Cars** (☎ 01753 677677). *By bus:* **Green Line** operates the frequent **702 service** seven days a week from Victoria Station (☎ 0870 608 7261; **greenline.co.uk**). Inclusive ticket and

THEME PARKS AND ATTRACTIONS

NOT TO BE MISSED AT LEGOLAND WINDSOR

Adventure Land
Wave Surfer
Dino Safari

Duplo Land
Fairy Tale Brook

Imagination Centre
Imagination Theatre

Kingdom of the Pharaohs
Laser Raiders

Knights Kingdom
The Dragon
Dragon's Apprentice

Land of the Vikings
Vikings' River Splash

Lego City
Pirates of Skeleton Bay
Digger Challenge
Pirates Landing
Pirate Falls Dynamite
Drench

Traffic
Driving School
Boating School

travel packages available. From London hotels, **Golden Tours** operates a daily service to the park, with collection from over 50 establishments (☎ 0844 801 7261).

OVERVIEW Opening in 1996, Legoland Windsor was the second Legoland theme park built after the original in Billund, Denmark. Located on approximately 150 ac (60 ha) on the site of a former animal safari park, Legoland Windsor is an easy commute from Windsor or London. The park is open approximately eight months of the year, from roughly April through November.

Like Alton Towers, Thorpe Park and Chessington World of Adventures, Legoland Windsor is owned by Merlin Entertainments Group. With Thorpe, Chessington and Legoland all within a few miles of each other, Merlin is actively focusing the set of attractions in each park towards a specific demographic. In the case of Legoland, that demographic is the preschool and primary-school set. Thus, you'll find nothing more than a handful of very mild roller coasters at Legoland, with no scary attractions, extreme thrill rides or anything inspired by the latest gory film franchise.

Legoland Windsor is similar to Disney-style theme parks in that it's organised into themed areas, or 'lands'. Architecture, ride selection and landscaping support the various themes, creating a collage of distinct environments. The thread that binds the themed areas is the basic Lego building block, writ large with Lego structures, fanciful Lego human and animal figures and even Lego buildings, both miniature and full-scale. Festooning the entire park, the sculptures and constructions are ambitious in their size and diversity. Some are simply jaw-dropping; all add immensely to the colour and upbeat spirit of the place. Topography likewise plays a major role in Legoland's gestalt. The park entrance is on the crest of a ridge that envelops the park's western side. In a great bowled valley below the ridge stretch the contiguous themed areas and their rides. Visitors can access the valley via a hill train (almost a funicular) or by pedestrian paths that descend in a series of switchbacks

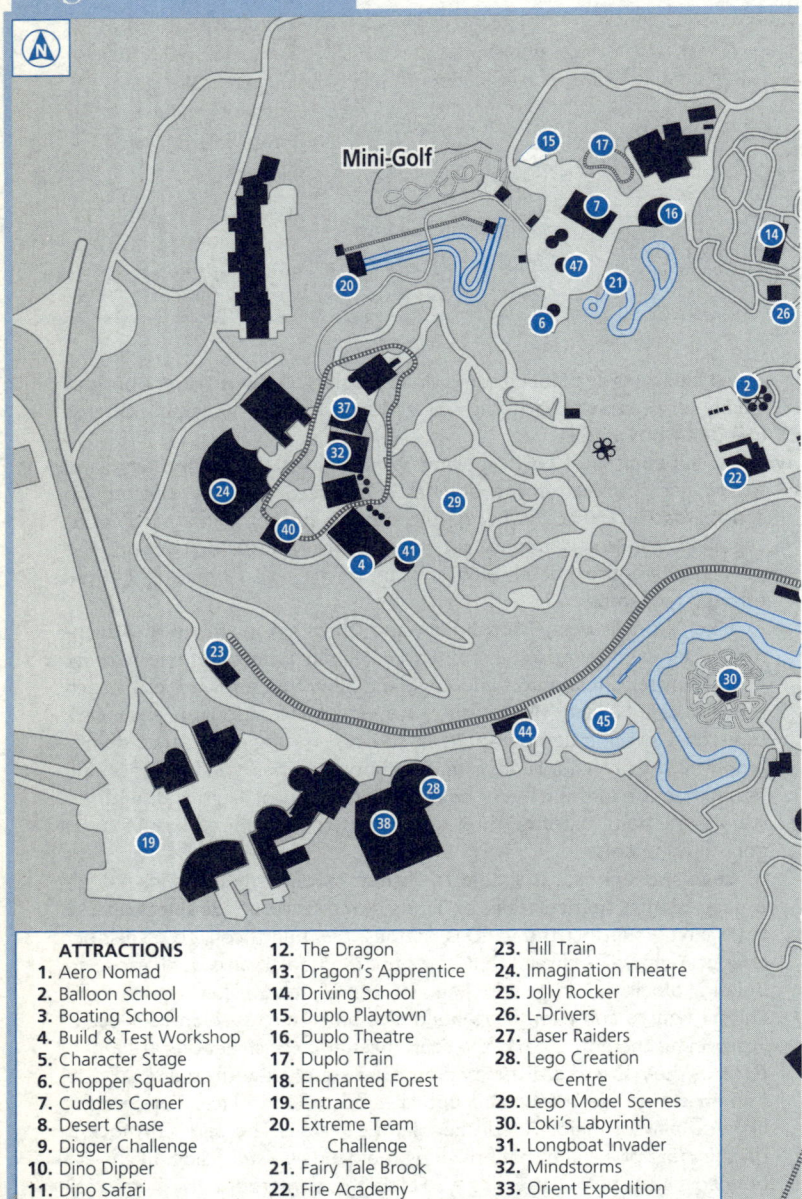

Legoland Windsor

Mini-Golf

ATTRACTIONS
1. Aero Nomad
2. Balloon School
3. Boating School
4. Build & Test Workshop
5. Character Stage
6. Chopper Squadron
7. Cuddles Corner
8. Desert Chase
9. Digger Challenge
10. Dino Dipper
11. Dino Safari
12. The Dragon
13. Dragon's Apprentice
14. Driving School
15. Duplo Playtown
16. Duplo Theatre
17. Duplo Train
18. Enchanted Forest
19. Entrance
20. Extreme Team Challenge
21. Fairy Tale Brook
22. Fire Academy
23. Hill Train
24. Imagination Theatre
25. Jolly Rocker
26. L-Drivers
27. Laser Raiders
28. Lego Creation Centre
29. Lego Model Scenes
30. Loki's Labyrinth
31. Longboat Invader
32. Mindstorms
33. Orient Expedition

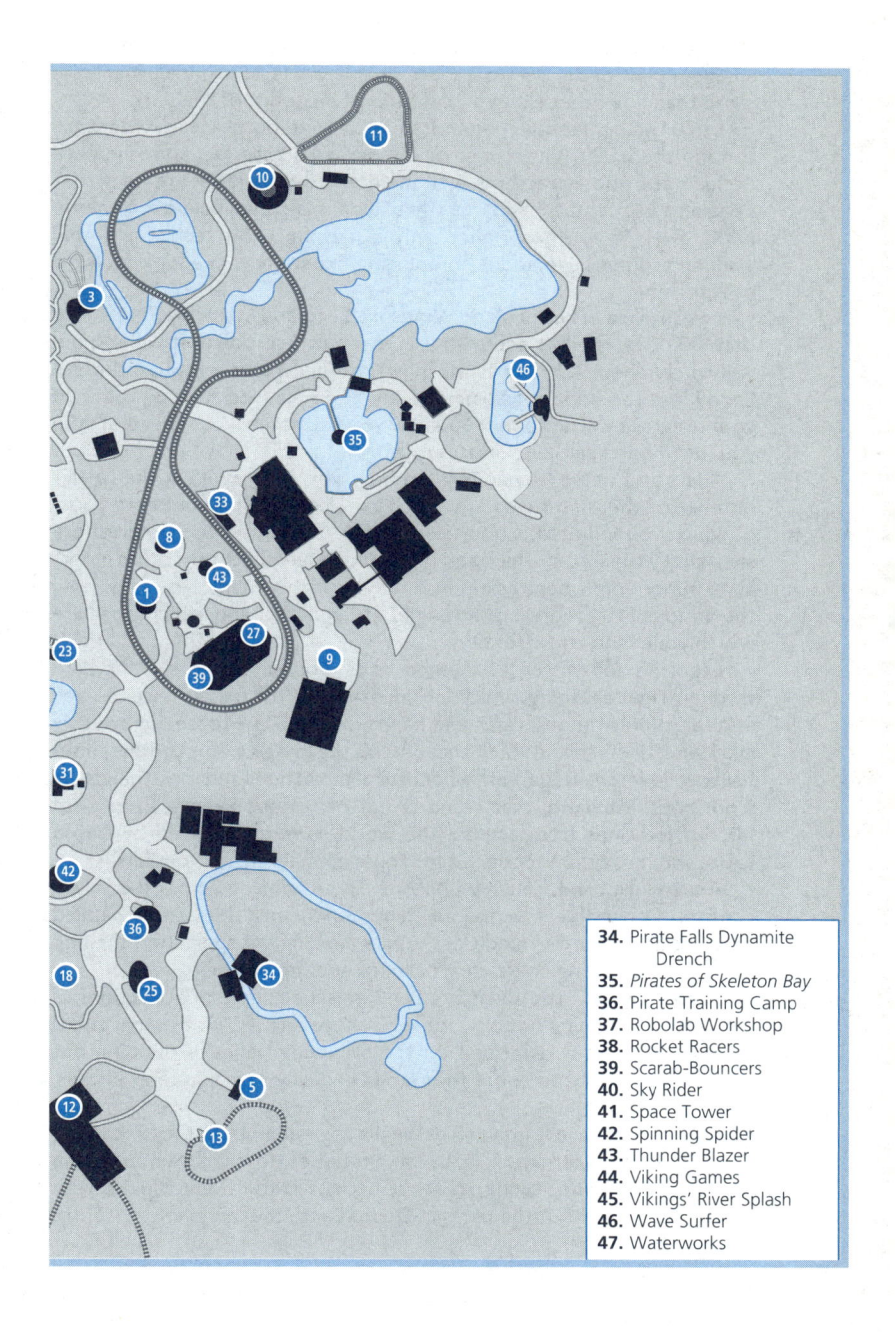

LEGOLAND WINDSOR MAP 155

34. Pirate Falls Dynamite Drench
35. *Pirates of Skeleton Bay*
36. Pirate Training Camp
37. Robolab Workshop
38. Rocket Racers
39. Scarab-Bouncers
40. Sky Rider
41. Space Tower
42. Spinning Spider
43. Thunder Blazer
44. Viking Games
45. Vikings' River Splash
46. Wave Surfer
47. Waterworks

and stairs. On a terrace just below the entrance is **Miniland,** a whole miniature world built of Lego blocks, where you'll find everything from a Lego replica of Big Ben to a space shuttle on its launch pad. Miniland, more than any other element, captures the essence of the park.

In 2012 Legoland will open its first on-site hotel, near Adventure Land in the back-right corner of the park. Add the fact that the park is clean and the attractions well maintained, and it seems clear that Legoland is intent on rising to the standard of the world's top theme parks. Even if you experience only a handful of attractions, simply walking around Legoland is an uplifting experience. We look forward to returning.

GETTING ORIENTATED The Legoland Windsor ('Legoland') park map lists more than 80 rides, exhibits and restaurants. Your first look at it will remind you of childhood Christmas mornings, dumping out a thousand-piece Lego kit in the hopes of turning it into the sibling-terrorising robot of your dreams by afternoon. You knew you had some work ahead of you; you just didn't realise it was this much.

The good news (depending on how you look at it) is that a fair number of the map items are snack bars, cafés and restaurants, most of which you won't visit on the same day. Other points of interest are speciality workshops, which can be visited at any time; others are ignorable, minor coin-operated rides. The rest of this chapter explains how the various attractions are arranged at Legoland, and which ones are worth your time and attention.

Legoland consists of 11 themed lands. You enter and exit the park through **The Beginning,** which includes most of the park services as well as a selection of shops, cafés and hands-on exhibits. Proceeding roughly clockwise, the first land you'll encounter is the **Imagination Centre,** about halfway down the ridge, with a handful of attractions and more hands-on workshops. **Miniland,** that grand layout of realistic Lego sculptures of famous locations from around the world, is next, followed by **Duplo Land,** with attractions designed for younger children and toddlers.

Adventure Land, roughly opposite The Beginning across the valley, consists of a handful of animal- and dinosaur-themed rides. An area called **Traffic** is nestled in the middle of the park, hosting transportation-themed attractions including boats, cars, balloons and fire engines.

Lego City, next to Adventure Land, hosts a couple of attractions as well as several dining options, souvenir shops and a Q-Bot virtual queuing kiosk (Q-Bot is described on the following pages). Rounding out Legoland's themed areas are **four lands** dedicated to pharaohs, pirates, knights and vikings.

PARK SERVICES Most are found at The Beginning and in Lego City, including first aid, park information, baby-care facilities, lost children and cash machines. A smoking section is at the back of Traffic. Rental lockers are dispersed throughout the park, in Duplo Land, the Imagination Centre and The Beginning.

Pushchairs are available for hire at a cost of £6.50 per day for a single and £10 for a double, plus an additional £5 refundable deposit. A

THEME PARKS AND ATTRACTIONS

ATTRACTIONS WITH Q-BOT AT LEGOLAND WINDSOR

Aero Nomads	Driving School	Orient Expedition
Balloon School	Extreme Team Challenge	Pirate Falls Dynamite Drench
Chopper Squadron	Fairy Tale Brook	Sky Rider
Desert Chase	Fire Academy	Spinning Spider
Dino Dipper	Imagination Theatre	Thunder Blazer
Dino Safari	Jolly Rocker	Vikings' River Splash
The Dragon	Laser Raiders	
Dragon's Apprentice		

limited number of wheelchairs are available as well, for a deposit of £20 per day. You'll need to bring proof of disability, such as a Disability Living Allowance book, Attendance Allowance book or Invalidity Benefit book. See Legoland's website for a complete list of acceptable documents for proof of disability.

Legoland has other benefits for guests with disabilities, including a guest-assistance card, which allows guests to queue in the exit queue if they're not able to stand in the regular queue. Check the Legoland Frequently Asked Questions list at **legoland.co.uk/Plan/FAQ** for a complete list of services.

PARENT SWAP (AKA 'SWITCHING OFF' OR 'CHILD SWAP') As with Alton Towers' Parent Queue Share (see page 271), Legoland Windsor offers a way for two or more adults with a small child to experience a ride without waiting in line twice. While Alton Towers uses a printed paper pass, guests at Legoland need only tell a queue attendant that they wish to 'switch off'. The attendant will instruct you on how to proceed. Switching off is used when your group has at least one child not yet old enough or tall enough to experience certain attractions.

Q-BOT This is an electronic virtual queuing system that 'saves' your spot in a queue while you're off doing other things. On a small hand-held computer, you select from Q-Bot's menu the attraction at which you want to queue, and Q-Bot tells you the time at which you should return to ride. In practice, Q-Bot is a computerised version of the paper-based Fastrack queuing system in use at other Merlin theme parks (see page 269 in the Alton Towers chapter for details). The main advantage of using Q-Bot is that you use the device to make reservations instead of having to walk to a central point to get paper-based tickets.

As with Fastrack, most Q-Bot–enabled attractions have a special Q-Bot queue, usually the ride's exit, through which you'll queue to board. Unlike Fastrack, which charges per person, one Q-Bot can hold spots for up to six members of your party. Q-Bot is significantly more expensive, however, and unlike Fastrack, there is no à la carte option if you want to use Q-Bot only for a couple of rides. Finally, the price to use Q-Bot varies by day and crowd level – from £10 per group per day on off-peak times to around £40 per day during busier times of the year. It's also possible to combine Q-Bot with Parent Swap – ask a ride attendant for details.

The Beginning

Enter and exit the park through The Beginning. At the top of a hill, and with fantastic views of the surrounding countryside, The Beginning holds many of Legoland's park services, as well as shopping and dining. The Beginning also hosts the **Lego Creation Centre,** where guests can view some of the most intricate Lego models ever made.

Hill Train ★★

What it is Outdoor train ride. **Scope and scale** Minor attraction. **Height requirement** Under 4'3" (1.3 m) must ride with an adult. **Fright potential** None. **When to go** Anytime. **Authors' rating** Better on your way out; ★★. **Duration of ride** About 6 minutes. **Average wait in queue per 100 people ahead of you** About 11 minutes. **Loading speed** Slow.

DESCRIPTION AND COMMENTS In the back-left corner of The Beginning, the Hill Train is the easiest path to get to the middle and back of Legoland. The train runs round-trip from a ridge-top terminus near The Beginning to a terminus at the centre of the valley near the intersection of Kingdom of the Pharaohs, Traffic and Land of the Vikings.

TOURING TIPS The train is usually inundated in the morning and right before closing. Best to walk to the valley in the 3 hours after opening.

Rocket Racers ★★★

What it is Hands-on driving simulator. **Scope and scale** Minor attraction. **Age requirement** Must be age 5 or older. **Fright potential** None. **When to go** Anytime. **Authors' rating** Better on your way out; ★★. **Duration of ride** About 3 minutes. **Average wait in queue per 100 people ahead of you** About 15 minutes. **Loading speed** Slow.

DESCRIPTION AND COMMENTS Rocket Racers is an attraction in two parts. First, you design your own race car, choosing from among various kinds of bodies, tyres and more. Then you board a miniature race car with built-in video game and race your created car around a simulated race track.

TOURING TIPS A good attraction to try when you're leaving for or returning from a midday break.

Imagination Centre

Going clockwise, Imagination Centre is the first land you encounter after The Beginning. It includes two attractions and an indoor movie theatre, as well as workshops for building advanced Lego models.

Space Tower ★★

What it is A vertical tower which you climb by pulling yourself up via rope. **Scope and scale** Diversion. **Height requirement** 3' (0.9 m); under 4'3" (1.3 m) must ride with an adult. **Fright potential** None. **When to go** Anytime. **Authors'**

rating A nice view of the park; ★★. **Duration of ride** Varies. **Average wait in queue per 100 people ahead of you** Varies. **Loading speed** Slow.

DESCRIPTION AND COMMENTS On Space Tower, riders sit on a small plastic bench connected to one end of a rope hanging from the top of a tower. You pull on the rope to climb the tower. Once at the top of the tower, you get a nice view of the area around Legoland. the other end of the rope contains a counterweight, which serves to provide a gentle descent, even if you let go of the rope suddenly.

TOURING TIPS Crowded first thing in the morning, as it's one of the first prominent attractions seen if walking this way through the park.

Sky Rider (Q-Bot) ★★½

What it is Elevated-train ride around Imagination Centre. **Scope and scale** Minor attraction. **Height requirement** 3' (0.9 m); under 4'3" (1.3 m) must ride with an adult. **Fright potential** None. **When to go** Anytime. **Authors' rating** Another nice view of the park; ★★½. **Duration of ride** About 4 minutes. **Average wait in queue per 100 people ahead of you** About 15 minutes. **Loading speed** Fast.

DESCRIPTION AND COMMENTS A slow-moving elevated-train ride around the perimeter of Imagination Centre. Set midway up the ridge, so you get some decent views of the area around the park.

TOURING TIPS Many folks get sidetracked by the Sky Rider, as it's one of the first attractions seen this way through the park. Save this attraction for late afternoon on your way out of the park.

Imagination Theatre (Q-Bot) ★★★½

What it is 3D film presentation with in-theatre special effects. **Scope and scale** Major attraction. **Height requirement** None. **Fright potential** A few of the effects may frighten some very young children. **When to go** As per the daily entertainment schedule. **Authors' rating** Better than expected; ★★★½. **Duration of show** About 15 minutes. **Loading speed** Fast.

DESCRIPTION AND COMMENTS An indoor theatre that shows several different 3D films each day, the Imagination Theatre is the premier attraction in the Imagination Centre and one of the better attractions in the park.

Guests sit on tiered concrete rows, so this is not a lavish venue. However, the films shown can be appreciated visually by the youngest children in the audience and as a complete story by older kids and adults. Several films are shown each day, and usually they're rotated so that no film is shown twice in a row.

Besides the 3D films, the theatre's other special effects include rain (from the ceiling), lightning and wind. It's possible that some very small children may be frightened by these, but we didn't see a single scared youngster during our movie viewings.

TOURING TIPS The theatre can hold around 200 people per show and is rarely crowded early in the morning. Check the daily entertainment schedule for show times, and be sure to see at least one of the films.

Miniland

This large landscaped area contains detailed replicas of famous sites from around the world. Highlights include a scale model of London's most famous buildings, a miniature Loch Ness (including Nessie) and the US space-shuttle launch complex in Cape Canaveral, Florida.

We're huge Lego fans, having grown up with the toys decades ago. Len even keeps a couple of the more advanced sets around the house for idle fun (for the children, of course). Even so, the architectural detail in these models has to be seen to be fully appreciated. While the scale of each exhibit varies, many of the buildings are as tall as an adult. Supposedly comprising more than 20 million Lego bricks, Miniland shows what you can do with these things if you have obsessive–compulsive disorder with a Lego fixation. We rate Miniland as a must-see.

TOURING TIP View Miniland either on your way out of the park or during a post-dinner stroll.

Duplo Land

Duplo is Lego's brand of plastic bricks for the preschool set, and the attractions in Duplo Land are designed specifically for preschool children. Including play areas and a theatre show, Duplo Land consists of seven attractions. There's also a good sit-down restaurant serving carved beef and fried chicken.

Duplo Playtown ★★½

What it is Large, colourful outdoor play sets. **Scope and scale** Diversion. **Height requirement** None. **Fright potential** None. **When to go** Anytime. **Authors' rating** Great way to spend some unstructured play time; ★★½.

DESCRIPTION AND COMMENTS A large, colourful collection of outdoor slides, small buildings and other playground equipment, Duplo Playtown is where to take the children when they're tired of queuing and touring and need some free time to run around.

One of thing things we parents like best about Duplo Playtown is that there's only one way in and out. This reduces the chance that a child may wander off into the rest of the park while Mum and Dad are enjoying a few minutes to themselves.

TOURING TIPS Gets moderately crowded in the early morning and afternoon, but there's enough to do here that kids will be happy just running from place to place.

Duplo Train ★★

What it is Small train ride around Duplo Playground. **Scope and scale** Diversion. **Height requirement** None. **Fright potential** None. **When to go** Anytime. **Authors' rating** Good only if there's no wait; ★★. **Duration of ride** About 1 minute. **Average wait in queue per 100 people ahead of you** About 23 minutes. **Loading speed** Slow.

DESCRIPTION AND COMMENTS A short train ride around the back of Duplo Playtown. Nothing special to see beyond Playtown itself, and the ride lasts only around 70 seconds. You'll spend that much time just getting seated.

TOURING TIPS Eminently skippable on any touring plan. May open an hour after the rest of the park on days of lighter attendance.

Extreme Team Challenge (Q-Bot) ★★½

What it is Short, gentle 2-person water slide. **Scope and scale** Minor attraction. **Height requirement** 3' (0.9 m) to ride; under 4'3" (1.3 m) must ride with an adult. **Fright potential** None. **When to go** Before 11 a.m. (if it's warm enough) or after 4 p.m. **Authors' rating** More fun than it should be. Also wetter; ★★½. **Duration of ride** About 15 seconds. **Average wait in queue per 100 people ahead of you** About 36 minutes. **Loading speed** Slow.

DESCRIPTION AND COMMENTS This pair of side-by-side water slides allows groups of four to race down a set of gentle, short flumes. There are a couple of turns but no giant hills or dips. Perfectly appropriate for anyone tall enough to ride, as long as they're willing to get wet. Expect to get soaked enough that it takes a few hours to dry off.

Although the signage says you must have two people in your party to ride, we found that the staff are perfectly willing to hop on a raft with anyone who shows up alone. We'd like to thank Sophie for donning her wetsuit early one brisk fall morning as part of our commitment to participatory journalism.

TOURING TIPS Not crowded during most of the day, especially morning. If you see more than 10 or 20 people in the queue, however, try again on your way out of the park or just after lunch.

Duplo Theatre ★★★½

What it is Puppet show held in outdoor covered theatre. **Scope and scale** Minor attraction. **Height requirement** None. **Fright potential** None. **When to go** As per performance schedule posted at theatre. **Authors' rating** Well done; ★★★½. **Duration of show** About 20 minutes.

DESCRIPTION AND COMMENTS Housed in a covered outdoor theatre with bench seating, the Duplo Theatre hosts puppet productions of classic children's stories such as 'Goldilocks and the Three Bears'. Immensely popular for their puppetry and storytelling, most shows play to packed houses. Tiered seating allows those in the back to see the stage, too. The best seats are the 16 or so directly up front, within 3 or 4 ft of the small stage.

TOURING TIPS To get a seat up front, arrive 20 minutes before the start of a morning show, or 25 minutes during afternoon shows or when the park is crowded.

Chopper Squadron (Q-Bot) ★★

What it is Gentle 2-person spinning, up-and-down helicopter ride. **Scope and scale** Minor attraction. **Height requirement** 3' (0.9 m) to ride; under 4'3" (1.3 m) must ride with an adult. **Fright potential** None. **When to go** Before 11 a.m. or after 4 p.m. **Authors' rating** Resist urge to quote *Apocalypse Now* while riding; ★★. **Duration of ride** About 2½ minutes. **Average wait in queue per 100 people ahead of you** About 21 minutes. **Loading speed** Slow.

DESCRIPTION AND COMMENTS A set of 12 two-person Lego-inspired toy helicopters. Each 'copter is mounted on a hydraulic shaft, which can be raised or lowered by the passengers. The helicopters can get 7–10 ft (2–3 m) high, and the passengers can also spin the helicopter from side to side.

TOURING TIPS Somewhat hidden by a row of tall hedges surrounding half the attraction, Chopper Squadron doesn't get busy until midday. Tour in the early morning or during dinner.

Waterworks ★★

What it is Interactive play area with water fountains. **Scope and scale** Minor attraction. **Height requirement** None. **Fright potential** None. **When to go** Anytime. **Authors' rating** Let's get soaked! ★★.

DESCRIPTION AND COMMENTS A large outdoor play area with plenty of places to climb, run through and get absolutely soaked. The water features include fountains that bubble up from the ground, tall steel 'flowers' that function as giant sprinklers, and a ring of random water jets that will wet any body parts that remain dry. On warmer days, strip your kids down to the legal limit and let them run wild.

TOURING TIPS As parents, we think the best time to visit Waterworks is right before leaving the park for a nap. This allows you to change the kids out of their sopping clothes and put on something dry for the rest of the day. If that can't be done, leave Waterworks for last thing in the day. At least you'll be able to control the temperature in the car on the drive home – something you can't do while you're in the park.

Fairy Tale Brook (Q-Bot) ★★★½

What it is Slow boat ride past scenes from childhood stories. **Scope and scale** Minor attraction. **Height requirement** Under 4'3" (1.3 m) must ride with an adult. **Fright potential** None. **When to go** Anytime. **Authors' rating** One of our favourites in the park; ★★★½. **Duration of ride** About 5½ minutes. **Average wait in queue per 100 people ahead of you** About 7 minutes. **Loading speed** Moderate.

DESCRIPTION AND COMMENTS Fairy Tale Brook is a calm, gentle boat ride past Lego-created storybook scenes, including Red Riding Hood, Sleeping Beauty, the Three Little Pigs and more. Most scenes are done on a nearly-life-size scale, almost completely out of Lego bricks. Besides the Legos, the background scenery includes a shaded, wooded area that keeps the ride cool during summer. One of the best attractions in the park.

TOURING TIPS One of the most efficient attractions in the park, Fairy Tale

Brook handles crowds well. Your waits should not be more than 20 minutes except on the busiest days.

Traffic

Traffic is Legoland's homage to most forms of transportation, including automobiles, boats and balloons. As Traffic is near the centre of the park, most of its attractions get crowded early in the day.

Besides the attractions, there's a small sandwich shop near the back of the land. If you're hungry, however, continue walking to Lego City. It's an extra minute or so but provides many more dining options.

Driving School (Q-Bot) ★★★½

What it is Miniature driving course through city streets. **Scope and scale** Minor attraction. **Age requirement** Ages 6–13. **Fright potential** None. **When to go** Before 11 a.m. **Authors' rating** The best we've seen of this kind of attraction; ★★★½. **Duration of ride** About 4½ minutes. **Average wait in queue per 100 people ahead of you** About 29 minutes. **Loading speed** Slow.

DESCRIPTION AND COMMENTS About one-fourth of Traffic's land is devoted to Driving School. Around two dozen children at a time get to drive their own small plastic battery-powered cars around a large set of city streets. The size of the track ensures kids don't spend most of their time in a giant scrum, although when they get to the far end of the track it can be hard to see them or get good photos.

We spent a good half-hour observing kids' reactions to the Driving School, and no one left unhappy.

TOURING TIPS Long queues develop almost from the time the park opens, so Driving School should be one of the attractions you see first thing in the morning. Our suggestion is to see Driving School and the rest of Traffic on the way towards attractions in the back of the park; those typically have larger capacities and thus shorter queues.

L-Drivers ★★½

What it is Miniature driving course through city streets. **Scope and scale** Minor attraction. **Age requirement** Ages 3–5. **Fright potential** None. **When to go** Before 11 a.m. **Authors' rating** A smaller version of Driving School; ★★½. **Duration of ride** About 3 minutes. **Average wait in queue per 100 people ahead of you** About 72 (yes, 72) minutes. **Loading speed** Slow.

DESCRIPTION AND COMMENTS A smaller version of Driving School for the preschool set, L-Drivers is notable only for its minuscule capacity. Besides the actual driving, children get a pre- and post-ride talk from the ride staff. Unfortunately, the staff get carried away and seem to ramble on forever, forgetting that there is an army of impatient kids in the queue. It's a lot of fun, and kids seem to enjoy it, but the consequence is that it's almost impossible to get more than a few dozen kids per hour through the attraction.

TOURING TIPS If your children are tall enough to experience Driving School, skip L-Drivers. Otherwise, be on hand at opening and ride L-Drivers in the first 30 minutes of operation. Above all, don't get stuck in the queue here. If the estimated time to board is more than 20 minutes, it's better to just write it off. You could also consider using Q-Bot. It's a relatively-expensive option but will help reduce time in the queue later in the day.

Boating School ★★½

What it is Miniature boats driven around a canal. **Scope and scale** Minor attraction. **Height requirement** Under 4'3" (1.3 m) must ride with an adult. **Fright potential** None. **When to go** Before 11 a.m. **Authors' rating** We love the smell of diesel in the morning; ★★½. **Duration of ride** About 6½ minutes. **Average wait in queue per 100 people ahead of you** About 10 minutes; assumes 24 boats operating. **Loading speed** Moderate.

DESCRIPTION AND COMMENTS Similar to Driving School, except here you steer miniature two-person boats around a small water course. Along with Driving School, Boating School occupies about half of Traffic's land, giving you some idea of how long these two courses are.

There's not much to see along the waterway, and nothing that can't be seen from the walkways around the attraction. As we've noted for other water rides, the big appeal is that the water adds a dynamic element to each visit, meaning no two trips down the canal are exactly the same.

TOURING TIPS Despite being water-based, Boating School handles many more people per hour than Driving School. See Driving School first (and L-Drivers before either), then Boating School.

Balloon School (Q-Bot) ★★

What it is Spinning, balloon-themed funfair ride. **Scope and scale** Minor attraction. **Height requirement** Under 4'3" (1.3 m) must ride with an adult. **Fright potential** None. **When to go** Before 11 a.m. or after 3 p.m. **Authors' rating** Would be much more fun if untethered; ★★. **Duration of ride** About 2½ minutes. **Average wait in queue per 100 people ahead of you** About 20 minutes; assumes all 6 balloons operating. **Loading speed** Slow.

DESCRIPTION AND COMMENTS Miniature hot-air balloons are suspended from arms hung from a central axis. The whole contraption turns, and pilots seated in each balloon's gondola can raise or lower their balloon using a control stick.

The balloons are pretty, and the ride structure is well themed. Still, this is a dressed-up version of a typical amusement-park ride.

TOURING TIPS Is one of the lowest-capacity attractions in the park but isn't usually popular enough to develop long queues for most of the day. See last in Traffic.

Fire Academy (Q-Bot) ★★★

What it is Do-it-yourself simulated fire-fighting. **Scope and scale** Minor attraction. **Height requirement** 3' (0.9 m) to ride; under 4'3" (1.3 m) must ride with an adult. **Fright potential** None. **When to go** Before noon or after 3 p.m. **Authors' rating** We predict that Ambulance Academy is next; ★★★. **Duration of ride** Just under 2 minutes. **Average wait in queue per 100 people ahead of you** About 33 minutes; assumes all 8 fire engines operating. **Loading speed** Slow.

> **DESCRIPTION AND COMMENTS** One of the funniest attractions we've seen in any theme park anywhere in the world. Parents and children team up to race one of eight fire engines down a small course, then hop out to spray water on a building that everyone pretends is on fire. Once the 'fire' is doused, everyone hops back in the fire engine to race back to the starting line.
>
> Parents and children operate a small two-person pump to move their fire engine. The funny thing about the attraction is that the parents (and by 'parents' we mean 'dads') inevitably view the whole thing as a competition to see who can finish first. It's hysterical to see men – erm, 'parents' – who are obviously not used to physical labour turn purple and sweat like hogs while aboard a miniature plastic fire engine. We were frankly surprised no one had a coronary on the warm day we were watching.
>
> **TOURING TIPS** The physical labour involved in the attraction scares off many people who would otherwise ride. Don't try Fire Academy right after eating.

Lego City

In the back corner of the park and roughly opposite the park entrance, Lego City is an oasis of restaurants and shopping for this side of Legoland. As far as the restaurants go, **City Walk** is an all-you-care-to-eat buffet, with pizza, pasta and salad. Many of Merlin Entertainments' parks have this kind of restaurant, and many of the families we've spoken to consider this the best dining value in Legoland.

Besides pizza and pasta, Lego City contains a café and an ice-cream parlour, as well as a souvenir shop. The **Xbox 360 Gaming Zone** houses a dozen or so two-person stations where kids and adults can try the latest Microsoft Xbox 360 games free. The building is air-conditioned and, with the video games, can become crowded after lunchtime. If your kids find an open station and want to relax here for a bit, grab a coffee next door and let them unwind.

Pirates of Skeleton Bay ★★★

What it is Live-action stunt show with singing. **Scope and scale** Major attraction. **Height requirement** None. **Fright potential** None. **When to go** See performance schedule for times. **Authors' rating** Frenetic and fun; ★★★. **Duration of show** About 20 minutes.

> **DESCRIPTION AND COMMENTS** One of the most enjoyable live-action shows in any of the theme parks we've visited, *Pirates of Skeleton Bay* follows the story of a pirate crew haunted by a pirate ghost who is seeking the key to his treasure chest.

Staged on a small lagoon, with special effects and set pieces that include a 2-storey lighthouse and rope bridges, *Pirates* is also one of the more elaborate settings we've seen. The sets are complemented by a group of performers who are clearly skilled at physical comedy – most of them run around, tumble and perform other gymnastic moves almost nonstop during the show. And of all the shows we've seen, the actors in *Pirates* deliver their lines most articulately, so even small children and guidebook authors understand what's going on.

TOURING TIPS It's possible to find shade for the midday performances along the walkway closest to Brick Brothers Souvenir Co.

Digger Challenge ★★★

What it is Kid-operated construction equipment. **Scope and scale** Minor attraction. **Age requirement** Ages 3–5 to operate the digger. **Fright potential** None. **When to go** Before 1 p.m. or after 5 p.m. **Authors' rating** The park needs more hands-on things like this; ★★★. **Duration of play** About 3 minutes. **Average wait in queue per 100 people ahead of you** About 45 minutes; assumes all 10 diggers operating. **Loading speed** Slow.

DESCRIPTION AND COMMENTS Children operate their own miniature hydraulic digger, using joysticks to manoeuvre the digger's metal scoop into picking up small plastic balls and depositing them in a bucket for counting. The more balls you scoop and deposit, the higher your score. No prizes are awarded, and the diggers are so far apart that no one really competes against anyone else.

It's a great amount of hands-on fun, and we were really itching to try this ourselves. Parents may need to go on twice, using their kids as a ruse on the second ride so they can try the digger themselves. One parent and one child fit in each digger.

TOURING TIPS The diggers struggle to handle more than 150 people per hour, so the ride has the potential to develop long queues during busier times of the year. Fortunately, this attraction is in the very back of the park, so many folk don't discover it until around lunchtime.

Orient Expedition (Q-Bot) ★★½

What it is Train ride through Lego City and parts of Traffic. **Scope and scale** Minor attraction. **Height requirement** Under 4'3" (1.3 m) must ride with an adult. **Fright potential** None. **When to go** Anytime. **Authors' rating** Okay if the queue isn't too long; ★★½. **Duration of ride** About 4 minutes. **Average wait in queue per 100 people ahead of you** About 7 minutes; assume 2 trains running. **Loading speed** Slow.

DESCRIPTION AND COMMENTS A somewhat relaxing train ride around the area between Lego City and Traffic. Two things make the ride a little frustrating: one is that it takes almost as long to load the train as it does for the actual train ride; the other is that there are various water features set up along the track to squirt unwary riders. There's nothing worse than closing your eyes for a little 30-second nap, only to be awakened by something squirting in your ear.

TOURING TIPS As long as two trains are running, Orient Expedition can handle crowds as well as almost any attraction in the park. And if this ride is crowded, it's virtually certain that everything else in the park will be too.

Adventure Land

It's a given that if an amusement park decides to organise its park into themed 'lands', one of those will be called 'Adventure Land'. Legoland is no exception. Here, Adventure Land consists of two dinosaur-themed attractions, a water-based variation on the standard funfair-style spinning ride, and two restaurants.

One of the restaurants is a burger joint, serving standard theme-park fare. The other is a Mexican cantina (evocatively called 'Mexican Cantina') whose only remarkable characteristic is, unfortunately, the slowness of the service. We're sure the staff are working as hard as they can on every order, but then again, Mexico achieved independence in roughly the same amount of time as it takes this place to cook up a burrito. It's not a good use of your time in the park unless you really need a long break and don't mind waiting for your food.

As we were going to press, Legoland's parent company, Merlin Entertainments Group, was rumoured have begun construction on a major new attraction in Adventure Land, set to open sometime in the second half of 2011. Dubbed 'Project Atlantis', the pyramid-shaped attraction supposedly combines a Sea Life marine aquarium with a ride system to transport guests through the aquarium's various exhibits. Other Merlin parks, such as Alton Towers, have Sea Life exhibits, so this partnership would be an extension of that arrangement. Besides the ride, we hear Atlantis will offer walk-through exhibits and shopping.

Wave Surfer ★★★½

What it is Fast-spinning boat ride, like teacups over water. **Scope and scale** Minor attraction. **Height requirement** 3' (0.9 m) to ride; under 4'3" (1.3 m) must ride with an adult. **Fright potential** None. **When to go** Before noon or after 4 p.m. **Authors' rating** Imaginative take on funfair spinning rides; ★★★½. **Duration of ride** About 2½ minutes. **Average wait in queue per 100 people ahead of you** About 17 minutes; assumes both sets of vehicles operating. **Loading speed** Slow.

DESCRIPTION AND COMMENTS Every amusement park and funfair contains some variation of a ride in which vehicles spin around a central axis. The ride mechanics are well established, and the only variation you see usually is in the paint job of the ride vehicles.

Wave Surfer is a different kind of spinning ride in that the ride vehicles are positioned in a small circular pool of water. Themed as two-person jet-ski pods, each vehicle pivots about two points on an arm extending from the centre of the ride. This allows passengers to steer the vehicles in the pool, creating huge plumes of water that soak riders and bystanders alike. This is the most creative adaptation of a standard ride we've seen in a long time. We're a bit surprised that it hasn't been copied elsewhere.

TOURING TIPS The ride is set up as two groups of six vehicles each. While Wave Surfer doesn't handle a huge number of guests per hour, its remote location and potential to soak tends to moderate crowds on all but the busiest, hottest days.

Dino Dipper (Q-Bot) ★★½

What it is Standard spinning amusement-park ride. **Scope and scale** Minor attraction. **Height requirement** 3' (0.9 m) to ride; under 4'3" (1.3 m) must ride with an adult. **Fright potential** None. **When to go** Before 11 a.m. or after 4 p.m. **Authors' rating** Pretty but excruciatingly slow to load; ★★½. **Duration of ride** About 2 minutes. **Average wait in queue per 100 people ahead of you** About 23 minutes; assumes all seats occupied for each cycle. **Loading speed** Very slow.

DESCRIPTION AND COMMENTS A set of nondescript train cars arranged in a connected circle, spinning around a central axis maybe 50 ft (15 m) in diameter. There are a couple of really gentle hills (not more than 3 ft/ 1 m high). For variety, the ride takes a turn spinning backwards. There's little difference between Dino Dipper and a hundred other similar rides at funfairs. Dino Dipper is, however, in a covered structure, so at least you're out of the direct sunlight while you wait to board.

TOURING TIPS Unbelievably slow to load if there's only one person working the attraction – by our count it takes the Dino Dipper staff member more than 9 minutes to load and unload passengers for each 2-minute ride. This reduces the ride's capacity immensely. If you see more than a few dozen people in the queue, come back later in the day.

Dino Safari (Q-Bot) ★★★

What it is Slow-moving ride past outdoor displays of dinosaurs. **Scope and scale** Minor attraction. **Height requirement** 3' (0.9 m) to ride; under 4'3" (1.3 m) must ride with an adult. **Fright potential** None. **When to go** Before 11 a.m. or after 4 p.m. **Authors' rating** Pleasant scenery if the wait isn't too long; ★★★. **Duration of ride** About 2 minutes. **Average wait in queue per 100 people ahead of you** About 12 minutes; assumes 10 cars running. **Loading speed** Fast.

DESCRIPTION AND COMMENTS Dino Safari consists of a set of small two-person trucks that follow a guided track on an outdoor path past scenes with static displays of different dinosaur species. Interesting, child-friendly facts are displayed in the queuing area and on the ride for each dinosaur, making the attraction at least tolerable for adults.

TOURING TIPS The building is well themed and positioned directly on a pretty walkway to Adventure Land, so long queues develop around late morning and continue throughout the day. One of the attractions to visit early or late.

Kingdom of the Pharaohs

An Egyptian-themed land between Lego City and the borders of Land of the Vikings and Pirates Landing, Kingdom of the Pharaohs contains **Laser Raiders,** one of Legoland's headliner attractions, and four small outdoor funfair-style attractions. Because they're on a main walkway between Lego City and the Pirates' and Knights' lands, these attractions are almost constantly inundated with guests. When you see long queues at these, it's almost certainly because of the amount of traffic going by, not because of the quality of the attractions.

Laser Raiders (Q-Bot) ★★★★

What it is Indoor ride-through shooting gallery. **Scope and scale** Headliner. **Height requirement** Under 4'3" (1.3 m) must ride with an adult. **Fright potential** The theme and noise may frighten some small children. **When to go** Before 11 a.m. or after 4 p.m. **Authors' rating** Loads of fun and not to be missed; ★★★★. **Duration of ride** About 2½ minutes. **Average wait in queue per 100 people ahead of you** About 6 minutes; assumes 10 ride vehicles operating. **Loading speed** Fast.

DESCRIPTION AND COMMENTS An indoor shooting gallery similar to Duel at Alton Towers or Tomb Blaster at Chessington, Laser Raiders is Legoland's premier attraction and is extensively themed. A pre-ride film explains the ride's premise – that you're joining an expedition to Egypt to help some adventurers. Of course, things go awry, and you must fight the villains with your hand-held laser gun.

More than 90 laser targets are spread throughout the ride. Shooting one earns you a varying amount of points, depending on how difficult the target is to reach. A score is displayed for each of the four riders in your vehicle.

Laser Raiders also contains the best-themed queuing area of any attraction in Legoland. Dark, long and visually rich, the area combines Lego-built figures, props and other artefacts into a comic-book-like Egyptian setting. A couple of sponsorship adverts are displayed on monitors, but they're integrated reasonably well into the overall theme. We rate this as the best attraction in Legoland Windsor.

TOURING TIPS One of the park's most popular attractions, and one for which guests make a beeline as soon as the park opens. The fastest way to get to Laser Raiders in the morning is to bear left at The Beginning and head down the stairs towards Miniland. Keep Miniland on your left until you reach the Orient Expedition railway tracks, then turn right. Look for a bridge over the tracks on your left, which will put you in front of Laser Raiders' entrance.

Scarab-Bouncers ★½

What it is Bouncing funfair-style ride. **Scope and scale** Minor attraction. **Height requirement** 3' (0.9 m) to ride. **Fright potential** None. **When to go** Right after

Laser Raiders, if you must. **Authors' rating** Nothing special; ★½. **Duration of ride** About 1½ minutes. **Average wait in queue per 100 people ahead of you** About 41 minutes; assumes both bouncers operating. **Loading speed** Slow.

DESCRIPTION AND COMMENTS Similar to Alton Towers' Frog Hopper. Riders sit in a row of seats that is then lifted about 10 ft (3 m) off the ground. Once suspended, the row begins to bounce its way back to the ground. Most variations, including this one, include a couple of quick trips back to the top before a final hop to the bottom.

Scarab-Bouncers is situated in a dark, recessed part of the Laser Raiders ride building. As such, it doesn't draw the crowds that it would if it were outdoors and easy to see.

TOURING TIPS This kind of attraction is guaranteed to process guests slowly at any location in any park. The good news is that because it's hard to see, most kids won't beg to ride it (or miss not riding it). If we had to choose between getting in a long queue for Scarab-Bouncers or throwing a few £2 coins on the ground as a temporary distraction, we'd reach for our pockets.

Thunder Blazer (Q-Bot)   ★★

What it is Small funfair-style swinging chair ride. **Scope and scale** Minor attraction. **Height requirement** 3' (0.9 m) to ride. **Fright potential** None. **When to go** Before noon or after 4 p.m. **Authors' rating** Good for little ones; ★★. **Duration of ride** About 2 minutes. **Average wait in queue per 100 people ahead of you** About 22 minutes; assumes all swings occupied for each cycle. **Loading speed** Slow.

DESCRIPTION AND COMMENTS Similar to flying carousels at many parks, but smaller, Thunder Blazer is a pint-size version of a typical funfair ride in which metal chairs are suspended from a rotating circular ceiling by long metal chains. What makes this version attractive for small children is that Thunder Blazer doesn't go as high or as fast as most other variations on the ride.

TOURING TIPS We wouldn't wait more than 10 or 15 minutes for this, especially if it's a warm day.

Desert Chase (Q-Bot)   ★★

What it is Small funfair-style merry-go-round. **Scope and scale** Minor attraction. **Height requirement** Under 3'5" (1.1 m) must be accompanied by an adult. **Fright potential** None. **When to go** Before noon or after 4 p.m. **Authors' rating** Good for little ones; ★★. **Duration of ride** About 2 minutes. **Average wait in queue per 100 people ahead of you** About 23 minutes; assumes all seats occupied for each ride. **Loading speed** Slow.

DESCRIPTION AND COMMENTS A small, 26-person merry-go-round with a desert theme. While the attraction is nothing special, there is a good bit of shade around the queuing area, which is welcome in warmer weather.

TOURING TIPS As with most of Kingdom of the Pharaohs attractions, see this one after Laser Raiders. If you're going to tour this land in one go, see Laser Raiders first and leave Scarab-Bouncers for last.

Aero Nomad (Q-Bot) ★★

What it is Small funfair-style Ferris wheel. **Scope and scale** Minor attraction. **Height requirement** Under 4'3" (1.3 m) must be accompanied by an adult. **Fright potential** None. **When to go** Before noon or after 4 p.m. **Authors' rating** Good for little ones; ★★. **Duration of ride** About 1½ minutes. **Average wait in queue per 100 people ahead of you** About 14 minutes; assumes all seats occupied for each ride. **Loading speed** Slow.

DESCRIPTION AND COMMENTS A 32-person Ferris wheel with a balloon theme. Another typical funfair-style ride.

TOURING TIPS Has a slightly-larger capacity than Thunder Blazer or Desert Chase, so may have shorter queues during busier times of day.

Land of the Vikings

Despite the name, the amount of Norse theming is pretty minimal in Land of the Vikings. You could just as easily throw a couple of animal skins around and call it 'Land of the Mongols' or 'Taxidermy Land'. Sadly, there's no restaurant here either, so we can't throw a tantrum and shout 'You call this mead, wench?'

Land of the Vikings is the first area you'll encounter if you walk straight back from the park entrance down the right-most path. The land's attractions are built into the hillside and overlook the valley farther down. **Vikings' River Splash,** a headliner attraction, lures crowds to Land of the Vikings early in the day by virtue of its popularity and proximity to the park entrance. Queues take longer to develop when the weather is cooler, but you still have to get here pretty early on to avoid substantial waits.

Vikings' River Splash (Q-Bot) ★★★

What it is River-raft ride. **Scope and scale** Headliner. **Height requirement** 3'3" (1 m) to ride; under 4'3" (1.3 m) must be accompanied by an adult. **Fright potential** None. **When to go** Before 11 a.m. or after 4 p.m. **Authors' rating** Fast and fun; ★★★. **Duration of ride** About 4½ minutes. **Average wait in queue per 100 people ahead of you** About 7 minutes; assumes 15 rafts operating. **Loading speed** Fast.

DESCRIPTION AND COMMENTS Up to six guests board a round inflatable rubber raft before setting out on a high-speed white-water trip through Viking country. There's no story and little theming to the attraction, but the views of the surrounding land from this hillside-based attraction are lovely. Note that you will get wet on Vikings' River Splash, but you probably won't get soaked.

TOURING TIPS One of the most efficient attractions in the park; we recommend visiting River Splash after Laser Raiders and Pirate Falls Dynamite Drench.

Loki's Labyrinth ★★½

What it is Hedge maze. **Scope and scale** Diversion. **Age requirement** Under age 7 must be accompanied by an adult. **Fright potential** None. **When to go** Anytime. **Authors' rating** One of the best hedge mazes we've seen; ★★½. **Duration of experience** Allow 10–15 minutes to get through and back.

DESCRIPTION AND COMMENTS A well-done hedge maze similar to Pleasure Beach Blackpool's Chinese Puzzle Maze (page 395), but less complicated to get through. At the middle of the maze is a 1-storey covered observation platform with nice views of the rest of the park. If you can get there with some snacks and your family intact, it'd be a nice place for a midday break. Despite it being easier to navigate than Pleasure Beach's maze, we still suggest hitting the loo before you head in.

TOURING TIPS Rarely crowded. Visit anytime.

Spinning Spider (Q-Bot) ★★

What it is Spinning-teacup funfair ride. **Scope and scale** Minor attraction. **Height requirement** 3' (0.9 m) to ride; under 4'3" (1.3 m) must be accompanied by an adult. **Fright potential** None. **When to go** Before noon or after 4 p.m. **Authors' rating** Motion sickness + bugs = fun? ★★. **Duration of ride** About 1½ minutes. **Average wait in queue per 100 people ahead of you** About 15 minutes; assumes all seats occupied for each ride. **Loading speed** Slow.

DESCRIPTION AND COMMENTS An insect-themed variation on the classic 'teacups' funfair ride. Guests sit in small circular ride vehicles and turn a metal wheel to spin their vehicle on a central axis. Groups of three ride vehicles spin in a larger circle, and the whole set of vehicles spins in yet another large circle. Not for those prone to motion sickness.

TOURING TIPS Outdoors and uncovered, which can make for some miserable waits during summer. Make sure everyone is properly hydrated before getting in the queue.

Longboat Invader ★★

What it is Side-to-side swinging-boat ride. **Scope and scale** Minor attraction. **Height requirement** 3' (0.9 m) to ride; under 4'3" (1.3 m) must be accompanied by an adult. **Fright potential** None. **When to go** Before noon or after 4 p.m. **Authors' rating** More fun that it may look; ★★. **Duration of ride** About 2½ minutes. **Average wait in queue per 100 people ahead of you** About 25 minutes; assumes all seats occupied for each ride. **Loading speed** Moderate.

DESCRIPTION AND COMMENTS Similar to Heave Ho! at Alton Towers. Riders board a miniature pirate ship that glides gently back and forth on a horseshoe-shaped track. The pirate ship also spins in a small circle while it swings.

TOURING TIPS Outdoors and uncovered, but not especially popular.

Pirates Landing

A swashbuckling land in the back-right corner of the park between Kingdom of the Pharaohs and Knights Kingdom, Pirates Landing is one of the best-themed areas in all of Legoland. Its signature attraction is the **Pirate Falls Dynamite Drench**, a log-flume ride that's guaranteed to make a smiling, soaking mess of your entire family. There is a handful of other rides and three decent take-away dining choices, plus a lovely (but small) picnic area named **Enchanted Forest.**

Pirate Falls Dynamite Drench (Q-Bot) ★★★½

What it is Outdoor log-flume ride. **Scope and scale** Headliner. **Height requirement** 3'3" (1 m) to ride; under 4'3" (1.3 m) must be accompanied by an adult. **Fright potential** The drop sequence may frighten some preschool children. **When to go** As soon as the park opens or after 4 p.m. **Authors' rating** Needs a catchy tune, but otherwise a lot of fun; ★★★½. **Duration of ride** About 3½ minutes. **Average wait in queue per 100 people ahead of you** About 11 minutes; assumes 24 boats operating. **Loading speed** Moderate.

DESCRIPTION AND COMMENTS An elaborate, heavily-decorated flume ride around the back corner of Legoland, Pirate Falls Dynamite Drench is one of the most popular attractions in the park.

There's no explicit story to Pirate Falls, but the scenery is lovely, shaded and relaxing. There is one fairly steep drop at the end, which is completely visible from the walkways around the attraction. If your children are hesitant to ride Pirate Falls, have them stand in front of the hot-dog stand and watch riders slide down, while you point out the faces of happy children when they're done.

TOURING TIPS Handles more than 500 guests per hour, making it one of Legoland's most efficient attractions. See early in the morning along with Laser Raiders and Vikings' River Splash. Ponchos are available near the end of the queue for around two quid. Money well spent, in our opinion.

Pirate Training Camp ★★★½

What it is Large pirate-themed play area. **Scope and scale** Diversion. **Age requirement** Must be 7 years old to play: **Fright potential** None. **When to go** Anytime. **Authors' rating** The ultimate backyard play-set; ★★★½. **Duration of play** Varies.

DESCRIPTION AND COMMENTS A massive log-fort complex with miniature pirate ships, bows, sterns and other ship parts to climb and explore. With the exception of Pirate Falls, this is the heart of Pirates Landing. It's possible for a couple of children to spend an hour here without any complaint whatsoever. Fortunately for parents, there's seating, shade and refreshments nearby, so they can relax while the kids do the running around.

TOURING TIPS Can get crowded around the middle of the afternoon, but the place is so big that there's always something to do. Tour anytime.

Jolly Rocker (Q-Bot) ★★½

What it is Swinging-boat ride. **Scope and scale** Minor attraction. **Height requirement** 3'3" (1 m) to ride; under 4'3" (1.3 m) must ride with an adult.

Fright potential Some small children are frightened by the height. **When to go** Before noon or after 4 p.m. **Authors' rating** It's part of the pirate code that every theme park must have one of these; ★★½. **Duration of ride** About 2 minutes. **Average wait in queue per 100 people ahead of you** About 13 minutes; assumes all 45 seats filled for each ride. **Loading speed** Slow.

> **DESCRIPTION AND COMMENTS** Similar to The Blade at Alton Towers, Jolly Rocker is a boat suspended from above by a set of long metal arms affixed to a central axis. The arms forming a triangular swing, and once under way the boat swings back and forth like a clock pendulum gone to extremes.
>
> This is a standard funfair and amusement-park ride, where the only thing that usually varies is the decoration on the ride vehicle. In this case, it's pirates instead of the Canadian wilderness or Viking fleet.
>
> **TOURING TIPS** Slow loading and unloading times mean long waits on busy days. If you see more than a few dozen people in the queue and only one employee working the ride, come back later; it's just too time-consuming for one person to do the unload, load and start of the ride.

Knights Kingdom

Set in the farthest corner of Legoland Windsor, Knights Kingdom contains two dragon-themed roller coasters and a castle-themed restaurant serving rotisserie-grilled meats and salads. The two coasters are fun and popular. And although this is one of the more remote locations in the entire park, the food is decent, and you can find enough places to sit to make for a pleasant meal.

The Dragon (Q-Bot) ★★★½

What it is Outdoor roller coaster. **Scope and scale** Headliner. **Height requirement** 3'3" (1 m) to ride; under 4'3" (1.3 m) must be accompanied by an adult. **Fright potential** The tight turns and speed may frighten some very young children, but the overall experience is mild. **When to go** Within the first hour the park is open or after 4 p.m. **Authors' rating** Not too scary for older primary-schoolers; ★★★½. **Duration of ride** About 2 minutes. **Average wait in queue per 100 people ahead of you** About 15 minutes; assumes 1 train running. **Loading speed** Slow.

> **DESCRIPTION AND COMMENTS** One of the park's headliner attractions, The Dragon takes riders on a medium-speed track around more than half of Knights Kingdom. There are no loops or inversions on the track, only tight turns. This makes the experience ideal for older primary-school children who are looking to graduate to bigger rides.
>
> The ride lasts about 2 minutes, and a considerable amount of that is spent hauling the dragon-themed train out from the boarding station and past a series of detailed Lego sets showing the inside of a castle and the eponymous dragon run amok. That, coupled with the time it takes to get up the first lift hill, composes most of the time you'll spend on the train. Still, you go through a number of tight turns and dips, and when the weather's nice you get a great view of the landscape around the park.

TOURING TIPS Riders sit in rows of two. If your group contains an odd number of people, decide before boarding which person gets the row to themselves. The Dragon is the ride on which we realised that if a UK theme-park sign says something like DON'T STAND UP ON THE RIDE OR YOU'LL HIT YOUR HEAD AND DIE, you shouldn't stand up on the ride. Because if you do, you'll hit your head. And die.

Dragon's Apprentice (Q-Bot) ★★★

What it is Tame outdoor roller coaster. **Scope and scale** Minor attraction. **Height requirement** 3' (0.9 m) to ride; under 4'3" (1.3 m) must be accompanied by an adult. **Fright potential** Shouldn't frighten anyone. **When to go** Within the first hour the park is open or after 4 p.m. **Authors' rating** Perfect for younger primary-schoolers; ★★★. **Duration of ride** About 1 minute. **Average wait in queue per 100 people ahead of you** About 17 minutes; assumes 1 train running. **Loading speed** Slow.

DESCRIPTION AND COMMENTS A smaller version of The Dragon, for kids not yet able or willing to ride the larger, faster coaster. Set in a mediaeval fair's tent, Dragon's Apprentice includes a slower, shorter track, with smaller ride vehicles and no large hills or dips to throw anyone into a tizzy. We observed children as young as age 4 experiencing Dragon's Apprentice without problems.

TOURING TIPS As with The Dragon, riders sit in rows of two. If your group contains an odd number of people, decide before boarding which person gets the row to themselves.

Legoland Windsor Touring Plans

Here we've included touring plans for parents with both older and younger children.

One-Day Touring Plan for Parents with Small Children under 3' (0.9 m)

1. The night before your visit, check **legoland.co.uk** for park hours and weather.
2. Arrive at the park entrance 30 minutes prior to official opening, with your admission in hand. Arrive 45 minutes early if you need to purchase admission.
3. As soon as the park opens, make your way to Traffic at the centre of the park and experience L-Drivers (for children aged 3–5), Driving School (aged 6–13) or both.
4. Try Balloon School, also in Traffic.
5. Take a spin on Boating School in Traffic.
6. From Boating School, head to Kingdom of the Pharaohs and experience Laser Raiders.
7. Ride Desert Chase in Kingdom of the Pharaohs.
8. Try Aero Nomad in Kingdom of the Pharaohs.
9. Take the Digger Challenge in Lego City.

10. Board the Orient Expedition for a train ride around Lego City.
11. Check the daily entertainment schedule for the next performance of *Pirates of Skeleton Bay* in Lego City and work lunch in around this show.
12. Eat lunch. Good nearby choices include City Walk in Lego City and the barbecue places in Pirates Landing.
13. If your children need some unstructured time, visit the Xbox 360 Gaming Zone in Lego City.
14. Make your way to Duplo Land and ride the Fairy Tale Brook boat ride.
15. Check the daily entertainment schedule for the next puppet show at the Duplo Theatre, and work this show in around time at the Duplo Playtown play area.
16. Play in the Duplo Playtown play area. Take a spin on the Duplo Train if the wait isn't more than 10 minutes.
17. If it's warm enough, splash through Waterworks at Duplo Land.
18. Check the daily entertainment schedule for the next show at the Imagination Theatre in Imagination Centre.
19. Tour the buildings of Miniland.
20. Eat dinner.
21. Make your way to Pirates Landing and see the Pirate Training Camp.
22. Tour the Enchanted Forest in Pirates Landing and Loki's Labyrinth in Land of the Vikings.
23. Repeat any favourite attractions or visit any missed steps.
24. Tour the Legoland Creation Centre on your way out of the park.
25. Depart Legoland Windsor.

One-Day Touring Plan for Parents with Older and Younger Children

1. The night before your visit, check **legoland.co.uk** for park hours and weather.
2. Arrive at the park entrance 30 minutes prior to official opening, with your admission in hand. Arrive 45 minutes early if you need to purchase admission.
3. As soon as the park opens, make your way to Traffic at the centre of the park and experience L-Drivers (for children aged 3–5), Driving School (aged 6–13) or both.
4. Take a spin on Boating School in Traffic.
5. From Boating School, head to Kingdom of the Pharaohs and experience Laser Raiders.
6. Have at least one adult and the older children ride Pirate Falls Dynamite Drench in Pirates Landing. Tell the ride attendant you'd like to use the 'parent swap' to ride. One other adult and the younger children should try the Pirate Training Camp nearby.
7. Ride Vikings' River Splash in Land of the Vikings. Adults and older

children should use the 'parent swap' technique again. Now would be a good time to take younger children on a snack or toilet break.
8. Ride the Longboat Invader in Land of the Vikings.
9. Try the Spinning Spider in Land of the Vikings.
10. Tour Loki's Labyrinth while you're there.
11. Eat lunch. We think Pirates Landing is the best option for take-away dining. Try to find a spot in the shade at Enchanted Forest to sit and eat.
12. In Adventure Land and ride the Dino Dipper.
13. Ride the Dino Safari in Adventure Land.
14. Also in Adventure Land, try the Wave Surfer.
15. Check the daily entertainment schedule for the next performances at the Imagination Theatre in Imagination Centre, the Duplo Theatre in Duplo Land and *Pirates of Skeleton Bay* in Lego City. See these shows in the order that best fits your schedule for the rest of the day.
16. Play in the Duplo Playtown play area. Take a spin on the Duplo Train if the wait isn't more than 10 minutes.
17. If it's warm enough, splash through Waterworks at Duplo Land.
18. Tour the exhibits at Miniland.
19. Visit any of the hands-on workshops in Imagination Centre or The Beginning.
20. If your children haven't yet had their fill of attractions, try the Orient Expedition in Lego City and continue with the next few steps in the plan.
21. Try Aero Nomad, Thunder Blazer and Scarab-Bouncers in Land of the Pharaohs.
22. Eat dinner.
23. Revisit any favourite attractions or see any missed ones.
24. If you're up for a little wet fun, try the Extreme Team Challenge in Duplo Land on your way out of the park.
25. Depart Legoland Windsor.

One-Day Touring Plan for Parents with Children over 3' (0.9 m)

1. The night before your visit, check **legoland.co.uk** for park hours and weather.
2. Arrive at the park entrance 30 minutes prior to official opening, with your admission in hand. Arrive 45 minutes early if you need to purchase admission.
3. As soon as the park opens, make your way to Knights Kingdom and ride The Dragon.
4. Ride Dragon's Apprentice.
5. Play Laser Raiders in Kingdom of the Pharaohs.
6. Ride Pirate Falls Dynamite Drench in Pirates Landing.

Legoland Windsor Recommended Attraction Visitation Times

AREA/ATTRACTION | BEST TIME TO VISIT

THE BEGINNING
Hill Train | Anytime
Rocket Racers | Anytime

IMAGINATION CENTRE
Space Tower | Anytime
Sky Rider | Anytime
Imagination Theatre | As per the daily entertainment schedule

MINILAND
All models | Anytime

DUPLO LAND
Duplo Playtown | Anytime
Duplo Train | Anytime
Extreme Team Challenge | Before 11 a.m. (if it's warm enough) or after 4 p.m.
Duplo Theatre | As per the daily entertainment schedule
Chopper Squadron | Before 11 a.m. or after 4 p.m.
Waterworks | Anytime
Fairy Tale Brook | Anytime

TRAFFIC
Driving School | Before 11 a.m.
L-Drivers | Before 11 a.m.
Boating School | Before 11 a.m.
Balloon School | Before 11 a.m. or after 3 p.m.
Fire Academy | Before noon or after 3 p.m.

LEGO CITY
Pirates of Skeleton Bay Stunt Show | As per the daily entertainment schedule
Digger Challenge | Before 1 p.m. or after 5 p.m.
Orient Expedition | Anytime

---

7. Ride Vikings' River Splash in Land of the Vikings.
8. Make your way to Traffic and try Driving School.
9. Ride Balloon School, also in Traffic.
10. Take a spin at Boating School in Traffic.
11. If your cardiovascular system is in good shape, do the Fire Academy in Traffic.
12. Eat lunch. You're in the centre of the park, so good dining options are no more than a few minutes' walk away. We think Pirates Landing is

AREA/ATTRACTION | BEST TIME TO VISIT

ADVENTURE LAND

Wave Surfer | Before noon or after 4 p.m.
Dino Dipper | Before 11 a.m. or after 4 p.m.
Dino Safari | Before 11 a.m. or after 4 p.m.

KINGDOM OF THE PHARAOHS

Laser Raiders | Before 11 a.m. or after 4 p.m.
Scarab-Bouncers | Right after Laser Raiders, if you must
Thunder Blazer | Before noon or after 4 p.m.
Desert Chase | Before noon or after 4 p.m.
Aero Nomad | Before noon or after 4 p.m.

LAND OF THE VIKINGS

Vikings' River Splash | Before 11 a.m. or after 4 p.m.
Loki's Labyrinth | Anytime
Spinning Spider | Before noon or after 4 p.m.
Longboat Invader | Before noon or after 4 p.m.

PIRATES LANDING

Pirate Falls Dynamite Drench | As soon as the park opens or after 4 p.m.
Pirate Training Camp | Anytime
Jolly Rocker | Before noon or after 4 p.m.

KNIGHTS KINGDOM

The Dragon | Within the first hour the park is open or after 4 p.m.
Dragon's Apprentice | Within the first hour the park is open or after 4 p.m.

the best option for take-away dining. Try to find a spot in the shade at Enchanted Forest to sit and eat.

13. Make your way to Adventure Land and ride the Dino Dipper.
14. Ride the Dino Safari in Adventure Land.
15. Also in Adventure Land, try the Wave Surfer.
16. Make your way to Land of the Vikings and ride the Longboat Invader.
17. Try the Spinning Spider, also in Land of the Vikings.

18. Tour Loki's Labyrinth while you're there.
19. Check the daily entertainment schedule for the next performances at the Imagination Theatre in Imagination Centre, the Duplo Theatre in Duplo Land and *Pirates of Skeleton Bay* in Lego City. See these shows in the order that best fits your schedule for the rest of the day.
20. Tour the exhibits at Miniland.
21. Eat dinner.
22. Visit any of the hands-on workshops in Imagination Centre or The Beginning.
23. If your children haven't yet had their fill of attractions, try the Orient Expedition in Lego City and continue with the next few steps in the plan.
24. Visit the Jolly Rocker in Pirates Landing.
25. Try Aero Nomad, Thunder Blazer and Scarab-Bouncers in Land of the Pharaohs.
26. Revisit any favourite attractions or see any missed ones.
27. If you're up for a little wet fun, try the Extreme Team Challenge in Duplo Land on your way out of the park.
28. Depart Legoland Windsor.

Paultons Park ★★★½

APPEAL BY AGE	PRESCHOOL ★★★★★	PRIMARY SCHOOL ★★★★★	TEENS ★★★
YOUNG ADULTS ★★		OVER 30 ★★★	SENIORS ★★★

Ower, Romsey, The New Forest, Hampshire SO51 6AL
☎ **02380 814 442; paultonspark.co.uk**

HOURS 10 a.m.–5.30 p.m. peak season. Earlier off-season.

COST £21 adults, children over 3'3"/1 m (£19.50 online); £18.50 senior citizens (£17 online); £60.50 family of 3 (£56 online); £80 family of 4 (£74 online); £100 family of 5 (£92.50 online).

GETTING THERE *By car:* In Ower, on the edge of the New Forest in Hampshire, a short distance from Junction 2 of the M27. Follow the brown tourist signs. Free parking. *By rail:* The nearest stations are Romsey and Totton, both about 4 mi (6.4 km) from the park, which would require a short taxi ride. Southampton Central Station is farther away, at 8½ mi (13.7 km), but is better served by mainline services and is across the road from the city bus terminus, where you can catch a bus to the park (**nationalrail.co.uk**). *By bus:* The **X7 Salisbury–Southampton service** (Monday–Saturday, except public holidays) stops at the Vine Inn in Ower, near the park driveway. During certain Wiltshire school holidays some journeys go to the park entrance. On Sundays and public holidays this service is numbered **X71**, and buses go to the park entrance during normal opening hours (**Wilts & Dorset Bus Company:** ☎ 01722 336855; **wdbus.co.uk**). (Route information: **transportdirect.info**.)

DESCRIPTION AND COMMENTS To children of a certain age, this Hampshire park named after a historic country estate is really Porky Park, not

Paultons. As the only theme park in the world with an area dedicated to the animated children's character Peppa Pig, there's a whole lot of porcine going on here, and the kids couldn't be happier. The addition of **Peppa Pig World** marks an important step for the former country park and bird garden, which has renovated gardens originally landscaped in the 1700s by Capability Brown.

Paultons is taking an aggressive stance in the family-theme-park market. It's not as flashy (and expensive) as Legoland, certainly, but it is comparable to Gulliver's, and has some nice touches you won't find there. For example, Paultons is peppered with the coin-operated rides usually found outside supermarkets, but here these can be ridden at no cost. And the toilets, long a sore point at other parks, are scaled to kid-sized, with steps up to the sinks and two-level toilet seats. Minor things, maybe, but they show a surprising attention to the needs of customers – something all too rare at other UK parks.

That said, you'll be disappointed by your initial impression of Paultons. The entrance way, with a few wooden buildings, is plain and unimpressive, not the grand statement you like to see if you're going to be forking out for admission. But your kids won't care, and this day out is really all for them – although you'll have to pay full price for entrance too.

As you enter the park you'll see woods in front of you, where the bulk of the animal and bird exhibits are located. There are rides diagonally behind you to the left and right. Peppa Pig World is back to the right, while the park's best coaster, **The Edge,** is found to the left. It nicely divides the crowd. If you're here for Peppa, go to the right and work your way around anti-clockwise. If thrill rides are more your interest, start at the left. Although queues aren't often a problem here, coaster fans will probably want several goes at The Edge.

Peppa Pig World, which opened in April 2011, offers seven rides and attractions in a fully-themed 3-ac (1.2-ha) land, where there's plenty of pink and bright colours. The rides aren't as imaginative as the carefully Peppa'd theming – but it's hard to resist the green dinosaur-shaped cars that run around a track on **George's Dinosaur Adventure Ride.** The 40-ft (12-m) **Windy Castle** ride uses cloud-shaped cars that gently rise and fall while the ride spins, and **Peppa's Big Balloon Ride** is similar. **Miss Rabbit's Helicopter Flight** is a mini–Ferris wheel, while **Daddy Pig's Car Ride** lets you tool around in mini vehicles, and **Grandpa Pig's Train Ride** circles a small area. And make sure to look for the animatronic ducks in the pond.

There's also a 12,000-sq-ft (1,115-m²) indoor play area called **George's Spaceship Playzone,** with an environmentally-correct grass roof. Among its many activities you'll find a recycling area, where you can practise vacuuming up coloured balls – just don't count on your kids begging to do housework when you get home. There's an outdoor play area called **Mr Potato's Playground** and a splash area called **Muddy Puddles.** You can grab a bite to eat at **Daddy Pig's Big Tummy Café.** And we're sure your charges aren't going to let you leave without a stroll through the country's largest Peppa gift shop.

Some kids, we know, are going to want to spend all day here. But there is a lot more to see. Just beyond Peppa's you'll find a display of live **meerkats** in their own manor, and to the left of Peppa's you'll see the fun **Trekking Tractors,** which let you drive stylised farm machinery around a landscaped farm track. You can take in the **Wave Runner** slide, which you descend on a dinghy. Then cut to the right, in front of Peppa's, to see the **Penguin Pool** and the tortoise house. Now head back to the rides for the swinging pirate ship and a 39-ft (12-m) **Jumping Bean** drop tower.

There's a spinning **Tea Cup** ride, followed by the unusual **Kontiki.** You and several dozen other riders board a large boat-shaped vehicle that begins to spin as it glides back and forth on a steel track. It's a miniature version of the park's best ride, The Edge. Next door is the not-too-menacing **Stinger,** a kiddie coaster that reaches about 20 mph (32 km/h) over its tangled 652 ft (199 m) length.

Now it's time for a breather. You've reached the park's zoo and garden section, where you'll find more than a dozen bird displays, and walk-through atriums. While children will enjoy the birds, they probably aren't going to get much out of the gardens, so the best strategy may be to divide and conquer. Let part of the party go ahead with the kids, while those who are interested stay and explore. In the first exhibit you'll encounter, **hornbills** and **toucans** look as if they just flew over from Peppa's world. Next come the more menacing **birds of prey,** and the garden aviary. Just as enticing are the gardens and ruins of the Paulton mansion. In the **Main Garden,** originally designed by Capability Brown, you can see cedar trees that are more than 160 years old, and pathways discovered during restoration. The **Rockery** has cellars from the old house, and makes a secluded spot for a picnic while the rhododendron and azaleas are in full bloom during spring. There's also a **Grass Garden,** with various varieties, and a **Japanese Garden** added in 1989.

Meanwhile, in the top left-hand corner of the park, you'll find the giant six-lane **Astroglide** slide, and the nearby **go-karts,** which carry an extra charge. If it's a nice day and it's starting to get hot, you'll probably want to find your way to **Water Kingdom,** a 8,500-sq-ft (790-m^2) splash park, which boasts it has 'more than 20 different ways of getting wet'. Suspects include water jets, giant tipping-buckets, fountains and super-soakers. And don't dry off just yet. Next door is the **Raging River Ride,** a log flume with two steep drops. The largest, from 36 ft (11 m), hits the water at 37 mph (60 km/h).

If you didn't pack a towel, you can probably dry off a bit on the **Magic Carpet,** a flat pendulum ride that will swing you (not too) high. Even tamer is the **Flying Saucer,** a flat spinning ride that tilts just enough as it rotates. Continuing towards the back of the area, you'll see the cute **Digger Ride** – colourful construction machines that ride around a small circular track.

The thrill-seekers will have been eying the **Cobra** all day. It's the park's longest and fastest coaster. The steel tangle climbs up over 54 ft (16.5 m) and reaches speeds of more than 30 mph (48 km/h). But the park's best ride is **The Edge,** a rare Disk'O coaster. Instead of boarding a train, you're strapped into a yellow disc facing out, which rotates as it progresses along a 295-ft (90-m) red steel track with a camelback hump in the middle. First the disc begins rocking between the first hill and the hump, and as it goes back and forth it gains speed, before finally topping the middle hump and flying down the other end of the track. You'll reach speeds of 43 mph (69 km/h) on this unusual and actually-thrilling ride.

TOURING TIPS Pack a towel and change of clothes if you plan on visiting Water Kingdom. There's really no way you can stay dry here. Peppa Pig World is often busy, and if your kids have pork on their mind, head there early. Although we usually suggest packing a picnic, the themed Daddy Pig's Big Tummy Cafe has great appeal to many young visitors. If you go, try to eat outside of traditional lunch hours, when the wait will be long, fraying the nerves of the little (and big) Peppa fans in your group.

Portsmouth Historic Dockyard ★★★★★

| APPEAL BY AGE | PRESCHOOL ★★★ | PRIMARY SCHOOL ★★★★ | TEENS ★★★★ |
| YOUNG ADULTS ★★★★★ | | OVER 30 ★★★★★ | SENIORS ★★★★★ |

Visitor Centre, Victory Gate, HM Naval Base, Portsmouth PO1 3LJ
☎ **0239 283 9766; historicdockyard.co.uk**

HOURS 10 a.m.–6 p.m. summer (last tickets sold at 4.30 p.m.); 10 a.m.– 5.30 p.m. winter (last tickets sold at 4 p.m.). A few attractions can close up to 2 hours earlier – check online before you visit and look for current closing times on your admission ticket. The entire Dockyard is closed 24–26 December.

COST £19.50 adults; £14 children (5–15), students; £16.50 senior citizens; £55 family of 5 (no more than 2 adults or senior citizens). Tickets can also be bought through the Tesco Clubcard rewards scheme.

GETTING THERE *By car:* The dockyards are less than 5 mi (8 km) from Junction 12 of the M27. Follow the brown HISTORIC WATERFRONT signs from the M275 into Portsmouth. Car parking is available on-site, or if the car park is full, an alternative car park is within a 5-minute walk. For those using satnav devices, the postcode of the dockyard car park is PO1 3LA. *By rail:* Portsmouth Harbour train station is less than 5 minutes' walk from the dockyard entrance (**nationalrail.co.uk**). Those travelling from London's Waterloo station can save £3.50 per ticket by purchasing a combined rail-and-dockyard ticket (☎ 0845 600 0650; **southwest trains.co.uk**). *By bus:* Many local and regional bus services stop at the Hard Interchange, adjacent to the dockyard entrance. (Route information: **transportdirect.info.**)

DESCRIPTION AND COMMENTS If Alton Towers is England's epicentre of roller coasters, then Portsmouth is its theme park of naval history. Here you'll find the country's most important ship, Admiral Lord Nelson's HMS *Victory*, along with other nautical monuments. When Britain ruled the seas in the nineteenth century, Portsmouth was where its power was based. A trip to the dockyards is one of the highlights of English tourism, thanks to the thoughtful presentation of these historic shrines. You can easily spend a day here – or even longer – which makes it fortunate that a dockyards ticket entitles you to visit for a year, although it allows only one entry to the HMS *Victory,* the *Mary Rose* Museum and the harbour tour.

The dockyard is part of an active naval station, but carefully separated to allow for daily visitors, which can number in the thousands. There's no charge to wander the dockyard, but you will have to pay to tour the ships, museums and interactive exhibits. A dockyard ticket includes admission to six major attractions: HMS *Victory,* the *Mary Rose* Museum, HMS *Warrior* (1860), the National Museum of the Royal Navy, Action Stations and the harbour tour.

The most popular (and crowded) tour is on **HMS Victory.** To avoid long queues, buy your ticket ahead of time and arrive when the attraction opens, or tour late in the day. You can visit the *Victory* on your own with an audio tour during the summer, but at other times of year you're scheduled for a 50-minute guided tour. These can fill up, so again, arriving early is key. *Victory* is the highlight of a dockyards visit, and you don't want to miss it. Put simply, the warship saved England's independence, leading the British fleet in attack on the French at the Battle of Trafalgar in 1805. This old ship is startlingly well preserved, looking ready to set sail. It stretches just 227 ft (69.2 m) long. When you see the cramped quarters below deck, you'll be surprised to learn it was home to 820 sailors.

HMS *Victory* is towards the back of the dockyards. If the crowds are light, we suggest first popping into the **National Museum of the Royal Navy,** a three-building complex near the *Victory.* You could spend all day here, but instead stop to catch the 15-minute walk-through multimedia presentation, **Trafalgar Experience.** The presentation will greatly enhance your *Victory* tour, helping you appreciate the significance and historical context of the ship. Instead of just touring an old boat, younger visitors will understand what all the fuss is about. The experience first takes you to a briefing room, where Lord Horatio Nelson and French emperor Napoleon explain their strategies for the battle. Next stop is a gun deck, complete with smoke and the sounds of battle. Then you'll encounter the bloody scenes where *Victory*'s wounded were treated, and Surgeon William Beatty discusses Nelson's death. The experience concludes with a huge panorama, a vivid painting of the battle enhanced by sound and light.

Now that you're up to speed on your history, it's time to visit the ship where it all took place. The six-decked *Victory* was commanded by Lord Admiral Horatio Nelson, who hatched the unorthodox plan of attacking the French off the coast of Spain by sailing straight at their ships instead of pulling up alongside them. When Nelson unleashed the *Victory*'s cannons, the French couldn't respond in kind, and the British prevailed – though at a price. Nelson was killed by a French sniper.

While touring the ship isn't nearly as arduous as living on it must have been, be prepared for narrow walkways, steep stairs and tight quarters with little headroom. You may emerge with a crick in your neck from the constant stooping. Imagine what it was like to live aboard.

As you start your tour on the **upper gun deck,** you'll reach **Nelson's cabin,** which was divided into three sections. It may seem luxurious, with its polished tables and black-and-white flooring, but all the furnishings could be folded up and readied for battle within minutes. It's said that Nelson wrote his final prayer before the Battle of Trafalgar at the circular table in the day cabin. The uniform on display is a replica of Nelson's. Elsewhere on the deck, you'll see **leg irons,** which helped keep discipline aboard ship. Miscreants were kept in these for days on end and had to live on a diet of bread and water. They were also required to make their own cat o' nine tails, which would be used to flog them later.

On the **quarterdeck,** you'll see where Nelson directed the battle, wearing a bright uniform to inspire his sailors – and make him an easy target. Look for the **plaque** marking the spot where he was felled by a sniper's shot from the French ship *Redoubtable* at 1.15 p.m. on 21 October. Heading down the **middle gun deck,** you'll begin to appreciate the living conditions sailors faced. Meals were prepared in the galley, and sailors strung hammocks overhead. The electric lighting is a modern luxury – the crew depended on small lamps and the weak stream of light from the gun ports.

Now climb down below the waterline to the **orlop,** where you can see the spot where England's saviour died, saying 'Thank God I have done my duty.' Look for a plaque in the surgical theatre marking the site of Nelson's death. Every year on the anniversary of the battle, a wreath is laid here in memory of him and others who perished, although recent research suggests Nelson's actual death might have occurred elsewhere on the deck, up towards the ship's bow.

After that drama, you'll emerge back to daylight. The ship next door, the 500-year-old **Mary Rose,** is under renovation until 2012. The vessel, Henry VIII's favourite warship, is scheduled to be open to the public in a new boat-shaped museum after a £35 million renovation. The ship sank in 1545 and was encased in mud off the English coast. It was raised in 1982 and has been undergoing restoration ever since. Until the new museum opens, you can see artefacts, watch a 15-minute film about the raising of the ship and learn about life at sea 500 years ago at the **Mary Rose Museum** near the dockyard entrance.

HMS Warrior, by contrast, stands in near-pristine condition, because it never saw battle. Launched in 1860, the first ironclad warship represented such a technological advantage that it served as a deterrent against naval battles. Although the ship, which held 705 men, became obsolete within a decade, it represented a huge leap in naval engineering. The 418-ft (127-m) vessel reached speeds of up to 13 k under sail, 14.5 k under steam. We recommend the £1 audio tours, but you're also free to wander the four-deck ship on self-guided exploration. You'll be struck by the contrast of the living quarters. Sailors slung hammocks over the guns and kept their few possessions in a small ditty bag. The **Captain's Cabin,** by contrast, resembles a Victorian parlour, with fine furniture. As you tour, you're free to sit at a mess-deck table and touch the cannons and artefacts. Crew and volunteers are on board to answer questions and, given half a chance, will offer detailed explanations and history.

Other minor attractions include a warehouse containing the largest remaining **sail** from the *Victory*. The massive topsail, protected from the elements, shows the damage inflicted during the battle by cannonball and chain shot. The **Dockyard Apprentice** exhibit focuses on the early 1900s, when battleships were constructed at the yard.

After all that history, even the most precocious child is going to get antsy. **Action Stations** to the rescue. This mini–hands-on science centre contains more than two dozen games and activities and a 27.5-ft (8.4-m) climbing wall. Even adults will be impressed by **Magic Planet,** England's only public 3D video-projection globe, which offers an astronaut's perspective on Earth from space. There's also a **virtual Trafalgar simulation,** showing how HMS *Victory* would have performed against the latest Royal Navy destroyer. The **Propulsion** exhibit demonstrates the science behind the technology that makes ships and planes move. In the **Dynamic Oceans** area, you can change the tides, discover how ships float and even see the effect global warming might have on Portsmouth Harbour. Other activities demonstrate how radar and sonar work. A series of **simulators** let you fly a naval helicopter, shoot down missiles and even feel what it's like to land on an aircraft carrier. There's also a 25-minute film, **Command Approved.** It's full of James Bond–inspired action and is meant to encourage naval recruitment. Not surprisingly, swabbing the decks doesn't get much screen time.

But who's to say what Nelson would make of it? He never had to rely on an all-volunteer navy to staff his ships.

Finally, it's time to get out on the water. Your ticket includes a 45-minute **narrated harbour tour,** leaving about hourly during the summer, 11 a.m.–4 p.m. (Tours aren't offered every day during the winter.) You may see active duty ships in the harbour, depending on the activities at the naval base. If you've arrived early at the dockyards, you can use the tour as transportation to **Gunwharf Quays** for lunch and then make the 15-minute walk back to finish your tour. Or you might want to end your dockyards visit with a trip to the quay's shopping and dining area, and the city's iconic **Spinnaker Tower.**

TOURING TIPS Before climbing aboard HMS *Victory,* make sure everyone in your party is able to navigate its narrow passages, low overhead and steep stairs. Plymouth's 558-ft (170-m) Spinnaker Tower offers sweeping views of the city and coast. It costs £7.25 for adults, £6.50 for senior citizens and students, and £5.75 for children aged 3–15, with discounts for local residents and online purchases (**spinnakertower.co.uk**).

The Portsmouth Historic Dockyard, ironically, is both an attraction that the whole family can enjoy and one where family members are frequently at cross-purposes. A person interested in history could spend 1 or 2 hours in each museum, gallery and ship. Those with a more topical interest will tour the dockyard more quickly. Our advice is to tour with someone whose level of interest is similar to yours. If your party is composed of people of varying ages and enthusiasm for the subject, pick a time and a place to meet later and then split up. If those less enamoured of the dockyard run out of things to see, there are other Portsmouth attractions, such as the **D-Day Museum** near Southsea Castle, the **Royal Garrison Church** and **Charles Dickens's birthplace.** For younger tastes there's the **Blue Reef Aquarium** (see page 147).

FARM EXPERIENCES

BECAUSE THE VARIOUS FARM EXPERIENCES are so similar (see page 13), we felt it unnecessary to provide individual profiles as we do with other types of attractions. Following is a selective list of South England farm experiences.

BERKSHIRE

BUCKLEBURY FARM PARK
Bucklebury Farm
Bucklebury, Reading
Berkshire RG7 6RR
☎ 0118 971 4002
buckleburyfarmpark.co.uk
**info@buckleburyfarm
   park.co.uk**

DORSET

ABBOTSBURY CHILDREN'S FARM
Church Street
Abbotsbury, nr Weymouth
Dorset DT3 4JJ
☎ 01305 871 817
abbotsbury-tourism.co.uk
info@abbotsbury-tourism.co.uk

FARMER PALMER'S FARM PARK LTD
Wareham Road
Organford, Poole
Dorset BH16 6EU
☎ 01202 622 022
farmerpalmers.co.uk
info@farmerpalmers.co.uk

HAMPSHIRE

LONGDOWN ACTIVITY FARM
Deerleap Lane
Ashurst, nr Southampton
Hampshire SO40 7EH
☎ 023 8029 2837
longdownfarm.co.uk
enquiries@longdownfarm.co.uk

OXFORDSHIRE

FARMER GOW'S
Longcot Road
Fernham, nr Faringdon
Oxfordshire SN7 7PR
☎ 0179 378 0555
farmergows.co.uk
enquiries@farmergows.co.uk

PART SEVEN

SOUTH WEST ENGLAND

WHILE MANY REGIONS OF ENGLAND GREET VISITORS with a gentle embrace, the South West is more likely to clap you heartily on the back. That sensation might be augmented by a bracing wind racing across the desolate **Devon Moors,** or a spray of Atlantic surf crashing against the rocky coasts of **Cornwall.**

You will never be far from the sea wherever you wander in England's south-westernmost counties; these areas occupy a long peninsula that juts into the English Channel to the south and the Atlantic Ocean on the north and comes to a breathtakingly dramatic finale at **Land's End,** the western edge of England. Altogether, some 650 mi of coastline skirt Devon and Cornwall alone. You'll soon come to associate **Devon** with wild moors, including those in Dartmoor National Park that inspired Sir Arthur Conan Doyle's *The Hound of the Baskervilles;* but desolate as the landscape can be, Devon offers plenty of civilized attractions, such as **Exeter Cathedral.** Cornwall is a place for walks along jagged coastlines (including the stretch at **Tintagel** of Arthurian legend), swims from golden sands and a pint or two in a cozy pub alongside a snug harbour.

South West England, in addition to Cornwall and Devon, also encompasses Bristol, Dorset, Somerset, and Wiltshire, with one of the world's greatest prehistoric treasures, **Stonehenge,** just north of Salisbury. In Somerset is **Bath,** founded by the Romans, a famous eighteenth- and nineteenth-century watering hole for high society, and now an architectural treasure-trove. In addition, the region is home to a broad variety of attractions ranging from the ear-splitting armoured battles of **The Tank Museum** to the fecund greenhouses of **Eden Project.**

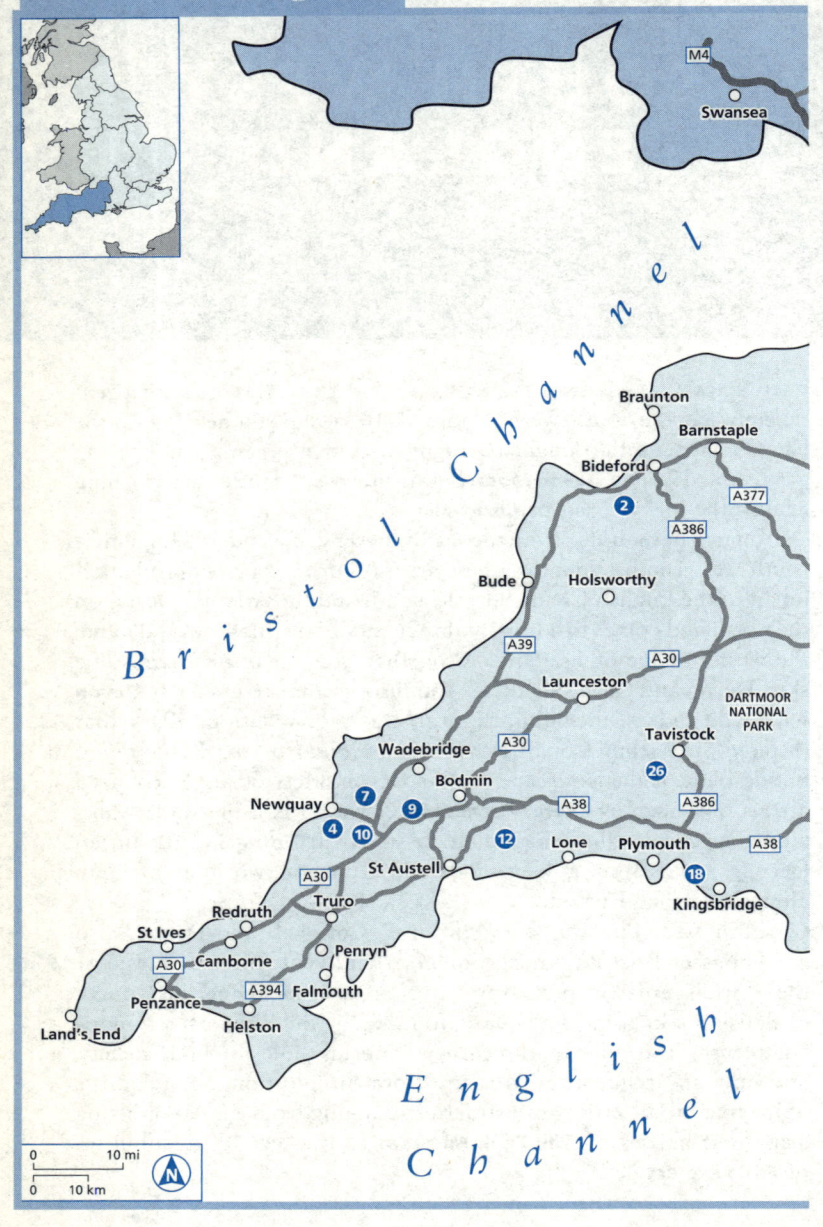

South West England

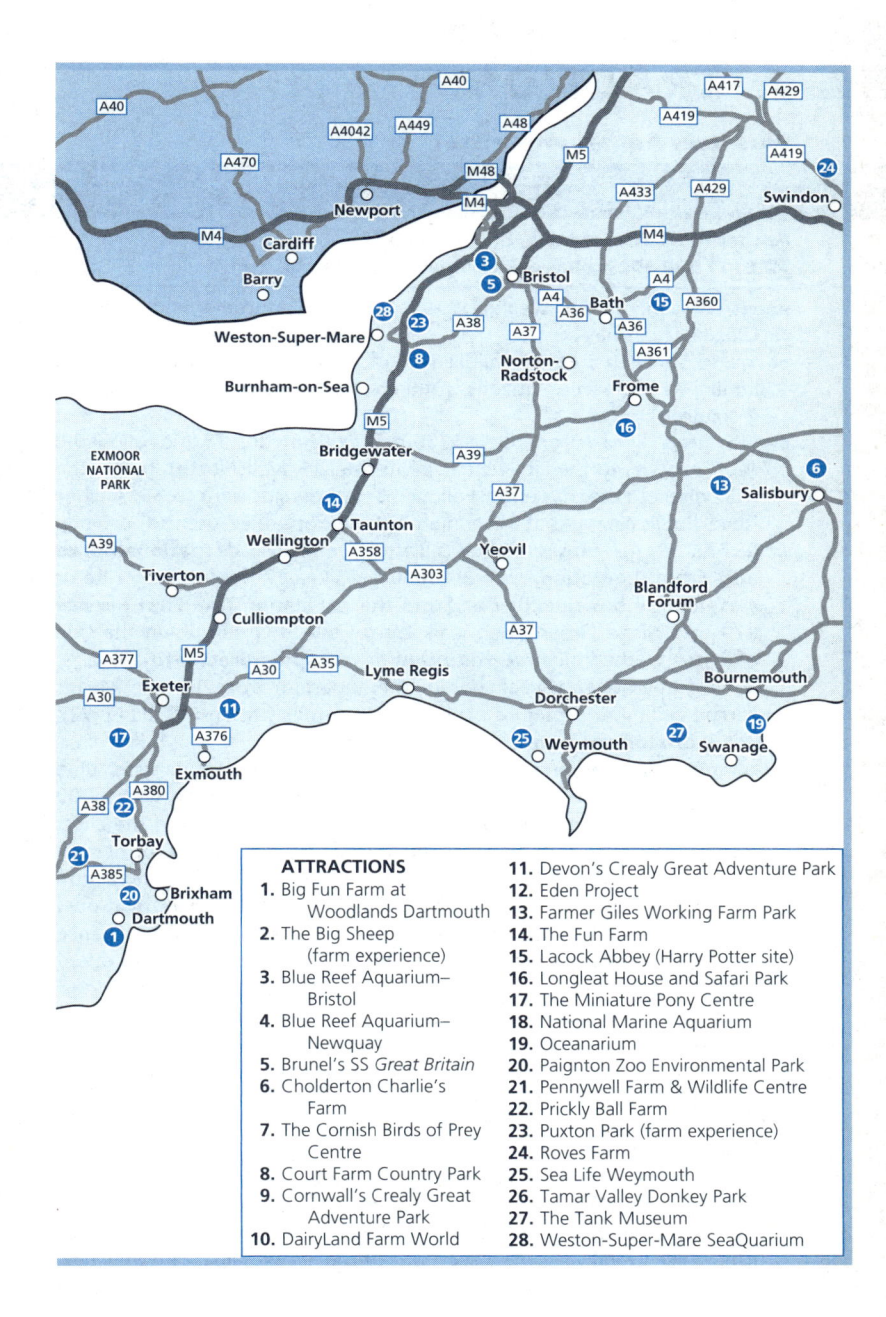

SOUTH WEST ENGLAND MAP

ATTRACTIONS

1. Big Fun Farm at Woodlands Dartmouth
2. The Big Sheep (farm experience)
3. Blue Reef Aquarium–Bristol
4. Blue Reef Aquarium–Newquay
5. Brunel's SS *Great Britain*
6. Cholderton Charlie's Farm
7. The Cornish Birds of Prey Centre
8. Court Farm Country Park
9. Cornwall's Crealy Great Adventure Park
10. DairyLand Farm World
11. Devon's Crealy Great Adventure Park
12. Eden Project
13. Farmer Giles Working Farm Park
14. The Fun Farm
15. Lacock Abbey (Harry Potter site)
16. Longleat House and Safari Park
17. The Miniature Pony Centre
18. National Marine Aquarium
19. Oceanarium
20. Paignton Zoo Environmental Park
21. Pennywell Farm & Wildlife Centre
22. Prickly Ball Farm
23. Puxton Park (farm experience)
24. Roves Farm
25. Sea Life Weymouth
26. Tamar Valley Donkey Park
27. The Tank Museum
28. Weston-Super-Mare SeaQuarium

THEME PARKS *and* ATTRACTIONS

Blue Reef Aquarium—Bristol ★★★

| APPEAL BY AGE | PRESCHOOL ★★★★ | PRIMARY SCHOOL ★★★ | TEENS ★★ |
| YOUNG ADULTS ★★ | OVER 30 ★★★ | | SENIORS ★★★ |

Anchor Road, Harbourside, Bristol BS1 5TT
☎ 0117 929 8929; bluereefaquarium.co.uk/bristol.htm

HOURS 10 a.m.–5 p.m. weekdays; until 6 p.m. Saturdays and Sundays. Closed Christmas Day.

COST £13.50 adults; £9.20 children 3–14 (must be accompanied by an adult); £12.50 senior citizens, students; £43.40 family ticket (2 adults, 2 children).

GETTING THERE *By car:* From the M5 (South), exit Junction 18 and follow the A4 (Portway) to the city centre. From the M4/M5 (North), follow the M32 direct to the city centre. Follow the Harbourside signs to A4/Anchor Road. Public car parks at Millennium Square. For satnav, use the postcode BS1 5LL. *By rail:* Closest station is Bristol Temple Meads (**nationalrail.co.uk**). From the station, it's a 20-minute walk, a 17-minute ferry ride or a 10-minute bus ride. *By bus:* From the rail station take **First Service 8/9** to College Green, then walk from College Green down the side of Bristol Cathedral (**firstgroup.com** or **transportdirect.info**). *By ferry:* Service operates on weekends to the aquarium from Temple Meads Ferry Landing, a 3-minute walk from the train station (☎ 0117 927 3416; **bristolferry.com**).

DESCRIPTION AND COMMENTS At nearly three times the size of its sister Blue Reef properties, Bristol's aquarium is truly bigger and better, with 7,000 fish from 250 species in 40 different attractions. Located in the city's historic Harbourside area, it was retrofitted into the site of a former science centre at a £4 million investment. It's the first Blue Reef attraction designed by the company – in the UK, Blue Reef has previously grown by acquiring and re-branding existing aquariums – so this is a chance for the chain to show off. You'll find a 60,000-gal (250,000-litre) open-topped tropical reef display, which you cross on a wooden footbridge. It's home to strange creatures like the giant humphead wrasse, which can grow up to 6 ft (1.8 m) long. You can also walk through the exhibit in one of the site's two underwater tunnels, and take in the sights through an unusual 'bubble helmet' – an indentation in the aquarium glass that lets you stick your head up into the display for a 360° magnified view of the exhibit.

Other exhibits re-create a Bristol harbour scene and a shipwreck. There's also an Amazon pool, a re-created South American fishing village and a glasshouse with tropical plants. Look for the strange archer fish, which literally shoots insects out of the air with a stream of water. The standout here, though, is an IMAX 3D theatre, which comes close to offering the ultimate aquarium experience – a trip under water. Recent showings included features on sharks, on whales and dolphins and on ocean sea-life diversity.

TOURING TIPS All feedings, educational talks and IMAX shows are announced 10 minutes in advance, to allow you sufficient time to locate the presentation venue. The IMAX shows, for which 3D glasses are provided, run about 45 minutes. The entire facility is accessible for pushchairs and wheelchairs.

(For more on aquariums, see page 10.)

Blue Reef Aquarium–Newquay ★★½

| APPEAL BY AGE | PRESCHOOL ★★★★ | PRIMARY SCHOOL ★★★ | TEENS ★★ |
| YOUNG ADULTS ★★ | OVER 30 ★★★ | | SENIORS ★★★ |

Towan Promenade, Newquay, Cornwall TR7 1DU
☎ **01637 878 134; bluereefaquarium.co.uk/newquay.htm**

HOURS 10 a.m.–4 p.m. November–February; to 5 p.m. March–October. Closed Christmas Day.

COST £9.20 adults, £7.20 children (3–14; must be accompanied by an adult); £8.20 senior citizens, students. Discounted family packages. Tickets allow in-and-out privileges.

GETTING THERE *By car:* Newquay is a 5-hour drive from London, off the A30. Park at the Manor car park or follow brown tourist signs to town-centre car parks. *By rail:* The nearest rail station is Newquay, a 10-minute walk. It's served through Par, Cornwall (**nationalrail.co.uk**). *By bus:* The nearest bus station is a 10-minute walk from Towan Beach, served by **Western Greyhound** (**westerngreyhound.com;** general info: **transportdirect.info**).

DESCRIPTION AND COMMENTS This chain of public aquariums has the fish business down to a science, and the location on the north coast of Cornwall has all the requisites, from walk-through glass tunnel to giant central tank to public feedings.

Some complain that the facility, with its 40 displays and more than 150 fish species, is small, but there's enough to keep visitors occupied for an hour or two – perfect for a rainy day. The attraction is geared towards families, with multi-level display windows. A café and gift shop also can keep you on-site (and spending).

In recent years, the aquarium has emphasised conservation, rehabilitation and breeding – finding success with jellyfish, sharks, clownfish and cuttlefish. You can see the offspring in a special **nursery exhibit.** The facility has even grown its own coral – but not without some challenges. In 2009, the aquarium made international tabloid news when a 4-ft (1.2-m) sea worm was discovered hiding under rocks in a coral display. The voracious worm, which likely arrived from another facility as a juvenile hidden in rocks, destroyed nearly half of the aquarium's coral and killed several fish before it was trapped.

Newquay's offerings include Cornish coast species you might find a few miles from the aquarium's front door, which overlooks Towan

Beach, as well as some colourful specimens from the Mediterranean and Caribbean.

The aquarium is built around a 55,000-gal (250,000-litre) **display** housing black- and white-tip reef sharks, giant groupers, moray eels, stingrays, angelfish, puffer fish and many others. The most interesting views come from the **walk-through tunnel.** Elsewhere, you can see displays of **garden eels, octopuses and giant crabs. Sea horses** are bred on-site and displayed in a striking column-shaped display. A standout, though, is the **freshwater-turtle display,** which includes Florida snappers, Australian pig-nosed alligator snappers, mud turtles and fly-river turtles. All in all, you'll leave with much more respect for reptiles and amphibians.

TOURING TIPS To get the most out of your visit, catch one of the daily presentations. A highlight is the **Pacific octopus enrichment,** daily at noon. These eight-legged wonders are notoriously smart, and guests see how Louis, one of the residents, has developed an attachment to a Mr Potato Head toy. (Though there are rumours of Louis being seen at Epsom Downs, he is not to be confused with the late Paul the Octopus in Germany, who famously picked winning teams in the 2010 World Cup.) Equally impressive is the **tropical ocean feed** at 11 a.m. and 4 p.m., when thousands of fish all swirl around in search of snacks. There's also **piranha and turtle feeding** in the Amazon displays at 10.30 a.m., and a **shark feeding** in the Tropical Lagoon area at 1 p.m.

(For more on aquariums, see page 10.)

Brunel's SS *Great Britain* ★★★★

APPEAL BY AGE	PRESCHOOL ★★★	PRIMARY SCHOOL ★★★★	TEENS ★★★
YOUNG ADULTS ★★★		OVER 30 ★★★★	SENIORS ★★★★

Great Western Dockyard, Bristol BS1 6TY
☎ **0117 926 0680; ssgreatbritain.org**

HOURS (26 March–31 October) 10 a.m.–5.30 p.m.; (1 November–25 March) 10 a.m.–4.30 p.m. Last admission 1 hour before closing.

COST £11.95 adults; £5.95 children (5–16); £9.50 aged 60 and over, unemployed, students aged 18 and over. Discounted family packages. Tickets allow repeat visits for 1 year. Open daily except for Christmas Eve, Christmas Day and 1 day in January.

GETTING THERE *By car:* On the waterfront in Bristol, amidst a tangle of streets and motorways. From the M4, take Junction 19 to the M32 and continue until the motorway ends. Stay in the left-hand lane and follow signposts for the SS *Great Britain.* Park at the pay-and-display car park, next to the ship. From the M5, exit at Junction 18 onto the A4 Portway into Bristol, about 4 mi (6.4 km). After passing under Brunel's Clifton Suspension Bridge, take the left exit, signposted for City Centre and Historic Harbour, and after the traffic lights, get into the right-hand lane. At the next set of lights get into the left lane, taking the first exit to cross the old swing bridge. Then fork left and within 110 yd (100 m) turn left onto Cumberland Road. Proceed .6 mi (1 km) and take a left into Gas Ferry Road. Follow the road into the pay-and-display car park, next to the ship. *By rail:* Bristol Temple Meads is the closest station (**nationalrail.co.uk**). From there you can walk or take a ferry or bus. *By ferry:* A ferry operates on weekends to the SS *Great Britain* from Temple Meads Ferry Landing (☎ 0117 9273416; **bristolferry.com**), which is a 3-minute walk from the train station. During the week, catch the ferry from the city centre. *By bus:* **Route 500** runs every 20 minutes between Temple Meads Station and the ship, as do red **City Sightseeing** open-top buses. (Route information: **transportdirect.info.**)

DESCRIPTION AND COMMENTS A monument to Britain's industrial heritage and its greatest engineer, Isambard Kingdom Brunel, this nineteenth-century passenger liner was the first major transatlantic iron steamship. Now it's Bristol's top-notch attraction, winning national awards including UK Museum of the Year.

The SS *Great Britain,* launched in 1843, served 43 years on the high seas, logging nearly 1 million mi (1,610,000 km). Its revolutionary use of a screw propeller changed nautical design. Eventually, though, the ship was damaged rounding Cape Horn and was sold, to become a floating coal-and-wool warehouse in the Falkland Islands before being abandoned in the 1930s. By the time the ship was rescued in 1970 and returned to the city where it was berthed, the once-glorious vessel was little more than scrap.

Now the meticulously-refurbished liner offers visitors an entertaining view (and smell) of a historic vessel, which will appeal to both lovers of maritime history and families looking for a diverting day out. Refreshingly, you won't encounter DO NOT TOUCH signs here.

A visit starts with a warning to hold your nose as you head 'under water' into the cleverly-designed dry dock, which is covered with glass and water and which protects the ship from decay. The under-the-sea illusion lets you examine the aged steel hull and the revolutionary screw propeller up close. It also offers a unique view of what appears to be a pristine vessel above, which seems ready to sail.

The tour moves on to an interactive **dockyard museum.** Kids can try on Victorian clothing, blow a ship's horn and practise steering a vessel. Audio-visual displays teach about the ship's engineering breakthroughs, with kids getting guidance from Sinbad, the ship's cat. For adults, there's a chance to learn about the extraordinary measures to rescue the ship in 1970, when it was floated 8,000 mi (13,000 km) back across the Atlantic. The liner was in such poor shape that mattresses were stuffed into a crack in the hull to keep it afloat. A crowd of 100,000 greeted the liner when it finally made it back up the Bristol River to the dock from where it was first launched more than a century earlier.

From the museum, the tour moves to the highlight: the ship itself, and an imaginary trip to Australia. (The ship made the trip 32 times, bringing scores of emigrants to Melbourne, and provided transport for the inaugural visit of the UK cricket team.) Guests can chose from four **audio guides,** free with admission, offering narration from the perspective of a first- or third-class passenger, a maritime archaeologist and, for kids, Sinbad the cat. The guides are structured to let you wander the ship's three decks and don't limit you to a specific route. Along the way, guests visit astoundingly-tiny steerage cabins, a 'working' 1,000-hp steam engine, the promenade deck and the first-class dining hall. Much of the narration derives from diaries and letters of Victorian-age passengers.

As you roam the ship you'll encounter mannequins and models, including a rat scurrying across a bed. Guests also discover the smells of the ship – from baked bread, to vomit in a steward's cabin, to manure in the livestock area populated by whinnying horses, to the comforting spicy scent of the barber's shop. Watch out for the mysterious talking toilet.

And of course, what visit would be complete without meeting engineer Brunel? He can be found lurking on his famous creation.

TOURING TIPS Take advantage of the unstructured ship-tour to wander the vessel at your own pace. If you visit on a dry day, you'll enjoy another highlight: sitting on the deck and enjoying the harbour view.

Cornwall's Crealy Great Adventure Park ★★★

APPEAL BY AGE	PRESCHOOL ★★★★★	PRIMARY SCHOOL ★★★★	TEENS ★★
YOUNG ADULTS ★		OVER 30 ★	SENIORS ★★

Tredinnick, Wadebridge, Cornwall PL27 7RA
☎ **01841 540 276; crealy.co.uk/cornwall**

HOURS 10 a.m.–6 p.m. holidays and high season. Closes earlier other times of year. Opening days limited to weekends and some holidays during winter (see website for details).

COST £8.95 over 3'3" (1 m) (£7.95 online); £10.50 for 3'–3'3" (.92 m–1 m) (admission good for 1 year); £6.95 senior citizens 60+ (£5.95 online); £7.95 group of 4 (apiece).

GETTING THERE *By car:* Between Newquay and Wadebridge on the A39, the park is well signposted with brown signs. *By rail:* With sparse service in the area, your best bet is to take a train to Newquay and catch the limited bus service from there (**nationalrail.co.uk**). *By bus:* **Western Greyhound 557** service from Padstow and St Columb Major stops in Newquay and at the park (☎ 01637 871 871; **westerngreyhound.com**). Receive a £1 discount on admission if you show your bus ticket.

DESCRIPTION AND COMMENTS This second park in the mini–Crealy empire doesn't match the scope of the original in Devon (page 198). Clearly aimed at the 3–12 set, it's part farmyard petting zoo and indoor playground. But it also sports several water-park attractions, and even a handful of thrill rides.

Crealy started in 1989 in Devon, when Angela Wright, a housewife-turned-entrepreneur, opened a park meant to re-create her country upbringing in the birthplace of Sir Walter Raleigh. (The name *Crealy* honours the original owners of the land that is now the Devon park.) In 2004 she expanded the family-owned business by purchasing a park in Cornwall and investing in improvements. The park says its average visitor spends 6 hours on-site (though that must include a very leisurely lunch and more than a few minutes in the loo), with time divided between several 'realms' – a fancy word to describe the indoor and outdoor playgrounds, water rides, thrill attractions and animal experiences. Older children will be drawn to the big funfair rides.

As you enter, you encounter a paddock with ponies, pigs and goats, setting the tone for the park. The property's quite small, and you're free to jump around from ride to ride as your whim dictates. If you have adventurers in your group, they'll want to rush to the **Morgawr** roller coaster, named after the local Cornish sea monster that has been spotted in Falmouth Bay over the centuries. The ride was added in 2010, and although it's more cute than scary, it will send the breeze through your hair as it makes its twisting rounds.

From there, head to **The Beast,** a 50-ft (15-m) drop tower, and the **Viking Warrior,** a swinging pirate ship, both in the **Wild Water Realm** on the left side of the park. Adjacent **Thunder Falls Log Flume** features two steep drops that will leave you wetter than a trout. And the nearby **Raging Rivers Water Coasters** offer that and more, as you descend a slide on a foam raft and end with a big fat splash. You may stop in your tracks when you see **Water Walkerz,** which cost an extra £3.50. Riders climb inside giant waterproof plastic bubbles and float, crawl and manoeuvre their way around a pool. Watching is as much fun and much less tiring than walking inside one.

The nearby **Adventure Realm** is dominated by the **Giant Twister and Triple Tubes,** a huge slide with plenty of opportunities for racing. Young ones will want to spend time in the **Haunted Castle** soft-play area. Although it claims to be geared towards adults and children, you'll probably find one trip down the Slide of Doom is enough, but the kids will want to run back and try it all afternoon. There's also a castle fort for climbing, and another extreme playground ride, the **Sheer Drop Slides.** Several other attractions are also built around slides, including **Towering Inferno,** which makes us think this park should have been named Slide World.

All in all, the more imaginative rides are aimed towards the younger ones. On the right side of the park you'll find the **Pony Express,** which offers a simulated horseback ride on a track. (No bookmaking, please.) Nearby, the indoor **Dragon Kingdom** soft-play area lets kids romp around ball pits, foam rooms and more slides, along with climbing nets and mazes.

If you have more energy to burn, head to **SwampBuster's Eco-Adventure,** with bridges and river crossings. It's presided over by a mascot that looks suspiciously like Shrek.

But it's in the Animal Realm near the front of the park where Crealy plays to its strength. At **MacDonald's Farm,** you can pay 50p for a bag of fruit or vegetables to feed the livestock. All will marvel at the kune kune pigs, a friendly and oh-so-cute New Zealand breed.

If you're a horse-lover, you'll eat up *All the King's Horses,* a performance with miniature ponies and full-size Shire horses. Crealy ups the ante with a special camping programme: stay for three nights and you get to 'adopt' a pony while you're at the park, feeding and caring for it. Campers can also help feed animals in the morning and round up the ponies. Plus they get early park entry. Cost: £20 per pitch, or an extra £5 for electric hook-ups.

TOURING TIPS Review ticket specials carefully. If you'll be spending a holiday in the region, some tickets and promotions may include entrance to the other Crealy's property, in Devon. Dining is surprisingly varied, including pasta, burgers, vegetarian options, smoothies and a coffee bar, with an emphasis on locally-sourced or Fair Trade goods. Those with infants will appreciate the baby-food warmers.

Devon's Crealy Great Adventure Park ★★★

APPEAL BY AGE	PRESCHOOL ★★★★★	PRIMARY SCHOOL ★★★★	TEENS ★★
YOUNG ADULTS ★		OVER 30 ★	SENIORS ★★

Sidmouth Road, Exeter, Devon EX5 1DR
☎ **01395 233 200; crealy.co.uk/devon**

HOURS 10 a.m.–6 p.m., holidays and high season. Closes earlier other times of year. Opening days limited to weekends and some holidays during winter (see website for details).

COST £9.95 over 3'3" (1 m) (£7.95 online); £10.50 for 3'–3'3" (.92 m–1 m) (admission good for 1 year); £6.95 senior citizens 60+ (£4.95 online); £8.95 group of 4 (apiece).

GETTING THERE *By car:* On the A3052, a few minutes from Junction 30 on the M5. *By rail:* The closest train stations are Exeter Central or Exeter St Davids (**nationalrail.co.uk**). *By bus:* **Stagecoach Bus 52A** or **52B** serves the park from Exeter Bus Station, a few minutes' walk from Exeter Central (**stagecoachbus.com**). Show your bus ticket to get a £1 discount on park admission. (Route information: **transportdirect.info**.)

DESCRIPTION AND COMMENTS The original Crealy park pulls in a half-million visitors a year, making it the South West's biggest family attraction. It has found success by catering to the 3–12 set, with farmyard petting zoos and soft-play areas. But it also makes a splash with water-park attractions and not-too-scary family coasters. Devon's Crealy offers a wider range of rides and is priced comparably to the Cornwall property. If given a choice, we'd opt for the original location; given the overlap of attractions, there's certainly no reason to visit both.

The parks are the creation of Angela Wright, who wanted to develop a park that offered some of the simple pleasures of her country upbringing. Today, despite the coasters and towering water rides, the rural farm experience remains at the core of the park. (Even the name, *Crealy*, is a nod to the rural past, and the original owners of the property). There's also a noticeable parent's perspective here. The large play areas have adjacent cafés, so you can relax while your child romps around. There's even WI-Fi. However, Crealy does include several activities – gold-panning, canoeing, pony rides and go-karting to name just a few – that carry an additional charge. Parents are often surprised to learn that it's really not one-price-covers-everything.

The 100-ac (40-ha) park offers lots of space for its 40-plus attractions. We suggest circling the property in a clockwise fashion. Starting at the entrance, cut to the left for the park's best thrill ride, the steel roller coaster **Maximus.** It has a Roman theme in honour of the forces that occupied the land 2,000 years ago, but we bet they didn't bring a contraption like this. It's near the **Queen Bess Pirate Ship,** a classic swinging-gondola ride. Then head towards the bottom left-hand corner for the **Dino Blaster** bumper boats, which are enhanced by the water-balloon slingshots around the edge. Just be ready to pay for your ammo (£2.50 for 8 balloons), or better yet, bring your own. That's next to the **Techno Race Karts,** which carry an additional charge of £4 and are only available to riders who are at least 10 years of age and 4'8" (1.42 m) tall. The adjacent **Driving School** costs £1 and is geared towards younger visitors. Or, for a completely new form of transportation, climb inside a plastic ball called **Water Walkerz** and crawl around in a pool. It's more fun than it sounds, and even more fun to watch. The experience, though, runs an extra £3.50.

Now it's time to get splashed. The **Soak Zone** features fountains, jets and sprays, which means you couldn't stay dry even if you tried. Let the under-5s play barefoot, and don't forget to bring a towel and an extra pair of dry underpants. Nearby are imaginative outdoor play areas, including **Crealy Construction Co,** where little ones don hard hats and start building in the sand. It's next to **Sahara Sands,** another area for building. You'll also find a kid-sized model village here and a tiny train, both geared for toddlers. For more playtime, step inside the **Magical Kingdom,** a multi-level indoor soft-play area with ball pools and climbing ramps. The attraction has a café attached, allowing you to have a bite while your kid burns off energy.

Refreshed, head off to the left for the **Woodlands Wilderness Wildlife Adventure Area,** with tree houses, bridges, mazes and paths that lead past goats, deer and reindeer.

For more action, head to the top left-hand corner of the park for the **Tidal Wave** log-flume ride, which ends with a 40-ft (12-m) drop and a soaking splash. Beyond it, find **Dragonfly Lake,** where you can see geese, ducks and swans and feed fish, and to the right you can take a pony ride for £3, or save some money and hop aboard one for free on the nearby **Victorian Carousel.**

Next comes something you don't normally see in a theme park – a call to social action. The **Roundabout PlayPumps** are playground roundabouts that have been installed across sub-Saharan Africa. As children play in their villages, the ride rotates and pumps clean water from wells. There's a model here that you can try out, a short movie on the project and a chance to donate to help install more.

Now that you have water on your mind, turn the corner to the **Vortex Watercoaster,** which is an elaborate slide on a raft down your choice of three tubes – Venom, Vertigo and Viper – the last being the longest, at 236 ft (72 m). Instead of being dank enclosures, the tubes have special-effects swirl lighting and sounds, offering a bit of flash with your splash. (Sorry, we couldn't resist.) Needless to say, if you like water slides, you'll want to do this one over and over and over.

The park's indoor play areas are a godsend when the weather's not great but are enticing enough to check out even on a nice day. The newest, **Dina's Lost World,** plays up its prehistoric theme with plenty of dinosaur models, an extinction-themed maze and even the small-scale **Meteorite Drop Tower,** the first time we've seen a ride like this inside. The indoor play area with the most activities, the **Adventure Zone,** offers a spectrum of slides: bumpy, twisty and what management likes to call mega-drop. There are also aerial walkways, climbing nets and rope swings. If it sounds like a monkey house at the zoo, you're not far off.

For more-low-key attractions, head to the **Animal Barn**, where staff members bottle-feed baby goats and milk cows. In the cuddly-pets area, there's a chance to snuggle up with guinea pigs, rabbits and chipmunks. But if you're wise, you'll steer away from the sales desk, where you could find yourself bringing home a souvenir that's hungry all the time and isn't house-trained: the park sells rabbits, guinea pigs and rats – and even goats, sheep and ponies. Unlike most keepsakes, which wind up on a shelf gathering dust, these require care and commitment. On reflection, that £3 pony ride seems like a much better deal.

TOURING TIPS Pack a swimsuit, towel and change of clothes. Review ticket specials carefully: if you'll be spending a holiday in the region, some tickets and promotions permit unlimited returns for the week, or even a year. Working parents might trade off time with the kids while the other takes advantage of the park's free Wi-Fi.

Eden Project ★★★★★

APPEAL BY AGE	PRESCHOOL ★★★	PRIMARY SCHOOL ★★★★	TEENS ★★★★
YOUNG ADULTS ★★★★★		OVER 30 ★★★★	SENIORS ★★★★

Bodelva, St Austell, Cornwall PL24 2SG
☎ **01726 811 911; edenproject.com**

HOURS Parking opens at 9 a.m.; gates at 9.30 a.m. Closing time varies from 4 to 9 p.m. based on the season. Last entry 90 minutes before closing. Closed 24–25 December.

COST £17.50 adults; £6 children 5–16, also under 18 if in full-time education and visiting as part of a family group (free November–mid-February); £10 students; £12.50 senior citizens 60+. Online purchases discounted by £1 per person. Receive a discount of £4 per ticket if you walk, cycle or take public transport to the site. Tickets can also be bought through the Tesco Clubcard rewards scheme.

GETTING THERE *By car:* Eden Project is well signposted from both the A30 from Exeter and the A391/390 from Plymouth. The car parks are on the ridge overlooking the site. A tram transports you from the car parks to the entrance. (Yes, you can walk, but it's a long way.) *By rail:* Eden is 4 mi (6 km) from St Austell station (**nationalrail.co.uk**), which has a bus service to the site. *By bus:* Eden is a 30-minute ride from St Austell railway station, 75 minutes from Newquay station and less than 30 minutes from Luxulyan station. **First Bus 101** serves Eden from St Austell railway station, as does **Western Greyhound** from Newquay and St Austell stations. (Route information: **transportdirect.info.**)

DESCRIPTION AND COMMENTS The world's largest greenhouse attracts nearly 2,000,000 visitors a year to what was once an abandoned clay quarry. It's now an artificial eco-paradise, with over 100,000 plants from more than 2,500 species. With gleaming domes and edgy sculptures, it has the look and feel of a science-fiction paradise.

The Project takes its green mission seriously, advocating carbon-neutral and sustainable living. The water used for plants and loos is all rainwater gathered from a subterranean drainage system below the bottom of a pit 50 ft (15 m) below the water table. The entire project runs on Green Tariff power generated by wind turbines in Cornwall.

Eden's two massive golf-ball-shaped geodesic domes dominate the landscape and set the tone for an otherworldly outing. It was all dreamed up in the early 1990s by landscape designer Tim Smit. Pulling together a team of horticulturists, Smit and the group were able to refine their vision into a sweeping proposal and have it accepted as one of the Landmark Millennium Projects that were being created to mark the year 2000. Working with promissory notes and plenty of pluck, Smit had the buildings designed by architect Nicholas Grimshaw. Construction lasted 2½ years, before it opened to headlines in 2001. Now it's the top tourist attraction in southern England.

Your enjoyment really depends on your expectations and interests. If you come with an open mind, curious about Smit's vision and interested in plants and ecosystems, you'll be mesmerised. But if that's not your cup of tea, you'll wander around scratching your head, wondering if you've just put out nearly 20 quid to visit a giant garden centre.

In any case, you're unlikely to have the site to yourself. As the massive 4,000-vehicle car park suggests, the Project was designed for heavy visitation – a tram serves the distant car parks. Walking down the hill to the entrance, you'll catch a view of the biomes, the geodesic domes that are the heart of the project. After paying admission, take a moment and admire the strange view from the overlook.

The area covers 32 ac (13 ha) – over 30 football pitches – and has two main biomes, one devoted to tropical plants, the other to temperate ones. The giant geodesic domes are constructed of steel tubing and covered with hexagonal clear plastic panels. The **Link** building connects the two structures, while the **Core** building to the right houses exhibits, a restaurant and a gift shop. There's even a giant climbing structure called **The Nest,** which will give young visitors a welcome break.

While several trails lead throughout the area, the straightest route to the biomes is, ironically, **The Zigzag,** a switchback path that passes a crop garden on the way down the hill. On the way you'll also see bizarre sculptures and a soaring white tent, called **The Stage,** which hosts concerts during summer evenings. Although the grade is slight, if you have trouble walking or want an easier route, you can take a right from the Visitor Centre and follow the relatively-flat path to the Core building, and then take a lift down. From that point it's a flat path to the biomes.

Or there's the **Land Train** tram, which connects the Visitor Centre to The Stage, just a short walk to the biomes.

The path will lead you to the **Link** building, which does exactly that – connects the two greenhouses. Once you arrive, you'll find toilets, a restaurant and places to sit. Take a left to access the **Rainforest Biome,** the headliner attraction here. The building covers 3.9 ac (1.56 ha) and measures 180 ft (55 m) high.

The first thing you'll notice is the heat and humidity. Although it's Cornwall outside, inside the biome you're in Malaysia, West Africa or Brazil. Temperatures can reach 30 °C (86 °F), which can be a delight on a winter's day. But make sure to dress in layers, because you'll quickly wilt if you're wearing a jumper and coat. In summer it can be downright scorching. You'll want to bring water along, and if the heat becomes unbearable, take advantage of the **cool rooms,** air-conditioned oases scattered through the area, where you can stop and refresh for a bit.

Although there's some chance to wander, you largely follow a path weaving through the greenhouse. It can feel crowded at times, as the paths aren't wide, and you may find yourself in a traffic jam reminiscent of the M1. About halfway through the biome, a steep path juts off to the left and climbs up a hill on the side. You'll get a nice view here and, often, a break from the crowd.

As you wander, you'll find **banana trees, bamboo, coffee, cocoa, mahogany, bromeliads, spices** and **ferns,** plus an 80-ft (24-m) **waterfall.** Several small exhibits explain the importance of these and other crops. As you walk through the biome, breathe in the smell of damp earth and wet plants, and look for tree frogs and tiny tropical birds. There's also a mini–**soya plantation** and **rubber trees.** Bridges cross streams, and in the undergrowth you'll see huts representing the structures used by the humans who live in the areas featured. You are, to all intents, in the jungle.

In 2010, the Project opened a new **Rainforest Lookout** at the top of the biome, which carries an additional £3 charge. Tickets can be purchased from the gift shop in The Link. From a vantage point higher than the Tower of London, you can look down at the canopy and marvel at the balsa and kapok trees that have nearly reached the biome roof. But as spectacular as the view is, don't expect to stay long to admire it: temperatures can reach 40 °C (104 °F).

Not as spectacular, but much more comfortable, is the **Mediterranean Biome,** which covers 1.6 ac (.65 ha). Here you'll find more-familiar plants, like **lemon and olive trees** and **grape vines.** During spring, a literal million **bulbs** will be in flower. It may feel like Greece, but the climate and ecosystem, you'll learn, are similar to ones found in California and South Africa. Thus, you'll see **poppies** and **lupines** blooming in the Californian grasslands, **red chilli peppers** and an array of huge South African proteas, which look as if they should be growing on Mars. Gnarled **cork trees** recall Portugal. Look for a gold mosaic in the middle of the path – called **Liquid Gold,** it's meant to represent olive oil. Cavorting in the vineyards are **bacchanalian sculptures** of gods at play. As you walk through this most pleasant of climates, you'll breathe in the scents of **lavender, thyme, rosemary, myrtle** and **citrus.**

Finally, there's the **Outdoor Biome,** which many people just breeze through on their way to and from the buildings. But stop to notice the scenery. You'll see a field of **lavender** and an area devoted to **Cornwall's ecosystem.** Also look for a **wooden ship** sailing through a sea of tea plants. Just as intriguing are the arresting **sculptures** scattered across the area, like **Adam,** a 19.7-ft (6-m) man clutching a rope of fibres, and **WEEE Man,** a statue created from waste electrical and electronic equipment. There's also an **Industrial Flame Plant,** a wry metallic take on a blossom that recalls a bird of paradise, and the **Giant Bee,** a huge cyborg pollinator made from recycled scrap. Another highlight is the **Cloud Chamber,** a walk-in stone hive where you can see images of moving clouds.

The last building to visit is **The Core,** an education centre with interactive displays reminiscent of a hands-on science museum. The design is dramatic, with curved wooden roof beams forming a web above, and clerestory windows offering outside light and a glimpse of the sky. The exhibits are compelling and provocative. You'll see the **world's largest nutcracker** – actually a huge interactive sculpture. It's meant to be a social commentary about the over-processing of plants, but for kids it's simply a fun machine they can operate by winding a handle. Other displays explain **photosynthesis,** describing how the so-called 'plant engine' makes human life possible. We particularly liked the **Wall of Fridges,** kind of a Speakers' Corner for the note-jotting set. Just record your thoughts on a piece of paper, and you can stick it on a fridge door with a magnet.

TOURING TIPS Given the green idealism at the heart of Eden Project, we were anticipating something utopian – a verdant, happy place. However, sculptures large and small peppered throughout Eden Project paint a darker, more dystopian picture. Many are (intentionally) grotesque and menacing; others capture man's most primitive animal instincts and behaviours, including orgiastic sexuality. Some larger pieces composed of junk metal and industrial parts stir recollections of the evil machines in the *Terminator* films. The art is glorious, make no mistake, but it engenders a response in us that balances uneasily between wonder and the willies, and thus colours the whole Eden Project experience. We learned a lot at Eden Project and were wowed by the diversity of plant life, but what we remember most vividly, and what haunt us still, are the sculptures.

If you're visiting on a cool day, dress in layers. You'll need to shed some clothes in the Rainforest Biome. If you really want to prove your green colours, consider making a day hike from the Luxulyan railway station to Eden Project. It's a 2½-mi (4-km) trek along the Saints Way, which crosses fields and old industrial landscapes, plus you'll earn a substantial discount on admission. You can find a brochure outlining the hike on the website. Given the popularity of Eden Project, time your visit carefully. Earlier in the day is always better, as is avoiding school breaks and bank holidays.

Longleat House and Safari Park ★★★★

| APPEAL BY AGE | PRESCHOOL ★★★ | PRIMARY SCHOOL ★★★★★ | TEENS ★★★★ |
| YOUNG ADULTS ★★★ | | OVER 30 ★★★★ | SENIORS ★★★★ |

Warminster, Wiltshire BA12 7NW
☎ **01985 844 328; longleat.co.uk**

HOURS House open 10 a.m.–5.30 p.m. during summer, with limited hours during winter. Closed Christmas Day. Safari opens at 10 a.m., with last entry varying from 4 to 5 p.m. mid-February–October. Other attractions open at 11 a.m., when the safari is open.

COST Longleat Passport (entry to safari park and all attractions): £24 adults; £17 children (3–13); £19 senior citizens 60+. Safari park only: £12 adults; £8 children (3–13); £9 senior citizens 60+. Book online for a 15% discount. Tickets can also be bought through the Tesco Clubcard rewards scheme.

GETTING THERE *By car:* Just off the A36 between Bath and Salisbury on A362 (Warminster–Frome Road). Car parking is free. If using satnav, ignore directions as you approach Longleat and follow the brown tourist signposts (many satnav units direct you to a dead end). *By rail:* The nearest train station, Warminster, on the Cardiff–Portsmouth line, is about 5 mi (8 km) from the park. Westbury station, on the Paddington–Penzance line, is approximately 12 mi (19 km) from the park (**nationalrail.co.uk**). Both stations are serviced by taxis, which will bring you directly to Longleat. *By bus:* No services available.

DESCRIPTION AND COMMENTS Longleat is an imposing mansion nestled deep in the Wiltshire countryside near Bath. It's home to Alexander Thynn, the seventh Marquess of Bath, who has transformed his vast estate into one of the top visitor sites in the UK, with a safari park and numerous other amusements. Longleat practically created the blueprint for British attractions in 1966, becoming the first stately home to open to the public, and starting what's believed to be the first safari park outside Africa. Today many know it from the BBC show *Animal Park*, the documentary programme about Longleat's animals and keepers.

It's just the latest bit of history for an already storied property. The house, built in the late 1500s by Sir John Thynne and designed by Robert Smythson, is one of the best examples of Elizabethan architecture in the nation. It's set in over 900 ac (364 ha) of parkland landscaped by the famous Capability Brown, and it's surrounded by 8,000 ac (3,237 ha) of woods and farmland.

You approach Longleat along a road surrounded by dense woodland, which then opens to reveal a magnificent honey-coloured house surrounded by gardens and lakes. At the entrance, you have the option of just paying for the safari park or buying a Longleat Passport, which provides entry to the house and a host of other attractions, including a maze, a railway and a safari boat trip. The Passport allows you into most attractions only once but is open-ended, giving you the option of splitting your visit over more than one day. You don't have to purchase Longleat Passports to visit the attractions, as they are all individually priced, most at £3 or £4, although a few are free, such as the Yin–Yang garden and the garden labyrinths. However, the passport is a worthwhile purchase if you want to take in more of Longleat, as it gives you the freedom to enjoy what you like without worrying about digging ever deeper into your wallet.

The safari is busiest at the beginning of the day, so we suggest leaving it until afternoon, when the queue dies down. You'll have plenty to keep you busy at the house and park base.

Parking is free, and since you may have had a long ride, we suggest you start with the **Adventure Castle,** a huge playground with bridges, nets, slides and swings. Young ones, aged 18 months–5 years, can roam in the **Little Lionheart Soft Play Tent,** while older visitors can sport around on the **Spiders Web,** a climbing area with stones and nets. If it's a nice day, you'll have a hard time avoiding **Splashpad,** a water-play area with interactive fountains and jets that are activated when you step on pressure pads. Make sure you have a towel in the car, because someone is going to get soaked. We recommend letting pre-schoolers play barefoot in their underwear (bring some extra dry pants). This is the only area you can revisit with the Passport, so you can always come back later.

The sixteenth-century Longleat House is more of an adult treat. A house tour includes the **Elizabethan Great Hall,** with coats of arms and a massive hunting scene painted in the 1730s. The tour continues to the **Red Library,** displaying many of the 40,000 books in the house. The ornate **Lower Dining Room** has family portraits from the sixteenth and seventeenth centuries, including a painting of Thomas Thynne, usually known as 'Tom of Ten Thousand', a reference to his annual income.

When you wander through the **State Dining Room**, know you're following in regal footprints. The first royal visitor was Queen Elizabeth I, in 1574, and the most recent was Queen Elizabeth II in 1980. The **Dress Corridor** has a collection of not-so-casual outfits worn in the latter half of the nineteenth century.

And then there's the optional tour of **Lord Bath's Murals** in the private part of the home where the Thynn family still lives. These images, created by the current Lord Bath, are by turns bright, dark, sexually explicit and whimsical. If you want to explore the eccentric owner's psyche – he admits to having 74 mistresses, or 'wifelets', as he calls them – arrange for a tour at the front desk. There's no additional charge, but it may have you shaking your head over the state of the aristocracy. If it's any comfort, Lord Bath announced in 2010 that he was retiring from the family business and turning it over to his son.

For a puzzle of a different sort, check out the incredible **Hedge Maze,** made from more than 16,000 English yews. The pathway stretches for 1.69 mi (2.72 km) and can keep you busy for more than an hour. You can also try more-mild amusements, like the tame **Tea Cup Ride** and the more-dynamic **Motion Simulators,** which offers either a racing-car run or an African safari experience. As veterans of these computerised rides can attest, you can expect much shaking and jerking around, all synchronised with the film projected in front of you. Not recommended if you're pregnant, have back problems or find being shaken like a martini disagreeable.

A must-do is the **Safari Boats.** These tour the large lake adjacent to the house, which is home to Longleat's collection of California sea lions. They and two resident hippopotamuses follow the boat closely. Visitors are given the chance to buy a pot of fish for £1 to feed the sea lions, which leads to a mass charge to the boat by every sea lion in the lake, accompanied by much noise and splashing. You can also take a water-borne tour around the island home of **Nico,** Longleat's gorilla, who has his own little house complete with television. The on-board commentary reports that nature documentaries are his favourite, and he is also a big *SpongeBob SquarePants* fan.

Elsewhere at Longleat, there is a narrow-gauge **steam railway** with a 1950s-style platform, period adverts and other props, and **Old Joe's Mine,** a dark cavern that holds a colony of fruit bats. You would be well advised to avoid this if you have the slightest aversion to bats, as they are not enclosed and swoop around your head as you walk through. They also defecate. The total bat experience is known as 'Swoop and Poop'.

You might want to stop for lunch at either the **Cellars Café** in the house, which offers a variety of home-made English dishes, such as beef cobbler at £7.25, and traditional cream teas for £4.40. There are also several snack bars across the site, and the **Central Café**, next to the car park, offers mains such as fish-and-chips and lasagne at £7.25 and sandwiches for around £3. Picnics are also a good option.

Now it's time for the **safari.** Longleat's animal experience is impressive. It's big and, unlike in other safari parks, you aren't next to busy roads or fields of grazing cattle. Instead, you're surrounded by trees, and it's easier to imagine yourself on a genuine safari. There is also the presence of keepers in every enclosure, which is reassuring when you are being eyed hungrily by the lions. The drive should take about 90 minutes, but allow more at busy times as you can get stuck in lines of traffic waiting for a turn at the best animal-watching spots.

The safari is split into different sections, and you initially drive into a picnic area where you can park, giving you a last chance to stretch your legs, use the loo or buy something from the Trading Post snack bar. You can also see wallabies and tapirs here. The next stop is the 60-ac (24-ha) **East African Reserve,** where you can see animals such as giraffes, zebras, camels and, improbably, llamas. You'll also pass through **Flamingo Valley,** home to Chilean flamingos, African spoonbills, sacred ibis, Carolina ducks and white-faced whistling ducks.

Soon you'll come to the **Big Game Park,** where the most impressive sight is the southern white rhinoceros herd. Also look for ankole cattle (an ancient breed of longhorns domesticated in Africa), Bactrian camels, Père David's deer and scimitar-horned oryx.

The **Deer Park,** which comes next, is also a historical attraction. The estate has had deer fencing since the 1540s. This is the only place on the safari where you can buy food for the animals and feed them from your car. You'll pass by the **Pelican Pond,** home to the first breeding population of pink-backed pelicans in the UK, and also the common eland and distinctively-striped bongo.

Then drive by tigers and lions – with your windows closed, natch. Finally comes the surprisingly-pretty **Wolf Wood,** where the Canadian timber wolves can be seen stalking through the forest – although they're more likely to be lounging.

After you exit the safari park, you have the option of leaving the site or heading back to the large main car park and returning to the house and park base.

TOURING TIPS Neither cars with soft or vinyl tops or sunroofs nor motorbikes are permitted in the Safari Park, but a limited daily **Safari Bus** service is available. Check with Visitor Information if you have an inappropriate vehicle or have arrived by public transport. The Safari Bus is subject to a surcharge and space is limited, so sign up as soon as you enter the park.

National Marine Aquarium ★★★½

APPEAL BY AGE	PRESCHOOL ★★★	PRIMARY SCHOOL ★★★	TEENS ★★★
YOUNG ADULTS ★★★		OVER 30 ★★★★	SENIORS ★★★★

Rope Walk, Coxside, Plymouth, Devon PL4 0LF
☎ **01752 600 301; national-aquarium.co.uk**

HOURS (April–September) 10 a.m.–6 p.m. (October–March) 10 a.m.–5 p.m. Last entry 1 hour before closing.

COST £11 adults; £6.50 children 5–15; £9 senior citizens, students; £30 family ticket (2 adults, 2 children). Discount of 10% for booking online. The 4D theatre costs an extra £2 per person. Admission can also be bought through the Tesco Clubcard rewards scheme.

GETTING THERE *By car:* In the Coxside area of Plymouth. Follow the brown-and-white fish signs, found on all entry roads into the city. The recommended route is the A38 to Marsh Mills (Sainsbury's), then along the A374 Embankment Road. The route for the aquarium and Barbican Car Park (main parking for the aquarium) is signposted from here. Pay-and-display parking costs £1.20 per hour. For satnav, use the postcode PL4 0DX. *By rail:* Closest station is Plymouth, 1 mi (1.6 km) from the aquarium (**nationalrail.co.uk**). *By bus:* The 25 bus stops a few minutes' walk from the aquarium. The site is also a 15-minute walk from the city centre, reached by all city bus routes. (Route information: **transportdirect.info.**)

DESCRIPTION AND COMMENTS Even though it has *National* in its name and is the UK's largest aquarium, the National Marine Aquarium isn't the country's premier fish house – that honour goes to The Deep, in Hull (see page 333). But with a 33-ft (10-m) tank, tied with The Deep for the deepest in Europe, it's still an impressive sight and worth a visit. The aquarium has 4,000 animals from 400 species, including 60 sharks and rays. The population increased in 2009, when the aquarium chartered a Boeing 767 jet to fetch 1,000 fish, including sharks, rays and tarpon, it had purchased from a Barbados aquarium that was shutting down. Tragedy struck the following year, when in late 2010 a power outage drained the Atlantic Reef tank and killed several hundred fish. The incident gave the attraction a chance to revamp the display, and it was expected to be fully populated and back in running order within a few months of renovations.

The aquarium is in Plymouth's historic Barbican harbour area. It overlooks Plymouth Sound, and you'll find gorgeous views from the building's café and coffee bar. (There's also a soft-play area outside the café, so you can have a bite while your youngsters get the wiggles out.) There's easy parking in an adjacent car park, and a ramp leads right to the entrance. Although you can wander the site at will, the aquarium provides a suggested route, leading from local species to the Atlantic and then around the world. We suggest following it, too.

After paying admission, you take a lift 2 storeys up and begin your visit in the **Shallow Water** area, which is devoted to specimens from the southwest coast. You'll see starfish, stingrays, a huge lobster and a common octopus named Bagpipe, who feeds himself by opening a jar that has been filled with crabs. Next, descend a ramp to the **Atlantic Reef** display, which lost most its inhabitants during the power outage. The cinema-screen-sized 121,000-gal (550,000-litre) tank provides views of creatures that live in the deeper waters off the southwest coast, including sea bass, pollack, bream and conger eels. From there, proceed to the small **Ocean Drifters** area, devoted to the beautiful (and sometimes painful) jellyfish, which gently float in dramatically-lit tanks.

Then head over to the ginormous 550,000-gal (2.5-million-litre) **Atlantic Ocean** tank, with 30 different species of Caribbean fish, many of them relocated from Barbados. The collection includes a trio of sand tiger sharks, named Enzo, Emily and Howardine (fish are one thing, but do the British really name their girl children Howardine?), each 8.2 ft (2.5 m) long. There are also barracuda, rays and tarpon. The tank can be seen from 2 storeys. Take the lift down to get a bottom-of-the-sea perspective, complete with a plane wreck circled by sharks. The aircraft, a replica Supermarine Walrus biplane, was used in World War II on search-and-rescue missions. The original launched from the nearby RAF Mount Batten station and crashed off-shore.

Backtrack past the Ocean Drifters area and head down the ramp to **Weird Creatures,** which delivers on its promise. You'll see longhorn cowfish and the venomous lionfish, along with clownfish, frogfish, sea horses and the diamond-shaped tassel filefish.

If you've purchased a ticket for the **4D Screen on the Sea** (and we recommend you do), you'll find yourself enveloped in a theatre with moving seats and its own weather system – snow and rain are distinct possibilities. But don't come expecting *Blue Planet*, which used aquarium staff as expert sources. The 15-minute animated production, *Turtle Vision*, has a smidgen of educational value, but it's largely for fun.

Finally, you'll exit through the **Coral Seas** exhibit, where you can watch Snorkel, the loggerhead turtle that starred in the 4D film, cruising the tank she shares with blacktip reef sharks and tiny coral catsharks, along with a colourful display of reef residents including unicornfish, a guineafowl pufferfish (which looks like a mini–beach ball with a face) and England's only spotted eagle rays.

TOURING TIPS If you haven't purchased admission online, you can still avoid the queue by buying your tickets from the nearby **Plymouth Tourist Information Centre, 3–5 The Barbican, Plymouth, PL1 2LR** (☎ 01752 306 330; **visitplymouth.co.uk**). The aquarium has talks and feedings throughout the day, from 11 a.m. to 4 p.m. Catching one will greatly enhance your visit. If the weather's nice, you can picnic in the aquarium's **Maritime Garden.**

(For more on aquariums, see page 10.)

Oceanarium ★★★

| APPEAL BY AGE | PRESCHOOL ★★★ | PRIMARY SCHOOL ★★★ | TEENS ★★★ |
| YOUNG ADULTS ★★ | | OVER 30 ★★★ | SENIORS ★★★ |

Pier Approach, West Beach, Bournemouth, Dorset BH2 5AA
☎ **01202 311 993; oceanarium.co.uk**

HOURS 10 a.m.–5 p.m. (last entry 1 hour before closing). Closed Christmas Day.

COST £8.95 adults (£6.25 online); £6.40 children 3–15 (£4.50 online); £7.75 senior citizens (£6.20 online); £7.95 students (£6.25 online); £6.70 disabled and carers (£5.35 online); £25.95 family ticket (2 adults, 2 children) (£20.75 online); £30.95 family ticket (2 adults, 3 children) (£24.75 online).

GETTING THERE *By car:* About 100 mi (160 km) southwest of London on the Dorset coast. From the A338 Wessex Way, follow the brown tourist signs to Oceanarium, Pier and beaches and the BIC (Bournemouth International Centre). Pay-and-display car parks are a few minutes' walk away at Bath Road South, Bath Road North and the BIC car park. *By rail:* The nearest rail station is Bournemouth, about 1 mi (1.6 km) from the aquarium (**nationalrail.co.uk**). *By bus:* Most buses from the train station lead to Bournemouth Pier, which is very close to the aquarium. (Route information: **transportdirect.info.**)

DESCRIPTION AND COMMENTS One of two UK aquariums owned by Parques Reunidos, a Spanish theme-park conglomerate. Although small, the site goes beyond sea creatures, featuring well-themed hands-on exhibits. We particularly like the **Interactive Dive Cage,** a virtual shark-dive in virtual water, with animated visuals and games. In one surprising encounter, you're swallowed by a blue whale and tour its digestive system until you're ejected through the blowhole. In another area, **Global Meltdown,** you explore the consequences of climate change. Watch as London becomes the new Atlantis when it floods with rising sea levels. You can calculate your personal carbon footprint, and at the end you're encouraged to record a video pledge to help the environment.

But you will find actual fish and wildlife here too. The **Amazon section** has piranhas and red-eared turtles, the **Marine Research Lab** displays porcupine pufferfish and the **Abyss** has an octopus, a nautilus, a Japanese spider crab and the strange flashlight fish, which has glowing organs.

TOURING TIPS Arrive early and experience the Interactive Dive Cage first. It can accommodate a fair number of guests, but the fewer the people the better, because you can view the action from several windows at once (when the cage is crowded, you're pretty much relegated to the window in front of you). If there's not room next to a window, try again later.

(For more on aquariums, see page 10.)

Paignton Zoo Environmental Park ★★★½

APPEAL BY AGE	PRESCHOOL ★★★	PRIMARY SCHOOL ★★★	TEENS ★★★★
YOUNG ADULTS ★★★		OVER 30 ★★★★	SENIORS ★★★

Totnes Road, Paignton, Devon TQ47EU
☎ **0844 474 2222; paigntonzoo.org.uk**

HOURS Opens at 10 a.m. Closing times vary by season, and last entry is usually 1 hour before closing. Closed Christmas Day.

COST £13.10 adults; £9.25 children (3–15); £10.80 senior citizens, students; £10.90 disabled adults; £7.20 disabled children (3–15); £8.95 disabled senior citizens, students (wheelchair pusher, attendant or nurse free); £41.25 family ticket (2 adults, 2 children). Admission charges include an optional 10% donation to the zoo, which you are not obliged to pay.

GETTING THERE *By car:* On the A3022 (Totnes Road), 1 mi (.6 km) from Paignton town centre. Once in Paignton follow the brown tourist signs, marked with an elephant and ZOOLOGICAL GARDENS. The zoo has a free car park for 1,110 cars on-site and an overflow car park a short walk away. *By rail:* The nearest station is Paignton, 1.3 mi (2 km) away (**nationalrail.co.uk**). *By bus:* **First Western** serves the zoo from Torquay and Plymouth (**firstgroup.com**). All visitors travelling to the zoo by bus receive a 10% discount on admission with a valid bus ticket. (Route information: **transportdirect.info.**)

DESCRIPTION AND COMMENTS For almost a century now, travellers to the West Country have included a visit to Paignton in their holidays. The Devon zoo is just a few miles from the beach, and even offers sea views from its slopes. It also has a botanical collection, allowing you to see cacti along with crocodiles and cheetahs. But from the beginning, Paignton has aimed to be more than a quick walk-through attraction.

Founder Herbert Whitley was a shy, eccentric millionaire with a deep interest in conservation. Even back when children could enter for a shilling (5p in today's money) and animals were kept in small cages, there was a concern about extinction and education, and the park was one of the first to combine a zoological and botanical garden in one site. Now the park is one of the largest zoos in England, with about 2,000 animals from nearly 300 species, including rarities like the Cuban crocodile and the impressive 6-ft (1.75-m) African wattled crane. It also cultivates some 1,600 different species of plants.

Another thing hasn't changed since the 1920s. The park's topography includes steep hills and winding paths. You'll leave the zoo well educated about animals, but with sore legs too. The park does hire powered scooters for those who have trouble with the terrain, though by the end of the day, the batteries begin to wind down as the electric cars struggle up slopes. Although the wooded setting is attractive, the signing isn't great. It's easy to get lost, and believe us, you don't want to do any unnecessary backtracking. Ask for a map, and refer to it often.

The zoo also offers a free audio guide on an MP3 download from its website. It's a great way to enhance your visit. You'll want to arrive at the zoo early for several reasons: the animals are active in the morning, the crowds will be smaller and, perhaps most importantly, you can get a parking spot close to the entrance. Like the zoo, the car park is on a hill, and the last thing you want to face at the end of the day is a long climb back to your vehicle.

The zoo's shaped roughly like an upside-down triangle, and you'll enter from the tip on the left side. As you arrive, check on feeding times. March–October a bird show is also offered several times in the afternoon. As you walk in, you'll see a lake circled by a miniature railway. The ride costs 70p and takes only a few minutes. It's really not worth the time, but it offers an overview of the front of the park, and if your young ones love trains, you may have no choice but to ride it anyway.

Otherwise, the first attraction you encounter is the **Wetland Habitat,** with **flamingos**, **pelicans**, **wood ducks** and **cranes.** The zoo has six species of cranes, including the largest, the African wattled crane, which can stand up to 5'9" (1.75 m) tall. To your left you'll see glasshouses holding reptiles and plants from the tropics and desert. The tropics area is quite warm and lush, the perfect environment for cold-blooded residents like **skinks, tortoises** and **tree frogs.** Look for the **anaconda,** one of the world's longest snakes, measuring up to 30 ft (9 m) long. You'll pass by an impressive stand of **giant bamboo** and then step into the **desert house,** which is actually cooler than the tropics. It's covered with sand and is home to desert birds, reptiles and an assortment of **cacti.** Look for the **stone curlew,** a bird that runs around on its long yellow legs like a roadrunner.

Walk past the **Island Restaurant,** and then loop back to the left. This is the **Primley** area, the oldest part of the zoo, named for Whitley's estate. You'll soon come across cuddly **red pandas.** The zoo has had success with breeding, and if you're lucky you may get to see a cub. You'll find separate enclosures for **owls** and **parrots** before you reach the top point of the property, home to one of the park's newest additions, **Crocodile Swamp,** where the zoo rather breathlessly proclaims you'll see 'the world's most aggressive crocodile, the world's largest crocodile and the world's longest snake'. They're not lying – at least not that we can prove. Look for the **Cuban crocodiles,** rare reptiles and the only ones in the UK. You'll also see the **saltwater croc,** the world's largest, which reaches lengths of up to a scary 23 ft (7 m). As for the snake, it's the **reticulated python,** which grows up to 33 ft (10 m) long. Now, with a new menagerie of creatures to populate your nightmares, you can stop to admire the **giant water lily.** Then take in a healthy dose of cute with the **black-tailed prairie dogs,** social creatures that still build entire towns in the western United States. On your right, you'll pass a small **baboon** troop, and a **ginkgo** (**maidenhair**) **tree.** Then take a left into the **Forest Habitat.** You'll pass **red-ruffed lemurs** and the **Monkey Heights** exhibit, which has raised walkways offering a clear view of the precocious primates. At the end of the walkway look for the **coast redwood** tree from California.

Now cross the pathway for the **Nocturnal House,** where the animals live on a reverse schedule so you can take a look at them. Look for **bats, sloths** and **nine-banded armadillos.** Any visiting Texan will be surprised to see living specimens of the latter, given that the weak-sighted creatures are most commonly seen flattened on highways in the US (there are even barbecue recipes for armadillo road kill). In the UK, however, they're quite rare – one of nature's oddities – and certainly worth a look. Heading for the far right-hand corner of the park brings you to the **Savannah Habitat,** where you'll pass **zebras** on the left and **red river hogs,** the surprisingly-cute porkers from Africa. Look for **Bactrian camels** (the two-humped ones) as you cut to the right at the far end of the park, and then head around the corner to the **Elephant and Giraffe House,** which lets you observe these iconic and fascinating creatures from an elevated gallery. The elephant's large ears, which are used to radiate heat, indicate these are the African variety. Now you'll pass a large **cheetah** enclosure on the left and an even larger field for **ostriches** on the right. Also on the right you'll see the **Badger Hide.** The zoo offers special programmes to watch the mischievous creatures at night, when they're out and active.

Following the path will eventually bring you to the **Ape Centre,** home to a group of five lowland gorillas, a critically-endangered species, and orang-utans. Next, cut down to the left (the bottom of the triangle) to **Lemur Wood,** a walk-through habitat starring the primates from Madagascar. They're free-ranging, which means you'll get an excellent up-close look at these fascinating, nimble creatures. Now walk past the **bongos** (not drums, but African antelopes with white stripes), and you'll find WCs and a kids' play area – a perfect place to get a snack and take a load off your feet while your charges burn off some energy.

Refreshed now, you can continue on the winding path back towards the entrance, passing the **Sumatran tigers** and **Asiatic lions** on your right. Then comes an aviary with a combination you'd never see in the wild: **egrets** and **wood ducks** living as neighbours with **hornbills** and **toucans.** Now you're back at the entrance, tired perhaps, but with an experience you can truly crow about.

TOURING TIPS Download the free audio tour from the zoo's website to your MP3 player. Check for feeding times and the bird show, which operates during high season. If you think you'll struggle climbing the zoo's hills, consider renting one of the zoo's electric scooters, which cost £5 with a £20 deposit. Call ahead to reserve one: ☎ 0844 474 2222.

THEME PARKS AND ATTRACTIONS

Sea Life Weymouth ★★½

APPEAL BY AGE	PRESCHOOL ★★★★	PRIMARY SCHOOL ★★★	TEENS ★★
YOUNG ADULTS ★★		OVER 30 ★★★	SENIORS ★★★

Lodmoor Country Park, Weymouth, Dorset DT4 7SX
☎ **0871 423 2110; visitsealife.com/weymouth**

HOURS 10 a.m.–4 p.m. (last entry 1 hour before closing). Closed Christmas Day.

COST £17.50 adults (£13.50 online); £14.95 children 3–14 (£10.95 online); £52 family ticket (2 adults, 2 children) (£42 online); £19 for 2 adult tickets (£34.50 online). Admission can also be bought through the Tesco Clubcard rewards scheme.

GETTING THERE *By car:* About 140 mi (225 km) southwest of London, in Dorset. Follow signs to Weymouth along the A352 and A353, then follow brown signs to Sea Life Park, which is on Preston Beach Road. *By rail:* The nearest rail station is Weymouth, about 1 mi (1.6 km) from the aquarium (**nationalrail.co.uk**). To walk to the aquarium, follow signs for the beach and stay on the promenade. *By bus:* From the train station, catch the **Number 4/4A bus** outside of the Cash Converters store. (Turn left out of the station, follow the road ahead and then bear to the right, and the bus stop will be straight ahead.) (Route information: **transportdirect.info**.)

DESCRIPTION AND COMMENTS You'll learn where sharks come from at a unique shark-breeding centre, where you can see shark eggs, youngsters and their parents, although none of them looked too cuddly to us. Unlike most aquariums, which are confined to a single building, you'll find a sprawling 7-ac (2.8-ha) waterfront attraction here. It's home to 1,000 creatures, including crocodiles, sharks, seals, otters, penguins and turtles. There's also a rainforest and ray pool.

But the centre treats the term *sea life* loosely. It aims for the young crowd, with **Adventure Island,** which has a quartet of children's amusements – a drop ride, tugboat, pirate ship and seal-themed roundabout. You'll also find pirate-themed crazy golf, a splash area and **Escape from Crocodile Creek,** a croc-inspired water flume ride.

TOURING TIPS Be sure to take in the feedings and educational programmes. Good for an hour or two – more if the kids take advantage of the play area and rides.

(For more on aquariums, see page 10.)

The Tank Museum ★★★

APPEAL BY AGE	PRESCHOOL ★★★	PRIMARY SCHOOL ★★★★	TEENS ★★★★
YOUNG ADULTS ★★★★		OVER 30 ★★★★	SENIORS ★★★★

Royal Armoured Corps Museum and Royal Tank Regiment Museum, Bovington Camp, Bovington, Dorset BH20 6JG
☎ **01929 462 359; tankmuseum.org**

HOURS 10 a.m.–5 p.m. daily. Closed Christmas Eve, Christmas Day, Boxing Day and New Year's Day.

COST £11 adults; £7.50 children (5–16); £9 senior citizens, disabled. Discounted family packages. Tickets allow repeat visits for 1 year.

GETTING THERE *By car:* The museum, about 125 mi (200 km) southwest of London, is signposted on major roads from Dorchester, Blandford, Poole, Bere Regis and Wool. *By rail:* The nearest rail station is Wool, on the main line between London Waterloo and Weymouth, where you can catch a bus to the station (**nationalrail.co.uk**). *By bus:* **Door-to-Dorset Bus Service 103/103A** operates between Wool Station and the Tank Museum, a distance of about 3 mi (4.8 km). Trips may need to be pre-booked at ☎ 0845 602 4547 (for general info: **transportdirect.info**). See the Tank Museum website for more info.

DESCRIPTION AND COMMENTS Lovers of military history and big machines that go *boom* will have a blast at the Tank Museum, the world's largest and most significant collection of armoured fighting vehicles. Unlike most military museums, where a visit involves a succession of dusty display cases and impressive, but static, machines, at Bovington the collection not only moves, it churns across fields and fires flames.

The museum is an official arm of the Royal Tank Regiment & Royal Armoured Corps, which has conducted manoeuvres on the grounds for nearly a century. This is where tanks were first used in training, and it was none other than Rudyard Kipling who is said to have suggested that the vehicles should be preserved in a museum. Even if you don't know a turret from a tambourine, the collection of about 200 displayed tanks from 26 countries is historically significant, and includes the world's first tank, a boxy vehicle known as **Little Willie**.

To get the most out of your visit, check the website and strive to come on weekdays during summer or the April, May or October school holidays for special **Tank Action Displays.** Surprisingly, these outdoor shows are free and can be viewed without purchasing museum admission.

Visitors take a seat in a mini-stadium at 1 p.m. for a 30-minute performance that's part history lesson, part army movie. First a reconnaissance vehicle speeds out onto the field, quickly followed by an armoured personnel carrier and then a battle tank. A narrator notes the significance of the vehicles and explains their battlefield roles. The cheers have hardly died out when a surprise attack comes from the Ruritanians (that is, the bad guys, not a men's civic organisation), who seize the Union Jack and plant their own flag in its place. The battle's on, and the crowd watches the vehicles they had seen earlier stage an attack. Combatants include eight volunteers equipped with replica AK-47s and rocket-propelled grenade launchers, who jump out of the personnel carrier to help regain the land for the British. (Volunteers are recruited inside the museum in the morning before the show. If you want to be considered, tell the ticket-taker at the entrance.) There's plenty of smoke and pyrotechnics, but thankfully no live ammunition.

Also, on certain days you can ride in a large tracked vehicle for an extra £2.50. The ride is in an M548 cargo carrier, converted to hold 16 people at a time, and offers a short bump-and-grind around the grounds. Think of it as a school bus with attitude. A few times a year it's also possible to ride in an actual tank. But that sells out months in advance and requires pre-booking. It's also quite pricey: £150 for a ride and a special half-day behind-the-scenes visit. Other specialised experiences, from birthday parties to private tours, can also be pre-booked.

But the museum itself has plenty to offer in its hanger-like halls. A visit starts in the new 50,000-sq-ft (4,645-m²) wing, dedicated by the Queen in 2009. The new exhibit, called **The Tank Story,** covers the museum's 30 most significant machines. It follows the invention and development of the tank, beginning with the earliest tracked machines and ending with the Challenger 2, Britain's most modern armoured vehicle. There are display panels and audio programming, and volunteer guides are often on hand to add a personal touch. Many visitors are drawn to one of four simulated firing ranges, where you can shoot a Vickers machine gun or an anti-tank weapon for £1. These look and operate like standard arcade video games, but somehow they seem more educational here.

Among the visitors are often soldiers in training at Bovington, and it's not uncommon to see civilians asking questions of the fighters and thanking them for their service. If you find you're developing a fascination with tanks, four other halls are filled with scores more, although there's not as much interpretation. But for most visitors, The Tank Story will be enough – the vehicles, as impressive as they are, can get to be overwhelming. However, do make sure to tour the **Trench Experience,** which re-creates the horrible conditions of World War I. As you survey the mud and misery, sounds of battle and even poetry written about the Great War play from hidden speakers. Eventually you encounter a British tank breaking through the barbed wire and attacking the German line. Tanks, we learn, saved the day.

Older visitors will be fascinated with the small exhibit devoted to **T. E. Lawrence** (Lawrence of Arabia), who briefly served at Bovington. If you're a fan, visit Lawrence's home, just 1.5 mi (2.5 km) away. Cloud's Hill is now a small museum maintained by the National Trust (Wareham, Dorset BH20 7NQ; ☎ 01929 405 616; **nationaltrust.org.uk/cloudshill.** Admission: £4.50 adults, £2 children).

The Gauntlet restaurant offers sandwiches, snacks and cakes, with hot food available from 11.30 a.m. until 3 p.m. You're also free to bring a picnic. And, of course, there's a gift shop packed with military history books and DVDs, along with T-shirts and caps. On summer evenings you may want to stick around for weekly outdoor concerts from military, swing and jazz bands. Tickets run £10 but do allow a 20% discount on museum admission.

TOURING TIPS As you enter the museum, enquire about guided tours. The free volunteer-led walks give visitors a chance to sit inside tanks from World War I and the Cold War era. Before your visit, you can download free tours from the museum's website without charge and play them on your personal MP3 player. As the museum historian described on one of the tours, the first soldiers assigned to tanks were 'working in conditions so utterly awful as to be almost unbearable'.

Weston-Super-Mare SeaQuarium ★★½

APPEAL BY AGE	PRESCHOOL ★★★	PRIMARY SCHOOL ★★★	TEENS ★★
YOUNG ADULTS ★★		OVER 30 ★★★	SENIORS ★★★

Marine Parade, Weston-Super-Mare, Somerset BS23 1BE
☎ **01934 613 361; seaquarium.co.uk/weston.php**

HOURS 10 a.m.–5 p.m. (last entry 1 hour before closing). Call ahead for winter hours. Closed 24–26 December.

COST £6.50 adults; £5.50 children 3–16; £7.75 senior citizens; £5.50 disabled (includes 1 carer free); £23 family ticket (2 adults, 2 children; £4.99 each additional child). Admission can also be bought through the Tesco Clubcard rewards scheme.

GETTING THERE *By car:* About 20 mi (32 km) southwest of Bristol. Exit the M5 at Junction 21, and follow the signs for either AQUARIUM or SEA FRONT. The site is between the sand dunes and the Grand Pier. You'll have to pay for beach parking, but there's free street parking a few streets inland. *By rail:* The nearest rail station is Weston-Super-Mare, about .5 mi (.9 km) from the aquarium (**nationalrail.co.uk**). *By bus:* Weston-Super-Mare is served by **First Group Routes X1/353/653** from Bristol (**firstgroup.com**). (Route information: **transportdirect.info**.)

DESCRIPTION AND COMMENTS SeaQuarium's setting alone is part of its charm. It sits on a seaside pier, which when it opened in 1995 was the first to be built in England in 85 years. And the location in Weston-Super-Mare, with its extreme tidal range, means it's surrounded by miles of beach and mudflats. The attraction is part of a mini-chain – its sister sites include Rhyl SeaQuarium and West Midlands Safari Park – and its design feels less corporate than its competition.

With about 25 displays, it's not huge, but you'll find the expected sharks, sea horses and rays. As you enter, ask for the **Discovery Trail Quiz,** which is designed for kids, but teens and adults can have fun, too, as they seek out answers on the various display boards. Try to time your visit to catch one of the daily feedings, at 11.30 a.m. and 2.30 p.m. Highlights include the **Tropical Reef Zone,** where you'll find moray eels and stonefish.

The **EvoZone** has the strange lungfish, which can breathe air and is the closest living relative to the first land animals. And the **Rainforest River Zone** includes freshwater stingrays, snakeneck turtles and glass catfish.

TOURING TIPS The Weston SeaQuarium is modest but well done. It's a double treat if you visit when the tide is out and you can explore the tidal pools accessible from the adjacent beach.

(For more on aquariums, see page 10.)

FARM EXPERIENCES

BECAUSE THE VARIOUS FARM EXPERIENCES are so similar (see page 13), we felt it unnecessary to provide individual profiles as we do with other types of attractions. Following is a selective list of South West England farm experiences.

CORNWALL

THE CORNISH BIRDS OF PREY CENTRE
(Specializes in birds of prey and falconry but also offers farm animals, playground and fishing)
Meadowside Farm
Winnards Perch, St Columb
Cornwall TR9 6DH
☎ 01637 880 544
cornishbirdsofprey.co.uk
info@cornishbirdsofprey.co.uk

DAIRYLAND FARM WORLD
Nr Newquay
Cornwall TR8 5AA
☎ 01872 510 246
dairylandfarmworld.com
info@dairylandfarmworld.co.uk

TAMAR VALLEY DONKEY PARK
St Ann's Chapel, Gunnislake
Cornwall PL18 9HW
☎ 01822 834 072
donkeypark.com
info@donkeypark.com

DEVON

PENNYWELL FARM & WILDLIFE CENTRE
Pennywell, Buckfastleigh
Devon TQ11 0LT
☎ 01364 642 012
pennywellfarmcentre.co.uk
info@pennywellfarmcentre.co.uk

PRICKLY BALL FARM
(includes a hedgehog hospital)
Denbury Road
Newton Abbot
Devon TQ12 6BZ
☎ 01626 362 319
pricklyballfarm.co.uk
enquiries@pricklyballfarm.co.uk

THE BIG SHEEP
Abbotsham, Bideford
Devon EX39 5AP
☎ 01237 472 366
thebigsheep.co.uk
info@thebigsheep.co.uk

THE MINIATURE PONY CENTRE
(Stud farm for the Keensacre miniature Shetland pony)
Wormhill Farm
Moretonhampstead, Dartmoor
Devon TQ13 8RG
☎ 01647 432 400
miniatureponycentre.com
**enquiries@miniature
    ponycentre.com**

**BIG FUN FARM AT WOODLANDS
DARTMOUTH**
Blackawton, Totnes
Devon TQ9 7DQ
☎ 01803 712 598
woodlandspark.com
fun@woodlandspark.com

SOMERSET

COURT FARM COUNTRY PARK
Wolvershill Road
Banwell, Weston-Super-Mare
Somerset BS29 6DL
☎ 01934 822 383
courtfarmcountrypark.co.uk
info@courtfarmcountry
   park.co.uk

THE FUN FARM
Priorswood, Taunton
Somerset TA2 8QJ
☎ 01823 270 289
thefunfarm.org
enquiries@thefunfarm.org

PUXTON PARK
Cowslip Lane
Hewish, Weston-Super-Mare
Somerset BS24 6AH
☎ 01934 523 500
puxton.co.uk
info@puxton.co.uk

WILTSHIRE

CHOLDERTON CHARLIE'S FARM
Amesbury Road
Cholderton, Salisbury
Wiltshire SP4 0EW
☎ 0198 062 9438
choldertoncharlies.com
(Email via form at website)

**FARMER GILES WORKING FARM
   PARK**
Teffont, Salisbury
Wiltshire SP3 5QY
☎ 01722 716 338
farmergiles.co.uk
farmergiles@farmergiles.co.uk

ROVES FARM
Sevenhampton
Highworth, Swindon
Wiltshire SN6 7QG
☎ 01793 763 939
rovesfarm.co.uk
info@rovesfarm.co.uk

PART EIGHT

The EAST of ENGLAND

TUCKED AWAY IN A CORNER OF BRITAIN to which many travellers never have much need to go, **East Anglia** is a world removed from London and, for that matter, from other, busier parts of Britain too. This is a land of rolling fields, skies full of fleecy clouds, meadows full of fleecy sheep, marshy fens and quiet villages that haven't changed too much since their mediaeval marketplaces and half-timbered houses were erected. East Anglia is not, however, an unsophisticated backwater. One of the finest universities in the world is here, at **Cambridge**, as are a number of fine, proud towns, such as **Bury St Edmunds** and **Norwich**, which have played their parts in English history.

The more east-central counties of Bedfordshire, Buckinghamshire and Hertfordshire, as well as Lincolnshire to the north, are also included in this chapter. Attractions include the **Imperial War Museum Duxford, Thrigby Hall Wildlife Gardens** and **ZSL Whipsnade Zoo.**

THEME PARKS *and* ATTRACTIONS

Adventure Island Sunken Gardens ★★★

APPEAL BY AGE	PRESCHOOL ★★★★	PRIMARY SCHOOL ★★★	TEENS ★★★★
YOUNG ADULTS ★★★		OVER 30 ★★	SENIORS ★★

Western Esplanade, Southend-on-Sea, Essex SS1 1EE
☎ 01702 443 400; adventureisland.co.uk

HOURS Opens at 11 a.m.; closing times vary throughout the year. Limited to weekends and some holidays during winter (see website for details).
COST Park entrance is free. Ride tickets cost £1.20 each, and some rides may require several. If you plan to go on more than a few rides, the best strategy is to purchase a wristband, which allows unlimited access

The East of England

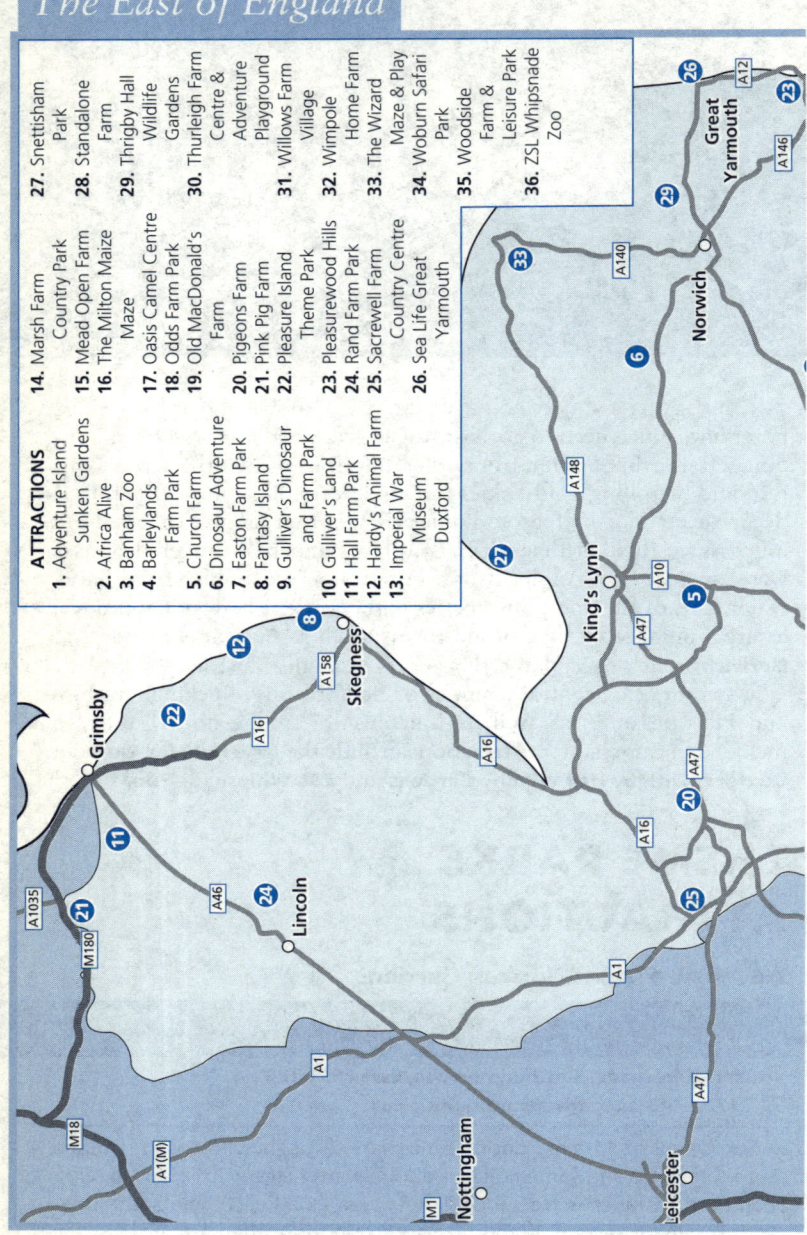

ATTRACTIONS
1. Adventure Island Sunken Gardens
2. Africa Alive
3. Banham Zoo
4. Barleylands Farm Park
5. Church Farm
6. Dinosaur Adventure
7. Easton Farm Park
8. Fantasy Island
9. Gulliver's Dinosaur and Farm Park
10. Gulliver's Land
11. Hall Farm Park
12. Hardy's Animal Farm
13. Imperial War Museum Duxford
14. Marsh Farm Country Park
15. Mead Open Farm
16. The Milton Maize Maze
17. Oasis Camel Centre
18. Odds Farm Park
19. Old MacDonald's Farm
20. Pigeons Farm
21. Pink Pig Farm
22. Pleasure Island Theme Park
23. Pleasurewood Hills
24. Rand Farm Park
25. Sacrewell Farm Country Centre
26. Sea Life Great Yarmouth
27. Snettisham Park
28. Standalone Farm
29. Thrigby Hall Wildlife Gardens
30. Thurleigh Farm Centre & Adventure Playground
31. Willows Farm Village
32. Wimpole Home Farm
33. The Wizard Maze & Play
34. Woburn Safari Park
35. Woodside Farm & Leisure Park
36. ZSL Whipsnade Zoo

EAST OF ENGLAND MAP   221

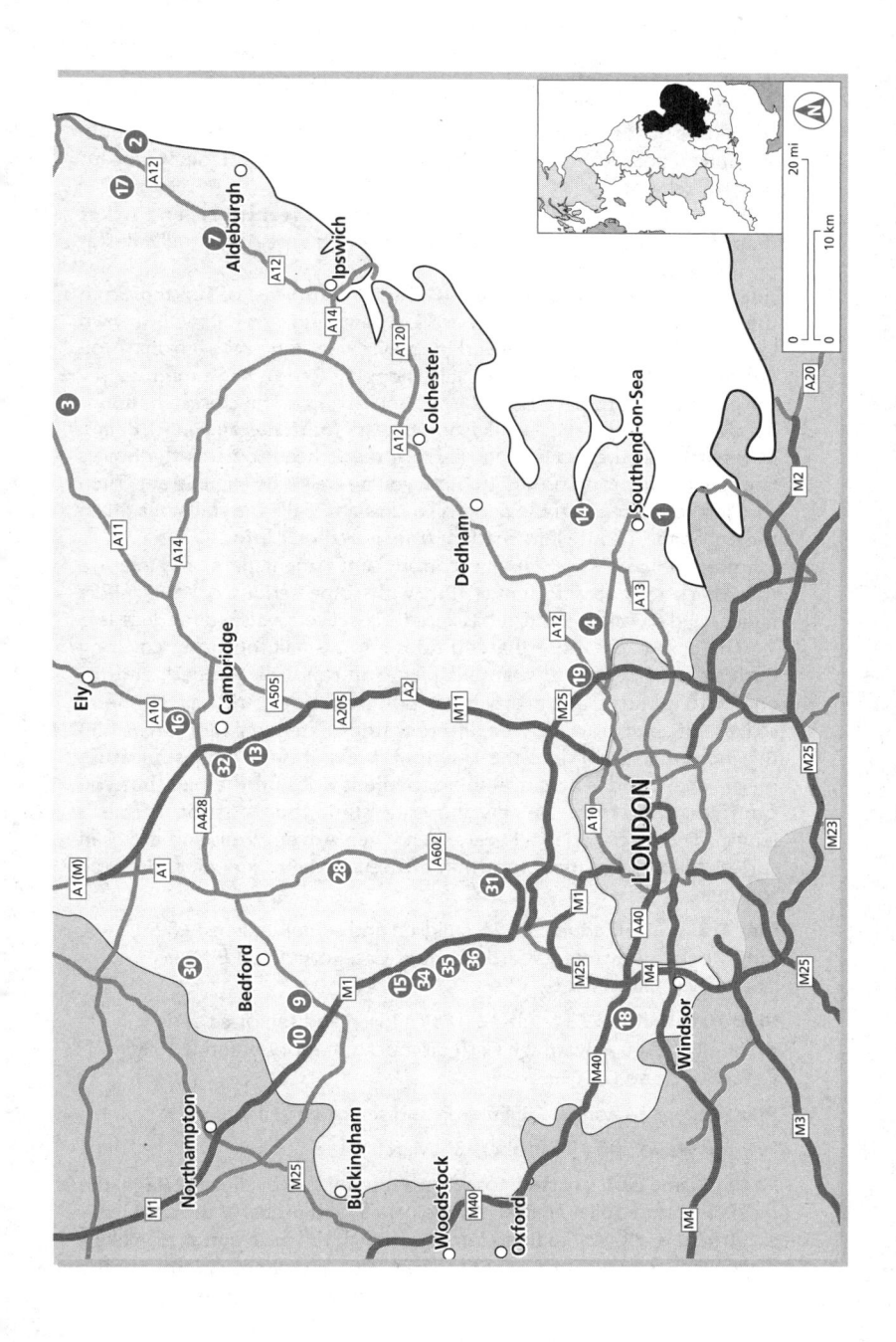

throughout the day. Wristbands: (peak season) £22 adults and children over 3'11" (1.2 m); £15 children 3'3"–3'11" (1–1.2 m); £8.50 children under 3'3" (1 m). (off-peak) £18 adults and children over 3'11" (1.2 m); £12 children 3'3"–3'11" (1–1.2 m); £6.50 children under 3'3" (1 m). On some days bands are half price after 6 p.m. Discounts available by booking online, and tickets can also be bought through the Tesco Clubcard rewards scheme.

Free rail travel is available through a special **Adventure Island Ticket** that can be bought at c2c or National Express East Anglia railway stations (see website for details).

GETTING THERE *By car:* The park is about 45 mi (73 km) east of London. From the M25, take either Junction 29 or 30 to Southend, and follow the brown tourist signs. Pay-and-display parking is available along the seafront if you can find it. Alternatively, the Royals Shopping Centre has a multi-storey car park. Expect to pay about £1 per hour. *By rail:* The closest station is Southend Central, a short walk from the park (**nationalrail.co.uk**). *By bus:* Buses arrive at the Travel Centre. From there, head towards the Royals Shopping Centre and turn right, until you arrive in the High Street. Then turn left to the sea, and the park will be in sight. Take the stairs or a lift to the esplanade. (Route information: **transportdirect.info.**)

DESCRIPTION AND COMMENTS This beachfront amusement park may seem a throwback to a seaside funfair. But with some serious coasters, short queues and a walkable size, it has kept thrill-seekers satisfied for decades.

The park packs more than 40 rides into a small footprint, covering both sides of Southend's famous pier. You can walk the park end-to-end in 10 minutes, and pretty much pop from ride to ride as the mood strikes. The pier, however, is a different story. Extending more than 1.33 mi (more than 2 km) into the Thames Estuary, it is the longest pleasure pier in the world. There are no amusement rides on the pier, but you can ride a train from the new shoreside station for most of the pier's length. The pier is open all year, even when Adventure Island is closed (prices follow). For more information see **southend.gov.uk** and search for 'pier'.

Pier Train: £3.50 adults; £1.75 children and senior citizens; £8.50 family ticket. Advantage Card discount Category A and B 10%; Category C and D 50%.

Pier Walk & Ride: £3 adults; £1.75 children and senior citizens; £7 family ticket. Advantage Card discount Category A and B 10%; Category C and D 50%.

Pier Fishing: £4 adults; £3 children and senior citizens.

Winter Walk: 50p (1 October–31 March)

At the theme park, coaster fans will want to make a beeline for **Rage,** the park's signature roller coaster. As the park's (and probably the city's) tallest structure, it's easy to find. Coming through the main entrance, make a diagonal to the southeast sector the park. (It's also directly in front of the east side main entrance.) Look for a yellow-and-purple tangle of steel, and listen for particularly-intense screams. The coaster takes riders straight up a 72-ft (22-m) hill, providing a brief but thrilling seafront view before plunging down a 97° angle into a loop and a disorienting succession of twists and helixes. Great fun.

Tucked next to Rage, you'll find **Sky Drop,** a 70-ft (21-m) drop tower tucked in next to Rage. And **Archelon,** a wave-swinger, is just a little farther east.

Also on the east side of the pier, **Green Scream** provides an excellent introduction to coasters for young riders. Available to guests over 3'3" (1 m) tall, the crocodile-themed ride climbs a modest lift hill and then smoothly swoops and turns past bushes and trees. It's thrilling, but not too scary, and after the first experience kids will want to head back to do it over again, which is why the purchase of unlimited-ride wristbands is probably a good idea.

And if your children aren't ready for coasters, they'll probably love the purple elephant **Flying Jumbos,** located next to the Green Scream.

The park's other steel coasters are found on the west side of the park, near the water. **Barnstormer** and nearby **Mighty Mini Mega** each stretch around 745 ft (222 m) and reach about 25 mph (40 km/h). They provide tight curves and helixes in a small footprint, giving a heightened sense of speed – and imminent decapitation. Although they're considered junior rides by the park, the Mighty Mini Mega in particular is intense at times. Coaster fans will find something to like in each of them.

Another notable ride, **Dragon's Claw,** near the front of the park on the west side, spins riders sideways and upside-down. Ride this one before lunch, or you'll be seeing your meal again. Other than those, the offerings are pretty standard here. You'll have to pay an extra fee for a few attractions such as crazy golf, tenpin bowling, go-karts and, of course, the prize stalls.

But if you're not a coaster fan or aren't accompanying young children, there's little to interest you, except perhaps for **Over the Hill,** back in the southeast corner of the park. It's a £1 million dark ride through a cemetery set, with computer animation effects. The imaginative ride was designed by animator Martin Clapp, who worked on the Oscar-winning film *Peter & the Wolf*. The various ghouls, skeletons and the like are more whimsical than scary, but the ride is very intimate, with all the action happening very close to the ride vehicles. The lighting effects, some of the best we've seen, are what really make this ghost train special.

TOURING TIPS Part of Adventure Island's appeal, of course, is the seafront holiday setting. Since a wristband's valid all day, you're free to leave the park and wander the waterfront, where you can have a bite to eat by the arcades. The park's food offerings are limited to three sit-down restaurants offering fish-and-chips, pizza and fast food, plus an array of snack and sweets stalls.

One of the main challenges is parking. Come early, before the park opens at 11 a.m., and sit on the beach before heading into the park. Time it right and you can get your thrills in during the early part of the day, have some time on the beach and then return in the evening, when the flashing lights and crowds make for a memorable holiday scene.

Africa Alive ★★★½

| APPEAL BY AGE | PRESCHOOL ★★★ | PRIMARY SCHOOL ★★★★ | TEENS ★★★ |
| YOUNG ADULTS ★★★ | | OVER 30 ★★★ | SENIORS ★★★★ |

White's Lane, Kessingland, Lowestoft, Suffolk NR33 7TF
☎ **01502 740 291; africa-alive.co.uk**

HOURS (Spring–October) 10 a.m.–5 p.m.; until 4 p.m. off-season. Last admission 1 hour before closing. Closed Christmas and Boxing days.

COST (Mid-March–October) £13.95 adults; £9.95 children (3–15), special needs and carers; £12.95 senior citizens. (off-season) £10.95 adults; £7.95 children (3–15), special needs and carers; £9.95 senior citizens. Tickets can also be bought through the Tesco Clubcard rewards scheme.

GETTING THERE *By car:* The park is 3 mi (5 km) south of Lowestoft. From the A12, take the White's Lane exit and follow signs. *By rail:* The nearest station is Lowestoft, served by **National Express East Anglia** (**nationalrail.co.uk**). *By bus:* **Routes 99** and **99A** run by the park from Lowestoft or Southwold, except Sundays (**firstgroup.com**).

DESCRIPTION AND COMMENTS If you want all Africa, all the time, this is the place for you. You'll encounter familiar creatures from the continent, such as giraffes, rhinos and lions, plus little-seen species such as aardvarks and striped hyenas. We kind of like the concept of a zoo with a theme, instead of a higgledy-piggledy collection of animals all thrown together. You visit by strolling through the exhibits in a walking safari of sorts, which is manageable during a several-hour visit. A train ride offers an overview.

Formerly known as Suffolk Wildlife Park, Africa Alive was taken over in 1991 by the Banham Zoo (see page 226), which began to develop its African theme. The property covers 100 ac (40 ha) of coastal parkland in East Anglia and would be notable for its natural beauty – with fields, marshes and lakes, graced with mature willows – even if it wasn't populated with monkeys and mongooses.

After parking you enter and quickly pass the gift shop, food court and play area. Make sure to pick up a schedule of feeding times and animal talks. Children should also grab a free guide booklet, which contains a map of the park and the **Passport Challenge,** a programme to collect stamps at various stations around the park. If they get all eight, the passport can be redeemed for a medal at the park reception area. It's open to children under age 16 but will be of greatest interest to those under 10.

The park is arranged like an upside-down figure of eight or bowling pin, with the larger loop on top of the smaller. We suggest that you turn left and begin your visit by first looping through the larger main portion of the park, which has expansive, wide-open animal habitats. Several of the areas have viewing shelters, allowing you to observe the animals unobtrusively. Save the park's bottom loop, with its concentration of smaller exhibits, train station and show arena, for the end of your visit, when your feet are tired and you won't be as willing to stroll across a few acres just to see a zebra or two. Some of the paths more remote from the entrance area are gravel and rock – not impossible, but certainly effortful, for pushchairs and wheelchairs.

Heading to the left from the entrance plaza, you'll pass the **addax,** a critically-endangered desert antelope with dramatic twisting horns. Then follow the ramp on your right up to **Lookout Lodge,** a viewing platform that looks like a stadium press box, offering a bird's-eye view of the **Kingdom of the Lion** area.

Continue your loop and pass **cheetahs** on your way to the heart of the park, the **Plains of Africa.** On a good day this wide-open field can look like the assembly point for Noah's Ark, with giraffes, rhinos, zebras, ostriches and blesbok, an antelope with purplish shading, all grazing in apparent harmony. One rhino has strange pincer-like horns that reminded us of what Mum said would happen if you didn't cut your fingernails regularly. You'll pass several vantage points and viewing areas as you loop through this area. Try out at least a few for the different perspective they offer. On the way you'll see the **Rhino House;** the **Zebra, Ostrich and Blesbok Stables;** and the **Giraffe House.** If you don't see these animals in the Plains, take a moment to explore the houses to see if you can find them indoors. For £15 per person (minimum age 6 years), you can take a guided jeep tour of the plains.

At the top of the park, the path crosses a stream leading to **ankole cattle,** with distinctive long horns; two subspecies of **lechwe,** a type of antelope; and **nyla,** reclusive forest antelopes. To say that the enclosures for these hoofed creatures are spacious is an understatement. With several acres allocated to each species, the animals are often found grazing 150 yd (137 m) or more from the pedestrian path

Continuing on the loop, take some time to watch the **lemurs,** which live on an island in the stream. The wildly-popular animals, which seem to be in every zoo in the world these days, are from Madagascar, which means they qualify as African, since the island nation is just off the continent's coast. (You can also see the lemurs up close in the seasonal **Lemur Encounters** area near the park entrance.) Just across the path, you'll find the considerably-rarer **bongo,** a red forest antelope with distinctive white stripes. Flanking the bongos is a serene **lake** that is home to free-ranging indigenous species, including many water birds.

Continuing back towards the entrance, you'll pass other less-familiar animals, including **Barbary sheep, Congo buffalo** and the **Somali wild ass.** Across from the Somali creatures, the young wild asses in your group can cut loose in a play area, with pioneer structures and an obstacle course. If the weather isn't conducive to outdoor play, the **Wild Zone** indoor play area is nearby.

Now you'll find yourself in the smaller loop of the figure of eight. Although the enclosures are much smaller, allow time to look around because there's plenty to see here. Along with the Lemur Encounters walk-through area, where the lemurs can come as close to you as they feel comfortable doing, there are additional exhibits of **fennecs, bat-eared foxes, mongooses, monkeys** and **chimps.** Make a quick pass through the **Bat & Reptile House,** a disappointing exhibit with only a few specimens.

Next are **aardvarks** and **porcupines,** two odd creatures that show God certainly has a sense of humour.

Farmyard Corner offers a chance for young ones to pet and feed some cuddly animals (mostly sheep). The cuteness factor doesn't let up with the **meerkats** and **otters,** but you probably won't be cooing at the nearby **striped hyenas.** Also catch a look at the rare **fossa,** a small carnivore from Madagascar that resembles a cross between a lynx and a mongoose, and the **serval,** which appears to have the head of a house cat imposed on a larger (more deadly) body.

While you're touring this area, make sure to check the park schedule. A **birds-of-prey show** and visiting African-themed entertainers are featured in the arena, which is in the centre of this small loop.

You can also catch the zebra-striped **road train** nearby during high season. It may be a welcome break if you (or your party) are beginning to flag.

TOURING TIPS The number of species at Africa Alive is not overwhelming, but you can walk yourself silly in this spacious park. It's important to check the map carefully, because you won't want to backtrack. Conversely, don't forgo exploration of the more-far-flung areas – these offer lakes, woods and exceptional natural beauty, in addition to the animals. A number of **'feeding talks'** are offered according to a daily schedule, all informative and worthwhile. Lions and cheetahs are usually fed back-to-back, making it easy to take in two talks with little effort.

You can get a variety of coffees, teas, panini, sandwiches and cakes at the **Limpopo Station Restaurant,** which has both indoor and outdoor seating. For children's meals, jacket potatoes and daily specials, there's the **Explorer's Food Hall** at the entrance, or picnic tables if you bring your own lunch. The park will also let you order a picnic box, saving the time of packing a lunch or queuing. Either call ahead (☎ 01502 740 291) or stop by Explorer's Food Hall the morning of your visit. The price is £6.95 for adults and £4.50 for children.

Banham Zoo ★★★★

APPEAL BY AGE	PRESCHOOL ★★★★	PRIMARY SCHOOL ★★★★	TEENS ★★★
YOUNG ADULTS ★★★		OVER 30 ★★★	SENIORS ★★★★

Kenninghall Road, Banham, Norfolk NR16 2HE
☎ 01953 887 771; banhamzoo.co.uk

- **HOURS** (October–spring) 10 a.m.–4 p.m. (closing times later during high season). Last admission 1 hour before closing. Closed Christmas and Boxing days.
- **COST** (mid-March–October) £13.95 adults; £9.95 children, special needs, carers; £12.95 senior citizens. (Off-season) £10.95 adults; £7.95 children (3–15), special needs, carers; £9.95 senior citizens. Tickets can also be bought through the Tesco Clubcard rewards scheme.
- **GETTING THERE** *By car:* About 25 minutes from Norwich and about an hour from Cambridge, between the A11 and A140 and well signposted from both roads, it's on the B1113. *By rail:* The nearest station is Attleborough

(**nationalrail.co.uk**). *By bus:* During summer, Route 200 connects the zoo with Norwich, Hethersett, Wymondham and Attleborough (**firstgroup.com**).

DESCRIPTION AND COMMENTS You're excused for harbouring doubts about the Banham Zoo. As you travel for miles and miles to what feels like the middle of nowhere, you've got to wonder if it's really worth the trip. What, after all, is a collection of exotic animals doing here? Don't worry. When you finally arrive after your journey through the Norfolk countryside, you'll discover a small but well-run zoo with a huge variety of primates, rare snow leopards and many other species that would be a surprise anywhere. The privately-owned attraction opened in 1968 with a collection of parrots and pheasants. Three years later, it brought in a colony of woolly monkeys and now has one of the most varied primate collections in Europe, with seven species of lemurs alone.

Although lacking elephants and lions, the beautifully-landscaped and immaculately-clean 25-ac (10-ha) zoo holds many surprises and can offer a full day out. There are also more than a half-dozen **special experiences** you can add on, from giraffe feeding, for £7.50 per person or £30 per family, to the **Fur and Feathers Experience Day,** which allows you to help out with the birds of prey and Amazing Animals shows. (That runs a cool £170 per person.) While many zoos sell similar premium opportunities, the breadth of offerings here is rare. The experiences make for a pricey but memorable day, and most participants received it as a gift or are celebrating birthdays, anniversaries or other special occasions. Think carefully before you sign up, assessing the person's actual interest in an in-depth experience that will keep him or her occupied for several hours at a minimum. It could be perfect for a budding mammal biologist . . . or a waste of time if the recipient has only a passing interest in raptors, for example.

As you approach the zoo and pay admission, you'll find yourself in a figurative maze. There's no obvious route through the zoo, and although it's well signed, you're likely to get lost if you don't follow your zoo map carefully. Check the schedule for **animal feedings and shows** – one touring strategy is to make your way through the park as you catch those that appeal to you. Otherwise, we suggest starting in an anti-clockwise fashion across the bottom of the zoo. Then you can catch the free tiger-striped **road train,** which will give you an overview of the park and a better idea of which other animals you'd like to see.

But if you have young ones, you won't have much trouble picking a route. The **Farm Barn** – a hands-on experience with pygmy goats, chickens, pigs, cows and other barnyard animals – is directly in front of the entrance. For other visitors, continue by the **mongooses, penguins, fur seals** and **parrots.** As you pass the **colobus monkeys,** look for the viewing station, an elevated perch offering a nice overview of the enclosure. Several such elevated vantage points are found throughout the zoo. Then look for the always-alluring **lemurs,** and you'll find yourself at the **Safari Roadtrain** station. This free 10-minute excursion is a good chance to take a break and get an overview of the zoo.

This area is also the entrance to the **Woodland Walk,** a lovely stroll past **flamingos,** more lemurs and even **red squirrels.** Although not exactly marquee animals like tigers or pandas, numbers of this once-common mammal have dropped precipitously in England due to the introduction of the eastern grey squirrel from North America. The zoo has been involved in a breeding programme to restore the species.

From this point, we suggest continuing a loop of the zoo. There's no shortage of cute in this corner, with adjacent exhibits of **red pandas, meerkats** and **otters.** Allow time for plenty of cooing at the creatures. Stroll by **Tiger Territory,** which is particularly engaging at feeding time. Keepers feed through the fence using tongs to hold meat high, forcing the felines to stretch and reach for their food.

Then head to the far upper corner of the property to take in the **deer park.** Rounding the bend, you'll begin walking across the top of the zoo. A viewing station offers a chance to gaze on the rarely-seen **Sri Lankan leopards.** Then cut over to the giraffe area, a zoo highlight. The **Zarafa Heights Walkway** will put you eye to eye with these fascinating creatures. The adjacent **Giraffe House** is a multi-level work of architectural genius. Here, too, you can look a giraffe in the eye. Then you'll pass another unique exhibit, where you can see **Poitou donkeys,** a bulky and strange-looking old French breed that reminds us of a nuclear horse, and majestic **shire horses,** a breed dating to medieval England. This 2,200-lb (1,000-kg) animal could carry a fully-armoured knight into battle. Look for long hair over the fetlocks and white feet.

The far corner holds **llamas** and the show areas. Try to take in both performances: **Amazing Animals** features meerkats, armadillos, kinkajous and ferrets, and the **birds-of-prey** show has free-flying raptors, with an owl, a caracara, a vulture and a bald eagle zooming over the heads of the audience, which is a real thrill. Between shows, the birds are tethered to perches at the nearby **Birds of Prey Centre.** With only a low barrier between you and the birds, you have a totally-unobstructed view from about 2½ ft (.7 m) away. It was the closest we Yanks had ever been to an American bald eagle. In addition to the Birds of Prey Centre, there are two owl exhibits along the path back to the zoo entrance. Unlike the tethered birds, however, these owls like their privacy and are often hard to spot. If Mr Big Eyes is not in plain sight, look for him in an open-sided wooden box mounted in the uppermost left or right rear corner of the cage.

Moving back down through the park in a zig-zag brings you past **maned wolves** and **Grevey's zebras.** Then comes **Tarzan Towers Play Area,** and even if you want to keep going, we bet someone in your party will welcome the break. Once the wiggles are out, you'll be much more appreciative of the rare and beautiful **snow leopard,** which lives in a fairly-posh habitat with a stream and a variety of rocks for climbing. It's all topped by a tent-like steel mesh, because these guys are great jumpers. Several cubs have been born here in recent years, and if you're lucky you'll see one of these cuddly (but dangerous) puffballs. The twisting route then leads to what could be called Primate Central. There are **marmosets,**

THEME PARKS AND ATTRACTIONS 229

tamarins, siamangs, spider monkeys and yet more lemurs. At this point, you'll be near the food hall and coffee shop. Have a seat – this little zoo in the middle of nowhere has probably worn you out.

- TOURING TIPS Food choices are better than you might expect, but supplies can be limited on busy days. A picnic is always a good choice here, and if it's raining there's a covered dining area near the parrots. If you're able to visit mid-week during the school year, you may have the animals to yourself.

If you drive and use the car park, be forewarned that the signs directing you to the zoo exit are very confusing. Many drivers make two complete laps around the zoo before sorting out how to access the main road.

Dinosaur Adventure ★★★

APPEAL BY AGE	PRESCHOOL ★★★★	PRIMARY SCHOOL ★★★★	TEENS ★★★
YOUNG ADULTS ★★		OVER 30 ★★★	SENIORS ★★★

Weston Park, Lenwade, Norwich, Norfolk NR9 5JW
☎ **01603 876 310; dinosauradventure.co.uk**

- HOURS (Spring–October) 10 a.m.–5 p.m.; until 4 p.m. off-season. Last admission 1 hour before closing. Open every day but Christmas and Boxing days.
- COST (Mid-March–October) £8.95 adults; £10.95 children (3–15); £8.95 senior citizens; £7.95 special-needs adults and carers; £9.50 special-needs children. (Off-season) £6.95 adults; £7.95 children; £6.95 senior citizens; £5.95 special-needs adults and carers; £6.95 special-needs children. Tickets can also be bought through the Tesco Clubcard rewards scheme.
- GETTING THERE *By car:* Located 9 mi (14 km) from Norwich, off the A1067, or can be reached from the A47. Signposted from both. *By rail:* Nearest station is Norwich (**nationalrail.co.uk**). *By bus:* The **X29 bus** runs from Norwich or Fakenham to Lenwade, a 20-minute walk from the park.
- DESCRIPTION AND COMMENTS In this era of holographic 3D imagery and virtual-reality video games, there's something delightfully retro about Dinosaur Adventure. At heart, it's just a pretty walk through lush woods populated by life-size dinosaur statues. Of course, the park tarts things up a bit with play areas, a petting zoo, crazy golf and a deer park, but still, it's all low-tech. And fun.

On 100 wooded acres (40 hectares) near Norfolk, the park is unabashedly aimed to the under-12 set. It helps if they like dinosaurs, but even if they don't, they'll probably enjoy a busy day out. Parking is free in a large grassy field, which can get soggy after rain. Neither it nor the park is geared for standard pushchairs, which may get stuck in the mud or gravel walkways.

As you pay admission, make sure to pick up a schedule of activities, demonstrations and talks. Children should also each grab a free park-guide booklet, which contains the **Passport Challenge,** a programme to collect stamps at various stations around the park. If they get all eight, the passport can be redeemed for a medal at the park reception area.

As you enter the park, a central path divides it into halves. On the left side of the main path is **Base Camp,** with shopping, guest information, food services and picnic facilities. A little farther along you'll pass by a new indoor play area, **Dinomite.** Down a bit and on the opposite side of the path is **Jurassic Putt** (a crazy-golf course) and **Raptor Races,** where kids race pedal karts. The main path now enters a wooded area called **Neanderthal Walk,** where Neanderthal family and hunting scenes featuring saber-toothed cats, cave bears, woolly mammoths and the like bracket the path. There are sound effects but no animatronics.

The trail ends in a lower area with another open field with picnic tables. You'll see donkeys and pygmy goats and can catch the seasonal **Deer Safari,** which carries an extra cost (£1.95 adults; £1.50 children). Riding on bench seats in the back of a 2.5-tonne canvas-topped army-style truck, you rumble through a paddock where several species of deer come running to claim snacks from the driver. The whole experience takes about 20–25 minutes, and a running commentary provides information on the animals. On days of high attendance, the truck can pull one or more trams.

Across from this area is a pretty walled area, where the **Secret Animal Garden** has donkeys, goats, turtles, llamas and wallabies. In the right rear of the walled area is the **Animal Encounters Barn.** Here, children can get personal with snakes, bugs, bunnies, guinea pigs, lizards and ferrets according to a daily activities schedule. In addition, there's a sandpit where kids can use shovels and brushes to uncover dinosaur bones. A second barn houses snakes and huge African spurred tortoises. Nearby, metal dinosaur sculptures are on display and for sale as well.

Let's start over back at the park entrance and catalogue the right side of the main path. Here you'll quickly confront the sprawling wooden **Adventure Play Area,** with slides coming from a dinosaur's belly and walls to climb. It's all set in several contiguous open fields, as big as four rugby pitches. Children under age 5 have their own playground, called **Tiny Terrorsaurs.** Don't even try to keep the kids off it, but do set a time limit – you could easily spend an hour here. Behind that, in the woods you'll find **Lost World A-Mazing Adventure** (more of a trail than a maze) and **Assault-o-Saurus,** another play area with a playground-style seated zip-line and an imaginative obstacle course with a climbing wall and a walk across a chain and suspended logs. Even eye-rolling teens who have been dragged along for the day will enjoy this area. Heading farther into the park, you'll find **Arachnophobia,** a fancy name for a web-shaped climbing net, and **Climb-a-Saurus,** a placid-faced hollowed-out dinosaur to explore, with portholes at the top. (Think that's enough dino puns? You ain't seen nothin' yet. The park's slogan proclaims: 'It's Time You Came-N-Saurus!')

Directly across from Climb-a-Saurus is the entrance to the **Dinosaur Trail,** the main attraction. The premise is simple: you're on a *Jurassic Park*-style trek through the wilderness to track *Tyrannosaurus rex*es. As you follow the path, which leads downhill, you'll encounter several of the beasts and other dinosaurs, many imaginatively situated. Your first sighting may just be a glimpse through the trees, and as you approach the creature on the path you'll get different views, as if you were really stalking it. Several of the beasts roar and screech on occasion. Along the way, you'll encounter a wrecked Land Rover, presumably damaged by the marauding dinos. There are also stations with field radios, allowing you to 'check in' with authorities, who are counting on your dino-tracking skills to save the day. Unfortunately, some of the dinosaurs are beginning to look like actual relics from the Cretaceous era, and could use a good scrubbing and a coat of paint. There are signs with information about the dinosaurs, but many of the signs are posted on the far side of a barrier rail and are difficult to read. Still, all in all, it's good fun if you can put yourself in the right mind-set.

Even if you're not big (pun intended) on dinosaurs, you'll savour the natural beauty of the trail. Laid out on a hill and extending to the valley below, it passes through old-growth forest of towering height, graced by fern gardens. We were so struck by the loveliness of the setting that we momentarily forgot the dinosaurs (which is not an easy thing to do).

TOURING TIPS The entrance to the Dinosaur Trail is not well marked. You have to divert to the right from the main path or you'll end up (as we did) at the end of the trail in the valley. You can walk the trail in reverse, of course, but doing so makes the story-line (tracking *T. rex*es) a non-starter. To find the trailhead, turn right across the lawn after passing the Arachnophobia climbing structure. The trailhead is at the edge of the woods, not far from the Climb-a-Saurus.

A limited selection of food is available, with the best served at the **Gardener's Cottage** near the end of the Dinosaur Trail. The park will also let you order a picnic box, either by calling ahead (☎ 01603 876 312) or by ordering at **Dippy's Diner,** near the park entrance. For such a big park we were surprised to find only two loos, neither located in a convenient place and both somewhat hard to find. We can only surmise that there's a lot of peeing going on in the woods.

The park is a sister attraction to Africa Alive and the Banham Zoo; if you have a season pass for the zoo, you get 50% off the admission price.

Fantasy Island ★★★

APPEAL BY AGE	PRESCHOOL ★★★	PRIMARY SCHOOL ★★★★	TEENS ★★★★
YOUNG ADULTS ★★★		OVER 30 ★★★	SENIORS ★

Sea Lane, Ingoldmells, Lincolnshire PE25 1RH
☎ **01754 615 860; fantasyisland.co.uk**

HOURS Daily, 10.30 a.m. to 9–11 p.m. during summer (closes 3–8 p.m. in early and late season). The market closes at 5 p.m.

COST Park entrance is free. Unlimited ride wristbands (bank holidays): £20 adults (£17 peak; £12 off-peak); £15 children under 12 (£11 peak; £6 off-peak). Discount of £1–£2 for online wristband purchases at least 24 hours in advance. Individual rides can be purchased for £1–£3. Also look for discount coupons in regional newspapers and at the tourist information offices in Skegness (☎ 01754 764 821) or Mablethorpe (☎ 01507 472 496).

GETTING THERE *By car:* The park is in Ingoldmells, 5 mi (8 km) north of Skegness. From the A1/M northbound take the junction to Lincoln (A46) towards Skegness (A158). At Skegness, take the A52 towards Mablethorpe and look for signs. Parking can run £6 for the day. Find a car park a few blocks away and the price will be much lower.

The most direct route to Fantasy Island is to turn east on Sea Lane off the A52. The problem is that after about 11 a.m., Sea Lane becomes gridlocked with bumper-to-bumper traffic extending all the way from the beach back to Ingoldmells. To avoid this mess, do the following: if you're coming from north of Ingoldmells, turn east on Anchor Lane and then, near the beach, go right (south) on Roman Bank Road. Roman Bank intersects Sea Lane east of most of the traffic. Go left (east) on Sea Lane a short way to parking garages. If you're coming from south of Ingoldmells, turn right (north) on Roman Bank Road and continue to Sea Lane. Here, turn right to park. Depart the area using the same route, avoiding Sea Lane west of Roman Bank Road. No matter from which direction you arrive, the question of where to park is confusing. There are a number of proprietary parking garages and outdoor car parks. Just choose one.

By rail: From London or Scotland, change at Grantham to connect to the Skegness station, about 3 mi (5 km) from the park (**nationalrail .co.uk**). *By bus:* Several bus routes serve the park from the bus stop adjacent to the Skegness railway station. (Route information: **transport direct.info.**)

DESCRIPTION AND COMMENTS It's rare that a theme park isn't all about rides, but Fantasy Island isn't your typical theme park. Near the English coastal town of Skegness, this is more of a seaside-entertainment free-for-all. Mixed in with some of the most ambitious rides in the country are a daily indoor–outdoor flea market, various bars and a bookmaker. Many of the guests are much more concerned with finding a knock-off Rolex than knocking around on a coaster. It's a park geared to holidaymakers of all persuasions.

Fantasy Island has evolved over the years to accommodate its various constituents with an unlimited-ride wristband scheme. Although you can buy rides by the token, it's more economical to purchase a band, which is really a high-tech device that's read like the Oyster card on the London Tube. All this means that shoppers don't have to pay an entrance fee to browse through the treasures and tat, and you can enjoy the convenience of an unlimited-ride park.

Everybody wins.

Well, sort of. All the shopping means that more people are crowding the park, and it can feel very claustrophobic at times. And the retail offerings aren't all family-friendly, to say the least. For example, along with stuffed toys, crafts and clothing, you can buy anatomically-correct lollipops. It's not the sort of thing you're going to want your toddler carrying around – trust us. The atmosphere is gloriously freewheeling, and it can be a lot of fun if you're in the right mood. But if that doesn't appeal, stay away. All that said, there are some incredible rides here for both thrill-seekers and youngsters, and as long as you avoid the busiest times, you can enjoy the day out.

The layout is like a traditional funfair, with no obvious path through the park. Because there's no admission charge for the park itself, there's no main entrance. Feel free to wander in at any point along Sea Lane. If you stand in Sea Lane facing the park, most of the outdoor rides are on the left (east) side of the park, though a couple of rides, including a headliner coaster, are on the far-right side. Amazingly, one coaster loads above the pavement right in front of the park on Sea Lane. Though there is a park map at **fantasyisland.co.uk/map,** printed maps are not available at the park. Our suggestion is to print the website map and bring it with you. The map, however, makes the layout look deceptively simple and fails to convey the utter confusion of the market; it also fails to show where the entrances and loading areas of the rides are. We spent 15 minutes walking under the track of the Odyssey roller coaster to find the entrance, which is tucked away in a cul-de-sac on the front-west side of the park.

For most theme parks, we advise you to arrive early and experience the more popular rides before the park becomes crowded. At Fantasy Island, however, most rides do not begin operating until demand builds ... whatever time that happens to be. On our visit, we arrived at 10 a.m. and no rides were operating; and as 11 a.m. came and went, still many rides remained closed. One coaster, once up and running, allowed you to board but was not dispatched until 15 minutes later, when enough riders had arrived to warrant a circuit around the track. As this example shows, ride operators exercise a lot of discretion, so you're pretty much at their mercy. On the other hand, operators of non-coaster attractions often reward you with an extra-long ride when business is slow. Bottom line: Try to catch the headliner rides a little while after they open but before queues begin to form. Next, if there are young 'uns in your party, proceed inside the pyramid, where many of the children's rides are located. Although it can get noisy, it's a wonderful way to pass a rainy day at the seaside.

A top priority on your must-ride list should be the **Jubilee Odyssey** (now simply **The Odyssey**), built for the Queen's Golden Jubilee in 2002, although you can bet she's never ridden it. The entrance for the custom steel coaster is outside the main cluster of rides – to the far right as you look at the park map. It resembles a giant abstract steel sculpture, with a red-and-yellow steel track supported by a forest of white beams and braces. The ride stands 190 ft (58 m) tall, making it the country's third tallest coaster. You'll experience five inversions over its nearly 3,000-ft (915-m) length, experiencing nearly 5 g's. The 3-minute ride, which reaches speeds of nearly 70 mph (115 km/h), has been upgraded and improved over the years. The coaster's momentum can be slowed by gusty seaside breezes, and initially the cars would stall along the track. That prompted the park to go back and modify some of the loops, although the ride still closes during windy periods. Royal connection or not, it's certainly no walk in the park, and one of the main reasons to visit.

Then walk east in Sea Lane in front of the park, near the McDonald's, for the **Millennium Roller Coaster.** After a long climb up a 150-ft (46-m) hill, it plunges towards park patrons and goes through three inversions but feels silky-smooth. While you're here, try the nearby **Amazing Confusion,** a spinning Frisbee at the end of a swinging pendulum. If you're seeking more thrills, look for **Volcanic Eruption** (**Volcanic Impact** on the web map) in the southeast corner of the park. Towering at 200 ft (61 m), the space-shot ride won't be hard to miss. It's right next to **The Beast,** a swinging-pendulum ride with spinning gondolas on one end. **Techno Jump,** also called **Jumping Frogs,** has you in a ride vehicle on the end of a long radial arm springing from a central axis. As you rotate around the axis, the ride vehicles also bounce up and down, first going forwards and then backwards, then forwards again, and so on.

Next look for the **Elephant Ride,** a Dumbo-inspired spin, and **Fantasy Flume,** a small, splashy log ride. Now you're next to the kiddie coaster, **Rhombus Rocket,** a neighbour to the more dynamic **Fantasy Mouse,** a spinning wild-mouse coaster that is one of the first rides to build a long queue.

Other outdoor rides in this area include a **carousel** and **dodgems.** If you have youngsters in your party, you should now find your way into the pyramid for an array of indoor child-themed rides. Even those not interested in kiddie rides should check to see if **Dragon Mountain Descent** is open. The water slide has you travelling on two-person rafts through tubes in an open flume on a curvy descent. Count on getting pretty wet.

Others will gravitate towards the gentle **Jellikins Coaster, Mini Dodgems** and **Balloon Ride,** a flat contraption in which you're placed in a basket suspended from the ride's arms, which gently rise and fall to mimic the flight of a hot-air balloon. On **Toucan Tours,** a monorail takes you on a Polynesian-themed ghost train past volcanoes, fountains, gods and, of course, tropical birds. Even more unthreatening is the **Jungle Ride.** You (or more likely your child) sit in a colourful train, motorbike or car for an open-air ghost-train ride past cartoonish African scenery. Maximum height for this ride is 4'7" (1.4 m). The **Magical Seaquarium** offers a dry, relaxing raft ride through whimsical, cartoon-like undersea-themed sets. Also in the pyramidal building, unexpectedly, is a shop that sells electrical convenience vehicles, walkers and a variety of other equipment for the ambulatory disabled.

TOURING TIPS The headliner coasters The Odyssey and Millennium close in windy conditions. If you have your heart set on them, call ahead to check if they're operating. Don't leave belongings like handbags or backpacks on the platform while you're on a ride – they may not be there when you get back. Unlike most theme parks, where you are confined to a specific area, this is not a closed park, and it's possible for members of your party to wander far off. Set a time and place to meet up if you get separated. The area isn't conducive to picnicking, but there

THEME PARKS AND ATTRACTIONS

are plenty of dining options – from kebabs, to Chinese, to pasta, to fish-and-chips, to burgers. Okay, it's not haute cuisine, but this is a seaside holiday park. Try to eat before midday or after 2 p.m., otherwise you may spend 30 minutes in a queue.

Gulliver's Dinosaur and Farm Park ★★★

PRESCHOOL ★★★★★	PRIMARY SCHOOL ★★★★	TEENS ★
YOUNG ADULTS ★	OVER 30 ★★★	SENIORS ★★★

Livingstone Drive, Milton Keynes MK15 0DT
☎ **01925 444 888; gulliverseco-park.org**

HOURS Open April–October. (peak season) 11 a.m.–6 p.m.; (off-peak) 10–11 a.m. to 4 p.m.

COST £8.95 adults and children; children under 2'11"/0.9 m, free; £7.95 seniors citizens 60+; £35 family ticket (4 people). Gulliver's Land is separate from Gulliver's Dinosaur and Farm Park, and entrance is not included in the price, although you can purchase a combination ticket for an extra £3.50 per person. Packages combining hotel and park admission are also available (**gullivers-shortbreaks.co.uk**).

GETTING THERE *By car:* Gulliver's Dinosaur & Farm Park is in Milton Keynes, not far from Junction 14 off the M1, from where it is well signposted. (Follow the signs carefully, as Milton Keynes is notorious for its unfathomable road layout.) It's about 1½ hours from central London, Oxford, Cambridge and Birmingham. Two large car parks provide free parking. *By rail:* The nearest station is Milton Keynes Central, 2.3 mi (3.7 km) from the park. Direct trains run from Euston in London (**nationalrail.co.uk**). *By bus:* Take the **Number 3 bus** from Milton Keynes Central to the Woolstone roundabout. It's a short walk to the park from there. (Route information: **transportdirect.info**.)

DESCRIPTION AND COMMENTS Although you'll find some rides here, this park isn't an excuse to zip about on dinosaur-themed roller coasters. Instead, the Dinosaur and Farm Park is a sincere attempt to educate visitors on ecological themes – reminiscent of what Walt Disney did when he planned the Epcot theme park in Florida, albeit on a much tinier scale. You won't find anything else quite like it in the UK. After all, how many parks celebrate Healthy Eating Week?

But like Epcot, Gulliver's has had to modify its plans over time. The park, next to Gulliver's Land (see next page), opened in 2007 as Gulliver's Eco-Park, with special areas devoted to Evolution, Land and Water. It proved a bit too high-concept for Gulliver's young demographic, though, and within two years the property changed its name to Gulliver's Dinosaur and Farm Park. You'll find many of the same attractions from the original park, though, with an emphasis on nature and natural history. A farm shop sells organic goods, and the restaurant has an emphasis on healthy food. Kids can even learn to cook. The park is just a short walk on a gravel path from the main theme park. You enter through a circular plaza decorated with stone-and-wood buildings and cooled with a natural climate-control system. The park is arranged linearly, with a path on the right connecting the major areas, although it's possible to move seamlessly between them as well. Start your visit in **Dinosaur Park,** populated with replicas of more than 30 dinosaurs and prehistoric figures. You can see many of the creatures on **Lost World Tours,** a floating trip through a not-too-scary Jurassic landscape. In keeping with the eco theme, the ride is solar-powered. Next find your way to the **Exploration Digs** area, where you can unearth and identify replica dinosaur bones. Finally, pretend you're burning up fossil fuels on the **Dinosaur Carts** driving ride, and work your way across a treetop walkway to spot even more prehistoric creatures. There's also a dinosaur simulator, a crafts pavilion and a play area. Now it's time to zoom 65 million years through time to the present. The next area, **The Farm Yard & Barn,** mixes cute but expected attractions, such as the **Big Green Tractor Ride,** with surprising offerings such as the **Farm House Cookery School.** Don't expect your kids to emerge having mastered cordon bleu, but they will get to see how cakes, pizza and soups are made. If that doesn't thrill your youngster, perhaps insects will. In **Bug City,** they can see tarantulas, stick insects and giant snails. Finally, don't miss **Gully's Musical Farm,** where you press buttons and start animal models singing 'Old MacDonald'. It may be a cacophony to adults, but to the ones pushing the buttons it's apparently great fun. Proceeding clockwise takes you to **Farmer Gully's Crops.** The highlight here is harvesting in the **Giant Vegetable Patch.** You take a menu and then dig in the soil to find the required ingredients. You'll also find singing vegetables, and you can plant crops in the **Poly Tunnel.** Then work your way to the **Farmer Gully's Animals** area, where you'll see real animals, including chickens, cows, goats, horses, pigs, sheep and even reindeer. In the **Cuddle Corner,** you can pet fluffy ones, such as bunnies and guinea pigs. And you can milk virtual ones in a **Milking Challenge.**

TOURING TIPS Ask for a schedule when you arrive, so you won't miss feeding times and other special programmes. Don't overlook package admission deals that include the theme park and the Splash Zone water park. If you're planning on making an overnight of it, check out the hotel–park admission packages available through **gullivers-shortbreaks.co.uk.**

Gulliver's Land ★★★

| APPEAL BY AGE | PRESCHOOL ★★★★★ | PRIMARY SCHOOL ★★★★ | TEENS ★ |
| YOUNG ADULTS ★ | | OVER 30 ★ | SENIORS ★ |

Livingstone Drive, Milton Keynes MK15 0DT
☎ **01925 444 888; gulliversfun.co.uk**

HOURS (Ticket booths open at 10 a.m.) 10.30 a.m. to 4.30–5.30 p.m., with special holiday hours. Open for school holidays in February, late March–early November and late November–December.

COST £14.75 adults and children; children under 2'11"/0.9 m, free; £13.75 senior citizens 60+; £57 family (4 people). Discounts for online purchases. Be aware that a nearby sister park, Gulliver's Dinosaur and Farm

Park, is separate from Gulliver's Land, and entrance is not included in the price, although you can purchase a combination ticket for an extra £3.50 per person. Wheelchairs are available for a £5 refundable deposit, and pushchairs are available for the same deposit and a further £2 per half day. Packages combining hotel and park admission are available (**gullivers-shortbreaks.co.uk**).

GETTING THERE *By car:* Gulliver's Land is in Milton Keynes, not far from Junction 14 off the M1. (Follow the signs carefully, as Milton Keynes is notorious for its unfathomable road layout.) It's about 1½ hours from central London, Oxford, Cambridge and Birmingham. Two large car parks provide free parking. *By rail:* The nearest station is Milton Keynes Central, 2.3 mi (3.7 km) from the park. Direct trains run from Euston in London (**nationalrail.co.uk**). *By bus:* Take the **Number 3 bus** from Milton Keynes Central to the Woolstone roundabout. It's a short walk to the park from there. (Route information: **transportdirect.info.**)

DESCRIPTION AND COMMENTS Like all the Gulliver's parks, the Milton Keynes version targets 3- to 12-year-olds. Teenagers unaccompanied by parents aren't allowed. And adults shouldn't dream of trying to show up without a child in tow, as we did one summer morning. You won't be allowed to buy a ticket.

Gulliver's Land opened in 1999 and is looking somewhat worn. Given the weather in England, it's not easy to keep a theme park looking smart, but fresh paint must be pretty far down on the priority list. That's not to say the park has been resting on its laurels. In 2010 it opened a water park and a camping/caravan site. That followed on the heels of Gully Town, a charming miniature village designed to let kids do things they'll probably hate as adults, such as buying groceries and mending a car.

Parking is free, and once inside the gates, children are immersed in a magical land populated by familiar characters such as Dora the Explorer and the park's own mascots, the Gully Gang. (The park pays licensing fees, and their presence is not assured for the long run. If they're important to your children, call ahead to make sure they're on duty.) Adults, by contrast, find a fairly drab-looking theme park with little of interest to anyone over the age of 12. But hey, you're there for the kids, right? Parents don't have the option of touring passively while the children spin. On many rides, an adult must accompany any child under 3'11" (1.2 m). Other rides require accompaniment for youngsters under 2'11" (0.9 m) or under 4'7" (1.4 m). And yet others exclude anyone over 4'11" (1.5 m). Bottom line: you'll have to check out each ride's requirements (and be ready to squeeze your bum into something about the size of your teenage knickers).

But remember, this park is not designed for you. Still, management understands that it needs to keep parents content. With about 50% of its attractions under cover, it is a good all-weather park, and there's more healthy food to be had here than at most parks. You get a free drink and salad with every main course, and options include sausage and mash, pasta and meatballs, and lasagne – all priced at £7.50 for adults and £5 for kids. At the Castle Food Court, things loosen up a bit, with pizza, jacket potatoes, burgers and hot dogs, ice-cream and fish-and-chips. Several snack bars are also dotted about the property.

Although the park offers more than 60 attractions, the property is quite small and can be easily navigated on foot. Given the size, you could walk the whole thing in about 20 minutes, so getting around is not a problem. However, a little train can be caught from Main Street Station, near the park entrance, with three stops dotted around the park where you can alight. However, you must tell the driver before you set off if you would like to be dropped off – the train does not stop automatically.

Walking into the park, the first area you encounter, **Main Street,** has a traditional carousel, a soft-play area for children under 5 and a theatre. At the end of each day, the park's mascots sing and dance in a farewell show here and pose for pictures before bidding you goodbye. Head to the left for **Lilliput Land,** where you'll find **Gulliver's Giant Tea Cups,** a familiar funfair ride with spinning cups. Several other spinning rides are here, and the fun **Cycle Monorail** has you pedal your way around a track. Unless you've got an energetic (and long-legged) child, you'll probably do most of the work. Closed-toe shoes are required, so dress accordingly. Also look for the **Amazing Journeys of Gulliver,** a gentle, Egyptian-themed simulator ride.

Cutting back to the centre of the park brings you to **Lilliput Land Castle,** home to a restaurant and several attractions. Here's where the park caters to princesses – with a princess-themed play area. But everyone (of a certain age) seems to like the interactive **Enchanted Forest,** where you press a button and trees tell stories. The gentle **Gulliver's Travels ghost train** tells the familiar tale, with some worn-out animated models. Finally, there's a small balloon-themed Ferris wheel. Older kids will flock to **Adventure Land,** located to the upper left of the castle. This is the biggest area in the park and has the most 'thrill' rides. Here you'll find **The Python,** a twisting steel roller coaster, which reaches a surprising 25 mph (40 km/h); the not-too-scary **Free Fall**; **Tree Tops Swing** (a flying carousel); a maze made of hedges; a ball pit and a tame **Jungle River Ride.** The **Flying Carpet** is a kiddie-scaled pendulum ride, and the **Monkey Climb** lets kids expend a bit of energy themselves.

At the top of the park, you'll find **Gully Town,** an imaginative indoor interactive experience. Kids get a kick out of shopping, cooking and performing on stage. There are also workbenches, a post office, and more soft-play and ball-pit areas. The town is sized for children and will keep some of them busy for hours. Continuing clockwise, in the top right-hand corner of the park, you'll find the **Junior Discovery Cove** with the **Junior Drop Tower,** as well as a spinning ride in vehicles shaped like boots. There's also a giant sand pit for digging and an Old West town for exploring.

Next you'll come to **Discovery Bay,** the park's second-largest area, where you'll find some more thrill(ish) rides such as the **Runaway Train,** a small steel coaster. Riders climb to 13 ft (4 m) and zoom around the track, narrowly missing obstacles. Normally riders get two or three laps. You'll also find a log flume ride, guaranteed to soak you. The popular **Silver Mine** is a short (well under a minute) but fun ghost train, allowing you to shoot at targets – a hit activates an animatronic character. The **Hard Luck Bear Jamboree** is a knock-off of Disney's *Country Bear Jamboree*. The animatronics, especially the arm and body movements of the bears, are stiff and jerky, but the show is upbeat, with some tunes that will stick in your head all day.

Finally, work your way down to **Toy Land,** just to the right of the entrance. Along with dodgems, miniature golf and a house of mirrors, you'll find rides such as the **Cheese Factory**. This indoor wild-mouse-style roller coaster is supposed to be in the dark, but there's enough lighting to keep things from getting too scary. You'll also find face painting and **The Tug Boat,** a mini–swinging pirate ship. **Diggers** has child-scaled backhoes that dig up balls from a pit, drop them and repeat. It's a children's attraction that, more times than not, dads will hijack.

TOURING TIPS When you first arrive, take a tour on the train that skirts the park, giving you a good idea of the layout and what's on offer. Rides stop half an hour before closing time, allowing you to watch the goodbye show in the Main Street area. If you're planning on making an overnight of it, check out the hotel–park admission packages available through **gullivers-shortbreaks.co.uk**.

Imperial War Museum Duxford ★★★★★

APPEAL BY AGE	PRESCHOOL ★★	PRIMARY SCHOOL ★★★½	TEENS ★★★★
YOUNG ADULTS ★★★★		OVER 30 ★★★★	SENIORS ★★★★½

Duxfield Airfield, Duxford, Cambridgeshire CB22 4QR
☎ **01223 835 000; duxford.iwm.org.uk**

HOURS 10 a.m.–6 p.m. (until 4 p.m. off-season). Last admission 1 hour before closing. Closed 24–26 December.

COST (Mid-March–October) £16.50 adults; children under 16, free; £13.20 students and senior citizens 60+; £8.25 unemployed (with proof of entitlement); £9.90 disabled (proof required; 1 carer per disabled visitor free). (off-season) £14.50 adults; children under 16, free; £11.60 students and senior citizens 60+; £7.25 unemployed (with proof of entitlement); £8.70 disabled (proof required; 1 carer per disabled visitor free). Tickets can also be bought through the Tesco Clubcard rewards scheme, except during air shows and special events.

GETTING THERE *By car:* Just south of Cambridge at Junction 10 of the M11. *By rail:* Stations at Cambridge, Royston or, closest, Whittlesford Park. (**nationalrail.co.uk**). *By bus:* **Stagecoach Cambridge City 7 bus** operates from Cambridge city centre (Emmanuel Street, bus stop E1) to the museum via Cambridge train station and Addenbrooke's Hospital. (Route information: **transportdirect.info**.)

DESCRIPTION AND COMMENTS You might think Heathrow is the centre of all aviation in Britain, but it's really nothing compared to Duxford. Sure, you can catch a nonstop to Abu Dhabi from the international airport, but at Duxford you can step aboard a Concorde, gasp at a B-52 Stratofortress with a wingspan of 185 ft (56.4 m) or even go flight-seeing in a pre–World War II bomber. Considered Europe's top aviation museum,

Duxford can be a full day out as you work your way through the seven hangars and exhibition buildings and try to take in 200 aircraft, tanks and military vehicles.

Duxford, as it's known, has a working runway and hosts four air shows a year. This can be the best (or worst) time to visit, depending on your interest. Crowds are huge during these shows, and the admission is more expensive. But it's thrilling to watch the spectacle of roaring jets and aerobatic feats. Still, if you visit during an air show, you won't have time to see the entire museum and will need to return to take in the many compelling exhibits.

Even without aircraft, the property itself would be significant – the grounds contain several dozen structures with listed-building status in recognition of their role in UK aviation history. The museum is built on the site of the Duxford Aerodrome, which was developed at the end of World War I and served as a Royal Air Force (RAF) fighter station during World War II. It played a key role during the Battle of Britain and later served as a US Air Force base. Some 30,000 American soldiers lost their lives on missions leaving from Britain, and they're now honoured in Duxford's grand American Air Museum. In 1976 the airfield was turned over to the Imperial War Museum, and it has grown steadily ever since.

The standard advice for visiting any museum is to wear comfortable shoes. It can't be overstated here, because instead of strolling marble hallways, you'll be hiking along a runway and walking through and around cavernous hangars. You'll also need to be prepared for the weather: dress as you would for an airplane-themed day hike. A shuttle bus does run the length of the museum, but there's no escaping a lot of walking. Two of the biggest attractions, AirSpace and Land Warfare, are about 0.6 mi (1 km) apart, at opposite ends of the property. So this is not a site you'll be able to breeze through – if you walk in and think you can knock it off in an hour or two, you're flat crazy.

While Duxford is a big draw for aviation nuts and propeller-heads, interactive and educational exhibits broaden its appeal. **AirSpace** has scientific stations to teach the fundamentals of lift and aeronautics; the **Land Warfare** hall includes walk-through exhibits that put you in the battlefield. There's even a playground to help get the wiggles out.

Arriving at the museum, you pass an idled Comet Tank and replica Hawker Hurricane plane by the car park and pay admission in the glass-walled Visitor Centre, where you'll find **The Mess Restaurant,** one of three eateries on-site. If you haven't already checked online, inquire about visiting hours for the **Concorde.** It's open on a limited schedule, usually from 10 a.m. to 3 or 4 p.m., but it can close as early as 2 p.m. off-season. The plane, Concorde No. 101, was the third built for test purposes. In 1974 it reached Mach 2.23 during the fastest flight of any Concorde to that date. The jet is inside the AirSpace building, directly to the left of the Visitor Centre. The museum's other don't-miss site is the Land Warfare Museum. In between, you'll want to visit **Hangar 2,** featuring British and American fighters from World War II; **Hangar 4,** with the Battle of Britain exhibit; and the **American Air Museum.**

While **Hangars 3 and 5** are worthwhile, they're not as compelling as the other sites.

The huge AirSpace building is a tribute to UK aviation history, with 30 historical British and Commonwealth aircraft. Opened in 2008 after it was redeveloped from the museum's unheated Superhangar, it contains 129,167 sq ft (12,000 m²) of floor space. Here you'll see military aircraft such as the **Avro Vulcan,** one of Britain's nuclear bombers, and the World War II–era **Short Sunderland,** a so-called flying boat which had on-board bunks, galley and workshop and was equipped with 14 machine guns. Other sights include the **Avro Lancaster,** the RAF's heavy bomber during World War II, and the **de Havilland Mosquito,** Britain's fastest and most versatile bomber during the conflict. AirSpace also has interactive science exhibits and the **Airborne Assault Museum,** honouring the Parachute Regiment and Airborne Forces, which served in Africa, Sicily, Normandy and Arnhem and, more recently, the Falklands, Kosovo, the Persian Gulf and Afghanistan. Exhibits include period films and displays showing jeeps and other heavy equipment as if being dropped from the sky. Another exhibit, the **Medal Display,** shows honours won in combat, including the Victoria Cross and the George Cross.

Once you've hit the highlights, head outside and continue to the next building. On the way you'll pass a playground – worth a stop if the weather's nice. In Hangar 2 you'll find a concentration of British and US craft that saw service during World War II, all of which still fly and are deployed during museum air shows. You can also watch mechanics working on and restoring planes in an open shop.

Continuing down the runway, you'll pass Hangar 3, which features maritime exhibits and a miniature submarine. Hangar 4 has the **Battle of Britain** exhibit. This was the actual site where air operations were conducted during Britain's 'finest hour' in 1940–41. Displays recount the heroism and terror of the bombings and blitz. Artefacts include a blackout clock and an **Anderson Bomb Shelter,** allowing you to see how British civilians hunkered down in back gardens during bombing raids. Aircraft displayed include a **Germany Messerschmitt Bf 109,** which crashed in a Sussex field in 1940. With the RAF battling back the attackers, a full-scale German invasion was prevented. As Prime Minister Winston Churchill said of the aircrews at the time, 'Never in the field of human conflict was so much owed by so many to so few.'

Hangar 5 has aircraft-conservation workshops, where you can watch workers painstakingly bring vintage aircraft back to life. Then comes the dramatic American Air Museum, a glass-fronted building with a sloping roof, designed by Sir Norman Foster. The museum was financed by US donors, the Heritage Lottery Fund and, improbably, the government of Saudi Arabia. The hall holds the largest collection of US aircraft outside America. It was literally constructed around the huge **B-52 Stratofortress,** with the building shaped to accommodate the wings. Aircraft here include the Cold War–era **F-4 Phantom.** Make sure to look for the restored **B-24 Liberator,** the most widely-produced US World War II heavy bomber, which saw action in Europe, the Pacific and Asia, and the only **SR-71 Blackbird** displayed outside the United States. The reconnaissance planes were never shot down, as pilots could use their Mach 3.2 speed to easily evade fire.

Finally comes the Land Warfare building, with a collection of tanks, military vehicles and artillery. The must-see here is the **Normandy Experience,** which puts you in the footsteps of combatants on D-Day. During the operation, more than 150,000 soldiers took part in the invasion of northern France, gaining a foothold in Continental Europe and ultimately forcing the Nazis into retreat. You can try to imagine the emotions a soldier might have experienced during the assault by stepping aboard a reconstructed landing craft. And you can try on a loaded pack to see how well you might have shouldered the load. Artefacts on display include an antitank gun, an ambulance, a jeep, a motorcycle, a command tank and a half-track.

The related **Monty** exhibit focuses on Field Marshal Bernard Law Montgomery, who was in charge of all Allied forces on D-Day. The exhibit traces the life and military accomplishments of England's most celebrated commander of the past century. You can see the three vehicles that made up his mobile tactical headquarters, including his bedroom, office and map caravans. Other exhibits focus on the **Forgotten War** in Burma during World War II, as well as scenes from more-recent conflicts in Korea, Northern Ireland, the Falklands and the Persian Gulf, and peacekeeping in Bosnia.

After an immersive experience like that, you may be ready to take flight. Luckily for you, a museum concessionaire, **Classic Wings,** offers trips taking off from Duxford's runway. Prices range from £99 for tours over Madingley and Cambridge in a Dragon Rapide, to £379 for a 20-minute flight in a T6 Harvard, a two-seater dive-bomber that you're able to pilot yourself for a brief moment. Find details at **goliathres.com.**

TOURING TIPS Take your time. Slow down and take it all in. Various food and beverage concessions (among other places) are about halfway between the AirSpace and Land Warfare buildings. This is a good place to take a break in the middle of your tour. If you're footsore, look for the shuttle travelling between exhibit buildings and hangars. If you want to catch an air show or other event (usually about eight each year), realise that you won't be able to see much of the museum. Food and drink aren't allowed inside the hangars, but you'll find picnic tables scattered around the museum grounds. Duxford is a good choice for rainy days, but bring an umbrella for those long hikes between the various buildings.

Pleasure Island Theme Park ★★½

APPEAL BY AGE	PRESCHOOL ★★★	PRIMARY SCHOOL ★★★	TEENS ★★★
YOUNG ADULTS ★★		OVER 30 ★★	SENIORS ★

Kings Road, Cleethorpes, North East Lincolnshire DN35 0PL
☎ 0844 504 0104; pleasure-island.co.uk

THEME PARKS AND ATTRACTIONS 243

- **HOURS** 10.30 a.m.–4 or 5 p.m., depending on time of year (check website for details). During off-season the park may operate rides on a schedule, so you can ride them only at certain times of day. Open daily in July and August and on weekends and some weekdays April–June, also in September and October. Open some days for skating only, late November–23 December.
- **COST** £17.50 adults and children over age 4; £10.50 senior citizens, disabled and carers; £64 family ticket (4 people). Discounts for online purchases. Park brochures offer a £2 per person coupon.
- **GETTING THERE** *By car:* In North East Lincolnshire, between Grimsby and Skegness. The park is signed from the M180/A180. *By rail:* Nearest rail station is Cleethorpes (**nationalrail.co.uk**). *By bus:* Coaches from Lincoln, Hull, Grimsby and Skunthorpe. (Route information: **transportdirect.info**.)
- **DESCRIPTION AND COMMENTS** For years Pleasure Island was the forgotten sibling of Flamingo Land park. Although under the same management, Pleasure Island never got the investment or attention of its affiliate. Things came to a head in 2010, when the park temporarily closed and then re-opened under the management of a separate company headed by one of Flamingo Land's directors. Now it seems to have a new lease of life. There has been substantial investment, especially in new shows, and renewed attention to a park that always had potential.

While small, its ride selection is well thought out, and there were hints of big plans, such as the custom soundtracks that play on a few rides and one of only two Boomerang-model coasters in the UK. So how much you enjoy your visit will really be based on expectations. If you come anticipating Alton Towers, you're going to leave disappointed. But if you figure that it's just a funfair by the sea, you'll be pleasantly surprised.

The park is built on the former Cleethorpes Zoo, so it's quite spacious. It has six loosely-themed areas – **Old England, Morocco, Africa, Spain, Kiddies Kingdom** and **White Knuckle Valley.**

You arrive in a large car park and make your way to the entrance. The park is built around a lake and shaped like a V, and you'll be entering at the bottom point. Once inside, you'll find yourself in **Old England,** which has mainly restaurants, shops and support services. It's also home to the carousel-inspired **Flying Chairs,** a spinning swing ride. Head to the outer edge of Old England towards the lake for **Shrieksville,** a dark ride introduced in 2010, taking the place of a former jungle-themed attraction. Your ride vehicle takes you through six scenes, including a graveyard and a haunted quarry. As spooky as the name and the promotion may appear, it's not too intense, as 7-year-olds are allowed to ride.

Moving on to the Spain section, look for **The Bird Show,** featuring performing parrots. Adults and older teens have probably seen this all before, but it will keep the attention of young visitors. The performances are at 11.30 a.m., 1 p.m. and 2.30 p.m., with an extra show at 4 p.m. on days the park is open until 5 p.m. Before or after the show, head directly across the street to **Tommy Tinkaboo's Sweet Adventure Water Ride.** It's a gentle watercourse where the aim is to amuse children and inspire them to buy sweets in the gift shop at the end – parents, you've been warned. The ride passes glow-in-the-dark characters making candies, priming the pump as it were.

You certainly won't want to be eating sweets before the next ride, the **Gravitron.** You step inside what looks like a flying saucer and arrange yourself against padded panels on the wall. As the ride begins to spin, you're thrust against the wall by centrifugal force. The speed can reach 24 rotations per minute, which creates forces of up to 3 g's. For a less taxing ride, head next door to the **Mini Dodgems.** This section also has a **theatre.** Although productions vary year to year, you can expect plenty of singing and dancing, with some razzmatazz. In 2010 the venue featured a musical revue called *High School Summer*, a fairly-blatant knock-off of Disney's *High School Musical* franchise.

Continuing along the edge of the park, you'll pass regular-sized **dodgems** and the **Galleon,** a swinging pirate ship. That will bring you to **Alakazam!,** a park favourite. It's shaped like a flat Ferris wheel, and you ride lying down on your stomach in a gondola. But as the ride begins to spin, the wheel begins to rise to the vertical. The sensation is something like flying. You might want a bit of a sit-down after that. Luckily, your next stop is the **Sea Lion Show** stadium, where performances are held at 12.15, 1.45 and 3.45 p.m., with an extra 4.40 p.m. show on days the park is open until 5 p.m.

Working your way back towards the lake, you'll come to the 130-ft (40-m) **Hydromax,** a pendulum ride that's the tallest in the park. It's essentially a propeller, with you and three others sitting in a pod at the end of the blade. The ride spins at 47 mph (75 km/h) at a g-force of 4.1. Nearby is **Hyper Blaster,** an 89-ft (27-m) drop tower that will subject you to 3 g's when you're shot up to the sky. If all that sounds a bit much, you might prefer to watch the action from the **Lake Boats,** cute swan-shaped pedal craft in which you can ride around on the water.

As you walk along the far side of the park (the open side of the V), you enter **Kiddie Cove,** a play area for children aged 2–7. They'll find opportunities for climbing, sliding, crawling and balancing on a pendulum swing. There are also sit-in spring autos, a climbing net and a giant slide. In the ride department there are several children's rides, as well as **Astra Slide,** a tall, camel-hump dry slide that you descend in a burlap bag.

Crossing a small bridge brings you to the other wing of the park, and the menacing-looking **Terror Rack.** The flying-carpet-type ride has you seated in a gondola that's connected to two pendulum arms. As the arms rotate, the gondola swings in circles and spins. You'll get only a blurry glimpse of the Lincolnshire countryside as it cycles through its motions. This leads to the park's headline coaster, **Boomerang.** After you're seated, the ride vehicle is pulled to the top of the steel track and then released, sending you flying back through the loading station, into a roll and then a loop. The ride climbs a hill, and then you go through the same process backwards.

For a breather, head over to **Paratower.** You load into a gondola for a pleasant ride up and a gentle glide down. It feels like an open-air lift, but the views are nice, as is the breeze. The ride doesn't operate in windy or inclement weather, though. You'll find more thrills on **Pendulus,** which simultaneously spins and swings. You're strapped inside a giant disc suspended at the end of a pendulum. The swinging arm eventually rises to a 90° angle as you spin around. Gentler rides include the giant **Clown Slide,** a small **monorail** and a **carousel.** There are also **go-karts** and a **train** that circles the entire section of the park. In 2010 the park also unveiled an **ice-skating rink.** Double-edge skates are available for those who aren't quite ready for the Olympics' freestyle competitions.

Your ride won't be quite as graceful on the **Obliterator,** another swinging, spinning pendulum ride. This time you face out, and the pendulum does a complete 360, leaving you spinning upside-down 100 ft (31 m) off the ground. It's programmed with multiple combinations, so it's unlikely that any two rides will be the same. Heading back towards the entrance brings you to the park's last performance space. Keeping to the Africa theme, the park has featured an **African acrobatic team** here in the past, and you're likely to encounter something similar.

TOURING TIPS Though Pleasure Island touts its 'white knuckle rides', we like it primarily as a 12-and-under park. The whole family will enjoy the shows and rides such as Tommy Tinkaboo's Sweet Adventure. Tots and tweens have lots from which to choose too. If the thrill rides beckon, experience Obliterator, Boomerang, Terror Rack, Alakazam!, Hydromax, and Hyper Blaster, in that order, as soon as the park opens. If one or another of the rides isn't online when you show up, experience the closest ride to it and circle back later. After you've had your fill of rides, plan the rest of the day around the various shows. The sea-lion and bird shows are both winners, but for incredible athleticism and fast-paced action, the African acrobatic show is hands-down the best live entertainment in the park.

Make sure to ask if rides will be open all day, and if not, request a schedule. The park tries to cut costs during slow periods by running rides only at certain periods. On the plus side, the queuing and operation seem to be more efficient during these limited-run periods. Also pick up a show schedule when you enter. Although the programming changes from year to year, the entertainment value is good enough to make it worth your while.

Pleasurewood Hills ★★½

APPEAL BY AGE	PRESCHOOL ★★★	PRIMARY SCHOOL ★★★	TEENS ★★★★
YOUNG ADULTS ★★★		OVER 30 ★★	SENIORS ★

Leisure Way, Corton, Lowestoft, Suffolk NR32 5DZ
☎ **01502 586 000; pleasurewoodhills.com**

HOURS (April–early July and most of September) 10 a.m.–5 p.m. Closes at 6 p.m. early July–early September; 4 p.m. in October. Open daily in July and August, and on weekends and some weekdays other months. Check website for details.

COST £16.50 adults; £14.50 children (aged 3–11); £10.50 senior citizens, carers and special needs. Discount for online purchases. Family tickets for 4–9 guests can be purchased online only. Tickets can also be bought through the Tesco Clubcard rewards scheme.

GETTING THERE *By car:* Just off the A12 between Lowestoft and Great Yarmouth. Signage to the park is fine from the A12 but very poor from all other points. Print detailed directions to the park from Google Maps or MapQuest before heading out. *By rail:* The closest station is Lowestoft (**nationalrail.co.uk**). *By bus:* **First Bus Routes X1** and **1A** serve the park from Great Yarmouth and Lowestoft (**firstgroup.com**). (Route information: **transportdirect.info.**).

DESCRIPTION AND COMMENTS Although not on most park fans' thrill-seeking radar, Pleasurewood Hills has quietly gone about the business of entertaining visitors to the English east coast since 1982. Catering to Suffolk seaside holidaymakers and a dedicated regional audience, it offers a few dynamic rides, three shows and some nice attractions geared for younger visitors.

Although it faced financial challenges in the 1990s, the park seems to be pottering along quite nicely now. It's been freshening up rides and play areas for its youngest visitors. Its mascot, a cuddly teddy in a sailor suit named Woody Bear, can often be seen roaming the park, giving hugs. All in all, Pleasurewood offers a day of diversions, largely free of big-park hassles.

The 59-ac (24-ha) park is in a nicely-wooded area near the coast, with ample parking. As you enter, check the times for the parrot, sea-lion and circus shows. All are well done and worth planning your day around. When you pass through the gates, you'll find yourself in a central plaza facing an exquisite **vintage carousel.** If anyone in your party is under age 5, this will likely be your first stop. You can also hop on the **Pleasurewood Express** train, which stops at several stations as it circles the park, although we suggest you wait until later in the day and first head to the rides before queues start to build.

On that note, thrill-seekers will want to turn left for the first of what's likely to be several runs on the park's headliner ride, **Wipeout.** The boomerang steel coaster stands 117 ft (36 m) tall and goes through three inversions, reaching almost 50 mph (80 km/h) and subjecting riders to more than 5 g's. Then it does it all backwards. It's surprisingly smooth, and a contender for best coaster in east England.

Although thrill-seekers can skip the detour, if you have pre-teens in tow, you can take a slow chairlift across a small lake or alternatively walk to the back corner behind the entrance to **Snake in the Grass,** a steel family coaster that's been around since the 1980s. You're taken up a 26-ft (8-m) lift hill inside a mountain, and then you descend through two figure of eights outside, covering 1,180 ft (400 m) before it's all over. The top speed of 22 mph (35 km/h) makes it perfect for those new to coasters. Older children will like a spin on **Dodgy Dodgems** before heading back towards the entrance plaza.

Others will want to cut back across the entrance area to **Shiver M' Timbers,** a swinging pirate ship that's the oldest ride in the park, dating to 1985. Then head to **Enigma,** a 1,968-ft (600-m) steel coaster featuring tight-banking turns but no inversions, and reaching 34 mph (55 km/h). It's also one of the slowest-loading coasters on the planet, meaning you can spend some very serious queue time here. Enigma is a runaway mine train with not so much as a shred of theming. But it's a smooth ride until the end: brace yourself for an abrupt stop.

Nearby is **Thunderstruck,** an unusual spinning ride that starts flat and then elevates to resemble a giant three-bladed windmill, with a cluster of ride vehicles at the end of each blade (it reminded Bob of an electric shaver). You're seated in a small 'thunder pod' that spins like a pinwheel while the ride itself spins. If you're getting dizzy reading this, imagine what riding it is like.

Perhaps the adjacent **Adventure Play** area is more your speed. The 23,600-sq-ft (2,200-m²) playground includes slides, tunnels, bridges, climbing ladders and monkey bars but lacks the thematic creativity so common to play areas in most UK parks. Nevertheless, Adventure Play is popular and can get crowded midday.

Before moving farther into the park, cut back to the left to **Tales of the Coast,** a 3D boat ride. About half of the tranquil float experience is outdoors, with not much to look at, but the other half through 'underground caverns' features Black Shuck, 'a savage dog the size of a calf' who menaces you in 3D. If, after the grisly creatures in the Harry Potter films, a dog the size of a calf doesn't sound too intimidating, it's because he isn't. Even so, Black Shuck is bad enough that you need to think twice before taking preschoolers on this ride. The story-line is a little convoluted, but the novelty of taking a moving ride wearing 3D glasses trumps all.

Then head to **Timber Falls,** a flume ride that's a park favourite. A chainsaw buzzes in the background, but that's pretty much the extent of the theming. The ride starts with a small initial drop and a steep final hill that ends with a splash. Perhaps it's unintentional, but you're now right next to the **Sea Lion Stadium,** where a 30-minute show provides plenty of splashing of its own. Show times are 12.15 and 3.15 p.m., with an extra 5.15 p.m. performance on days the park closes at 6 p.m. Now head to **Wizzy Dizzy,** a ride with a name that offers truth in advertising. It's a spinning pendulum ride that will subject you to nearly 5 g's. If you're still wet from Timber Falls, you'll likely be spun dry by the time the ride ends. Next you'll find yourself in the park's maritime-themed **Main Street** area, with restaurants, shops and services. It's close to **Le Mans,** a go-kart ride that carries an extra £3 charge.

In the far corner of the park you'll find **Kite Flyer,** a flat spinning ride that can offer an unfamiliar sensation to park-goers: relaxation. You climb into a vehicle and lie down on your stomach, like a hang-glider. As the ride rotates, the sensation is more a gentle rocking than an intense spin.

Working your way down the far side of the park brings you to **Wave Breaker,** a water slide that proves that simple is sometimes best. You load two to a raft and zoom down a double-dip slide, leaving, it may feel, your stomach somewhere behind you. Nearby, **Kidzone** is a soft-play area that charges extra admission. Working your way back around the far side of the park brings you past **Sky Hooks,** a flying swing ride, and then down to the **Circus and Street Art Show,** an unexpected treat. The programme changes from year to year but includes international performers in a condensed circus with a ringmaster, acrobatics, break-dancers and a BMX rider doing tricks. Show time is 2 p.m., with a second 3.45 performance on days the park closes at 6 p.m. Cutting back to the centre of the park brings you to the **Parrot Show,** another perennial favourite that will keep even jaded teens entertained. Show times are 11.15 a.m., 1.15 p.m. and 4.15 p.m.

TOURING TIPS If you have a choice, visit Pleasurewood Hills on a weekday, when crowds are smaller. Almost all rides have low hourly capacities, resulting in long queues. Whenever you go, especially if you like the thrill rides, arrive before opening and be among the first to enter the park. Hit the rides in this order:

1. Wipeout
2. Enigma
3. Thunderstruck
4. Wizzy Dizzy
5. Timber Falls
6. Shiver M' Timbers
7. Tales of the Coast
8. Snake in the Grass

The numerous children's and family rides are mostly low-capacity and slow-loading. If you want to experience the thrill rides, get them in the rear-view mirror before starting in on the rides for the younger set. Alternatively, split the group, with someone accompanying the children to the kiddie and family rides while the rest of the group tackles the thrill rides. If you're primarily invested in showing the 8-and-unders a good time, head first for the Snake in the Grass corner of the park and then work your way up the left side of the property to the top of the park.

The shows at Pleasurewood Hills absorb a surprising percentage of the crowd, so the best time to hit the rides is first thing after park opening or when a show is in progress. Conversely, when a show concludes, the exiting crowd will inundate nearby attractions. If you bump into this, your best bet is to head for another area of the park. The way the performances are scheduled allows you to see the shows in sequence, with just enough time to walk from one show venue to another.

Food selection is fairly limited. Your best bet is to bring a picnic. But for a guilty pleasure, visit **Woody's Candy Cabin,** with a wide variety of sweets. If you overindulge, note that Pleasurewood Hills would be our pick of all UK theme parks for someone with a dodgy stomach – you won't believe how many WCs there are.

Sea Life Great Yarmouth ★★½

APPEAL BY AGE	PRESCHOOL ★★★★	PRIMARY SCHOOL ★★★	TEENS ★★
YOUNG ADULTS ★★		OVER 30 ★★★	SENIORS ★★★

Marine Parade, Great Yarmouth, Norfolk NR30 3AH
☎ **01493 330 631; visitsealife.com/great-yarmouth**

HOURS Monday–Thursday, 10 a.m.–3 p.m.; Saturday–Sunday, 10 a.m.–4 p.m. Last entry 1 hour before closing. Closed Christmas Day.
COST £13.95 adults; £10 children aged 3–14; £12 senior citizens and students; £40 family ticket (2 adults, 2 children). Discounts for online purchases. Combination tickets including admission to Hunstanton Sea Life Sanctuary (not covered in this guide), about 80 mi (130 km) away,

cost an additional £4–£5. Admission can also be bought through the Tesco Clubcard rewards scheme.

GETTING THERE *By car:* Follow the A47 from Norwich into Great Yarmouth, then follow the brown tourist signs to Sea Life; or follow the A12 from Lowestoft into Great Yarmouth and then follow the brown tourist signs. Pay-and-display parking is available on Marine Parade and at the seafront car parks. *By rail:* The nearest rail station is Great Yarmouth (**nationalrail.co.uk**). Follow signs to the seafront, and you'll find the aquarium situated next to Wellington Pier. *By bus:* **National Express** and **First Bus** offer service to the area (☎ 01493 846 346). (Route information: **transportdirect.info**.)

DESCRIPTION AND COMMENTS African dwarf crocodiles and a colony of Humboldt penguins help set this site apart from the other Sea Life centres. You'll also find something perhaps just as rare: a performing-shark show. The staff have trained four of the predators to respond to unique coloured sign boards and collect food on demand, which is demonstrated during the popular shark feeds. Also unique is Winkle, a 6.6-lb (3-kg) lobster caught 5 mi (8 km) off-shore, and donated by the fisherman who caught it. The creature is 18" (45 cm) long and is believed to be at least 20 years old.

TOURING TIPS Generally representative of all Sea Life Aquariums, this version is one of many tourist attractions along the colourful Great Yarmouth beachfront. Check it out on an inclement day.

(For more on aquariums, see page 10.)

Thrigby Hall Wildlife Gardens ★★★½

| APPEAL BY AGE | PRESCHOOL ★★★ | PRIMARY SCHOOL ★★★★ | TEENS ★★★ |
| YOUNG ADULTS ★★★ | | OVER 30 ★★★ | SENIORS ★★★ |

Filby Road, Thrigby, Great Yarmouth, Norfolk NR29 3DR
☎ **01493 369 477; thrigbyhall.co.uk**

HOURS 10 a.m.–5 p.m. (until 6 p.m. during summer)
COST £9.50 adults; £7.50 children (aged 4–14); £8.50 senior citizens. A coupon on the website gives a 50p discount apiece for up to 6 people.
GETTING THERE *By car:* Located 8 mi (13 km) outside Great Yarmouth, south of the village of Filby. Follow the brown road signs from the A47 at Acle, or from the A149 at Caister-on-Sea. *By rail:* Closest stations are Great Yarmouth and Acle (**nationalrail.co.uk**). *By bus:* Service from Acle and Great Yarmouth. (Route information: **transportdirect.info**.)
DESCRIPTION AND COMMENTS Nearly three centuries ago, when nobleman Joshua Smith, Esquire, built his estate near Great Yarmouth, few if any Englishmen had ever heard of pandas and pythons, let alone seen them. Now they're on display at this historical home and garden, where the combination of exotic animals and landscaped country estate works surprisingly well together. Although the property is relatively small, it makes for a pleasant day out amid beautiful surroundings. And it offers unexpected thrills, allowing you to get surprisingly close to dangerous creatures.

Smith built **Thrigby Hall** in 1736, though it's believed that Thomas Ivory, who designed the Norwich Assembly Rooms, was the architect of the home and the Summer House. Make sure to study the building as you walk past. But you'll also be walking through history as you tour. The grounds were laid out in the style of King William III, with a dramatic avenue of yews. Later landscapers created the famed **Willow Pattern Garden,** basing the design on the Chinese scenes depicted on the iconic blue china created by English artist Thomas Turner in the late eighteenth century. The garden brings the ceramic scene to life, with plants, water and a bridge, and is home to cranes and other waterfowl. The property served the family for 150 years until then-owner Squire Daniels remodelled the hall in 1876. A century later, in 1979, Ken Sims, a former Malaya rubber-planter, poisonous-snake farmer and crocodile keeper, opened it to the public as a wildlife park, with the goal of preserving endangered species, particularly those from Asia.

As you enter the property, you'll find parking an informal affair on dirt and grass. But if you're travelling with a wheelchair or pushchair, don't worry. The gardens themselves are well laid-out, with paved paths making it easy to tour. Make sure to pick up a park map, as it outlines a suggested route taking in all the sights. Also check on feeding times. In summer, feeding usually begins with leopards at 2.30 p.m., followed by tigers at 3, monkeys at 3.30 and otters at 4. If the weather is hot enough to keep them active, the crocodiles are fed at 3.30.

Thrigby Hall is the most straightforward to navigate of all the UK's zoological parks. After paying admission, turn right down the stately **Yew Avenue.** Your first stop will be the extremely-rare **Amur leopard.** Walk up the adjacent stairs for a good view. The feline is native to the Amur-Ussuri region that links Russia, China and Korea, and there may be less than three dozen of these creatures left in the wild. Next pass the tiny **Summer House,** which looks out at the **red pandas.** The exhibit is slightly below ground, giving you a good perch from which to watch them. See if you can detect their nimble fingers, used to grasp bamboo and snare the unsuspecting mouse that may cross its path. Next come the **gibbons,** tailless lesser apes, followed by the **monkeys.** You can see both by walking up a ramp which leads to walkways that circle and go over the enclosures, providing more good views. One particular gibbon enjoys performing, but only if you're watching. He'll tap or gesture to get your attention – when he's sure he's got you, he launches into his acrobatic routine. Just off the path are the **Asian small-clawed otters,** which can be easily watched zipping through the water as their enclosure is at eye level. They're natural entertainers and will keep you amused with their antics.

That leads to the interconnected 2-storey **Swamp and Forest Houses,** real park highlights. Both are well executed, but there's not much differentiation, with the Forest House being about as swampy as the Swamp House. The huge habitats are kept at tropical temperatures, which means the cold-blooded saltwater and marsh **crocodiles** and **American alligators** are more likely to be active. For humans, it quickly becomes uncomfortably hot and humid during the summer, but it can be a real delight on a chilly day. You can get distressingly close to the crocs by crossing over their pond on a bridge surrounded by double wire fencing, while you're separated from the alligators only by a short glass wall that's easy to peer over. There are also reticulated and Burmese **pythons,** and other, less menacing reptiles.

Pass by the café, toilets and gift shop, and Thrigby Hall itself, which is topped by a huge stork's nest. Then make your way past the Pool Garden to the **babirusas,** Indonesian pigs. The males have large swooping tusks and, like kangaroos, they 'box' for dominance.

Continue on the main path to the **Tiger Tree Walk and Tunnel,** another park highlight. You're given three ways to see the tigers, all worthwhile if you're brave enough. The most thrilling is the walk. You climb up to a bridge, which is a narrow elevated walkway. You're not in danger of falling, though, because walls, which again are double-fenced, come up like a V on each side of the walk, protecting you from the felines. The route feels precarious as you work your way directly over the enclosure, where you can watch the tigers at play or sleep. You can also walk up a ramp, which will take you only inches from a log where the tigers often sunbathe. It's the closest you'll probably ever get to a man-eating mammal – at least we hope. Finally you can see them from ground level through glass. One section of glass pane is shaded blue, meant to mimic how a deer sees the world, illustrating how easily the ruminants can miss seeing the tigers. From a deer's perspective, the carnivores are largely camouflaged and aren't spotted until it's too late.

The **Walk-Through Aviary,** by contrast, is much less menacing but still entertaining. You'll see a variety of songbirds, including magpie robins and fairy bluebirds. These are frugivores (a great crossword-puzzle word meaning 'fruit eaters'). There are also Java sparrows, or rice birds, a species once considered a pest and now threatened. Heading back towards the entrance, you'll pass the mediaeval **St Mary's Parish Church,** surrounded by an ancient country graveyard. Virtually abandoned, it holds just one service per year. Take a close look at the heads carved into the fourteenth-century doorway. The tower has the remains of an oven in its base, where communion bread may have been baked. Finally, proceed to the Willow Pattern Garden, which is best seen from the **Lime Tree Lookout,** a tower that provides an aerial view of the garden, making it easier to see and appreciate the patterns and design.

TOURING TIPS The Wildlife Gardens offer a pleasant half-day outing. Laid-back, easy to navigate and nicely landscaped, the park offers the excitement of a zoo and the tranquillity of a garden. The park's **Cockatoo Cafe** has fairly reasonably-priced sandwiches, and there's a picnic pavilion near the yew avenue, plus a small playground.

Because a number of animals are not transferred to their daytime viewing enclosures until 30–45 minutes after Thrigby Hall opens, we recommend arriving about 11 a.m.

Woburn Safari Park ★★★½

APPEAL BY AGE	PRESCHOOL ★★★	PRIMARY SCHOOL ★★★★	TEENS ★★★
YOUNG ADULTS ★★★	OVER 30 ★★★★		SENIORS ★★★★

Woburn Park, Bedfordshire MK17 9QN
☎ 01525 290 407; woburn.co.uk/safari

HOURS 10 a.m.–5 p.m. (last safari entry); Leisure Area: (peak season) 11 a.m.–6.30 p.m. (closes earlier in off-season). Open weekends only from early November to early March. Check website for details.

COST (Peak season) £18.50 adults; £13.50 children (aged 3–15); £15.50 senior citizens; £58 family ticket (2 adults, 2 children). (off-season) £12.95 adults; £8.95 children (aged 3–15); £10.95 senior citizens; £34.95 family ticket (2 adults, 2 children). Online discount: 10% on single tickets and £6 off family tickets. Must be purchased by midnight the day before your visit. Tickets can also be bought through the Tesco Clubcard rewards scheme.

GETTING THERE *By car:* South of Milton Keynes, near the village of Woburn. Follow signs from the M1 Junction 12 or 13. From the west, take the A5 and follow signs to Woburn. The park is signposted from there. *By rail:* Closest station is Woburn Sands (**nationalrail.co.uk**). *By bus:* From Woburn Sands train station, take the coach towards Leighton Buzzard and get off at Woburn; then walk about 25 minutes to the park (**transport direct.info**).

DESCRIPTION AND COMMENTS Woburn was the second arrival on the UK safari-park scene when it opened in 1970, following in the paw-prints of Longleat. It now covers 3,000 ac (1,214 ha) and boasts that it's Europe's largest private park dedicated to the conservation of animals.

The park is part of the Duke of Bedford's Woburn estate, and you drive through wooded parkland before paying for entry. Here you have the option of buying a guidebook for £5 or an audio CD guide for £6.50. They both provide information about the animals and the park itself, but they're expensive given that plenty of information boards are around. However, an animal-spotter's guide at £1 is good fun for kids.

Entrance includes all attractions, with the exception of **Go Ape** – a chain of treetop adventure sites that let visitors play at being Tarzan for the day. Although on the Woburn site, this is a separate facility and requires pre-booking, with prices starting from £20.

The grounds themselves are home to **Woburn Abbey,** founded by the Cistercians in 1145. It was seized in 1547 by Henry VIII, who presented it to John Russell, first Earl of Bedford. In the early nineteenth century, the sixth Duke of Bedford hired the famous landscaper Humphry Repton to construct a garden and menagerie. It included peacocks, swans, antelopes and llamas. Later, the eleventh duke became president of the Royal Zoological Society and continued the abbey's tradition of housing and breeding exotic animals. The other significant claim to fame is that this is purportedly where the tradition of afternoon tea was begun in the 1830s by Duchess Anna Maria, wife of the seventh duke. She would entertain friends in the Abbey's Blue Drawing Room, serving a meal during that intolerably-long wait between lunch and dinner. Today you can have tea in the abbey, then tour the home and the adjacent deer park. These all carry a separate admission charge from the safari park. Admission is £3 or less, while the safari is considerably more, proving, it seems, that the cost of maintaining a historical home is peanuts compared to looking after a herd of elephants.

The park began its evolution from royal retreat to roadside attraction following World War II. Instead of turning over the expensive and deteriorating estate to the National Trust, the thirteenth duke opened it to the public in 1955 and began adding amusements. While it may have horrified fellow nobles, the park has been a success, and the property remains in private ownership. At one point, the grounds were considered for the home of a major theme park. But instead project developers chose another site, which became Alton Towers.

Perhaps it's just as well. The safari park offers a lovely drive through English countryside, populated not by squirrels and the odd crow but a range of free-roaming wild creatures. We suggest that you park first and visit the **Leisure Area** for the **Foot Safari** – a fancy name for zoo. Then when traffic dies down in mid-afternoon, you can begin your driving adventure.

When you enter the park base, you'll park in front of a restaurant and gift shop on a hill overlooking the Foot Safari area. Additional parking is in a field parallel to the entrance road. Your first or last stop should be the delightful **Rainbow Landing,** a lorikeet aviary. It's worth buying a cup of nectar to have the colourful birds treat you as a perch as they slurp up their snack. Then head to the top path and look for the **Australian Walkabout,** which is hidden off in the trees and somewhat hard to find even with a park map. Here you can meet wallabies and rheas, and participate in a daily wallaby feeding at 2.45 p.m. There are also feeding sessions for the penguins, river hogs, lemurs and monkeys. These present a great opportunity to learn more about the animals. Times vary, so check the schedule and time your safari drive accordingly.

Roughly opposite the walkabout is **Sea Lion Cove,** with daily talks and demonstrations. Next look for **Monkey Business,** a first-class elevated treetop exhibit. In this aviary, squirrel monkeys will swing above and around you.

Nearby is the **Tree Tops Action Trail,** a play zone where the wild creatures scrambling through the trees are children. During inclement weather, look across the path for the indoor **Mammoth Play Ark,** an exceptional soft area with slides, ball pits and trampolines for children aged 5–12, as well as a separate area for younger ones. The area is fully supervised, so parents can relax in the adjacent **Two by Two** snack bar and watch the kids play. It's along the main path leading from the entrance and will keep kids busy for a long time.

Back on the Foot Safari, look for the **sheep and goat paddock** and, next door, the **Animal Encounters** area, home to free-ranging **marmosets,** along with **lynx, lizards** and **turtles.** Then come the always-popular

Humboldt penguins – feedings in their glass-walled pool are held twice daily. Continue to the **Land of Lemurs.** You pass through the area on an elevated walkway. Look for three species of the cuddly creatures hanging from the trees above. Finally, there's **Bobcat Run,** a large six-run sack slide for kids and adults (must be over 3'11"/1.2 m to ride).

Cycling back towards the lake, you'll reach the station for the **Great Woburn Railway.** The train tours the **camel paddock,** which also houses wild asses and zebras – an area you'll see on the road safari. Pedal-operated **swan boats** can be taken out for a 10-minute tour of the lake.

Now it's time to hit the safari. During high season you can take the park's lorry trip through the herbivore section for £4 per person, but you'll probably want to hop in your own vehicle to get the full experience. Be careful: although the destructive primates have been removed, rhinos have been known to do a number on vehicles as well. The roadway has two lanes, and you're free to stop as long as you like to take photos or watch the animals. Just make sure that there's room to pass. If you run into any trouble, do not get out of your vehicle – sound your horn and a ranger will assist you.

As you enter the safari, you'll first see **Asian elephants,** and if you're lucky, they'll be giving themselves a mud bath. Then you'll pass **elands, buffalos, oryx, zebras** and the odd **Przewalski's horse,** a rare and endangered undomesticated equine. There are also **white rhinos.** Signs everywhere offer more information about the animals and their habitats. Eventually you'll reach the secured **tiger enclosure,** where you'll have to queue for entrance. Soon after come **wolves** and **black bears,** not common sights in the UK. You're not supposed to stop here, as bears can snap off your wing mirrors. And you might also want to keep your windows up and doors locked because you'll soon approach the 32-ac (13-ha) **lion enclosure.**

The following area, the **African Forest,** isn't so scary though. It's home to **giraffes, addax antelopes** and **bongos,** African's rarest antelopes. Finally, you'll cruise by the two-humped **Bactrian camels** and **Somali wild asses.** As you exit the safari, you can return to the park base or head back to the entrance and go on safari again.

TOURING TIPS More than at other safari parks, Woburn has an extensive roster of feedings and animal talks. Consult the schedule when you arrive, and plan your visit around the ones that appeal to you.

Be aware that the lemurs and marmosets running free in walk-through exhibits are infamous for taking liberties with visitors.

On the safari drive, making the transition from one area to another through double gates is painfully slow and results in releasing vehicles into each new habitat in bunches. The upshot is that you're relegated to proceeding in lockstep with the other cars that process through with you. If you resign yourself to a basically-inefficient process and understand that you'll have little freedom of movement on the drive, you'll better relax and enjoy the animals. Better for your blood pressure too.

If, like most visitors, you park in the field, it's a little difficult to get your bearings as you begin your tour. We suggest heading for the amphitheatre in the centre of the park and navigating according to the park map from there.

Food – expensive and unremarkable – is not Woburn's greatest strength. Bring a picnic.

ZSL Whipsnade Zoo ★★★★

| APPEAL BY AGE | PRESCHOOL ★★★★ | PRIMARY SCHOOL ★★★★★ | TEENS ★★★ |
| YOUNG ADULTS ★★★ | | OVER 30 ★★★ | SENIORS ★★★ |

Dunstable, Bedfordshire LU6 2LF
☎ 01582 872 171; zsl.org/zsl-whipsnade-zoo

HOURS Opens at 10 a.m., with closing time varying by season, usually until 7 p.m. on Sundays and bank holidays (mid-March–early October) and 4–6 p.m. other times of year. Closed Christmas Day.

COST (peak season) £19.50 adults; £14.50 children (aged 3–15); £16.50 senior citizens 60+, students and disabled; £59 family (4 people, if purchased online). Slight discounts during mid-winter and winter season. All prices include a £1.80 donation per ticket to the Cheetah Action Programme, which can be refused (although being British, most visitors don't). Price to bring car into zoo: £15, but free during winter. Tickets can also be bought through the Tesco Clubcard rewards scheme.

GETTING THERE *By car:* About 30 mi (48 km) northwest of London, just to the south of Luton. The zoo is signposted from the M1 (Junctions 9 and 12) and all major roads. If you choose not to drive into the zoo, parking costs £4. *By rail:* The nearest stations are Luton Parkway and Hemel Hempstead Boxmoor, both about 10 mi (16 km) away (**nationalrail.co.uk**). *By bus:* Served by **Centrebus Route X31**, linking Luton Rail Station, Luton Town Centre, Dunstable and Hemel Hempstead with the zoo at 2-hour intervals Monday–Saturday, with extra services at peak times (**centrebus.co.uk**). (Route information: **transportdirect.info.**)

DESCRIPTION AND COMMENTS Whipsnade may be expensive, but once you're in, it provides an excellent zoo experience. It's big, with plenty of space for animals and visitors alike, and there is plenty to see and do. The zoo advertises itself as home to the 'Whipsnade Big Five' of elephants, lions, rhinos, giraffes and bears, along with chimpanzees, cheetahs, hippos and wolves, as well as an indoor Discovery Centre, which houses tropical creatures such as crocodiles and turtles. A free map helps you navigate, and signposts are dotted about the site, pointing the way to the most popular enclosures.

The site started in the 1930s as a satellite location for the London Zoo, which still operates it. (ZSL stands for Zoological Society of London.) During World War II, animals from the London Zoo were brought here for safety. The plan largely worked, expect when the Luftwaffe bombed the property and literally frightened a 3-year-old giraffe named Boxer to death. Several of the ponds at the zoo are actually bomb craters. In our opinion, Whipsnade is better than its London counterpart. It's bigger and houses larger animals, such as elephants and giraffes, which you no longer find at London Zoo. It's easier to reach, is less busy and has a more relaxed atmosphere.

The views of the surrounding countryside are excellent. Whipsnade stands on the crest of a hill overlooking the fields and woods of south Bedfordshire, with the Chiltern Hills stretching to the north. The site itself is nicely landscaped and blends well with the surrounding area – there are lots of trees, and a woodland bird walk near the entrance makes for a pleasant diversion, although it is not recommended for wheelchairs.

Disabled access to the zoo is reasonable, and non-motorised wheelchairs are available with a refundable £25 deposit. Ramps enable access to the enclosures, and wheelchairs can be taken onto the bus and train. Pushchairs are available to rent for £5 plus a £25 deposit, although no prams are available. For both wheelchairs and pushchairs, the zoo advises visitors to call in advance to book the hire. Some minor paths crisscrossing the site are not suitable for either.

The zoo has two restaurants: the **Wild Bite Café** in the centre of the property and the **Look Out Café** on the north-eastern edge, which offers spectacular views across the countryside. Neither gets great reviews. They serve dishes such as lasagne, fish cakes, roast chicken and sandwiches. Hot meals run £6.95–£8.95, with sandwiches £3–£4. More-kid-friendly fare is available at the kiosk to the side of the Wild Bite and at the small café in the play area next to the train station. An outdoor barbecue also runs throughout the summer at the Wild Bite, serving from midday until the park closes. A coffee bar near the entrance sells snacks and hot drinks, and vending machines are also dotted around the site.

One lovely feature of the zoo is that some smaller animals, such as wallabies, peacocks and muntjac deer, roam free around the property, although visitors are asked not to feed them. In fact the zoo adopts a surprisingly-accessible attitude towards many of its animals. The fences around some enclosures could just be vaulted over, except for the likes of lions, tigers and bears. However, with this in mind it would be wise to keep an eye on the more-adventurous children in your party, lest you turn around to find one of them on the back of a reindeer. It really is that easy to get close to some of the bigger creatures.

At 600 ac (242 ha), Whipsnade takes some walking around. However, for £15 the zoo offers a surprising option: you can drive your car into the property and use an exterior road. (Car entrance is free during winter.) An auto lap around the park takes about an hour, but some enclosures are in the interior of the property and can't be reached by car. Pedestrians share the road with the cars, so if you're walking, remember to check over your shoulder. Alternatively, a double-decker bus offers free transport, and a narrow-gauge train passes through the Asia area.

Without the benefit of a vehicle, a visit to Whipsnade takes at least 3 hours, and longer if you take in the live shows, which we recommend. Walkers should follow the road around a complete circuit of the zoo, before dipping into the centre to see the rest of the animals.

If you decide to park, you'll reach the zoo through a tunnel under the main road and enter at a modest plaza, where you'll find a restaurant, toilets and customer service. Your first stop is **Wild Wild Whipsnade,** which features animals now extinct in Britain. Following the car/pedestrian path, you'll zigzag to both sides of the road, first passing **European lynx** on your right and **wild boar.** Then on the left side of the road, take the pedestrian path to circle around the **chimps** (which did not live in the UK!), which may be at play in their extensive indoor-outdoor 'chimpnasium'. Also look for **European bison.** Back on the right there are more former local species, such as **brown bears** and **wolverines,** and to the left **moose** and **wolves.** While it's sobering to realise that these creatures are extinct here, at least you don't have to worry about running into them on the way home from the pub at night. When you're over on the left side, which is the interior of the park, look for the **giraffes,** part of Whipsnade's big five.

Farther off to the right, you'll find a **penguin pool,** where Humboldts and rockhoppers star in a daily afternoon feeding (times vary). Moving back into the park, look for the rain shelter, an important landmark in inclement weather, and then seek out the **bongos** and **white rhinos** at the top-right corner of the park. As you circle this portion of the zoo, you'll pass the **roan antelopes,** Africa's largest antelope species. Then keep an eye out for **oryx** and the zoo's expansive **Lions of Serengeti** area, inspired by Tanzania's Serengeti National Park. The viewing area, shaped like a traditional hut, is built with windows almost 10 ft (3 m) tall, which often provide an up-close view of the predators.

On the opposite side of the path you'll see the **common hippo.** If you're near this area in the late morning, catch the zookeeper talk about this surprisingly-dangerous animal. Now you should be approaching **Cheetah Rock,** a 43,000-sq-ft (4,000-m²), £1 million exhibit. Part of the expense was for special heated 'rocks', so the fleet residents will perch atop a fake stone formation for your viewing pleasure. You can watch the felines from an African-style hut with floor-to-ceiling glass windows. The males and females are often separated but are allowed to look at each other. It's kind of like a singles bar, as zoo staff watch their interactions and pair them up for breeding. Apparently the matchmakers know what they're doing. The London Zoo was the first Western zoo to have cheetahs, and over the last 40 years, the zoo has produced more than 130 cubs.

Next on your left, you'll pass **Grévy's zebras, flamingos** and **egrets.** On your right, see if you can catch a view of the Asian animals, including **yaks,** several species of **deer, rhinos** and **elephants.** Entrance through this area is limited to cars and the **Jumbo Express train,** which you can catch ahead of you on the left. On the way, follow the loop on your right, leading past the lovable **sloth bears,** the odd-looking **Przewalski's horses,** two-humped **Bactrian camels, tigers** and **onagers,** which look part horse, part donkey. Now you can get the train – a historical attraction in its own right, powered by steam locomotives or, on some days, a couple of diesels. Cost is £2.75 for adults, £2.25 for children, and tickets can be purchased at the station.

Next, dip down to the **children's farm,** where goats, turkeys and other farmyard creatures roam freely and can be petted by visitors. This seemed to be a huge hit with little children, although perhaps less enjoyable for some of the animals. When we visited, the turkey being chased by a tribe of screaming 4-year-olds certainly didn't seem overly keen on the concept. While here, make sure to look for the very hairy and large **Poitou donkeys,** which are also perfectly pettable.

Above the farm, you'll find other speciality areas, which host shows during high season. **Birds of the World** has raptors in free flight in late-morning and early-afternoon shows. The adjacent **Splashzone** is home to sea-lion shows at midday. When we visited, all the keepers were superb, keeping everyone amused with a running commentary and interacting well with the animals. In fact, the staff in general were very friendly. Heading back towards the entrance you'll find the **Discovery Centre,** filled with reptiles and various creepy-crawlies, which you can get to know better during a daily question-and-answer section with the keepers.

Finally, cross over to **Lemur Island** to see the always-popular primates in action. You'll probably want to take one home. And that's why you'll find stuffed versions in the gift shop near the exit.

TOURING TIPS Double-check times for shows and keeper talks. They're very worthwhile but require planning. The zoo is so large that you won't be able to reach one on the spur of the moment.

With its expansive grounds (and unremarkable food service), Whipsnade is perfect for a picnic – the area between the penguin enclosure and the Lookout Café offers plenty of picnic benches and wide-open spaces where you can have a bite to eat and enjoy the view.

Bear in mind that Whipsnade is purely a zoo; there are no rides or similar attractions, although there is a large playground.

Given the size of the site, losing children is a real possibility – decide on a prearranged meeting-spot in case this happens.

While plenty of rain shelters are dotted around the site, the only truly indoor exhibit is the Discovery Centre. If a prolonged downpour is forecast, the zoo is probably best left for another day.

FARM EXPERIENCES

BECAUSE THE VARIOUS FARM EXPERIENCES ARE SO SIMILAR (see page 13), we felt it unnecessary to provide individual profiles as we do with other types of attractions. Following is a selective list of farm experiences in the East of England.

BEDFORDSHIRE

MEAD OPEN FARM
Stanbridge Road
Billington, Leighton Buzzard
Bedfordshire LU7 9HJ
☎ 01525 852 954
meadopenfarm.co.uk
info@meadopenfarm.co.uk

THURLEIGH FARM CENTRE &
ADVENTURE PLAYGROUND
Cross End, Thurleigh
Bedfordshire MK44 2EE
☎ 01234 771 597
thurleighfarmcentre.co.uk
office@thurleighfarmcentre.co.uk

WOODSIDE FARM & LEISURE PARK
Woodside Road
Slip End, Luton
Bedfordshire LU1 4DG
☎ 01582 841 044
woodsidefarm.co.uk
maria@woodsidefarm.co.uk

BUCKINGHAMSHIRE

ODDS FARM PARK
Wooburn Common Road
Wooburn Common, High Wycombe
Buckinghamshire HP10 0LX
☎ 01628 520 188
oddsfarm.co.uk
oddsfarm@oddsfarm.co.uk

CAMBRIDGESHIRE

SACREWELL FARM COUNTRY CENTRE
Thornhaugh
Peterborough PE8 6HJ
☎ 01780 782 254
sacrewell.org.uk
info@sacrewell.org.uk

PIGEONS FARM
*(Typical farm experience –
not about pigeons)*
Wisbech Road, Thorney
Peterborough PE6 0TD
☎ 01733 271 020
pigeonsfarm.co.uk
info@pigeonsfarm.co.uk

THE MILTON MAIZE MAZE
*(Usual farm experience plus huge maze
with a different theme every year)*
Rectory Farm Shop, Milton
Cambridgeshire CB4 6DA
☎ 01223 860 374
themiltonmaizemaze.co.uk
**enquiries@themiltonmaizemaze
.co.uk**

WIMPOLE HOME FARM
*(A National Trust site featuring
Wimpole Hall and gardens dating from
1643, as well as the farm experience)*
Old Wimpole Road
Arrington, Royston
Hertfordshire SG8 0BW
☎ 01223 108 987
wimpole.org
wimpolehall@nationaltrust.org.uk

ESSEX

**BARLEYLANDS FARM PARK &
CRAFT VILLAGE**
Barleylands Road; Billericay
Essex CM11 2UD
☎ 01268 532 253
barleylands.co.uk
info@barleylands.co.uk

MARSH FARM COUNTRY PARK
Marsh Farm Road
South Woodham Ferrers, Chelmsford
Essex CM3 5WP
☎ 01245 321 552
marshfarmcountrypark.co.uk
marshfarm@essex.gov.uk

OLD MACDONALD'S FARM
Weald Road
Brentwood
Essex CM14 5AY
☎ 01277 375 177
oldmacdonaldsfarm.org.uk
info@omdfarm.co.uk

HERTFORDSHIRE

STANDALONE FARM
Wilbury Road
Letchworth Garden City
Hertfordshire SG6 4JN
☎ 01462 686 775
standalonefarm.com
info@standalonefarm.com

WILLOWS FARM VILLAGE
Coursers Road
London Colney, St Albans
Hertfordshire AL4 OPF
☎ 0870 129 9718
willowsfarmvillage.com
info@willowsfarmvillage.com

LINCOLNSHIRE

HALL FARM PARK
Thornton Road
South Kelsey, Market Rasen
Lincolnshire LN7 6PS
☎ 01652 678 822
hallfarmpark.co.uk
enquiries@hallfarmpark.co.uk

HARDY'S ANIMAL FARM
Anchor Lane
Ingoldmells, Skagness
Lincolnshire PE25 1LZ
☎ 01754 872 267
hardysanimalfarm.co.uk
(Email via form at website)

PINK PIG FARM
Holme Hall
Holme, Scunthorpe
North Lincolnshire DN16 3RE
☎ 01724 844 466
pinkpigfarm.co.uk
shop@pinkpigfarm.co.uk

RAND FARM PARK
Rand, Lincoln
Lincolnshire LN8 5NJ
☎ 01673 858 904
randfarmpark.com
office@randfarmpark.com

NORFOLK

CHURCH FARM
Stow Estate Trust
Stow Bardolph, nr Kings Lynn
Norfolk PE34 3HU
☎ 01366 382 162
churchfarmstowbardolph.co.uk
enquiries@churchfarmstowbardolph.co.uk

SNETTISHAM PARK
(Undergoing expansion – limited operations)
Snettisham, Kings Lynn
Norfolk PE31 7NQ
☎ 01485 542 425
snettishampark.co.uk
info@snettishampark.co.uk

THE WIZARD MAZE & PLAY
(Farm experience with maize maze)
Hall Farm; Metton
Norfolk NR11 8QU
☎ 01263 761 255
wizardadventuremaze.co.uk

SUFFOLK

EASTON FARM PARK
Easton, Woodbridge
Suffolk IP13 0EQ
☎ 01728 746 475
eastonfarmpark.co.uk
info@eastonfarmpark.co.uk

OASIS CAMEL CENTRE
(Yep, this is a weird one: usual farm experience plus camels and llamas)
Orchard Farm
Linstead, Halesworth
Suffolk IP19 0DT
☎ 07836 734 748
oasiscamelcentre.co.uk
info@oasiscamelcentre.co.uk

PART NINE

EAST *and* WEST MIDLANDS

THE EAST AND WEST MIDLANDS REGION COMPRISES middle central England, including Derbyshire, Gloucestershire, Herefordshire, Leicestershire and Rutland, Northamptonshire, Nottinghamshire, Shropshire, Staffordshire, Warwickshire, the West Midlands, and Worcester.

This section of England encompasses not only the middle part of the country but also incorporates cities and towns where much of that quality we associate with 'Englishness' took root. Shakespeare was born here, in **Stratford-upon-Avon.** What's more, here in this swath of England, you'll see the great variety of past and present that constitutes British life – dark Victorian remnants, modern business complexes, popular tourist haunts and sleepy villages.

Britain's largest theme park, **Alton Towers,** is in this region, as are the **National Space Centre,** the charming riverside enclave of **Bourton-on-the-Water** and the splendidly-preserved **Warwick Castle.**

THEME PARKS *and* ATTRACTIONS

Alton Towers ★★★★★
Alton, Staffordshire ST10 4DB
☎ **0871 222 3330; altontowers.com**

HOURS The park opens at 10 a.m., with closing time varying by season. Usually it's open to 7 p.m. high season but can close as early as 5 p.m. during spring and autumn. Check the website for details. The park opens with selected rides and attractions for February half-term and for the main season in late March. It usually closes by early November.

COST £38 adults (£30.40 online); £29 children 4–11 (£23.20 online); £19 disabled and carers (£15.20 online); £81 family of 3 with no more than

262 PART 9 EAST AND WEST MIDLANDS

East and West Midlands

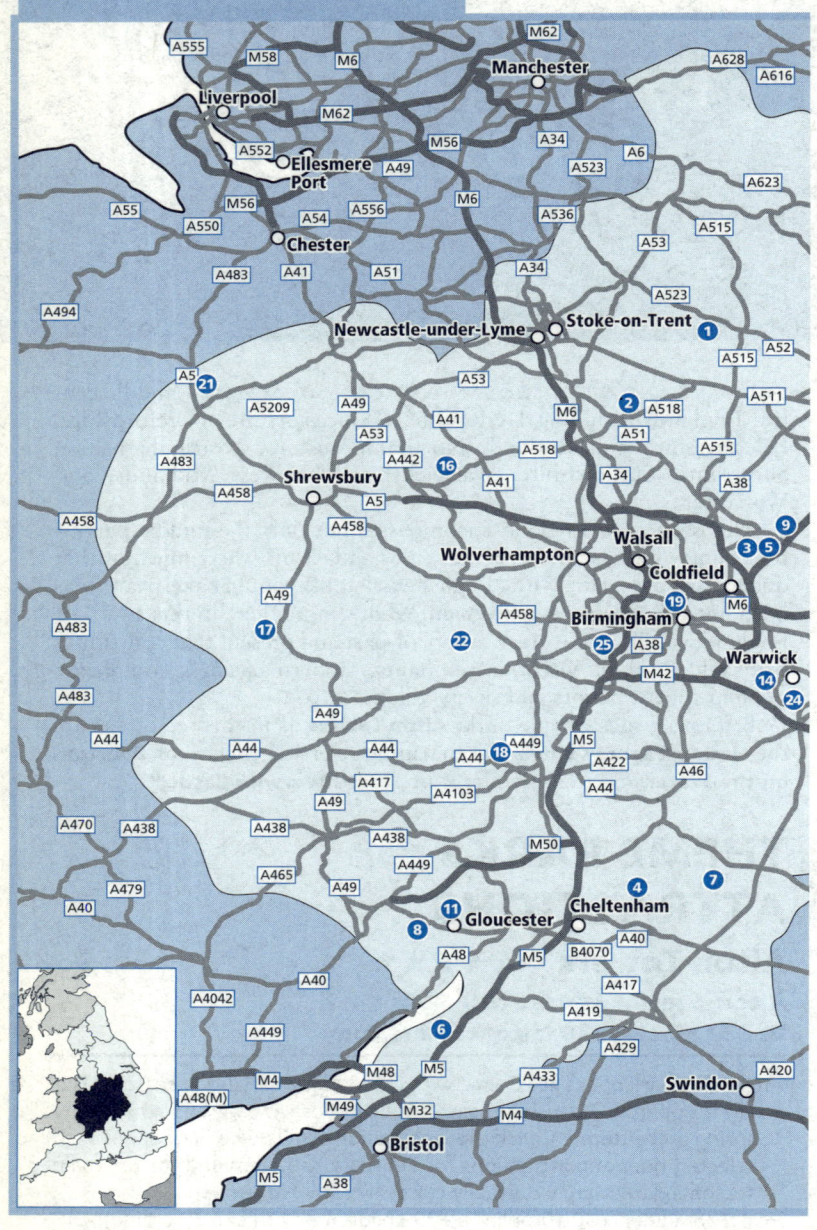

EAST AND WEST MIDLANDS MAP

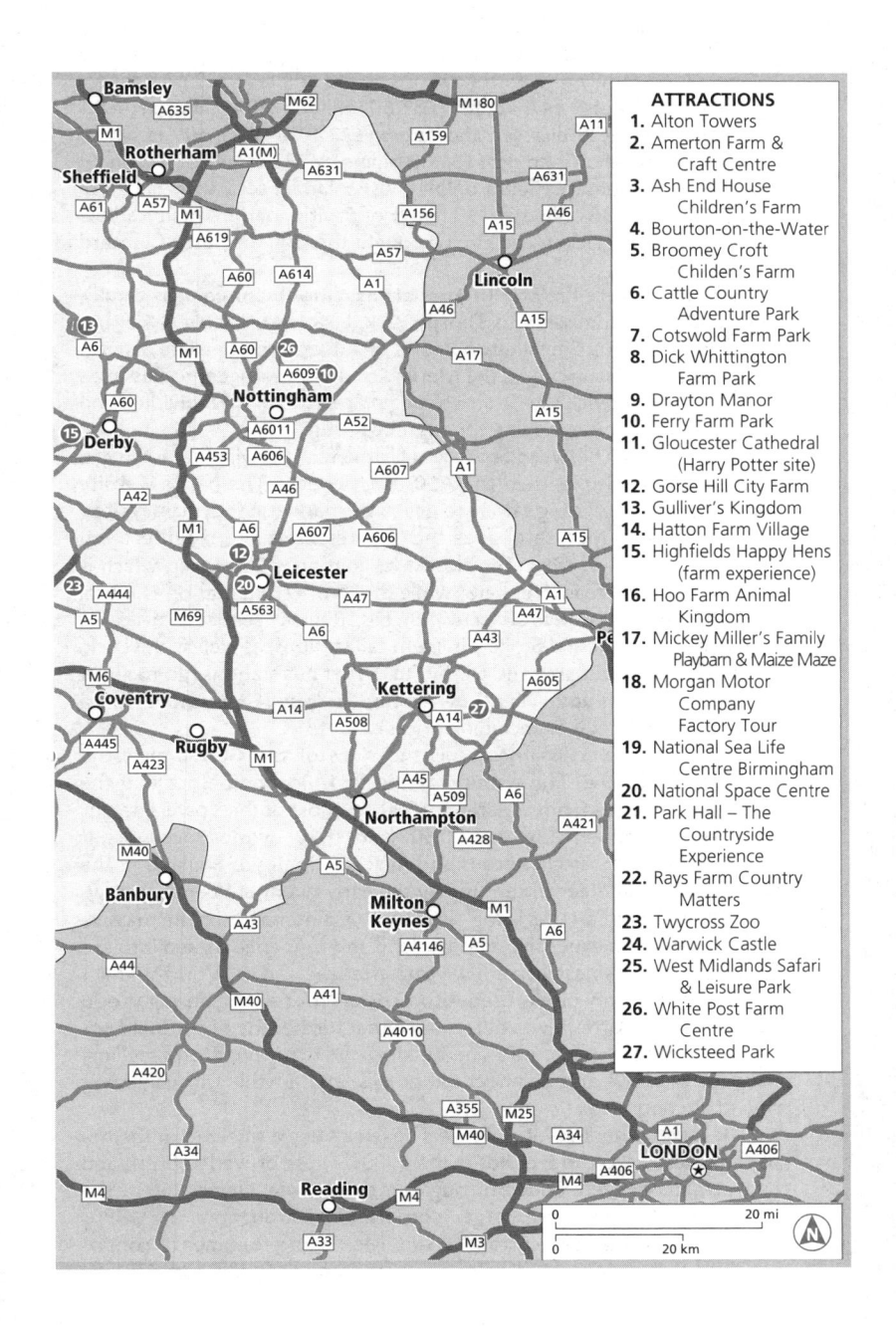

ATTRACTIONS
1. Alton Towers
2. Amerton Farm & Craft Centre
3. Ash End House Children's Farm
4. Bourton-on-the-Water
5. Broomey Croft Childen's Farm
6. Cattle Country Adventure Park
7. Cotswold Farm Park
8. Dick Whittington Farm Park
9. Drayton Manor
10. Ferry Farm Park
11. Gloucester Cathedral (Harry Potter site)
12. Gorse Hill City Farm
13. Gulliver's Kingdom
14. Hatton Farm Village
15. Highfields Happy Hens (farm experience)
16. Hoo Farm Animal Kingdom
17. Mickey Miller's Family Playbarn & Maize Maze
18. Morgan Motor Company Factory Tour
19. National Sea Life Centre Birmingham
20. National Space Centre
21. Park Hall – The Countryside Experience
22. Rays Farm Country Matters
23. Twycross Zoo
24. Warwick Castle
25. West Midlands Safari & Leisure Park
26. White Post Farm Centre
27. Wicksteed Park

2 adults (£64.80 online); £108 family of 4 with no more than 2 adults (£86.40 online); £135 family of 5 with no more than 2 adults (£108 online); £162 family of 6 with no more than 3 adults (£129.60 online).

Two-day tickets: £47 adults (£37.60 online); £34 children 4–11 (£27.20 online); £28 disabled and carers (£22.40 online); £99 family of 3 with no more than 2 adults (£81.60 online); £132 family of 4 with no more than 2 adults (£108.80 online); £165 family of 5 with no more than 2 adults (£136 online); £198 family of 6 with no more than 3 adults (£163.20 online). Tickets can also be bought through the Tesco Clubcard rewards scheme.

You can also use the **Merlin Annual Pass** (**merlinannualpass.co.uk**), which provides admission to Thorpe Park, Legoland Discovery Centre, Legoland Windsor, Chessington World of Adventures, Sea Life Sanctuaries, Dungeons attractions, the Merlin London Eye, Madame Tussauds London and Warwick Castle. Prices begin at £150 for an individual and drop in price if you're buying for a family group.

GETTING THERE *By car:* Between Stoke and Uttoxeter. If driving, take the M6 to the A500 to Stoke, then the A50 to Uttoxeter. The park's website notes that if you're using satnav to get to the park, use the 'main routes' or 'fastest' navigation setting, as the 'shortest' setting may direct you to a cow pasture. *By train:* The closest rail station is Uttoxeter, which is 6.5 mi (10.4 km) from the park, while Stoke-on-Trent station is 18 mi (29 km) away (**nationalrail.co.uk**). *By bus:* Regular service is available from the Uttoxeter and Stoke-on-Trent rail stations, as well as the Leek, Nottingham Broadmarsh and Derby Full Street bus stations (go to **alton towers.com/plan-your-visit/how-to-find-us/public-transport** for a complete bus timetable, including prices).

OVERVIEW Alton Towers' namesake is the ruins of the Gothic ancestral home of the Earls of Shrewsbury, dating to 1406, and before that the site of various forts from as early as 1000 BC. Most of the Towers' major construction happened between 1800 and 1850. By most accounts, it was among the most glamorous and majestic homes in England at the middle of the nineteenth century. By the early twentieth century, however, the current Earl was living elsewhere. Maintenance of the massive home proved too expensive, and the land and residence passed into the hands of local businessmen a few years after the end of World War I.

The British Army briefly used Alton Towers for training during World War II, but soon after it was determined that further use of the buildings was not financially practical. The buildings were stripped of panelling, fixtures, windows and architectural details, and anything of value was sold at auction.

The local owners of Alton Towers began adding a small set of theme-park attractions to the grounds in the 1980s. These proved popular, and new attractions were added throughout the decade. Ownership of the land passed between ever-larger corporations throughout the 1990s and into the 2000s. The current tenant, Merlin Entertainments, continues to add attractions. Merlin also operates many other UK-based theme parks, though Alton Towers is the most popular.

THEME PARKS AND ATTRACTIONS

In our opinion, Alton Towers is the most 'Disney-like' of the UK's theme parks. The various 'lands' that make up the park are differentiated by elaborate sets and landscaping inspired by stories or themes that enhance the overall experience.

Several sit-down restaurants accompany the usual fast-food offerings. And as at Disney's theme parks, while it's possible to see the highlights of Alton Towers in one day, we think a two-day visit is the most relaxed, practical way to see everything.

Tip: A **Merlin Annual Pass** (see previous page) gets you one year of admission to every theme park and attraction owned by Merlin Entertainments, including Alton Towers, Legoland Windsor, Thorpe Park and Chessington World of Adventures, among others. If you're visiting these parks for more than a few days, the annual pass pays for itself quickly. Pass-holders also get a substantial discount (around 20%) on food inside the parks.

HOTELS Alton Towers operates two hotels: the **Alton Towers Hotel** and **Splash Landings.** The latter is the newer property, opened in 2003, and features a Caribbean theme with lots of bright pastel colours and tropical décor. Splash Landings also has a small indoor water park called **Carriba Creek,** a restaurant serving breakfast and dinner and a nearby crazy-golf course named **Extraordinary Golf.**

The Alton Towers Hotel opened in 1996 and carries a vague 'eccentric inventor' theme, with an odd, gadget-filled fountain welcoming guests at the entrance, and a hot-air balloon near the restaurant and bar on the bottom floor. The hotel has one restaurant, serving a buffet breakfast and a regular menu for dinner. A bar serves a limited menu of sandwiches and salads for lunch.

Other on-property amenities include a small spa, popular with guests looking to shed tension built up over long days of theme-park visiting, as well as a small conference centre between the hotels and connected via covered walkways. Service at the spa is good.

The one advantage of staying at an Alton Towers hotel is that guests get into the park an hour earlier than regular guests. However, you can stay within a 30-minute drive at a B&B, hotel or motel in either Alton, Stafford or Stoke-on-Trent for a fraction of the cost, in rooms of comparable or better quality, and use the savings to purchase Fastrack tickets (see page 269) for popular attractions to make up for the lost hour. This will almost certainly be our strategy during our next visit.

> *unofficial* **TIP**
> Having stayed on-site at Alton Towers, we think both hotels are overpriced. Soundproofing between the rooms and hallways is almost non-existent, so you're likely to hear the screams of children and tired adults until late at night. While the staff are friendly and helpful, the rooms are small, sparse and not particularly well maintained. Rooms do not feature air-conditioning, but come with an oscillating electric fan to keep things cool at night during warmer months.

ARRIVING If you're driving to Alton Towers, you'll be directed to one of the car parks, each referenced by a letter, such as *A* or *B,* allowing you to

Alton Towers

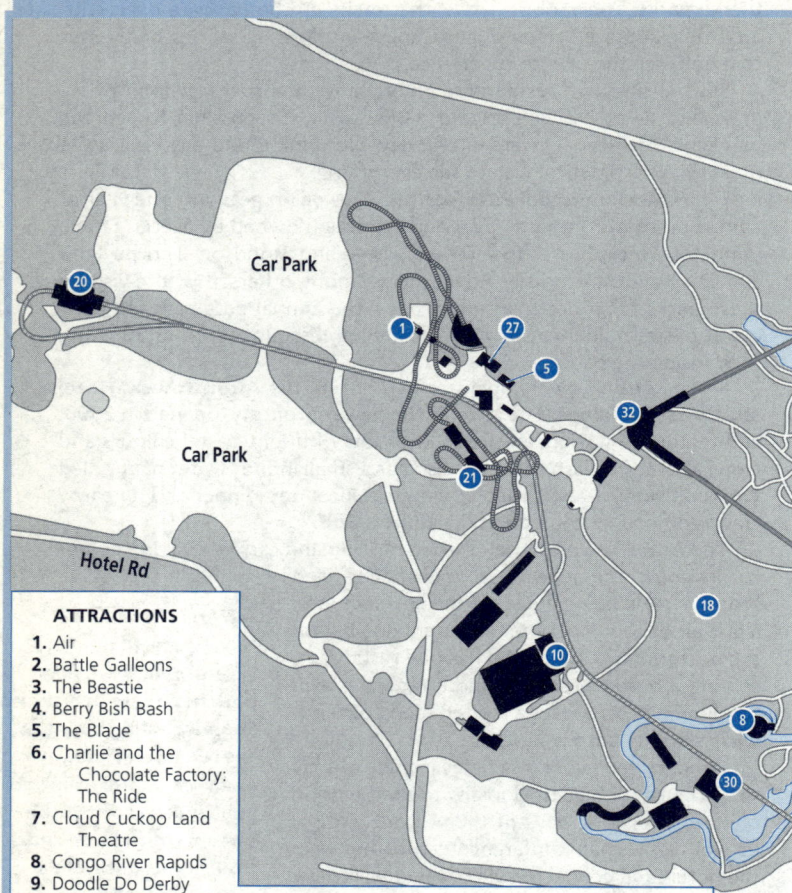

ATTRACTIONS

1. Air
2. Battle Galleons
3. The Beastie
4. Berry Bish Bash
5. The Blade
6. Charlie and the Chocolate Factory: The Ride
7. Cloud Cuckoo Land Theatre
8. Congo River Rapids
9. Doodle Do Derby
10. Duel – The Haunted House Strikes Back
11. Enterprise
12. The Flume
13. Frog Hopper
14. Gallopers Carousel
15. The Gardens
16. Heave Ho!
17. Hex – The Legend of The Towers
18. Haunted Hollow
19. Marauder's Mayhem
20. Monorail Station
21. Nemesis
22. Oblivion
23. Old MacDonald's Singing Barn
24. Old MacDonald's Tractor Ride
25. Peugeot Driving School
26. *The Pirate of Sharkbait Reef*
27. Ripsaw
28. Riverbank Eye Spy
29. Rita
30. Runaway Mine Train
31. Sharkbait Reef Aquarium
32. Skyride
33. Sonic Spinball
34. Squirrel Nutty Ride
35. Submission
36. There's Something in the Dung Heap
37. The Towers
38. THI3TEEN
39. Twirling Toadstool
40. Wobble World

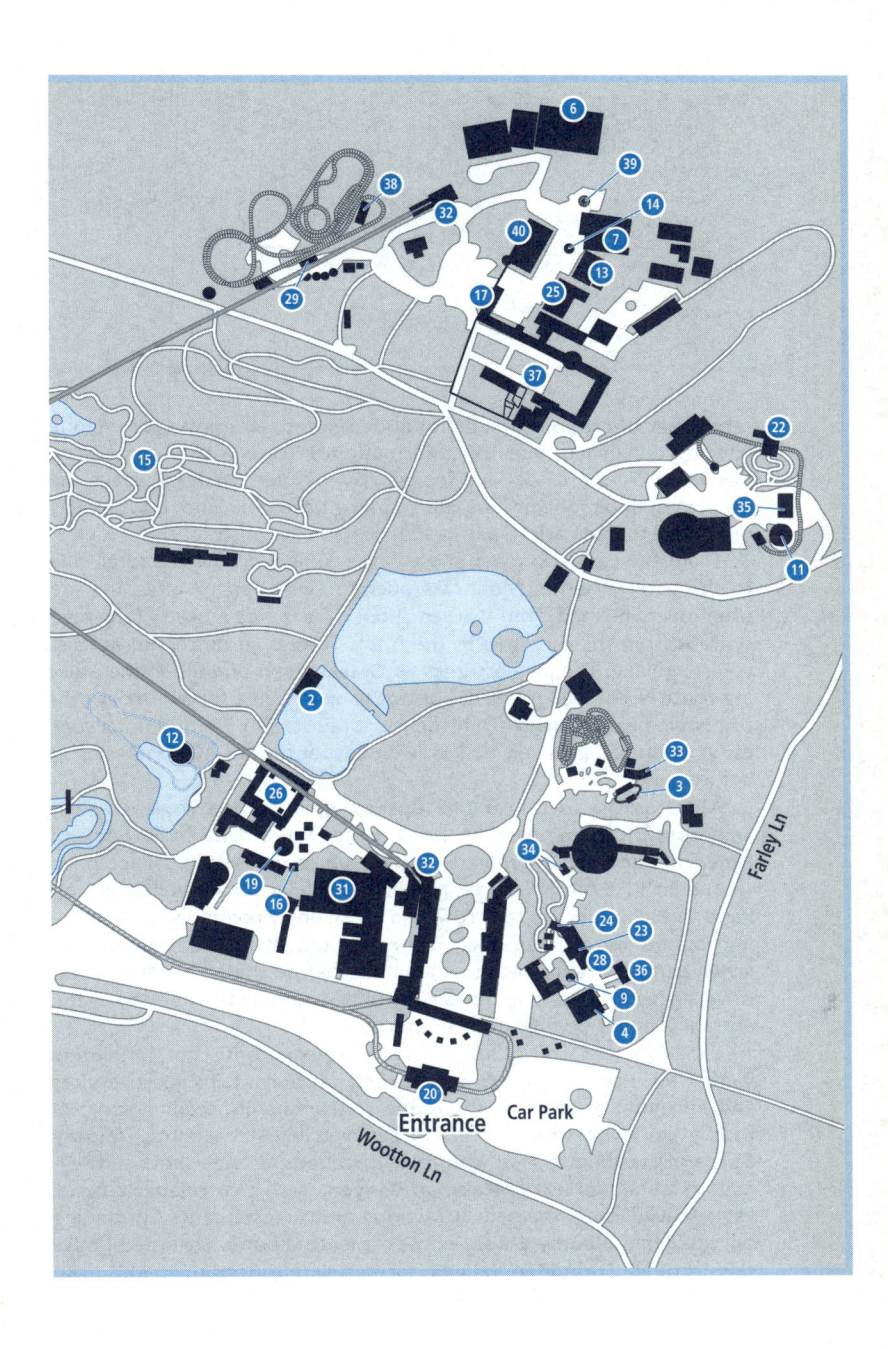

ALTON TOWERS MAP

NOT TO BE MISSED AT ALTON TOWERS		
Katanga Canyon Congo River Rapids	**The Towers** Hex	**Forbidden Valley** Air Nemesis
Mutiny Bay Battle Galleons	**Cloud Cuckoo Land** Charlie and the Chocolate Factory: The Ride	**Gloomy Wood** Duel
Adventure Land Sonic Spinball	**Dark Forest** Rita	
X-Sector Oblivion	TH13TEEN	

remember where you parked. (It's also useful to text-message someone else in your group with this information, in case you forget.) Alton Towers charges a £5 parking fee per day, payable when you leave the car park, or look for coin-operated parking ticket machines on your way out of the theme park to pay in advance.

From the car park, most guests will take a 5-minute monorail ride to the park entrance. Monorails operate every few minutes and are often overwhelmed from 9.30 to about 11 a.m. It's a pretty long haul on foot from the car parks to the Alton Towers entrance, but at least you're moving. The park assumes you'll take the monorail, so the walking route is not well marked; but not to worry: just follow the stream of people heading away from the monorail station. Returning to your car via monorail is usually no hassle except for the last 40 minutes or so before closing.

More visitors are on hand for opening time at Alton Towers than at any other UK theme park. Much as at the Disney parks in Europe and America, hundreds arrive early and queue at the park entrance prior to opening. At Alton Towers, however, far fewer ticket-sellers are on hand to accommodate the crowd, so we strongly recommend purchasing your admission in advance. During the busier times of year, plan to arrive at the entrance at least 30 minutes before the park opens. If you drive, arrive at least 45 minutes early to park and make your way to the entrance, either on foot or by monorail.

GETTING ORIENTATED Once in the park, Alton Towers consists of 13 themed lands. You enter through **Towers Street,** which contains guest services and a handful of souvenir shops and restaurants. Proceeding approximately clockwise from Towers Street, you'll first encounter **Mutiny Bay,** a pirate-themed land with four attractions, a stage show and several restaurants. Next is **Katanga Canyon,** with two relatively-tame, vaguely-wilderness-themed attractions and a restaurant. Continuing on, you'll find **Gloomy Wood,** whose main attraction is a haunted-house ride-through; **Forbidden Valley** is farther, with four of the park's main thrill rides and a handful of food stands.

In the middle of the park is **The Gardens,** a winding, stair-filled

THEME PARKS AND ATTRACTIONS

FASTRACK AT ALTON TOWERS

Air	The Flume	Ripsaw
Battle Galleons	Heave Ho!	Rita
Congo River Rapids	Hex	Runaway Mine Train
Charlie & The Chocolate Factory: The Ride	Marauder's Mayhem	Sonic Spinball
Duel	Nemesis	Submission
Enterprise	Oblivion	TH13TEEN

walk through the gardens and forest of the ancestral Alton estate. At the opposite end of the property from the park entrance is **Dark Forest,** which holds two more of the park's most popular thrill rides. Next to it is **Cloud Cuckoo Land,** one of three park areas dedicated to children.

Past Cloud Cuckoo Land is **The Towers,** the long-abandoned home and hunting lodge of the Earl of Shrewsbury, with one attraction and a small landscaped garden incorporated into the ruin. If you're on the north or northwest side of the park, The Towers is a useful reference point for determining your location.

Next is **X-Sector,** whose unpublished theme, we're convinced, is 'rides that make anyone over 30 vomit'. **Adventure Land** and **Old MacDonald's Farmyard** round out the lands, with both of these dedicated to animal-themed kiddie attractions.

PARK SERVICES Most are found on **Towers Street.** Pushchairs are available for hire at a cost of £5 per day for a single and £9 for a double, plus a £5 refundable deposit. A limited number of wheelchairs are available as well, for a deposit of £20 per day. You'll need to bring proof of disability, such as a Disability Living Allowance book, Attendance Allowance book or Invalidity Benefit book, or face an additional £10 per day. See **altontowers.com** for a complete list of acceptable documents for proof of disability.

FASTRACK Available at several Merlin Entertainments theme parks in England, Fastrack is a pay scheme that allows you to bypass the standby queue at some of the park's most popular attractions. Fastrack is available for everything from a single ride on 1 attraction to unlimited riding for an entire day on almost 20 attractions. The per-person cost ranges from £2 for a single ride on Flume up to £80 for the unlimited plan. Most of the popular attractions cost £4–£5 per person per ride.

Fastrack can be purchased both in advance and on the day of your visit; check **altontowers.com/plan-your-visit/fast-track** for package details. Save your receipts, as you'll need to show these prior to boarding each ride.

> **unofficial TIP**
>
> In our experience, the opening Fastrack return time (2.30 p.m. in our example) is strictly enforced, so you cannot arrive early to ride. The closing return time (3.30 p.m.) is not enforced, so you're able to come back any time after the first time listed on your Fastrack. We were able to use 'expired' Fastrack receipts on every attraction up until the park closed.

In most cases, you cannot immediately use your Fastrack after purchase. Rather, each Fastrack receipt lists a time window, such as 2.30–3.30 p.m., when you're asked to return and ride. This allows Alton Towers to smooth out spikes in demand, manage each attraction's capacity and prevent even longer standby queues.

Because each Fastrack's return time is based on the ride's capacity and the park's attendance that day, the later in the day you purchase your Fastrack, the later your return time will be to ride. Thus, you're better off buying Fastrack in advance or very early upon arrival. Once a ride's Fastrack capacity for the day has been sold, your only option is the standby queue that everyone else uses.

When using Fastrack, you enter a dedicated Fastrack queue separate from the standby queue. (Sometimes the Fastrack entrance is also the ride's exit. Whichever the option, the signage is clear on which way to go.) Both the standby and Fastrack queues merge very close to the attraction's boarding area.

At the boarding area, the attraction's operators favour Fastrack guests by allocating more of each attraction's capacity to guests in the Fastrack queue than in the standby queue. For example, 15 of the 20 seats on Rita may be allocated to Fastrack guests, with only 5 seats left for standby guests. The actual ratio of Fastrack guests to standby guests is at the discretion of each attraction's operators, but the policy is the same on every Fastrack ride. In short, Fastrack provides preferential treatment to those willing to shell out a few more quid per ride.

Long waits in queues are possible even with Fastrack. Enough people are willing to drop £5 per ride for Rita, for instance, to make the wait in the Fastrack queue up to 30 minutes long during peak summer days when the standby queue hits 2½ hours.

In our experience, Fastrack is useful only on a small number of attractions, and then only during busier times of the year. Our Alton Towers touring plans avoid much of the wait from these attractions, too, removing a lot of the need for Fastrack. If you arrive after park opening, however, or simply want to experience certain attractions multiple times, then Fastrack may be useful. In those situations, we'd recommend Fastrack for Air, Nemesis, Oblivion, Rita and TH13TEEN. All but TH13TEEN have a free single-rider queue, too, described in the next section.

SINGLE-RIDER QUEUES The best way to ensure a theme-park ride is running at full capacity is to put a guest in every seat of every ride vehicle before it leaves the loading area. It happens, however, that you often find an empty seat here or there because the next group in the queue may not have exactly the right number of people to fill all of the seats. To maximise capacity on the most popular rides, most theme parks use a simple solution: the 'single rider' queue.

At the loading point, visitors are taken from the single-rider queue one at a time and directed to empty seats. Because these empty seats appear at random times, one or more ride vehicles may depart without taking anyone from the single-rider queue. Families with small children are discouraged from using this queue, as it's virtually guaranteed that the group will be split amongst different ride vehicles, sometimes many minutes apart. For teens, adults and small groups who don't mind a little separation in exchange for shorter waits, though, single-rider queues are often useful.

Six attractions at Alton Towers have single-rider queues: Air, Nemesis, Oblivion, Rita, Sonic Spinball, and and TH13TEEN. Most of these are also the attractions for which we think Fastrack is most useful. Thus, if you've got a small group, the single-rider queue is an inexpensive alternative to Fastrack.

PARENT QUEUE SHARE (AKA 'SWITCHING OFF', 'CHILD SWAP' OR 'PARENT SWAP')
Several attractions have minimum height and/or age requirements. Some families with children too small or too young forgo these attractions, while others take turns queuing to ride. Missing some of Alton Towers' best rides is an unnecessary sacrifice, and waiting in a standby queue twice for the same ride is a tremendous waste of time.

Instead, take advantage of Alton Towers' free Parent Queue Share pass, available at Guest Services on Towers Street. To use the pass, your group must comprise at least two adults and at least one child under 1.2 m tall. The entire group will head for the standby queue at an attraction. When you reach an Alton Towers ride attendant, say you want to use the Parent Queue Share. The ride attendant will direct the non-riding adult, as well as the non-riding members of the group, to a location near the ride's exit where they can meet up with the riding adult. The ride attendant will also tell the non-riding adult how to access the attraction without waiting again in the standby queue (for example, by telling the non-riding adult to use the Fastrack queue instead of the standby queue).

Once everyone has met up, the next parent takes the Parent Queue Share pass and enters the alternate queue as directed. Everyone meets up near the ride's exit, as before, and the entire group proceeds to the next attraction.

The Parent Queue Share pass works especially well for large groups of adults and children. Some non-riding adults decide to take non-riding children on nearby age-appropriate attractions that aren't otherwise interesting for the rest of the group. This allows everyone to experience their favourite attractions without unnecessary queuing.

The one downside to the Parent Queue Share pass is that some areas of Alton Towers have no child-friendly attractions anywhere near their thrill rides. You're forced either to walk to another section of the park or have small children stand around until the riding parent is done. For example, Forbidden Valley (home to Air, Nemesis, The Blade and Ripsaw) has no attractions appropriate for small children. The nearest kid-friendly rides are the Runaway Mine Train and Congo River Rapids in Katanga Canyon, near the opposite end of the park.

Mutiny Bay

This pirate-themed area is immediately to the left of Towers Street. It consists of six attractions, a live show and three restaurants. Before the entrance to Mutiny Bay is the **Skyride** station, which connects to Forbidden Valley and Cloud Cuckoo Land and saves quite a bit of walking if you're trying to get between the front and back of the park.

Of the Mutiny Bay restaurants, we prefer the **Courtyard BBQ and Bar.** Menu items cost between £8 and £10 and include rotisserie chicken, burgers and BBQ ribs. Vegetarian burgers and children's meals are available, as is beer. Seating is outdoors under a large canopy, which is fine most of the year. When it rains, however, hordes of dripping-wet guests will crowd around your table, seeking shelter from the storm.

Courtyard Hot Dogs, Pasties and Pancakes serves exactly what it says. All of the food is take-away. The hot dogs and pasties aren't bad, especially on cooler days. If you can find a seat near the corner of Mutiny Bay, you'll have a nice view of the lake while you dine.

The other restaurant is the **Mexican Cantina** (entrée range £3–£8). While the service is friendly enough and the portions are large, the food is bland, with nary a Mexican flavour to be found. Our chicken burrito tasted more like Italian chicken Parmigiana wrapped in a tortilla.

Battle Galleons (Fastrack) ★★★

What it is Outdoor boat ride. **Scope and scale** Minor attraction. **Height requirement** 3' (0.9 m) to ride; under 3'5" (1.1 m) must ride with an adult. **Fright potential** None. **When to go** Between 11 a.m. and 4 p.m. **Authors' rating** Real pirates don't wear ponchos; ★★★. **Duration of ride** About 6 minutes. **Average wait in queue per 100 people ahead of you** About 11 minutes. **Loading speed** Slow.

DESCRIPTION AND COMMENTS There's a saying for parents along the lines of 'If kids are crabby, put them in water'. Nothing better illustrates this than the Battle Galleons, a group of miniature pirate ships that 'sail' on top of an underwater track around a small section of the lake. Each pirate ship has a set of water cannons that spray bystanders and other ships when riders turn a small crank on the cannon. The faster you turn the crank, the farther the water travels. The track layout guarantees that ships get close enough to each other for a few water fights.

Bystanders have their own land-based armaments, and the result is that anyone within shouting distance of the ride gets completely soaked. In the times we observed the Galleons, we saw grumpy teens and tired parents transformed into laughing, drenched families. It's proof that you don't have to spend £10 million on the latest technology to end up with an entertaining ride.

TOURING TIPS Battle Galleons is usually not crowded in the early morning. Try just before lunchtime or around dinner. Large drying stations are available for £2 just outside the ride, but these don't seem to work very well. Wear a mac if you must, landlubber.

Marauder's Mayhem (Fastrack) ★★

What it is Funfair-type spinning ride. **Scope and scale** Minor attraction. **Height requirement** 3' (0.9 m) to ride; under 3'5" (1.1 m) must ride with an adult. **Fright potential** None, but may induce motion sickness. **When to go** Before 11 a.m. or after 4 p.m. **Authors' rating** We asked for hazard pay after riding; ★★. **Duration of ride** About 2½ minutes. **Average wait in queue per 100 people ahead of you** About 11 minutes. **Loading speed** Slow.

DESCRIPTION AND COMMENTS If you've ever wondered what it's like to be a pair of socks in an electric clothes dryer, then this is your chance to find out. Four or five riders sit in a circular vehicle, modelled after a pirate ship's gunpowder keg. Each keg has a small metal wheel in the middle. Turning the wheel spins the keg around, and the faster you turn the wheel, the faster the keg spins. Further, each keg spins in a small circle with two other kegs. The entire group of 12 kegs spins in a much larger orbit, so it's circles within circles within circles.

Needless to say, teenagers love to ride Marauder's Mayhem with unsuspecting adults and tormentable siblings. With a bit of advance preparation, parents, it's possible to identify discreet places near the attraction where you can throw up after riding.

TOURING TIPS Not usually crowded (go figure!) until mid-afternoon. Check to see if there's only one operator running the ride. If so, the time it takes to load and unload guests from the kegs can be about twice as long as the ride itself.

Heave Ho! (Fastrack) ★★

What it is Side-to-side swinging-boat ride. **Scope and scale** Minor attraction. **Height requirement** 3' (0.9 m) to ride; under 3'5" (1.1 m) must ride with an adult. **Fright potential** None, but may induce motion sickness. **When to go** Before 11 a.m. or after 4 p.m. **Authors' rating** Alton should sell Dramamine-flavoured snacks on the side; ★★. **Duration of ride** About 1½ minutes. **Average wait in queue per 100 people ahead of you** About 11 minutes. **Loading speed** Slow.

DESCRIPTION AND COMMENTS Riders board a miniature pirate ship that swings back and forth on a track on the ground. The pirate ship also spins in a small circle while it swings. Heave Ho! is much like a smaller, less intense version of The Blade in Forbidden Valley (which doesn't spin), and is appropriate for small children.

TOURING TIPS Part of Heave Ho!'s popularity comes from the fact that it's outdoors, without a roof or enclosure, and thus easily visible to small children. We suggest riding first thing in the morning or around dinnertime.

The Flume (Fastrack) ★★

What it is Water-flume ride. **Scope and scale** Major attraction. **Height requirement** 3' (0.9 m) to ride; under 3'5" (1.1 m) must ride with an adult. **Fright potential** Smaller children may be frightened by the drop at the end of the ride, visible from the queue. **When to go** Between 11 a.m. and noon or after 4 p.m. **Authors' rating** Like a shower in the forest; ★★. **Duration of ride** About 5 minutes. **Average wait in queue per 100 people ahead of you** About 11 minutes. **Loading speed** Slow.

DESCRIPTION AND COMMENTS A traditional water-flume ride, with an odd bathtub-and-shower and farm theme. The bathtub-shaped ride vehicles hold three people.

Though the ride lasts nearly 5 minutes, most of it consists of floating past the wooded area surrounding the track. There's no story or theme to the ride, and no compelling visuals through most of the ride to keep you interested.

The Flume has three relatively small drops, none of which should be frightening to most children. The major source of fear seems to be from the screams of riders during the last drop, which is visible from Mutiny Bay and the queue. It's not as bad as it seems, however, and most kids get a kick out of it.

TOURING TIPS Usually opens at 11 a.m. While everyone will get wet, riders in the front will get soaked. Bring ponchos or macs unless you need to cool off.

The Pirate of Sharkbait Reef ★★

What it is Live-action show. **Scope and scale** Minor attraction. **Fright potential** Low. There's a skeleton on stage, some play fighting, and small bursts of flame as special effects. **When to go** Check the posted entertainment schedule for show times. **Authors' rating** Combined with a cold drink, makes a nice break in the afternoon; ★★. **Duration of show** About 15 minutes.

DESCRIPTION AND COMMENTS Performed near Courtyard BBQ and Bar, *The Pirate of Sharkbait Reef* combines singing, jokes and a bit of stage fighting into an entertaining live performance. The story follows the kidnapping of beautiful Emily by pirate Sharktooth Jack, and her eventual rescue by Billy the deckhand.

The show's dialogue and jokes are done at a fairly rapid pace that may confuse smaller children. There are enough visual elements going on during the show, however, to keep their attention.

TOURING TIPS The audience stands during the show. Arrive about 10 minutes early, grab a drink and get a spot up front.

Skyride ★★½

What it is Suspended cable car ride. **Scope and scale** Minor attraction. **Fright potential** Not for those with a fear of heights. **When to go** Anytime. **Authors' rating** Beats walking; ★★½. **Duration of ride** About 4 minutes per segment. **Average wait in queue per 100 people ahead of you** About 4 minutes. **Loading speed** Moderate.

DESCRIPTION AND COMMENTS Riders board an enclosed, windowed car, suspended via long cables attached to towers, and travel between the front and back of the park. Boarding stations are just before the entrance to Mutiny Bay, Forbidden Valley and the border of Cloud Cuckoo Land and Dark Forest.

The ride is gentle and relaxing, with wonderful views of the park. The experience is punctuated occasionally by the screams of riders on some of the attractions you pass between stations. Also, the segment between Cloud Cuckoo Land and Forbidden Valley takes you fairly high over the woods, and there's a decent chance you'll be stopped here to allow riders in the cars ahead to unload at the Forbidden Valley station.

If you're afraid of heights and haven't exercised in a while, you'll have to choose between 4 minutes of potential terror here or 10 minutes of sweat-inducing hiking through The Gardens. We suggest the Skyride.

TOURING TIPS A great way to get between the front of the park to Dark Forest, Cloud Cuckoo Land or The Towers. Take the Skyride back to the front of the park to end your day.

Sharkbait Reef Aquarium ★★★½

What it is Walk-through aquarium and aquatic exhibits. **Scope and scale** Major attraction. **Fright potential** None. **When to go** Anytime. **Authors' rating** Plenty of live, colourful fish exhibits. Don't miss it; ★★½. **Duration of presentation** Allow 20–30 minutes for a full walk-through.

DESCRIPTION AND COMMENTS Opened in 2009, Sharkbait Reef is a large, detailed walk-through exhibit of marine life, including sharks, rays and hundreds of colourful fish. Besides a large aquarium, there are dozens of smaller displays dedicated to various species. All are presented with short, educational written descriptions of the creatures' habitats and special adaptations to it. In addition to the displays, regular live presentations are held at some of the larger exhibits. Ask a member of staff for the schedule.

TOURING TIPS Don't miss the display areas that jut out from the main rooms, under the water. It feels like you're standing on the ocean floor.

The tour can get crowded during late afternoon, and it has a number of twists and turns along the way. Keep an eye on the little ones, as kids can get lost whilst everyone's watching the fish.

Katanga Canyon

This themed area sits between Mutiny Bay and Forbidden Valley in the lower-left corner of the park. Unlike Mutiny Bay, Katanga Canyon doesn't have a coherent, unifying theme to tie together its rides (we'd call it 'Adventure-ish'). Both of the attractions are worth visiting, though.

Katanga Canyon also has the **Explorers Pizza and Pasta Buffet,** an all-you-care-to-eat restaurant serving a variety of dishes, as well as a salad bar. Indoor and outdoor seating is available, and the cost is around £9 per adult and £6 per child. Most of the families we spoke with thought Explorers was the best dining value in the park.

If you're looking for a filling meal on a budget, or you have picky eaters, we'd have to agree.

Congo River Rapids (Fastrack) ★★★★

What it is White-water raft ride. **Scope and scale** Major attraction. **Height requirement** 3' (0.9 m) to ride; under 3'5" (1.1 m) must ride with an adult. **Fright potential** None. **When to go** Opens at 11 a.m. Visit between 11 a.m. and noon or in the last hour the park is open. **Authors' rating** Well done; ★★★★. **Duration of ride** About 5 minutes. **Average wait in queue per 100 people ahead of you** About 3 minutes; assumes more than 25 rafts operating. **Loading speed** Fast.

DESCRIPTION AND COMMENTS A white-water raft ride around most of Katanga Canyon, Congo River Rapids is a relaxing ride for the whole family. There's no story to follow while on the ride, but the scenery is lovely, with lush plants, rock outcroppings, waterfalls and a couple of bridges to float under.

The appeal of most raft rides comes from the water itself. Due to the currents, waves and splashes can't be predicted, and each ride is a different experience. It's entirely possible that half your family will stay dry and the other half will be wet to the bone. Ride twice to even out the odds.

TOURING TIPS When running at full capacity, Congo River Rapids can handle more than 2,000 riders per hour, one of the highest capacities of any attraction in any UK theme park. Don't be dissuaded by long queues right before the Rapids opens, as these will usually be dispatched within minutes of the ride starting.

Runaway Mine Train (Fastrack) ★★★½

What it is Small roller coaster. **Scope and scale** Minor attraction. **Height requirement** 3' (0.9 m) to ride; under 3'5" (1.1 m) must ride with an adult. **Fright potential** None. **When to go** Before 11 a.m. or after 4 p.m. **Authors' rating** Charming and well themed; ★★★½. **Duration of ride** About 4 minutes. **Average wait in queue per 100 people ahead of you** About 11 minutes; assumes 1 train running. **Loading speed** Slow.

DESCRIPTION AND COMMENTS Runaway Mine Train is a relatively-gentle introduction to roller coasters for young children. Decorated in the style of an abandoned mine, with lots of tied wood logs, fence posts and the like, it's one of the best-themed attractions in the park. It also runs past part of the Congo River Rapids, in case you need a quick glimpse into how wet you might get on that.

The Mine Train's track is short, and one lap takes little more than a minute. Because of this, most rides consist of two or three laps around the track. At the end of your first lap, when the ride operator asks over the public-address system whether anyone wants to go round again, don't expect you've really been given an option.

TOURING TIPS Riders sit in rows of two, so families with small children and an odd number of members should decide in advance who is sitting with whom.

Gloomy Wood

This area connects Mutiny Bay with Forbidden Valley. **Haunted Hollow,** listed as an attraction on park maps, is a wooded walking path beginning at Mutiny Bay that makes up half of the things to see in the Wood. The Hollow has a couple of moderately-interesting effects, but nothing that should be frightening to most children, and nothing that would make us consider this an 'attraction' in the proper sense. See Haunted Hollow on your way out of the park or on your second day at Alton Towers. The other attraction in Gloomy Wood is **Duel,** described below.

Duel – The Haunted House Strikes Back (Fastrack) ★★★

What it is Combination haunted house and indoor shooting gallery. **Scope and scale** Major attraction. **Height requirement** Under 1.1 m must ride with an adult. **Fright potential** Frightening to many children, with skeletons, ghosts and other effects. **When to go** Anytime. **Authors' rating** Entertaining and well themed; ★★★. **Duration of ride** About 5 minutes. **Average wait in queue per 100 people ahead of you** About 4 minutes; assumes 25 ride vehicles operating. **Loading speed** Fast.

DESCRIPTION AND COMMENTS Duel combines the visual elements of a traditional haunted house – mostly ghosts and skeletons – with an indoor shooting gallery. Each person in Duel's five-seat ride vehicles gets an electronic laser gun, used to shoot at light-sensitive targets on the ghoulish inhabitants along the ride.

The ride's story involves a doctor who once used to live in the house and whose hobby involved bringing people back from the dead. Not surprisingly, the doctor's experiments go wrong and the house becomes filled with zombies. The story-line becomes vague when trying to explain what you're supposed to be doing there. Our guess is that you've been sent by desperate real-estate agents trying to maintain the property values of the neighbourhood. Let us know if you come up with something better.

Duel has the potential to frighten almost any child. Besides the creepy theme, darkness, strobe lighting and scream-filled soundtrack, the ghosts and ghouls can be terrifying to look at. In addition, there are so many of them, and they're presented at such a frenetic pace, that Duel is bound to test almost anyone's limits.

TOURING TIPS Each ride vehicle has a row of two seats and a row of three seats. Families with small children and an odd number of members should decide in advance who is sitting with whom. In front of each seat is a scoring system with a display. Two tips for achieving a high score: If you see both yellow and green targets to shoot at, go for the yellow ones first, since they're worth more. Also, try to ride with as few people as possible, because everyone in the car with you, as well as the cars before and after you, is essentially shooting at the same targets.

Forbidden Valley

Sitting on the leftmost part of the park, Forbidden Valley is home to four of Alton Towers' most popular thrill rides. It also has one of the park's three **Skyride** stations. From here you can take a cable car to the **Mutiny Bay–Towers Street** area at the front of the park, or to the **Dark Forest–Cloud Cuckoo Land–Towers** area at the back.

Forbidden Valley contains two restaurants. One is a **Burger King**, serving burgers, chicken sandwiches and fries either for dine-in or take-away. The other, **Fresh Fish and Chips**, serves, well, fish. And chips. Both will do in a pinch, but neither is memorable or worth crossing the park to find. A couple of other snack kiosks are here, too.

Ripsaw (Fastrack) ★★★

What it is Like riding an oversized washing machine. **Scope and scale** Minor attraction. **Height requirement** Riders must be between 3'5" (1.1 m) and 6'4½" (1.95 m). **Fright potential** The height and spinning can frighten many children and adults. **When to go** Anytime. **Authors' rating** Great on a warm day; ★★★. **Duration of ride** Just under 2 minutes. **Average wait in queue per 100 people ahead of you** About 10 minutes. **Loading speed** Slow.

DESCRIPTION AND COMMENTS Imagine you're sitting comfortably on your sofa at home, when suddenly two giant robot arms burst through the walls and clamp on to either end of your couch, lifting you into the air and spinning the couch on its axis as both arms make a giant circle over what remains of your house. Now imagine that when they burst through the walls, these arms ruptured the neighbourhood's water pipes, which now spray you every couple of times the robot arms circle you around.

Add in a couple of shoulder restraints, and you've got Ripsaw. (You've also got half the plot to another Bruce Willis movie, but that's another book.) While there's lots of spinning and circling, the ride is pretty smooth. The experience takes place above a small pool of water, where pressurised fountains shoot water at key points during the ride to either warn you of what's to come or give you a thorough soaking. Very popular on warm days, especially with teens.

TOURING TIPS No seat is protected from getting wet. Wear a poncho. How wet you'll get depends on your height – the taller the wetter.

The Blade ★★★

What it is Swinging-boat ride. **Scope and scale** Minor attraction. **Height requirement** 3' (0.9 m) to ride; under 3'5" (1.1 m) must ride with an adult. **Fright potential** The height and sensation of weightlessness can frighten some children. **When to go** Anytime. **Authors' rating** Mild, fun zero-gravity experience; ★★★. **Duration of ride** Just under 2 minutes. **Average wait in

queue per 100 people ahead of you About 9 minutes; assumes all 45 seats filled. **Loading speed** Slow.

DESCRIPTION AND COMMENTS Riders board a boat-like vehicle that is suspended from above. The boat starts off with gentle gliding back and forth before progressing quickly to swift half-circle swings. Riders at either end of the boat experience strong, brief sensations of weightlessness at the top and bottom of each swing. Sit in the middle of the boat for a less-intense experience.

TOURING TIPS Most guests bypass The Blade to get to Nemesis and Air. Long queues don't usually develop until mid-afternoon.

Nemesis (Fastrack) ★★★★

What it is Suspended roller coaster. **Scope and scale** Headliner attraction. **Height requirement** 4'7" (1.4 m) to ride. **Fright potential** An intense ride that can frighten children and adults alike. **When to go** As soon as the park opens, in the last hour before the park closes or use Fastrack. **Authors' rating** Alton Towers' best thrill ride; ★★★★. **Duration of ride** Just under 2 minutes. **Average wait in queue per 100 people ahead of you** About 7 minutes; assumes 2 trains running. **Loading speed** Moderate.

DESCRIPTION AND COMMENTS Nearing 20 years old, Nemesis is still consistently ranked as one of the best thrill rides in the UK. This is almost entirely due to the ride's never-goes-out-of-style design of tight high-speed turns, three rolls and one complete loop. Despite a complete ride time of just under 2 minutes, you're in constant, fast motion almost the entire time, and rarely going straight and level for more than a few tenths of a second.

Riders' seats are suspended from above, so your legs dangle throughout the ride. This accentuates the g-forces generated in turns and loops and makes it seem that Nemesis is faster than it really is. By far the best seats are up front. A separate queue exists just for these seats, and waits can be double those for the rest of the ride. If you can get to Nemesis first thing in the morning, seats up front are worth the extra short wait.

There's supposed to be a story attached to the ride, but it's hardly noticeable. Because the ride has to meet the local town's sight and noise ordinances, part of Nemesis is set into the ground. The ride's designers made the most of this, putting part of the standby queue in a tight canyon wall within the ride itself. Through a combination of speed and air pressure from the confined space, passing ride vehicles generate enough wind to knock the hats off guests in the queue.

Finally, note that Alton Towers' Nemesis ride is a similar design to the Nemesis Inferno ride at Thorpe Park outside London (see page 133).

TOURING TIPS Nemesis operates in light-to-moderate rain, but the experience is like riding a motorcycle in a downpour without a helmet.

Despite the height requirement, Nemesis is one of the most popular attractions in the park. Long queues develop as soon as the first wave of guests is able to make the walk from the entrance.

Air (Fastrack) ★★★★

What it is Suspended roller coaster. **Scope and scale** Headliner attraction. **Height requirement** 4'7" (1.4 m) to ride. **Fright potential** Can frighten children and adults alike. **When to go** As soon as the park opens, in the last hour before the park closes or use Fastrack. **Authors' rating** A smooth flight; ★★★★. **Duration of ride** About 1½ minutes. **Average wait in queue per 100 people ahead of you** About 9 minutes; assumes 2 trains running. **Loading speed** Moderate.

DESCRIPTION AND COMMENTS Like Nemesis, Air is a suspended roller coaster featuring high speeds, tight turns and upside-down rolls. The first major difference is that Air has no loops. The second is that Air riders begin in a sitting position, and then the floor drops away and the seats rotate forwards 90°, with riders' legs clamped into safety harnesses, so that everyone is facing the ground during the ride. The idea is that this position gives a better sensation of flying.

Of the approximately 90 seconds of Air's ride time, about 40 seconds is spent climbing the first hill. Still, Air's overall experience is great. The track is smooth and the layout gets you close enough to treetops and the ground that it actually does feel like you're flying. Surprisingly, the face-down position makes for better views throughout most of the ride. Since you're only able to see slightly ahead and down, you concentrate on the things you hope you don't smash into. For that reason, it's not as necessary on Air as on Nemesis to sit up front to get a good view.

We like Air quite a bit. We have to confess, however, as the floor dropped away and we were rotated forwards, backsides in the air for our ride, the first thought that popped into our heads was, 'This must be how they inseminate livestock on an industrial scale.' We laughed so much we missed most of the ride and had to get in the queue again.

TOURING TIPS Along with Nemesis, Air is one of the most popular attractions in the park. Most guests see Nemesis first, and that funnels away some of the demand for Air. You're not allowed to wear hats or even glasses on Air. And be forewarned that when you're rotated to the bum-up position, the ride's restraints will put a lot of pressure on your front trouser pockets and shirt pockets. It's best, therefore, to give anything fragile like cameras or glasses to the operators when you board; they'll store them for you until you retrieve them after the ride.

The Gardens

The Gardens is a lush, landscaped refuge almost in the middle of the park. While we've joked that its primary purpose is as a physical barrier for out-of-shape theme-park guests, it's one of the loveliest gardens we've seen anywhere, and an attraction in its own right.

The Gardens straddle a small valley in the middle of the park, and there are several sets of stairs to navigate to get from one side to the other if you're on foot. Most of the landscaping, fountains, sculpture and buildings in The Gardens are adjacent to Gloomy Wood, sparing you the necessity of clambering down into the valley bottom. And though you can cross the valley to access the other side of the park, most folks opt for the Skyride cable car. Buildings include a set of glass-domed houses, a pagoda, and a Greek monument with a bust of the Earl of Shrewsbury. A set of arches made from yew trees more than a century old lines one of the walkways inside the Gardens. While many families choose the area around the lake for a mealtime picnic, we think the Gardens is a much more scenic experience.

Dark Forest

Almost directly across from Towers Street, the Dark Forest land sits at the back of the park. Here you'll find two of the park's most popular thrill rides (**Rita** and **TH13TEEN**), plus a **Skyride** station. If you're coming from Gloomy Wood or Forbidden Valley, the Skyride saves a walk through The Gardens.

Dark Forest has two restaurants: **Woodcutter's Bar and Grill** and **Forest Feast.** Woodcutter's is one of the more popular on-site restaurants, serving hearty meals of ribs, burgers, steaks and sandwiches. Vegetarian and children's meals are also available, as is beer. Most main courses run £8–£10. The décor is a little dark, in keeping with the forest theme, but service is prompt and friendly.

Forest Feast serves take-away hot dogs, jacket potatoes, pies and the like. The food's decent, but it can be difficult to find seating nearby. Most items cost £8–£10.

Rita (Fastrack) ★★★★

What it is High-speed roller coaster. **Scope and scale** Headliner. **Height requirement** 4'7" (1.4 m) to ride. **Fright potential** The launch scares some small children. **When to go** As soon as the park opens, in the last hour before the park closes or use Fastrack. **Authors' rating** Like being shot from a sling; ★★★★. **Duration of ride** About 1 minute. **Average wait in queue per 100 people ahead of you** About 5 minutes; assumes 2 trains running. **Loading speed** Moderate.

DESCRIPTION AND COMMENTS Rita is a fast-launching roller coaster. With tight turns and dips but no loops or rolls, its most notable feature is its initial launch, which takes you from standing still to more than 60 mph (96 km/h) in less than 3 seconds. You'll cover Rita's 2,000 ft (610 m) of track in under a minute. Those of you without teenage drivers in the house are almost certainly not used to such acceleration. If you've missed your morning tea or coffee, Rita will get your heart racing just the same.

TOURING TIPS The front row of the coaster is wildly popular, with a separate queue. There's also a single-rider queue available, but it doesn't appear to go much faster than the regular standby queue. While Rita's official opening time is usually the same as when the park opens to the general public, the ride is frequently running 10–20 minutes beforehand. Guests staying at Alton Towers' hotels can sometimes get a ride in before heading to TH13TEEN.

TH13TEEN (Fastrack) ★★★★

What it is High-speed roller coaster. **Scope and scale** Headliner attraction. **Height requirement** Riders must be between 3'11" (1.2 m) and 6'5" (1.96 m) to ride. **Fright potential** Moderate. The queue and soundtrack are spooky, and a couple of ride elements are surprising. **When to go** As soon as the park opens, in the last hour before the park closes or use Fastrack. **Authors' rating** Proof that a coaster doesn't have to loop to be great; ★★★★. **Duration of ride** About 2 minutes. **Average wait in queue per 100 people ahead of you** About 5 minutes; assumes 3 trains running. **Loading speed** Moderate.

DESCRIPTION AND COMMENTS TH13TEEN, opened in 2010, combines high-speed turns with a relatively-rare feature for roller coasters: a backwards-running segment.

Set in a heavily-wooded section of the park, and so far back from the rest of the attractions that the ride track is hardly visible, TH13TEEN has a theme (as far as we can tell) along the lines of 'This forest is haunted.' A creepy soundtrack at the queue entrance reinforces the atmosphere.

Heavily hyped on park maps and in television commercials, the actual ride is somewhat anti-climactic from the build-up. It begins with an uphill lift common to most coasters, and quickly follows with fast, banked turns, S-curves, dips and hills. About a minute into the ride, you pull into what looks like an abandoned unloading station. The vehicle stops here, something moderately surprising happens (we won't give it away), and you're sent backwards along the track to finish the ride.

While the ride isn't themed at all, TH13TEEN is a fun, fast coaster. We don't think it's as exciting as Nemesis, but it's longer and better than Oblivion (especially at night) and on a par with Air.

TOURING TIPS As it's the park's shiny new coaster, long queues develop from the minute the first guests are allowed in. Our advice is to ride first thing in the morning or just before the park closes, or use the single-rider queue or Fastrack. Also, TH13TEEN's queue has to be one of the longest, most convoluted paths we've ever seen in a theme-park attraction. We're pretty sure we saw families camped out along the way, resting and gathering strength for the remainder of the journey.

Cloud Cuckoo Land

Adjacent to Dark Forest at the back of the park, Cloud Cuckoo Land is one of three areas dedicated to children's rides at Alton Towers. Cloud Cuckoo Land holds six attractions, two restaurants and a toy-shop. The architecture, signage and landscaping fit together nicely, and the wide, open paths are a welcome contrast from the Towers and Dark Forest areas.

Cloud Cuckoo Land has two restaurants with indoor seating. A **Burger King** serves the usual burgers and chicken sandwiches, and the **Wobble World Café** serves coffee and tea, sandwiches, ice-cream and cakes. (Shouldn't something named 'Wobble World' be a bar serving strong adult drinks?)

Peugeot Driving School ★★½

What it is Slow-moving electric cars on simulated city streets. **Scope and scale** Minor attraction. Height/age requirement Riders must be at least 4 years old and between 3'3" (1 m) and 4'7" (1.4 m) to ride. Children between 4 and 6 should love it. **Fright potential** None. **When to go** As soon as the park opens, during lunch or dinner or in the last hour the park is open. **Authors' rating** Fun to watch kids get behind the wheel for the first time, but almost unbearably slow-loading; ★★½. **Duration of ride** Just over 3 minutes. **Average wait in queue per 100 people ahead of you** About 44 minutes; assumes 16 cars running. **Loading speed** Slow.

DESCRIPTION AND COMMENTS At Peugeot Driving School, young drivers pilot tiny, colourful plastic cars around miniature city streets. (Upon reflection, couldn't we say the same about actual Peugeot drivers?) Sixteen children at a time get a turn in a car. There's enough space for everyone to move freely, but invariably the kids end up in a giant scrum in one of the turns, as if drawn to each other by some unseen magnet.

The ride's operators stage short briefing and de-briefing sessions before and after the ride, which most kids either ignore or don't comprehend and which only serve to reduce the number of kids who can ride in any hour. That said, the ride is exceedingly charming, and most preschoolers love it.

TOURING TIPS If you think there's any chance your child might enjoy this ride, get here as soon as possible in the morning. According to our calculations, no more than 130 children can ride in an average hour, making this Alton Towers' lowest-capacity attraction.

Twirling Toadstool ★★½

What it is A flying-carousel spinning ride with chairs suspended from long chains. **Scope and scale** Minor attraction. **Height requirement** Riders must be at least 3'11" (1.2 m) to ride. **Fright potential** The height scares some small children. **When to go** Anytime. **Authors' rating** A tame introduction to this kind of ride; ★★½. **Duration of ride** About 2½ minutes. **Average wait in queue per 100 people ahead of you** About 13 minutes; assumes all 51 seats filled. **Loading speed** Slow.

DESCRIPTION AND COMMENTS Twirling Toadstool is a colourful variation of the classic funfair 'swinging chair' ride. Individual seats are suspended via long chains from the bottom of a circular roof (in this case, shaped like a giant mushroom). Once riders are seated, the roof raises a few feet off the ground and begins to spin, taking the riders with it.

Besides the spinning, Twirling Toadstool's roof oscillates up and down, like a spun penny about to settle on a tabletop. Thus, during one complete spin around the base, riders go up and down while swinging around. Most children tall enough to ride seem to take all of this in stride – we didn't see any frowns or tears while observing the ride.

TOURING TIPS Perhaps because variations of this ride can be found at many funfairs, we didn't observe long queues at any time during the three summer days we visited. Visit anytime.

Frog Hopper ½

What it is Bouncing funfair-style ride. **Scope and scale** Minor attraction. **Height requirement** 3' (0.9 m) to ride; under 3'5" (1.1 m) must ride with an adult. **Fright potential** None. **When to go** As soon as the park opens. **Authors' rating** Not worth the time in queue; ½. **Duration of ride** About 1 minute. **Average wait in queue per 100 people ahead of you** About 33 minutes; assumes all 6 seats used. **Loading speed** Slow.

DESCRIPTION AND COMMENTS Frog Hopper is a relatively simple attraction. Six riders sit in a row of seats, which is then lifted about 10 ft (3 m) off the ground. Once suspended, the row begins to bounce its way back to the ground. Most variations, including this one, include a couple of quick trips back to the top before a final hop to the ground.

Frog Hopper is visually appealing to small children because all of the activity takes place outdoors. The display of bouncing legs, laughing and shrieking adds to the excitement of riding.

TOURING TIPS The Frog Hopper ride has the second-smallest capacity of any Alton Towers attraction, barely handling 180 riders per hour. Variations on this attraction can be found at almost any theme park, so don't feel bad about skipping it if more than a few people are in the queue ahead of you. If riding is essential to your child's happiness, however, ride as soon as the park opens and just after visiting the Peugeot Driving School.

Charlie and the Chocolate Factory: The Ride (Fastrack) ★★★½

What it is Short boat ride and 360° presentation inspired by the film. **Scope and scale** Major attraction. **Height requirement** 3' (0.9 m) to ride; under 3'5" (1.1 m) must ride with an adult. **Fright potential** Some children are frightened by the lift scene at the end. **When to go** Before noon or after 4 p.m. **Authors' rating** Well done; ★★★½. **Duration of ride** About 7 minutes. **Average wait in queue per 100 people ahead of you** About 11 minutes; assumes 8 boats running. **Loading speed** Moderate.

DESCRIPTION AND COMMENTS Charlie and the Chocolate Factory is an indoor boat ride and standing film presentation that follows the story of the reclusive chocolatier Willy Wonka, his chocolate factory and a group of children who are invited to tour the factory after winning a contest. If you've missed seeing the two film versions of this Roald Dahl story over the last few decades, it goes something like this: As the kids tour the factory, each child's vice (greed, gluttony, watching too much television, excessive gum chewing, etc.) causes him or her to do something dangerous in the factory. The consequence for each child is that he or she is forced to leave the tour, in ways befitting his or her vice's consequences. At the end, only well-behaved Charlie remains, and he inherits the entire factory from Wonka.

The initial part of Alton Towers' book adaptation consists of a boat ride through the first few children's mistakes. The boat ride ends, and riders walk to a small room for a quick film presentation of the fate of all but one of the remaining children. The final part of the ride takes place in a simulated stand-up lift 'inside' the chocolate factory. Film projections on all four walls make it seem as if you're in the lift with Charlie and Willy as they zip up, down and sideways through the factory and beyond, as Willy shows Charlie all that he's won.

If you've seen either version of the film, each of the ride's scenes will be instantly recognisable, as will the children's fates. None of the scenes is as detailed or colourful as those in the original 1971 film, and that's a bit disappointing. The lighting is also fairly dark throughout, giving the attraction a less light-hearted feel than the movie.

TOURING TIPS Long queues develop around mid-afternoon. If you're spending the morning in Cloud Cuckoo Land, we advise seeing Charlie after the Peugeot Driving School, Frog Hopper and Galloper's Carousel.

Galloper's Carousel ★★

What it is Small horse-themed carousel. **Scope and scale** Minor attraction. **Height requirement** Under 4'3" (1.3 m) must ride with an adult. **Fright potential** None. **When to go** Before 11 a.m. or after 4 p.m. **Authors' rating** Very colourful and well maintained; ★★. **Duration of ride** About 2½ minutes. **Average wait in queue per 100 people ahead of you** About 21 minutes; assumes all 32 seats filled per ride. **Loading speed** Slow.

DESCRIPTION AND COMMENTS A pretty, colourful classic carousel, with shiny horses and carriages. The horses rock gently back and forth and go up and down. Most children love it, and it's a bit of shade for parents who have to stand next to them.

TOURING TIPS A complete load-ride-unload cycle of the Carousel takes about 6½ minutes on average, limiting the Carousel to just under 300 people per hour. Experience the Carousel after the Peugeot Driving School and Frog Hopper.

Wobble World ★★

What it is Enclosed room with air-inflated bouncy castles and the like. **Scope and scale** Minor attraction. **Height requirement** Under 3' (0.9 m) for the smaller areas; between 3' (0.9 m) and 3'11" (1.2 m) for the large. **Fright potential** None. **When to go** Anytime. **Authors' rating** Good for letting kids blow off some steam; ★★. **Duration of play** 10 minutes is the (unenforced) limit per visit. **Average wait in queue per 100 people ahead of you** 10 minutes; assumes all rooms filled. **Loading speed** Slow.

DESCRIPTION AND COMMENTS Wobble World is an indoor play area themed with mushrooms and 2D forest scenes. Kids can bounce around inside air-inflated castles or jump into a giant ball-filled pit. It's great for letting small children run around after standing in queues for a couple of hours. Grab a drink and a snack at the nearby Wobble World Café, and let the kids do their thing.

TOURING TIPS Seating is available outside Wobble World, from which all of the attraction's entrances and exits can be watched. This makes it easy to take a break while keeping an eye on the kids.

Because there's no ride or film, waits throughout the day are usually less than 15 minutes. We were told that each child is limited to 10 minutes of playtime before being asked to leave, but we never saw this policy enforced even once.

Cloud Cuckoo Land Theatre ★★★★

What it is Elaborate stage show with puppets. **Scope and scale** Minor attraction. **Fright potential** None. **When to go** See the daily performance schedule for show times. **Authors' rating** Much better than the outside of the theatre would suggest; ★★★★. **Duration of show** 25 minutes.

DESCRIPTION AND COMMENTS The Cloud Cuckoo Land Theatre stages an elaborate live-action show several times per day. While the show usually changes every year or so, the basic recipe is the same: a bit of dialogue, lots of singing and some on-stage special effects. This year's show theme is along the lines of 'anything you can dream is possible', but you'd be hard-pressed to remember how that's different from anything presented before.

None of that will make a bit of difference to the young children for whom the presentation is staged. With the show's oversized props, zippy stage lighting and effects, a good sound system and plenty of catchy songs, most kids are too busy clapping along to notice the plot.

TOURING TIPS Arrive about 10 minutes before show time to get a decent seat, 20 minutes to get a good one up front.

The Towers

While few relics remain from Alton Towers' heyday as an estate, theme-park guests can still walk through some of the abandoned ruin, from the ground floor to the tower itself. Because it's enormous and built of brick, the interior of the home can remain comfortably cool well into a hot summer's day. If you're willing to climb to the rooftop or tower, you'll have an almost-constant refreshing wind and unparalleled views of the entire countryside. Inside is also a unique (and uncrowded) place to have lunch.

As visiting Americans, we were initially surprised that Alton Towers' management lets guests walk through what is essentially a condemned building. While there are no blatantly-dangerous areas in the Towers, there are narrow, darkly-lit paths, a few creaky wood staircases, and enough broken mortar bits and other debris to ensure you'll need to look carefully where you're going. If the Towers were in the US, we think it would take about 5 minutes for someone to trip over an old brick, find a lawyer and sue for emotional distress. We also hope that Alton Towers' management doesn't change a thing and tells us to keep our litigious American opinions to ourselves – walking through the Towers is a real treat!

Hex – The Legend of the Towers (Fastrack) ★★★

What it is Indoor ride and optical illusion. **Scope and scale** Major attraction. **Height requirement** 3' (0.9 m) to ride; under 3'5" (1.1 m) must ride with an adult. **Fright potential** Frightening to children of all ages. **When to go** Before 1 p.m. or after 4 p.m. **Authors' rating** Don't look for equilibrium; ★★★. **Duration of ride** About 9½ minutes, including 7-minute pre-show. **Average wait in queue per 100 people ahead of you** 13 minutes; assumes all 80 seats filled for each ride. **Loading speed** Slow.

DESCRIPTION AND COMMENTS Hex is the only attraction in the park housed inside the former Alton Towers ruin. It's a great use of the Towers' immense Gothic space, and not bad as far as the story-line goes.

Upon entering the queue, guests are shown a video in which the team responsible for preserving Alton Towers' buildings and heritage stumble across evidence of an old curse that befell one of the previous earls who owned Alton Towers. The story continues to unfold in subsequent video presentations as you wind your way through the queue and deeper into the old home. We won't spoil the story for you, but the end result is that guests are seated in a cathedral-like room, on long rows of seats, where they get to view evidence of the curse.

While you're sitting there, you notice that the room has begun to sway back and forwards. The seats are moving, and it appears you're being swung higher and higher towards the ceiling. Through a very clever visual trick, it seems as if your seat does a complete loop around the inside of the room. As you're thus made dizzy, the curse is satisfied, the seats stop swinging, and whatever supernatural spirits that uphold the curse get ready for the next wave of guests.

All in all, Hex has the potential to be a really great ride. As we note previously, it's a perfect use of the Towers' ruins, it's consistent with the theme of the building and the ride mechanism is well done. The story is just a bit weak, however, and one ride seems to be enough for most folk.

TOURING TIPS Most people pass by the entrance to Hex on their way to Dark Forest or Cloud Cuckoo Land. For this reason, Hex doesn't usually get busy until the afternoon. Be aware that the ride area is in the far back of the main hallway, and the hallway (the queue) holds hundreds of people.

X-Sector

With attractions named **Oblivion** and **Submission,** X-Sector clearly doesn't contain fluffy bunnies and prancing unicorns. We can't figure out what, exactly, X-Sector's theme is (if anything), but if we had to guess, it's something along the lines of technology-gone-bad space travel.

Besides Oblivion and Submission, X-Sector contains **Enterprise** – a paean to human centrifuge experiments – and a surprisingly-popular **KFC** restaurant. Oblivion is a relatively-new thrill ride for the park and opens an hour early for Alton Towers Hotel guests, before the general public is admitted. If you're in the park in the morning and hear screaming, it's probably coming from Oblivion.

The KFC offers a wide variety of chicken meals. Ours were served hot, fresh and fast. Not surprisingly, then, KFC gets mobbed around lunchtime. Many people choose to take away their food and eat either on the grass around the lake or in the shadow of the towers.

Submission (Fastrack) ★★★

What it is A goes-upside-down twist on the classic funfair swinging-boat ride. **Scope and scale** Minor attraction. **Height requirement** 3'11" (1.2 m) to ride. **Fright potential** Frightening to many small children. **When to go** Anytime. **Authors' rating** We surrender! ★★★. **Duration of ride** About 2½ minutes. **Average wait in queue per 100 people ahead of you** 20 minutes; assumes both sides operating and all 20 seats filled for each side. **Loading speed** Slow.

DESCRIPTION AND COMMENTS Submission is a modern variation on the classic swinging-pirate-boat funfair ride. Instead of being suspended from cables at either end of the boat, however, Submission's 20-seat vehicle has a pivoting metal arm just below the middle of the boat. (Imagine a Ferris wheel with just one gondola, which spins in its own circle while the Ferris wheel turns.) At various points (not coincidentally, mostly while you're upside-down) the spinning stops, allowing riders to ponder their place in the universe from a different perspective.

TOURING TIPS Not as popular as Oblivion, perhaps because guests get to see up close exactly what it is they're in for. During our visit during the busy summer holidays, we rarely saw waits of more than 20 minutes here.

Enterprise (Fastrack) ★★½

What it is Fast-spinning funfair ride. **Scope and scale** Minor attraction. **Height requirement** 3' (0.9 m) to ride; under 4'7" (1.4 m) must ride with an adult. **Fright potential** Frightening to many small children and those prone to motion sickness. **When to go** Before noon or after 4 p.m. **Authors' rating** We haven't been this dizzy since pound-a-pint night; ★★½. **Duration of ride** About 2 minutes. **Average wait in queue per 100 people ahead of you** 14 minutes; assumes all 20 ride vehicles filled for each cycle. **Loading speed** Slow.

DESCRIPTION AND COMMENTS Another variation on a classic funfair attraction. In Enterprise, one or two riders sit in enclosed metal capsules that spin around a central axis. Enterprise's twist is that the central axis is actually a movable metal arm that pivots from flat on the ground to nearly vertical. Riders go from spinning perpendicular to the ground to looping up and down on a high-speed wheel before the metal arm pivots back down to the ground.

We rode Enterprise early in our visit to Alton Towers, before we'd had a chance to see how the arm moved. We figured something was up when we noticed we were spinning at an ever-increasing angle to the ground instead of just around in circles. In the split second it took us to figure out what was going on, we're pretty sure our shouting set a linguistic record for profanities per syllable.

TOURING TIPS Both Enterprise and Submission have about half the capacity of Oblivion, but Oblivion is far more popular. See Enterprise after Oblivion and Submission – if you're still able to walk straight.

Oblivion (Fastrack) ★★★½

What it is High-speed vertical-drop roller coaster. **Scope and scale** Headliner. **Height requirement** 4'7" (1.4 m) to ride. **Fright potential** Hell, it frightens everyone. **When to go** As soon as the park opens, in the last hour the park is open or use Fastrack. **Authors' rating** That first step is a doozy; ★★★½. **Duration of ride** About 1½ minutes. **Average wait in queue per 100 people ahead of you** 7 minutes; assumes 3 ride vehicles operating. **Loading speed** Moderate.

DESCRIPTION AND COMMENTS Opened in 1998, Oblivion was one of the world's first roller coasters to incorporate a nearly-vertical drop into its track layout. And what a drop it is!

Most of the ride's 90-second experience is spent getting you to the top of the hill. As you turn slowly through the first two corners, however, you get a glimpse of the ride's steep drop-off into a giant hole in the ground.

Just as your ride vehicle nudges over the drop-off's edge, it stops and you hang, momentarily, looking straight down into a black abyss (or more prosaically put, a big concrete hole in the ground). If you had more than a moment to think, you'd try to cut a deal with the deity of your choice, where in exchange for not having a heart attack you'd vow to live a more sober life, curse less in front of the kids and call your mum more often. Alas, the moment passes quickly, the brakes let loose and you go hurtling into the dark. It's for the best, as your vow about cursing wouldn't have lasted this far into the ride anyway and the kids are right next to you.

Your ride vehicle levels out and emerges from a tunnel a few dozen yards beyond the hole for a couple of short high-speed turns before returning to the station. It's over in a matter of seconds, but the adrenaline rush lasts much longer.

TOURING TIPS Screams from riders draw crowds as soon as the park opens. If you're staying at an Alton hotel, note that Oblivion usually opens an hour before TH13TEEN and Rita. It's possible to get in a quick ride here before queues for the other two get too long.

Adventure Land

Another land whose theme we can't quite make sense of, Adventure Land features a small roller coaster for children; a nausea-inducing, wild spinning coaster; and a gentle ride aboard a giant acorn on an elevated track. We haven't seen Alton Towers' souvenir DVD from this section of the park, but we bet it's a couple of chickens shy of something Fellini would have directed. (And the chickens are in Old MacDonald's Farmyard next door.)

Sonic Spinball (Fastrack) ★★★½

What it is Roller coaster whose ride vehicles spin 360°. **Scope and scale** Major attraction. **Height requirement** Between 3'11" (1.2 m) and 6'4½" (1.95 m) to ride. **Fright potential** Moderate – the spinning frightens young and old alike. **When to go** As soon as the park opens, in the last hour the park is open or use Fastrack. **Authors' rating** A little bumpy but a lot of fun; ★★★½. **Duration of ride** About 1½ minutes. **Average wait in queue per 100 people ahead of you** About 12 minutes; assumes 6 ride vehicles operating. **Loading speed** Moderate.

DESCRIPTION AND COMMENTS A novel coaster, with short drops, big curves and tight spins. The interesting thing is that your ride vehicle can also spin 360°. As you've got no control over the spin – it depends on how the ride was programmed – some really tight turns become gentle glides because you spin with the turn, while others become bone-jarring endurance experiments if you happen to spin against the force of the turn. We heard more grunting in our ride vehicle than in an entire hour of watching the World's Strongest Man competition.

TOURING TIPS Outdoors and highly visible from the front of the park, Sonic Spinball draws large crowds as soon as the park opens. Try first thing in the morning, in the last hour before the park closes or use Fastrack.

The Beastie ★★

What it is Small roller coaster for children. **Scope and scale** Minor attraction. **Height requirement** Under 3'11" (1.2 m) must ride with an adult. **Fright potential** Almost none. **When to go** Anytime. **Authors' rating** Another good introduction to the roller-coaster genre; ★★. **Duration of ride** Just under 2 minutes. **Average wait in queue per 100 people ahead of you** About 18 minutes; assumes all 24 seats filled per ride. **Loading speed** Slow.

DESCRIPTION AND COMMENTS The Beastie is a small dragon-themed roller coaster for children. Virtually the entire track is visible from the queue, so it's easy for kids to see what they're signing up for. Most children love it.

TOURING TIPS Because the coaster holds only around 24 people per ride, long queues can develop on busy days. Try riding in the first 2 or last 2 hours the park is open.

Squirrel Nutty Ride ★★★

What it is Slow-moving elevated-track ride around Adventure Land. **Scope and scale** Minor attraction. **Height requirement** Under 3'5" (1.1 m) must ride with an adult. **Fright potential** None. **When to go** First hour the park is open or last hour before the park closes. **Authors' rating** Almost inexplicably charming; ★★★. **Duration of ride** About 5 minutes. **Average wait in queue per 100 people ahead of you** About 19 minutes; assumes 10 ride vehicles operating. **Loading speed** Slow.

DESCRIPTION AND COMMENTS Squirrel Nutty Ride is a lovely, quaint ride aboard a giant acorn, on an elevated track that circles much of Adventure Land. There are no high-speed turns, loops, 0-g dips or possessed arboreal creatures waiting to jump out at you. The views of Adventure Land are quite good. We loved it, and you and your children should too.

TOURING TIPS As everyone knows, squirrels can't carry a whole lot. This means that long queues develop for Nutty Ride almost as soon as it opens. Ride early in the morning or try to jump on just before the park closes.

Old MacDonald's Farmyard

We think Old MacDonald's Farmyard reflects the agrarian roots of the countryside surrounding Alton Towers. The Farmyard has six attractions. Two of them – **There's Something in the Dung Heap** (!) and **Berry Bish Bash** – are better classified as interactive play areas, and one – **Old MacDonald's Singing Barn** – is a static display of singing robotic farm animals. If you've got small children, however, you'll want to see the three remaining attractions early in the day. Most of them hold very few people, and long queues develop by lunchtime.

There's Something in the Dung Heap ★★

What it is Walk-through educational farm exhibit and play area. **Scope and scale** Diversion. **Height requirement** Varies by play area, but most are designed for small kids. **Fright potential** None. **When to go** Anytime. **Authors' rating** Holy s––! ★★.

DESCRIPTION AND COMMENTS Our choice for the 'What were they thinking?' prize based on the name of the attraction alone, Dung Heap is a cul-de-sac off the side of Old MacDonald's Farmyard. True to its name, it contains a life-sized simulated dung heap that shows the various bacteria, plants, insects and other creatures that digest and break down farm manure into fertiliser and food for others.

The other part of Dung Heap is a children's play area, with climbing bars, a short zip-line and other things to climb, jump and run on. We saw relatively few children using this area during any day of our visit, but the zip-line was particularly popular. Falls are mostly benign on the moist, squishy, mysterious surface of the playground ...

TOURING TIPS See anytime.

Berry Bish Bash ★★½

What it is Interactive play area with air-powered cannons shooting foam balls. **Scope and scale** Diversion. **Height requirement** 3' (0.9 m). **Fright potential** None. **When to go** Anytime. **Authors' rating** Turn the kids loose, stand back and watch; ★★½. **Duration of play** Each group gets about 10 minutes. **Average wait in queue per 100 people ahead of you** About 40 minutes; assumes 25 people per 10-minute play period.

DESCRIPTION AND COMMENTS A 2-storey interactive play area that lets kids gather colourful round foam 'berries', then shoot them at their friends using low-pressure air cannons. Adults are allowed to accompany their children into the play area, but we didn't see many takers during our visit. That's all just as well – kids were running around like chickens, and the adults wouldn't stand a chance of keeping up. We also didn't see a single person actually get hit with one of the foam berries. We think the kids are just excited to collect them and see them pop out of the air cannon.

TOURING TIPS Grab some video if you can. See anytime.

Riverbank Eye Spy ★★½

What it is Slow-moving boat ride past various farm animals. **Scope and scale** Minor attraction. **Height requirement** Under 3'3" (1 m) must ride with an adult. **Fright potential** None. **When to go** First 2 hours the park is open. **Authors' rating** A lovely but short ride; ★★½. **Duration of ride** About 6½ minutes. **Average wait in queue per 100 people ahead of you** About 17 minutes; assumes 5 boats operating. **Loading speed** Slow.

DESCRIPTION AND COMMENTS A slow-moving boat ride past groups of (mostly) wood cut-outs of various farm animals. Small speakers emit the stereotypical sounds of each animal. Simple rhymes are shown with each group, where the last word of the rhyme is the name of the animal. However, children don't need to be able to read to name the animals – it's obvious.

Besides the wood cut-outs, there are a few plush live chickens pecking around the beginning of the attraction. Saying 'Ohhh, they look so real!' is just bound to confuse other parents in the boat.

TOURING TIPS Each boat holds nine people, in three rows of three. If you've got more than three people in your party, decide before boarding who is riding with whom.

Doodle Doo Derby ★★½

What it is Small farm-themed merry-go-round. **Scope and scale** Minor attraction. **Height requirement** Under 3'3" (1 m) must ride with an adult. **Fright potential** None. **When to go** First 2 hours the park is open and after other attractions in the Farmyard. **Authors' rating** No great shakes; ★★½. **Duration of ride** Just under 3 minutes. **Average wait in queue per 100 people ahead of you** About 11 minutes; assumes all 35 seats filled each ride. **Loading speed** Slow.

DESCRIPTION AND COMMENTS Another merry-go-round, this one composed of various farm animals. It's nothing special, but there's no reason not to ride it either.

TOURING TIPS Can handle more people than anything else in this area. See after all of the other attractions in the Barnyard.

Old MacDonald's Tractor Ride ★★½

What it is Slow-moving tractor ride. **Scope and scale** Minor attraction. **Height requirement** Under 3'5" (1.1 m) must ride with an adult. **Fright potential**

None. **When to go** First hour the park is open, during mealtimes or the last hour before the park closes. **Authors' rating** We wanted to buy one; ★★½. **Duration of ride** Just over 4 minutes. **Average wait in queue per 100 people ahead of you** About 27 minutes; assumes all 4 tractors operating. **Loading speed** Slow.

DESCRIPTION AND COMMENTS A slow-moving tractor ride through a simulated farmyard, complete with barn, haystacks and fields. The colourful tractors have names like 'Chuggy' and 'Huffy' and move at a near-glacial pace around a fixed track on the ground. Kids get to 'steer' their tractor past all manner of farmyard obstacles. The tractors seem to hold some sort of visceral appeal to kids, all of whom seemed quite content in the middle of their 30-minute waits to ride.

TOURING TIPS One of the longest waits in the entire park. Use the toilets and grab a snack before queuing.

Old MacDonald's Singing Barn ★★½

What it is Singing animatronic animals. **Scope and scale** Diversion. **Height requirement** None. **Fright potential** None. **When to go** Anytime. **Authors' rating** Not worth more than a glance; ★★½.

DESCRIPTION AND COMMENTS A walk-through attraction showing a handful of robotic animals singing the familiar children's tune. Nothing special.

TOURING TIPS See anytime.

Alton Towers Touring Plans

We've included touring plans for parents with small children, as well as plans for adults and teens. We think it's possible for parents with small children to see most of the park's age-appropriate attractions in one day. Because there are a larger number of thrill rides, though, adults and teens who wish to experience everything the park has to offer should plan to spend two days at Alton Towers. Alternatively, we've included a one-day touring plan for adults; this makes use of Fastrack to avoid queues at some of the more popular attractions in the afternoon.

One-Day Touring Plan for Parents with Small Children Under 3' (0.9 m)

1. The night before your visit, check **altontowers.com** for park hours and weather.
2. Arrive at the park entrance 30 minutes prior to official opening.
3. As soon as the park opens, make your way to Cloud Cuckoo Land in the back of the park. Experience the Peugeot Driving School.
4. Ride the Galloper's Carousel, also in Cloud Cuckoo Land.
5. See Charlie and the Chocolate Factory: The Ride.
6. Using The Towers as a landmark, walk from Cloud Cuckoo Land to Old MacDonald's Farmyard. As you pass Adventure Land, ride the Squirrel Nutty Ride.
7. In the Farmyard, ride Old MacDonald's Tractor Ride.
8. Take the Riverbank Eye Spy boat ride.

9. Ride the Doodle Doo Derby.
10. Turn your kids loose at the Berry Bish Bash.
11. If time permits, walk past the animals at Old MacDonald's Singing Barn.
12. Walk through There's Something in the Dung Heap and nearby play area.
13. Eat lunch. Good nearby choices include the KFC in X-Sector and the restaurants on Towers Street.
14. Ride The Beastie in Adventure Land.
15. Check the entertainment schedule for the next showing of *The Pirate of Sharkbait Reef*. Work in this show around Heave Ho! in the next step.
16. Experience Heave Ho! in Mutiny Bay.
17. If your kids are up for it, experience Duel in Gloomy Wood.
18. Take the Skyride to Dark Forest, then walk to Cloud Cuckoo Land.
19. In Cloud Cuckoo Land, check the entertainment schedule for the next showing of *The Wonderful World of Cloud Cuckoo Land* in the Cloud Cuckoo Land Theatre. Work in this show around Wobble World in the next step.
20. If you haven't already done so, experience Wobble World.
21. Tour The Towers.
22. Experience as much of The Gardens as desired.
23. See any missed attractions or repeat any favourites.
24. Depart Alton Towers.

Combined One-Day Touring Plan for Families with Children Over and Under 3' (0.9 m)

Note: See our description of Alton Towers' Parent Queue Share pass on page 271.

1. The night before your visit, check **altontowers.com** for official park hours and weather.
2. Arrive at the park entrance 30 minutes prior to official opening.
3. As soon as the park opens, obtain a Parent Queue Share pass from Guest Services on Towers Street.
4. At least one adult and the small children should walk to Old MacDonald's Farmyard. As you pass Adventure Land, ride the Squirrel Nutty Ride. In the Farmyard, ride Old MacDonald's Tractor Ride.
5. The other adults and older children should make their way to the Dark Forest to ride TH13TEEN.
6. The entire group should rendezvous in Old MacDonald's Farmyard. The adults who have not experienced TH13TEEN should do so now, using the Parent Queue Share pass. The remaining adults and small children should ride the Riverbank Eye Spy boat ride and the Doodle Doo Derby. If time permits, turn the kids loose at the Berry Bish Bash.
7. Have the entire group meet at the Runaway Mine Train in Katanga Canyon. Ride the Mine Train.

THEME PARKS AND ATTRACTIONS

8. Take the Congo River Rapids raft ride.
9. Check the daily entertainment schedule for the next showing of *The Pirate of Sharkbait Reef*. Work the show in around lunch and the next few rides in Mutiny Bay.
10. Eat lunch. A good nearby location is the Courtyard BBQ and Bar.
11. Ride Marauder's Mayhem.
12. Experience Heave Ho!
13. Fight with other scurvy dogs on Battle Galleons.
14. Ride The Flume.
15. If your kids are up for it, experience Duel in Gloomy Wood.
16. Take the Skyride to Dark Forest, then walk to Cloud Cuckoo Land.
17. See *Charlie and the Chocolate Factory:* The Ride.
18. Using The Towers as a landmark, have the adults and older children walk to X-Sector and ride Oblivion. The remaining adult(s) and the small children can see the next show at the Cloud Cuckoo Land Theatre, ride the Galloper's Carousel and bounce in Wobble World in Cloud Cuckoo Land.
19. Meet back at the entrance to Oblivion and switch groups so that the second set of adults can ride Oblivion. The remaining adults and small children should walk to Adventure Land and ride The Beastie.
20. If time permits, tour The Towers.
21. Experience as much of The Gardens as desired.
22. See any missed attractions or repeat any favourites.
23. Depart Alton Towers.

One-Day Touring Plan for Adults, Teens and Children Over 3' (0.9 m)

1. The night before your visit, check **altontowers.com** for official park hours and weather.
2. Arrive at the park entrance 30 minutes prior to official opening.
3. As soon as the park opens, make your way to the Dark Forest and ride TH13TEEN.
4. Take the Skyride to Gloomy Wood and make your way to Forbidden Valley. Ride Air.
5. Experience Nemesis.
6. Try Ripsaw, also in Forbidden Valley.
7. Ride The Blade.
8. Try Duel – The Haunted House Strikes Back in Gloomy Wood.
9. Eat lunch.
10. On days of peak attendance you may want to consider purchasing Fastrack tickets now for Oblivion, Submission, Sonic Spinball or Enterprise. A Fastrack booth is near Ripsaw in Forbidden Valley and also in Mutiny Bay. Alternatively, consider the single-rider queues.
11. Ride the Runaway Mine Train in Katanga Canyon.
12. Take the Congo River Rapids raft ride.

Alton Towers Recommended Attraction Visitation Times

AREA | ATTRACTION | BEST TIME TO VISIT

ADVENTURE LAND

Sonic Spinball | As soon as the park opens, in the last hour before park closing or use Fastrack

Squirrel Nutty Ride | First hour the park is open or last hour before the park closes

The Beastie | Anytime

CLOUD CUCKOO LAND

Charlie and the Chocolate Factory: The Ride | Before noon or after 4 pm

Cloud Cuckoo Land Theatre | As per entertainment schedule

Frog Hopper | As soon as the park opens

Galloper's Carousel | Before 11 a.m. or after 4 p.m.

Peugeot Driving School | As soon as the park opens, during lunch or dinner, or in the last hour the park is open

Twirling Toadstool | Anytime

Wobble World | Anytime

DARK FOREST

Rita | As soon as the park opens, in the last hour before park closing or use Fastrack

TH13TEEN | As soon as the park opens, in the last hour before park closing or use Fastrack

FORBIDDEN VALLEY

Air | As soon as the park opens, in the last hour before park closing or use Fastrack

Nemesis | As soon as the park opens, in the last hour before park closing or use Fastrack

Ripsaw | Anytime

The Blade | Anytime

GLOOMY WOOD

Duel – The Haunted House Strikes Back | Anytime

AREA | ATTRACTION | BEST TIME TO VISIT

KATANGA CANYON

Congo River Rapids | Between 11 a.m. and noon, or in the last hour the park is open

Runaway Mine Train | Before 11 a.m. or after 4 p.m.

MUTINY BAY

Battle Galleons | Between 11 a.m. and 4 p.m.

Heave Ho | Before 11 a.m. or after 4 p.m.

Marauder's Mayhem | Before 11 a.m. or after 4 p.m.

Sharkbait Reef Aquarium | Anytime

Skyride | Anytime

The Flume | Between 11 am and noon, or after 4 pm

The Pirate of Sharkbait Reef | As per entertainment schedule

OLD MACDONALD'S FARMYARD

Berry Bish Bash | Anytime

Doodle Doo Derby | First 2 hours the park is open and after other attractions in the Farmyard.

Old MacDonald's Singing Barn | Anytime

Old MacDonald's Tractor Ride | First hour the park is open, during mealtimes or the last hour before the park closes.

Riverbank Eye Spy | First 2 hours the park is open

There's Something in the Dung Heap | Anytime

THE TOWERS

Hex – The Legend of the Towers | Before 1 p.m. or after 4 p.m.

X-SECTOR

Enterprise | Before noon or after 4 pm

Oblivion | As soon as the park opens, in the last hour before park closing or use Fastrack

Submission | Anytime

13. Check the daily entertainment schedule for the next showing of *The Pirate of Sharkbait Reef*. Work the show in around the next few rides in Mutiny Bay.
14. Ride Marauder's Mayhem.
15. Fight with other scurvy dogs on Battle Galleons.
16. Ride The Flume.
17. Walk to X-Sector and ride Submission.
18. Also in X-Sector, take a spin on Enterprise.
19. Ride Oblivion.
20. Walk to The Towers and experience Hex – The Legend of the Towers.
21. Ride Rita in Dark Forest.
22. Experience Charlie and the Chocolate Factory: The Ride, in Cloud Cuckoo Land.
23. Eat dinner. Nearby dining locations include a Burger King (next to Charlie and the Chocolate Factory) and Woodcutter's Bar and Grill.
24. In Adventure Land, try Sonic Spinball.
25. Tour the rest of Adventure Land and Old MacDonald's Farmyard.
26. See any missed attractions or repeat any favourites.
27. Depart Alton Towers.

Two-Day Touring Plan for Adults and Teens
DAY ONE
1. The night before your visit, check **altontowers.com** for official park hours and weather.
2. Arrive at the park entrance 30 minutes prior to official opening.
3. As soon as the park opens, make your way to Forbidden Valley and ride Air.
4. Ride Nemesis, also in Forbidden Valley.
5. Ride Ripsaw.
6. Experience The Blade.
7. Ride Duel – The Haunted House Strikes Back, in Gloomy Wood.
8. Eat lunch. Good nearby locations include the Explorers Pizza & Pasta Buffet and Courtyard BBQ.
9. Try the Runaway Mine Train in Katanga Canyon.
10. Take the Congo River Rapids raft ride.
11. Check the daily entertainment schedule for the next showing of *The Pirate of Sharkbait Reef*. Work the show in around the next few attractions.
12. Try The Flume, in Mutiny Bay.
13. Take a spin (yes, after lunch – sorry!) on Marauder's Mayhem, also in Mutiny Bay.
14. Get soaked on Battle Galleons.
15. Take a quick walk through the Haunted Hollow. Return to Mutiny Bay when done.
16. See Hex – The Legend of the Towers, in The Towers.

17. Experience Charlie and the Chocolate Factory: The Ride.
18. Tour The Towers.
19. If you're tired of walking, take the Skyride from Dark Forest to the front of the park.
20. Tour The Gardens.
21. Depart Alton Towers.

DAY TWO
1. The night before your visit, check **altontowers.com** for official park hours and weather.
2. Arrive at the park entrance 30 minutes prior to official opening.
3. As soon as the park opens, make your way to Dark Forest and ride TH13TEEN.
4. Ride Rita, also in Dark Forest.
5. Walk to X-Sector and ride Oblivion.
6. Try Submission.
7. Take a spin on Enterprise.
8. Eat lunch. The nearest dining location is the KFC in X-Sector.
9. In Adventure Land, ride Sonic Spinball.
10. We know it's for children, but try the Squirrel Nutty Ride. Don't be too cool to enjoy it.
11. Tour Old MacDonald's Farmyard, if only to ask 'What were they thinking?' at There's Something in the Dung Heap.
12. See any missed attractions or re-visit any favourites.
13. Depart Alton Towers.

Bourton-on-the-Water ★★★½

SOMETIMES AN AGGREGATION of smaller attractions adds up to a big day out. Such is the case with Bourton-on-the-Water, a village of some 4,000 in the Cotswolds, Gloucestershire. Sometimes called the Venice of the Cotswolds, Bourton-on-the-Water sits astride the 40-ft-wide (12-m-wide) River Windrush, as it runs through the centre of the village. The Venice reference comes from the numerous small pedestrian bridges that resemble bridges over the canals in Venice. The river was channelled in the seventeenth century to provide a sustained flow of water to three local mills.

Drawing on Saxon words, the town's name means a fort or camp (*burgh*) beside a village (*ton*, or town). Evidence of human habitation dates back to the Stone Age and Bronze Age. Iron Age currency bars excavated in the twentieth century can be seen in the British Museum. Close by to the west is the A429, originally a Roman road that for a time formed the border between Roman Britain to the east and Celtic Britain to the west.

Tourists began arriving in numbers in 1881, when the town became accessible by rail. Today Bourton is a picturesque streamside village with a thriving tourism business. Restaurants and pubs abound, a number of them offering alfresco dining, and the retailers tailor their inventory to the tastes of visitors. The lovely historical buildings include the Parish Church of St Lawrence, built on the site of a Roman temple. A Saxon church built of wood occupied the site until a Norman stone church was built around 1110. The present church combines a fourteenth-century chancel, a Georgian tower and a Victorian nave. Depending on how much time you have, it's easy to spend a whole day seeing the village and its various attractions.

We've profiled Bourton-on-the-Water's more worthwhile gated (paid-admission) attractions, starting on the east side of the village and moving sequentially to the west side. Each is within easy walking distance of the others.

GETTING THERE *By car:* Bourton-on-the-Water is almost due east of Gloucester and Cheltenham, in Gloucestershire. From either city take the A40 east to the A436, crossing the A429 and following the signs to Bourton-on-the-Water. Parking is a bit iffy. We used the car park of a pub where we'd eaten lunch and then struck out on foot from there. *By rail and bus:* Use Moreton-in-Marsh Station (the nearest station) from London (Paddington) or Cheltenham Spa if coming from the southwest, Midlands and the north of England. From Moreton-in-Marsh Station, walk to the centre of the village (5 minutes) and catch **Pulhams Bus 801** or **855** to Bourton-on-the-Water. From Cheltenham Spa catch a bus to Cheltenham Royal Wells and then Pulhams Bus 801 to Bourton-on-the-Water.

Birdland Park and Gardens   ★★★

APPEAL BY AGE	PRESCHOOL ★★★	PRIMARY SCHOOL ★★★	TEENS ★★½
YOUNG ADULTS ★★★	OVER 30 ★★★		SENIORS ★★★

Rissington Road, Bourton-on-the-Water, Gloucestershire GL54 2BN
☎ **01451 820 480; birdland.co.uk**

- **HOURS** (April–October) 10 a.m.– 6 p.m.; (November–March) 10 a.m.– 4 p.m. Open daily except Christmas.
- **COST** £6.50 adults; £4.25 children (3–15); £5.50 senior citizens; £19.80 family ticket (2 adults, 2 children). Dogs are allowed, provided they're kept on a leash at all times.
- **DESCRIPTION AND COMMENTS** Birdland is a 7-ac (3-ha) park laid out on a meander loop of the River Windrush. Tropical birds are housed in aviaries and cages, while others, such as flamingos, pelicans, rheas, cassowaries and waterfowl, are displayed in simulated natural habitats. A 5-minute walk from the centre of Bourton-on-the-Water, Birdland is attractively landscaped, incorporating riverscapes, ponds, grassy lawns and marshy areas, all augmented by a small forest of poplars. Highlights include the king and Humboldt penguin exhibit (with daily feeding at 2.30 p.m.), the Marshmouth nature walk, through a natural area reclaimed from a builder's dump site, and the Discovery Centre, where close encounters with birds and reptiles add a personal touch to your visit.

THEME PARKS AND ATTRACTIONS

The Model Village ★★

| APPEAL BY AGE | PRESCHOOL ★½ | PRIMARY SCHOOL ★★ | TEENS ★★ |
| YOUNG ADULTS ★★ | | OVER 30 ★★½ | SENIORS ★★½ |

Old New Inn, Rissington Road, Bourton-on-the-Water, Gloucestershire GL54 2AF; ☎ 01451 820 467

HOURS (April–October) 10 a.m.–5.45 p.m.; (November–March) 10 a.m.–3.45 p.m. Open daily except Christmas.

COST £3.50 adults; £2.75 children (3–13) for Model Village. £1 for all ages for the miniature-scene exhibit.

DESCRIPTION AND COMMENTS The Model Village, jammed into the back garden of the Old New Inn, is a $1/9$-scale reproduction of the village as it was in 1937. Created from authentic building materials, the model faithfully reproduces the village's buildings, bridges and roads. The $1/9$ scale makes for awkward landscaping – almost too large for bonsai or the type of landscaping associated with model railways, and too small for trees, plants and shrubs at their natural size. The buildings are interesting but redundant, lacking the colour and freshness of the real village. You can walk the miniature streets and look into shop windows, churches and the like. Unlike model railway villages, there is no sign of life – no miniature vehicles or human or animal figures built to scale. This, coupled with the unremitting grey of the stone buildings, conjures up bleak sci-fi scenarios – 'Spock, it's as though the town was frozen in time . . . but what happened to all the people?' And speaking of sci-fi, it stands to reason that if the real village has a building with a miniature village in the back garden, then the model village should also . . . and it does. And so does the model of the model of the model village, and so on, in Russian-doll fashion.

Though cleverly executed and displaying a high level of craftsmanship, the model buildings have not been well maintained. Signage and shop-window treatments are likewise drab and worn. In addition to the Model Village, which is all outdoors, there is an indoor exhibit of miniature scenes, on about a $1/20$ scale, which are expertly crafted. Unfortunately, there is an additional £1 charge to view them. Adding this to the already steep admission for the Model Village, you begin to feel like the workman who forked over a day's wages 'to see the varmint'. Bottom line: you'll enjoy the Model Village if you don't mind feeling shaken down a little bit. If you're keen about getting your money's worth, however, spare yourself the irritation and find something else to do.

Bourton Model Railway Exhibition ★★★½

| APPEAL BY AGE | PRESCHOOL ★★★ | PRIMARY SCHOOL ★★★½ | TEENS ★★★½ |
| YOUNG ADULTS ★★★½ | | OVER 30 ★★★ | SENIORS ★★★½ |

Rissington Road, Bourton-on-the-Water, Gloucestershire GL54 2AN ☎ 01451 820 686; bourtonmodelrailway.co.uk

HOURS (June–August) 11 a.m.–5.30 p.m. daily; (September–May) 11 a.m.–5 p.m. weekends only (excluding January).

COST £2.50 adults; £2 children (3–15); £2 senior citizens; £7.50 family ticket (2 adults, 2 children).

DESCRIPTION AND COMMENTS Attached to a model-and-toy shop, the Model Railway Exhibition is first-rate, with just under 50 trains running automatically on three large OO/HO and N-gauge layouts. The various displays, covering some 500 sq ft (46 m²), feature villages, cities with buses, suburbs, industrial sites, mountains, rivers, rail yards, numerous bridges and tunnels, a lighted stadium and even a funfair with dodgems and a roller coaster, all rendered and landscaped in exquisite detail. Trains can be activated by pressing buttons on control panels mounted in front of the displays. Some layouts even alternate between night and day, with appropriate lighting for each. You can linger over the layouts for hours, taking in the subtleties and clever design elements. Supplementing the working layouts is an extensive collection of HO/OO locomotives and a wealth of model-railway and railway memorabilia.

Cotswold Motoring Museum ★★★

APPEAL BY AGE			
PRESCHOOL ★½	PRIMARY SCHOOL ★★	TEENS ★★½	
YOUNG ADULTS ★★★	OVER 30 ★★★	SENIORS ★★★½	

Corner of High Street and Sherbourne Street, Bourton-on-the-Water, Gloucestershire GL54 2BY
☎ **01451 821 255; cotswold-motor-museum.co.uk**

HOURS (Early February–early December) 10 a.m.–6 p.m. daily.
COST £4.10 adults; £2.70 children (4–16); £12.20 family ticket (2 adults, 2 children).

DESCRIPTION AND COMMENTS If there's a square inch of the Cotswold Motoring Museum that's not bulging with vintage cars, caravans dating from the 1920s, bicycles, motorcycles, mechanics' tools, signs for long-extinct products, model cars and old-fashioned toys, we can't find it. Though you can blast through this busy museum in 30 minutes, it would probably take a day to eyeball everything. Not all the stuff fits exactly with the concept of a motoring museum, but somehow it doesn't seem out of place. Touring the museum is like a safari in Granny's attic, or in this case Granny's garage. The car collection features a number of 1920s and '30s Rileys, a multi-decade assortment of Austins (but no Austin Healeys), a 1948 Jaguar MK V, and a sporty Jaguar 1954 XK 140 two-seater, our choice for best of show. Brum, a 'little superhero car' whose adventures can be seen on the BBC, also makes the museum his home. There's a quirky and eccentric dimension to the collection as well, epitomised by two-dimensional cardboard cut-outs of celebrity heads hanging behind the steering wheels (Audrey Hepburn is in a Fiat Topolino), and a totally-wacky video of a motorcycle football game (we watched the whole thing twice). The Motoring Museum is a bit on the adult side, though a vintage-toy collection appeals to younger visitors.

THEME PARKS AND ATTRACTIONS

Drayton Manor ★★★★½

APPEAL BY AGE PRESCHOOL ★★★★★ PRIMARY SCHOOL ★★★★★ TEENS ★★★★
YOUNG ADULTS ★★★★ OVER 30 ★★★ SENIORS ★★

Tamworth, Staffordshire B78 3SA
☎ **0844 472 1950; draytonmanorplus.co.uk**
Thomas Land: thomaslanduk.co.uk

HOURS (Mid-March–November) Park and zoo open 9.30 a.m., rides at 10.30 a.m. Closes 5–6 pm; open later bank and August holidays and during Fireworks, Halloween or Christmas celebrations. (Late November–early January) Open for limited hours (see website). Closed 24–26 December. Discount tickets for 15% savings can be purchased through the Tamworth Tourist Information Centre, 29 Market St, Tamworth, Staffordshire; ☎ 01827 709 581. Tickets can also be bought through the Tesco Clubcard rewards scheme.

COST £28.00 adults; £24 children (4–11); £14 senior citizens; £19.00 disabled and helper; £69 family of 3; £92 family of 4; £115 family of 5. Discounts for online purchase, plus no queuing. Bring your printed voucher, which will allow access to the park through any entrance. Online purchases not available for day of visit and limited to buyers with a UK postcode.

GETTING THERE *By car:* On the A4091, close to Junctions 9 and 10 of the M42, well marked with signs. *By rail:* The nearest station is Wilnecote, 1.5 mi (2.4 km) from the park (**nationalrail.co.uk**). *By bus:* Take Route 110 (between Birmingham and Tamworth) and get off at Fazely, a 10-minute walk from the park. (Route information: **transportdirect.info**.)

DESCRIPTION AND COMMENTS Clement Attlee was living at 10 Downing Street and England was just a few years removed from the war when this countryside park opened its doors in 1949. Since then Drayton Manor has had its ups and downs, but it got a major new lease on life in 2008 thanks to an animated train. Thomas Land put Drayton Manor on the map for every 5-year-old in love with the cheeky tank engine. This compact children's section is one of the more-masterly-themed amusement-park areas in Britain, and reason enough for many to visit. It has helped boost attendance to record levels and propel the park back into the top league.

The rest of Drayton is a little tired-looking, but it does feature a few top-notch thrill rides, a ghost-boat ride inspired by Disney's Pirates of the Caribbean, and a high-definition 4D cinema. A 150-room park hotel (with Thomas-themed rooms, natch) is scheduled to open in 2011, proving that even as it enters its seventh decade, Drayton still has surprises and no shortage of ambition.

The park, in the West Midlands, was built on the site of Drayton Manor, the home of Robert Peel (1788–1850), prime minister and creator of London's Metropolitan Police Force. The house is long gone now, replaced by the theme park. Visitors will find ample free parking, but make note of your parking area, because after a day of spinning at multiple g's it's easy to get turned around. As you approach the main entrance you'll see the looming, looping coils of roller coasters, which should get hearts pumping for the thrill-seekers in your party. (A second entrance gate, easily accessible from the hotel and the camping and caravan site, has you entering in the middle of the park, closer to the zoo and Central Plaza.)

If you arrive when the park opens at 9.30 a.m., the only thing open will be the zoo, at the opposite end of the park from the main entrance. It's more of an after-thought for most visitors, but you can keep yourself entertained while you wait, watching **meerkats, marmosets, penguins, tigers, leopards, chimps** and **parrots**.

The aptly-named **Action Park** is just off to the right of the main entrance. Head here for Shockwave, Splash Canyon, Maelstrom and Stormforce 10. But those who have come for **Thomas Land** will be dragged off to the left. The self-contained park-within-a-park is faithful to the spirit of the Rev W. V. Awdry's mechanical characters but manages to sneak in a few thrills for pre-teens too. It's also a model of family-friendliness, at least compared with most other parks. Many rides here openly offer an 'Infant Rider Swap' option, allowing adults to queue together but take turns riding while the other holds the baby. Even in Thomas Land, many rides have a height minimum of 3 ft (.9 m).

The park is designed to be Thomas's town of Sodor, and part of the fun here is to take in the elaborate theming and catch an appearance by the **Fat Controller** (or, more formally, **Sir Topham Hatt**), dressed in top hat and tails, who gladly poses for pictures. The area covers just a few acres (.6 hectares) and can get crowded. It holds a dozen rides, the most daring being the **Troublesome Trucks Runaway Coaster,** a smooth, well-designed kiddie coaster, and **Cranky's Drop Tower,** a not-too-scary introduction to the genre. Other stand-outs include **Sodor Docks, Jeremy's Flying Academy** and **Harold's Heli Tours & Engine Shed.** Although most are simple rotating flat rides, each is well thought out and not just a generic funfair spin-around decorated with train stickers. However, since the rides can only take about a dozen children per cycle, queues do build up. The indoor **Emily's Adventure Play** area offers shelter from the rain, but visits are limited to 30 minutes.

The area even has a suburb of sorts, **Spencer's Activity Park,** which is reached by a **miniature train,** pulled by Thomas or his friends. The stations are carefully decorated, and once you arrive there are picnic tables, a huge playground and **Father McColl's Farm,** with a handful of exotic animals like **ostrich, emu** and **reindeer,** and a **dinosaur trail.** But watch the crowds here, because you have to queue up for a return train trip (or hike back). If your timing's poor, this little excursion could eat up a good chunk of your day. Finally, what would a licensed theme-park area be without a licensed-product store? The merchandise may be adorable at the **Thomas Land Shop,** but it's not cheap. Set a spending limit before your visit, and keep your kids (or spouse) to it.

For those who aren't in search of railway nirvana, you'll want to take a right at the entrance to enter **Action Park.** Working around the area, start with **G-Force,** a tangle of steel roller coaster with an unfamiliar design that will keep your head spinning. The ride vehicles, called X-Cars, look like lunar modules with seats attached. Unlike traditional steel coasters, which use shoulder restraints, this one holds you in the car at the hip, which provides more freedom of movement – and vulnerability – when you hang out of the car. The 40-second ride starts with a drop, leading to a roll. It then plunges into a loop reaching 44 mph (70 km/h), and soon comes to a very tight loop, followed by another curvy section of track that resembles a figure of eight bent in the middle at 180°.

If you haven't lost your breakfast – or nerve – then quickly move on to **Shockwave,** Europe's only stand-up roller coaster, and a doozy at that. Riders are perched on what resembles a bicycle seat, and held in place by shoulder restraints. The ride starts with a 120-ft (37-m) lift hill, then sends you into a loop, followed by a period of weightlessness and two corkscrews. The ride lasts 90 seconds, stretches for 1,640 ft (500 m), and reaches 53 mph (85 km/h). In total there are four inversions. You can expect to be shaken up a bit. To minimise headaches, hold your head back in the restraint.

In this area you'll also find **Splash Canyon,** a deservedly-popular river-rapids ride. The course is scenic, and there are no big drops, only swift currents. You might be splashed a little but probably not soaked. On your way out, to your left you'll see **Maelstrom,** a rotating-pendulum ride with riders facing out. It looks something like a toilet-bowl cleaner – with you serving as the bristles. Right across from this you'll see **Stormforce 10,** a flume ride that purports to re-create the story of a water rescue, and which was launched with the cooperation of the Royal Navy Lifeboat Institution. The park says it's the world's first charitable ride, and it collects donations on-site. It's a good cause, no doubt, but as far as we can tell it's largely an excuse to get soaked. The boat descends through three drops, two facing forwards and one backwards, as you reach speeds up to 40 mph (64 km/h) One of just a few such rides in the world with multiple drops, Stormforce 10 is our choice of the best outdoor flume ride in the UK. Adding to the novelty are electric driers at the exit that run £2 for 3 minutes. We didn't use the driers at Drayton Manor, but we've had very limited success with them at other parks. Their effectiveness is very much correlated to what you're wearing, with cotton clothing being the most difficult to dry. There are often long queues, allowing you the indignity of waiting in lines both before and after the ride. If you're intent on staying dry, you can also purchase ponchos for £2 at the shop underneath the ride or a vending machine in the queue. Some friendly riders have been known to hand off theirs when they complete the ride. Another option is to bring along an extra-large plastic bin-bag with a hole cut in the top for your head. Yes, you'll look like a sack of potatoes, but you'll stay pretty dry. Also don't forget your shoes. We've found that putting both feet in a plastic grocery bag works well.

You may be content to spend all day in this area, but there are other thrills to be had. Walking towards the centre of the park, with a long, rectangular lake on you right, brings you to **The Bounty,** a swinging pirate ship. At the end of the lake take a right and proceed to **Aerial Park** and look for the looming tower. **Apocalypse** is one of the country's best drop rides, giving you three choices of how to scare yourself to death. Different entrances allow you ride seated, standing, and standing without a floor – known as the 'Fifth Element'. To add to the thrill, the standing riders are tipped out to a 15° angle before they're shot downward 177 ft (54 m) in 4 seconds, subjecting them to 4 g's in the process. The side-by-side swing **Pandemonium,** while not nearly as imaginative, will send you upside-down as it whirls through its paces.

After all that excitement, it's time for a nice peaceful movie – well, not exactly. The **4D Cinema** features a short version of the animated Hollywood film *Happy Feet,* starring dancing penguins. You'll line up outside and enter for a pre-show to set the stage for the film. Then the doors open, and while the previous audience exits, you move into the 152-seat auditorium. The customised Art Deco–styled theatre offers a high-definition film experience, complete with numerous special effects, like seats that move, water spray, air blasts, leg-ticklers, aroma and even smoke and soap bubbles. You wear 3D glasses for this fun, entertaining and at times startling experience. You're likely to exit with a smile on your face. The queue frequently billows out of the theatre onto the pedestrian plaza, but not to worry – the theatre is large enough that usually everyone waiting is admitted to the show. You can also keep yourself busy in this area with typical funfair rides as well as arcade games, which carry an extra charge and appear to be unwinnable.

Roughly behind the 4D Cinema is **The Haunting,** a walk-through haunted mansion ending with a combination ride and optical illusion in a room that seems to spin upside-down. We like this treatment for its originality – very different from the typical ghost train or walk-through spook house. The entrance to The Haunting is a little hard to find. From the 4D Cinema walk in the direction of Peel Plaza, turning left on a path between two buildings. To see this ride concept more fully realised, check out Hex at Alton Towers (see page 287).

After getting your fill of Aerial Park rides, head over to the Pirate Cove area for **Pirate Adventure,** a ghost-boat ride that's so similar to Disney's Pirates of the Caribbean, you've got to wonder if park managers have had visits from Disney lawyers. Perhaps Disney knew it had nothing to worry about. The various scenes are pretty good (though not up to Disney standards), but the animatronics seem amateurish. The ride's unlikely to launch a hit film series or interest Keith Richards, but it's still a pretty elaborate dark ride. Taken on its own terms, we'd give it three stars. Unfortunately, Pirate Adventure borrows so heavily from the Disney version that comparisons are inevitable. When you judge it in that light, it comes across as an inferior knock-off. On the bright side, queues are usually short.

TOURING TIPS The park opens a full hour before the rides do. If you arrive early, you can visit the zoo, which opens at 9.30, and then be ready promptly at 10.30 to ride G-Force, Shockwave, Stormforce 10, Splash Canyon, Maelstrom, Apocalypse and The Haunting, in that order. Next sample the remaining rides in Aerial Park and take in the 4D Cinema. If your family is too young for the coasters and thrill rides, head for Thomas Land first thing, or wait until mid- to late afternoon (nap time for the biggest Thomas fans), when crowds begin to thin.

Though Drayton Manor has two entrances, only the main entrance affords quick access to Thomas Land and the thrill rides in Action Park. Likewise, wheelchairs and pushchairs are available for hire only at the main entrance. Smoking is prohibited in queues, shops, restaurants, buildings, WCs and on rides throughout the park.

Hot dogs, burgers, pizza and chicken pieces are available throughout the park. For a broader selection (including vegetarian options), try the **cafeteria and licensed restaurant** in Peel Plaza. Beer, wine and snacks can be purchased at the **Park Inn Bar and Patio,** also in Peel Plaza.

Gulliver's Kingdom ★★★

APPEAL BY AGE	PRESCHOOL ★★★★★	PRIMARY SCHOOL ★★★★	TEENS ½
YOUNG ADULTS ½	OVER 30 ½		SENIORS ½

Temple Walk, Matlock Bath, Derbyshire DE4 3PG
☎ **01925 444 888; gulliversfun.co.uk**

- **HOURS** Gates generally open at 10.30 a.m.; closing time ranges from 4.30 to 7 p.m., with special holiday hours. Open for school holidays in February, late March–early November and late November–December.
- **COST** £13.95 adults, children (under 2'11"/.9 m free); £12.95 senior citizens 60+; £53 family of 4. Discounts for online purchases.
- **GETTING THERE** *By car:* Exit the M1 at Junction 28 and follow the signs. If approaching from the south on the M6, take the A38 towards Lichfield, and then follow the signs. Parking is free on a hilly and sometimes crowded car park, and the later you arrive, the higher up the hill you'll have to park. *By rail:* Closest station is Matlock Bath train station (**nationalrail.co.uk**), a 10-minute walk to the park. Follow the river on the left until you reach the Fishpond Pub, and take the path up the hill. *By bus:* The **Transpeak** bus (**transpeak.co.uk**) from Manchester to Derby runs through Matlock Bath. Get off at the Fishpond Pub and take the path up the hill. From Chesterfield take the **17 bus** to Matlock and then catch the Transpeak or **R61** to the Fishpond Pub. If you're not accustomed to being surrounded by thousands of hyper-giddy kiddies, you can fortify yourself at the pub before continuing to the park. (Route information: **transportdirect.info.**)
- **DESCRIPTION AND COMMENTS** Some parks try to be all things to all people, but not Gulliver's. This mini–entertainment empire knows its audience: 3- to 12-year-olds, the younger the better. Teenagers unaccompanied by parents aren't allowed, and adults shouldn't dream of trying to show up without a child in tow. You won't be allowed to buy a ticket.

  The family-owned Gulliver's began in 1978, when it opened its first property here in Matlock Bath in Derbyshire. Gulliver's Kingdom is the smallest of the chain, with fewer attractions than the other two (see pages 236 and 377), but it established what became the model for the other locations. What makes the park stand out is its unique wooded setting on a steep hill. Luckily, the planners included a budget for a chairlift – which you'd be wise to use if you can tolerate the queue. Still, you can expect to get a good workout shoving prams and pushchairs up the grades, making it easier to justify a mid-afternoon treat of crepes or doughnuts. On the plus side, the park offers beautiful vistas of the Peak District countryside – which is only enhanced from some of the tall rides. From the lift, for example, you'll get a bird's-eye view of the village of Starkholmes. If you're interested, the **Heights of Abraham** tourist attraction offers great ridge-top views and guided tours of caverns and mines (**heightsofabraham.com**).

Most of Gulliver's rides will be familiar from funfairs, but there are enough quirks and unique touches to keep them interesting. Scattered throughout the park, for example, are play areas, with tricycles and go-karts left for kids' cruising pleasure. You'll find some imaginative rides and theming here, but like the rest of the Gulliver's theme parks, the place seems to suffer from a lack of upkeep, with rides and public areas looking a little worn around the edges. Also like the other Gulliver's parks, the site's dominated by a none-too-enthralling castle smack-dab in the middle of the park. Adult perceptions aside, the castle will delight all but the most cynical princes and princesses.

Warning: This is not a park where adults shift from foot to foot and watch kids do stuff. On many rides, an adult is required to accompany any child under 3'11" (1.2 m). Other rides require accompaniment for youngsters under 2'11" (.9 m) or under 4'7" (1.4 m). And yet others ban anyone over 4'11" (1.5 m). Bottom-line (pun intended): you'll have to check out each ride's requirements and be ready to manoeuvre your posterior into kiddie-sized seats. But remember, this park is not designed for you. Still, management understands it needs to keep parents content. About 50% of its attractions are under cover, making rainy-day visits an option.

The park's signature characters, the **Gully Gang,** wander the property throughout the day, performing and liberally dispensing hugs and posing for photos. Since 2009, they've been supplemented by Nickelodeon characters Dora and Diego from *Dora the Explorer*. The park pays licensing fees, and their presence is not assured for the long run – if they're not there when you arrive, be prepared to tell your disappointed little ones that Dora is off exploring.

But your first challenge will be navigating the hillside car park. Once you're inside the park, it's a free but winding hill-climb up, and you may find yourself doing some hiking to reach the main entrance. We recommend taking advantage of gravity whenever possible. Take the chairlift to the top, and over the course of your visit work your way back down to the entrance. That does require studying the map and any special show times carefully to avoid backtracking. (There's also a secondary, top entrance to the park, which will have you start your visit near the hilltop, avoiding the need for the chairlift.)

Although meant as transportation, the modest chairlift may scare some small visitors. Treat it as just another ride, and remind them of the excitement awaiting them at the top. Your destination is the **Fantasy Terrace** area. Rides here include a drop tower, dodgems and one of the many soft-play areas you'll find scattered across the property. In the covered **Ball Shoot,** children get to fire ball cannons at each other and unsuspecting parents.

Then cut over to **Western World,** an Old West–themed area, where you'll find a log-flume ride. On the **Silver Mine Ride** is a ghost train that lets you shoot at targets with a toy laser. When activated, the targets may spring to life or shoot out water. There's no score-keeping, but after all, we don't want our children to be too competitive, right? At **Old Macdonald's Farm,** you press buttons and activate noisy animal models. It may sound like a barnyard KISS concert to adults, but kids eat it up. There's also gold-panning, or actually **Mineral Panning** – don't expect to find any ingots here. Finally, **Diggers** has child-scaled backhoes, permitting them to dig up balls from a pit, drop them, and do it all over. Sometimes avid dads even let their child operate the controls.

Heading back towards the centre of the hill brings you to the **Party House,** which sounds suspiciously like a place you'd find at university. The appeal here, though, includes a sizable **Desert Sand Pit,** a collection of pedal tractors and **Jumping Star,** another scaled-down drop tower. Next, cut back to the castle to enter **Lilliput Land.** Here you'll find **Amazing Journeys of Gulliver's,** a simulator attraction with a pre-show. Some say it's so bad it's good, but our advice is to find humour anywhere you can. On the other hand, some children will be amused by the silly *Hard Luck Bear Jamboree* show. The **Millennium Maze** offers a 2-storey challenge. You can play chess with giant pieces and, for low-key entertainment, cross a small body of water on Stepping Stones – don't be surprised if someone 'accidentally' slips into the shallow pool. Overlapping with this area is the rather small **Dinosaur Kingdom.** Here you can tour around in vintage cars like Victorians on an expedition, looking for dino models in the woods.

Now you'll cut diagonally back to the left (as you're looking up the hill), to reach **Palais Royale,** home to the park's two coasters. The **Switchback,** a steel coaster, climbs to 46 ft (14 m) and takes a minute to wind its way along about 770 ft (235 m) of track. The neighbouring steel **Log Roller Coaster** has been offering pink-knuckle thrills since 1986. Then look for the fun **Cycle Monorail,** which has you pedal your way around a track at treetop level. Unless you've got an energetic (and long-legged) child, you'll probably do most of the work, though. Closed-toe shoes are required, so dress accordingly. There are also **Moonbuggies,** pedal karts your kids can zip around in while you take a load off your feet. The area includes a flat flying-elephant and biplane ride, along with a mini–ladybird coaster and a special ride area for under-5s. The two-level **Jubilee Carousel** is a nostalgic favourite, while **Gully's Jousting Castles** is a clever name for a scrambler ride in castle-shaped vehicles.

Finally, find your way to the **Bourbon Street** area near the entrance. Although the name might suggest otherwise, this is not the place for your children to meet their first drag queen. Instead, expect a gentle

Lazy River Ride, a Ferris wheel in balloon cars, a carousel, swinging pirate ship, miniature golf and several play areas. Look for the **Fire Engine Ride,** which lets standing riders man a water hose and spray a building while their platform slowly rises and falls.

TOURING TIPS Watch the time, because rides stop at least half an hour before closing time, allowing you to catch the goodbye show in the Entrance Plaza. If you're planning on making an overnight of it, check out the hotel–park admission packages available through **gullivers-shortbreaks.co.uk.**

Morgan Motor Company Factory Tour ★★★★

| APPEAL BY AGE | PRESCHOOL ★★ | PRIMARY SCHOOL ★★★ | TEENS ★★★★ |
| YOUNG ADULTS ★★★★ | | OVER 30 ★★★★★ | SENIORS ★★★★★ |

Pickersleigh Avenue, Malvern Link, Worcestershire WR14 2L
☎ **01684 584 580; morgan-motor.co.uk**

HOURS 8.30 a.m.–5 p.m. Monday–Thursday; until 3.30 p.m. Friday. Tours must be pre-booked by phoning or emailing (**angela.hymas@morgan-motor.co.uk**). Tours are unavailable during the factory's 3 annual shutdowns, usually the last week of April, the last week of July and during the Christmas and New Year's holidays.

COST £10 (under age 10 free).

GETTING THERE *By car:* About 15 minutes from M5 Junctions 7 and 8. Proceed into Malvern and join the A449 to Malvern Link. If you use satnav, be aware that the postal code is for the factory on Pickersleigh Avenue. The Visitor Centre is on a side road that connects Pickersleigh Avenue with Spring Lane. Travelling south from the town centre and the A449, turn left off Pickersleigh just before you reach the factory. The Visitor Centre will be the first building on your right. *By rail:* Closest station is Malvern Link. Turn left out of the station, head down Worcester Road and turn right onto Pickersleigh Avenue (**nationalrail.co.uk**). *By bus:* Regular service from Worcester Crowngate Bus Station. (Route information: **transportdirect.info.**)

DESCRIPTION AND COMMENTS Even if you know nothing about cars, you will be immediately impressed by Morgan. The company makes hand-crafted sports cars that look like something James Bond would drive on weekends off. They're slick and fast, with a design both space-age and classic. Simply put, there's nothing else like them on the road, because no one else builds cars like this anymore. The company, the world's oldest private car-maker, produces about 700 vehicles a year, crafting their bodies from steel, aluminium and ash wood. That's right – wood is a major component. The engine is manufactured by others, but the car is all Morgan.

You have to make certain sacrifices to drive a Morgan, though. In the so-called 'Morgan environment', you may encounter a suspension so stiff that, it's been said, if you run over a coin you can tell whether it's heads or tails. In some models, the windows don't roll down – they have to be removed and placed in the back. And cars sometimes leak in the rain.

But customers will join a waiting list of a year or more just for the privilege of buying one. If you just can't wait, the company will help you find a used model, which may run anywhere from £4,000 for a three-wheeler that seems to be nothing more than a glorified go-kart to £130,000 for a sleek Aero 8, an ultra-high-end super-car. This popular model was originally built for royalty: commissioned by Prince Eric Sturdza, a descendant of the Moldavian royal family and president of a private Swiss bank. Indeed, all cars are built to order, with 70% manufactured with left-hand drive for overseas customers. This is clearly not the vehicle to use if you need to hop down to the market for a carton of milk.

The third-generation family-owned manufacturer can trace its roots back a century, when automobiles were little more than horseless carriages. H. F. S. Morgan, the son of a Herefordshire clergyman, was a railway draughtsman who had a fascination with cars. He founded a local bus company and in 1909 built his first car, a three-wheeled runabout powered by a Peugeot engine. Interest was so high that he launched a business with his father, and the family has never looked back.

You can see the earliest Morgans and trace the product lines in a factory museum, but unless you're a crazed sports-car fan or an incurable gear-head, you probably shouldn't bother going out of your way just for the exhibits. However, if you can schedule a factory tour, it's worthwhile spending an afternoon taking in this unique slice of British industrial history.

Whether taking the tour or just stopping by the museum, you'll start at the **Visitor Centre,** which opened for the company's centenary in 2009. You'll find gleaming displays of early **three-wheelers** – look for the dark-green model resembling a giant rolling gherkin. At the time they were produced, their using just three wheels (two in the front, one in the back) offered a significant tax savings for owners, because the vehicle was considered a motorcycle. The company stopped production of the car in 1952 but announced plans to revive the three-wheeler in 2011.

You'll also see several Morgan **4/4s,** which have been in production for more than 70 years. Elsewhere are roadsters, photos and artefacts chronicling the family history. Make sure to catch the Morgan-history film, which will have you zooming through the countryside. With their wood frame, Morgans are extremely light, which means they move extremely fast. All said, you'll get much more out of your factory visit with this Visitor Centre introduction.

The 2-hour tour itself is run by former employees and takes you through every step of the production cycle. As you proceed through brick factory buildings – **'The Works'** as Morgan calls them – you'll watch craftsmen shaping cars in front of you, and mechanics painstakingly putting the pieces together. Particularly astonishing is watching woodworkers craft the ash-wood chassis, which makes up a significant proportion of the fabric of the car. But sheet-metal workers show just as much attention to detail when they deploy hand-operated tools to create the distinctive louvres on Morgan bonnets.

And even diehard environmentalists will have a hard time suppressing a gasp when they encounter the **Aero SuperSport,** which Charles Morgan, grandson of the founder, calls 'a luxurious flamboyant sports car'. It's powered by a 4.8-litre BMW V8 engine and a six-speed transmission, with prices beginning at £108,000 plus VAT.

As there's no traditional production line, cars are hand-rolled from stage to stage. Throughout the tour, you'll experience a barrage for the senses: smells of a wood shop, clanging from the body works, the glare of welding torches and the hissing of paint guns.

If you think you're ready for the 'Morgan Environment', you don't have to put down thousands in deposit to purchase a vehicle: the factory hires out cars. Day rental starts at £120, with weekly hire for a roadster reaching £1,200. Renters must be between 25 and 70 years old, have more than three years' driving experience and have no more than three penalty points on their licence.

TOURING TIPS Make sure to arrive about an hour before your factory tour is scheduled to allow ample time to take in the museum. Wear closed-toe shoes, as this is a working factory, and not flip-flop-friendly.

National Sea Life Centre Birmingham ★★★

APPEAL BY AGE	PRESCHOOL ★★★★	PRIMARY SCHOOL ★★★	TEENS ★★
YOUNG ADULTS ★★	OVER 30 ★★★		SENIORS ★★★

The Waters Edge, Brindleyplace, Birmingham B1 2HL
☎ **0121 643 6777;** visitsealife.com/Birmingham

HOURS 10 a.m.–5 p.m. weekdays; 10 a.m.–6 p.m. weekends and bank holidays. Last entry 1 hour before closing. Closed Christmas Day.

COST £17.50 adults (£13.50 online); £14 children 3–14 (£10 online); £54.95 family ticket (2 adults, 2 children) (£44 online). Admission can also be bought through the Tesco Clubcard rewards scheme.

GETTING THERE *By car:* Take the M6 to Junction 6 or the M5 to Junction 3 and follow signs for the city centre and the NIA (National Indoor Arena). *By rail:* The nearest rail station is New Street (**nationalrail.co.uk**), then follow signs for the ICC (International Convention Centre) and the NIA. *By bus:* Take any bus to Birmingham city centre and follow signs for the ICC and NIA. (Route information: **transportdirect.info.**)

DESCRIPTION AND COMMENTS This chain location offers more than the basic aquarium run-through. The multi-level attraction, with over 60 displays and 1,000 creatures, has electric eels and plenty of sharks. The 'touch pool' is open all day, allowing you to hold a crab or pet a starfish for as long as you like (this admittedly gets old after the first 3 or 4 hours). But the highlights come about halfway through your visit. Make sure to catch the clever 4D movie, a turtle adventure featuring sights, sounds, smells, movement and more.

Elsewhere, you'll also see a talking animated turtle and two real ones, giants named Molokai and Gulliver. Towards the end of your visit, you descend to a dramatic walk-through ocean tunnel to see what the aquarium says are the only hammerhead sharks in Europe. They're impressive, but young and small now, especially in the expansive 260,000-gal (1-million-litre) tank. We're not sure what a hall of mirrors has to do with sea life, but it's a fun diversion near the exit and soft-play area.

TOURING TIPS One of Sea Life's better aquariums, and a good place to spend a rainy morning or afternoon. Be sure to catch one or more of the live demonstrations, programmes or feedings.

(For more on aquariums, see page 10.)

National Space Centre ★★★★½

APPEAL BY AGE	PRESCHOOL ★★★	PRIMARY SCHOOL ★★★★	TEENS ★★★★
YOUNG ADULTS ★★★★		OVER 30 ★★★★	SENIORS ★★★★½

Exploration Drive, Leicester, Leicestershire LE4 5NS
☎ **0845 605 2001; spacecentre.co.uk; email info@spacecentre.co.uk**

HOURS (Peak season) 10 a.m.–5 p.m. daily (last admission 4 p.m.); (off-peak) 10 a.m.–4 p.m. Tuesday–Friday, 10 a.m.–5 p.m. Saturday and Sunday, closed Monday.

COST £13 adults (17 and up); £11 children, senior citizens, students; £41 family of 4 (max 2 adults); £51 family of 5 (max 2 adults). Tickets are available in advance online or at the centre entrance.

GETTING THERE *By car:* The National Space Centre is just off the A6, 2 mi (3.2 km) north of Leicester city centre, midway between Leicester's inner and outer ring roads. Brown road signs with a distinctive rocket logo will direct you from the arterial routes around Leicester. *By rail:* **East Midland Trains** and **Cross Country Trains** serve Leicester Station. From here you can either take a bus or a taxi to the centre. Taxis will meet trains by prior arrangement. *By bus:* **First Bus 54** runs every 10 minutes throughout the day Monday–Saturday, and every 20 minutes on Sunday from Charles Street, a short walk from the station, running from 9.30 a.m. **First Bus 70** runs from Belgrave Gate every 20 minutes, Monday–Saturday, to Abbey Lane. The Space Centre is just a short walk along Exploration Drive.

DESCRIPTION AND COMMENTS The National Space Centre was co-founded in the 1990s by the University of Leicester (known for space research) and the Leicester City Council, with funding from the Millennium Commission. The museum is as cutting-edge as the science it celebrates, with clever interactive exhibits, space-travel simulations, lectures and demonstrations, and a jaw-dropping planetarium show. Though British contributions to space exploration and space science are acknowledged, the National Space Centre largely chronicles the achievements of man in space irrespective of nationality.

The museum consists of two buildings. The main exhibit area is in a cavernous rectangular building, with the **Space Theatre** (planetarium) in the centre and six major galleries arrayed around it. The second building is the **Rocket Tower,** resembling an enclosed launcher gantry, and housing the **Blue Streak,** the largest rocket ever built in Britain, and a **Thor-Able,** precursor to modern Delta series rockets, the workhorse rocket for launching satellites. Exhibit galleries surround the rockets on three floors.

Galleries in the main building each focus on a subject central to astronomy and space exploration. **Gallery 02 – Into Space** deals with the challenges of living in space and features a full-size replica of the **Columbus Module** of the International Space Station, complete with a sleeping compartment and shower. Other gallery highlights include a Mercury capsule; artefacts from the career of the UK's first astronaut, Helen Sharman; and a number of interactive and experiential exhibits. There's also a space toilet that recycles urine for drinking water, but sadly it's not one of the interactive experiences.

Next, moving left to right, is **Gallery 03 – Exploring the Universe.** One of our favourites, Gallery 03 is like a fun crash-course in astronomy and astronomical physics. Topics tackled here include the Big Bang, the power of gravity, black holes, the life and death of stars and, of course, everyone's favourite – alien life. One of the most clever exhibits is **Aliens on Earth,** which deals with the astonishing variety of life forms on earth. You'll note pretty quickly that many of our most appalling film aliens were inspired by critters that surround us every day. **Grand Tour to the Giants** is a video presentation about the Voyager missions. A mini-theatre provides the welcome option of sitting during the show. Another video, **How the Universe Ends,** is a big hit with pessimists. A subsection of Gallery 03 is **Near Earth Objects,** which explains (among many other things) how the Earth might be destroyed or flung unceremoniously into nuclear winter by a meteor. Another exhibit looks at Mars and Martians and how we've depicted them in art, literature and film.

Moving from the universe to something closer to home takes us to **Gallery 4 – The Planets,** an expansive and beautifully-executed introduction to all things planetary, including man's past, present and future efforts to explore them.

Gallery 05 – Orbiting Earth looks at Earth from an environmental perspective, delving into such topics as weather, electromagnetic waves, greenhouse gases, temperature changes and the ozone hole. An interactive feature, the **Weather Studio,** allows you to become a television weatherman for a few minutes (it's harder than it looks). Impressively on display is **MOP-4,** the fully-functional flight spare of the Meteosat 7 weather satellite, part of the series of geostationary satellites that have provided images of Earth and data for weather forecasts since 1977. The MOP-4 flight spare is the most valuable item in the collection, with a value of £3 million.

Gallery 06 – Space Now is a never-ending work in progress presenting news on the latest space exploration, breakthroughs in science, and astronomical events. The **Space Now Stage** hosts live demonstrations and offers a glimpse of the new-generation virtual 3D holographic technology. There are also interactive exhibits. A standout is **Mars Yard,** which hosts development models of the ExoMars Rover on simulated Martian terrain.

Gallery 07 – Tranquillity Base is a training centre for those aspiring to crew on space stations as well as on base stations established on other planets and moons. It's 2025 at a lunar base, and you're challenged to test yourself as an individual and a team player in a totally-immersive experience. There is no particular order as far as experiencing the various training exercises and tests goes – when you see something that appeals, just jump right in. The training is supposed to culminate in a 3D simulated space flight from Earth's moon to the ice-moon Europa, but you can enjoy the simulator ride without doing any training tests or exercises. Memorable moments include the obligatory near-miss with an asteroid and a 'We're Going In!' *Star Wars*–like romp through Europa's ice canyons. Running full-tilt, the simulator can handle about 120 riders an hour, with the ride itself lasting about 6 minutes. To avoid queues, we recommend riding as soon after the centre opens as possible. As a footnote, the simulator has been fraught with technical problems and was inoperable for much of last year's busy season.

In the middle of the main exhibit building is the planetarium, known as **Space Theatre.** The technology here is superb, with 3D animation and 180° surround video in addition to traditional planetarium effects. The layout is theatre-style, with the audience facing the staging area as opposed to in-the-round seating typical of planetariums. As of this writing, nine different shows have been produced for the Space Theatre. The show we reviewed had a wag-the-dog feel, as if the production's primary goal was to show off the theatre's spiffy techno capabilities rather than delve in depth into the subject matter. That said, the technical dimension alone makes the presentation enjoyable and worthwhile. The theatre seats 167 people, and most presentations run about 20 minutes.

When you purchase your Space Centre admission, whether at the gate or through **spacecentre.co.uk** in advance, you will be asked to select one of several show times at the Space Theatre. The particular show time you choose will be printed on your ticket, showing that a seat has been reserved for you for that performance. No muss, no fuss, no queues. Just arrive at the theatre entrance about 10 minutes before show time.

The Rocket Tower, a separate but contiguous building, can be accessed by ascending stairs from Galley 02 – Into Space to a mezzanine walkway, thence to the first floor of the tower. A handout map of the Space Centre will help you with this bit of navigation but is not sufficiently detailed to be of much help with anything else. While commuting along the mezzanine, be sure to check out the USSR *Soyuz* space capsule suspended from the ceiling.

Exhibits in the tower trace in chronological order man's efforts to explore space. You begin on the first floor (Deck 2) with **New Frontiers,** advancing to **Leaving Earth: 1942–1962,** on the second floor (Deck 3), and culminating with **Destination Moon: 1962–1975** on the third (Deck 4). All three levels can be accessed by stairs or lift. On display are hardware and other artefacts of the so-called Race to Space between the Soviet Union and the West, most notably the United States. The centrepieces for all three floors are the upright Thor-Able and *Blue Streak* rockets.

The Space Centre's approach to presenting information is often playful and humorous. This is especially true in the Rocket Tower's mini-theatre showing of Georges Melies's 1902 narrated film classic *Le voyage dans la lune* (*A Trip to the Moon*), often cited as the first science-fiction movie. In it, a group of scientists board a bullet-shaped capsule that is fired from a cannon. It's one of the silliest films you'll ever see but also provides a telling retrospective of how space travel was envisioned at the turn of the twentieth century. The only realistic part involves the earthlings promptly murdering the moon people's leader (some things never change). We watched the 14-minute movie twice and could easily have stayed for another showing.

TOURING TIPS Humour, interactive exhibits, mind-tickling doomsday scenarios, generous use of video and a real gift for storytelling make the National Space Centre the most educational yet entertaining museum we cover in this guide. While there's a fair amount of display signage to read (but never too much at once), the message is almost always conveyed in a fun and creative way through puzzles, games, hands-on experiential displays, videos and live presentations. Plus, the collection of gear, hardware, artefacts and rocketry is second-to-none.

Though the centre makes learning fun and sets a new standard for engaging visitors, there's *sooooo* much to see and do. Believe us – this is not a museum that you can romp through in an hour. A cursory visit requires at least a couple of hours, and a more comprehensive inspection will take the better part of a day. We dislike being prescriptive when it comes to age, but the nature of the subject and the stamina required for a meaningful tour suggest that the centre is best suited for children age 8 and up. If, however, you have a preschooler in tow, there's an under-5s play area in the Planets gallery.

Though our description of the main galleries is straightforward enough, one needs to understand that each gallery is essentially a museum unto itself, crammed to the point of rupture with things to see and experience. The centre map illustrates the location of the galleries but offers no hint of how convoluted their layout is. At any particular time you're likely to have exhibits in front of you, behind you, to each side and sometimes even overhead. This makes for a museum where it is very easy for your group to become separated, or to lose a child or two. A child simply stepping to the opposite side of a display can remove him or her from your field of vision. It's essential, therefore, to have a contingency plan for being separated. Designate a particular easy-to-find spot, such as the bottom of the stairway in the main building, or the Thor-Able viewing point on the first floor of the Rocket Tower, to re-group.

As mentioned numerous times, many of the exhibits are hands-on. If it's your hands instead of someone else's that concern you, try arriving early in the day before the interactive exhibits become crowded. Because only a couple of ticket-sellers service the centre, you're better off purchasing your admission in advance online. If you do so, you'll print a ticket that can be exchanged for a daily pass at Advance

Ticketing in the museum lobby. Usually the queue for Advance Ticketing is shorter than the one for the ticket-sellers.

If you drive, parking is £2. There's food and drink to be had at **Boosters Restaurant** on the ground floor of the Rocket Tower. Boosters is not within the gated (paid-admission) part of the centre, so if you leave the museum to eat and you want to be re-admitted, make sure to hang on to your admission tickets. Finally, the loos at the museum are pretty well hidden and not well signed. Chances are you'll have to ask centre staff for directions. Once you've found the WC, be sure to try the space-age hand-washing system. It's like a car wash for hands: When you put your hands in the machine, it squirts soap on them and then pauses to let you rub it around. Next it rinses your hands and then blows them dry. As we went to press, there were rumours of a new robot that administers sponge baths.

Twycross Zoo ★★★½

APPEAL BY AGE	PRESCHOOL ★★★	PRIMARY SCHOOL ★★★★	TEENS ★★★
YOUNG ADULTS ★★★	OVER 30 ★★★★		SENIORS ★★★★

Burton Road, Atherstone, Warwickshire CV9 3PX
☎ **01827 880 250; twycrosszoo.org**

HOURS (British Summer Time) 10 a.m.–5.30 p.m.; (Standard Time) 10 a.m.–4 p.m. Closed Christmas Day.

COST The zoo requests that you make a 10% contribution for conservation, and its default prices reflect the donation. Admission without the fee: £11.82 adults; £8.18 children (3–16); £10 senior citizens, students with NUS card; £7.27 special-needs adults; £6.36 special-needs children; £36.36 family ticket (2 adults, 2 children); £25.45 family ticket (1 adult, 2 children).

GETTING THERE *By car:* On the A444, which can be accessed via the A5 and the M42. *By rail:* The nearest station, Polesworth, is 4 mi (6 km) away (**nationalrail.co.uk**). *By bus:* Service 7 leaves from Market Street in Ashby de la Zouch. It operates in the other direction from Nuneaton bus station. Service 29 and 29A serve Ashby from Leicester (**leics.gov.uk**; search for 'Twycross').

DESCRIPTION AND COMMENTS We guarantee you'll go ape over the Twycross Zoo. With the largest collection of primates outside Japan, this is the only place in England where you can see four species of apes and bonobos. It has one of the largest collections of gibbons outside Southeast Asia, and more monkeys, lemurs, chimps and tamarins than you can shake a banana at. If the zoo had been around in Darwin's day, he would have called it the ultimate family reunion.

The zoo's primates first reached national attention in the iconic PG Tips tea adverts, which continued for decades. The 'Tipps Family' chimps dressed in clothing and were cast as everything from rock musicians to housewives. Why this inspired consumers to drink PG Tips we never quite understood, but you can't argue with success. The fees from using and training the chimps financed the growth of the zoo, which is now a leading supporter of primate conservation around the world. And, to this day, in cold weather the chimps are still served warm tea.

It's been a long evolution for the zoo, which began as a private collection of animals owned by two rival pet-shop owners. The women joined forces and lived together with chimps on the grounds of a Victorian home, Norton Grange, which eventually became the zoo grounds. The home, now surrounded by chimp houses, has been restored and refurbished and hosts conferences. Eventually, the private collection became a charitable trust. Now it's home to more than 1,000 animals from more than 200 species. It has slowly expanded from primates to include rare cats, elephants, sloths and reptiles. Though the apes and their kin get top billing, Twycross boasts one of the better Asian-elephant exhibits in the UK, and the first in the world to theme a Sri Lankan–elephant habitat.

Although there's plenty of parking, drive slowly as you enter the property, because the gravel road has potholes. After parking in one of the ample lots (make note of your parking area), you first encounter the impressive **Himalaya Welcome Centre,** a single-storey grass-roofed building which serves as both a conduit to the zoo entrance and as a central feature within the zoo. A multi-functional venue, the welcome centre assists tourists with visits to the National Forest and to the various attractions within Leicestershire and the surrounding counties. The building additionally houses prayer-flag-draped shops and a 300-seat restaurant overlooking a Himalayan mountain scene populated with rare snow leopards. Free to enter 364 days a year, the restaurant offers a great opportunity to enjoy lunch with the big cats. It's a beautiful space with exotic architecture – a welcome centre that's actually welcoming. You'll want to sit down and take in the scene, but don't linger too long; there's plenty to see in the property itself. To the left of Himalaya, you'll find **Wetlands** and the **Native Waterway Walk,** which teach about local environmental issues, as opposed to the global ones addressed in the rest of the zoo.

The property has a main horizontal axis, which serves as the principal corridor. To visit all the exhibits, you'll have to loop through both the upper and lower halves. Make sure you have a zoo map, and orient yourself often as it's easy to get turned around.

As you pay admission, also request a free timed ticket for a tour of the **Tropical House** (more about this later – depending on the schedule, you may need to modify your touring plans so that you don't have to backtrack). Also check on feeding times and talks. Continue down the main axis, passing the **meerkats** and the first **chimpanzee** enclosure. As you view the chimps (and you will view lots of chimps), see if you can spot the dominant male. The chimps live in family groups of about five. Take note of their facial expressions – like humans, they show their emotions – and listen to their range of calls. Take a right and then a left to pass through the **Monkey House,** which may feel a bit like a scene from *Planet of the Apes,* since on many days you'll probably be the minority species. On the other side of the house you'll pass vocal **howler monkeys,** and then head back towards the axis to the **giraffe house.** Then catch the **Monkeys of the Amazon** and the **Gorilla House** before continuing on the axis and dipping down to see the **elephants.** Then you'll go back a few dozen yards to the **Mary Brancker Waterways,** a delightful stroll past reeds and a water garden with exotic waterfowl like cranes, egrets and storks. As you follow the path, you'll cross an elaborate bamboo bridge, pass through and aviary and end up at the **Borneo Longhouse,** a replica of the island's typical residences.

Winding your way back to the centre of the zoo will lead you by **Scottish wild cats, sea lions** and **owls,** then cut back by a play area and over to the **Humboldt penguins.** Now head back to the centre walkway, and you'll find yourself facing the **Tropical House.** When it's time for your tour, a guide takes you through a rainforest environment, with exotic plants and free-ranging animals like **sloths, marmosets** and **iguanas,** and few (thankfully) confined ones, like a **blue poison-dart frog, spiders** and **boa constrictors.**

As you leave the house, continue away from the entrance to visit the extremely-rare **bonobos,** which are sometimes called pygmy chimpanzees since they resemble their larger cousins. They live in female-dominated groups of between 50 and 200 and are amongst the few non-human species that have sex for fun and friendship, not just breeding. Continuing to the top of the zoo, you'll pass **hornbills, dholes** (rare wild dogs), **hyenas** and **otters.**

Now loop down to see the very rare **Amur leopards,** with only about 40 still in the wild; **orang-utans**; and **dusky langurs,** small monkeys with white rings around the eyes. Other animals and exhibits in this centre area worth a visit are the **prairie dogs,** the **colobus monkeys** and the **gibbon complex,** where the apes swing effortlessly through an activity area. If that inspires your bound-to-be-restless youngsters, swing over to the corner of the park for the **Little Explorers** play area for toddlers and the more challenging **Adventure Playground** for older ones. Other kid-friendly exhibits here include a **train,** a **reindeer** and the clever **Pets at Twycross** area, with rabbits and chinchillas, goats, alpacas and miniature donkeys. Along with cuddly animals, you'll find a strong educational component about the responsibility of owning a pet. And if you're the one in charge of walkies at home, it might be a good time to reinforce the concept of help from other family members.

TOURING TIPS Ask if there are any babies in the **nursery.** Nearly all creatures are adorable when they're young, and they may be the highlight of your visit. The guidebook is nicely done but may be out-of-date. Check before dishing out £2.99 for it – the free map and *What's On* guide may be of more help. If you bring a picnic (which is recommended), you can leave it in your car and retrieve it at lunchtime. Just ask for a wristband allowing re-entry to the zoo.

Warwick Castle ★★★★½

APPEAL BY AGE	PRESCHOOL ★★★★	PRIMARY SCHOOL ★★★★½	TEENS ★★★★½
YOUNG ADULTS ★★★★½		OVER 30 ★★★★½	SENIORS ★★★★½

Warwick, Warwickshire CV34 Q4U
☎ **0871 265 2000; warwick-castle.com**

HOURS (2 April–3 October) 10 a.m.–6 p.m.; (4 October–1 April) 10 a.m.–5 p.m. Closed Christmas Day.

COST One-day ticket *excluding* the castle dungeon: £19.95 adults; £11.95 children (4–16); £13.95 senior citizens (60+); £12.95 students; £8.95 disabled/carer; £5.00 disabled children; £55.00 family ticket (2 adults, 2 children). One-day ticket *including* the castle dungeon: £25.45 adults; £17.50 children (4–16; not recommended for under-10s); £19.45 senior citizens (60+); £20.45 students; £8.95 disabled/carer; £5.00 disabled children; £80.00 family ticket (2 adults, 2 children). Discounts of up to 20% can be obtained by purchasing tickets online.

You can also use the **Merlin Annual Pass** (**merlinannualpass.co.uk**), which provides admission to Alton Towers Resort Theme Park, Thorpe Park, Legoland Discovery Centre, Legoland Windsor, Chessington World of Adventures, Sea Life Sanctuaries, Dungeons attractions, the Merlin London Eye and Madame Tussauds London. Prices begin at £150 for an individual and drop in price if you're buying for a family group.

GETTING THERE *By car:* In central Warwick. From the M40, take the A429 into Warwick and follow the signs for the castle. The main entrance and car parks are off Stratford Road/West Street/A429 about half a mile (.8 km) southwest of central Warwick. Because the main-entrance car parks are such a long hike to the castle, we recommend going into central Warwick on West Street/A429 and turning right on Castle Street to access Castle Lane, which runs along the castle-grounds wall. Try to find a parking space on or near Castle Lane and then use the Warwick town portal to access the entrance to the castle. If you can find a spot on the street, parking on Castle Lane will save you about 25 minutes of walking. If you can't find a street slot, use the Stables pay car park (£8) off Castle Lane near the castle admission centre. *By rail:* Warwick Station is approximately 1 mi (1.6 km) from the Castle. Direct service into London Marylebone (1 hour 45 minutes) or Birmingham Snow Hill is available (**centraltrains.co.uk** or **chilternrailways.co.uk**). *By bus:* Almost all Warwick bus routes pass through central Warwick, affording easy access to the castle from every direction (**warwickdc.gov.uk/WDC/Roads-parking-and-transport/Public+transport**).

DESCRIPTION AND COMMENTS When Bob was a boy, his favourite and most evocative plaything was a miniature castle with crenellated towers, ramparts, a courtyard and a lofty keep, all populated by toy knights and ladies. He never dreamed that he would one day stroll through the portals of a real castle similar in every way. This is Warwick Castle.

Atop a hill overlooking the River Avon, Warwick Castle has eight towers and a great house, all connected by battlements. The tallest of the towers, **Guy's Tower,** rises 128 ft (39 m) and has 5 storeys. Three gates provide access. Adjacent to the castle is a stables complex that serves as the ticketing centre and main entrance to the castle proper. Surrounding the castle are grassy activity areas, an elaborate playground and a lovely Victorian rose garden, as well as a conservatory fronted by the **Peacock Garden,** designed by the Victorian landscape gardener Robert Marnock. The River Avon runs northeast to southwest along the south side of the castle. On the opposite side of the river from the castle is an area that hosts jousting and trebuchet demonstrations.

The history of Warwick Castle dates to the Norman Conquest, when William the Conqueror ordered the building of a motte-and-bailey fort in 1068. William's fort consisted of a large earth mound with timber stockades in concentric circles around both the base and top. In the late twelfth century stone structures began replacing wooden ones, and by the end of the fourteenth century Warwick Castle was one of the most formidable fortifications in Britain.

Following the Third English Civil War (1649–1651), the castle was incrementally converted from a fortification to primarily an opulent residence. Chief among the renovations was the addition of the **State Dining Room,** and the **Red, Green** (with wax figures of Henry VIII and all of his wives) and **Cedar Drawing Rooms.** The **Great Hall,** first constructed in the fourteenth century, was rebuilt in the seventeenth century and restored in 1871. The Great Hall and **State Rooms,** with their extensive collection of art and period furniture, are open daily for tours. For those interested in history, the tour of the Chapel, Great Hall and State Rooms will be the high point of their day. Of special note is the late-sixteenth-century field armour that graces the walls of the barrel-ceilinged Great Hall. Even more impressive are re-creations of knights in full battle regalia mounted on armoured warhorses.

In 1088 William II created the first Earl of Warwick. From then to 1978, Warwick Castle remained in the hands of the 36 sequential Earls of Warwick, except for two periods when the castle became Crown property. (The first such period was from 1499 to 1547, under Henry III and Henry VII, and the second from 1589 to 1604, under Elizabeth I and James I.) The eighth Earl of Warwick, Fourth Creation (thirty-sixth in succession), David Greville, Lord Brooke, sold the castle in 1978 to Madame Tussauds of wax-museum fame, which performed major restorations and opened Warwick Castle to the public. In 2007, Madame Tussauds was acquired by Merlin Entertainments, the British entertainment and theme-park conglomerate.

Merlin turned Warwick Castle into a mediaeval-themed tourist attraction, adding elements that appeal to more-sensational tastes, such as a **dungeon** with realistic depictions of torture and a bedroom and boudoir tour called **Secrets and Scandals of the Royal Weekend Party** (set in 1898, for some inexplicable reason). Both the dungeon and Secrets and Scandals make use of wax figures and live actors to tell their story. The dungeon, for which there's an additional charge, features executions, scenes from the plague, a 'Labyrinth of Lost Souls' and torture using such everyday tools as tongue-tearers, jaw-breakers, castrators and, of course, the hook and the claw. The 40-minute guided tour is grisly in the extreme and probably best left to teens and other less-sentient beings. Secrets and Scandals, on the other hand, is fun and only mildly salacious, plus, unlike the dungeon, it's included in your castle admission. The tour moves stepwise through the salons and sleeping quarters in the left wing of the main castle and provides a look at the lifestyle of royals in the late nineteenth century. Of special note are the art, furnishings and décor of the rooms.

Other Merlin additions include an audience participation version of the Arthurian **Sword and the Stone** story, and a **Princess Tower** in the Disney tradition, where children can meet and be photographed with a princess. Warwick Castle has its own royalty, Princess Arabella, who holds courts supported by ladies-in-waiting and lesser princesses. The Princess Tower is open 11 a.m.–1 p.m. on weekdays and 10 a.m.–4 p.m. on weekends. To keep queues manageable, 'timed tickets' are required. Obtainable from Molly the Maid or one of the supporting princesses at the base of the tower, the ticket states a specific time to return and tour the tower. Visits to the Princess Tower are not available without a ticket.

On the lower levels of the left wing is another walk-through exhibit, **The Kingmaker**. Here Richard Neville, the Earl of Warwick, also known as the Kingmaker, prepares his household for the Battle of Barnet in the War of the Roses, in 1471. Once again the story is told by live actors supplemented by wax figures. The preparations for battle are interesting, but so too is the glimpse of the inner workings of the castle and the daily lives of the servants, craftsmen, cooks, armourers and clerks.

Extending downhill outside the western wall of the castle is the **Pageant Field,** where a number of shows, demonstrations and activities are held daily according to a posted schedule. Among these are falconry and archery demonstrations, organised activities for children, mock battles, jousting and demonstrations of a trebuchet, a mediaeval siege machine that (in this case) catapults fiery balls. Both the trebuchet-firing and jousting are staged on the far side of the River Avon, while guests watch from a hill on the castle side of the river. There's much blathering filler and very little jousting (about 2 minutes of a 30-minute show) or trebuchet-firing; still, the demonstrations are worthwhile and held in a truly-magical setting. There's a story-line about King Henry and his knights fighting barbarians that goes with the jousting and ensuing hand-to-hand combat. The trebuchet-firing, though doctored up with some pomp and pageantry, is more straightforward.

Back up the hill towards the castle is a **Knight School,** offering introductory lessons in sword-fighting and archery (with both bow and a crossbow). Enrolment costs £5 per person over and above your admission. Nearby a jester leads kids (and some adults) in various courtly games (one corpulent mum came perilously close to cardiac arrest whilst feverishly spinning a dinner plate on a stick). Just beyond the jester's domain is the falconry-demonstration venue.

TOURING TIPS Warwick Castle has a lot to offer. Allocate about 4–6 hours for a comprehensive visit. Plan your time around the daily entertainment schedule, touring the castle towers, buildings, grounds and battlements between performances. Take time to walk around the exterior of the castle and see **The Mound,** the oldest part of the castle.

The castle grounds are generally wheelchair- and pushchair-accessible, but the buildings are not.

If you use the main entrance, there are ten car parks in total, with No. 10 being the most remote and No. 1 being the closest. Just continue driving towards the castle in hopes of scoring a spot in one of the closer ones. Especially if you arrive after lunch, chances are good that early-arriving visitors will have completed their visit and vacated their close-in parking spaces. Exits to the car parks are controlled by token-operated gates. When you pay your parking fee you'll be given a token for the gate – put it someplace safe.

Food can be purchased at the eighteenth-century **Coach House,** the mediaeval **Undercroft Restaurant,** the **Riverside Pavilion** and several seasonal concessions. If you bring your own food, lovely picnic areas abound.

West Midland Safari & Leisure Park ★★★★

APPEAL BY AGE	PRESCHOOL ★★★★	PRIMARY SCHOOL ★★★★	TEENS ★★★
YOUNG ADULTS ★★★★		OVER 30 ★★★★	SENIORS ★★★★

Spring Grove, Bewdley, Worcestershire DY12 1LF
☎ 01229 402 114; wmsp.co.uk

- **HOURS** Opens at 10 a.m. (9 a.m. bank holidays). Closing varies, but generally at 3 p.m. during winter, 4 p.m. off-peak summer, and 5 p.m. peak season. On many nights in August the last safari entry is 7 p.m., offering a chance to see the animals at twilight. Open daily mid-February–early November, and weekends during winter.
- **COST** £9.99 adults; £7.99 children (3–15); £8.99 senior citizens, disabled, students. £32.36 family ticket (2 adults, 2 children). Discounts of £1 per ticket for online purchases. Ride wristbands: £11 adults; £10.50 children (3–15); £10.50 senior citizens, disabled, students. £38.70 family wristband package (2 adults, 2 children). Wristband for Cubs Kingdom rides only: £7.75. Individual ride tickets run £2 apiece, with a minimum purchase of 3 tickets. Some rides require 2 tickets. Park admission (but not wristbands) can also be bought through the Tesco Clubcard rewards scheme.
- **GETTING THERE** *By car:* The park is 45 minutes southwest of Birmingham. Take the A456, following park signs through Kidderminster to Bewdley. From the south (Bristol): Take the M5 north to Exit 6 and follow the A449 to Kidderminster, and then the A456 to Bewdley. From the south (Liverpool/Manchester): Take the M6 south to Exit 8 and the M5. Continue to Exit 3 and follow the A456 through Kidderminster to Bewdley. *By rail:* The nearest station is Kidderminster, 4 mi (6 km) from the park (**nationalrail.co.uk**). The bus station is .5 mi (.8 km) away *By bus:* Take

the **Kidderminster–Bewdley coach.** There's a stop on both sides of the road outside the park entrance. The reception area is a 10-minute walk, a portion uphill. (Route information: **transportdirect.info.**)

DESCRIPTION AND COMMENTS Many theme parks have a small zoo attached, and many zoos feature a few amusement rides. West Midland does both. The two-dozen-plus rides include coasters, log flumes and a pendulum. They cost extra, though, and a day out can get quite dear.

That said, you come here for the animals. The park offers a superb 4-mi (6-km) safari experience, allowing you to feed giraffes, camels and other creatures from your car window. You'll also see unusual predators like white lions and African hunting dogs. Plus, the park base has a cluster of exhibits with animal talks, and an amazing hippo-viewing area, which allows you to feed the behemoths by tossing them cabbages. It looks like a Monty Python arcade game and is one of the strangest sights we've seen in a park anywhere.

On the grounds of an eighteenth-century manor house, the 200-ac (81-ha) park is set in rolling wooded Worcestershire countryside. The property was once owned by Samuel Skey (1726–1800), a former apprentice grocer in Bewdley who made a fortune manufacturing dyestuffs and sulphuric acid. Skey and his heirs lived in the commanding sandstone manor, **Spring Grove House,** which was landscaped by Lancelot 'Capability' Brown. The property opened as a safari park in 1973. Decades later, on Christmas Eve 2006, fire nearly destroyed the home, and firefighters were forced to draw water from the Hippo Lake to get the blaze under control. After a £5-million refurbishment, the former Georgian home has been re-imagined as a luxurious African colonial residence and has opened for corporate and private events. The new, tented **Treetops Pavilion** also hosts private events.

As you enter the property, you'll ascend a long driveway and queue at a drive-through ticket booth. Hawkers offer a worthwhile £4 guidebook, but the key to enjoying the **driving safari** is to choose your visiting time carefully. During busiest periods, you'll find yourself sitting in exhaust fumes, breathing in the smell of burning brakes and clutches. The park uses a 'lock' system to separate animal reserves, so you must wait in line for a gate to open. Then you pull up to the next gate while the first one closes behind you. Finally the front gate opens and you're ready to drive into the next section. While it's quicker than navigating a canal, it does create queues. Expect to spend 75 minutes at a minimum making your way across the park. During busy times, it can take 2 hours.

So head to the park base first. You'll pass through an African-themed main street flanked by gift shops and restaurants. This is the **Discovery Trail** area, where you can see **snakes, sea lions, cheetahs** and, directly to your right, **bats.** Enter the **Twilight Cave** and give your eyes a few minutes to adjust. It's almost too dark to see anything. Soon, however, you'll realise you're not alone. Bats are in free flight all around you – look for the **Rodrigues fruit bats,** with wingspans of nearly 3 ft (1 m). There are also the much smaller **Seba's bats, Madagascar jumping rats** and rare **aye-aye lemurs.** Next door you'll find the **Creepy Crawlies** exhibit, also very dark, with the **goliath bird-eating spider,** the world's largest **tarantula;** plus **leaf-cutting ants** and **giant locusts.** Crossing the plaza, you can visit an excellent **leopard exhibit,** one of the best we've seen, with huge glass viewing windows. Then in the back left corner, find **Mark O'Shea's Reptile World,** an exemplary herpetarium with oodles of written information about the inmates posted on the exhibits and supplemented with videos. There are even interactive educational games. Although you're unlikely to see the TV star himself, you can shiver at the sight of venomous **poison-dart frogs, reticulated pythons, cobras** and **rattlesnakes.** Catch a scheduled talk in front of the building, along with the 15-minute **sea-lion show,** held in the 525-seat stadium.

By now, some in your group have probably fallen under the gravitational pull of the **amusement area.** The layout's straightforward. You first encounter rides appealing to older children and thrill-seekers. (Rides for younger visitors are in **Cubs Kingdom,** in the back of the park.) If you want to experience more than a couple of the rides, you'll want wristbands, sold in an office on your left. Tickets for individual rides are available at coin-operated machines near the Snack Shack. Then head to the right, where the most intense rides are clustered.

You'll first encounter **Black Fly,** a 46-ft (14-m) pendulum with a wicked spinning base. Next comes the short **Wild River Rafting** ride, which starts as a slide and eases into a bubbling waterway. There's no theming, and in fact nothing aesthetically appealing about this ride. It's next door to the 141-ft (43-m) **Venom Tower Drop,** which hauls you to the top for a 10-second stall. In theory, you have a great view of the park, but you're really just worried about when you'll be shot down to earth – at speeds that reach 37 mph (60 km/h) in less than a second. This cycle continues for a long 90 seconds. You're now near back-to-back coasters. The first, **Rhino Rollercoaster,** is a short, family-friendly ride with a front car shaped like a sleepy rhino; the second, the wild-mouse-style **Twister Coaster,** has ride vehicles that spin as they zip through the course. The last big ride is **Zambezi Watersplash,** a two-dip water flume. Once again it's not themed – just a labyrinth of half-pipes. Other rides include **Dr Umboto's Catacombs,** a ghost train with more bloody body parts than a lion attack.

Now walk to the back of the area and look behind the kiddie coaster, **African Big Apple.** Here's where you'll find the **Hippo Lakes** viewing platform. Not only does it overlook the country's largest hippo family, but you can feed the members with cabbages available from a vendor. When the hippos feel like a snack, they'll float in your direction and open their mouths. Your job is to shot-put one of the cabbage heads down the hatch. Don't try to make their vegetable last longer by throwing leaves; the hippos won't be bothered. They may come over for a half cabbage, but it's the whole thing they're after.

After that, any ride would be a let-down, but preschoolers in your party will want to sneak across the bridge to **Cubs Kingdom,** with flat rides featuring rhinos, caterpillars, pandas and the like. By now, if it's mid-afternoon or a low-attendance day, the traffic should have died down on the safari route. You can walk back to the entrance or take the Safari Express Train. First, though, make a toilet stop – once you're on the 4-mi (6-km) safari drive, there won't be a chance. Then leave the park base and find your car. The exit to the safari entrance isn't well marked – you'll find it on the far side of the car park.

If you haven't purchased animal food, now's the time. The feed is £3 a bag and is suitable for most of the non-carnivores you'll encounter. You should also consider taking the **safari bus,** which costs £3.50 per person. This saves your car from possible damage. (You're advised before entering the park to remove externally-mounted spare tyres and covers, because animals will attack them. And tigers have been known to gleefully urinate on cars and into open windows.) The vehicle, which is like a Land Rover, will take you off-road and close to animals, offering great photo opportunities and narration from the driver. Space is limited – if you're interested, check availability when you arrive.

Once on the hilly road, you'll first enter the **African Reserve** and come across a crash (as a grouping is called) of **white rhinos.** This is the largest and most sociable of the species, weighing in at 5,070 lb (2,300 kg). There are also **zebras, wildebeests, elands, red lechwe** and **ankole cattle,** easily recognised by their distinctive long horns. All can be fed, but the animal most likely to stick its head into your car is the **giraffe.** Don't feel you have to distribute all the food now, as you'll be passing through the reserve two more times. Next, go down under to the **Wallaby Reserve.** The white **Bennett's wallabies** hopping around here have royal pedigrees, being descendants of a mob given to the Queen in 1962 during a state visit to Australia. Next you'll move from cuties to canines. The **Wolf Reserve** houses **North American wolves,** which can reach speeds of 40 mph (64 km/h). To enter the predator area, you pass through a set of double gates – rather like boats going through a set of locks. This has the effect of bunching up the vehicles that pass through the gates at the same time. Our advice is to drive swiftly through the Wolf Reserve and achieve some separation between you and the gaggle. This will liberate you (for the moment) and net you some independence of movement.

You'll now enter the **Asian Reserve,** home to a spectrum of creatures, from **blackbuck antelopes,** weighing 77 lb (35 kg), to the ginormous **Asian buffalo,** at a cool 2,200 lb (1,000 kg). You'll also see **samba** and **barasingha deer,** and the extremely-rare **Philippine spotted deer.** Look for the odd **Przewalski's horse,** the only true remaining species of wild horse. And what would a trip to Asia be without spying a **yak**?

Next come cats and dogs – and more of the traffic-snarling double gates. First drive by **Bengal tigers,** followed by **cheetahs.** Then you'll see the fascinating and colourful **African wild dogs.** These methodical killers are why you're warned to remove your spare tyre: the dogs can rip one to pieces while you sit helplessly in your car. Finally you'll encounter the **African lions** and **white lions,** which are so rare that the wild population is limited to one spot: South Africa's Timbavati Game Reserve. The lion area is the safari's most notorious bottleneck (more gates) and a very good reason to drive the safari in mid- to late afternoon, when there are fewer cars on the route.

Next you'll make your way to the **Eurasian Reserve,** home to two-humped **Bactrian camels.** Although there are millions of domesticated camels around the world, fewer than 1,000 remain in the wild, in northwest China and Mongolia. You'll also find **nilgai,** Asia's largest antelope, and **banteng cattle.**

The route then loops through the **African Elephant Reserve.** This species is larger than the Asian elephant, tipping the scales at 9,920 lb (4,500 kg). The females are highly social and have been known to greet each other by intertwining trunks.

TOURING TIPS Check the time of the last entry to the safari park, which can be as early as 3 p.m. during winter. Pack a towel and antimicrobial gel – if you feed animals, you *will* be slobbered on. Heed the signs and warnings on the safari. In some areas, it's safe to put down the windows; in others, you must roll them up and (if you're really paranoid) lock your door for extra measure. If you run into any trouble, honk your horn and wait for help from a ranger.

Animals wander onto the road hoping to be fed, sometimes blocking one or both lanes. Compounding the problem are visitors with food who neglect to pull off the road as they dole out goodies. This results in a long train of vehicles that can't continue until the car at the very front decides to move on. The animals are hip to the scene and post themselves at the front of the car queue like toll-takers. Though there are park staff nearby, they decline to intervene. Towards the end of the driving safari it gets worse, as visitors run out of animals before they run out of food. The upshot is car after car trying to unload their remaining grub onto two or three animals before departing the preserve. *Crikey!*

Most people don't have the time, but you can drive the safari more than once if you please.

For the record, many safari parks avoid these traffic problems by having staff man single gates instead of the double-gate arrangement. This permits relatively free-flowing traffic. Also expediting affairs is providing three lanes instead of two, and prohibiting the feeding of animals.

If you visit the base and amusement areas before doing the driving safari (recommended) and you use the car park, it's not obvious how to reach the entrance to the safari. Simply drive to the far side of the car park opposite the base area and turn right. You'll reach an intersection where you can bear left to exit the park or continue straight to the safari entrance.

Wicksteed Park ★★★½

APPEAL BY AGE	PRESCHOOL ★★★	PRIMARY SCHOOL ★★★★	TEENS ★★★
YOUNG ADULTS ★★★★		OVER 30 ★★★★	SENIORS ★★★★

Barton Road, Kettering, Northamptonshire NN15 6NJ
☎ **01536 512 475; wicksteedpark.co.uk**

HOURS The park opens at 9 a.m. and rides open at 10.30 a.m. Closing times vary (see website for details). Grounds open every day but Christmas. Rides not open from November to mid February.

COST Park admission is free, but wait till you see how much parking costs! Unlimited ride wristband: £11 adults (£10 online); £16 children (16 and under) (£15 online); £8 senior citizens. Children under 2'11" (.9 m) and wheelchair users, free. Wristbands discounted off-season. If you don't have a wristband, each ride requires from 1 to 4 tickets. £1 single-ride ticket; £11 sheet of 12 tickets – equivalent to 92p per ticket (online £10; equivalent to 83p per ticket); £22 sheet of 30 tickets – equivalent to 73p per ticket (online £20; equivalent to 66p per ticket). Wristbands and tickets can also be bought through the Tesco Clubcard rewards scheme.

GETTING THERE *By car:* About 1 hour from Milton Keynes, Cambridge and Birmingham, just under 2 hours from central London. From the north, exit the M1 at Junction 19 and join the A14. Then exit at Junction 10 and follow the brown signs. From the south, leave the M1 at Junction 15 and join the A43, then take the A14 (Junction 8) east to Junction 10 and follow the brown signs. Parking £6; late afternoon (1 hour before closing), £3. *By rail:* The closest station is Kettering, which is 1.2 mi (3.2 km) away (**nationalrail.co.uk**). You can take a taxi or walk to the park. *By bus:* **Stagecoach buses** stop outside of the park on Barton Road, with service from Burton and Kettering (**stagecoachbus.co.uk**). (Route information: **transportdirect.info**.)

DESCRIPTION AND COMMENTS Very rarely is a day in a theme park really a day in a park. Wicksteed, believed to be the oldest amusement park in England, is a lovely exception. Situated on 147 ac (59 ha) of landscaped English countryside, it offers 35 rides over three separate areas.

The founder, Charles Wicksteed, started out in 1921 to build a model village with open space and parkland for residents. He noticed many local children played in the street because they didn't have gardens at home, and his new development included the country's largest free playground. Perhaps Wicksteed had an ulterior motive – he owned a company that manufactured playground equipment for public parks, and the development would be a great showcase for his work. But what he created at Wicksteed has aged gracefully, attracting amusement-park-goers, along with picnickers and dog-walkers drawn by the huge, open green space. More than a quarter of a million guests come per year to ride the park's iconic narrow-gauge railway. It was the last feature added by Charles Wicksteed, who died two weeks before it opened to the public at Easter in 1931. The park is now owned by a charitable trust.

Rides are distributed around four sections – **The Fairground, The Playground, The Lakeside** and **The Arena.** The Fairground and The Playground are next to each other in the main section of the park – near the car park and the visitor's centre. There is quite a lot of walking involved in a trip to Wicksteed, particularly as children are likely to zip around between the different areas, but the site is quite flat and the paths are in good condition. Wheelchairs are available from the first-aid office next to the visitor's centre for a £5 refundable deposit, although pushchairs are not. You are advised to book in advance for a wheelchair, as availability is limited.

How long you spend at Wicksteed depends on the age of your party – it probably won't hold much interest for children over 13, especially if they're used to the thrills and spills of Alton Towers or Chessington, but there's plenty to keep younger children occupied. Its wide open spaces and free playground offer a further benefit in that you could take a picnic and a football and enjoy a typical family day in the park for nothing.

Entrance to the park is free, although a £6 fee is charged for car-parking – a somewhat unavoidable cost, as the park is out of town and there is no free parking nearby. You then pay to go on the rides either by purchasing a wristband that allows for free entry onto all rides all day, or by way of a ticket system. The tickets can be bought at stands across the park. The price of tickets goes down if bought in bulk, and they are open-ended, so they can be used on repeat visits.

As you enter the property, you'll find yourself confronted with an unfamiliar theme park site: free attractions. Wicksteed still has one of Europe's largest playgrounds, which includes swings, see-saws, slides, zip-lines and a play castle. These may keep your little ones busy for a while – and leave your wallet untouched. But if you've sprung for a wristband – the smart choice if the weather's nice and you're planning on spending several hours – you may want to steer them to the ticketed rides, since you've already paid for them. The ride options aren't too surprising. The compact **Playground** and **Fairground** areas have a swinging pirate ship and a classic **Carousel** and lighthouse-shaped **drop tower.** There's also **crazy golf, dodgems** and **Lazer Tag.** (In this interactive game you step into a dome, wearing a special vest that lights up when a direct hit is scored.) Other attractions include a **giant slide** and spinning **Cups & Saucers.**

While you're in the area, take a quick walk through the lovely **Sunken Memorial Garden,** where you'll find the Charles Wicksteed memorial. Fittingly, this is near the station for the **Wicksteed Park Railway,** which circles the lake. When first built, it was intended to be just one of many attractions, but it has continually ranked as a visitor favourite. The trains are usually hauled by one of two diesel locomotives shaped to look as if they're steam-powered. The park takes a paternal pride in its engines and even names them. For years, a 40-hp train dubbed 'Cheyenne' did most the work, but in 2010 the park added a new member to the family, named 'Merlin'. It cost £75,000 and is now the principal hauler.

The other sections are spread around the park and linked by pathways. The **Lakeside** is at one end of the park's 30-ac (12-ha) lake and offers a monorail, a few spinning flat rides and a small water flume called the **Waterchute,** which is not only a thrill ride but a bona fide historic attraction. When Mr Wicksteed built the ride in 1926, it was one of the few water-amusement rides in the world. The ride itself is a simple affair: You climb some stairs, are strapped in a boat and descend a chute with a mighty splash, which is enhanced by the fins on the front of the vessel. Then the boat's hauled back up to the top of the tower by a permanently-attached rope, ready for the next riders. The old-timey atmosphere continues with **Mr Wicksteed's Veteran Cars,** which offer a quick jaunt in scaled-down antique motors. As you toddle around the track, look for the breakdown vehicle towing away a car; it's one of the Mini Cars from the original driving attraction, removed in 2005 after more than 50 years of service. These rides blend nicely with more-traditional park activities, like **rowing boats, canoes** and **pedalos,** which can be taken out onto the lake. There is also a small **aviary** full of parrots and other brightly-coloured birds. Finally, there's a free **sandpit,** and a **model-boating lake,** which is fun to watch.

Along the water from the Lakeside is **The Arena,** by far the busiest area, with the best rides. The top draw here is the **Wicksteed Racers** – little petrol-driven cars that can be raced around an impressively-long track, reaching speeds of up to 15 mph (24 km/h). They're great fun, although drivers must be at least 5'3" (1.6 m) tall. There is an excellent log flume, **Rocky River Falls,** which includes a 36-ft (11-m) drop, the expected splash, and a drier at the exit for those who get soaked. You'll also find a steel roller coaster with the imaginative name of **Roller Coaster.** It stretches 1,066 ft (325 m) over its figure-of-eight track and reaches speeds of 28 mph (45 km/h). You'll also find the very gentle **Ladybird Coaster,** and the **Paratrooper,** a spinning umbrella ride. For more-low-key amusements, there's a **fishing lake** and a 1.3-mi (2-km) **Nature Trail.**

TOURING TIPS Wicksteed gets very busy during school holidays, so arrive early and take in The Arena first, as that is where queues are longest, particularly for Wicksteed Racers, Roller Coaster and Rocky River Falls. However, note there are no toilets at The Arena, with the nearest about 900 ft (275 m) away along the path to The Waterside. Also, as the park has very few covered attractions, it's best avoided on a wet day. While you'll find plenty of restaurants and places to grab a snack, it would be hard to find a prettier place for a picnic; there are plenty of benches and barbecue grills around the property.

FARM EXPERIENCES

BECAUSE THE VARIOUS FARM EXPERIENCES ARE SO SIMILAR (see page 13), we felt it unnecessary to provide individual profiles as we do with other types of attractions. Following is a selective list of farm experiences in the East and West Midlands.

DERBYSHIRE

HIGHFIELDS HAPPY HENS
(Complete farm experience but big on chickens)
Highfields Farm
Heage Lane
Etwall, Derby
Derbyshire DE65 6LS
☎ 01283 732 083
highfieldshappyhens.co.uk
**happyhens@happyhens
    .force9.co.uk**

GLOUCESTERSHIRE

COTSWOLD FARM PARK
Guiting Power, Cheltenham
Gloucestershire GL54 5UG
☎ 01451 850 307
cotswoldfarmpark.co.uk
info@cotswoldfarmpark.co.uk

DICK WHITTINGTON FARM PARK
Blakemore Park
Little London, Longhope
Gloucestershire GL17 0PH
☎ 01452 831 000
dickwhittington.org
info@dickwhittington.info

CATTLE COUNTRY ADVENTURE PARK
(Features American bison in addition to the usual suspects)
Berkeley Heath Farm
Berkeley
Gloucestershire GL13 9EW
☎ 01453 810 510
cattlecountry.co.uk
info@cattlecountry.co.uk

LEICESTERSHIRE AND RUTLAND

GORSE HILL CITY FARM
Anstey Lane
Leicester LE4 0FJ
☎ 0116 253 7582
gorsehillcityfarm.org.uk
gorsehillcityfarm@live.co.uk

NOTTINGHAMSHIRE

FERRY FARM PARK
Ferry Farm
Boat Lane
Hoveringham
Nottinghamshire NG14 7JR
☎ 0115 966 4512
ferryfarm.co.uk
enquiries@ferryfarm.fsnet.co.uk

WHITE POST FARM CENTRE
(Features reptiles, insects and wallabies in addition to barnyard critters)
Mansfield Road
Farnsfield, Newark
Nottinghamshire NG22 8HL
☎ 01623 882 977
whitepostfarmcentre.co.uk
hello@whitepostfarm.co.uk

SHROPSHIRE

HOO FARM ANIMAL KINGDOM
(Offers a variety of non-indigenous wildlife including wallabies, alpacas, ostriches, and in a singular twist, armadillos)
Preston upon the Weald Moors
Telford
Shropshire TF6 6DJ
☎ 01952 677 917
www.hoofarm.com
info@hoofarm.com

MICKEY MILLER'S FAMILY PLAYBARN & MAIZE MAZE
(Includes a 6-ac maize maze)
Oakfield Farm
Watling Street, Craven Arms
Shropshire SY7 8DX
☎ 01588 673 800
mickeymillers.com
mickey@mickeymillers.com

PARK HALL – THE COUNTRYSIDE EXPERIENCE
(Features various driving experiences for children and a classic-car museum for adults)
Park Hall Farm
Oswestry
Shropshire SY11 4AS
☎ 01691 671 173
parkhallfarm.co.uk
rachel@parkhallfarm.co.uk

RAYS FARM COUNTRY MATTERS
(Satnavs have trouble finding the farm if using the postal code; farm is signposted off B4363)
Billingsley, Bridgnorth
Shropshire WV16 6PF
☎ 01299 841 255
raysfarm.com

STAFFORDSHIRE

AMERTON FARM & CRAFT CENTRE
Amerton Farm
Stowe by Chartley, Stafford
Staffordshire ST18 0LA
☎ 01889 270 294
amertonfarm.co.uk
office@amertonfarm.co.uk

ASH END HOUSE CHILDREN'S FARM
Middleton Lane
Middleton, nr Tamworth
Staffordshire B78 2BL
☎ 0121 329 3240
childrensfarm.co.uk
contact@childrensfarm.co.uk

WARWICKSHIRE

BROOMEY CROFT CHILDREN'S FARM
Bodymoor Heath Lane
Bodymoor Heath, Kingsbury
Warwickshire B76 0EE
☎ 01827 873 844
broomeycroftfarm.co.uk
info@broomeycroftfarm.co.uk

HATTON FARM VILLAGE
Dark Lane
Hatton
Warwickshire CV35 8XA
☎ 01926 843 411
hattonworld.com
hatton@hattonworld.com

PART TEN

YORKSHIRE

MOST VISITORS WILL BRING SOME SORT OF preconceived notion to Yorkshire. There are, of course, the rugged moors where Heathcliff brooded in *Wuthering Heights,* the green valleys that veterinarian–author James Herriott describes in his appealing representations of English country life, even the gloomy graveyard on a hill above the sea in Whitby that allegedly inspired Bram Stoker's *Dracula.*

Whatever expectations you bring to Yorkshire, your journey up north will be well rewarded. At the centre of this swath of northern England is the richly-historic and remarkably-attractive walled city of **York.** To the west are the deep, luxuriant river valleys of the **Yorkshire Dales,** and to the east and north are the rugged, heather-covered **Yorkshire Moors.** In these landscapes are literary shrines (notably, **Haworth,** where the Brontë sisters wrote their masterpieces); ruined abbeys (the most spectacular are those at **Bolton** and **Rievaulx**); isolated but lavish country houses (aside from a royal palace or two, **Castle Howard** may well be the grandest home in England); and charming towns and villages (our favourite is seaside **Whitby**). Given the riches that await you in Yorkshire, it would be a shame to not make the journey north. We suggest that you make York your base and set out on easy day trips from there.

Attractions in Yorkshire range from the ghoulish **York Dungeon** and the sprawling **National Railway Museum** to **The Deep,** Britain's finest aquarium.

THEME PARKS *and* ATTRACTIONS

The Deep ★★★★★

APPEAL BY AGE	PRESCHOOL ★★★	PRIMARY SCHOOL ★★★★	TEENS ★★★★
YOUNG ADULTS ★★★★★	OVER 30 ★★★★★		SENIORS ★★★★½

Tower Street, Hull, East Yorkshire HU1 4DP
☎ 01482 381 000; thedeep.co.uk

Yorkshire

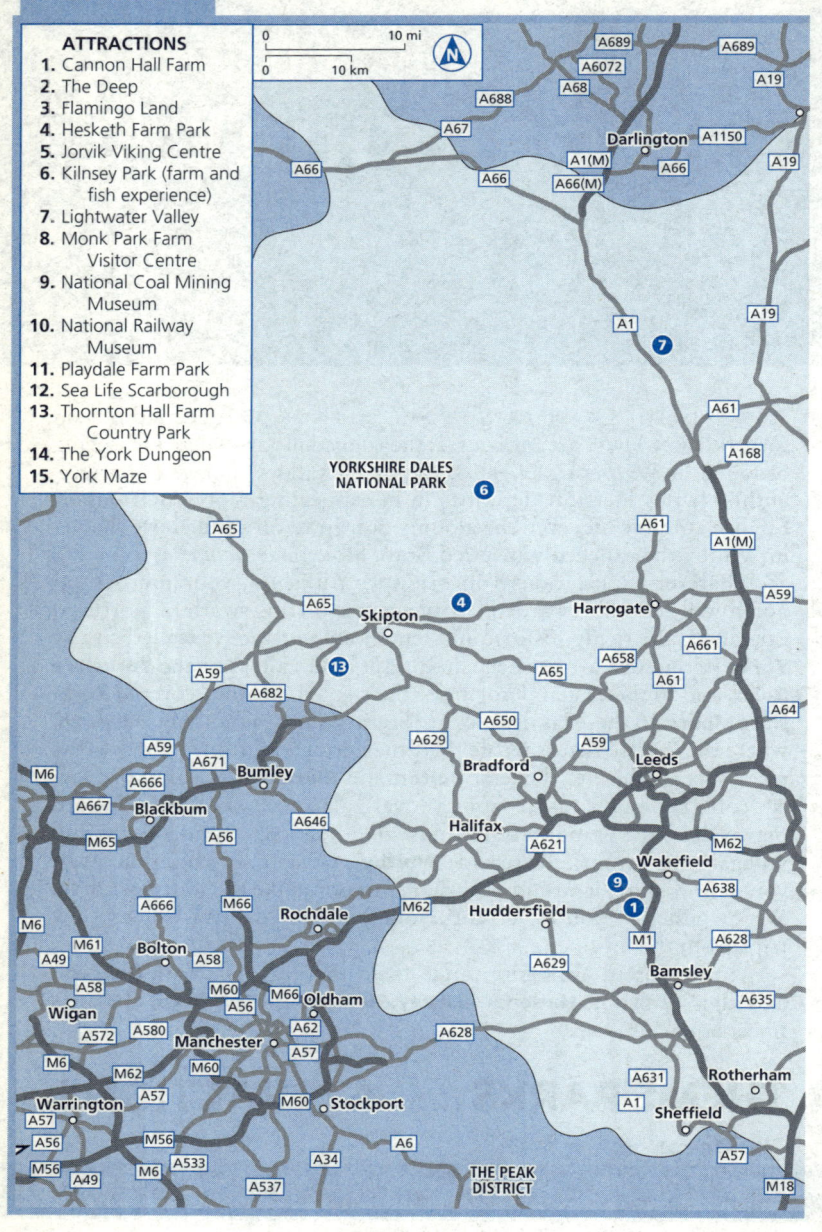

ATTRACTIONS
1. Cannon Hall Farm
2. The Deep
3. Flamingo Land
4. Hesketh Farm Park
5. Jorvik Viking Centre
6. Kilnsey Park (farm and fish experience)
7. Lightwater Valley
8. Monk Park Farm Visitor Centre
9. National Coal Mining Museum
10. National Railway Museum
11. Playdale Farm Park
12. Sea Life Scarborough
13. Thornton Hall Farm Country Park
14. The York Dungeon
15. York Maze

YORKSHIRE MAP 335

HOURS 10 a.m.–6 p.m. (last entry 5 p.m.); closed Christmas Eve and Christmas Day.

COST £9.50 adults; £7.50 children (aged 3–15; must be accompanied by an adult); £8 senior citizens and students; £30 family of 4 (maximum 2 adults); £36 family of 5 (maximum 2 adults). Tickets purchased online allow you return entrance for a year.

GETTING THERE *By car:* One hour from York, Leeds, Lincoln and Sheffield. Follow the signs to Hull, then local signs. *By rail:* Direct trains from London take 2¾ hours. Taxis from the station cost about £4.50. *By bus:* The nearest stop is under Myton Bridge (for schedule: ☎ 01482 222 222). *By foot:* A 15-minute walk from Hull city centre and 20 minutes from the Paragon Transport Interchange by pedestrian footbridge.

DESCRIPTION AND COMMENTS The best aquarium in Britain makes quite an impression before you even step inside. The spectacular angular glass building, designed by Sir Terry Farrell, rises like a shark's fin from Hull's waterfront. It opened as a Millennium Project in 2002 and immediately became the port city's top attraction and symbol – it has even been featured on a Royal Mail stamp. Fortunately, the building's exhibits live up to the splashy packaging. But as with most aquariums, you do need to invest some time and energy to get the most out of your visit. Stop and read the signs and monitors. Spend some time at the interactive video screens. Check for scheduled feedings and talks. It's all time well spent. You'll leave with a greater appreciation for the wonders of the sea – and feel that you've gotten your money's worth.

The Deep calls itself a 'submarium', a made-up name to convey that you'll be gazing upon sea life living far under water. The idea is reinforced by the layout, which has you starting at the top of the building and slowly working your way down to the creatures far below.

If you drive, you'll find plenty of room in the car park. The £3 charge is annoying, but hold on to your receipt – it's good for a £2 credit at the gift shop or cafeteria, or use it towards an audio guide and booklet.

Once you reach the building, you'll take a lift up to the exhibition area and proceed through a walk-through pre-admission exhibit that aims to put our oceans, which cover two-thirds of the planet, into perspective. You'll pass by the café, which has an adjoining balcony. If the weather is nice, step outside for a sweeping view of the Humber River estuary. If you're lucky you may catch a glimpse of porpoises during the spring, or seals year-round. Once you pay admission, you have few choices to make. Unlike many other aquariums, this one has a prescribed course and traffic flow that will have you passing through or by all the exhibits. First stop is the **Introduction Theatre,** where it's explained that The Deep is 'the story of the world's oceans told through time'. Unfortunately, the ambient echo and the relatively-low volume of the video presentation make it almost impossible to hear. **Timeline: The Evolving Seas** is next. Simply follow the ramp leading down into the building. The handrail on your right is meant to convey your progression through the Earth's 3.5-billion-year history, which is illustrated by fossil replicas embedded in the rock face wall. Each 0.3" (1 cm) you move is the equivalent of 1 million years. At this scale, it's only when you reach the last few inches (or about 10 cm) of the exhibit that man emerges on the planet. Stop to look at the monitors along the way. You can design a prehistoric sea monster and see if it will survive Earth's changing conditions.

As you continue your 3-storey ramp descent, your journey is punctuated by numerous videos on monitors supplementing the marine and static exhibits. It's all very engaging, but you did pay to see an aquarium, and just when you begin to wonder if there are any fish here, you finally get to see some water. Turning the corner leads you to the **Lagoon of Light,** a tank with living coral and brightly-coloured creatures such as the Picasso triggerfish, which looks as if it just swam off the Spanish surrealist's canvas. Around the corner, the **Coral Realm** provides a scuba-eye view of the action when you climb a ladder leading into a glass bubble, where you're surrounded by tropical scenery. A nearby periscope offers a similar experience. As you continue to work your way into the building, make sure to duck into the **Kingston Communications Discovery Corner.** It's designed for kids but is fun for everyone. Its touch pool, which is open intermittently throughout the day, features animals from the British coast, including crabs, starfish and sea anemones.

Finally comes your first good look at **Endless Ocean,** a 550,000-gal (2.5-million-litre) capacity tank that contains 187,000 lb (85,000 kg) of salt. You'll find several dozen sharks, of course, and strange creatures such as the blue-and-gray potato grouper. But try to spot schools of jacks. The iridescent fish travel in packs as a defence mechanism, because in open water there's nowhere to hide.

The tank is big enough that you can see how light begins to change as you descend. Thirty-three feet (10 metres) down, colours fade to blue because most light waves can't penetrate the water. While you won't see dolphins in the tank, you can hear recordings of their clicks and whistles on headsets. Standouts include the green moray eel; the 6½-ft (2-m) humphead wrasse, which looks like a giant indigo goldfish but has jaws that can crunch through snails; the spotted wobbegong, resembling a brown camouflage-covered shark that blends seamlessly into the background; and the green sawfish.

Hope it's been a while since lunch because now it's time to get grossed out. **Slime** is devoted to the marvels of mucus, which you'll learn is a mixture of sugar and protein employed by a variety of land and sea creatures. Here you'll take in frogs, snails and slugs – and learn that clownfish protect themselves from the sting of sea anemones with a thick coating of goo. Down the ramp from Slime is an open area offering 3D films on various subjects, including the life cycle of sea turtles. The films are excellent, but nearby display lights compromise the necessary darkness and detract from the quality of the images on the screen – much as when a cinema forgets to dim the house lights before starting the feature film.

Acknowledging that England isn't exactly tropical, the **Industrial Seas** exhibit showcases cold-water fish such as cod and addresses industrial uses of the sea, including shipping and oil exploration. The exhibit doesn't pull punches, discussing the devastating effect pollution has had on sea life.

Next comes the **Twilight Zone,** which covers the area between surface and sea bottom – from 656 to 3,281 ft (200 to 1,000 m) down. It's an alien world where animals have adapted to live with low oxygen, cold temperatures and crushing pressure. The stars here are giant Japanese spider crabs, wolf eels and, a favourite, the giant Pacific octopus. The Twilight Zone is the only non-linear part of your tour, requiring you to turn left as opposed to continuing straight to the **Kingdom of Ice.** Not to worry: an anti-clockwise circuit of the Twilight Zone will bring you back to the passage to the Kingdom of Ice, where the walls literally are encased in ice. In this tribute to the polar seas, you'll see Arctic jellyfish and learn about the impact of global warming.

Little ones will appreciate **Hullabaloo,** a soft-play area for preschoolers that comes just in time for tired feet. The tour ends in **Deep Blue 1,** a mock submersible research station that bears a striking resemblance to the deck of the Starship *Enterprise*. The exhibit asks you to pretend that it's 2050 and you're a trainee working 2½ mi (4 km) under water, exploring deep sea vents and observing glowing jellyfish and swift-moving squid.

Not to knock any of the displays, but perhaps the most exciting part of a visit is your exit. First you walk through the deepest underwater-viewing tunnel in Europe, at the bottom of the main aquarium. At the end of the tunnel, a transparent lift rises directly through the main ocean tank, giving you a plankton-eye view of the huge exhibit. Queues are sometimes 15 minutes long, but it's worth the wait. But all's not lost if you take the stairs, which have windows looking into the tank. In fact some prefer this route, since you can take your time and enjoy the view.

TOURING TIPS When you enter, check for feeding times and talks. The **Dive Presentation,** at 2 p.m. daily, is particularly engaging, letting you watch the dive team prepare for their tank visit. Arrive as early as possible, and try to avoid school holidays. Sunday mornings are particularly quiet. If you're visiting on the weekend and are looking for an engaging night out, try the 'dining with the sharks' programme at the aquarium's **Two Rivers Restaurant** from 7 p.m. While you feast on contemporary Mediterranean food, you can gaze at the sharks and fish gliding through the tanks (reservations required: ☎ 01482 382 883).

Flamingo Land ★★★★

APPEAL BY AGE	PRESCHOOL ★★★★	PRIMARY SCHOOL ★★★★★	TEENS ★★★★★
YOUNG ADULTS ★★★★		OVER 30 ★★★	SENIORS ★★★

Kirby Misperton, Malton, North Yorkshire YO17 6UX
☎ **0871 911 8000; flamingoland.co.uk**

HOURS (Mid-March–October 31) 9.30 a.m.– 4 p.m. or 6 p.m., depending on season; rides start 10 a.m.

COST £25 adults and children over age 4; children aged 3 and under, free (proof of age may be required); £12.50 senior citizens, disabled and carers (official proof required); £90 family ticket (2 adults, 2 children). Purchase online for discounts of about 10%.

GETTING THERE *By car:* From the A64 or A170 take the A169 (Malton Road) to Kirby Misperton Road. *By rail:* From the York rail station, you can catch the **Yorkshire Coastliner bus** (☎ 01653 692 556 or 0113 244 8976), which drops off at Flamingo Land. The closest rail station is Malton, about 8 mi (13 km) from the park. For more information, call ☎ 08457 484950.

DESCRIPTION AND COMMENTS Although not quite Disney's Animal Kingdom, Flamingo Land does an admirable job of mixing zoo and theme park. The enterprise started several decades ago with a flock of flamingos, which is now the largest in Britain. Over the years, the property has changed hands and morphed into a full-blown theme park. Now, along with wild rhinos and elephants, you'll find wild roller coasters, some quite good – including a world-record holder. Several other rides are quite clever and appealing, not the typical funfair offerings. Flamingo Land is also a sprawling resort, with camping, cabin rentals and live shows with big-name entertainers. The shows and concerts aren't really for families, but the park as a whole certainly is and will keep you busy for a good long day.

The theme-park component of Flamingo Land offers some exhilarating rides with very small carrying capacities and, with one exception among the biggies, short ride times.

The park is set in a hilly, bucolic area of North Yorkshire, and after paying admission you enter the **Metropolis** portion of the park, where you're immediately greeted with family and kiddie rides, including a wave-swinger. But straight ahead you'll find something unfamiliar: the **Cycle Monorail.** As on an airborne paddleboat, you're provided the power to move a small vehicle around an elevated track. It's worth trying this at the beginning of your visit, because at the end of the day, you'll be too exhausted to power it. Nearby you'll find a pair of junior coasters, **Runaway Mine Train** and **Dragon Coaster,** which has the lowest height restriction of all the coasters.

More exciting is **Velocity,** a rare cycle-style roller coaster. You straddle a replica motorbike and zoom along the track. Acceleration is 0–60 mph (96 km/h) in 2.8 seconds. Try that in a Ferrari.

Turning left takes you to the **Corkscrew.** One of the park's first coasters, it still packs a wallop, inverting riders twice as it twists for almost 2 minutes through its nearly-0.5-mi (0.75-km) length. And with a minimum height requirement of just 4 ft (1.2 m), it's an equal-opportunity nausea machine. It surrounds the **Wild Mouse** coaster and **dodgems.** There is also a concentration of children's rides in this area, including the ubiquitous flying elephants and a beginner roller coaster, among others.

Continuing in a clockwise direction leads you to the **Seaside Adventure** area, where the emphasis is on children's rides. This is where you can catch the cute cow-themed **People Moover,** which can whisk you off to the Mucky Duck Farm children's area, back near the park entrance.

But thrill-seekers should check out **Cliff Hanger** – the looming 180-ft (55-m) lighthouse-themed tower you'll have seen from the moment you entered the park. It ties with Bomber Mark 2 at M&D's in Scotland as the tallest tower-drop ride in Britain, and passengers must be at least 4'4" (1.3 m) to ride. The ride cycles through several modes. The standard experience launches you to the top for a free-fall, and then again launches halfway up for another drop. In the combo mode, the ride vehicle stops at the top, and screaming passengers are literally left hanging as they're suspended in mid-air, waiting to be launched downwards. Cliff Hanger is super-slow-loading and develops long queues.

Continuing to the back of the park towards the **Adventure Land** area, you'll find **Mumbo Jumbo,** the world's steepest coaster, with a record-setting 112° drop. For those of you who forgot your geometry, that means that as you drop, you're actually partially upside-down and, if not for restraints, you'd fall out of the car. The steel coaster reaches a height of 98 ft (30 m) and subjects riders to 4 g's. It has a wild-mouse design and is a true crowd-pleaser, ranking 158th in the world on a steel-coaster poll. Just as thrilling is **Kumali,** named for one of the zoo's lions. The double-inverted looping coaster has you suspended in your seat, leaving your feet dangling as you twist over a lake at 56 mph (90 km/h). Want to relive the ride over and over? You can purchase a DVD of your ride as you exit. Loading and unloading for Kumali can best be described as glacial.

Nearby is **Voodoo,** a pirate-ship ride, and the **Bongo Warriors** stage, offering dancing, acrobatics and contortions to a pulsing jungle beat. The fast-paced show runs three or four times a day and boasts a sound system that would make Metallica cringe. Too bad you can't watch the performance from 300 yd away.

Across the walkway from the Bongo Warriors is where you can catch the **Lost River Ride,** a clever water adventure that starts as a floating zoo tour and wraps up with a literal splash. The trip takes you through animal habitats, passing near hippos, rhinos, lions, zebras, giraffes and ostriches. (If you don't have the time or inclination for the ride, you can see all of the animals from surrounding walkways.) Boat-mounted speakers provide sound effects and information on the animals. Then comes the 60-ft (18-m) drop at the end. Lost River Ride carries the dubious distinction of having the longest queues in the park, partly because the ride has a very low hourly carrying capacity, but also because most riders eat up 4 minutes or so donning rain-gear (provided by the park). After finally having been dispatched from the loading platform, each boat is halted and held again for about 4 minutes before being released to take the big drop and finish the course. From beginning to end the float lasts 11½ minutes. Even with the rain-gear, you can count on getting wet.

If that whets your appetite for water thrills, you'll love **Splosh!,** a water playground near Adventure Land that has palm trees and water jets. On **Splash Battle,** a unique interactive water ride, you take a seat in a submarine-themed vehicle and man battle stations in the form of water cannons. If you don't hit designated targets, you'll get soaked. But the interactivity doesn't stop there. You're also free to shoot at people walking near the ride – and they're free to fire at you with water cannons based on land. As you'd expect, mayhem and soaking are the order of the day, and most of those who ride wear rain-gear. **Flip Flop,** a top-swing pendulum ride, flies over a lake, offering a chance to be soaked too, as a water volcano erupts every 20 minutes. The splashing even continues indoors in the nearby **SpongeBob SquarePants 4D** presentation, a goofy 4-D film about SpongeBob chasing down a pickle for a hamburger. It's a slick production where the theatre itself packs a few surprises (including seat movements that are very jarring and unpleasant) – if, that is, you can locate the theatre. The entrance is anything but obvious. Look for the building to the rear of the HMS Bouncy indoor play area.

Finally you reach the **zoo,** where the whole park started. Although an afterthought for many ride-obsessed guests, it's certainly worth a visit to this side of the park. You can get a relaxing overview on the cable-car ride that crosses the area, but on foot you can linger and watch lions, giraffes, hippos, storks and more. The walk-through **aviary** is worthwhile, as is the **white rhino** habitat. Try to time your visit around the **sea-lion and parrot shows,** long-time favourites. There are also **lemurs, meerkats, baboons** and a **bat house.** Back near the front of the park, you can access the elevated **Treetop Walkway,** with views of emus, kangaroos, tapirs, rheas, alpacas and, of course, flamingos, descendants of the original flock that started the park years ago. In 2010 a well-designed penguin exhibit was added as an extension of the walk. The zoo offers a bird show and a sea-lion show, both fun and informative.

Lastly comes **Mucky Duck Farm.** Yes, every park seems to have a farm-based petting-zoo area, but the **Tractor Ride** makes this area stand out. Little ones can drive their own vehicle on a designated path, taking in the scenery and their favourite farmyard animals along the way. It really does feel and look like a drive-through farm. The area's also home to a ghost train, **Mischief Mansion,** with cartoonish ghouls and goblins.

There are four scenic rides. **Cable Cars** connect the Lost Kingdom section of the park with the zoological section. The **Daktari Express** is a miniature train that circles the Lost Kingdom, while the **Zoo Monorail** provides an aerial view of meerkats and baboons. Finally, decked out like the hide of a Friesian cow, the **People Moover** will transport you from the Seaside Adventure section of the park to Mucky Duck Farm.

TOURING TIPS Flamingo Land is a multi-dimensional theme park with modern, extremely-appealing rides diminished by their low carrying capacity and inefficient loading. To avoid excruciating queues, buy your admission in advance and arrive 15–30 minutes before the park opens. When admitted, experience the rides in this order:

1. Velocity
2. Cliff Hanger
3. Mumbo Jumbo
4. Kumali
5. Lost River Ride

After Lost River Ride, experience the other coasters and thrill rides in whatever order you find most convenient. Save the zoological exhibits, shows and scenic rides until you've had your fill of the thrill rides. If one or more of the rides are not open when you arrive, skip to the next open ride. Return to the closed ride 15 minutes before it begins operating.

Another, more expensive, approach is to use Flamingo Land's jump-the-queue scheme, which will notify you by mobile when you can zoom to the front of the line. The so-called **Q-Busters** are available on ten attractions. You purchase credits at the kiosk in the main plaza near the entrance, and then you text with the associated Q-Code, followed by a space and the number of riders. A moment later you should get a text with your allotted time and a booking confirmation code. When the appointed time arrives, you enter through the exit ramp and show your text message to jump the queue.

Mumbo Jumbo requires three Q-Buster credits and its code is MUMBO; Kumali (KUMALI) and Velocity (VELOCITY) require two credits, while Wild Mouse (MOUSE), Cliff Hanger (CLIFF), Splash Battle (SPLASH), Lost River Ride (LOST), SpongeBob 4D (SPONGE), Corkscrew (CORK) and Mischief Mansion (MANSION) each require one credit.

So is it worthwhile?

Queues aren't normally terribly long here, but on busy July and August weekends, the Mumbo Jumbo can have a 2-hour wait. Our advice: check line lengths before purchasing credits, and use the service sparingly. On all but the busiest days, for example, you should never face a long wait for *SpongeBob SquarePants 4D* because the theatre can hold many guests.

If you have young children in your party, get the adult rides finished and then turn to the kiddie rides.

Finally, be advised that credit cards can be used only for admission and shop purchases – all food and drink are sold on a cash-only basis. A cash machine is just beyond the ticket booths and to the left.

Jorvik Viking Centre ★★★½

| APPEAL BY AGE | PRESCHOOL ★★★ | PRIMARY SCHOOL ★★★★ | TEENS ★★★ |
| YOUNG ADULTS ★★★ | | OVER 30 ★★★★ | SENIORS ★★★★ |

15–17 Coppergate Walk, York, North Yorkshire YO1 9WT
☎ **01904 543 400; jorvik-viking-centre.co.uk**

HOURS (April–November) 10 a.m.–5 p.m. (last admission); (November–April) last admission 4 p.m. Closed 24–26 December.

COST £8.95 adults; £6 children; £7 concession; £26 family of 4; £29 family of 5. Pre-book to avoid the queue (☎ 01904 615 505; **jorvikbookings.com**; or text VIKING + space + your name to ☎ 60777). Various package prices include admission to York Archaeological Trust's other attractions. Tickets can be bought through the Tesco Clubcard rewards scheme but cannot be pre-booked or used for packages that include other Trust sites.

GETTING THERE *By car:* In the city centre, in the Coppergate shopping centre. Once in the city, follow the pedestrian green-and-gold fingerpost signs for CASTLE AREA, then signs for Jorvik. Nearest parking is the Castle car park, a 5-minute walk away. Traffic is often congested, so consider the **Park & Ride** programme (**york.gov.uk/parking/ride**), offering free parking on the outskirts of the city centre. *By rail:* The centre is a 10-minute walk from the main station. *By bus:* The nearest stop is on Tower Street, a 2-minute walk away.

DESCRIPTION AND COMMENTS A millennium ago, the busy city of York wasn't much different than it is today. Shopkeepers sold goods, neighbours gossiped and – as snickering schoolchildren will be delighted to discover – people went to the loo. All this happened in Jorvik, the most important Viking settlement in Britain, which eventually became York. Through a combination of luck and careful planning, a large section of the village was excavated in the late 1970s before the area was developed as the open-air Coppergate shopping centre. The lucky part was that the area had boggy, peaty soil, which preserved a huge array of artefacts, including clothing, tools and homes.

Now people queue every day to visit this part museum, part ghost-train ride devoted to the ancient settlement. Run by the York Archaeological Trust, it offers an entertaining look at history (complete with smells) that lies literally beneath your feet. But don't be fooled: this is meant to be an educational experience, not a funfair ride. If you don't make the effort to read the exhibits and spend time exploring the video-screen presentations, you'll leave feeling disappointed and ripped off. If you're travelling with youngsters, it can be a tricky balancing act. They'll enjoy the 'ride' and indeed will learn something, but they'll want to hurry through the rest of the site. Our advice is to realistically assess your group. You may want to split up, so those interested in taking time to absorb Jorvik won't feel rushed. But that will mean having to accept that some will be done with the £9 attraction in 45 minutes. Also, it's important to come when crowds are small; otherwise you'll literally pushed through the attraction by the patrons behind you. Plus, if you come at a busy time, you may spend more time in the queue than the attraction itself.

But if you do find yourself waiting to enter, the Jorvik staff do their best to keep you entertained, or at least dry, providing umbrellas if it's raining and sending out Viking re-enactors to interact with the crowd. After paying admission, you enter a large **glass-floored gallery** built on top of the re-created Jorvik excavation. Members of the trust spent five years on the dig, which covered an area of 10,764 sq ft (1,000 m^2). They unearthed a surprising 29.5-ft (9-m) layer of artefacts, including the famous Coppergate Helmet, on display at the Yorkshire Museum (a replica is displayed here). They even found seeds, plants and human-parasite eggs, which gave researchers new data on the diet and health of the ancient residents. Look carefully at the exhibits, which include many artefacts from the dig, including timbers that once were part of homes. And take your time at the video monitors, which give detailed explanations on the site and Viking history, including who they were, how they got to Britain and how they lived.

Next it's time for what for many is the highlight of the site, a **ride through Jorvik,** circa AD 975. Take a seat and adjust your headsets.

Narration is available in several languages, along with a children's version. When the many animatronic characters address you, they're speaking in actual Old Norse, voiced by York University graduate students. Your first stop is the riverbank, where you'll be greeted with fish smells and an explanation of the Viking diet. Next comes a farmyard, complete with more smells, and then Sigurd the antler-worker. His products were used to make combs, both for grooming and to remove head lice. Notice his missing finger, lost in a saw accident. The ride continues past the smell of burning logs to an amber-worker's home, a blacksmith and a wood-turner. You'll smell molten iron through this area. The ride then passes by builders constructing a 2-storey home, foreign traders and a gossiping woman and a fishmonger. The next smell is roasting boar, which leads to a Viking house interior, a leather stall, a misbehaving child and a couple arguing over what to have for dinner. You'll smell the market as you pass through it, and see fighting dogs. Finally comes the home stretch, with a backyard scene and, ending with a bang, the Viking WC, which of course is occupied. The locals, you may or may not want to know, used moss or rags as toilet paper when they visited their backyard privies. The various sets that the ride passes through are detailed and well executed, but the movements of the animatronic figures are jerky and not very realistic.

As the ride ends, you'll find yourself in an exhibit hall with more artefacts, video screens and Viking re-enactors. The **Are You a Viking?** section explores how the people's language and influence is still felt today. In the **Viking Ghosts** and **Artefacts Alive** sections, holographic images describe some of the objects on display. In the **coin-striking area,** you can make a penny, worth a barrel of beer or 16 chickens – before being adjusted for inflation. And finally in the **Unearthed area,** you can meet an actual Viking, or at least his bones, which date to the tenth and eleventh centuries. Then it's over. You step through a curtain and find yourself in a gift shop.

TOURING TIPS By all means avoid school and bank holidays. Come early or late, but not midday. First thing Sunday morning is often good. Because of the design of the centre, a crowd can ruin your visit, rushing you through Jorvik and blocking signs and displays.

The York Archaeological Trust runs several other attractions in town, including **Barley Hall,** a mediaeval house once home to the mayor of York; **Mickelgate Bar,** a museum in the ancient city walls; and **DIG,** an interactive archaeological experience geared to youngsters. Guests dig up 'artefacts' from a sandbox and learn how archaeologists analyse their findings.

Lightwater Valley ★★★½

APPEAL BY AGE	PRESCHOOL ★★★★	PRIMARY SCHOOL ★★★★	TEENS ★★★★
YOUNG ADULTS ★★★		OVER 30 ★★★	SENIORS ★★★

Lightwater Farm, North Stainley, Ripon, North Yorkshire HG4 3HT
☎ 0871 720 0011; lightwatervalley.co.uk

HOURS 10 a.m.–4.30 p.m. or later, depending on season (rides start at 10.30 a.m.)

COST £19.45 adults and children over 4'3" (1.3 m); £16.95 children under 4'3 (1.3 m); children under 3'3" (1 m), free; £10.95 senior citizens and disabled. Family packages available, beginning at £49.50 for family of 3. Online tickets are one price: £15.95 over 3'3" (1 m), plus £1.50 booking charge for each order. Tickets can also be bought through the Tesco Clubcard rewards scheme.

GETTING THERE *By car:* About an hour from York. Exit the A1 onto the A61 towards Ripon; then take the A6108 for 2.5 mi (4 km). Follow the brown tourist signs. *By rail:* The nearest train station is Thirsk, about 8 mi (13 km) away. *By bus:* Ripon is served by **Harrogate Coach Travel** from York (**swiersnet.co.uk/hct**). From there, transfer to a **Dales and District bus** to the park (**dalesanddistrict.co.uk/dales.php**; schedules at **yorkshiretravel.net**).

DESCRIPTION AND COMMENTS Lightwater Valley gets it half right when it claims to be a theme park. On one hand, there's no theme here aside from a collection of funfair rides, but the 175 ac (71 ha) of North Yorkshire countryside feels like an honest-to-goodness park. Rides are spaced far apart, with trees and fields in between. On warm days, you'll find people sunbathing and relaxing in the open countryside. Try that at other theme parks, which typically are collections of rides plopped down on a sea of concrete and asphalt.

That said, Lightwater is still largely regional, with most attractions geared to the under-12 set, supplemented by seven thrill rides, including one of the longest roller coasters in the world and the best dark ride in the country. There's also a birds-of-prey centre, which carries an extra admission, and strangely enough, the park complex is home to a retail-outlet shopping centre. Taken as a whole, if you pack the right attitude, this can be a fun day out, with something to keep most everyone in your party reasonably happy.

Parking is rarely a problem, and as you approach the nondescript entrance, you pass a crazy-golf course and then find your way to the admission queues. Immediately you enter a covered arcade area that feels like a mock village high street. Games here carry an extra charge, so our advice is to make your way quickly into the park. Rides are split into three categories: **Nippers** are for the youngest visitors (under 3'3" [1 m]). **Whipper Snappers** are family rides and attractions for those over 3'3" (1 m), and **Jaw Droppers** have varying height requirements but are the headliner thrill rides. Staff are strict about the height limitations, so measure at home and consider thick-soled shoes for young visitors who may be just that tiny bit short for a ride.

The handout park map is of only marginal use in finding your way around. Fortunately, however, Lightwater Valley has some of the best directional signs we've seen in any park. Use the signs to navigate and the map for ride names and information.

As you enter the park, proceed in an anti-clockwise direction. On the left side of the main plaza go straight ahead along a tree-canopied walkway that curves right to **Eagles Claw** – a twisting pendulum ride with six sets of four seats hanging from the end of an arm that swings and turns. We suggest having a light breakfast, or you're likely to see it again. Continue working your way towards the back of the park. On your way, consider a stop at the **Amazing Maze** if you have young ones in your party. Strangely enough, this low-tech maze, sponsored by a fence company, seems to captivate young visitors. No flashing lights, spinning discs or plunges. Go figure.

But the rest of you thrill-seekers will want to dash to **Raptor Attack,** a subterranean roller coaster that is essentially a remake of the long-popular Sewer Rat ride. Raptor shows what a difference good theming makes. The fun begins as you queue up for what appears to be the entrance to a mine, complete with industrial warning signs. On the way in, old newspaper stories posted on the wall explain how more than a century ago, miners found something mysterious while they were digging. The staff are dressed like miners too, and as you descend you appear to enter a dilapidated mineshaft. These dark, dank tunnels with what looks like dinosaur fossils embedded in the walls set the right atmosphere for what comes next: a mine-train roller coaster that sends you hurtling through the darkness and perhaps into the jaws of a prehistoric raptor. The theme detail in the set-up, the mine (actually constructed in a quarry) and the ride itself make Raptor Attack a strong candidate for best dark ride in the UK. The ride lasts 83 seconds, and the queue is slow, with ten guests admitted every 4 minutes. Because it's new and because it's very popular, try to ride during the first hour the park is open.

Next, make your way to **The Ultimate,** the towering roller coaster you've seen ever since you entered the park. This is a mammoth ride that put Lightwater on the map when it opened in 1991 as the world's longest roller coaster. (It is now merely the longest ride outside of Japan, having been dethroned in 2000.) The 1.5-m (2.4-km) ride was designed by the park owner at the time, and British Rail helped lay some of the track. The ride lasts a good 6 minutes and reaches speeds of 50 mph (80 km/h). With two lift hills reaching more than 100 ft (30 m), you'll get commanding views of the park and the surrounding countryside. But there is a price to pay. The Ultimate has a split personality: the parts that you see from the loading area look like a typical roller coaster, with a steep initial drop followed by roly-poly hills. But what you don't see is that when the ride drops out of sight into dense woods, all hell breaks loose. It becomes a bumpy, bruising, jarring ride – something akin to being in a car wreck. We've covered theme parks and roller coasters for 30 years and can't recall a more violent ride. Many rides have warnings posted for pregnant women, persons with back and neck problems, heart problems and the like. On The Ultimate, take them seriously. In fact, consider that The Ultimate might *cause* some of these problems. Bob, who suggests that the ride be renamed Blunt Force Trauma, exited with bruised ribs from being slammed into the side of the car.

THEME PARKS AND ATTRACTIONS

Working your way back towards the centre of the park, find your way to **The Twister,** a spinning wild-mouse-style coaster with a lot of back and forth but not much up and down. After exiting, walk straight ahead to **Ladybug,** a polka-dotted kiddie coaster, and then ride **Wild River Rapids,** a 2-minute raft ride added in 2009 that offers a splashy spin down a flume. Unlike most flume rides this one has no big drop, so getting drenched is unlikely, though you'll probably get the seat of your pants wet from water left on the seats by previous riders unloading. Look to the edge of the park for **The Wave,** a large swinging pirate ship. Now moving back towards the park centre, check the queue for the **Grand Prix Go Karts.** If it's not too long, stop for a drive, but if there's a crowd, you may want to keep moving. The queue is notoriously slow. Next to the go-karts is the **Buffalo Express,** a kiddie train ride. One of the slowest rides we've ever seen, the train would be overtaken by an adult walking at normal speed.

Your next stop is the giant spinning wheel, **Black Widow's Web,** a variation on the Enterprise ride described on page 19. At first glance it looks like a horizontal Ferris wheel, but it rises to a near-vertical position so that passengers are at times suspended upside-down in their closed compartment. Continue to the **Falls of Terror,** another flume ride. Here you're in a dinghy and choose from one of three pipes for your wet and rapid descent. For a milder water-based experience, the **Swan Lake Pedal Boats** offer a relaxing and scenic chance to tool around a pond in a giant swan. Many find it a nice break from the jolts and bumps of the rides.

Not described here are 12 or more kiddie rides, including two junior coasters, a miniature Ferris wheel and a bevy of spinning platform rides. Some of these you can ride with your child, but a few cannot accommodate adults. In the lower left corner of the park is a play area with a large sand pit.

Now work your way to **Trauma Tower** in the corner of the park. Despite its colourful name, the tower-drop isn't too menacing. Finally, a fine **Ferris wheel** offers great views of the Swan Lake and the countryside beyond the park.

You can go back for another lap in the park or get your hand stamped to leave the park and visit the **Birds of Prey Centre** – £1.50 if you've already paid park admission. The free-flying falconry show is a crowd-pleaser that's offered several times a day. Also see one of the largest golden eagles in the country and pose for a picture with Gizmo, the centre's tiny owl. The centre also has **Creepy Crawly** and **Reptile Cave,** with tarantulas, frogs, rats and Murphy, a 10-ft (3-m) Burmese python.

TOURING TIPS As with most parks, the food offerings are fast-food-style at sit-down prices, but Lightwater has a few surprising options. The appropriately-named **The Pub in the Woods** is a cosy hideaway with pub food and drinks. Or get your hand stamped and step outside to the shopping area, where **The Granary Restaurant** and **Jo's Coffee Shop** both offer substantial meals for little more than you'd pay for a hot dog and chips in the park. While out here, you'll want to visit **Sweet Memories,** a shop packed floor to ceiling with sweets.

The other option is to bring food and stash it in a rented locker until lunchtime. With the beautiful countryside, there are plenty of places to settle down for a picnic.

National Coal Mining Museum ★★★★★

| APPEAL BY AGE | PRESCHOOL ★★★ | PRIMARY SCHOOL ★★★ | TEENS ★★★★ |
| YOUNG ADULTS ★★★★★ | | OVER 30 ★★★★★ | SENIORS ★★★★★ |

Caphouse Colliery, New Road, Overton, Wakefield WF4 4RH
☎ **01924 848 806; ncm.org.uk**

HOURS 10 a.m.–5 p.m. Last admission 1 hour before closing. Closed 24–26 December and 1 January.

COST Free. Mine train costs £1. Must be at least 5 years old to take underground tour.

GETTING THERE *By car:* The museum is on the A642 Wakefield–Huddersfield road, roughly halfway between the two towns. It's signposted from the M1 motorway. From the north, take the M1 and exit at Junction 40 towards Wakefield. Take the first right after the traffic lights (on Broadway). The Malt Shovel pub will be on your right. At the end of Broadway turn right onto the A642 to Horbury and Huddersfield. The museum is about 5 mi (8 km) ahead on your right. From the south, leave the M1 at Junction 38 (A637) and stay on the road through West Bretton and Flockton. At the Blacksmith's Arms roundabout, take the third exit towards Horbury (A642). The museum is about 2 mi (3.2 km) ahead on the left. *By rail:* The nearest station is Wakefield Westgate (**nationalrail.co.uk**). *By bus:* Take the **Yorkshire Traction Bus 232** from Wakefield Bus Station (**arrivabus.co.uk**). It stops outside the Reindeer Inn, a short walk from the museum. The **128 service** also runs from Wakefield to Dewsbury past the museum.

DESCRIPTION AND COMMENTS The rolling green countryside of Yorkshire once hid a valuable secret. Some of the richest coal deposits in the UK were found beneath the fields, and for centuries miners hauled out the rock that fuelled England's industrial revolution. Generations of laborers lived (and died) working the seams at places such as the Caphouse Colliery, which operated 1789–1985, eventually done in by depleted supplies, the violent national miners' strike and the government's pit-closure programme. Some workers still hold former prime minister Margaret Thatcher personally responsible for the closing, but you're sure to hear a variety of views from former miners who now serve as tour guides taking visitors underground to see their former workplace.

It's an exciting, informative and eye-opening look at a way of life that's largely disappeared. As at Wales's Big Pit: National Coal Museum (see page 439), you see historical buildings and follow in the boot-steps of former miners, acquiring an education you'll never get from watching a documentary on the telly. For example, it's hard to appreciate the importance of the pithead baths, added to the mine in 1938, until you see the dirty conditions underground. The museum's 75-minute underground tour is such an unusual experience that young visitors will be fascinated, while older ones will appreciate the importance the mine played for generations of local families. In short, it's a great day out for a multi-generational group.

The museum, recognised as an anchor point of the European Route of Industrial Heritage (**erih.net**), is actually home to two pits. You'll tour Caphouse, while the Hope Pit can be reached by a short walk or seasonal mining 'paddy' train ride. The pit is home to several historical mine buildings with minor exhibits. On a nice day, it's worth checking out, but it's not the highlight. Although you'll find picnic grounds on the site, the café's worth a visit for Yorkshire puddings, tea, cakes and the museum's ale, Collier's Ruin.

Upon arrival, you check in at the front desk and gift shop for your free **underground tour.** It's best to come early, because the mine is popular with school groups and tours can fill up by midday. Children under the age of 14 must be accompanied by an adult, and those under age 5 are not permitted underground. Surprisingly, the tour can accommodate wheelchairs, but you must phone ahead. Before heading underground, you'll need to hand over anything you're carrying that has a battery, because a stray spark could be dangerous. The front desk will hold on to your mobiles, electronic keys, cameras and iPods – even children's trainers with flashing lights aren't allowed. You're then outfitted with a miner's hat, lamp and a battery belt weighing 4.4 lb (2 kg). Your guide will lead you to the lift, and you descend 459 ft (140 m). The tour covers a lot of ground, showing you how coal was first removed by hand in the eighteenth century and how technology was later employed to drill out the valuable fuel. You'll see the conditions where children as young as age 4 worked for up to 12 hours a day pushing coal wagons, and where horses (so-called pit ponies) spent much of their lifetimes. The tour guides often relate tales from their own careers, and this can make the visit.

Back above ground, you'll find several exhibit areas putting the mine into context. The **Mining Lives Gallery** has re-created a 1940s mining-family kitchen and displays artefacts about unions, community sports, galas and brass bands. The **1842 Victorian Exhibit** explores the lives of women and children who worked underground. The conditions were so appalling that they led to the creation of the 1842 Coal Mines Act. This act prohibited hiring women and children under the age of 10 to work underground – a radical change for the era. Dickens, it's clear, didn't have to exaggerate. Gearheads in your group will want to visit the **Steam Engine Winding House,** which dates to 1876. It houses the machinery that lifted coal up the shaft for nearly a century. They'll also enjoy the 1980s **control room,** which coordinated mining operations until the pit closed. Others in your party will be drawn to the **stables,** where you can meet the type of horses that laboured on the site. Residents include Finn, a Clydesdale heavy horse, who joined the museum in 2010. Similar animals pulled heavy loads of coal and machinery around the site for most of its history. One of the spookiest sites at the mine is the **Caphouse baths,** where miners washed off the coal dust and grime they gathered at work every day. The showers and lockers look as though they're still ready to use. Nearby is the **wages office,** where miners started and ended their workday, and the **medical centre,** where a pit nurse tended to minor injuries. Of course, such facilities could do little in the case of huge disasters such as the Oaks Explosion, which killed more than 361 miners and their rescuers in 1866 at a mine just 12 mi (19 km) away.

There's also the **coal interface gallery,** packed with mining machinery such as coal cutters, and the **drift mouth,** where coal was brought to the surface by conveyor belt. Despite the site's heavy industrial use, the museum has a short nature trail through mixed woodlands, ending at settling ponds designed to contain and treat the polluted orange, iron-rich mine water. You can also walk to the adjacent **Hope Pit** or take a ride on a mine train (£1). Here you'll see more-specialised sites such as the compressor building, fan house and winding-engine house, which operated the shaft lift until 1985.

TOURING TIPS Dress warmly, as it's chilly underground – about 12 °C (53.6 °F). Although you won't be digging out coal, it can get muddy and dirty on the site – don't wear your best clothes. For in-depth information on the above-ground galleries and buildings, rent the worthwhile audio tour from the gift shop.

National Railway Museum ★★★★

APPEAL BY AGE	PRESCHOOL ★★★	PRIMARY SCHOOL ★★★★	TEENS ★★★½
YOUNG ADULTS ★★★½		OVER 30 ★★★★	SENIORS ★★★★

Leeman Road, York, North Yorkshire YO26 4XJ
☎ **0844 815 3139; nrm.org.uk**

HOURS 10 a.m.–6 p.m. Closed 24–26 December.

COST Free (£3 donation suggested). Additional charge for special events, simulator and miniature railway.

GETTING THERE *By car:* The museum is clearly signposted from all approaches to York. *By rail:* Located 600 yd (540 m) from the York railway station. Visitors can access the museum by footbridge. *By bus:* **Rawcliffe Park & Ride bus** (**firstgroup.com**) connects the museum to York Minster, the Mansion House and York Theatre Royal. The Road Train tram offers direct service from Duncombe Place (next to York Minster) every 30 minutes daily, 11.15 a.m.–4.15 p.m., April–October, with limited service off-season. One-way fare: £2 adults; £1 children.

DESCRIPTION AND COMMENTS If you're a trainspotter, a visit here is heaven. That's a given. But even if you're not, this attraction will still be a favourite. One of only two national museums outside of London (and the most-visited museum outside of London), it has one of the largest collection of trains and train memorabilia in the world – more than 100 locomotives and 200 railway carriages. Named European Museum of the Year in 2001, it hasn't let up since, continuing to develop exhibits and sponsor special events, from Thomas the Tank Engine rides to Diesel Days, a celebration of locomotives.

And here's the shocker: general museum admission is free!

You'll certainly see lots and lots of locomotives and train carriages here, but the appeal is broader. Interactive, historical and explanatory exhibits bring the artefacts to life. As you're next to a working rail yard, you can watch trains on the move and see how elaborate signalling systems keep riders safe. Still, the museum does take an investment of time. While you could breeze through it in 90 minutes, if you stop to read signs and absorb the exhibits, your visit will be much richer and more enjoyable. In short, you may come expecting to spend an hour or two, but don't be surprised if that stretches into half a day or even longer.

Most visitors come by train – natch – or via a seasonal road train from York city centre. If you drive, you'll have to pay for the experience – parking runs a cool £7. The museum is split in two by a road, and the main entrance has you starting your visit at the **Station Hall,** near the working railway. The car park leads to a secondary entrance, on the other side of the road. That will have you visiting the Great House and Warehouse side first. But don't forget to cross the road through the underground tunnel and catch the exhibits that you've missed.

Although entrance is free, you still need to queue for admission, and the staff do ask for a £3 donation. It's up to you – no one will look askance if you decline or offer less. You'll pass a gift shop and lockers on the way into the Station Hall, a faux mid-twentieth-century railway station re-created from an old goods depot. It's smartly executed, with piped-in sounds of whistles, bells and chugging engines. You're quickly confronted with an array of coaches, dining cars, carriages and wagons with sleeping compartments. An optional audio tour covers the highlights, but just about everyone makes it to the exhibit of **Royal Trains.** Follow the red carpet to peer inside carriages used by Britain's kings and queens. The Royal Family began travelling by rail in 1842 and still enjoy it. Check the front of the royal train here: it carries four headlamps, making it instantly recognisable to signalmen and train officials. The highlight is Queen Victoria's personal saloon car. The **Day Saloon** has plush furniture, padded ceilings and walls and a dining room. In the other half of the car, the **Night Saloon,** there's a bedroom and even a loo, complete with a bath. It was built by London & North Western Railway to Her Highness's particular specification, for a (then-enormous) £1,800 after she complained about the old royal coach. Talk about travelling in style – flying first-class out of Heathrow is steerage compared with this.

Elsewhere in the hall you'll see **commuter trains** and learn how they literally changed the country's landscape, paving the way for suburbs. Originally trains were used for hauling goods, and only as an afterthought did industrialists realise that they could carry passengers too. With the advent of commuting, the railway and then the country had to develop a standard time, so that when it was 5.15 in London, it was the same time in Birmingham, Manchester and York. You'll also see **tank cars, freight cars** and **sleeping cars** on display here.

On a nice day, you'll want to duck outside to the **South Yard,** where a **miniature railway** offers a brief 0.6-mi (1-km) trip for 50p. It runs through a garden resembling a scaled-down British landscape, designed by students from a nearby college. Also available is a 5- to 10-minute ride around the yard on a steam-locomotive-powered train. A train-themed outdoor **play area** adds to the area's kiddie appeal. Also look for the **Learning Platform,** where daily live shows attempt to bring railway science and engineering to life – The Energy Show, for example, shows how a Brazil nut could power a train. Other exhibits let kids learn how friction, track layout and streamlining affect a train's efficiency and speed. On weekends, the **Platform 4 Theatre** group performs here. Check the schedule; the troupe's short train-inspired productions are often hilarious. Outside, also look for the **Depot,** home to a fleet of fully-operational historical locomotives. To the right of the Depot is a children's playground.

Now you'll want to backtrack to cross under the road to the second half of the museum. (If you entered from the car park, this is where you'll start.) The **Great Hall,** a former locomotive shed, is the centre of the institution, a bright, airy space packed with historical trains. Look for a yellow vehicle with a towering white smokestack that looks like a tractor on steroids. This is a replica of **Stephenson's Rocket,** one of the first steam engines. Built in 1829, it won a then-fabulous £500 prize for its revolutionary design that brought water to the boil more quickly by running heated pipes through it.

Highlights here include the stunning art deco **Duchess of Hamilton** and the **Shinkansen (Japanese Bullet Train),** one of the few non-British pieces on display. You can step aboard the train, take a seat and watch a short film. The train, you'll learn, was a marvel of engineering, reaching unheard of speeds of 130 mph (210 km/h) when it made its debut in 1964. These days, France's TGV has followed in Japan's train tracks, clocking speeds of 320 mph (515 km/h). The **Topaz & Wainwright D Class No. 737** offers something for everyone. Rail fans will delight in the Wainwright D-class engine, while the rest of us will enjoy the posh Pullman carriage.

Not everything is stationary in the hall. The **turntable,** used to turn locomotives around, was installed in 1954 and used in the hall for decades, when it served as the York North shed for locomotive repairs and maintenance. A working steam locomotive has been cut open so you can see the moving parts and even begin to understand how it works. A section of the **Channel Tunnel** shows a video of the historical handshake between British and French officials when the two tunnelling segments met.

For virtual thrills, there's a **simulator.** The £3 'ride' will provide an engineer's-eye view of a London–Brighton train run at 765 mph (1,230 km/h). Although a little off-theme, other simulator options include a roller coaster, a space mission and a time-travel expedition to meet dinosaurs.

At one end of the hall you can climb up a set of stairs to the **Workshop Gallery,** which overlooks the museum's busy train workshop. Here you can watch craftsmen labouring over exhibits, most notably the famed **Flying Scotsman** steam locomotive, which the museum purchased in

2004 and has been working on ever since. Built in 1923, the Scot was the first train to reach speeds of 100 mph (160 km/h) and travelled 2 million mi (3.2 million km) before leaving service in 1963. The area also has a surprisingly-interesting exhibit on signalling, called **The Working Railway.** It provides a live feed of the East Coast Main Line signalling screens. After taking that in, you can step outside to a viewing platform overlooking the York rail yards and main line to see it happening live.

Underneath the gallery, an 0-scale **model railway** runs at scale speed on a specified timetable and will keep some visitors entranced all day.

As in most museums, some of the most interesting holdings aren't on display. But in the **Warehouse,** you can peer at thousands of pieces of train memorabilia and artefacts in well-labelled open storage, from railway china to promotion posters to tickets to signs. There are also uniforms, watches, furniture and even the gold-bullion box involved in the 1855 First Great Train Robbery. It's absorbing and addicting.

TOURING TIPS If you're greeted by a long queue at the main entrance, head up the road to the second entrance for visitors coming from the car park. Avoid Sundays and school holidays if possible – you will encounter not only crowds but also high decibels, as the large shed and hall are noisy to begin with. Unless it's particularly warm, pack a jumper, as the stations aren't insulated and can get quite nippy.

The museum has an unremarkable restaurant and the charming **Brief Encounter** café, the latter inspired by a train-station snack bar. It's worth a stop for tea and cakes. There are also indoor and outdoor picnic tables if you bring your own lunch.

Sea Life Scarborough ★★½

| APPEAL BY AGE | PRESCHOOL ★★★★ | PRIMARY SCHOOL ★★★ | TEENS ★★ |
| YOUNG ADULTS ★★ | | OVER 30 ★★★ | SENIORS ★★★ |

Scalby Mills, Scarborough, North Yorkshire YO12 6RP
☎ **01723 373 414; visitsealife.com/scarborough**

HOURS 10 a.m.–4 p.m. Last admission 1 hour before closing. Closed Christmas Day.

COST £14.50 adults; £10.75 children aged 3–14; £47.50 family ticket (2 adults, 2 children). Discounts available online. Admission can also be bought through the Tesco Clubcard rewards scheme.

GETTING THERE *By car:* On the North Sea coast, about 45 mi (72 km) northeast of York via the A64. Follow tourist signs into Scarborough and then follow the signs for North Bay Leisure Parks or Sea Life. Pay-and-display parking is directly outside the aquarium. *By rail:* The nearest rail station is Scarborough, about 1.5 mi (2.4 km) from the aquarium (**nationalrail.co.uk**). *By bus:* **Service 3A** terminates at the aquarium. (Route information: **transportdirect.info.**)

DESCRIPTION AND COMMENTS The big attraction here is actually quite small – strange leafy sea dragons from Australia. They're relatives of the sea horse and experts at camouflage. The centre has 150 different species of fishes, and a turtle sanctuary where you can see adults, babies and eggs in incubation. At an outdoor display, you can see otters, penguins and rescued seals – the centre is responsible for saving more than 350 of them, and if any are in hospital at the time of your visit, you can watch them on the road to recovery. The resident seals include Bubbles, a partially-sighted male, and his two sons, Ed and Sherbet. Extras include free craft activities, such as badge-making, and there's also an outdoor pirate-themed attraction where you can pan for gold, which runs an extra £2.

TOURING TIPS Be sure to take in the feedings and educational programmes. Good for an hour or two, especially on a rainy day.

(For more on aquariums, see page 10.)

The York Dungeon ★★★

APPEAL BY AGE	PRESCHOOL ★	PRIMARY SCHOOL ★★★	TEENS ★★★★
YOUNG ADULTS ★★★		OVER 30 ★★★	SENIORS ★★

12 Clifford Street, York, North Yorkshire YO1 9RD
☎ **01904 632 599; the-dungeons.co.uk**

HOURS Opening times vary from 10 to 11 a.m., closing from 4 to 5.30 p.m. (check website for details).

COST £15 adults; £11 children aged 4–15; £14 senior citizens and students; £48 family ticket (2 adults, 2 children). Discounts available online; all online tickets include priority entrance. Tickets can also be bought through the Tesco Clubcard rewards scheme. While there are no age limits, management does advise that 'the Dungeon is not suitable for people of a nervous disposition or very young children'.

You can also use the **Merlin Annual Pass** (**merlinannualpass.co.uk**), which provides admission to Alton Towers Resort Theme Park, Legoland Discovery Centre, Legoland Windsor, Thorpe Park, Sea Life aquariums and sanctuaries, Dungeons attractions, Merlin London Eye, Madame Tussauds London and Warwick Castle. Prices begin at £150 for an individual and drop in price if you're buying for a family group.

GETTING THERE *By car:* Located in the city centre. Closest car parks are St George's Field and Castle. Traffic is often congested, so consider the **Park & Ride** programme, offering free parking on the outskirts of the city centre (**york.gov.uk/parking/ride**). *By rail:* Closest station is York, a 10-minute walk along Station Road to the Dungeon (**nationalrail.co.uk**). *By bus:* The nearest stop is on Tower Street, a 2-minute walk away. (Route information: **transportdirect.info**.)

DESCRIPTION AND COMMENTS With Roman invaders, marauding Vikings, revolutionaries and highwaymen, York has had its share of scoundrels over the millennia. The York Dungeon uses these themes as a jumping-off point for an entertaining and spooky attraction. As at the other Dungeons (found across the UK and in Amsterdam and Hamburg, Germany), you'll wander through a haunted house of sorts, devoted to the unspeakable history that the city fathers would probably rather forget. Most of the Dungeons have the same base – rooms devoted to the plague, a cheeky judge, torture and a mirror maze. But each also has rooms about local legends and miscreants. York's Dungeon also stands out because its actors deliver consistently enthusiastic, frightening and funny performances. You won't find rides here, as at the London and Edinburgh Dungeons, but you probably won't feel cheated. Queues can be bad here, but if you come early – or late – you should be able to minimise your waiting time. If you find yourself in a queue, the Dungeon does send out a plague victim to horrify and harass the captive audience standing in line. (The Jorvik Viking Centre does something similar, and we applaud them both for doing their best to keep their customers entertained.) The dungeon itself can be intense for young children – preschoolers certainly, but also primary-schoolers. Some do fine, but you might want to visit the Dungeon's website to see how they react. It's not all thrills and chills, though – you can expect some laughter too.

As you enter the Dungeon, you're separated into small groups, in which you'll travel from scene to scene. You're greeted by a hologram offering scary tales of **Clifford's Tower,** the keep of York Castle, before you find yourself in the gruesome **Plague** scene. A doctor menaces the group with descriptions of how the disease ravaged Europe and the horrific 'medical' treatment victims received. As in most of the scenes, the actor selects a volunteer to help with the demonstration. If you look overly eager, you probably won't be picked, but if you try to hide in the back, you're sure to be on the list. You've been warned. The volunteer will be strapped down for 'surgery' – and a scare. The next scene is devoted to York native **Guy Fawkes** and his treasonous plot to blow up the king and Parliament. But the show switches from history to creepy when it shows Fawkes's fate – to be hanged, drawn and quartered. The **Ghosts of York** scene, set in what seems to be a cosy pub, makes a quite convincing case that the ancient streets outside are packed with spirits. Next comes the **Labyrinth of the Lost Legion,** which uses York's Roman past as an excuse for a dimly-lit hall of mirrors, where a centurion just might be found around any corner.

The next menace consists of the **Bloody Vikings,** including the most unpleasant Eric Bloodaxe. Expect a lot of yelling, blood and more scenes of torture. To lighten things up, you'll move on to the **Judgement of Sinners.** Here you'll find a very exuberant actor picking out ne'er-do-wells in the audience. It's usually the parents who get a stiff talking to here, and the crimes – bad dancing at a wedding? – are always big laugh-lines at the expense of the volunteer. If you're picked on, don't worry. All will be forgotten in the next **Torture** room, where you get to see demonstrations of devilish devices, clearly the works of twisted minds. The ninth scene is devoted to another local boy – **Dick Turpin,** the famed highwayman known for thievery and murder. You're witness to his execution – death by hanging – which is lovingly re-enacted. Finally comes **Witches: Burned Alive.** This scene also relies on a spirited volunteer, who is accused and convicted of witchcraft and burnt at the stake, complete with simulated flames, smoke and a corpse, which, thankfully, you won't have to provide.

TOURING TIPS Buying online from the Dungeon's website offers free priority entrance.

FARM EXPERIENCES

BECAUSE THE VARIOUS FARM EXPERIENCES ARE SO SIMILAR (see page 13), we felt that it was unnecessary to provide individual profiles as we do with other types of attractions. Following is a selective list of farm experiences in Yorkshire.

NORTH YORKSHIRE

HESKETH FARM PARK
Hesketh House
Bolton Abbey, Skipton
North Yorkshire BD23 6HA
☎ 01756 710 444
heskethfarmpark.co.uk
info@heskethfarmpark.com

KILNSEY PARK
(Not your typical barnyard experience, but one of the most beautiful farm parks in the UK. You can't feed lambs, but you can feed giant rainbow trout – cool, but low cuddle factor)
Skipton
North Yorkshire BD23 5PS
☎ 01756 752 150
kilnseypark.co.uk
info@kilnseypark.co.uk

MONK PARK FARM VISITOR CENTRE
Bagby, Thirsk
North Yorkshire Y07 2AG
☎ 01845 597 730
monkpark.co.uk
enquiries@monkparkfarm.co.uk

PLAYDALE FARM PARK
Killerby Grange
Station Road
Cayton, Scarborough
North Yorkshire YO11 3TL
☎ 01723 586 351
playdalefarmpark.co.uk

THORNTON HALL FARM COUNTRY PARK
(Using postal code on satnav will only get you to the village)
Thornton-in-Craven, nr Skipton
North Yorkshire BD23 3TJ
☎ 01282 841 148
thorntonhallcountrypark.co.uk
sandra@thorntonhallfarm.fsnet.co.uk

YORK MAZE
(Big place with several mazes, including a mini-putt in a maze)
Springfield, Heslington
York YO19 5LT
☎ 01904 607 341
yorkmaze.com
info@yorkmaze.com

SOUTH YORKSHIRE

CANNON HALL FARM
Bark House Lane
Cawthorne, Barnsley
South Yorkshire S75 4AT
☎ 01226 790 427
cannonhallfarm.co.uk
cannonhallfarm@btconnect.com

PART ELEVEN

NORTH WEST ENGLAND

THIS REGION COMPRISES CHESHIRE, LANCASHIRE, Greater Manchester, and Merseyside. The industrial revolution exploded in and around **Manchester** and other cities in this region, and, it seems only fair to mention, The Beatles burst onto the international scene from their humble roots in **Liverpool. Blackpool,** one of Britain's oldest and most fabled seaside resorts is located here, home of **Pleasure Beach,** the amusement park that originated the ghost-train genre of dark rides. Also in northwest England are the quirky **British Lawnmower Museum** and the labyrinthine **Chester Zoo** – arguably Britain's best.

THEME PARKS *and* ATTRACTIONS

The Beatles Story ★★★★

APPEAL BY AGE			
PRESCHOOL ★★	PRIMARY SCHOOL ★★★	TEENS ★★★★	
YOUNG ADULTS ★★★★	OVER 30 ★★★★★	SENIORS ★★★★★	

Britannia Vaults, Albert Dock, Liverpool, Merseyside L3 4AD
Satellite location: Pier Head, Mersey Ferries Terminal Building
☎ **0151 709 1963; beatlesstory.com**

HOURS 9 a.m.–7 p.m. daily (last admission 5 p.m.). Closed Christmas and Boxing days.
COST £12.95 adults; £6.50 children (5–16); £8.50 students, senior citizens, unwaged.
GETTING THERE *By car:* From the south follow the M6 north to Junction 21A, turning left onto the M62 towards Liverpool. At the end of the M62 (the Rocket), follow signs for the City Centre, where you'll see signs for Albert Dock. From the north, take the M6 to Junction 26 and then follow signs for the M58 to Liverpool. At the end of the motorway, follow signs for the A59 to Liverpool. Follow A59 City Centre, then follow

North West England

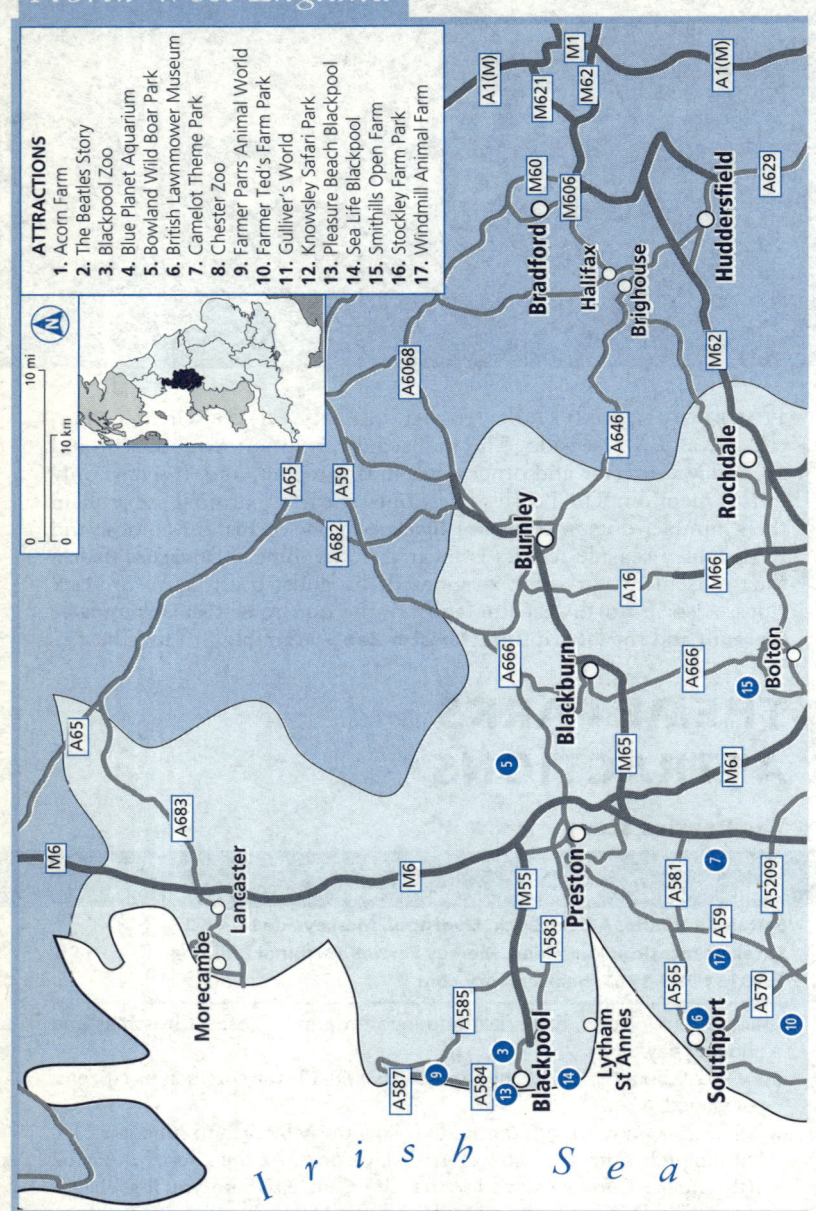

ATTRACTIONS
1. Acorn Farm
2. The Beatles Story
3. Blackpool Zoo
4. Blue Planet Aquarium
5. Bowland Wild Boar Park
6. British Lawnmower Museum
7. Camelot Theme Park
8. Chester Zoo
9. Farmer Parrs Animal World
10. Farmer Ted's Farm Park
11. Gulliver's World
12. Knowsley Safari Park
13. Pleasure Beach Blackpool
14. Sea Life Blackpool
15. Smithills Open Farm
16. Stockley Farm Park
17. Windmill Animal Farm

NORTH WEST ENGLAND MAP 359

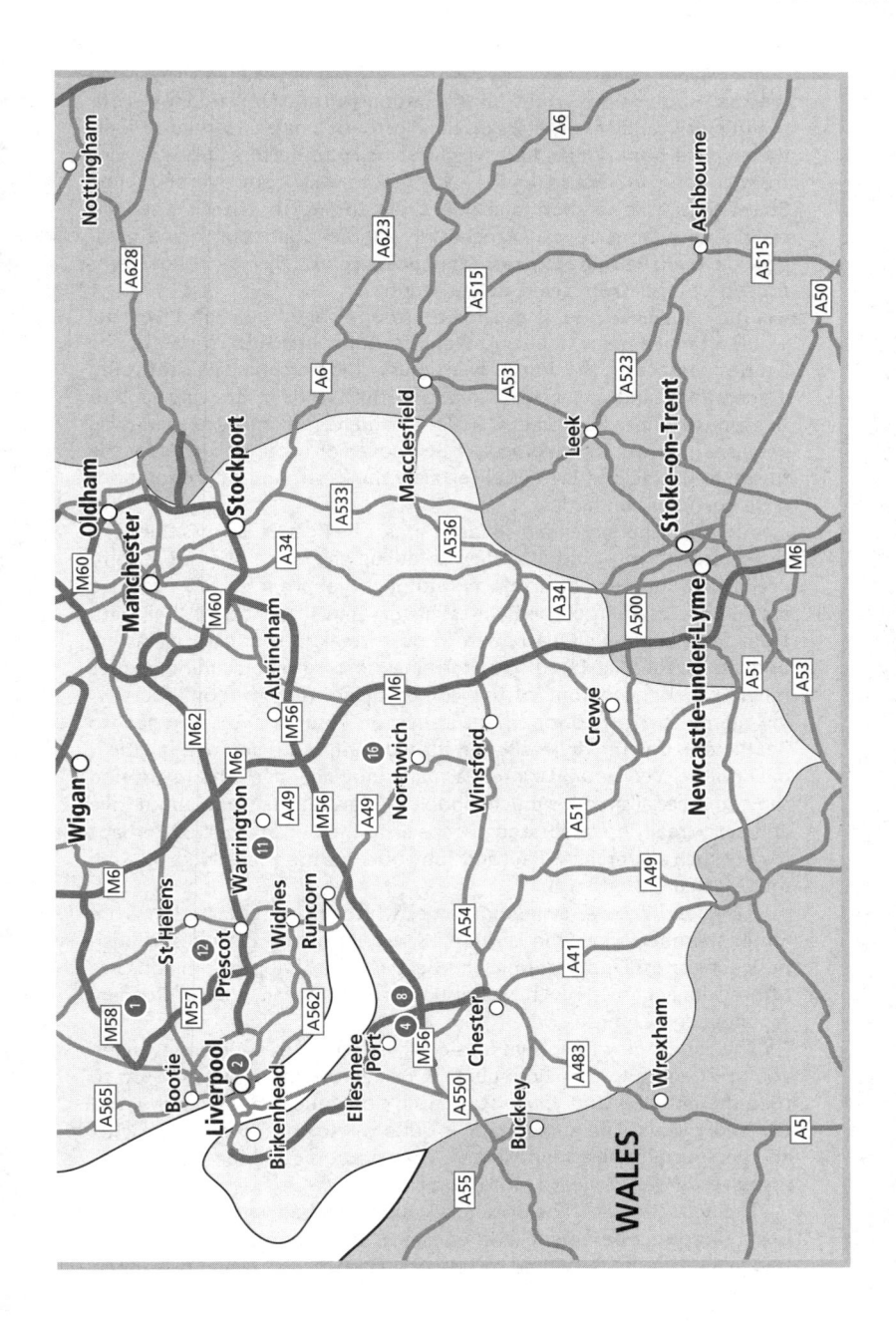

signs for Albert Dock. Parking's available in a car park adjacent to The Beatles Story, Albert Dock. *By rail:* Nearest **Merseyrail** (**merseytravel.gov.uk**) stations are James Street Station (on the Wirral Line), a 10-minute walk, and Moorfields (on the Northern Line), a 15-minute walk. By mainline train, **Virgin Rail** (**virgintrains.co.uk**) offers hourly service from London, a 2-hour trip. It's a 15-minute walk from Liverpool Lime Street Station, or a short taxi ride. From the north, there's a regular train service from Leeds, Manchester, Sheffield, Edinburgh and Glasgow on **TransPennine Express** (**tpexpress.co.uk**). *By foot:* Follow signs for Albert Dock from Liverpool city centre.

DESCRIPTION AND COMMENTS If not for the mop-topped quartet, Liverpool wouldn't make many holiday-travel lists. But it's hard to overstate The Beatles' impact on the world. Their music and personalities captivated a generation and changed history, and they've been drawing fans to this industrial city for decades. Will the band be remembered as musical geniuses in centuries to come, like Beethoven or Mozart? That's for the future to decide, but Liverpool certainly thinks so. And city reputations have been built on far less.

Although there are many Beatles sites, The Beatles Story is the city's major attraction – and *attraction* is indeed the word. It's not a comprehensive museum of artefacts (although you'll find a few); instead it's an immersion into The Beatles' history and snapshots of their path from John Lennon's Quarrymen to post-breakup solo careers. A second site at the Pier Head ferry terminal hosts an entertaining Beatles movie experience. None of this comes cheap, though. You'll be paying theme-park prices for what's at best an hour or two's voyage into Beatledom. If you're a Beatles fan it's worth it, but if you're a fanatic it may not be. You're unlikely to learn anything new here and might find the commercialism a bit much. Should the group that sang about love and peace really be celebrated in a specially-themed Starbucks? Perhaps it's not such a stretch. As Paul and John once harmonised, 'Now give me money, that's what I want.'

All guests receive an audio guide, which includes narration from family members like John Lennon's sister, Julia, and friends and business associates. Underscoring The Beatles' global appeal, versions are offered in English, French, Spanish, German, Italian, Polish, Russian, Japanese and Chinese.

The rooms play their own music, which can be overwhelming when you're listening to the audio guide. Our advice: take it slowly. Stop to read the timeline, and you'll be amazed how much happened in just a few short years. The audio guide is quite worthwhile, offering insights and perspectives new to most fans. Your ticket is good for 48 hours, so if you really want to learn more, you can return.

The attraction is in the Britannia Vaults, so when you arrive you follow a ramp to a basement-level entrance. The group's familiar story is told in a series of 18 themed rooms, or vignettes, connected by vaulted brick hallways lined with posters, television screens and a few artefacts, like George Harrison's guitar. After you pay admission, your visit starts in **wartime Liverpool,** when the Beatles members were born. Another room traces how 1950s rockers like Elvis and Buddy Holly changed the world of music and influenced a few Liverpool teens.

Next comes a re-creation of the **Woolton Parish Church Garden Fete,** where the man who would become Sir Paul McCartney recalls how he met mate John Lennon, his collaborator and later adversary. But that was a decade to come. For now, you can peer at some of the original instruments played by John and his band, the **Quarrymen,** at the 1957 gig. Here you can ponder the hand of fate and read up on some of the most forgotten men in rock history, John's former band mates: Colin Hanton, Red Davis, Eric Griffiths, Peter Shotton and Len Garry.

In short order, you visit Liverpool's leading rock venue of the era, the **Casbah Coffee Club.** Then you're off to the German city of **Hamburg**'s red-light district, where you visit the **Star-Club,** one of the strip joints where the group performed and mastered their rhythms and harmonies. The whole attraction is child-appropriate, although you might not want to focus on the mannequin–prostitute leaning against the wall. Then it's back to Liverpool for a walk down a re-created Matthew Street to a full-size replica of Liverpool's famous **Cavern Club,** a small, dark brick room enhanced by nightclub smells and a Beatles drum kit on a makeshift stage.

Another room includes Beatles manager **Brian Epstein**'s office at the cluttered NEMS Record store. You can re-live the British Invasion of America by sitting in a mock **747 jet** en route to New York in February 1964, and visit the **Abbey Road** recording studio, where you'll hear how Sir George Martin nearly declined to sign the mop-tops to a record contract. For a can't-miss photo op, you can pose in front of a picture of the famed crosswalk. Trust us, it's much safer to do it here than in the middle of the London street, where a friend almost got flattened by a bus.

There's even a giant **yellow submarine** to stroll through as you soak up sounds and images from the psychedelic era, along with a tribute to the *Sgt. Pepper's* album cover. Throughout, you'll find the theming and decorating thorough and well done, with obvious attention to detail.

Finally, the story gives the band's messy break-up a quick gloss-over and then explores each member's post-Beatles career in four separate '**Going Solo**' areas. Many find John Lennon's stark white *Imagine* **Room** particularly moving, with his glasses left in a glass cube on top of a white piano, making it seem as if he has just left a moment earlier. It looks like a scene from the song's video, filmed with Yoko Ono. White curtains blow as if caught in a breeze, and some visitors even bring roses. If you find yourself tearing up, you won't be the only one.

In another sweet irony, these rebellious rockers star in the **Discovery Room,** an education-themed area for children. If it's not filled with school groups, you're invited to visit to mock-up a newspaper, create Beatles-inspired artwork and jump around on a giant piano keyboard. There are even activities linked to Britain's national school curriculum.

And of course, there's a huge gift shop, the **Fab4Store,** where you'll find just about anything Beatles-inspired – music certainly, but shirts, posters, kitchen aprons, bookmarks and about anything else that will hold still long enough to print a Beatles image on it. Some of the souvenirs will be hard to find anywhere else, but the CDs can be bought at shops in town at a lower price.

That's not it either. Grab a free shuttle, or if it's a nice day, walk to The Beatles Story's satellite location at Pier Head ferry terminal for a **4D Beatles movie** – admission is included in your ticket. You'll be given funny glasses to get three-dimensional effects, while the theatre itself provides the fourth dimension, with bubbles, shaking seats and other surprises. The site also hosts temporary exhibits and another **Fab4Store**.

Even day-trippers will be tempted by Liverpool's other Beatles sites. The **Magical Mystery Tour,** a 1¾-hour bus tour, will take you away to Strawberry Fields, Penny Lane and other sites The Beatles made famous. Tickets are £14.95 – book through Cavern City Tours (☎ 0151 236 9091; **beatlestour.org**). In addition, the **childhood homes of John Lennon and Sir Paul McCartney** are preserved by the National Trust and open for touring from February to November. Neither home can be visited by car or on foot, making the minibus tour the only way to see them. Tours are £16.80 for adults; £3.40 for children 5–16. Tours sell out, so reservations are required (☎ 0151 427 7231; **nationaltrust.org.uk/beatles**).

TOURING TIPS The Beatles Story is a leading city attraction, and you can expect crowds, particularly during summer months. Plan a late-afternoon visit and you'll find the exhibits much less crowded. A free shuttle connects the main Albert Dock site to the 4D theatre at Pier Head terminal, but the wait can get long, and it's just a 15-minute walk. If the weather is nice, it's worth strolling over.

Blackpool Zoo ★★★½

APPEAL BY AGE	PRESCHOOL ★★★	PRIMARY SCHOOL ★★★★	TEENS ★★★
YOUNG ADULTS ★★★	OVER 30 ★★★		SENIORS ★★★★

East Park Drive, Blackpool, Lancashire FY3 8PP
☎ **01253 830 830; blackpoolzoo.org.uk**

HOURS Open 10 a.m.; closing varies by season, ranging from 3.45 to 5.45 p.m. (last entry 45 minutes before closing). Open every day but Christmas.

COST £14.50 adults; £10.25 children (3–15); £12.50 students, senior citizens. Discount of 10% for booking online, but check first for coupons, which are frequently available from area hotels and B&Bs. Family-discount packages available. Tickets can also be bought through the Tesco Clubcard rewards scheme, but the vouchers cannot be used to purchase family discount packages.

GETTING THERE *By car:* Follow the M6 to Junction 32 and take the M55 to Junction 4, then follow signs. Parking costs £2.50, coins only, no change available. *By rail:* Blackpool North Station is a 10-minute walk from Blackpool Tower, from which you can catch a bus to the zoo (**thetrainline.com**). Blackpool South Station is about 3 mi (4.8 km) from the zoo, and taxis are usually available. *By bus:* **Blackpool Transport Service Bus 20** runs from the south side of the Blackpool Tower (bus stop next to

Peacocks, just off the Promenade). Service varies by season (**blackpool transport.com**).

DESCRIPTION AND COMMENTS Over the last several years, Blackpool Zoo has turned a corner. Once tired and run-down, it has seen more than £10 million invested since 2003, when the city turned it over to private management. Now it's owned by Parques Reunidos, a major European park operator, and is tallying record numbers of visitors. If you haven't been here since the 1990s, you'll immediately notice changes. The entrance area is dramatically improved, and while some additions, like the silly Dinosaur Safari, don't add much, others, such as a rebuilt sea-lion pool, make it a much more pleasant place to spend the day.

The mid-sized zoo covers 32 ac (13 ha) and has 1,500 animals from more than 400 species. While not as ambitious as the Chester Zoo, about 45 mi (72 km) away, it does an admirable job. The zoo, 2 mi (3 km) from the seafront, was once the city airport and during World War II hosted the RAF, which assembled bombers and conducted parachute training on the site. Then from 1953 to 1971 it served as the home of the Royal Lancashire Agricultural Show. It's this long, varied history that leads some to believe the grounds are haunted.

The first feature you encounter inside the zoo is **Dinosaur Safari,** a nicely-landscaped walk around a pond inhabited by 32 plastic dinosaurs, some of which need a good scrubbing and some new paint. A water-erupting volcano adds a whimsical touch, but the whole thing seems odd, given the zoo's otherwise-sincere interest in conservation and education. Young dino-lovers might get a kick from the stroll, but the whole area seems like a throwback. Take in the prehistoric mock animals if you like, but make sure to get the day's schedule of feedings and talks, which occur roughly every half-hour throughout the zoo. If you did nothing but bounce from one presentation to another, you'd finish the day with sore feet, perhaps, but also with a wealth of information on everything from spider monkeys to camels. Not bad for a day out.

Heading clockwise around the zoo, you'll encounter noisy **king colobus monkeys.** Look for signs, because the map uses dozens of icons to identify animals, making it difficult to decipher. You'll pass **capybaras,** the huge South American rodents, and then you'll find the cats: **meerkats** and **lions.** The updated **lion enclosure** is called the Pride of Blackpool. (Clever, these zookeepers.) The often-lethargic cats are particularly active during feeding times. Apparently between meals, in a creative effort to get the lazy kings and queens of the jungle off their behinds, the zoo provides them with large cardboard boxes to chew on and rip apart. The newest male, however, prefers to romance the lionesses and has several cubs to show for it. Nearby are **porcupines, tapirs** and ever-playful **otters.** A platform puts you at **giraffe** height, offering an unfamiliar eye-to-eye perspective on the creatures.

From here you can catch a miniature train (an extra £1.50, return) for a 5-minute journey to the other side of the park, home to the Children's Zoo. It's probably the best suggestion if little ones are already beginning to flag. Otherwise keep going.

In the zoo's bottom corner, you'll find the free-flight **aviary.** Try to time your visit to this area to coincide with the **sea-lion show,** offered several times a day. If you're a little early, there's plenty to keep you occupied here. At **Gorilla Mountain** you can watch western lowland gorillas climbing and playing in their own isolated habitat. There is also a very respectable orang-utan exhibit. The nearby **Penguin Pool,** a recent addition, offers underwater views of entertaining African penguins. And if you still have a little time to kill, there's a playground here where you can park the kids. But don't wait too long, as you'll want to arrive for the sea-lion show at least 5 minutes early. Although the enclosure is the largest of its type in England, it still fills up, and you'll likely be turned away if you arrive just as the performance begins. The stands hold 250 guests, who are separated from the action by sheets of glass. The show includes the expected hoop-jumping, ball-balancing and flipper-clapping but also an explanation of how the animal's anatomy helps it survive in the wild.

Continuing clockwise, pass the **Zebra and Bongo House,** where you can marvel at Mother Nature's use of stripes. Soon you'll reach **Wallaby Walk-Through,** which will put you within petting distance of the bouncy Aussie natives. (Compare them with the kangaroos, which are on the other side of the Children's Zoo.) Likewise, **Lemur Wood**'s walkway offers close encounters of the furry kind with three different species of the Madagascar natives. The **Children's Zoo** is nicely done and very hands-on, with bunnies and barnyard animals, along with nearby **aardvarks** and **small primates.**

Rounding the corner back towards the entrance, stop to admire the elephants, but try to steer the kids away from the **Playbarn,** a typical soft-play area that carries an extra £3 charge per child, although discounts are often available.

Nearby, you'll find the memorable **Creepy Crawlies Corner,** which improbably occupies part of the elephant house. It's long on insects, but the reptiles are in short supply, especially snakes. Many exhibits are low to the ground, perfect for shorter children but awkward for adults. It might give some adults nightmares, but kids seem eager to hold tarantulas, snakes and various reptiles. In fact the zoo is frequently asked to offer special sessions for guests who suffer from phobias. Management hasn't been sympathetic. 'We are not trained psychologists', the website curtly notes. 'If you do suffer from a phobia, we advise you to speak to your GP, who should be able to offer help.' Another recent addition, the domed **Amazonia** exhibit, offers a walk-through rainforest experience, complete with curious squirrel monkeys. The staff often tries to deter them with water guns, but they have been known to jump on visitors' backs.

TOURING TIPS Though pleasant and modern, Blackpool Zoo is not without its deficits. As mentioned earlier, the park map uses animal symbols instead of identifying text on a very cluttered map. Signage is not great, either in terms of finding your way around or for identifying and providing information about the animals in their respective enclosures. The main demonstration and lecture area, roughly across from the Dinosaur

Safari, is not well marked. We searched all over the park before locating it, walking right past it three times in the process. Many visitors mistakenly turn up at a stage to the right of the elephant house, where they wait in vain until it becomes apparent that there's no demonstration forthcoming.

The zoo has a lot of elbow room, and many of the habitats are quite large. This is a euphemistic way of saying that it's easy for the animals to hide if they want to. Try to catch as many of the feedings and talks as possible. Food's unremarkable, so pack a picnic if possible. You'll probably have the best chance to pet a lemur late in the day. A £2 souvenir booklet has plenty of factoids about the animals but is hardly necessary for a visit.

Blue Planet Aquarium ★★★★

APPEAL BY AGE	PRESCHOOL ★★★	PRIMARY SCHOOL ★★★★	TEENS ★★★★
YOUNG ADULTS ★★★	OVER 30 ★★★		SENIORS ★★★★

Longlooms Road, Ellesmere Port, Cheshire CH65 9LF
☎ **0151 357 8804; blueplanetaquarium.com**

HOURS 10 a.m.–5 p.m.; until 6 p.m. Saturdays.

COST £14.75 adults; £10.75 children (14 and under); £12.75 students, senior citizens. £2 discount for booking online. Family-discount packages available.

GETTING THERE *By car:* At Junction 10 of the M53. If travelling from the M6, join the M56 at Junction 20, then head towards Ellesmere Port and turn onto the M53 at Junction 15. Follow the signs. *By rail:* The nearest station is Ellesmere Port on **Mersey Rail** (**merseyrail.org**) from Chester or Liverpool, about 2 mi (3 km) away. The aquarium's Shark Shuttle runs from the station late March–September. Call for details. *By bus:* Regular service from Liverpool, Chester, Ellesmere Port and North Wales. From Liverpool take **Bus 1** from Sir Thomas Street. From Chester take **Bus 1** or **Bus 4** from the central bus station.

DESCRIPTION AND COMMENTS It's hard to get a handle on Blue Planet. It's large and has Europe's biggest collection of sharks. But it's pricey and can be seen in just an hour or two. Bottom line: if you like aquariums and animal attractions, it's certainly worth a visit, but it's going to cost you.

The £12 million building, part of the Cheshire Oaks shopping centre, isn't your typical box-in-a-parking-lot. It sports a unique concrete roof, recalling a crashing wave. The Queen herself opened the attraction in 1998. At the time, it was Britain's largest aquarium (a title now held by the National Marine Aquarium in Plymouth).

But aside from a few standout exhibits, you'll find many familiar features from other aquariums. There's a touch tank with rays, a glass tunnel leading through a giant tank, and a variety of talks and feedings which enhance any visit. There are **six themed areas** but no set route through the attraction, so you may wander a bit at first. And a few exhibits are hard to track down – you've got to sneak out a door in the back of the gift shop to reach the playground and otters, for example.

Blue Planet's centrepiece, a 1.1-million-gal (3.8-million-litre) **Caribbean Reef** display, is what makes the place special. It's home to an astonishing assortment of **sharks** – 15 species at last count. The star attractions are the 353-lb (160-kg), 10½-ft (3.2-m) sand tiger sharks. With 250 needle-like teeth, these predators definitely look vicious. Although they rarely attack humans, they'll certainly hold your attention and make you thankful that there's thick glass separating you from them. Other species measuring in at more than 10 ft (3 m) include nurse and lemon sharks. You'll also see black- and white-tip reef sharks and bamboo, Port Jackson and zebra sharks, plus the bizarre bearded wobbegong shark. You get the best view by taking a 233 ft (70 m) moving walkway through the **Aquatunnel.** Don't be shy about going back again and again – it's really a remarkable sight to see these guys gliding past you.

You can also watch shark feedings at the **Aquatheatre,** which fronts a section of the reef tank. Presented by an announcer outside the tank and divers inside, the show is short but impressive. Afterwards, many are inspired to sign up for a 'diving with the sharks' experience, which must be booked ahead and runs £199.

Like many aquaria, Blue Planet has concluded that fish and sea mammals aren't enough to keep their audience happy. That's why you can find an assortment of dangerous **amphibians,** such as the deadly golden dart frog, used by Amazon Indians to poison their arrow tips. Each frog has enough poison on his skin to kill more than ten humans. And then there's the strange satanic leaf-tailed gecko from Madagascar, so named because the endangered animal has horns.

One exhibit lumps together spiders, fish and other sea life in a not-too-subtle collection called **Venom.** Along with stinging jellyfish, vipers and poisonous lionfish, there's a tower crawling with dozens of Guyanese pink-toed tarantulas. For an arachnophobe's nightmare, you can step inside an acrylic enclosure called **Tarantula Tower** and literally find yourself surrounded by the creatures. The exhibit also includes rare species such as a stonefish, the world's most venomous fish, and a 6" (15-cm) tree-dwelling tiger spider from India, known for its speed and aggressive behaviour. Bet you won't walk around barefoot for a while after visiting.

Other attractions are devoted to **Lake Malawi,** which is home to more than 1,000 species of fish, including 350 that are unique to the lake. The lake itself, Africa's third largest, stretches 400 mi (645 km) long and reaches 2,300 ft (700 m) in depth. Nearby are exhibits devoted to the **Amazon,** with piranhas; a **mangrove swamp,** with catfish crabs and terrapins; and the **Coral Bay** touch tank, with bat fish and manta rays.

Blue Planet also makes an attempt to feature native **freshwater fish,** which, it notes, were largely wiped out during the industrial revolution and have only begun to revive in the last 50 years. The pike, which can reach almost 6 ft (1.8 m) and is Britain's largest predatory freshwater fish, is impressive, but truth is that cold-water fish aren't nearly as colourful as tropical species. Local species are also featured in the **Rocky Shoreline** touch tanks.

Before you make your exit, look for a door in back of the gift shop. Go outside and find a spacious **otter enclosure,** one of the country's largest, which features playful Asian short-clawed and less-familiar Canadian otters. During the summer, they're fed a frozen concoction of mackerel, trout and squid, which the staff call fishy ice lollies. Yum. The area's also home to an elaborate **pirate-themed playground.**

TOURING TIPS Aquarium mascot Charlie the Clownfish tries to make younger visitors feel at home. Otherwise, Blue Planet plays up its scary, toothy and dangerous animals, which may be a tad overwhelming for preschoolers.

British Lawnmower Museum ★★½

APPEAL BY AGE	PRESCHOOL ★	PRIMARY SCHOOL ★	TEENS ★
YOUNG ADULTS ★★	OVER 30 ★★		SENIORS ★★★

106–114 Shakespeare Street, Southport, Merseyside PR8 5AJ
☎ **01704 501 336; lawnmowerworld.co.uk**

HOURS 9 a.m.–5.30 p.m. Closed Sundays and bank holidays.
COST £2 adults; £1 children; includes audio tour.
GETTING THERE *By car:* From the south, take the M6 to exit 26; take the M58 to Ormskirk, and then the A570 to Southport. From the north, follow the A59 from Preston (exit 31 from the M6) and then follow signs. *By rail:* **Merseyrail** (**merseyrail.org**) runs a regular service from Liverpool, about an hour away. **Northern Rail** (**northernrail.org**) runs from Manchester. *By bus:* **National Express** (**nationalexpress.com**) and **Merseytravel** (**merseytravel.gov.uk**) both serve Southport.
DESCRIPTION AND COMMENTS Okay, we don't suggest building your holiday around a visit, but you have to admit there's something charming, engaging, eccentric and, dare we say, a little British about a museum devoted to the humble lawnmower. But this unique collection, over a garden-equipment and lock store in Southport, teaches that the lawnmower wasn't always a humble machine. Its invention in 1830 might not match the importance of that of the steam engine, but it took a creative mind and perseverance to realise that we needed a machine to tend the little swathes of Eden that were sprouting up in front of the homes of England's emerging middle class.

The museum's patron saint, creator Edwin Beard Budding, fashioned the first mower from a tool used to trim nap from cloth woven for guardsmen's uniforms. Townsfolk thought him nuts, forcing him to tinker and test his machine in the middle of the night so he wouldn't be disturbed.

The museum takes this all very seriously but does seem to have its tongue firmly in cheek when it brags to visitors that it's 'mower interesting' and features a musical ode to lawnmowers on its website. The owners also deal in antique garden equipment and are considered worldwide authorities.

Must-sees include mowers of the rich and famous, including models owned by Prince Charles and the late Princess Diana, Alan Titchmarsh and Hilda Ogden of *Coronation Street* fame. But you can bet they never spent a sweaty afternoon pushing one around before heading down to the pub for a pint. There's also a solar-powered mower, a Rolls-Royce–powered mower and a 2" (5-cm) mower on exhibit. Many of the 200 or so machines on display have been rescued from scrapyards and restored to their original condition. There are also rare toy lawnmowers, vintage lawnmower adverts and special mowers designed for racing. (Why does this sound like a bad idea?)

And what self-respecting museum lacks a gift shop? Browse through such unique souvenirs as *Lawnmower World* DVDs, children's books and pewter mower miniatures, which run a cool £49.99. You can even pick up an antique mower of your own. But prices aren't posted, which suggests that, like so many lovely things in life, if you have to ask, you can't afford it.

Who knows what Mr Budding would make of all the hoopla. The inventor did have his moment of fame but is now largely forgotten. Perhaps it's understandable. Thanks to him, the world can tally billions of ruined weekends spent tending lawns when we'd rather be in front of the telly watching football.

TOURING TIPS If you're driving, the little brown-and-white PLACES OF INTEREST signs will get you close, but because the museum is on the first floor of a garden-equipment store, you'll probably drive right past. Look either for the street number, 106–114 Shakespeare Street, or for the intersection of Shakespeare Street and Bentham Street – the museum is on the southwest corner. Because the museum is not exactly a tourist magnet, you'll most likely have to collar a salesperson in the garden shop to buy your admission. Then it's up the steps you go. The museum is laid out in four rooms. Over the stairwell is a flat-screen television showing a nicely-produced introduction to the museum and its exhibits, as well as to the history of the lawnmower. As you wander the museum, it's a real challenge to locate the various mowers that the video is discussing, so we just watched the video and then, with a little background absorbed, began exploring the rooms.

As it turns out, the lawnmower was a precursor to a whole raft of other machines and imponderables, including early robots and any number of belt-driven inventions. You'll also learn the difference between a lawnmower (blades rotating around a horizontal axle) and what we mostly have today (blades rotating horizontally around a vertical axle), which is actually a lawn *cutter*. All of the mowers on display were used for cutting grass and none for agricultural purposes, though quite a few agricultural machines have a lawnmower in their ancestry. The mowers presented were variously propelled by humans, horses, internal combustion engines, electricity and steam. One of our favourite items was a set of overshoes for horses so that they wouldn't make hoof depressions in finely-manicured lawns.

The rooms are so jammed with machines and memorabilia that it makes your head swim, but they are arranged so that your attention is drawn to the more interesting items. We spent about 40 minutes seeing the museum but could have devoted twice the time. How long you spend will probably correlate with your mechanical aptitude and your penchant for tinkering.

Look for director Brian Radam, a walking encyclopaedia of lawn-mower lore who is always eager to share his knowledge.

Camelot Theme Park ★★★½

| APPEAL BY AGE | PRESCHOOL ★★★★ | PRIMARY SCHOOL ★★★★ | TEENS ★★★ |
| YOUNG ADULTS ★★ | | OVER 30 ★★ | SENIORS ★★★ |

Park Hall Road, Charnock Richard, Chorley, Lancashire PR7 5LP
☎ **0871 663 6400; camelotthemepark.co.uk**

HOURS (April–mid-September) Opens 10 a.m.; closing varies by season.
COST £22 adults and children over age 3'3" (1 m); £13.50 senior citizens, disabled. Family tickets for groups of 4–6. Discount of at least 15% for booking online.
GETTING THERE *By car:* Between Preston and Wigan. From the M6 northbound, take Junction 27, or if southbound, take Junction 28. From the M61, take Junction 8. Then follow signs to Camelot and Park Hall. *By rail:* The closest train station is Chorley (**thetrainline.com**). *By bus:* Bus service to the park runs every day but Sunday (**stagecoachbus.com**). Call Camelot's **Traveline** for details (☎ 0871 200 2233).
DESCRIPTION AND COMMENTS One of the country's few theme parks with an actual theme – King Arthur's legends of Camelot – this park appeals to younger kids, with a few energetic rides to keep teens and thrill-seekers happy. The tree-shaded setting is nestled in a pleasant pastoral valley amidst rolling hills. The park has rare on-site lodging – the **Park Hall Hotel** (☎ 0871 663 6510; **parkhall-hotel.co.uk/camelot.aspx**) – although there's not enough here to warrant spending more than a day.

If arriving by car, you'll park to the side and can see the rides behind trees as you walk around to the front. The park is divided into five lands, which in order are **King's Realm** (water and family rides), **Knight's Valley** (shows and a few family rides), **Merlin's Playground** (kids' rides), **Land of the Brave** (thrill rides) and **Squire Bumpkin's Friendly Farm** (petting zoo). Long queues are rarely a problem, so follow your bliss and wander and ride at whim. Guinevere would certainly approve.

The layout of the park is linear, beginning at the entrance area on a ridge, descending steeply to a long narrow terrace, then down into a wooded valley and up a hill to the farthest outpost, where most of the thrill rides are located. Navigating isn't visually simple because of the hills and valleys, but there's no way to get lost, and if you keep to the main pedestrian thoroughfare it will lead you through all of the theme areas. Speaking of which, theme execution is minimal throughout.

After paying admission at a castle-gate entrance, you immediately encounter a boxy white building loosely disguised as a castle, which holds an **entertainment centre** with a soft-play area, dodgems and arcade games. Unless it's raining, you'll want to put this off until later. Instead proceed to the right and enter **King's Realm,** where the standouts are two water rides – a **log flume** and **Pendragon's Plunge,** a splashy raft ride with choice of three chutes. No lane is wrong, but do expect to get wet. There's also a **kiddie coaster,** plus nine-hole **mini-golf** and **Formula-K Go-Karts,** both of which carry an extra charge.

Continue straight ahead to **Knight's Valley,** the show area, which in many ways is the heart of the park, and Camelot's unique selling point. You'll want to visit the stadium, which claims to be the UK's only dedicated full-time **jousting arena.** (We have to wonder if during the Middle Ages they were once as common as Burger Kings.) Crowds love cheering on Lancelot and his galloping compatriots as they take on the evil Black Knight with lances, broad swords and flaming maces. Expect plenty of pomp and circumstance, with blaring trumpets, pronouncements from a cheerleading Arthur and comic relief from windy, not-so-funny jesters, who monopolize and drag out the entire production. The jousting and knightly skill demonstrations are the best we've seen in England, but sitting through purgatory with the prattling jesters was almost more than we could bear. Afterwards, youngsters can line up to pet the horses. Nearby, at the indoor King Arthur's Castle theatre, Merlin and his assistant Scoop present two magic shows daily, with chances for audience members to participate. There's also a twice-daily interactive **School of Wizardry,** where kids can learn a few magic tricks themselves. Probably the best souvenir – and at no extra charge.

This area is also home to **Dragon Flyer,** one the strangest rides in theme-park lore. It's a diesel-powered roller coaster that some days barely seems to have enough horsepower to climb the pipsqueaky hills. Set on an elevated oval track, it does offer a nice view of the park, though, and gives riders two laps at speeds reaching 25 mph (40 km/h), enough to feel the breeze in your hair. Enjoy the scenery, but remember to hold your breath when you pass through the exhaust fumes. More-familiar rides in this area include a **swinging pirate ship,** a **flying carousel** with seats in mock hot-air-balloon gondolas, and a small Ferris wheel.

Backtracking to the centre of the park brings you past a food court with a Wimpy, a chip shop and a coffee shop. It's adjacent to **Merlin's Playland,** which has several flat children's rides designed for the little Lancelots in your group. Most will look familiar from any funfair, but with different names, like Cup and Sorcerer, Junior Jousting Horses and Human Cannon Ball. Don't worry, they all deliver a more gentle experience than their names might imply. There's also **Junior Dragon Coaster** – which the park calls a 'pink knuckle' ride. It chugs around a small oval at the far end of the park. You also can take a break and let kids romp around an indoor play area or send them to **Bertie Bassett's Driving School,** a ride that lets little ones chauffeur a double-decker bus or fire engine around a miniature town, for an extra charge.

Coaster fans, though, will quickly find their way to **Land of the Brave** in the back section of the park, which is home to Camelot's few true thrill rides. The headliner is **Knightmare,** a steel coaster that ranked 8th in the UK and 122nd on the planet in a recent worldwide poll. The £3-million runaway-mine-train coaster opened in 2007, representing a substantial investment in the park. The German-made ride, which was purchased from a park in Japan, is composed of a snarl of track that seems to threaten decapitation as it zooms through the 0.5-mi (.8-km) course. The ride carriages each seat 14 people and reach speeds of up to 43 mph (69 km/h). It's smooth in the front and a little bumpy in the back, but what grabs everyone's attention is the 5-g forces on one of the curves, nicknamed 'psycho drop'.

You'll also find the **Whirlwind,** a steel coaster with spinning vehicles. The ride's surprisingly long, and as the vehicle spins you'll find you're taking drops facing forwards and backwards. Riders must be balanced in the car by weight and size, and no more than two adults can sit in each vehicle. Unfortunately, there's no theming on this ride – it doesn't pretend to be anything more than a roller coaster. Another ride for the brave, **Excalibur 2** is a modified pendulum ride with a flat spinning platform on the end. If you savour the idea of spinning whilst upside-down, this ride's for you. If not, there's another reason to hang out here: pocket change. You'll find it showering down to the ground with almost every ride cycle.

Finally comes **Squire Bumpkin's Friendly Farm,** with goats, lambs, piglets, ponies and chicks to pet. It's not exactly in theme, but certainly there were farms in Arthur's vast kingdom, and little ones will adore it.

TOURING TIPS Dining options are limited here, and the food court fills up right after the midday jousting show. So if you're going to buy lunch on-site, either eat early or grab something during the show. Otherwise you may find yourself queuing for a half-hour to buy mediocre food at theme-park prices. Or bring a picnic.

Socks must be worn in all soft-play areas, and they aren't available for sale in the park. So either wear them in or pack a few pairs in a bag.

The jousting and magic shows operate according to the posted daily entertainment schedule. Plan your day around the shows you want to see. The jousting stadium can accommodate large numbers in a covered grandstand. The indoor magic venue, near the boarding area for the diesel coaster, is much smaller. The shows draw large numbers of visitors from the ride queues, so experiencing the more popular rides while a show is in progress is a good strategy for cutting queuing time.

The on-site Park Hall Hotel often offers discount packages, which include bed-and-breakfast and park admission for families.

Chester Zoo ★★★★★

APPEAL BY AGE	PRESCHOOL ★★★★	PRIMARY SCHOOL ★★★★★	TEENS ★★★★
YOUNG ADULTS ★★★★★		OVER 30 ★★★★★	SENIORS ★★★★

Upton-by-Chester, Chester, Cheshire CH2 1EU
☎ **01244 380 280; chesterzoo.org**

- **HOURS** Opens at 10 a.m.; closing varies by season. Open every day but Christmas and Boxing days.
- **COST** (Mid-July–September) £15.35 adults; £11.30 children (3–15); £13.85 senior citizens, students, disabled, carers; £50 family ticket (2 adults, 2 children). Mid-season (early September–October) prices about £1 less; low season, about £2 less. Discount of 15% for arriving on bicycle (with

voucher from website). Discount of 10% for booking online, but cannot be combined with bicycling discount.

GETTING THERE *By car:* About an hour from Manchester and a 10-minute drive north of Chester. From the M63, take the A56 exit west and then the A41 north and follow the signs. *By rail:* The zoo is a few miles from the Chester Station, served by **Virgin Trains, Arriva Trains Wales, Northern Rail** and **Merseyrail,** which offers a discount package including transportation and zoo admission (for packages, see **merseyrail.org**; for general tickets, **thetrainline.com**). A free shuttle bus runs from the station every 20 minutes during high season. Alternatively, the zoo is 2 mi (3 km) by taxi. *By bus:* **First Bus 1** runs from Chester Bus Exchange every 20 minutes Monday–Saturday, every 30 minutes on bank holidays and every hour on Sundays (**firstgroup.com**).

DESCRIPTION AND COMMENTS Chester boasts Roman history, a towering castle and a grand cathedral. But in our view, the best reason to visit is its zoo. It's the country's finest, and it can take an entire day or more to see all on offer in its 111 ac (45 ha). Top draws here include orang-utans, bats, butterflies, Asian elephants, jaguars and a long list of other endangered or threatened species. Plan on taking your time and savouring the sights, sounds and surroundings. You can learn a lot in what is truly a world-class attraction.

Animals aside, the zoo itself is noteworthy. It was created by George Mottershead, a nurseryman's son who began collecting the exotic insects and reptiles that arrived in shipments with his father's plants. (Now do you understand why the customs folk seize your fresh fruit at the airport?) It was a childhood experience visiting a Manchester zoo in the early 1900s and seeing a shackled elephant cramped in an iron cage that led Mottershead to vow to build a different kind of animal habitat – 'a zoo without bars'.

Even after being injured during World War I, Mottershead kept his promise, purchasing the Oakfield Manor House, a Grade II–listed building in the Chester suburb of Upton. The 9-ac (3.6-ha) property opened in 1931 with a revolutionary concept. Indeed, there were no bars and cages: animals were kept in open, naturalistic settings, separated from visitors only by moats and unobtrusive fences. It was based on the new zoo theories propagated by the German Carl Hagenbeck. Neighbours were quite concerned when the zoo opened a lion habitat enclosed by just a fence. An even bigger gamble came when it opened an island monkey habitat that used just a canal to separate visitors from the primates. No one knew if monkeys could or would swim away and wreak havoc in the Roman-era town. But they didn't, and the zoo's primate collection is now among the finest in the world, allowing an entire colony of chimpanzees to live in a complex social setting similar to what they'd have in the wild.

Over the years, the zoo has stuck to its motto 'Always Building'. It now includes 111 ac (45 ha) of exhibit space – nearly 500 ac (202 ha) in total when you include the car park, support buildings and surrounding fields. The collection numbers more than 7,000 animals from

400 species. Seeing the highlights is a daylong undertaking. The zoo's divided in half by a public cycle path, which can be crossed by two bridges. The award-winning grounds are an attraction in themselves, with sunken, water and Roman gardens.

The zoo has tried to make things easy for visitors by providing a suggested route to see the major exhibits. Although it covers nearly 2 mi (3.2 km) of walking, it still misses many highlights. We suggest you use this route with a few added sub-routes, which will allow you to loop through several rewarding areas you'd otherwise miss. You also may want to deviate from the route if there's an animal talk that interests you – pick up a map at the entrance. As you tour, look for signs and follow the map closely to make sure you know where you are, and don't be afraid to ask for directions. (Yes, men, this means you.) Navigation is anything but intuitive here, and with more than 11 mi (17 km) of paths, you can go far astray. Even with the zoo map, the layout is confusing and strangely organised. You don't want to waste your time and energy backtracking.

The zoo has two entrances: a main gate and a pedestrian entrance. The latter is almost directly on the opposite side of the property from the main gate. You'll probably be entering through the main gate. (If not, pick up the suggested tour halfway through and follow along from there.) After paying admission and grabbing the day's schedule of animal talks, you enter an open plaza with cafeteria and gift shop, and wheelchairs and pushchairs for hire. You might be tempted to start a visit with a lap on the monorail to get an overview of the property and animals, but the ride stops halfway through its route, forcing you to buy another ticket for the return route. A £4 round-trip tab on top of an already-pricey admission seems a bit much.

Instead, take a right and head to the **mongoose and warthog enclosure** – the latter has a face only a mother could love. It's part of the **Tsavo Black Rhino Experience,** an area dedicated to preserve a rare subspecies. In 1980, there were 60,000 black rhinoceros in Kenya, but their horns proved irresistible to poachers. Now there are only 500, representing 85% of the global population. Several of the animals you see here were born at the zoo. The mongoose exhibit is representative of the zoo's penchant for novelty and innovation. Here, children and adults can wind through a burrow that pops up under a Plexiglas display right in the middle of the mongooses' front garden.

Now that you have a taste for Africa, head through the **Tsavo Bird Safari,** showcasing fowl from the same area of the continent. Then you'll pass cranes as you loop by unusual **antelopes,** such as the Kafue Flats lechwe, gemsbok and dik-dik. Take a moment to look to your right after you pass the scimitar-horned oryx. The **spectacled bears,** a short-faced South American species, make a memorable sight with light, almost raccoon-like colouring on their faces. Now loop back towards the entrance, where you can start the zoo's suggested route.

Your next stop is the **monkey house and islands,** where you'll find a colourful quartet of primates: mandrills, Colombian spider monkeys and Sulawesi crested and lion-tailed macaques. During summer months, they prefer to play outside. Other times of year they'll be cozy inside the monkey house, while you – the supposed advanced species – are shivering outdoors.

From here continue on the suggested route to the **Fruit Bat Forest,** one of the strangest zoo exhibits we've encountered. A word of caution: if you're skittish about bats, you might want to move on, because once you step into the darkness, you are literally in the realm of the bats. Three fruit-bat species – Livingstone's, Rodrigues and Seba's – are in free flight here and will swoop near your head as you stumble through the near-darkness. As if bats aren't enough, the dark exhibit also includes Madagascar hissing cockroaches. Nothing's easy to see in this exhibit. We recommend stepping inside and just chilling out for a minute or two while your eyes adjust to the dark.

Now head over to the **cheetahs,** nature's version of the Formula One race car. These cats seem to have two speeds: rest and full-throttle. Unlike other animals, the females are solitary, while males live in groups called coalitions. The zoo has such a group with three males. While you're in a feline mood, head across a canal to see the critically-endangered **Asiatic lions,** which are reduced to less than 500 specimens in the wild in India. Chester is a leader in breeding to preserve this unique subspecies.

Now it's time to venture off the suggested route again. Proceed towards the pedestrian entrance, admiring **bush dogs, kangaroos, cassowaries** and **yellow mongoose** on the way. Your goal is the **red pandas.** The zoo's had recent success in breeding this beautiful rare species, and if there are babies on display, you'll be doing plenty of cooing at the cuties. They're most active in the mornings and late afternoon. Nearby you'll also find buildings with parrots and owls. An added bonus is that many visitors overlook this area, and if it's a crowded day, you'll welcome the break from the masses. If you've brought a picnic, this is a great place to stop. The **Little Acorns Play Area** will keep children occupied while adults take a breather. Nearby is the **Children's Fun Ark,** a large wooden play area with ladders, slides, climbing nets and towers.

But don't get too comfortable. There's still some great stuff ahead, like the rare **Sumatran tigers,** which number less than 500 in the wild. If you come during feeding time, it's a treat to watch the carnivores at work. Keepers hide the food around the enclosure – on the top of a pole, in containers and even in a floating raft – which lets the predators hunt down their meal as they would in the wild. Loop down from here to visit the large **aviary, Mongoose Mania** and especially **Islands in Danger.** The reptile exhibit includes the closest thing to a mythical creature this side of Harry Potter – the deadly Komodo dragon, which can reach speeds of up to 11 mph (18 km/h) and can kill humans. To even the score, it shares display space with **Caribbean iguanas,** which are eaten by humans. To each his own, we guess.

Circle back towards the Fun Ark to see (and hear) the boisterous **giant otters,** a South American carnivore. Next comes everyone's favourite, the always-natty **penguins.** Chester boasts a colony of 50 Humboldts, which are used in breeding programmes throughout Europe.

All this is a warm-up for one of the zoo's newest and most impressive exhibits, **Realm of the Red Ape,** devoted to Sumatran and Bornean orang-utans. The area replicates an Indonesian rainforest, complete with tropical birds like the scissor-billed starling and Timor sparrow. It's recognised as one of the world's best orang-utan habitats, and apparently the primates feel at home, having reproduced several times in recent years. Because it's so authentic, spotting the inhabitants can be tricky. Take your time to survey treetops and look in corners. Also on display is the **reticulated python,** the world's longest snake species, topping out at over 30 ft (9 m), as well as gibbons and giant walking-stick insects. And for those of you who are finally catching your breath after braving the bat house, you might want to know that the reticulated python is one of the few snakes known to eat humans. Like several of Chester Zoo's more elaborate habitats, Realm of the Red Ape consists of both indoor and outdoor enclosures. If the inside enclosures are empty, check outside and vice versa. If both are empty, check again – the orang-utan is second only to the octopus when it comes to hiding.

Now take a quick detour to the bottom corner of the zoo to visit **Spirit of the Jaguar,** which Chester simply calls 'the largest and best Jaguar enclosure in the world'. (There's a reason for that: the exhibit was financed by the Jaguar car company.) The species has adapted to live in two vastly-different habitats – savannah and rainforest – both of which are represented here. As with the tigers, these felines need to work for their food. Meals are dragged around to create scent trials and then hidden under bark and leaves or tucked into rock crevasses. Look for the **leaf-cutter ants** too; although they occupy the other end of the food chain, they're just as industrious, and it's fascinating to watch them carry vegetation as big as their bodies back to their nest in an artificial tree trunk. As with Realm of the Red Ape, this exhibit has inside and outside areas, and no guarantee you'll see a jaguar in either. Outside the jaguar house and to the right is the **Jaguar Coffee House,** with both indoor and outdoor seating. Rarely crowded, this is a good choice for lunch or a break on busier days.

Your next stop promises shenanigans. The **chimpanzees** live in one of the world's largest zoo colonies of primates. Following instinct, they have formed their own complex society as they would in the wild. They're fascinating and worth taking time to study. See if you can pick out the leaders, the ambitious adolescents, the breeding females and the elder statesmen. It's kind of like school with all the accompanying drama. Parents be warned, though: this might be the day you have to give the birds-and-bees talk to your little ones. Chimps may be our closest relatives, but they are uninhibited, to say the least.

In the last several years, it seems as if every zoo has fallen in love with **lemurs.** You'll find a particularly-good exhibit here, confined to its own island, where ring-tailed and red-ruffed lemurs bound through trees and take time to groom each other. Next come the descriptively-named **Visayan warty pigs,** an extremely-rare Filipino species seen only in a few zoos around the world. Deviating from the path for a moment, take in the **Secret World of the Okapi,** an African species related to the giraffe that's so elusive it was discovered only in the last century. Nearby is the giant anteater, not as rare but still fascinating.

Backtrack by the dwarf forest buffalo and take in the **onagers** and **camels.** Although they are familiar from bazaars and manger scenes, it's fascinating to see the beast of burden without a saddle placed awkwardly on its hump. Across the path, you'll find the **Condor Cliffs Aviary,** a building devoted to the huge predator and black vultures. The aviary allows the birds to be in free flight, an inspiring sight. For us, the Andean condor was a highlight of our visit. The aviary is at one end of and adjacent to the **Elephants Bridge,** the most central and noteworthy landmark at the zoo. On the zoo's busiest walkway, the bridge is a great place to meet if your party gets separated.

Contrast the raptors in the aviary with the creatures flying next door at **Butterfly Journey.** The legions of insects flutter around and will even perch on you if you stay still.

If you're starting to feel like Noah, don't worry; your journey through the animal kingdom is nearly done. Last stop is **Elephants of the Asian Forest,** home to a herd of six females and one male. They're part of a conservation programme. The mammals are highly intelligent and social. The females have the run of the expansive grounds, while the male is kept in a private enclosure because, well, his hormones get the best of him occasionally.

TOURING TIPS The main gate and ticket kiosks are pretty congested in the morning. If you encounter long queues waiting to purchase admission, turn right and follow a wooden rail down to the Group Ticket kiosks. The four ticket windows there are not usually crowded, and though tickets are ostensibly for groups, vendors will happily sell them to individuals. Available with your admission is a park map and a schedule of 'Animal Talks', about 12 such spread throughout the day, from 10.30 a.m. to 4.30 p.m. Subjects of the talks vary somewhat from day to day, with the weekend talks being the most interesting. All are worthwhile, but the elephant talk stands out as especially edifying.

Once you're inside, lockers, first aid, as well as wheelchair and pushchair hire, are to the right. Guest services is in the middle of the plaza. The park is abuzz with pushchairs (double and single models available). These work fine outside but create unfathomable congestion in indoor exhibits like the aquarium, the fruit-bat exhibit, Islands in Danger and the Butterfly Journey. We were trapped on several occasions by pushchairs in front and to the rear of us.

For a civilised break from touring, have afternoon tea on the terrace of **Oakfield Manor.** The historic house, near the pedestrian entrance, is now a restaurant and is a pleasant place to take a breather. Surrounding the manor are several lovely gardens that are also worth a look.

The monorail and a boat ride through the canals aren't mandatory, but they offer a chance to relax and take in the scenery.

If you choose to Gift Aid your admission, you'll receive a 10% discount card that can be used on some items in gift shops and restaurants.

Gulliver's World ★★★

APPEAL BY AGE	PRESCHOOL ★★★★★	PRIMARY SCHOOL ★★★★	TEENS ★
YOUNG ADULTS ★		OVER 30 ★	SENIORS ★

Camp Road, Burtonwood, Warrington WA5 5YZ
☎ **01925 240 085; gulliversfun.co.uk**

HOURS Gates open at 10.30 a.m.; closing time ranges from 4.30 to 7 p.m., with special holiday hours. Open for school holiday in February, late March–early November and late November–December.

COST £14.75 adults, children (under 2'11"/.9 m free); £13.75 senior citizens 60+; £57 family of 4. Discounts for online purchases. Be aware that a nearby sister park, Gulliver's SplashZone, is separate from Gulliver's World, and entrance is not included in the price. Packages combining hotel and park admission are available (**gullivers-shortbreaks.co.uk**).

GETTING THERE *By car:* Midway between Liverpool and Manchester; take the M62 to Junction 8 or 9 and follow the signs. From the M6, exit at Junction 21A onto the M62 to Liverpool; then exit at Junction 9 and follow the signs. *By rail:* Warrington Central is 1.5 mi (2.4 km) away (**nationalrail.co.uk**). *By bus:* From Warrington Central train station, exit to the left, go around the corner to the bus station and catch **Bus 18** or **18A** to the top of the park's driveway. It's a 5-minute walk to the park entrance.

DESCRIPTION AND COMMENTS Some parks try to be all things to all people, but not Gulliver's. This mini–theme park empire knows its audience: 3- to 12-year-olds – the younger the better. Teenagers unaccompanied by parents aren't allowed in. And adults shouldn't dream of showing up without a child in tow, as we did one summer morning. You won't be allowed to buy a ticket.

Gulliver's World is the chain's flagship park, with more than 80 attractions across 8 themed lands. In 1995, it got the attention of the British coaster world when it opened **Antelope,** a UK-designed wooden roller coaster that still attracts fans on pilgrimage. Most of the other rides will be familiar from funfairs, but there are enough quirks and unique touches to keep things interesting. Scattered throughout the park, for example, are play areas, with tricycles and go-karts left for kids' cruising pleasure. Gulliver's World is also the site of the company's latest expansion – a dedicated park hotel. You'll find some imaginative rides and theming at this park, but like the rest of the Gulliver's properties, it seems to suffer from a lack of upkeep. The rides and public areas could all use a fresh coat of paint.

And parents won't be able to sit back passively. On many rides, an adult will have to accompany any child under 3'11" (1.2 m). Other rides required accompaniment for youngsters under 2'11" (.9 m) or under 4'7" (1.4 m). Yet others ban anyone over 4'11" (1.5 m). Bottom line: you'll have to check out each ride's requirements and be ready to squeeze yourself into many kiddie-sized seats.

Parking is free, and once inside the gates, children are immersed in a magical land populated by familiar characters such as Dora the Explorer and the park's own mascots, the Gully Gang. (The park pays licensing fees for these characters, and their presence is not assured for the long run. If they're not there when you arrive, be prepared to tell your disappointed little ones that Dora's on holiday.) The site's dominated by a clunky-looking castle perched in the middle of the property, which will delight all but the most cynical princes and princesses in your group. Adults may not be so charmed. But remember, this park is not designed for you. Still, management understands that it needs to keep parents content. It notes that 50% of its attractions are under cover and can still be visited in the rain. And it brags about serving healthy food, which it does to a degree, although you probably won't find the crepes on any diet.

The 100-ac (40-ha) park is situated in a nicely-wooded area. You enter through a main plaza where you're greeted by a statue of Gulliver standing in front of quite a lovely lake. Here you can catch a 5-minute ride on **Gulliver's Railroad** for a quick round-trip.

But if you're a coaster fan, we suggest you head straight to the back of the park to the **Smugglers Wharf** area to ride **Antelope**. The ride is slow-loading, and queues inevitably build up throughout the day. This twisting, dipping coaster has a graceful design, but as you're flying through its paces, you may not have time to appreciate it. Although designed for youngsters, it's still a jarring ride, lasting nearly 2 minutes. It has two large drops and a hill that offers air-time. Some riders love it and will take in half a dozen trips over the course of a day. While you're here in the area, there's a classic **pirate-ship ride** and a **climbing wall.**

Now you'll circle back towards the park entrance in an anti-clockwise direction, stopping at **Circus World,** where children can do gymnastics and learn tricks of the trade in the kid's gym and **Clown School.** Face-painting is available at an additional charge. You can also take a trip through **Aladdin's Circus Ride,** a rudimentary ghost train. There are several soft-play areas, a playground and some very simple children's funfair-style rides. A short walk back towards the front of the park leads to **Western World,** an Old West–themed area. The standout here is the **Runaway Train Coaster,** a miniature wild-mouse-style ride that lasts about 90 seconds. It offers a breeze through your hair, but not much excitement. The silly *Hard Luck Bear Jamboree* show will keep some kids amused. Familiar junior-sized rides include the pendulum-style **Indian Creek Flying Raft,** the spinning **Barrel Ride** and **Billy Bob's Bi-Planes,** a flat ride that lets you control a plane's height as you rotate. The **Pony Express** ride lets little ones go for a ride on an elevated track, while the Pump Carts eke their way around a track under kid power.

Cutting back to the centre of the park brings you to **Alice's Wonderland.** What's this tale doing in the middle of Gulliver's World, you may ask? Well, Alice author Lewis Carroll was born in nearby Daresbury. In his honour, you can wander the **Maze of Cards** – a wooden maze with walls only about 3'3" (1 m) high, so it's hard to lose your children. The **Veteran Cars** ride lets your young ones take you for a spin, for a change, on a scenic track. The **Joker**'s a scaled-down, but still attention-getting drop tower, while the **Mad Hatter's Tea Party Ride** is a fancy name for spinning teacups.

Now you'll head back to the entrance and then proceed down the main walkway to **Lilliput Land.** Look for the fun **Cycle Monorail,** which has you pedal your way around a track at treetop level. Unless you've got an energetic (and long-legged) child, you'll probably do most of the work, though. Closed-toe shoes are required, so dress accordingly. There are also **Moonbuggies,** pedal karts your kids can zip around in while you take a load off your feet. For the adventurous, the **Ghost House** is a seriously-creepy walk-through haunted house, with corpses, skulls and body parts. We're sure many a parent faced weeks of nightmares after a visit here. Finally, find an old-fashioned **Horses Carousel, Dodgems** and another play area.

You're making a figure of eight to see the whole park, so your next destination is the back right-hand corner for **Adventure World,** home of the **Wild Mine Ride,** a smooth but unthemed 50-ft (15-m) wild-mouse coaster. The ride lasts about 80 seconds – watch out for the abrupt stop at the end. Another highlight is **Tomb Raider,** a ghost train that lets you shoot at targets with a toy laser. When activated, the targets may spring to life or shoot out water. There's no score-keeping, but that doesn't stop it from being fun. **Tree Tops Swing** is a flying carousel, and **Jeep Safari** offers a journey through the jungle in your own vehicle. In the covered **Ball Blast,** children get to fire ball cannons at each other and unsuspecting parents. But you can exact your revenge by sending them scrambling about the **Tarzan's Climb** playground. Finally, take a break with a gentle ride through **Calamity Canyon** on a raft.

There's a lot more splashing to be found in Water World, with the **Alpine Log Flume** and a **water-play area.** You can get the full beach experience digging around in a giant sand pit, and drive around in a tractor as well. Finally, **Diggers** has child-scaled backhoes, allowing you to dig up balls from a pit, drop them and do it all over. Great fun for 6-year-old boys – and their fathers.

Next you'll find **Gully Town,** an imaginative indoor interactive experience added in 2009. Kids get a kick out of shopping, cooking and performing onstage. There are also workbenches, a post office, and more soft-play and ball-pit areas. The town's sized for children and will keep some of them busy for hours. In the Fire Brigade ride, kids can even shoot a fire hose at a building from their own fire engine, while their platform slowly rises and falls.

End your tour in the dinosaur-themed **Lost World. Flight of the Pteranodon** is a spinning ride that you experience like a hang-glider, in a prone position, on your stomach. **Dino Safari Tour** offers a ramble through dino-infested forests in your own jeep. You can see baby dinosaurs emerging from eggs in the **Incubation Unit.** And you can learn where dinosaurs, and all human life, for that matter, came from in the **Carousel of Evolution,** where park mascot Gully Mouse and a professor explain Darwin's theory. Pretty heady stuff for a theme park.

TOURING TIPS Watch the time, because rides stop at least half an hour before closing time, allowing you to catch the goodbye show in the Entrance Plaza. If there's an attraction your kids have their heart set on, don't leave it until the late afternoon. If you're planning on making an overnight of it, check out the hotel–park admission packages available through **gullivers-shortbreaks.co.uk**.

Ticket kiosks are pretty jammed in the morning, so book your admission in advance online or by phone (☎ 01925 444 888; a £3 booking charge applies).

Knowsley Safari Park ★★★★

APPEAL BY AGE	PRESCHOOL ★★★★	PRIMARY SCHOOL ★★★★★	TEENS ★★★★
YOUNG ADULTS ★★★★★		OVER 30 ★★★★★	SENIORS ★★★★

Prescot, Merseyside L34 4AN
☎ **01514 309 009; knowsleysafariexperience.co.uk**

HOURS (March–October) 10 a.m.–4 p.m. (last entry); (November–February) 10.30 a.m.–3 p.m. (last entry).

COST £14 adults; £10 children (3–15), senior citizens; £7 pedestrians. £37 family ticket (2 adults, 2 children or 2 senior citizens).

GETTING THERE *By car:* Located 8 mi (13 km) from Liverpool city centre. Take the M62 to the Junction 6 exit to M57, then exit at Junction 2. At the roundabout follow the brown safari signs. *By rail:* Nearest train station is Prescot, about 1 mi (1.6 km) from the park (**nationalrail.co.uk**).

DESCRIPTION AND COMMENTS More windscreen wipers and aerials have been lost along a short stretch of road outside Liverpool than anywhere else in Britain. The culprit? Menacing packs of baboons that gleefully attack cars navigating Knowsley's safari drive. For some (usually kids who don't have to make car payments), it's the highlight of their visit – and even their childhood. For the rest of us, it's a trip of trepidation. Luckily, there's also a 'Safe Way', a route that avoids the baboons but allows you to observe the animals (and destruction) from behind a secure fence.

Knowsley Safari Park's baboon route is deservedly famous, and perhaps a fitting tribute to Edward Smith-Stanley, thirteenth Earl of Derby, who clearly appreciated the appeal of exotic animals. The former MP kept a private zoo on the property in the mid-1800s, gathering specimens from as far away as Central America and Africa. But assembling them wasn't simple. Often the animals were transported on long sea voyages, and some fell prey to illness, starvation and, in one case, the appetite of a hungry crew. Eventually, Lord Stanley's collection reached more than 400 animals, including alpacas, alligators, lemurs and zebras, and was ranked as one of the largest zoos in the world at the time. Paintings of the animals were published in a two-volume set, *Gleanings from the Menagerie and Aviary of Knowsley Hall,* which includes works by famous nonsense poet and natural-history artist Edward Lear, author of 'The Owl and the Pussycat'.

The 2,500-ac (1012-ha) Knowsley Estate has been in the Stanley family since 1385 and now belongs to The Rt Hon Edward Richard William Stanley, the nineteenth Earl of Derby. The earliest part of Knowsley Hall dates back to 1495, although a building has stood on the site since the twelfth century. The estate home combines a Georgian facade and Jacobean, Baroque and Victorian interiors, and the grounds were landscaped in the 1770s by the famed Sir Lancelot 'Capability' Brown. The home is open to the public five days a year and for charity functions. The property also has a spa and is rented out for conferences and team-building activities.

Thus when the eighteenth Earl of Derby opened the property as one of the country's first safari parks in 1971, it seemed quite natural to have exotic animals wandering the northern England countryside. The park has evolved over the years, and the route now looks like a plate of spaghetti. As you enter the park, you'll come to a roundabout. For the safari drive, bear right –but we suggest turning left and hitting the park base first, where you'll find **amusement rides, shows** and **animals.** Later in the day, when traffic dies down, you can hit the safari route.

After parking, head to the park base. As soon as you enter, you'll find yourself in a **mini-funfair,** with rides geared mainly to children under age 12. The cost is £1.50 per ride or £9 for an unlimited-ride wristband. Look over the offerings first and then do the simple math: if you expect you or a child will want to take more than six rides, spring for the band. The line-up includes several gentle rides, like the **swinging carousel** and **swinging pirate ships** that greet you at the entrance. The rides are all concentrated in this area, and if it's a summer day or a school or bank holiday, we suggest you visit these early in your visit before long queues develop. Other notable rides include **a carousel, a bouncy castle,** the **Ranger Patrol,** a jeep-style go-kart ride on a guided track and the **Rattlesnake,** a not-too-scary kiddie coaster. There are also **dodgems** and the **Stardancer** parachute drop. If it starts to rain, an **amusement arcade** offers shelter to the right of the entrance.

Now that you've got some of the wiggles out, you can begin exploring – but first, check the time of the **sea-lion show** and the **falconry flying display,** both on the left side of the park. The former features three resident California sea lions, Biffo, Max and Arthur, doing all sorts of things sea lions never do in the wild, like ball-balancing and ring-catching. Nevertheless, it's a perennial crowd-pleaser. The falconry show provides a chance to see raptors in flight, with hawks, owls and eagles soaring over the park.

And some – you know who you are – will go gaga over the nearby **Bug House,** which is packed with all manner of creepy-crawlies. More than two dozen species of invertebrates, amphibians and reptiles are on display, including Madagascar hissing cockroaches, emperor scorpions and Himalayan crocodile newts, to name a few. Also on this side of the park you'll find the 7-ac (2.8-ha) **Mizzy Lake Farm,** a walk-through barnyard area, and **Woodland Walk,** which offers a 15-minute educational stroll through the countryside. Staff are usually on hand to point out the flora and fauna in the area, from red squirrels to foxgloves to more than a half-dozen species of trees. Even if your party doesn't have young ones, it's a pretty walk.

Also in this area is **Aerial Extreme,** an elaborate and challenging adventure/ropes course. There are several levels of difficulty to choose from, but all include zip-lines, various tricky bridges and climbing structures. The greater the level of difficulty, the higher the course, with the most difficult course reaching heights of 45 ft (14 m). All participants are fitted with a pelvic climbing harness and are clipped in at all times. Costs range from £14 to £19 for children aged 15 years and younger, and £14 to £24 for adults. Estimated time to complete the courses ranges from 45 minutes to 2 hours.

You can get an overview of the animals on the right side of the park by taking the **miniature train.** The scenery doesn't differ from what you'll see walking around, but kids love trains and it's a good chance to have a seat. On foot, you'll first encounter **meerkats,** and then **red river hogs,** which look like little orange elephants from the side. There are also **marmosets** and **otters. Giraffes** and **African elephants** can be seen from a viewing platform as well as from on the safari drive. If you're on the drive, the elephants have their own spacious area next to the giraffes at the end of the drive. You can admire both while driving past or park and view them from a pedestrian viewing area.

Hopefully, that's whetted your appetite for animals, because now it's time to head back to the car park and load up your vehicle for the **safari drive,** which takes about an hour to navigate. First, a few rules: Pets aren't allowed, even in cars. If you've brought one, you can place it in one of the free kennels at the park base. Also, once you're out on the drive, don't get out of the car. *Ever.* If you break down, sound your horn and wait for the park patrol to come to your aid. Remember: out here, you're the one in a cage (your car), while the animals are roaming freely. But do take time and stop if something catches your eye. There are several lanes, and those behind you can pass if they want to move at a faster pace. At least that's the way it's supposed to work – in practice, animals in the middle of the road and visitors stopping dead without pulling over are common occurrences. And no littering or feeding animals. Some visitors have been known to put bananas on their roofs to attract baboons. It's not good for the animals or your car, and if the park patrol catches you, you're likely to be ejected. As for your transportation, choose your wheels carefully. Don't bring a convertible, and because your windows should remain closed, a car with air-conditioning will be welcome during warm months. And if you plan to brave the baboon route, don't bring your new Jaguar. A beaten-up car that you don't mind getting scratched, prodded and pummeled is a much wiser choice.

The 5-mi (8-km) route twists and turns and doubles back on itself. The map can give you a headache, so just follow the traffic and signs. The first animals you're likely to encounter are **bison, ostrich, forest buffalo** and the graceful **guanacos.** The **white rhinos** in this area have almost 100 ac (40 ha) to wander in. They seem to feel right at home and have become one of the best breeding groups of the species in Europe. Look at them carefully. In their native Africa, oxpecker birds eat bugs off their backs. Here, starlings and wagtails have taken up that role. You'll also pass **eland,** the largest species of antelope – a subspecies, the giant eland, was kept at the estate during the 1800s and is known as the Lord

Derby eland. The common elands here now, though, are of similar size. Both sexes have spiralled horns, and the males can reach 6 ft (1.8 m) at the shoulders and can weigh up to 2,200 lb (1,000 kg).

Rounding the corner takes you past a variety of antelope and deer species, eventually leading to the impressive **Cape buffalo.** These grazers, known as 'the black death', are extremely dangerous, with some reports claiming they're responsible for more human fatalities than any other African animal. They defend themselves against most predators – lions must work together to bring one down. For comic relief, glance to the right side of the road. The ostrich-like **rheas** look like a Lewis Carroll creation, particularly when they're in full gallop. Crossing a gated bridge takes you through several predator sections. You'll see rare **African wild dogs, tigers** and **lions.** The lion section is the best of any zoo or safari park in the UK. There is a multitude of lions, all habituated to cars in their kingdom and not at all reticent to come and check you out. This is where we had to carefully work our way past two lions sprawled in the middle of the road and another six on the shoulder, about three feet to our left. Here, more than anywhere else, it truly felt as if we were on an African safari.

After twisting through the area, you'll pass by **wallabies,** impressive **bongos** – antelopes with distinctive white stripes – and **nilgai,** the largest antelope species in India, which are considered sacred by local cultures. The route now doubles back by the hooved animals, but check to the right for the **wildebeest,** a strange antelope that looks like a cross between a buffalo and a horse. Plentiful in the wild, wildebeest are rare in UK zoos and safari parks. Knowsley has one of the largest herds in captivity.

Now comes the moment you've been anticipating (or dreading) – the **baboons.** If you're game, follow the well-signed route to the right. Others take the 'Safe Way', which will still allow you to watch the primates from a distance. Once you enter their domain, you'll be astounded by the sheer number of them – more than 125, in fact. They clearly have you outnumbered, so drive slowly – there have been baboon fatalities caused by drivers speeding through the area. Despite your caution, you may very well find the creatures jumping on your car. They seem to relish windscreen wipers – some visitors even remove them pre-emptively before taking the drive. They also can break off aerials and hood ornaments and dismantle rear tail lights. Don't enter with a car-top luggage carrier either. In 2009, the park created a video that went viral, showing how the baboons could break into a carrier in a matter of seconds and gleefully remove the luggage and clothes inside. The video was a set-up of sorts – the park purchased the carrier on eBay, and the clothes were donated by staff members – but there was nothing made-up about the baboons' systematic vandalism.

At the end of the ride, you will want to pull over and assess the damage to your car. Then you might consider picking up an 'I've Been Babooned' souvenir at the gift shop. You've earned it.

TOURING TIPS We recommend touring the pedestrian section of the park and seeing the sea-lion and birds-of-prey shows (both very worthwhile) before tackling the driving safari. We began our drive at about 3.30 p.m. on a summer Sunday, and there was very little traffic congestion. Remember to check your watch. The safari drive closes to entering vehicles at 4 p.m. during the summer, and 3 p.m. during winter months. In the main, the safari road is three lanes wide, and traffic flows better than at any other safari park we visited. If a dozen lionesses block the road, however, or if there are so many baboons on your car bonnet and windscreen that you can't see to drive, you may be stuck for a while. The site for the park doesn't resemble Africa, but the behaviour of the animals is totally consistent with what you'd experience on safari in Kenya or South Africa. This is in part due to the sheer number of animals. Where at most zoos or safari parks you'll find two to three representatives of each species, at Knowsley you'll encounter sizable herds.

Food options are nothing special, and they're pricey. There are plenty of picnic areas, including one next to Aerial Extreme where you can watch adventurous souls navigating the course, so feel free to pack a hamper. But do watch out for the peacocks and geese patrolling the area – they'll be on your lunch as quick as a baboon on a Honda.

Pleasure Beach Blackpool ★★★★★
525 Ocean Boulevard, South Shore, Blackpool, Lancashire FY4 1EZ
☎ **0870 444 5566; blackpoolpleasurebeach.com**

HOURS The park usually opens at 10 a.m. but can open as late as 11 a.m. during low season. Closing times vary from 5 p.m. low season to 8 p.m. high season. Open most days May–October, mainly weekends February–April and in November.

COST Pleasure Beach offers several admission ticket options. If you're going to experience more than half a dozen attractions, an 'unlimited ride' wristband is the best choice. Prices vary by season, but typical one-day rates range from £10 for adults during winter, to £25 per adult during summer. A two-day wristband is available and typically saves £5 off the cost of 2 one-day wristbands. Unlimited wristbands for children cost around £10 during winter, to £20 during summer. A two-day wristband for children also saves around £5 off the cost of 2 one-day wristbands.

Without wristbands, it's possible to pay cash for almost all of the attractions in the park. Most cost between £2 and £5 per person, per ride. A small number of attractions (mainly walk-through mazes) are free. Wristbands can also be bought through the Tesco Clubcard rewards scheme.

PARK-OPENING HOURS VERSUS RIDE-OPENING HOURS Pleasure Beach Blackpool often admits guests a full hour or more before all of the attractions begin operating. When this happens, a handful of attractions will run when the park opens (the Flying Machines is a safe bet), a few more attractions will open 30 minutes later, and most of the rest will open an hour later. A few stragglers, such as the monorail, may not begin operating until noon. Our touring plans take this staggered opening into account and direct you to the attractions most likely to be open as your morning unfolds.

GETTING THERE *By car:* Blackpool is a 4-hour drive from London, and around 3 hours from Nottingham or Birmingham. From the end of the M55 motorway (Junction 4), follow the Pleasure Beach signs. Six car parks surround the park: one each on the north, south, east and west sides of the park, plus one at the event arena at the corner of Bond Street at Watson Road, and one at the railway station (near the Big Blue Hotel). Car-park charges apply and vary based on the season. The railway and Bond Street locations are the easiest to get in and out of. *By rail:* Pleasure Beach Blackpool has a dedicated train station. It's about an 0.5-mi (1-km) walk from there to the park entrance, and you'll be able to see the park to your right as soon as you disembark from the train (**nationalrail.co.uk**). *By bus:* There's service from major cities around northwest England. (Route information: **transportdirect.info.**)

BLACKPOOL This is a complete resort city, with many large and small hotels fronting the sea and an astonishing number of bed-and-breakfasts, inns and small self-catering hotels lining the side streets that run perpendicular to the waterfront. The part of Blackpool most popular with tourists is the area between the North Pier and Pleasure Beach Blackpool theme park. Lodging properties facing the sea are on the east side of the coastal road, the **A584,** locally known as **The Promenade** and farther south as **Ocean Boulevard.** Along this stretch are three amusement piers: the aforementioned **North Pier,** the **Central Pier** and, close to Pleasure Beach, the **South Pier.** All three feature pay-as-you-go rides, souvenir shopping, food and beverage concessions and funfair sideshow games. In addition to Pleasure Beach Blackpool and the piers, there's lots to do. For more information see **visitblackpool.com.**

Broad pavements line the east side of the main road, and an even wider pedestrian promenade lies on the opposite side, paralleling the beach. A tram runs down the middle of the pedestrian promenade, charging varying but affordable fares depending on how far you ride. The tram runs every 8 minutes or so and makes commuting to the theme park from the side-street hotels quick and easy – just walk to the promenade and head for the closest tram stop.

OVERVIEW The 42-ac (17-ha) Pleasure Beach Blackpool was founded in 1896, making it one of the six oldest amusement parks in the United Kingdom. Some attractions, such as the Flying Machines, date back to the early days of the park and are still in operation. Others, such as Grand National and River Caves, influenced theme-park designers for years after their introduction. The park has been owned and operated by the Thompson family since the beginning of the twentieth century. Because the family continues to invest in new rides and the upkeep of classic attractions, Pleasure Beach is one of the UK's most popular tourist destinations. The family also operates the **Big Blue Hotel** (**bigbluehotel.com**), one of the nicest hotels in the area, on the amusement park's grounds.

Pleasure Beach Blackpool

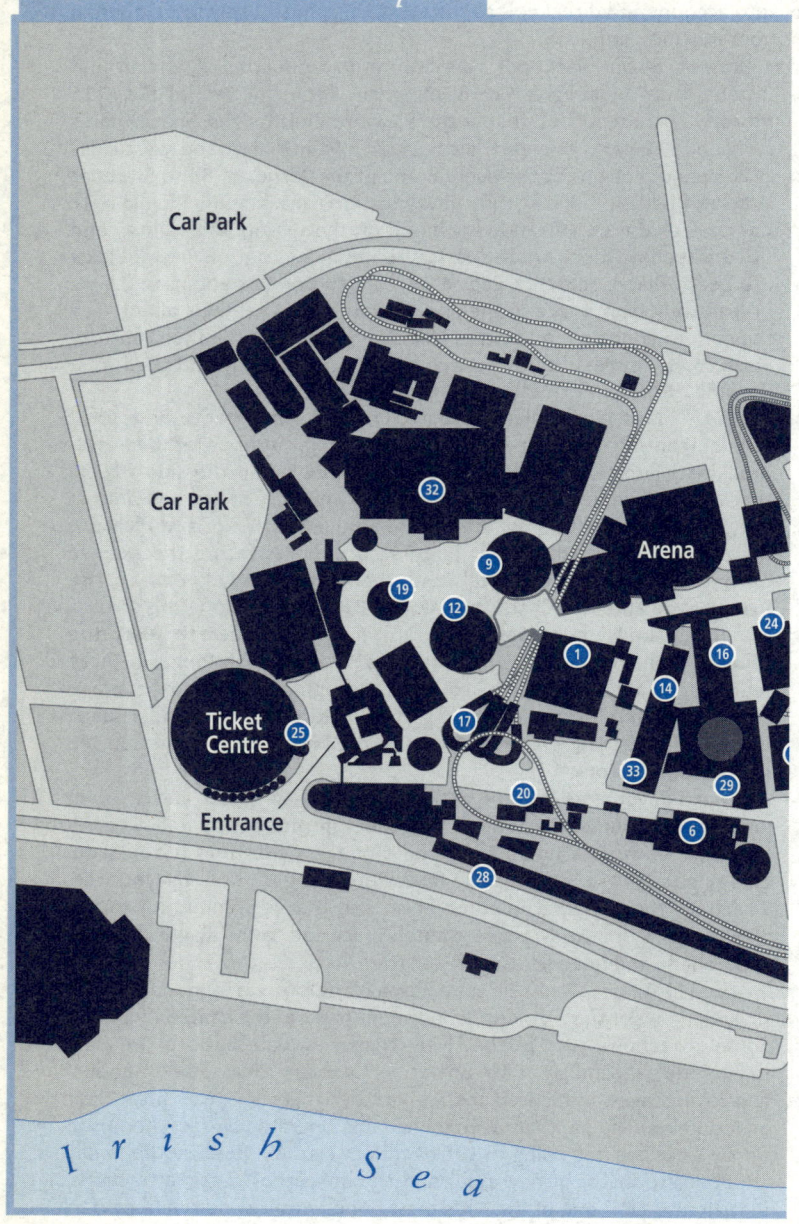

Car Park

Car Park

Arena

32
9
19
12
1
16
24
25
17
14
33
29
20
6
28

Ticket Centre

Entrance

Irish Sea

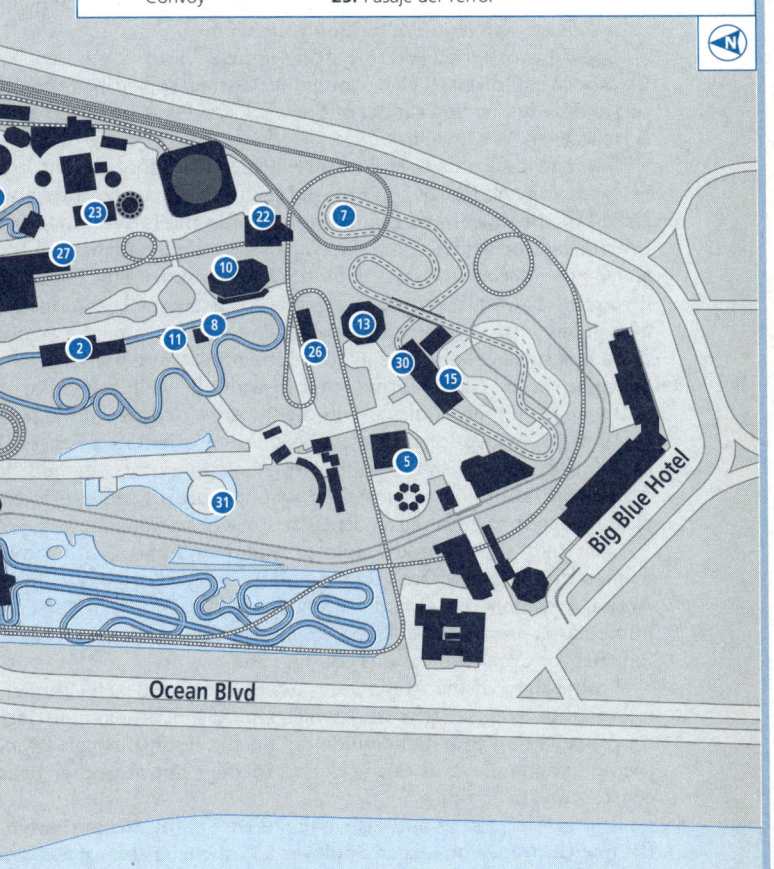

PLEASURE BEACH BLACKPOOL MAP

ATTRACTIONS
1. Alice Ride
2. Avalanche
3. Beaver Creek Children's Theme Park
4. The Big Dipper
5. Bling
6. Bowladrome
7. Chinese Puzzle Maze
8. Convoy Ride
9. Derby Racer
10. Dodgems
11. Eddie Stobart Convoy
12. Flying Machines
13. Gallopers
14. Ghost Train
15. Go Karts
16. Gold Mine
17. Grand National
18. Grand Prix
19. Ice Blast
20. Impossible
21. Infusion
22. Irn Bru Revolution
23. Magnus Mini Dodgems
24. Monorail
25. Pasaje del Terror*
26. Pepsi Max Big One
27. Pleasure Beach Express
28. Ripley's Believe It or Not! Museum*
29. River Caves
30. Steeeplechase
31. Swamp Buggies
32. Valhalla
33. Wild Mouse

Separate admission

> **NOT TO BE MISSED AT PLEASURE BEACH BLACKPOOL**
>
> | | | |
> |---|---|---|
> | Avalanche | Irn Bru Revolution | Steeplechase |
> | The Big Dipper | Pepsi Max Big One | Valhalla |
> | Infusion | River Caves | Wild Mouse |

Today, Pleasure Beach Blackpool operates approximately three dozen attractions, with a good mix of child-friendly and thrill rides. On summer days when the park is open at least 10 hours, it's possible to see almost everything in a single day. During the off-season, the park may be open for as little as 6 hours a day. Check the official website (**blackpoolpleasurebeach.com**) for opening times. That website also has on-board ride videos for most of the major attractions, allowing you to see exactly what you're getting yourself into.

Speaking of what you're getting yourself into . . . be aware that Blackpool could very well be the punk, Gothic, spiked-hair, henna, tattoo and body-piercing capital of the world. At Pleasure Beach every day is Halloween. We love it.

We spent five days at Pleasure Beach Blackpool during our first research visit and thoroughly enjoyed each day. Whatever the attractions lack in theme, they more than make up for in thrills. We found Pleasure Beach clean and well run, and the employees friendly and helpful. If you're anywhere in the area, it's worth a visit. We recommend the Big Blue Hotel if you're staying in Blackpool overnight. Arguably the best lodging in the area, it has large, stylish rooms (including suites for families), a good restaurant, a small yet effective gym with treadmills, and friendly staff.

GETTING ORIENTATED Most visitors enter Pleasure Beach Blackpool from the entrance off Ocean Boulevard, in the lower-left corner of the park.

With few exceptions, such as the children-orientated Beaver Creek, Pleasure Beach doesn't organise its attractions into themed 'lands'. Attractions are generally installed where there's adequate space and clearance, not to advance a particular story or narrative.

That said, there are a couple of useful landmarks within the park to help determine where you are and where you're going. One is the **Arena,** between the Grand National and Big Dipper roller coasters. Immediately beyond the Arena to your left is the **Beaver Creek** area. Past Beaver Creek are various coasters and mazes.

To the right of the Arena are most of Pleasure Beach's funfair-style indoor ghost trains (dark rides), which typically involve a small ride vehicle propelled along a metal guide rail on the floor, through an indoor, themed venue. Beyond this area and to the right are other headliner coasters and thrill rides.

PARK SERVICES Ticket sales and cash machines are at the **Ticket Centre,** near the main entrance on Ocean Boulevard. Pushchairs are not available for hire, but a limited number of wheelchairs are. Wheelchairs require a £20 deposit and £5 rental charge per day. Call in advance (☎ 0871 222 1234) to ensure availability.

Storage lockers are at the park entrance. Other lockers are on the left side of the Arena, inside the park near Derby Racer and also near Pepsi Max Big One.

Missing children can be found at the **Lost Child Centre** inside the park, on the corner opposite the right side of the Arena on the far-left corner of the Monorail. (If we have one complaint about Pleasure Beach, it's that it's really difficult to find things on the park map. Both the map and the map icons use the same colours, so sometimes it's like an in-park game of Where's Wally?)

DINING Pleasure Beach has its fair share of quick-service restaurants, cafés and coffee bars, so it's possible to sip and snack throughout your day. There's a large, efficient **Burger King** next to Bling in the lower right of the park, and the **Magnolia Café** (next to Ghost Train and near the Arena) is popular with anyone looking for fried chicken. Other restaurants serve pizza, Cornish pasties and fish-and-chips. We don't think any of the self-service restaurants stand out from the crowd, so our advice is to find something that appeals to everyone and has the shortest queue.

The Attractions

As noted earlier, with the exception of the Beaver Creek area, Pleasure Beach's attractions are not organised into themed 'lands'. Our attraction descriptions, therefore, follow the pattern of Pleasure Beach's theme-park map, which categorises attractions into three groups: 'White Knuckle Rides', 'Family Rides' and 'Beaver Creek Children's Theme Park'. First up are the 'White Knuckle Rides'.

Pepsi Max Big One ★★★★

What it is One of the fastest, tallest roller coasters you'll ever ride. **Scope and scale** Headliner. **Height requirement** 4'4" (1.32 m). **Fright potential** Scares everyone – every single person who's ever ridden or thought of riding, including motorists simply driving by the park. **When to go** As soon as it opens or in the last hour the park is open. **Authors' rating** Don't miss it. Also, take pictures and tell your friends; ★★★★. **Duration of ride** About 3 minutes. **Average wait in queue per 100 people ahead of you** About 8 minutes. **Loading speed** Moderate.

DESCRIPTION AND COMMENTS There's an old wartime saying that 'There are no atheists in foxholes.' And judging by the out-loud prayers we heard behind us as we went up the first hill, there are no atheists on the Big One either. The good news is that the Big One's first hill is so tall that when you decide it's time for you and God to talk, you're so close to heaven that you only have to whisper.

The Big One is Pleasure Beach's signature ride. Opened in 1994, it's one of the tallest, longest and fastest roller coasters in Europe. Unlike many modern coasters, which rely on loops, rolls and tight turns to deliver thrills, the Big One is all about speed and height. The initial trip up the first hill seems to take an eternity – enough for you to question several times what, exactly, you were thinking by getting on this ride –

and the initial drop of 200 ft (61 m) down at a tilt of over 60° propels you more than 70 mph (113 km/h).

Along with the first drop, the second hill provides spectacular views of the ocean and surrounding city (and probably, for that matter, a decent look at New York City), but we were too terrified to do anything but look straight ahead. The Big One's steel track runs more than half the length of the park, down Ocean Boulevard towards the Ticket Centre, before a turn brings you back the other way.

The Big One relies on a couple of interesting visual tricks to enhance the sensation of speed and height. If you keep your eyes open, notice that whenever your ride vehicle comes out of a tunnel, you're usually sent up a hill almost immediately after. By constraining your vision inside the dark tunnel, then providing an immediate contrast by pointing you skyward, the effect is to make the whole ride seem higher and more open.

The Big One is one of our favourite rides in the United Kingdom and the first thing we spoke about with friends back home when discussing Pleasure Beach. It's also a fantastic ride at night, especially during the city's autumn Illuminations festival. If we had one complaint about the Big One, it's that the ride is rough. Because of the speed, you get tossed from side to side quite a bit. It didn't keep us from riding again, though.

TOURING TIPS The fact that it's a scary ride keeps many people from riding. Still, our advice is to ride the Big One as soon as it opens or in the first hour the park is open. May open an hour after the park.

Avalanche ★★★½

What it is Alpine-themed sledge ride. **Scope and scale** Major attraction. **Height requirement** 3'8" (1.12 m). **Fright potential** The screams may frighten some small children, but the ride is relatively mild. **When to go** First hour the attraction is open or the last 2 hours the park is open. **Authors' rating** More fun than it looks; ★★★½. **Duration of ride** About 2 minutes. **Average wait in queue per 100 people ahead of you** About 11 minutes. **Loading speed** Moderate.

DESCRIPTION AND COMMENTS Set in a faux Alpine ski lodge, Avalanche is a snow-themed, wheeled sledge ride down an Olympic-style luge track. The ride's thrills come from its tight, high-banked turns. A novel feature is that the ride vehicles aren't on a track during much of the ride – they actually roll down on wheels. This makes your trajectory somewhat variable in the turns and means every ride is slightly different. We liked Avalanche quite a bit. Not enough to buy lederhosen or a goofy green cap, but still, a lot.

We don't think there's much in Avalanche to frighten children who are tall enough to ride. You'll hear screams from people already on the ride, but those are screams of happiness, not terror.

TOURING TIPS Almost smack-dab in the middle of the grounds, Avalanche is often overlooked by guests running to the coasters on the perimeter of the park. If you're anywhere near it midday, have a quick check at the waiting times to see if it's still undiscovered. May open an hour after the park.

Bling ★★★

What it is Spinning-arm ride. **Scope and scale** Major attraction. **Height requirement** 4' (1.22 m) **Fright potential** Frightens children and adults alike. **When to go** First hour the attraction is open or the last 2 hours the park is open. **Authors' rating** Like riding an out-of-control Cuisinart; ★★★. **Duration of ride** About 2½ minutes. **Average wait in queue per 100 people ahead of you** About 17 minutes. **Loading speed** Slow.

DESCRIPTION AND COMMENTS Very similar to Samurai at Thorpe Park. If you've ever wondered what it's like for cake batter to get spun around on the end of an electric mixer, Bling will give you an idea.

Six groups of five riders each sit in seats that extend starfish-like from a large metal arm. Once everyone is strapped in, each row of seats rotates you head-over-feet on its central axis, while all six rows of seats spin in a giant circle. And as that's going on, the metal arm swings in an arc as well. It's sort of like a three-dimensional version of a classic funfair 'spinning teacup' attraction.

Velocity builds up fairly fast, and you can go through a number of revolutions in a short amount of time. This isn't for the faint of heart or anyone who's just had lunch and wants to keep it.

TOURING TIPS Situated near the back of the park, Bling doesn't draw huge crowds. If long queues develop, it's almost certainly because of the ride's relatively-low capacity, not a surge of sudden interest from park guests. We recommend visiting Bling after completing the headliner attractions. May open 30 minutes after the park.

The Big Dipper ★★

What it is Wooden roller coaster. **Scope and scale** Major attraction. **Height requirement** 3'10" (1.17 m). **Fright potential** Not really frightening, but the ride can be painful. **When to go** First hour the attraction is open or the last 2 hours the park is open. **Authors' rating** Bone-jarring and violent; ★★. **Duration of ride** About 3 minutes. **Average wait in queue per 100 people ahead of you** About 21 minutes; assumes 2 trains running. **Loading speed** Moderate.

DESCRIPTION AND COMMENTS A classic wooden roller coaster with nice hills and decent speed, and no loops and inversions. If this were a smooth, modern steel roller coaster, the Big Dipper would be a fun attraction for most of the family. Because of its old wooden track, however, the ride is so harsh as to be completely unpleasant. We were frankly amazed that the world record for roller-coaster-riding (2,000 hours) was set on this thing. We wouldn't want to ride it twice.

TOURING TIPS May open 30 minutes after the park itself. Because of this, and the Big Dipper's low hourly capacity, you may want to try riding as soon as it opens. Otherwise, try after all the headliners or during mealtimes.

Grand National ★★★

What it is Wooden side-by-side roller coasters. **Scope and scale** Major attraction. **Height requirement** 3'10" (1.17 m). **Fright potential** Not really frightening, but the ride can be painful. **When to go** First 2 hours the attraction is open or the last 2 hours the park is open. **Authors' rating** Great track layout but a *very* rough ride; ★★★. **Duration of ride** About 2½ minutes. **Average wait in queue per 100 people ahead of you** About 11 minutes; assumes 4 trains running (2 per track). **Loading speed** Slow.

DESCRIPTION AND COMMENTS Another classic wooden roller coaster with nice hills and decent speed, and no loops or inversions. The novelty of Grand National is that it features two side-by-side tracks and runs one train on each track simultaneously. Both trains launch at the same time and 'race' through the track.

As with the Big Dipper, Grand National is an older wooden coaster. And like Big Dipper, this results in an extremely-rough ride, with guests being shaken from side to side for the duration. While there are no loops or inversions on the track layout, and there are some nice views from the tops of the hills, it's an unpleasant experience overall.

*If you decide to ride both Grand National and Big Dipper, send us an email (**unofficialguides@menasharidge.com**) to let us know whether you did them right after each other or whether you waited in between. We'd like to know whether riding these coasters consecutively is worse than spacing them out.*

TOURING TIPS Because it's got two trains running simultaneously, Grand National is one of the more efficient attractions in the park. It's also not a headliner, so you should be able to avoid long waits either in the morning or late at night.

If you elect not to ride but are waiting for a riding member of your party to exit, be aware that riders exit on the opposite side of the ride from where they boarded. If you board on the right side you'll exit on the left side, and vice versa.

Ice Blast ★★½

What it is Vertical ascent and free-fall. **Scope and scale** Minor attraction. **Height requirement** 4'4" (1.32 m). **Fright potential** Frightens children and adults alike. **When to go** First 2 hours the attraction is open or the last 2 hours the park is open. **Authors' rating** Good for would-be astronauts in training; ★★½. **Duration of ride** About 50 seconds. **Average wait in queue per 100 people ahead of you** About 18 minutes; assumes all seats occupied for each ride. **Loading speed** Moderate.

DESCRIPTION AND COMMENTS Ice Blast's ride structure consists of a vertical square tower to which 16 seats are attached, 4 per side, around each side of the tower. Once riders are strapped in, they're launched vertically to a height of 180 ft (55 m), before free-falling back most of the way down. If you've ever wanted to know what it's like for a circus performer to be shot out of a cannon, this may be the closest you'll get.

TOURING TIPS May open 30 minutes after the park itself. Because it's almost in front of the park's main entrance, Ice Blast tends to draw more visitors around late morning and lunchtime. If the wait is more than 20 minutes, try back around dinnertime or in the last 2 hours the park is open.

Infusion ★★★½

What it is Suspended looping roller coaster. **Scope and scale** Headliner. **Height requirement** 4'4" (1.32 m). **Fright potential** Frightens children and adults alike. **When to go** First hour the attraction is open or the last 2 hours the park is open. **Authors' rating** Lots of fun and not to be missed; ★★★½. **Duration of ride** About 1½ minutes. **Average wait in queue per 100 people ahead of you** About 8 minutes; assumes 2 trains operating. **Loading speed** Moderate.

DESCRIPTION AND COMMENTS Infusion is one of the park's headliner roller coasters. A modern steel track and padded shoulder harnesses mean Infusion's ride is smoother and much more fun than those of Pleasure Beach's wooden coasters.

Infusion, with ride vehicles suspended from above, zips through five loops and two rolls. Because your legs are allowed to swing from the seats, the overall sensation of speed and gravity-force is enhanced, making the ride feel more extreme than it is. Another good design feature is that the ride track snakes past the Big One's, with high-speed dips and turns near the ground, over water and through a forest of steel ride-support beams. Lots of stuff goes whizzing by you in the 90 seconds you're on-board.

TOURING TIPS May open an hour after the park itself. Infusion is one of the most efficient attractions in the park; we'd recommend trying it after Big One and some of the wooden coasters.

Irn Bru Revolution ★★½

What it is Looping roller coaster. **Scope and scale** Minor attraction. **Height requirement** 4'3" (1.3 m). **Fright potential** Frightens some small children. **When to go** Anytime. **Authors' rating** Looks more intimidating than it is; ★★½. **Duration of ride** About 1 minute. **Average wait in queue per 100 people ahead of you** About 14 minutes; assumes all seats filled for each ride. **Loading speed** Moderate.

DESCRIPTION AND COMMENTS Revolution is the most straightforward of roller coasters. You're launched in a straight line towards the track's single loop. After that, you coast to a stop and are re-launched, backwards, in a straight line through the same loop.

The appeal of the ride is that the track is suspended fairly high off the ground, affording a good view of the area.

TOURING TIPS May open an hour after the park itself. Situated in a back corner of the park, Revolution doesn't usually get too crowded until afternoon.

Valhalla ★★★½

What it is Indoor boat and flume ride. **Scope and scale** Headliner. **Height requirement** 3'10" (1.17 m). **Fright potential** The darkness and fire frighten many small children. **When to go** Anytime. **Authors' rating** The UK's best water-flume ride; ★★★½. **Duration of ride** About 6½ minutes. **Average wait in queue per 100 people ahead of you** About 12 minutes; assumes 8 boats operating. **Loading speed** Fast.

DESCRIPTION AND COMMENTS A Viking-themed indoor boat ride, Valhalla, named after the concept of the Viking afterlife, is one of the largest indoor boat rides in the world. Riders float through scenes festooned with icons of Norse mythology, including traps, obstacles and other dangers of life after death. Special effects include enough fire to spit-roast a pig, as well as simulated lightning and thunder. The darkness and the fire are the big draws in the attraction – the story is secondary.

Besides the effects there are several drops inside the ride, and most riders get quite wet. Ponchos are sold from a booth at the outside queuing area.

TOURING TIPS May open an hour after the park itself. Valhalla doesn't get crowded until a few hours after the park is open.

Wild Mouse ★★½

What it is Small wooden roller coaster. **Scope and scale** Minor attraction. **Height requirement** 4'4" (1.32 m). **Fright potential** Not really frightening. **When to go** As soon as the ride opens or in the last hour the park is open. **Authors' rating** Worth riding once just for the historical value; ★★½. **Duration of ride** About 1½ minutes. **Average wait in queue per 100 people ahead of you** About 25 minutes; assumes 4 ride vehicles operating, 2 people per vehicle. **Loading speed** Slow.

DESCRIPTION AND COMMENTS A small wooden roller coaster. You're seated in what can best be described as a wooden bathtub on wheels, then propelled around a twisting hill- and dip-filled track. Because of the ride vehicles' design and seating, it's difficult for riders to see down, meaning some of the ride's dips and turns come as complete surprises.

The turns aren't banked, so the lateral forces make the ride pretty rough; there's no scenery to speak of; and there's no story or theme at all. The main reason to ride Wild Mouse is that it is one of the best examples of its kind in the world, and the genre served as the inspiration for other world-famous roller coasters, such as Disney's Space Mountains.

TOURING TIPS Opens 30 minutes after the park itself. Wild Mouse has one of the smallest capacities of any Pleasure Beach attraction. While it's not very popular, long queues can still develop even on days of moderate attendance. Visit after you've got through the park's headliners and major attractions.

Family Rides

Blackpool has 15 of these, described following.

Alice Ride ★★★½

What it is Indoor dark ride. **Scope and scale** Minor attraction. **Height requirement** None. **Fright potential** Nothing especially frightening, but some of the scenes are very dark. **When to go** As soon as the attraction opens. **Authors' rating** One of Pleasure Beach's best indoor rides; ★★★½. **Duration of ride** About 4 minutes. **Average wait in queue per 100 people ahead of you** About 23 minutes; assumes 6 ride vehicles operating. **Loading speed** Slow.

DESCRIPTION AND COMMENTS Pleasure Beach's Alice Ride is a ride-through adaptation of the Lewis Carroll novel. Every major scene, from Alice going through the rabbit hole, to the mad tea party, to the Queen's croquet and more, is reproduced here. Each is remarkably detailed, with animatronic characters in most and other special effects that enhance the story.

If you visit other Pleasure Beach dark rides such as Ghost Train first, you may be tempted to skip the Alice Ride as more of the same. Don't do this; the Alice Ride is one of the best child-friendly rides in the park.

TOURING TIPS As with Wild Mouse, Alice develops long queues because of its low capacity, not because of overwhelming popularity. If you've got small children, make this one of your first stops in the morning.

Chinese Puzzle Maze ★★

What it is Outdoor garden maze. **Scope and scale** Minor attraction. **Height requirement** None. **Fright potential** None. **When to go** Anytime. **Authors' rating** My kingdom for a hedge clipper! ★★. **Duration of ride** Allow 20 minutes.

DESCRIPTION AND COMMENTS One of the few no-cost attractions in the park, the Chinese Puzzle Maze is an elaborate walk-through garden attraction with high hedges and a smattering of Chinese artefacts scattered around the grounds. The maze's hedges are well over 6 ft (2 m) tall, making it impossible to get a view of the entire maze.

We spent a good 20 minutes wandering through the maze. Our first two pieces of advice are to use the toilets before you enter, and to make sure you've got a drink or a snack first. It can easily take half an hour or more to get through. Finally, if you've got small children, make sure they don't run ahead of you. It's almost as difficult to find separated family members as it is to find your way through the maze.

TOURING TIPS The maze is rarely crowded. Visit anytime.

Derby Racer ★★½

What it is Warp-speed carousel. **Scope and scale** Minor attraction. **Height requirement** 4'4" (1.32 m). **Fright potential** None. **When to go** Anytime. **Authors' rating** Very pretty; ★★½. **Duration of ride** About 4½ minutes. **Average wait in queue per 100 people ahead of you** About 15 minutes; assumes all ride vehicles used for each cycle. **Loading speed** Slow.

DESCRIPTION AND COMMENTS A pretty, detailed indoor merry-go-round with a horse-racing theme. The horses are larger than on most similar rides, but the real kicker is how fast the platform revolves around the central axis. Not a carousel for tots. Very well done.

TOURING TIPS Usually opens when the park opens. Tour anytime.

Dodgems ★★½

What it is Indoor bumper cars. **Scope and scale** Minor attraction. **Height requirement** 4' (1.22 m). **Fright potential** None. **When to go** Anytime. **Authors' rating** Who doesn't love the smell of burnt electronics? ★★½. **Duration of ride** About 3 minutes. **Average wait in queue per 100 people ahead of you** About 13 minutes; assumes all ride vehicles used for each cycle. **Loading speed** Slow.

DESCRIPTION AND COMMENTS Typical funfair-style bumper cars, with a bit more space than most. This allows drivers to get up quite a bit of speed. During our observations, we didn't see anyone leave with anything less than a huge grin on their face.

TOURING TIPS Usually opens an hour after the park itself. Can handle more people per hour than most Pleasure Beach attractions. Good to see during mid-afternoon, when the headliner attractions are filled.

Eddie Stobart Convoy ★★

What it is Small lorries driving around a track in the ground. **Scope and scale** Minor attraction. **Height requirement** 4' (1.22 m). **Fright potential** None. **When to go** Just after lunch or try around dinnertime. **Authors' rating** Bring your trucker cap; ★★. **Duration of ride** About 3 minutes. **Average wait in queue per 100 people ahead of you** About 30 minutes; assumes all ride vehicles used for each cycle. **Loading speed** Slow.

DESCRIPTION AND COMMENTS Children get the chance to drive miniature 18-wheelers around a road course. The lorries are guided by a small track in the ground, so it doesn't matter how the children steer. Note that adults ride in the rear two seats of the four-seat lorries. Now would be a good time to practise your back-seat-driving skills.

TOURING TIPS Don't be deceived by a short queue for the Convoy. The attraction struggles to process more than 200 people per hour. Every 20 people ahead of you means at least 6 minutes' wait, and there's not a lot of shade nearby to keep you or your family cool.

Flying Machines ★★½

What it is Rocket ships revolving around a central axis, suspended from long chains. **Scope and scale** Minor attraction. **Height requirement** None. **Fright potential** Not for those with a fear of heights, fear of flying or motion sickness. **When to go** First hour the park is open, during mealtimes or in the last hour the park is open. **Authors' rating** A funfair-style classic; ★★½. **Duration of ride** About 11 minutes. **Average wait in queue per 100 people ahead of you** About 19 minutes; assumes all ride vehicles filled for each cycle. **Loading speed** Slow.

DESCRIPTION AND COMMENTS If you are prone to any of the warnings above, this ride (a) spins round and round; (b) goes much faster than you'd think; and (c) goes much higher than it looks. That being said, the views at night are very pretty.

TOURING TIPS Usually opens first thing in the morning with the rest of the park. Flying Machines is directly in front of the main entrance, so it draws a crowd as soon as people are let into the park. If you see a queue of more than a hundred people, try again during lunch or dinnertime.

Gallopers ★★½

What it is Traditional horse-themed merry-go-round. **Scope and scale** Minor attraction. **Height requirement** None. **Fright potential** None. **When to go** Anytime. **Authors' rating** Colourful and sparkling with lights; ★★½. **Duration of ride** About 3 minutes. **Average wait in queue per 100 people ahead of you** About 7 minutes; assumes all seats filled for each cycle. **Loading speed** Moderate.

DESCRIPTION AND COMMENTS Another traditional horse-themed merry-go-round and similar to the faster Derby Racer on the other side of the park. The main difference between the two, other than speed, is the colour scheme, with Gallopers done in festive red, yellow, white and blue. Also, each horse can accommodate one child and one adult, making it a wonderful shared experience.

TOURING TIPS May open up to 2 hours later than the park itself. Situated in the back of the park between some of the major thrill rides, and well away from other child-friendly attractions, Gallopers rarely has long queues.

Ghost Train ★★½

What it is Ride-through haunted house. **Scope and scale** Minor attraction. **Height requirement** None. **Fright potential** The ghosts, skeletons and other sights frighten many small children. **When to go** As soon as the attraction opens or the last hour the park is open. **Authors' rating** Not worth more than a few minutes' wait; ★★½. **Duration of ride** About 4 minutes. **Average wait in queue per 100 people ahead of you** About 19 minutes; assumes 12 ride vehicles operating. **Loading speed** Slow.

DESCRIPTION AND COMMENTS Situated in the left-centre of the park across from the Arena, Ghost Town is an expanded ride-through version of a typical funfair haunted house. Each two-person ride vehicle is guided from room to room through the house, past the usual sights of skeletons, zombies, decaying bodies, devils, giant spiders and the like. There are some tight turns and a couple of dips in the track, but the focus is on the sights instead of the ride.

The name of the attraction and the fact that many gruesome scenes are visible from the outdoor queue means that many small children are simply too frightened to try the ride. For this reason, we didn't see any small children getting off the ride who were obviously traumatised from the scenes inside. Even so, this isn't an attraction we'd recommend for young children.

TOURING TIPS May open 30 minutes later than the park itself. See after the Alice Ride and the attractions in the Beaver Creek area.

Grand Prix ★★½

What it is Drive-'em-yourself miniature cars. **Scope and scale** Minor attraction. **Height requirement** 4' (1.22 m). **Fright potential** None. **When to go** As soon as it opens or in the last hour the park is open. **Authors' rating** May be faster to actually teach kids how to drive; ★★½. **Duration of ride** About 5 minutes. **Average wait in queue per 100 people ahead of you** About 43 minutes; assumes 7 cars operating. **Loading speed** Slow.

DESCRIPTION AND COMMENTS Near the centre of the park, Grand Prix's colourful open cars draw a lot of attention as they putter slowly down and back on their track. And unlike most rides of this genre, Pleasure Beach's Grand Prix doesn't just run on flat terrain – a spiral 2-storey faux parking garage serves as the beginning and end of each journey.

Grand Prix's track runs the length of the Avalanche's track, on the same piece of land, which provides some nice scenery for drivers. There are enough turns and twists to make the drive interesting for older passengers, too, even if you're travelling at 3 mph (5 km/h) on a guided track.

TOURING TIPS May open 30 minutes later than the park itself. Has one of the smallest capacities of any attraction in the park, so ride early or late in the day to avoid crowds.

Impossible ★★½

What it is Walk-through display of optical illusions and other oddities. **Scope and scale** Diversion. **Height requirement** 4' (1.22 m). **Fright potential** None. **When to go** First 2 hours the park is open. **Authors' rating** Interesting but easily crowded; ★★½. **Duration of experience** Allow 20–30 minutes. **Average wait in queue per 100 people ahead of you** About 20 minutes.

DESCRIPTION AND COMMENTS A staple of funfairs around the world, Impossible presents a collection of strange facts, optical illusions and other curiosities in a series of small walk-through rooms. Many of the exhibits are hands-on, allowing children to see how the effects actually work. Because it's a self-guided tour, however, long queues and traffic jams can appear out of nowhere, turning your little area into a hot, crowded mess. Fortunately, there's an exit about halfway through the tour.

TOURING TIPS May open an hour or more later than the park itself. If you see any sort of queue forming outside the attraction, skip it. By the time queues form outside, the inside of the attraction is gridlocked.

Magnus Mini Dodgems ★★½

What it is Miniature bumper cars for small children. **Scope and scale** Minor attraction. **Height requirement** None. **Fright potential** None. **When to go** First

2 hours the park is open. **Authors' rating** Rubber baby buggy bumpers! ★★½. **Duration of ride** Around 2 minutes. **Average wait in queue per 100 people ahead of you** About 40 minutes; assumes 10 cars operating. **Loading speed** Slow.

> **DESCRIPTION AND COMMENTS** A miniature version of the adult-sized Dodgems also found in the park, Mini Dodgems is designed for children. In fact, many adults simply won't fit into the cars. Naturally, the cars go slower than their larger counterparts. Kids love them.
>
> **TOURING TIPS** May open an hour later than the park itself. One of the lowest-capacity attractions in the park. Handles 10 children at a time, and the average ride takes around 4 minutes, including loading and unloading. Thus, if you see 20 people in the queue ahead of you, expect a total wait of around 8 minutes.

Monorail ★★½

What it is Elevated train ride around the perimeter of the park. **Scope and scale** Minor attraction. **Height requirement** None. **Fright potential** None. **When to go** Anytime. **Authors' rating** Scenic and relaxing; ★★½. **Duration of ride** Around 10 minutes. **Average wait in queue per 100 people ahead of you** About 28 minutes; assumes all monorail cars used for each trip. **Loading speed** Slow.

> **DESCRIPTION AND COMMENTS** A scenic tour around the entire park and beyond, the Monorail is a relaxing way to take a break during a busy day. The tour takes you past most of the major attractions in the park, and the elevated track means you get to see quite a bit of the town around the park. Especially good at night, when the promenade is lit.
>
> **TOURING TIPS** May open up to 2 hours later than the park itself and close an hour earlier. One of the lowest-capacity attractions in the park, as it takes a long time to load people into the small monorail cars. Use the toilets before queuing, and bring a drink.

Pleasure Beach Express ★★½

What it is Train ride around the perimeter of the park. **Scope and scale** Minor attraction. **Height requirement** None. **Fright potential** None. **When to go** Anytime. **Authors' rating** Another scenic and relaxing tour of the park; ★★½. **Duration of ride** About 10 minutes. **Average wait in queue per 100 people ahead of you** About 33 minutes; assumes all train cars used for each trip. **Loading speed** Slow.

> **DESCRIPTION AND COMMENTS** Similar to the monorail, the Pleasure Beach Express is a scenic tour around the entire park and beyond. And, as with the monorail, the Express is a relaxing way to take a break during a busy day.
>
> **TOURING TIPS** May open up to 2 hours later than the park itself. Also like the Monorail in that it's one of the lowest-capacity attractions in the park. We think the Monorail is a better experience, and unless you're desperate to see everything in the park, there's no reason to ride both. Use the toilets before getting in the queue, and bring a drink.

River Caves ★★★½

What it is Dark boat ride. **Scope and scale** Minor attraction. **Height requirement** None. **Fright potential** Other than some dark sections, nothing really frightening. **When to go** Anytime. **Authors' rating** One of the best attractions in the park; ★★★½. **Duration of ride** About 6 minutes. **Average wait in queue per 100 people ahead of you** About 11 minutes; assumes 10 boats operating. **Loading speed** Fast.

DESCRIPTION AND COMMENTS A hidden gem buried near the middle of the park, River Caves is a remarkably-well-detailed long boat ride past scenes depicting exotic locations from around the world and throughout history. Each 'cave' holds a different scene, from Egypt to Africa to dinosaurs. River Caves is a remarkably-imaginative ride now more than a century old. Its influence on other boat-themed attractions around the world extends to Disney's Pirates of the Caribbean and It's a Small World, among others.

There's a small outdoor drop at the end of the ride. It's not scary, but it does offer the opportunity for those in the front seat to get soaking wet.

TOURING TIPS May open up to 90 minutes later than the park itself and close up to 2 hours earlier. However, River Caves can handle crowds as well as almost any other attraction in the park. Even if the indoor queue is completely full, your wait to board shouldn't exceed 15 minutes.

Steeplechase ★★★½

What it is High-speed race aboard a track-guided horse. **Scope and scale** Major attraction. **Height requirement** 4'2" (1.27 m). **Fright potential** Scares children and adults alike. **When to go** Anytime. **Authors' rating** Insane. Also a lot of fun; ★★★½. **Duration of ride** About 1½ minutes. **Average wait in queue per 100 people ahead of you** About 8 minutes; assumes 12 horses operating. **Loading speed** Fast.

DESCRIPTION AND COMMENTS Steeplechase is essentially a roller-coaster ride for which the ride vehicles are horses similar to the ones seen on Pleasure Beach's merry-go-rounds.

One rider boards each horse, which rolls around an elevated steel track through the back corner of the park and past the Big Blue Hotel. The track includes a number of hills, dips and tight turns, and the whole experience is one of a fast ride through the countryside.

We happened to be staying at the Big Blue Hotel in a room that faced the Steeplechase track, and the first time riders whizzed by us we thought we were seeing things. Other than a safety belt, there is virtually nothing to keep you from falling off the horse and the elevated track as you speed along at up to 30 mph (48 km/h). In the US, this kind of attraction would have been banned or sued out of existence decades ago. We're pleasantly surprised to see something like this survive in the UK.

TOURING TIPS May open up to an hour later than the park itself. Because it loads and unloads riders quickly, Steeplechase is one of the most efficient attractions in the park.

Beaver Creek Children's Theme Park

Beaver Creek is a small area in Pleasure Beach Blackpool dedicated exclusively to rides for small children. Most of these are variations on spinning carousel rides, indoor train rides and the like, although there is a small roller coaster and water-flume ride.

Beaver Creek is scheduled for a major refurbishment in 2011 that will convert most of the attractions into SpongeBob SquarePants–themed rides. If you've not seen this popular (and hilarious) kids' programme, ask your children for a quick explanation. We don't expect any of the attractions to be altered significantly from a ride-experience or mechanical perspective.

Thor's Turnpike ★★

What it is Miniature cars driving around a small track. **Scope and scale** Minor attraction. **Height requirement** None. **Fright potential** None. **When to go** As soon as the attraction opens, or not at all. **Authors' rating** The Grand Prix ride for little ones; ★★. **Duration of ride** About 3½ minutes. **Average wait in queue per 100 people ahead of you** About 55 minutes; assumes 5 cars operating. **Loading speed** Slow.

DESCRIPTION AND COMMENTS Children drive small cars around a paved track. A guide rail on the ground keeps the cars going straight and provides the illusion that the kids are steering.

Thor's Turnpike has the smallest hourly capacity of any attraction in any major UK theme park. On a bad day it would struggle to handle 100 children per hour. If you see more than a handful of people queuing, skip the attraction for something else.

TOURING TIPS May open up to an hour later than the park itself and close up to an hour earlier. If you see more than a handful of people in the queue, do whatever you can to distract your children from riding.

Magic Mountain ★★

What it is Indoor train ride around storybook scenes. **Scope and scale** Minor attraction. **Height requirement** None. **Fright potential** None. **When to go** Anytime. **Authors' rating** Colourful and pleasant; ★★. **Duration of ride** About 4 minutes. **Average wait in queue per 100 people ahead of you** About 41 minutes; assumes all train seats occupied for each ride. **Loading speed** Slow.

DESCRIPTION AND COMMENTS Miniature pirate ships spin around a small carousel. There's a small hill in the track, so the ships go gently up and down as they spin around in the circle. Although there are many similar attractions in the park, the kids coming off this one were all smiles.

TOURING TIPS May open up to 30 minutes later than the park.

Helicopters ★½

What it is Aviation-themed merry-go-round. **Scope and scale** Minor attraction. **Height requirement** None. **Fright potential** None. **When to go** As soon as it opens. **Authors' rating** Nothing special; ★½. **Duration of ride** About 3 minutes. **Average wait in queue per 100 people ahead of you** About 31 minutes; assumes all seats occupied for each ride. **Loading speed** Slow.

DESCRIPTION AND COMMENTS Miniature helicopters spin around a small carousel. There are half a dozen similar attractions within spitting distance.

TOURING TIPS May open up to an hour later than the park and close an hour earlier. Located behind the Beaver Creek Log Flume, so it gets missed by a fair number of people.

Fruit Shoot The Ride ½

What it is Small vertical bouncing ride. **Scope and scale** Minor attraction. **Height requirement** None. **Fright potential** None. **When to go** As soon as it opens. **Authors' rating** Ho-hum; ½. **Duration of ride** About 30 seconds. **Average wait in queue per 100 people ahead of you** About 21 minutes; assumes all 10 seats occupied for each ride. **Loading speed** Slow.

DESCRIPTION AND COMMENTS Similar to Frog Hopper at Alton Towers, Fruit Shoot is essentially a set of bucket seats attached to a horizontal rail. The seats are hoisted to the top of a short vertical tower, then lowered in short bouncing bursts back to the ground. A staple of amusement parks and funfairs everywhere.

TOURING TIPS May open up to 30 minutes later than the park and close an hour earlier.

Beaver Creek Log Flume ★½

What it is Small outdoor flume ride. **Scope and scale** Minor attraction. **Height requirement** None. **Fright potential** None. **When to go** As soon as it opens. **Authors' rating** An excuse to get very, very wet; ★½. **Duration of ride** About 3½ minutes. **Average wait in queue per 100 people ahead of you** About 20 minutes; assumes 5 boats running. **Loading speed** Slow.

DESCRIPTION AND COMMENTS A small outdoor log-flume ride. Theming and scenery are minimal, and there's really only one hill and drop in the entire short attraction. Shouldn't frighten children unless they're deathly afraid of baths. Note that much of the queue is outdoors and can get quite warm during summer.

TOURING TIPS May open up to an hour later than the park and close an hour earlier.

Tetley Tea Cup Ride ★½

What it is Spinning-teacup ride. **Scope and scale** Minor attraction. **Height requirement** None. **Fright potential** None. **When to go** As soon as it opens.

Authors' rating You'll need a drink when you're done; ★½. **Duration of ride** About 2 minutes. **Average wait in queue per 100 people ahead of you** About 17 minutes; assumes 6 cups running. **Loading speed** Slow.

DESCRIPTION AND COMMENTS Another funfair staple in which you're seated in oversized teacups that spin in circles, with the whole attraction spinning in another, larger circle. The interesting variation at Pleasure Beach is that the Tea Cup Ride's cups move in a figure-of-eight pattern, not circles. You'll be nauseated anyway, but it's something to ponder as you try not to black out.

TOURING TIPS May open up to an hour later than the park and close an hour earlier.

Veteran Carousel ★½

What it is Small merry-go-round. **Scope and scale** Minor attraction. **Height requirement** None. **Fright potential** None. **When to go** As soon as it opens. **Authors' rating** Hey, another carousel! ★½. **Duration of ride** About 2 minutes. **Average wait in queue per 100 people ahead of you** About 16 minutes; assumes all 30 seats filled. **Loading speed** Slow.

DESCRIPTION AND COMMENTS Another merry-go-round, in case you haven't had your fill.

TOURING TIPS May open up to an hour later than the park and close an hour earlier.

Zipper Dipper ★★½

What it is Small roller coaster for children. **Scope and scale** Minor attraction. **Height requirement** None. **Fright potential** None. **When to go** First or last 2 hours the attraction is open. **Authors' rating** The most fun in this area; ★★½. **Duration of ride** About 1 minute. **Average wait in queue per 100 people ahead of you** About 13 minutes; assumes all 20 seats filled each ride. **Loading speed** Slow.

DESCRIPTION AND COMMENTS A small wooden roller coaster designed especially for small children. The ride is mild, with a few gentle hills, dips and turns. Zipper Dipper is actually a nice break for adults from the vastly more harsh coasters in the rest of the park, too.

TOURING TIPS May open up to an hour later than the park and close an hour earlier.

Lunar Carousel ★½

What it is Merry-go-round. **Scope and scale** Minor attraction. **Height requirement** None. **Fright potential** None. **When to go** Anytime. **Authors' rating** In case you missed any of the others; ★½. **Duration of ride** About 2 minutes. **Average wait in queue per 100 people ahead of you** About 6 minutes; assumes all 72 seats filled each ride. **Loading speed** Slow.

DESCRIPTION AND COMMENTS Another carousel, this one with some space-themed vehicles. It handles four times as many riders per hour as Helicopters, and more than twice as many as the Veteran Carousel.

TOURING TIPS May open up to an hour later than the park and close an hour earlier.

Pleasure Beach Blackpool Touring Plans

We've included touring plans for parents with small children, as well as plans for adults and teens. Even when the park is open for 8 or 9 hours, it's fairly straightforward for both groups to see most of the park in a single day.

One-Day Touring Plan for Parents with Small Children

1. The night before your visit, check **blackpoolpleasurebeach.com** for park hours and weather.
2. Arrive at the park entrance 30 minutes prior to official opening. If possible, have your admission in hand before you arrive. Otherwise, arrive 15 minutes earlier and send one member of your party to obtain admission at the Ticket Centre.
3. As soon as the park opens, experience the Flying Machines near the main park entrance.
4. Ride Derby Racer, behind Flying Machines.
5. Walk to the Beaver Creek area and experience Fruit Shoot The Ride.
6. Take a spin on the Pirate Ride, also in Beaver Creek.
7. As soon as the rest of Beaver Creek opens, ride Thor's Turnpike.
8. Take a ride on Magic Mountain.
9. If your children are up for it, try the Zipper Dipper roller coaster.
10. See the Beaver Creek Log Flume. Leave this attraction for last if you don't want to get wet.
11. Leave Beaver Creek and see the Alice Ride.
12. Check the queue for the Grand Prix. If the wait is less than 20 minutes, get in queue now. Otherwise, try again during the last 2 hours the park is open.
13. Eat lunch.
14. Experience the Magnus Mini Dodgems.
15. Ride the Eddie Stobart Convoy if the queue isn't long.
16. See the River Caves boat ride.
17. In Beaver Creek, try the Lunar Carousel and the Veteran Carousel.
18. Take a tour of the park on the Monorail.
19. Try the Grand Prix if you've not already done so.
20. Eat dinner.
21. If time permits, try the Chinese Puzzle Maze.
22. Ride the Gallopers carousel.
23. See any missed attractions or repeat any favourites.
24. Depart Pleasure Beach Blackpool.

THEME PARKS AND ATTRACTIONS

One-Day Touring Plan for Parents with Older Children and Younger Children

1. The night before your visit, check **blackpoolpleasurebeach.com** for park hours and weather.
2. Arrive at the park entrance 30 minutes prior to official opening. If possible, have your admission in hand before you arrive. Otherwise, arrive 15 minutes earlier and send one member of your party to obtain admission at the Ticket Centre.
3. As soon as the park opens, experience the Flying Machines near the main park entrance.
4. Adults and younger kids should ride Derby Racer, behind Flying Machines. Older kids and willing adults can try Ice Blast, also near Flying Machines.
5. Adults and younger children should walk to the Beaver Creek area and experience any open attractions. Older kids and willing adults: ride the Pepsi Max Big One. The entire group should meet again at the Zipper Dipper in the Beaver Creek area.
6. Eat lunch.
7. Ride the Zipper Dipper.
8. Experience the Alice Ride.
9. See the River Caves Boat Ride.
10. Adults and older children should try Valhalla while other adults and younger children experience the Pleasure Beach Express. The entire group should meet back at the Monorail.
11. Take a tour of the park on the Monorail.
12. Try the Grand Prix.
13. Ride Gallopers.
14. If time permits, try the Chinese Puzzle Maze.
15. Eat dinner.
16. See any missed attractions or repeat any favourites.
17. Depart Pleasure Beach Blackpool.

One-Day Touring Plan for Teens and Adults

This touring plan minimises your queuing time by having you walk between key popular or low-capacity attractions for the first few hours the park is open. Compared with most theme parks, Pleasure Beach is relatively small, and the incremental 2 or 3 minutes of walking per attraction will easily save you many times that in queuing time.

1. The night before your visit, check **blackpoolpleasurebeach.com** for park hours and weather.
2. Arrive at the park entrance 30 minutes prior to official opening. If possible, have your admission in hand before you arrive. Otherwise,

Pleasure Beach Blackpool Recommended Attraction Visitation Times

ATTRACTION | BEST TIME TO VISIT

Pepsi Max Big One | As soon as it opens or in the last hour the park is open

Avalanche | First hour the attraction is open or the last 2 hours the park is open

Bling | First hour the attraction is open or the last 2 hours the park is open

The Big Dipper | First hour the attraction is open or the last 2 hours the park is open

Grand National | First 2 hours the attraction is open or the last 2 hours the park is open

Ice Blast | First 2 hours the attraction is open or the last 2 hours the park is open

Infusion | First hour the attraction is open or the last 2 hours the park is open

Irn Bru Revolution | Anytime

Valhalla | Anytime

Wild Mouse | As soon as the ride opens or in the last hour the park is open

Alice Ride | As soon as the attraction opens

Chinese Puzzle Maze | Anytime

Derby Racer | Anytime

Eddie Stobart Convoy Ride | Just after lunch, or try around dinner time

Flying Machines | First hour the park is open, during mealtimes or in the last hour the park is open

arrive 15 minutes earlier and send one member of your party to obtain admission at the Ticket Centre.

3. As soon as the park opens, experience the Flying Machines near the main park entrance.
4. Ride the Wild Mouse as soon as it opens.
5. Head back towards the Flying Machines and experience Ice Blast.
6. As soon as it opens, ride the Pepsi Max Big One.
7. Experience Infusion, near the front of the park.
8. Try The Big Dipper.
9. Ride Bling, near Burger King at the back of the park.
10. Eat lunch, if your stomach is able to keep food down.
11. Experience Avalanche.
12. Ride the Grand National.

ATTRACTION	BEST TIME TO VISIT
Gallopers	Anytime
Ghost Train	As soon as the attraction opens, or the last hour the park is open
Grand Prix	As soon as it opens or in the last hour the park is open
Impossible	First 2 hours the park is open
Magnus Mini Dodgems	First 2 hours the park is open
Monorail	Anytime
Pleasure Beach Express	Anytime
River Caves	Anytime
Steeplechase	Anytime
Thor's Turnpike	As soon as the attraction opens, or not at all
Magic Mountain	Anytime
Helicopters	As soon as it opens
Fruit Shoot The Ride.	As soon as it opens
Beaver Creek Log Flume	As soon as it opens
Tetley Tea Cup Ride	As soon as it opens
Veteran Carousel	As soon as it opens
Zipper Dipper	First or last 2 hours the attraction is open
Lunar Carousel	Anytime

13. Ride Steeplechase.
14. Take a spin on Irn Bru Revolution.
15. Try the Dodgems bumper cars.
16. Float through the River Caves boat ride.
17. See Ghost Town if the queue isn't too long.
18. Experience Valhalla.
19. Eat dinner.
20. Take a tour of the park on the Monorail.
21. Try the Grand Prix if the queue isn't too long.
22. If time permits, try the Chinese Puzzle Maze.
23. See any missed attractions or repeat any favourites.
24. Depart Pleasure Beach Blackpool.

Sea Life Blackpool ★★

APPEAL BY AGE	PRESCHOOL ★★★★	PRIMARY SCHOOL ★★★	TEENS ★★
YOUNG ADULTS ★★	OVER 30 ★★★		SENIORS ★★★

Promenade, Blackpool, Lancashire FY1 5AA
☎ **01253 622 445; visitsealife.com/Blackpool**

HOURS 10 a.m.–4 p.m. (last entry 1 hour before closing). Closed Christmas Day.

COST £13.95 adults (£9.95 online); £10.95 children 3–14, (£6.95 online); £11.95 senior citizens, students (£7.95 online); £41 family ticket (2 adults, 2 children) (£27.50 online). Admission can also be bought through the Tesco Clubcard rewards scheme.

GETTING THERE *By car:* Leaving the M55, follow the brown tourist signs to the main town car park. *By train:* The nearest rail station is Blackpool North (**nationalrail.co.uk**). Turn right outside the station to the Promenade and then left to the aquarium. *By bus:* Blackpool is served from major cities around northwest England. *By tram:* Take any seafront tram to the Central Pier stop, where the aquarium is located. (Route information: **transportdirect.info.**)

DESCRIPTION AND COMMENTS This modestly-sized location engages young visitors with its pirate theme – but it really sets itself apart with its sharks. The varied collection includes the cartoonish bowmouth guitar shark, and Willy and Wonka, a pair of white-tip reef sharks. Look for the Japanese spider crabs, which seem straight out of a horror movie, and Nobby, a giant lobster found off the coast of Fleetwood by a fisherman. Also check in on Ollie the Octopus, named after Blackpool FC's colourful manager, Ian Holloway.

TOURING TIPS Even though situated at a major tourist destination, the aquarium is rarely crowded. A great choice if rain precludes enjoying the beach, the amusement piers and Pleasure Beach.

(For more on aquariums, see page 10.)

FARM EXPERIENCES

BECAUSE THE VARIOUS FARM EXPERIENCES ARE SO SIMILAR (see page 13), we felt it unnecessary to provide individual profiles as we do with other types of attractions. Following is a selective list of farm experiences in northwest England.

CHESHIRE

STOCKLEY FARM PARK
Arley, Northwich
Cheshire CW9 6LZ
☎ 01565 777 323
stockleyfarm.co.uk
enquiries@stockleyfarm.co.uk

LANCASHIRE

BOWLAND WILD BOAR PARK
(Name notwithstanding, this park provides the usual farm experience coupled with wildlife viewing that includes wild boar)
Lower Greystoneley Farm
Chipping, Preston
Lancashire PR3 2QT
☎ 01995 61554
wildboarpark.co.uk
wildboar6@o2.co.uk

FARMER PARRS ANIMAL WORLD
(Usual crowd plus ferrets, wallabies, alpacas, and llamas, with reptiles and rodents thrown in for good measure)
Rossall Lane
Fleetwood, Lancashire FY7 8JP
☎ 01253 874 389
farmerparrs.com
enquiries@farmerparrs.com

FARMER TED'S FARM PARK
Flatman's Lane
Downholland, Ormskirk
Lancashire L39 7HW
☎ 0151 526 0002
farmerteds.com
farmerted@farmerteds.com

SMITHILLS OPEN FARM
Smithills Dean Road
Bolton
Lancashire BL1 7NS
☎ 01204 595 765
smithillsopenfarm.co.uk
info@smithillsopenfarm.co.uk

WINDMILL ANIMAL FARM
Red Cat Lane
Burscough
Lancashire L40 1UQ
☎ 01704 892 282
windmillanimalfarm.co.uk
info@windmillanimalfarm.co.uk

GREATER MANCHESTER AND MERSEYSIDE

ACORN FARM
Depot Road
Kirkby
Merseyside L33 3AR
☎ 0151 548 1524

PART TWELVE

NORTH EAST ENGLAND

CENTRED ON THE COALY TYNE, northeast England encompasses County Durham, Tyne and Wear and Northumberland. There are a number of famous film locations in this region, including the castle of the Duke of Northumberland, where several Harry Potter movies were shot. Attractions include **Blue Reef Aquarium–Tynemouth** and several farm experiences.

ATTRACTION

Blue Reef Aquarium–Tynemouth ★★½

APPEAL BY AGE	PRESCHOOL ★★★★	PRIMARY SCHOOL ★★★	TEENS ★★
YOUNG ADULTS ★★	OVER 30 ★★★		SENIORS ★★★

Grand Parade, Tynemouth, Tyne & Wear NE30 4JF
☎ **0191 258 1031; bluereefaquarium.co.uk/tynemouth.htm**

- **HOURS** 10 a.m.–4 p.m. (last admission). Closed Christmas Day.
- **COST** £8.30 adults; £5.95 children 3–14 (must be accompanied by an adult); £7.20 senior citizens, students; £26.50 family ticket (2 adults, 2 children); £31.50 family ticket (2 adults, 3 children).
- **GETTING THERE** *By car:* Tynemouth is on the North Sea coast, about 9 mi (14 km) from Newcastle. Follow the A19, taking the A1058 (Coast Road) signposted to Tynemouth. Follow signs towards Tynemouth Seafront. Parking is by meter on the street. *By rail:* The nearest rail station is Newcastle (**nationalrail.co.uk**). From there, take the **Metro** to Cullercoats and walk 10 minutes along the seafront (**nexus.org.uk**). *By bus:* Buses serve Tynemouth from Newcastle's Haymarket station on **Arriva Northumbria** (**arrivabus.co.uk**). (Route information: **transportdirect.info**.)
- **DESCRIPTION AND COMMENTS** This chain aquarium offers all the expected basics and a few standout exhibits. Its outdoor seal cove has a tank of more than 100,000 gal (500,000 litres). The indoor otter enclosure gives the playful

North East England

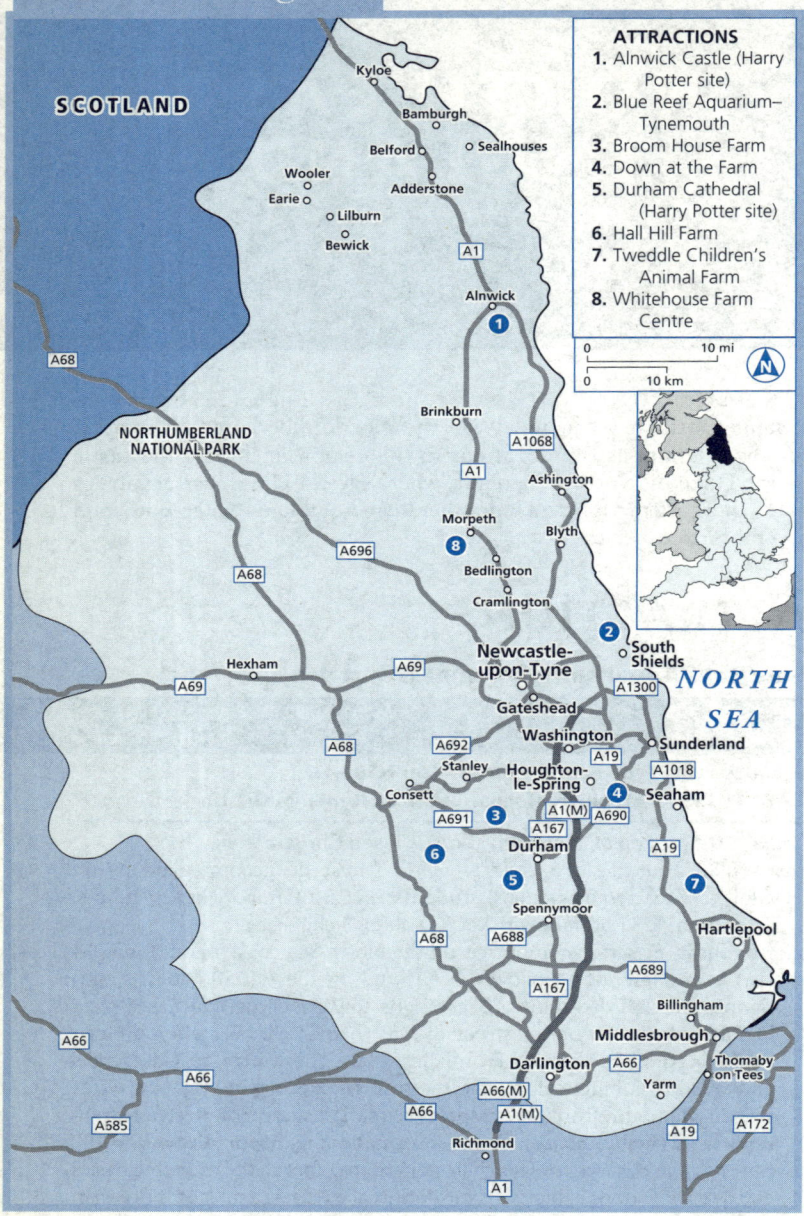

ATTRACTIONS
1. Alnwick Castle (Harry Potter site)
2. Blue Reef Aquarium–Tynemouth
3. Broom House Farm
4. Down at the Farm
5. Durham Cathedral (Harry Potter site)
6. Hall Hill Farm
7. Tweddle Children's Animal Farm
8. Whitehouse Farm Centre

critters lots of room to roam, but you may be put off by the strong musky odour. You'll also find poison dart frogs and a miniature-monkey display, including pygmy marmosets and cotton-top tamarins.

TOURING TIPS To get full value, allow time for feedings and talks. Parking near the aquarium can be problematic.

(For more on aquariums, see page 10.)

FARM EXPERIENCES

BECAUSE THE VARIOUS FARM EXPERIENCES ARE SO SIMILAR (see page 13), we felt it unnecessary to provide individual profiles as we do with other types of attractions. Following is a selective list of farm experiences in northeast England.

COUNTY DURHAM

BROOM HOUSE FARM
Witton Gilbert
County Durham DH7 6TR
☎ 0191 371 9697
broomhousedurnham.co.uk
(Email via form at website)

DOWN AT THE FARM
Stoneygate Lane
Houghton-le-Spring
Sunderland DH5 8JG
☎ 0191 584 1873
downatthefarm.co.uk
bookings@downatthefarm.co.uk

HALL HILL FARM
Lanchester
County Durham DH7 0TA
☎ 01388 731 333
hallhillfarm.co.uk
(Email via form at website)

TWEDDLE CHILDREN'S ANIMAL FARM
Fillpoke Lane, Blackhall Colliery
Durham TS27 4BT
☎ 0191 586 3311
tweddlefarm.co.uk
denise@tweddlefarm.co.uk

NORTHUMBERLAND

WHITEHOUSE FARM CENTRE
(Large variety of animals including rare breeds of pigs and sheep plus reptiles, insects, llamas and skunks)
North Whitehouse Farm
Morpeth
Northumberland NE61 6AW
☎ 01670 789 571
whitehousefarmcentre.co.uk
whitehousefarmcentre@tiscali.co.uk

PART THIRTEEN

CUMBRIA *and the* LAKE DISTRICT

WILLIAM WORDSWORTH, WHO SPENT HIS ENTIRE LIFE in the Lake District, captured the area's essential appeal when he wrote in his *Guide through the District of the Lakes* that these landscapes of craggy mountains and still, mist-shrouded waters were to be treasured by 'persons of good taste . . . [with] an eye to perceive and a heart to enjoy'. The poet rambled and climbed through almost every square mile of this region, wedged into a small corner of the northwest coast near the Scottish border, and he lobbied to protect it as a national property. Almost exactly a hundred years after Wordsworth's death, in 1951 the British parliament established the **Lake District National Park,** which covers nearly 800 sq mi (2,072 km^2).

The bracken-covered peaks of the Lake District are not particularly tall (none more than 3,000 feet), but they are beautiful nonetheless. In the wooded valleys beneath these mountain landscapes are the famous meres, or lakes – long, slender bodies of sparkling water that reflect the crags, forests, and meadows above them. Many visitors follow, quite literally, in Wordsworth's footsteps and explore the region on foot, and you should partake of this experience too while in the Lake District. You'll also want to visit any number of historic homes (including two where Wordsworth lived); explore the towns and small villages built of slate and stone that seem to blend into the landscape; and simply enjoy this part of the world that is both beautiful and quintessentially English.

Good bets for family days out in Cumbria and the Lake District include the **Lakes Aquarium** and the **South Lakes Wild Animal Park,** as well as a number of farm experiences.

Cumbria and the Lake District

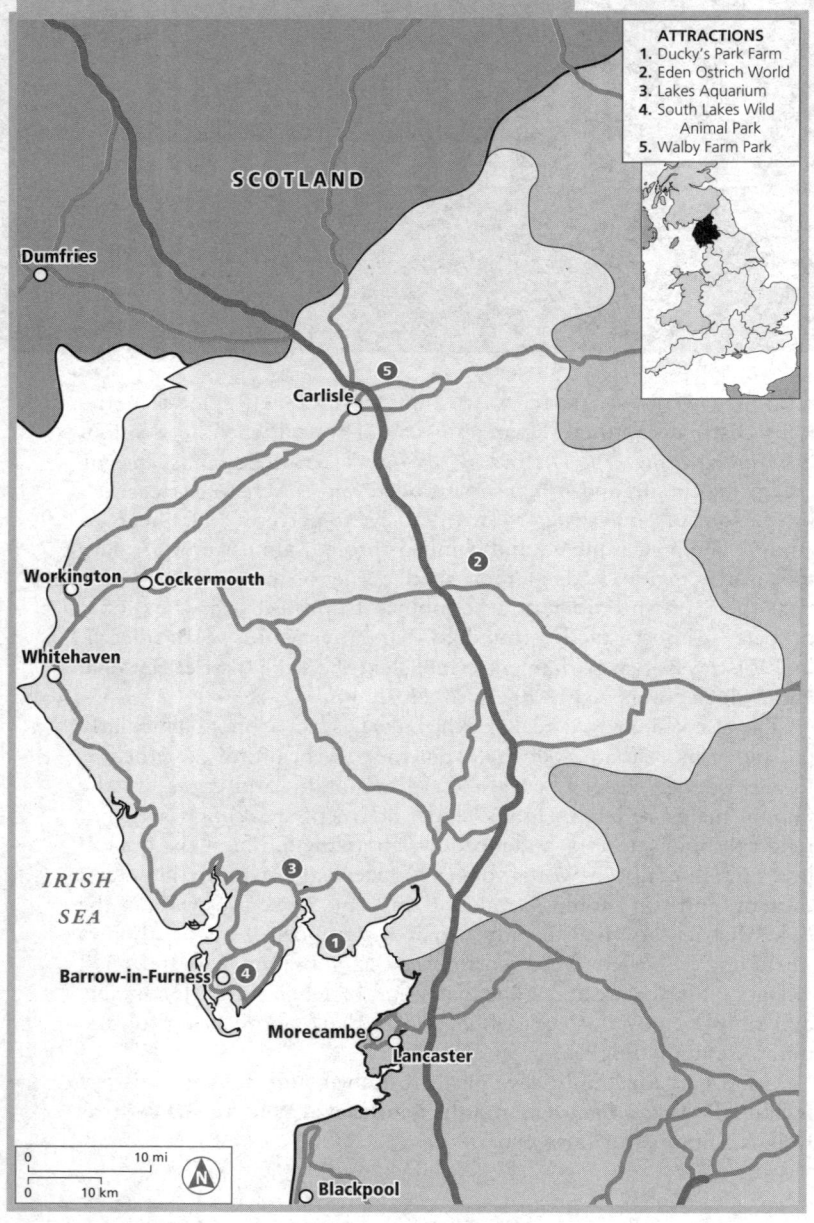

ATTRACTIONS
1. Ducky's Park Farm
2. Eden Ostrich World
3. Lakes Aquarium
4. South Lakes Wild Animal Park
5. Walby Farm Park

ATTRACTIONS

Lakes Aquarium ★★★

APPEAL BY AGE	PRESCHOOL ★★	PRIMARY SCHOOL ★★★	TEENS ★★
YOUNG ADULTS ★★		OVER 30 ★★★	SENIORS ★★★

Lakeside, Newby Bridge, Cumbria LA12 8AS
☎ **01539 530 153; lakesaquarium.co.uk**

HOURS 10 a.m.–5 p.m. (last entry 1 hour before closing). Closed Christmas Day.

COST £9.15 adults (£7.30 online); £6.10 children 3–15 (£4.85 online); £7.75 senior citizens (£6.55 online); £7.15 disabled adults; £4.60 disabled children; £27.65 family ticket (2 adults, 2 children) (£23.50 online); £32.95 family ticket (2 adults, 3 children) (£28 online). Discounts for combined tickets with Windermere Lake Cruises and Lakeside & Haverthwaite Railway.

GETTING THERE *By car:* On the southern shore of Lake Windermere in Cumbria, the aquarium is signposted from M6 Junction 36. Follow the fish symbols along the A590 to Newby Bridge. Take the first right after the roundabout, over the bridge, and follow the road to Hawkshead for approximately 1 mi (1.6 km). There is a large pay-and-display car park. *By steam train or boat:* The **Haverthwaite Steam Railway** runs from Haverthwaite to the aquarium Easter–October, with limited service throughout the year (☎ 01539 531 594; **lakesiderailway.co.uk**). To arrive by boat, catch a sailing from Bowness or Ambleside on **Windermere Lake Cruises** (☎ 01539 443 360; **windermere-lakecruises.co.uk**). *By train:* The nearest rail station is Windermere, about 9 mi (14 km) from the aquarium (**nationalrail.co.uk**). *By bus:* **Travellers Choice Bus 618** from Windermere serves Newby Bridge, which is about 1 mi (.6 km) from the aquarium (**cumbria.gov.uk/roads-transport**). (Route information: **transportdirect.info.**)

DESCRIPTION AND COMMENTS This small Lake District aquarium with about 30 exhibits offers gorgeous views onto Lake Windermere. It's one of two UK aquariums owned by Parques Reunidos, a Spanish theme-park conglomerate. Unlike the typical shark-and-clownfish collection, the aquarium features freshwater creatures and focuses on the region, although you'll find some saltwater displays too. It also has well-themed interactive exhibits. The aquarium is perhaps best included with a lake cruise and railway outing – it shares its location with both Windermere Lake Cruises and the Haverthwaite Steam Railway.

You start your aquarium visit by passing through an **underwater tunnel** meant to re-create the lake, where you'll see carp, perch and huge 6-ft (1.8-m) catfish – later you'll cross over the same tank for a view from above and a chance to watch diving ducks. Next comes an exhibit on the **Leven Estuary,** home to Arctic char, a remnant of the last Ice Age. A **rainforest exhibit** includes pygmy marmosets, caimans and boa constrictors. And to take you farther afield, a **virtual dive bell** provides encounters with a shark, crocodile and charging hippo, all brought to you through the magic of microprocessors. The **Asian exhibit** stars a pair of short-clawed otters, named Mia and Smudge, which are fed daily at 10.30 a.m. and 3 p.m. There's also a keeper talk at noon. Finally, you'll reach a **three-tiered tank** devoted to the Lake District, with (occasionally-jumping) brown trout, polecats and tiny harvest mice.

TOURING TIPS Be forewarned that the steam train and the excursion boat both deliver visitors to the aquarium in large numbers. Whenever one or the other arrives, ticket-sellers and the entrance area can be inundated. If you arrive on the boat or train, buy the discounted ride–aquarium combo ticket and try to be among the first to disembark. If accessing the aquarium by car, bus or on foot, check the train and boat schedules so you can avoid arriving at the same time as they do.

(For more on aquariums, see page 10.)

South Lakes Wild Animal Park ★★★★

APPEAL BY AGE	PRESCHOOL ★★★★	PRIMARY SCHOOL ★★★★	TEENS ★★★★
YOUNG ADULTS ★★★★		OVER 30 ★★★★	SENIORS ★★★

Broughton Road, Dalton-in-Furness, Cumbria LA15 8JR
☎ **01229 466 086; wildanimalpark.co.uk**

HOURS (April–October) 10 a.m.–5 p.m.; (November–March) 10 a.m.–4.30 p.m. (last admission 45 minutes before closing). Closed Christmas Day.

COST £11.50 adults; £8 children (3–15), senior citizens. Tickets can also be purchased through the Tesco Clubcard rewards scheme.

GETTING THERE *By car:* Take the M6 to Junction 36 and follow signs for Barrow-in-Furness until you see brown elephant signs to the park. *By rail:* Nearest station is Dalton-in-Furness. The park's a 20-minute uphill walk. Discounted rates from **A1 Taxis** (☎ 01229 838 383).

DESCRIPTION AND COMMENTS Nestled in the south end of the Lake District, this small zoo is not your typical animal-based attraction. It gives you the chance to literally rub shoulders with several exotic species that wander around the zoo freely. You can pet giraffes, meet monkeys and marvel at lemurs lounging in pathways. It also takes its preservation mission seriously, serving as the home to two international registered charities – The Wildlife Protection Foundation and The Sumatran Tiger Trust – and also supporting lemur conservation in Madagascar and red-howler-monkey conservation in Colombia. In short, it's a place where you can have a good time – and feel that you're doing good at the same time.

The park is the creation of David S. Gill, an animal nutritionist who started the park in 1993 on converted farmland, building the first enclosures by hand. The park boasts gorgeous views, and many a driver has been surprised rounding a corner in this quintessential British landscape only to spot giraffes sticking their heads above trees.

For all this, the park entrance doesn't seem to promise much. Many visitors mistake the winding park road for a wrong turn and are under-whelmed by the small car park, with overflow parking in a field. Walking down to the entrance, you may begin to question whether the place is worth your time and money. Even when you've stepped inside and walked 30 yd (27 m) or so, it's still not clear which way to go.

The park is roughly bisected by a miniature-train track. The areas on the right are mainly devoted to **African animals** in large, open paddocks and fields, which require the most walking to see. The section to the left of the tracks, the upper slope, is devoted to **Australia** and **South America,** and the exhibits are more densely concentrated. Our advice: start with the open areas on the right while you're fresh, and end your visit with the remaining part of the park, which will require less walking. Unless you fancy miniature railways, there's really no need for a ride. The park is small enough that you won't have any trouble getting around.

The park, built around several hills dotted with ponds, is compact and rather jumbled for the most part. Landscaping, especially on the right side, is minimal, while on the more-verdant left side erosion and drainage seem to be a problem. Navigation is by trial and error and requires a fair amount of backtracking. Although signage is adequate, there is no obvious, orderly way to see everything. There's also no handout park map. The only way to obtain a map is to buy a 133-page souvenir guidebook, which details the zoo's various conservation projects but doesn't offer much information about the zoo itself.

A standout feature is the elevated walkways, which provide a view of the animals without bars or a fence blocking the way. Generally there's a path underneath the walkways giving a ground-level perspective, but the two views are often redundant. We suggest using the elevated walkways when possible and returning to see animals from the ground only if you have a keen interest. If you can't spot the animal from the walkway, however, a quick trip to ground level often reveals that he's been directly below you and out of sight.

Unlike some zoos, where the keepers determine where their charges spend the day, at South Lakes the animals decide. On a rainy day, for example, you're more likely to find a critter in his indoor enclosure.

The first African animals you'll encounter as you enter are the **pygmy hippos** and **mandrills** on the right. Then come the **giraffes,** and you get an eye-to-eye view from a raised platform. Twice a day, at 11.30 a.m. and 3.45 p.m. (all times subject to change – check the posted schedule in the park), you can even have a chance to hand-feed them. Next comes the **Maki Restaurant.** Even if you don't want a full meal or you've packed a picnic, check out the back deck, which overlooks the giraffe, rhino and baboon enclosures.

Continuing around the outer rim of the park, make sure to visit the **rhinoceros house.** The park specialises in **white rhinos,** which weigh up to 6,615 lb (three tonnes), making them the world's second largest mammal by mass after the African elephant. Also keep an eye out for the hamadryas baboons.

The back corner of the park is devoted to **African lions,** which you can also see from a raised platform. In the biblical spirit of lions lying down with sheep, it's interesting to note that the lion enclosure is bordered by private farms populated by sheep and cattle. (We don't know whether the lions invite their neighbours over for tea.) Try to come for the feedings at 4.25 p.m., a visitor favourite. Food is placed on top of a 20-ft (6-m) pole, which the predators have to climb if they want to eat. It's thrilling to see the normally-sluggish felines at play. The same technique is used at the tiger and jaguar enclosure at 2.30 p.m. Try to arrive early for both, as the elevated walkways can get crowded during the busy summer months.

Continuing anti-clockwise brings you to **South American animals** like the **Andean bear, lowland tapir** and **capybara,** the world's largest rodent, which weighs in at more than 100 lb (45 kg).

Then you'll reach the busy **primate area**, with **Colombian spider monkeys, gibbons, macaques** and **brown capuchin monkeys,** which prowl their enclosure and swing through a climbing area that resembles a circus flying trapeze set-up. You'll get tantalisingly close, as you're separated only by a thin electric fence. Continue walking and look for the **Humboldt penguins.** Some visitors make the trip to the park just to take part in the daily 3 p.m. hand-feeding sessions. Next door is the **tiger enclosure,** which has both Amurs (Siberians) and Sumatrans on display. The Sumatran tiger, native to Indonesia, is particularly rare and is the focus of a park-sponsored charity, the world's leading fund-raiser for the animal. Over nearly 20 years the park has donated more than £1 million towards its preservation.

Crossing over the train tracks brings you to the **lemur** area, another park speciality. While these furry climbers from Madagascar have become the rage at many zoos, South Lakes boasts more than 100 of them, including eight species: black, belted ruffed, white-fronted, Alaotran gentle, ring-tailed, red-ruffed, mongoose, black-and-white ruffed, and oversexed – just kidding about that last one. Try to stop by at 2 p.m., when you can help the keepers feed the primates. The lemurs made national news in 2008 when several dozen died in a fire. Many former visitors wrote letters of sympathy, recounting fond memories of their encounters with the animals.

Next door is the **Australia** area, which is one of the park's top attractions – and one of the more memorable walk-through areas you'll encounter in a zoo. You step inside an enclosed area and stroll amongst a rather surprising number of **kangaroos, wallabies** and, most memorably, **emus.** (The shrieks you've been hearing from across the park all day probably weren't from animals, but from guests startled to find themselves face-to-face with a 6½-ft [2-m] flightless bird.) The area is also wallaby central, with Europe's largest collection of the marsupials. You can see unfamiliar species like the river sand and swamp wallabies, the only ones in Britain, and the white-throated wallaby, which was once thought extinct.

As you head back to the entrance, make sure to stop in at the **aviary,** home to the so-ugly-they're-cute **king vultures,** which are fed daily at 3.20 p.m., and **Andean condors,** the largest flying bird in the world, with a wingspan of more than 10 ft (3 m).

Finally, don't overlook the snake house on the way out. Here's your chance to pet a **Burmese python.** We dare you.

TOURING TIPS Parking is free. Allocate 2–3 hours for a comprehensive visit. You'll find plenty of places for picnics, but no lockers to stash your basket, so you'll have to keep it in your car until you're ready for lunch – the park provides passes out.

FARM EXPERIENCES

BECAUSE THE VARIOUS FARM EXPERIENCES ARE SO SIMILAR (see page 13), we felt it unnecessary to provide individual profiles as we do with other types of attractions. Following is a selective list of farm experiences in Cumbria and the Lake District.

DUCKY'S PARK FARM
Moor Lane
Floorburgh, Grange-over-Sands
Cumbria LA11 7LS
☎ 015395 59293
duckysparkfarm.co.uk
info@duckysparkfarm.co.uk

WALBY FARM PARK
Walby, Crosby-on-Eden
Carlisle
Cumbria CA6 4QL
☎ 01228 573 056
walbyfarmpark.co.uk
enquiries@walbyfarmpark.co.uk

EDEN OSTRICH WORLD
(Nope, doesn't sound like a farm, but it is; in addition to ostriches, features daily sheep-milking)
Langwathby Hall Farm
Langwathby, Penrith
Cumbria CA10 1LW
☎ 01768 881 771
ostrich-world.com
enquiries@ostrich-world.com

PART FOURTEEN

SCOTLAND

THE BEAUTY AND ASTONISHING VARIETY of Scotland's natural landscapes make a lifelong impression on all who visit. Though small, the country boasts a striking range of compelling vistas, from the peaks of the **Cairngorms** to the gentle undulating hills of **Dumfries** and **Galloway,** and from the jagged coastlines of the north-east to the misty lochs of the heartland and the subtropical gardens of **Wester Ross.**

Scotland is the place to go for kilts, salmon, thistle, bagpipes, tartan, golf and, of course, malt whisky. Though not exactly the theme-park or tourist-attraction capital of Europe, it's not lacking in that department either. Sadly, Scotland's most beautiful park, **Loudoun Castle Theme Park,** built on the grounds of the haunting ruin of Loudoun Castle, closed its doors in 2010 after only 15 years of operation. But there are other parks, as we shall see, and farm experiences, aquariums and zoos too. We doubt they'll be what brings you to Scotland, but they will spice your visit nonetheless.

THEME PARKS *and* ATTRACTIONS

Blair Drummond Safari and Adventure Park ★★★½

APPEAL BY AGE	PRESCHOOL ★★★★	PRIMARY SCHOOL ★★★★	TEENS ★★★
YOUNG ADULTS ★★★		OVER 30 ★★★	SENIORS ★★★

Blair Drummond, by Stirling FK9 4UR
☎ **01786 841 456; blairdrummond.com**

HOURS 10 a.m.–5.30 p.m. Last admission is 1 hour before closing.
COST £11.50 adults; £8 children (aged 3–14; must be accompanied by an adult), senior citizens, disabled and students with ID.
GETTING THERE *By car:* An hour's drive from Edinburgh and Glasgow. Take Junction 10 off the M9 and follow the signs. *By rail:* The nearest train

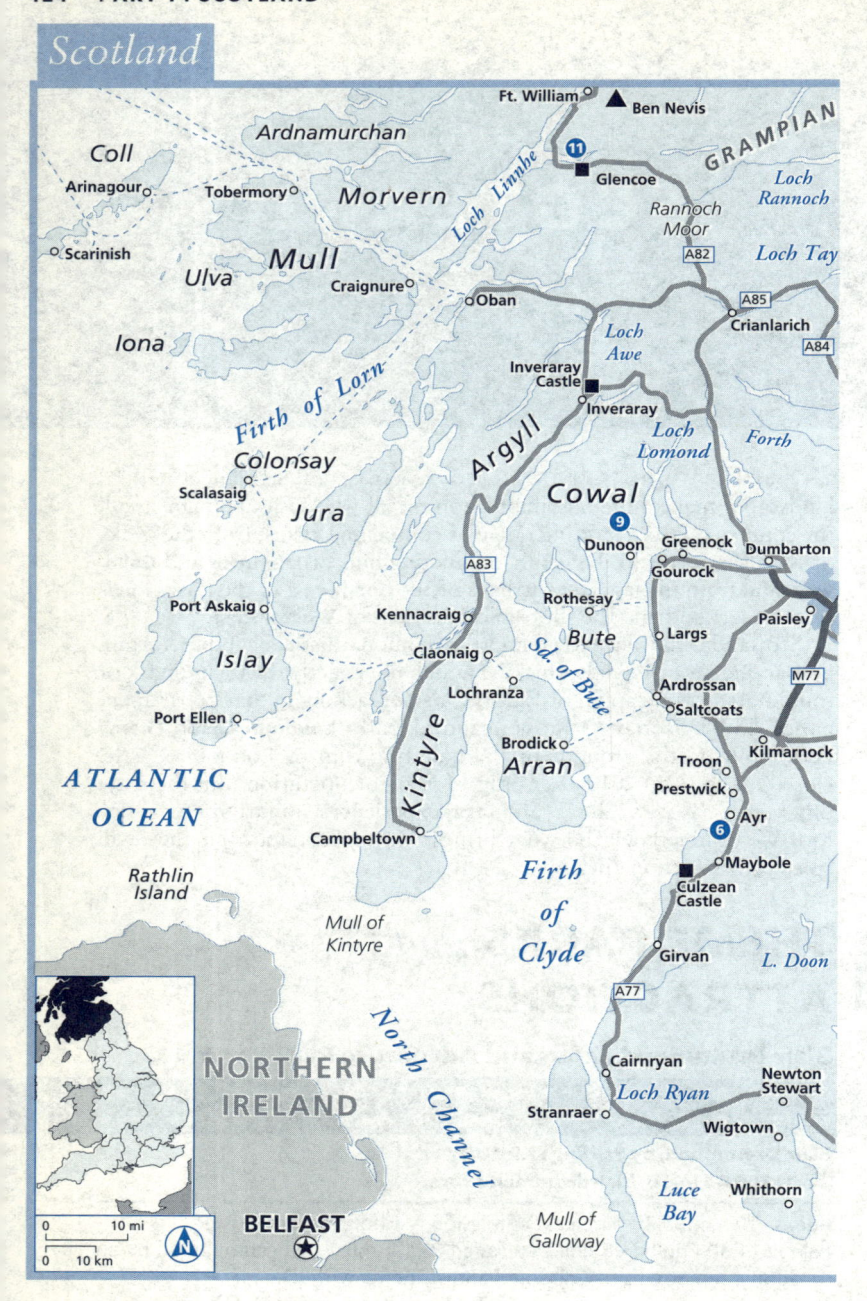

Scotland

SCOTLAND MAP

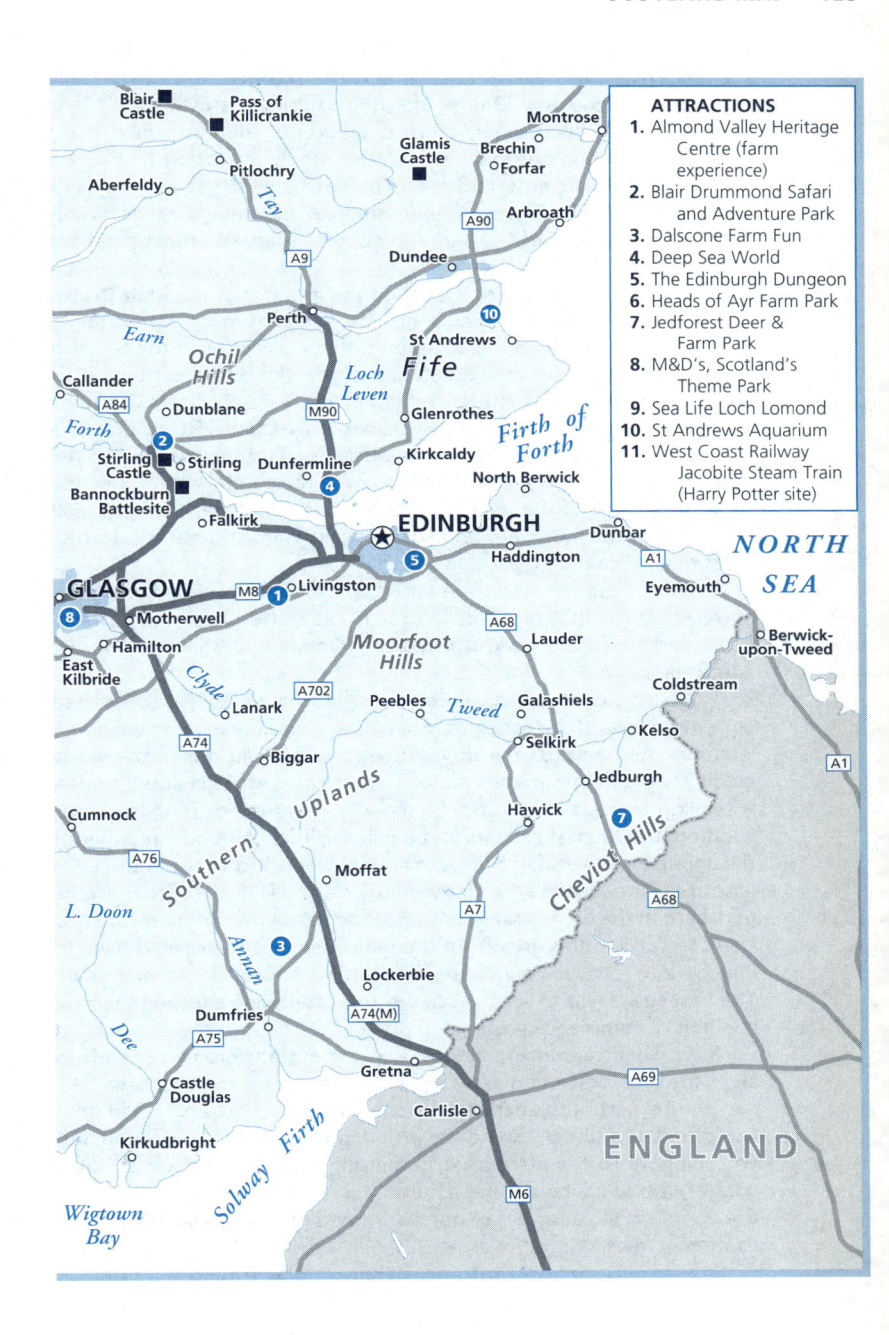

ATTRACTIONS
1. Almond Valley Heritage Centre (farm experience)
2. Blair Drummond Safari and Adventure Park
3. Dalscone Farm Fun
4. Deep Sea World
5. The Edinburgh Dungeon
6. Heads of Ayr Farm Park
7. Jedforest Deer & Farm Park
8. M&D's, Scotland's Theme Park
9. Sea Life Loch Lomond
10. St Andrews Aquarium
11. West Coast Railway Jacobite Steam Train (Harry Potter site)

station is Stirling. *By bus:* Regular **First Bus** service runs from Stirling past the safari park (☎ 08708 727 271; **firstgroup.com**).

DESCRIPTION AND COMMENTS One of the first safari parks in the UK, Blair Drummond has been showing off its version of the bush since 1970. Now it's a leading, but low-key, Scottish family attraction that offers surprising value and entertainment. You'll struggle to get a whole day's visit, but it makes for a good 4-hour outing. A real irritant is the unavailability of a free map of the park. To obtain a map, you must purchase a souvenir book.

The 120-ac (48-ha) park is built on the grounds of the **Blair Drummond House,** once the residence of Scottish philosopher Henry Home, Lord Kames. Home was a leader and influential figure of the Scottish Enlightenment during the second half of the eighteenth century. Blair Drummond House was entirely rebuilt in 1868–72 by James Campbell Walker and again in 1921–23 by James Bow Dunn after a fire. The house, with its many spires and its castle-like facade, was sold to the Camphill Trust in 1977 and is now a home for adults with disabilities. Though not part of the safari park, the house dominates the landscape and is one of the more intriguing of the many ruins and historical structures that grace theme parks in the UK.

Originally the attraction was based on a drive-through safari experience. Although that remains, the focus has shifted over the years to a zoo and adventure park, with many children's rides included in the admission price.

The park is divided into three areas: (1) a base area; (2) an isolated pedestrian area that features a boat ride, a zip-line experience and a lemur exhibit; and (3) the drive-through safari, laid out in the valley below the Blair Drummond House. The base area offers children's rides, a sea-lion show, a birds-of-prey show, a playground, funfair games, additional zoological exhibits and picnic facilities. A goodly number of the animals on the safari drive can also be viewed from the contiguous base area. The second area mentioned is along a lake en route from the park base to the driving safari entrance and has its own modest car park. You can walk to this area from the park base, but then you'd have to hike back to retrieve your car before heading out for the driving safari. The best strategy is to see the second area after you've toured the base and before commencing the safari drive.

After paying admission at kiosks on the entrance road, bear left to all of the park's different areas. First encountered is the base area. The 'adventure' part of the park mainly consists of a collection of mild rides you'd find at a funfair. Some are included in your park admission, but you will have to pay extra for experiencing the dodgems, a kids' roller coaster, a bouncy house and a carousel. Tokens run about 50p, with discounts available for larger purchases, and most rides cost from two to three tokens.

Kids will also be drawn to an **elaborate playground** featuring an impressively-large wooden castle with mazes, very serious 2-storey slides and a climbing mesh. Owing primarily to the steep slides, you'll find tweens as well as little ones here. There's also a jumbo wooden whaling ship complete with mast and crow's nest, a big sand pit with buried treasure to discover and toys for castle building. Many youngsters would stay all day if permitted.

Animal enclosures at the base are relatively small but ample enough to offer a chance to see animals in a naturalistic setting, without cramping them. Exhibits are well signed with the name and order of the species, its lifespan, its country of origin and a summary of salient information. Species on display include meerkats, lemurs, otters, penguins, bears and birds of prey. A **petting zoo** sounds promising, with horses, wallabies, goats, a pot-bellied pig, donkeys, Shetland ponies and llamas, but a 3½-ft (1-m) wire-mesh fence makes petting a challenge. Also accessible from the base are elevated wooden walkways from which giraffes, zebras, lions, tigers and bears can be observed. Extending from the playground area is a path to the rhino house and elephant exhibit several hundred yards distant.

Most of the park's food and beverage services, as well as the gift shop and picnic facilities, are situated here. The park base is linear, with a bear exhibit and the sea-lion theatre anchoring one end, and the playground and self-catering barbecue pavilion the other. The birds-of-prey show, a birds-of-prey exhibit and some well-hidden collared peccaries are situated at some distance across the car park and the main road.

Though both the **sea-lion shows** (three or four shows per day) and the **birds-of-prey show** (three shows per day) are worthwhile, the latter stands out because of its hilltop setting, overlooking a large lake with forest and mountains in the background. While the sea-lion show is indoors, the bird show is in an uncovered amphitheatre subject to gusty winds coming across the lake. If you want to see the birds, don't wait until the last minute – it's a good 5- to 10-minute hike. In between shows you can visit the birds at the adjacent exhibit. Both shows fill up quickly on busy days, so aim to arrive 15 minutes before the performance begins. The first and last scheduled shows of the day are the least crowded.

Departing the park base in the direction of the driving safari, you'll come upon a lakeside area where there is a boat ride to **Chimpanzee Island.** Each boat holds just over 40 passengers, and the wait to board gets longer as the day progresses, so try to hit this attraction early or after 2.30 p.m., when the rush is over. The boat captain puts out food for the chimps, so you're practically guaranteed a good view. But watch out: there's mesh on one side of the boat for a reason – the primates have been known to throw food and stones at their visitors. However, don't write off these mammals as brutes, as there's another side to them too. In 2010 research scientists published a paper documenting how the park's chimps cared for an ailing elderly member of their group and mourned her subsequent death for more than a month.

A bridge just upstream of the boat dock leads to **Lemur Land,** a walk-through habitat that allows surprisingly-close access to a cuddly colony of ring-tailed and brown lemurs.

Across the road from the boat dock is the **elephant enclosure,** a formidable structure that's home to three African elephants, a real treat in that most zoos and safari parks feature the more-mannerly Indian elephant. Check out the pachyderms now, because there won't be any elephants on the driving safari.

Not far from the Lemur Land bridge is the **Flying Fox,** a zip-line experience in which you glide across a narrow lake on a swing-type seat attached to a cable. It's fun because it's simple and resembles the basic but effective transport you might find deep in a jungle.

Next is the **drive-through safari.** If you have a convertible or pickup truck, or you arrived without a car, you can make arrangements for a free bus ride through the safari at the park base. A two-lane roadway allows drivers to stop and enjoy the view without holding up traffic. The safari is divided into three sections, the first and last showcasing herbivores, with the middle section featuring lions and Amur (Siberian) tigers. Even here the enclosures aren't expansive, as in most safari parks, but the good news is that the critters can't dance off to the outer limits of their habitat where they're all but invisible. Also, the smaller areas serve to habituate the animals to humans and the vehicles so they don't get spooked when you come near. Highlights of the safari drive include the southern white rhino and an impressive herd of American bison (improbably sharing a field with Bactrian camels that think biting the bison on their backs is great sport). There are always a few baby or juvenile animals to ooh and aah over. Our faves were a baby rhino and some baby ostriches.

TOURING TIPS Most visitors take the safari drive first, so our advice is to save it for last, preferably after 2.30 p.m., by which time the traffic will have thinned considerably. Be aware that it takes the park staff some time in the morning to move animals from their nighttime enclosures to their daytime habitats. If you arrive before 11 a.m., you might find a lot of empty enclosures.

If you play your cards right, you can avoid busting the bank at Blair Drummond. Some of the park's most imaginative experiences, such as the Chimpanzee Island boat ride, are included in your admission. Other free experiences include the zip-line, pedal boats and a giant slide.

The park is surprisingly accommodating, providing free dog kennels and even barbecues – just make sure to request one when you arrive, and bring your own charcoal and food. Otherwise you'll find typical snack food readily available.

Deep Sea World ★★★★

APPEAL BY AGE	PRESCHOOL ★★★★	PRIMARY SCHOOL ★★★★	TEENS ★★★½
YOUNG ADULTS ★★★½		OVER 30 ★★★½	SENIORS ★★★½

Battery Quarry, North Queensferry, Fife KY11 1JR
☎ **01383 411 880; deepseaworld.co.uk**

HOURS Monday–Friday, 10 a.m.–5 p.m.; Saturday–Sunday, 10 a.m.–6 p.m. Last admission 1 hour before closing.

COST £12 adults; £8.25 children aged 3–14; £10.25 senior citizens, students and carers; £38.50 family ticket (2 adults, 2 children); £35 family ticket (2 senior citizens, 2 children). Discounts available online.

GETTING THERE *By car:* Located 1 mi (1.6 km) from the M90, a 20-minute drive from Edinburgh, 50 minutes from Glasgow. From the south, follow the signs for Forth Road Bridge and, once across, take the first exit and follow the signs. From the north, exit the M90 at Junction 1 and follow the signs. Free parking. *By rail:* A short walk uphill from the North Queensferry station, reached from Edinburgh's Waverley and Haymarket stations on the Fife Circle Line. North Queensferry is the first station after crossing the Forth Rail Bridge. *By bus:* **Stagecoach Route Fife/55** from Edinburgh's St Andrew Square Bus Station (**stagecoachbus.com**) drops off outside the aquarium. (Route information: **transportdirect.info.**)

DESCRIPTION AND COMMENTS Here's why to come to Deep Sea World: the UK's longest transparent underwater-viewing tunnel. The walk-through tube has a moving walkway and stretches an impressive 367 ft (112 m), providing up-close views of sharks, stingrays, eels and 2,000 other creatures living in a 1-million-gal (4.5-million-litre) home. It's quite a sight and is the highlight of this aquarium. In fact, the other exhibits may be anti-climactic after this spectacular introduction (some visitors feel that they've seen everything within an hour). But check on scheduled feedings and talks, and read the explanatory signage on the exhibits, and you'll feel better about your investment of time and money and get much more out of your visit.

Take the **red-bellied-piranha feedings.** The predators aren't particularly impressive until you see a school of them swarming around a meaty piece of bait. Trust us – it may be a while before you settle calmly into a bath after watching this. As feedings are just weekly, it's probably not worth a special trip just to watch someone hang some meat into a pool of fish, but if you can work a visit around a feeding, you'll enjoy it. The creep show continues at the **Jaws** exhibit, devoted to all things toothy. Exhibits include alligator snapping turtles, a horned frog that can eat prey twice his size and the goliath tiger fish. Found in Africa's Congo River, it's the fastest freshwater fish and grows up to 51" (1.3 m) long. It has razor-sharp teeth, hunts in packs and has been known to prey on humans.

An **amphibian exhibit** has one of the largest collections in the UK, including the rare and highly-poisonous golden arrow frog. You'll also find pools of seals, some being rehabilitated before being released into local waters. Three rock pools feature sea life native to the Scottish coast. Once again, try to visit during a scheduled talk to get much more from the experience.

You'll also find a wide selection of bright tropical fish in tanks devoted to geographic areas such as Lake Malawi and Krakatoa. Finally, don't overlook the finger-long **mantis shrimp.** This little guy packs a kick like a mule. It flicks out a multi-hinged front leg to deliver a blow equivalent to a .22 bullet and has been known to break aquarium glass. After taking a peek, we bet you won't be ordering a shrimp cocktail for a while.

TOURING TIPS Many visitors are drawn to the aquarium by its location, underneath the famous Forth Rail Bridge. And indeed, the aquarium draws water from the Firth of Forth to fill its tanks, which explains why the water is a bit murkier than that found in other such attractions.

A stationary platform runs parallel with the moving walkway, where you can step off and linger over anything that interests you. Just don't use it to backtrack to the exhibit's entrance. Whether on the walkway or the platform, traffic is one-way.

Admission is purchased just inside the main entrance, near the exit of the cafeteria and gift shop. This makes for some congestion, with departing visitors elbowing their way out through the middle of the ticket queue. Though Deep Sea World can be enjoyed at any time of day, arriving either early in the morning or late in the afternoon will minimise your wait in the queue to purchase admission.

The Edinburgh Dungeon ★★★

APPEAL BY AGE	PRESCHOOL ★	PRIMARY SCHOOL ★★★	TEENS ★★★★	YOUNG
ADULTS ★★★		OVER 30 ★★★		SENIORS ★★

32 Market Street, Edinburgh EH1 1QB
☎ **0131 240 1000; the-dungeons.co.uk**

HOURS Opening times vary from 10 a.m. to 11 a.m., closing 4–7 p.m. on weekdays. Opens 10 a.m. weekends (check website for details).

COST £15.50 adults; £11.50 children aged 4–15; £15 senior citizens and students; £49 family ticket (2 adults, 2 children). Discounts and priority entrance tickets available online. Tickets can also be bought through the Tesco Clubcard rewards scheme. While there are no age limits, management does advise that 'the Dungeon is not suitable for people of a nervous disposition or very young children'. Admission to the Dungeon is included in the **Edinburgh Pass** (**visitscotland.com**; enter 'Edinburgh Pass' in the search bar). The pass provides admission to more than 30 attractions. Prices begin at £26.50 for adults for one day and £17 for children aged 5–15.

You can also use the **Merlin Annual Pass** (**merlinannualpass.co.uk**), which provides admission to Alton Towers Resort Theme Park, Legoland Discovery Centre, Legoland Windsor, Thorpe Park, Sea Life aquariums and sanctuaries, Dungeons attractions, Merlin London Eye, Madame Tussauds London and Warwick Castle. Prices begin at £150 for an individual and drop in price if you're buying for a family group.

GETTING THERE *By car:* In the city centre, the Dungeon has limited parking, from £2 per hour, with a maximum stay of 3 hours. Nearby car parks include Waverley Station, Greenside Place or St James Centre. *By rail:* Within 330 ft (100 m) of Edinburgh Rail Station (**nationalrail.co.uk**). *By bus:* Served by **Routes 36** and **X48** and city-centre buses. (Route information: **transportdirect.info**.)

DESCRIPTION AND COMMENTS Dungeons, torture, murder and a funfair ride or two might sound like a dubious basis for a business. But for decades now, The Dungeons have found a niche scaring and entertaining visitors across the UK and in Europe. The different locations employ many of the same scenes and even seem to use the same scripts for their performances. But each city nods to local history and lore by specialising its attraction. In Edinburgh, that means national hero William Wallace and the remarkably-gruesome serial murderers William Burke and William Hare get a good examination. But if you've been to one Dungeon, there's probably no reason to visit another.

Here's the Dungeon blueprint: after what can be a long wait, you enter a dark corridor and pose for a picture in the stocks, with one in your party wielding an axe over the other's head. Then you're broken into small groups and, over the course of an hour or so, are led from one scene to another. Many of these experiences rely on actors, who really can make the show. There's a mixture of humour, history and maniacal laughter. There's also a good chance for embarrassing willing (or unwilling) volunteers in various demonstrations and proceedings. You'll want to go with a group if you can because there can be plenty of giggles, particularly if someone in your party finds themselves singled out in the torture chamber or picked for an autopsy.

If you enter with the right attitude (discount tickets help), you'll find that you've learned a bit of history while you had a good fright and a laugh. Although there are no set age limits, management warns the Dungeon is not for people of a 'nervous disposition'. (You know who you are.) In addition, some primary-schoolers will be terrified by the waxwork corpses and splattered-blood decorations, while others will find them amusing. Know your child well and look at the Dungeons' website before your visit to gauge their reaction to the spooky music and gruesome scenery.

In Edinburgh, your visit starts with a **Judgement of Sinners,** a funny scene that breaks the tension that has been building ever since you entered the dark attraction. Here a crazed judge picks someone out of the audience (if you're dreading the experience, it will probably be you) and accuses him or her of a silly crime such as having an ugly girlfriend. Then you're escorted to the **Torture** chamber, where you'll get a disturbingly graphic and enthusiastic description of the tools used to inflict misery. One audience member is placed in a chair as the group hears about tongue clippers and devices to impale prisoners.

It's only in the third scene that the Dungeon nods to local history. **The Cave of Sawney Bean,** named for a cannibal from the Middle Ages, involves a boat ride of the kind you'd find in a funfair ghost house. Once you're settled in the vessel, the lights go out and you hear about Sawney Bean and his murderous clan. During the ride, which travels only a very short distance, there are various flashes and unexpected encounters. The experience itself is anti-climactic, but the dark heightens the tension, and there's plenty of nervous laughter. Next stop is to **Burke and Hare,** Scotland's notorious nineteenth-century murderers, who sold their victims' corpses to a medical teacher for dissection. Burke was arrested and sentenced to death, and his 1829 hanging is said to have attracted a crowd of 25,000. In this scene, you journey through a graveyard and watch an assistant extract body parts during an autopsy. Serious fans can even become part of the attraction:

in 2010 the Dungeon invited visitors to bequeath their skeletons for eventual display here.

Now you move on to **Mary King's Ghost,** a scene devoted to Edinburgh's plague epidemic. An actress describes the disease in gory detail and complains how victims were abandoned and left to die. Next comes **William Wallace,** Scotland's national hero. You step into a thirteenth-century castle and learn how the patriots defeated the English in 1297 at the Battle of Stirling Bridge. Then you learn of Wallace's inevitable betrayal and execution in London, where he was hanged, drawn and quartered. Finally, the scene ends with a video urging Scots to continue their battle against the English. Playing Wallace is former baggage-handler John Smeaton, who helped prevent a terrorist attack at the Glasgow International Airport in 2007.

After this you're escorted to the Dungeon's second funfair-style ride: **Extremis,** which is limited to guests at least 3'11" (1.2 m) tall. But this drop tower has such ghoulish theming that it's a completely different experience from what you'd find at an amusement park. You're strapped into a seat and raised up to the level of a hangman's noose. You've apparently been convicted of an awful crime, and as a judge reads your sentence, the tension builds until the tower drops and you plummet to the ground. Finally, you end your visit with the **Labyrinth of the Lost Souls,** a cleverly-designed mirror maze that will keep you wandering and bumping into your reflection – and an occasional unexpected actor.

TOURING TIPS Purchase your tickets online or find a discount coupon. While fun, the price is steep, and you're much more likely to enjoy your visit if you've found a deal.

M&D's, Scotland's Theme Park ★★

APPEAL BY AGE	PRESCHOOL ★★	PRIMARY SCHOOL ★★★	TEENS ★★½
YOUNG ADULTS ★★★		OVER 30 ★★	SENIORS ★

Strathclyde Country Park, Motherwell, Lanarkshire ML1 3RT
☎ **0870 112 3777; scotlandsthemepark.com**

HOURS Theme park open mid-March–mid-October; indoor attractions open year-round. Opens either 11 a.m. or midday, depending on the season, with closing time ranging 4–8 p.m. Check website for details. Last admission 1 hour before closing.

COST £15.75 unlimited wristband for children more than 4'5" (1.35 m); £11.75 for children under 4'5" (1.35 m); £49 family ticket (4 people). Discounts available online. Otherwise, individual rides are priced by tokens, 50p each, with discounts for bulk purchases.

GETTING THERE *By car:* From Glasgow, take the M8 and exit at Junction 8 to M73 Carlisle/M74. Exit at Junction 5 to A725, and take the second exit. From Edinburgh, take the M8 to the A8, and exit at A725. Follow signs to the park, on left. *By rail:* The nearest station is Bellshill, 1.4 mi (2.25 km) from the park (**nationalrail.co.uk**). *By bus:* About 10 mi (16 km) from Glasgow. Express bus service is available from Glasgow Buchanan bus station. Return tickets (£6 adults; £5 children) can be redeemed for £3 off unlimited-ride wristbands at the park.

DESCRIPTION AND COMMENTS More funfair than theme park, M&D's offers a motley collection of thrills. You'll find a few good coasters and some entertaining kiddie rides, but theming and landscaping here are minimal. Many of these rides are recycled from bigger UK parks – that doesn't mean they don't offer thrills, but if you think you've seen a ride before, you probably have.

Like most funfairs, the park charges by the ride. If you're planning on spending a day, your best bet is to buy an unlimited-ride wristband. But if you're only going to take in a few rides or are just along for the company, don't bother. Not included in the wristband are the park's numerous indoor attractions, which include glow-in-the-dark bowling, a carousel, a games arcade and a build-a-teddy-bear gift shop. Miniature golf also carries an extra fee, as does **Amazonia,** an indoor rain-forest attraction featuring monkeys, reptiles, bats, snakes, butterflies and spiders displayed in a tropical setting. Ambient lighting makes it difficult to see some of the critters, especially the tarantulas. Leaf-cutting ants are definitely the hardest-working denizens of Amazonia. In a very clever display, the ants cut leaves from one side of a passageway and carry them via a thick overhead rope to their abode on the opposite side. Another highlight is the fruit-bat exhibit. In some instances, displayed species have nothing to do with the Amazon, a case in point being the hissing cockroach, which actually comes from Madagascar. Admission seems a bit dear (£5.25 adults age 16 and older; £4.25 children and senior citizens; family tickets from £15.45; open daily, 10 a.m.–6 p.m.; **ama-zone-ia.com**). It's probably best left to a rainy day, when you need a break from the weather.

Many M&D's rides are the types you'd see in a travelling funfair, but they're based here semi-permanently. The park's best ride is **Tsunami,** the only inverted coaster in Scotland. Instead of sitting on a track, the cars hang from it and riders sit on a padded seat with their feet dangling in the air. The coaster takes riders through two inversions over its 2,132-ft (650-m) length, reaching speeds up to 40 mph (64 km/h). Next on the hit parade is **Wave Swinger,** a flying carousel distinguished more by its vintage art and lighting than by the ride itself. Perhaps M&D's is most notorious for **Tornado,** a wild steel coaster that was so rough that the park management had to modify the design, removing a corkscrew length of track and replacing it with a banked curve. Even so, each ride still feels like a crash-dummy test. But M&D's doesn't back away from the bad boy's reputation. A sign in front of the queue acknowledges that it's 'a very boisterous ride', and the park's website gleefully tells prospective customers: 'Don't forget to bring new underwear'. Consider yourself warned.

The most inefficient ride is **Bungee,** consisting of a globe-shaped ride vehicle containing seats for only two people. The globe is attached to bungee cords in a configuration resembling a slingshot. When the sling is released, you're shot upwards, spinning 360° within the globe.

According to M&D's, launch speed is 164 ft (50 m) in 1.2 seconds. We figure that Bungee can handle about 12 people an hour, about 3 people less than the average pay toilet.

Young ones have a couple of winning options here, and since they'll be so taken by the flashing lights and whirling rides, they're unlikely to notice the bare surroundings. Although it carries an extra 50p charge, the **Krazy Congo** indoor play area will keep preschoolers entertained with foam climbing structures. In the park itself, the **Big Apple** coaster is described as a 'pink knuckle' ride that will thrill, not terrify, young ones – but with three lift hills and subsequent drops over the 984-ft (300-m) track, it will keep their attention. The **Flying Jumbos,** by contrast, is a never-fail flat, spinning elephant ride – with each pachyderm connected by an arm to a central hub. Other family-friendly rides are fun but nothing remarkable: a splashy log flume, a 115-ft (35-m) Ferris wheel and a flying-carpet ride much beloved by adolescent males for its scantily-clad-harem-girl statuary.

TOURING TIPS Almost like on an amusement pier, there are a surprising number of dining options, plus a sports bar, a pool hall, a mini-putt and a beer garden. One outdoor dining area even has heat lamps – a blessing in nippy weather, which you'll often find here, particularly in late spring. On a nice day, pack a picnic to enjoy by the loch in surrounding Strathclyde Country Park.

The main car park is along the left side of M&D's, making for a bit of a trek to the main entrance. There is also disabled and family parking directly in front of the entrance. If you arrive a few minutes before opening, chances of scoring a family parking slot are good. The downside of arriving early, however, is that M&D's is pretty tardy about getting its rides up and running. We wandered around for a while just after opening looking for something to ride.

There is no admission to the park per se, but a ticket office to the outside rear of the entrance building sells ride tokens and wristbands. There are also automated ride-token machines. Various wristband packages are available, both for individuals and families, but only the 'White Knuckle' package includes Bungee. Free park maps are available but aren't particularly good for navigation.

Sea Life Loch Lomond ★★

APPEAL BY AGE	PRESCHOOL ★★★	PRIMARY SCHOOL ★★	TEENS ★★
YOUNG ADULTS ★★	OVER 30 ★★		SENIORS ★★★

Loch Lomond Shores, Balloch, West Dunbartonshire G83 8QL
☎ **0871 423 2110; sealifeeurope.com**

HOURS Daily, 10 a.m.–5 p.m. Last admission is 1 hour before closing. Closed Christmas Day.

COST £12 adults; £9 children aged 3–14; £10.75 students and senior citizens. Discounts available online.

GETTING THERE *By car:* A 20-minute drive from Glasgow. Take the A82 to Balloch and follow signs to Loch Lomond Shores. *By rail:* It's a 5-minute walk from the Balloch train station. *By bus:* From Glasgow Central Rail Station, take the First Bus 204 or 215 (**firstgroup.com**) to Balloch. (Route information: **transportdirect.info.**)

DESCRIPTION AND COMMENTS 'Sharks in a shopping mall' might sound like a sequel to *Snakes on a Plane,* but this aquarium, adjacent to a retail complex on the southern edge of Loch Lomond, is no B-movie flop. Although modest in size, it commands a beautiful view of the deep-blue loch and has enough to offer that it's worth a stop as you head to **Loch Lomond** and **The Trossachs National Park,** or as part of a day trip from Glasgow.

The aquarium itself is set within **Drumkinnon Tower,** a striking building inspired by ancient Scottish castles and connected to shopping and the National Park Gateway Centre in the Loch Lomond Shores centre. The complex also has a cinema and restaurants.

Sea Life–brand aquariums across the UK – yes, we're afraid they're a brand, like Burger King – make it a priority to include local species in their displays. That's why in many of the aquarium's 26 exhibits you'll find freshwater minnows, perch, trout and eels, along with cod, bass, skate and rays. But there's no shortage of crowd-pleasing, colourful tropical species. The company says that it was one of the first major commercial partners with Greenpeace, suggesting that it takes environmental concerns seriously.

Guests are routed on an imaginary journey through Scottish waters, beginning with the Falls of Falloch, and then passing by exhibits based on the Loch. Eventually the path heads through the Clyde estuary and around the world. The final walk-through features the 77,000-gal (350,000-litre) **ocean tank.** The transparent tunnel is decorated to look like a grotto, and includes mood lighting and music to help set what's supposed to be an otherworldly ambience. There's also a 350-seat giant-screen cinema featuring a film on predators, a ray pool and displays with sea horses and jellyfish.

In 2010 Sea Life added 154-lb (70-kg) **Cammy, a green turtle** from the Cayman Islands, the first in Scotland. But the stars here are probably mammals. Three **Asian short-clawed otters,** Roma, Shona and Mons, romp and play and usually have a small crowd – you'll get a lot more out of your visit if you catch the daily Otter Madness talks at 11 a.m. or 2.30 p.m. The **shark collection** is impressive too, including hammerhead, black-tip, nurse and guitar species. One zebra shark is named Sir Bobby Robson, in homage to the late Newcastle United and England football manager. As with most aquaria, talks and guided visits can add greatly to your enjoyment. If you catch the **touch pool talk** at midday, though, be warned: those who look too eager are often recruited as volunteers and will soon have starfish clinging to their hands. This could be a highlight for some, but not all, visitors.

TOURING TIPS Try to catch the talks and feedings; otherwise your visit won't last more than an hour. Make sure that you get your hand stamped so you can leave for lunch and come back later.

St Andrews Aquarium ★★

| APPEAL BY AGE | PRESCHOOL ★★★ | PRIMARY SCHOOL ★★ | TEENS ★★ |
| YOUNG ADULTS ★★ | OVER 30 ★★ | | SENIORS ★★ |

The Scores, St Andrews, Fife KY1 69AR
☎ 01334 474 786; standrewsaquarium.co.uk

HOURS Daily, 10 a.m.–5 p.m.; only open on weekends in January.

COST £7.10 adults; £5.20 children aged 3–15; £5.80 senior citizens; £6.10 students; £5.10 special needs. Family rates from £22.20 (2 adults, 2 children).

GETTING THERE *By car:* About 80 mi (130 km) north of Glasgow, 50 mi (80 km) north of Edinburgh. Take the A92 to the A915 to St Andrews. The aquarium is on the West Sands, adjacent to the Royal & Ancient Golf Club. Parking is nearby at West Sands Golf Museum, £1 Easter–October; free other times. *By rail:* The closest rail station is Leuchars, 6.6 mi (10 km) away (**nationalrail.co.uk**). It has taxi service (about £10) and bus service to St Andrews. *By bus:* **Stagecoach Routes 94, 96** and **99 Fife** connect Leuchars to St Andrews (**stagecoachbus.com**), and the aquarium is a short walk away. (Route information: **transportdirect.info**.)

DESCRIPTION AND COMMENTS Not all the hazards in St Andrews are on the links. This modest aquarium features sharks, piranhas and poisonous frogs that make the sand traps at the adjacent Old Course look tame by comparison.

Like a good golf hole, the stone building is deceptive; constructed alongside a seaside cliff, it's much larger than it appears. The exhibit areas are built in layers down towards the shore. Visitors will find 30 exhibition tanks and a few standout displays, such as Tyson, the **largest catfish in Scotland,** who weighs in at 66 lb (30 kg).

The most popular resident, though, is **Hardy the harbour seal**, who lives in an outdoor cliff-side pool, easily seen from an observation area. His story reads like a marine-mammal romance novel: Hardy and roommate Laurel were brought to the aquarium as pups, having been abandoned at separate areas near Oban, on Scotland's northeast coast, in 1991. Seals in the area were suffering from distemper at the time, so the aquarium kept them safely quarantined. But by the time the disease had subsided, the two were acclimated to humans and unable to return to the wild. For 18 years they frolicked together and – like their comedy namesakes – delighted audiences who came to watch them in their seaside pool. Sadly, though, Laurel was washed out to sea in a freak storm in 2010. Hardy seems to have adjusted to bachelorhood, seal specialists say. He's still a crowd-pleaser too, and you'll want to time your visit to catch one of the two daily feedings at midday or 3 p.m.

There's also a chance to explore an indoor touch pool with the twice-daily **Rockpool Ramble** at 11.30 a.m. and 2.30 p.m. And if you're wondering what's lurking out on the horizon, take a look at the **Coastal Cousins** exhibit, which is devoted to local sea life. All told, a visit will take about an hour, allowing time to take in sea horses, lobsters and lionfish, among others.

TOURING TIPS We've never understood why aquariums have restaurants specialising in seafood. It would seem that after seeing our undersea friends, you'd be reluctant to eat them. But clearly we're in the minority. The aquarium is home to **Catch,** quite a nice restaurant, with a spectacular seaside setting and terrace. You don't even have to pay aquarium admission to visit.

If you're driving, a combination of one-way streets and the inability to see the aquarium from the road make finding it tricky. The best landmarks are the St Andrews Links on one side of Golf Place/Bruce Embankment Road and the British Golf Museum on the opposite side. Heading towards the coast, turn right into the pay-and-display car park next to the Golf Museum. From the car park, the aquarium is about 60 yd (55 m) distant.

St Andrews is one of the most interesting towns in the UK. A great walking town, it has enough ruins, castles and reformation history – not to mention the University of St Andrews (third oldest in the Kingdom behind Cambridge and Oxford), as well as shopping and, of course, golf and the seashore – to keep you busy for several days. Amongst such distinguished company, the aquarium is a lesser constellation for sure, but well worth a visit, especially on a rainy day.

FARM EXPERIENCES

BECAUSE THE VARIOUS FARM EXPERIENCES ARE SO SIMILAR (see page 13), we felt that it was unnecessary to provide individual profiles as we do with other types of attractions. Following is a selective list of farm experiences in Scotland.

ALMOND VALLEY HERITAGE CENTRE
Millfield, Livingston
West Lothian EH54 7AR
☎ 01506 414 957
almondvalley.co.uk
info@almondvalley.co.uk

DALSCONE FARM FUN
Dalscone Farm
Edinburgh Road
Dumfries DG1 1SE
☎ 01387 254 445
dalsconefarm.co.uk
dalscone@btconnect.com

HEADS OF AYR FARM PARK
Dunure Road
Alloway, Ayr
Ayrshire KA7 4LD
☎ 01292 441 210
headsofayrfarmpark.co.uk
craig@headsofayrfarmpark.co.uk

JEDFOREST DEER & FARM PARK
Mervinslaw Estate
Camptown, Jedburgh
Scottish Borders TD8 6PL
☎ 01835 840 364
jedforestdeerpark.co.uk
info@jedforestdeerpark.co.uk

PART FIFTEEN

WALES

WALES IS A BEAUTIFUL AND DIVERSE COUNTRY. From the thriving capital city of **Cardiff** with its world-class rugby and football, to the summit of **Mount Snowdon,** where Sir Edmund Hillary trained for his attempt on Everest, to the long-dormant coal mines of the **Rhondda Valley,** Wales is a country rich in history and tradition. Like Scotland, it's not known for its tourist attractions, but they are there in ample number and variety. Some are just for fun while others, such as farm experiences, mix entertainment with education. Still others, such as **Big Pit: National Coal Museum,** tell a story of country-wide hardship, loss and resilience.

THEME PARKS *and* ATTRACTIONS

Big Pit: National Coal Museum ★★★★★

| APPEAL BY AGE | PRESCHOOL ★★★ | PRIMARY SCHOOL ★★★ | TEENS ★★★★ |
| YOUNG ADULTS ★★★★★ | | OVER 30 ★★★★★ | SENIORS ★★★★★ |

Blaenavon, Torfaen NP4 9XP
☎ **01495 790 311; museumwales.ac.uk/en/bigpit**

- **HOURS** (March–November) 9.30 a.m.–5 p.m. Last admission is 1 hour before closing. Limited hours during winter.
- **COST** Admission is free. Visitors must be at least 5 years old and at least 3'3" (1 m) tall.
- **GETTING THERE** *By car:* From the M4, exit at Junction 26 eastbound or Junction 25 westbound and follow the signs for Big Pit on the A465. Ample free parking is on-site. *By rail:* Newport is the nearest mainline railway station (**nationalrail.co.uk**). *By bus:* A bus runs several times a day from Newport. (Route information: **transportdirect.info**.)

North Wales

ATTRACTIONS
1. Rhyl Seaquarium
2. Welsh Mountain Zoo

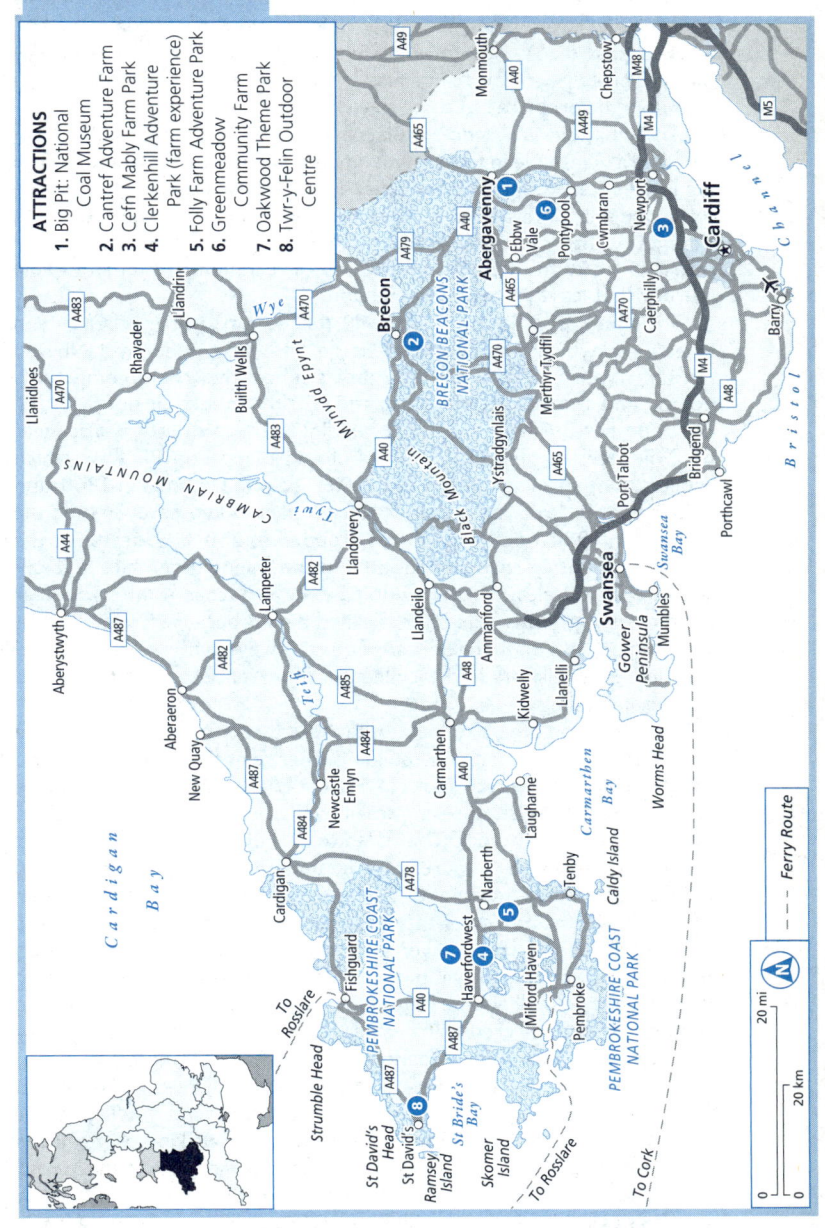

NORTH AND SOUTH WALES MAPS 441

South Wales

ATTRACTIONS
1. Big Pit: National Coal Museum
2. Cantref Adventure Farm
3. Cefn Mably Farm Park
4. Clerkenhill Adventure Park (farm experience)
5. Folly Farm Adventure Park
6. Greenmeadow Community Farm
7. Oakwood Theme Park
8. Twr-y-Felin Outdoor Centre

DESCRIPTION AND COMMENTS In the late 1970s, Wales was in crisis. Its mines, which had fuelled the industrial revolution and the region's economy for centuries, were being shut down. Generations of families who had worked (and died) underground suddenly faced the loss of their way of life. This huge social change also left huge scars on the land, leaving abandoned workplaces to rust away.

And what did Wales do? In Blaenavon, at least, they turned an eyesore and a giant hole in the ground into a brilliant tourist attraction. The Big Pit: National Coal Museum tells the story of Wales's coal heritage – not through an interactive museum but on a field trip to the actual site. You get outfitted with more than 10.4 lb (5 kg) of safety gear and are sent 295 ft (90 m) underground to tour a real mine. It's a memorable journey that leaves a lasting impression.

The museum is located about 30 mi (48 km) north of Cardiff in Blaenavon, which is a World Heritage Site recognised by UNESCO for the important role that the area's innovative coal-mining technology and techniques played in the world's industrial heritage. Big Pit alone has 39 listed historical buildings. The property is also near the volunteer-run heritage Pontypool and Blaenavon Railway, which expects to open a line directly to Big Pit. The mine opened in 1860, and at its height in 1908 more than 1,100 people worked here. By the time it closed in 1980, employment had dropped to 250. It is located at the end of a mountain road and situated in the rolling green hills and valleys of South Wales, which couldn't be more bucolic – until you near the museum grounds. The mine is called Big Pit because it was the first constructed with enough room for two tramways, with shafts 18 ft (5.5 m) wide. Now visitors find a collection of warehouses, rail tracks and industrial buildings.

The reception area, like most other structures on-site, is housed in a preserved and renovated mine building. There's nothing showy or grand about the entrance. It still looks like a workplace, although you may be tempted by the gift shop selling small bags of coal and figurines carved from the sedimentary rock. You're led to a waiting room with WCs that you'd be wise to visit, because you'll be underground for an hour. Then you'll be greeted by a volunteer guide – quite often an ex-miner – then equipped with mandatory safety gear before you can descend into the earth: a helmet with lamp powered by a heavy battery and a re-breather, an emergency filter that will provide safe air for about an hour during an emergency. You'll also be required to turn off or leave behind mobile phones, battery-powered watches and cameras – anything powered by electricity – because a single spark could set off an explosion.

All kitted out, you then pack into an industrial wire-cage lift and go down. You step out into the realm of the miner, and you'll discover that little has been sanitised for visitors. You'll be walking over uneven surfaces and up and down slopes, crouching in some areas to make your way through. Water seeps from the walls and is routed to a ditch, but walkways will still be slippery. (Even so, wheelchair users can be accommodated with prior arrangement.) The roof is held up by steel bands and supports, and the gas monitors and emergency telephones you see aren't props. Soon you'll see the actual working areas, where miners crawled with picks and axes to remove the coal that fuelled Britain's rise to industrial might. Children as young as age 5 worked down here on 12-hour shifts, opening and closing doors to let coal pass through. At least the children got to leave at the end of the shift. You'll also see stables still bearing the names of horses, such as Dragon, Patch, Tiger and Albert. At the mine's height, 72 of the animals lived down here hauling coal cars and were brought to the surface for only two weeks a year. The last horses weren't retired until 1972. At one memorable moment, everyone turns out their headlamps, and you're plunged into complete darkness.

But it's the ex-miners who bring the tours to life. Depending on their mood and personality, you may hear stories of camaraderie, bravery and the horrors faced underground. Others will rail at former Prime Minister Margaret Thatcher for her role in shutting down the mines.

Back on the surface, the tour is hardly over. You can visit restored buildings, including an engine house, a blacksmith's workshop, a lamp room and the renovated historical **Pithead Baths,** with towels still hanging on pegs. It's hard to imagine what an impact these showers had on miners' lives, we're told. Until they were installed, workers had to travel home filthy with coal dust and try to clean up there. When the baths were added, each miner had a 'clean' locker for his regular clothes and a 'dirty' locker for his work ones. After his shift, his filthy work clothes would be dried for his next shift by hot air that constantly blew through the lockers. In the medical centre, you can see how a doctor treated minor wounds and injuries. Sometimes it was woefully inadequate. In 1913 Britain's worst mining disaster occurred around 50 mi (80 km) away, at Senghenydd, where 439 men died.

Walk up a hill from the main pit to the **Mining Galleries,** where you can view a 20-minute multimedia presentation about how coal mining worked and evolved. You're led through exhibits showing mining from the 1950s, when workers used an undercutting machine – a huge chainsaw – to rip the coal from the earth, while other workers placed wooden posts to hold up the roof. Then the mined coal was placed on a conveyor belt by hand. Next you see how by the 1970s much of the work was automated, with conveyors, hydraulic roof supports and a tungsten-tipped cutter attached to a revolving drum. All is explained with sound, light and humorous narration.

The topic gets much more serious in the **Heroes or Villains?** exhibit, which explains how Wales's coal industry collapsed. Screens replay scenes from the coal strike of 1984 under Margaret Thatcher, which eventually led to the end of the industry in Wales. The South was particularly hard hit, and harsh feelings persist even decades later.

TOURING TIPS Arrive early in the day. Tours are limited in size, and you may end up waiting for more than an hour for your trip underground. Pack a jacket or jumper even on a summer's day. It's cold and damp underground. Big Pit is considered an anchor point for the European Route of Industrial Heritage (**erih.net**), which links more than 50 sites around the continent. While you're here, consider other industrial tours in the area, including Blaenavon's heritage railway (**pontypool-and-blaenavon.co.uk**), which plans to open a spur to Big Pit. Also nearby are the Blaenavon Ironworks and fascinating industrial walks exploring old worksites that are now overgrown (**world-heritage-blaenavon.org.uk**).

Oakwood Theme Park ★★★★

APPEAL BY AGE	PRESCHOOL ★★★	PRIMARY SCHOOL ★★★★	TEENS ★★★★★
YOUNG ADULTS ★★★★		OVER 30 ★★★	SENIORS ★★

Canaston Bridge, Narberth, Pembrokeshire SA67 8DE
☎ **01834 861 889; oakwoodthemepark.co.uk**

HOURS (September–October and April–mid-July) 10 a.m.–5 p.m. (mid-July–August) 10 a.m.–6 p.m. Closed November–March.

HOURS £19.95 adults and children aged 13 and older; £14.25 children aged 3–12; £12.25 senior citizens and disabled; £63 family ticket (2 adults, 2 children); £76.65 family ticket (2 adults, 3 children); £93.50 family ticket (2 adults, 4 children). Discounts available online.

GETTING THERE *By car:* The park is signposted on brown tourist-information signs from the end of the M4 and throughout Pembrokeshire. From South Wales follow the M4 West until Junction 49 and take the A48 to Carmarthen. From Mid Wales follow the A40 to Carmarthen. From North Wales follow the A487 from Machynlleth, then the A478 Cardigan to Tenby Road, and then turn right at the Penblewin roundabout onto the A40. *By rail:* The nearest station is Narberth, 5 mi (8 km) from the park (**nationalrail.co.uk**). Because Oakwood is not on a bus route, you need to book a taxi to reach the park. Return transport from the station for up to 4 people costs £42 (contact Jeff Cabs on ☎ 0800 783 4199).

DESCRIPTION AND COMMENTS Oakwood Park has come a long way since the late 1980s, when it was a Welsh dairy farm struggling to get by. The owners decided that coasters offered more promise than cows and carefully planned a theme park, aiming to maintain the country atmosphere and preserving as much tree cover as possible. Over the next two decades, it built some of the UK's most innovative rides and developed a manic following amongst coaster fans.

But in 2008, the founding family sold out to Spanish theme-park conglomerate Aspro Group. Although there haven't been many park updates since, the property still packs in visitors, many on a quest to experience the **Oakwood Big Four:** the **Speed** and **Megafobia** coasters, the **Bounce** drop tower and the **Hydro** water ride. By and large, the rides still deliver. And other, more-tame rides will keep you busy if you'd rather not be shot into the air, spun upside-down and doused in water.

As in most major parks, there's ample parking and a tram to haul you to the entrance. Take it – you'll want to save your energy for the park. Ticket queues can be long here, providing another reason to buy your admission on Oakwood's website. The major rides are distributed around the park, and adrenaline junkies would be wise to do a circuit and hit them first before the inevitable queues build.

The first stop is **Speed** (sometimes called Speed: No Limits), a steel coaster that features a 97° drop – yes, that's more than vertical, meaning you'll be hanging out of your seat as you plunge downwards 110 ft (35 m). The 90-second ride also includes a loop, helix and barrel roll and reaches speeds of 60 mph (95 km/h). The ride ranked as the third-best steel coaster in the UK in a recent international poll. It offers plenty of air-time and isn't as scary as it looks, some fans say. You'll have to make that decision for yourself.

Next hoof it over to **Bounce,** which is just to the right of Speed if you take the path behind the Waterfall ride. This 154-ft (47-m) drop tower holds 24 riders at a time (6 on each side of the tower) and shoots them up at 44 mph (71 km/h), which will subject you to 4 g's. Part of the appeal is the random nature of the ride. Sometimes you're shot up the tower immediately; other times you're raised slowly and then suddenly dropped. After the free-fall, the pattern continues, and you're never sure when the next shot up (or fall down) is coming.

Now make your way to the top of the park to that massive wood structure you've been eying ever since you arrived. **Megafobia** is the ride that made Oakwood and put it on the map. When it opened in 1996, it was the first of the new era of twister-style wooden coasters, and it soon became one of the favourite rides in all of the UK. It's said that if you took the whole thing apart and laid out the wood, it would stretch to London and back. The nearly-2-minute ride covers about 0.6 mi (1 km) and reaches speeds of about 50 mph (80 km/h). Some say that the ride is faster on a wet day; others suggest taking it towards the end of a hot day. The first drop plunges 82 ft (25 m) and delivers nearly 3 g's as you pass right under other sections of track. Between the speed, turns and the threat of decapitation, it's a ride that will keep your attention. A recent international poll ranked it as the top wooden coaster in the UK and twenty-ninth in the world. As with most wooden coasters, the ride is jarring, and because you're secured only by a lap bar, your upper body is bounced around a lot.

If you still have any nerves left, it's time to get wet. Head over to the far-right side of the park for **Hydro.** It's amongst the biggest water coasters in the world, and the tallest in Europe. The final plunge is down 118 ft (36 m) into a 1-million-gal (4.5-million-litre) pool, which creates a 45-ft (13.7-m) wave. Even if you're not brave (or foolhardy) enough to ride it, you can still get a full soaking by standing on a bridge over the plunge. But we think that if you're going to be drenched, you should earn it with your heart in your throat. If you want to keep dry, though, ponchos are for sale in the gift shops. If you don't want to spring for the poncho, bring a large plastic refuse bag with a hole cut for your head. Bring a smaller plastic bag for your feet unless you want to walk in soaked squishy shoes the rest of the day. Will people laugh at you? Only at the beginning of the ride. By the time you unload, they'll think you're the smartest person in Wales.

The other extreme thrill ride here is **Vertigo,** a free-fall swing under an enormous metal arch that costs an extra £33 for a solo flight. These rides are often seen at funfairs, and we think that you're already paying enough to visit. If you want to save a little cash, three people can be dropped together at once for £11 each. Make sure that you're good friends (or want to be), because you will all become very close as you face what feels like a near-death experience together. Vertigo can only accommodate a handful of riders per hour. If more than ten people are in the queue ahead of you, forget it.

After you've hit the Big Four, there's plenty more to keep you busy at the park.

Make your way back across the park behind Bounce to the cute **Treetops** coaster. Although it's kids' stuff after what you've been through, the 1,181-ft (360-m) steel coaster is quite fun and scenic as it weaves through the treetops. Not only is this a nice aesthetic touch, but it also enhances the ride. The trees block your view of the coaster track, so you're never quite sure where you're heading next. Plus there's the constant fear of whacking into a branch to keep you on edge. The 1-minute ride reaches speeds of 22 mph (35 km/h), making it a perfect family coaster.

Head back towards Bounce for another popular family ride: **Snake River Falls.** This water chute ride sends you zooming down in small rubber boats. You choose from four lanes: two closed tubes – called The Cobra and The Python – that cross-twist and turn as they descend, and two open bumpy slides. In theory your boat will bounce along the water at the bottom, taking you to a dry area to disembark. Don't count on it.

Similar is **Waterfall,** which you'll find right next door. It's a two-lane water slide in sledges. You'll stay above the water as you descend but may capsize in the pool at the bottom. If you want to avoid this fate, lean forwards when you hit the water. If you'd rather appreciate getting wet, lean back. The other popular family ride here is the **Bobsleigh,** an alpine toboggan slide in the centre of the park. This refreshingly-low-tech experience puts you in a sledge that's hauled up a hill on a track. You then control your descent with a handbrake. Yes, you, and not a ride computer, are in charge. You can ride by yourself or in pairs.

Young visitors will enjoy the mini–fairground thrills in the **Play Town Rides** area and the elaborate **Lost Kingdom** indoor soft-play area. If there's any aggression in your child, you'll soon discover it in the **Wacky Factory,** where everyone has a chance to fire plastic balls at each other.

Elsewhere you'll find standard park rides, from a swinging pirate ship to **Plane Crazy,** a flying carousel with the seats shaped like small planes. A rather ghoulish ghost ride, **Spooky 3D,** does manage to offer a few scares. But you can't leave without trying **Brer Rabbit's Burrow,** a scenic train ride that you'll either find charming or disturbing, with rather poor models of fairytale rabbits that appear to be drunk in some scenes and ready to hop into bed in another. We guess it just depends how you define the phrase *thrill ride.*

TOURING TIPS Remember to pack a swimsuit, towel and poncho if you don't want to be damp all day. Food here is nothing special, so a picnic would be a good idea. Remember your parking area – perhaps even text it to yourself. You don't want to spend an hour wandering around the car park looking for your vehicle. If you have a dog, the park kennels will hold it for free.

If you come for the thrill rides, arrive with admission in hand at park opening and ride Speed, Bounce, Megafobia and Hydro, in that order. Don't forget your bin liners.

Rhyl SeaQuarium ★★

| APPEAL BY AGE | PRESCHOOL ★★★★ | PRIMARY SCHOOL ★★★ | TEENS ★★ |
| YOUNG ADULTS ★★ | | OVER 30 ★★★ | SENIORS ★★★ |

East Parade, Rhyl, Denbighshire LL18 3AF
☎ **01745 344 660; seaquarium.co.uk/rhyl.php**

- **HOURS** 10 a.m.–5 p.m. Last admission 1 hour before closing. Closed 24–26 December.
- **COST** £7.99 adults; £6.99 children aged 3–16, senior citizens, students and disabled (disabled carer free); £27.99 family ticket (2 adults, 2 children; £6.49 each additional child). Admission can also be bought through the Tesco Clubcard rewards scheme.
- **GETTING THERE** *By car:* About 30 mi (48 km) northwest of Chester. Exit the A55, and turn at the A525 into Rhyl, where you'll take the A548 along the coast. There is often parking along the promenade. *By rail:* The nearest rail station is Rhyl, about 0.5 mile (0.9 kilometre) from the aquarium (**nationalrail.co.uk**). *By bus:* **Arriva** offers service to Rhyl from across the region (**arrivabus.co.uk**). (Route information: **transportdirect.info.**)
- **DESCRIPTION AND COMMENTS** This former Sea Life Centre on the North Wales coast is now owned by a mini-chain – its sister sites include Weston-Super-Mare SeaQuarium and West Midlands Safari Park – and its design feels less corporate and commercial than its competition. The smallish attraction has about 30 exhibits, all laid out in a clear path. As you enter, ask for the **Discovery Trail Quiz,** which is designed for kids, but teens and adults can have fun too as they seek out answers on various display boards.

  The SeaQuarium features the longest underwater tunnel in Wales. The highlight, though, is **Sealion Cove,** a performance area with a 33,000-gal (150,000-litre) pool – look for the giant sea-lion sculpture. The cove is home to 15-minute sea-lion and seal shows at 1 and 3 p.m., and a harbour-seal feeding occurs at midday. Along with the popular eels, rays and octopuses, you can see the small but strange axolotl, the so-called walking fish that's actually an endangered salamander species that never undergoes metamorphosis. For those in your party not interested in evolutionary quirks, there's always the aquarium's **Sharky Shack Fun Zone,** an amusement arcade.
- **TOURING TIPS** Not an attraction that you'd plan a day around, but fine for an hour or so if you're in the area. Sealion Cove is outdoors, so bring your brollies.

  (For more on aquariums, see page 10.)

Twr-y-Felin Outdoor Centre ★★★★

| APPEAL BY AGE | PRESCHOOL ★ | PRIMARY SCHOOL ★★★ | TEENS ★★★★★ | YOUNG ADULTS ★★★★★ | OVER 30 ★★★★★ | SENIORS ★★★ |

1 High Street, St David's, Pembrokeshire SA62 6SA
☎ **01437 721 611; tyf.com**

HOURS Half-day classes begin at 9 and 11 a.m. or 1.30 p.m. Call to check on times for full-day and weekend classes. Classes are offered year-round in all types of weather. If a class has to be cancelled, you'll be offered the choice of a refund or rescheduling.

COST (July–August) Half day of coasteering, kayaking, surfing or rock climbing: £60 adults; £40 children aged 16 and under. Whole-day Coastal Explorer package (includes coasteering, sit-on sea kayaking, snorkelling and often fishing): £100 adults; £75 children aged 16 and under. (September–June) Half day of coasteering, kayaking, surfing or rock climbing: £55 adults; £35 children aged 16 and under. Whole-day Coastal Explorer package (includes coasteering, sit-on sea kayaking, snorkelling and often fishing): £95 adults; £70 children aged 16 and under. Lunch available by pre-order: £5. The centre says that it takes customers aged 8–80, but you should realistically assess your level of fitness and ability to handle the activity you choose. The same Coastal Explorer prices apply to a full day of one or two activities. Get a 10% discount on all outings if you arrive by bus or rail and present your ticket.

GETTING THERE *By car:* From London, the Midlands, Bristol and the east, follow the M4 motorway to the end, then take the A48, and then the A40, following signs to Haverfordwest. From there follow the A487 to St David's. From Manchester and the north, head towards Wrexham and then south past Welshpool on the A470 and A489 to Aberystwyth and then Cardigan. From there take the A487 through Fishguard and then to St David's. Two car parks are near the office. The centre is situated opposite the National Trust shop and next door to Barclays Bank, just above the Cross Square. *By rail:* The closest station is Haverfordwest (**nationalrail.co.uk**). *By bus:* From Haverfordwest, take the **Richards Brothers 411 bus** to St David's, a trip of about 30 minutes (**richardsbros.co.uk**; **transportdirect.info**).

DESCRIPTION AND COMMENTS The south-west corner of Wales has some of the wildest and most beautiful scenery in the UK. Although there are stunning scenic drives in the region, you can also experience the craggy coastal setting in a more active way.

The Twr-y-Felin Outdoor Centre provides an easy way to get out near and on the water and explore the Pembrokeshire coastline. It offers half-day, full-day and weekend programmes for sea kayaking, rock climbing and surfing, but what makes it stand out is a full-body experience called coasteering, which lets you explore the ledges, cliffs, bays, caves and waters of this windswept corner of the country.

Coasteering (pronounced 'coast-earring') may be the town's most popular year-round pastime. The activity, which was invented here in the 1990s, mixes rock-climbing and cliff-jumping with swimming. Once your guide sets you loose, you'll be jumping around like a character in a video game, clambering over the forbidding landscape from land to sea and back. (The owners like to say that they didn't invent coasteering – they're just offering you the chance to try the same type of activity that has kept local children amused for centuries.) As you meet your guide, you're kitted out with a wetsuit, helmet and buoyancy belt, which give you the appearance of having just stepped out of a Monty Python skit. Then you're taken to a cliff side, where you'll clamber up and down the rocks and along the water's edge. You jump across boulders, crags and gullies, but at some point the path gives out, or a wave strikes, and you find yourself taking a leap of faith into the drink. Next thing you know, you're bobbing in the water.

Coasteering embraces this exciting zone between land and water. You see rocks, kelp and other sea life as you flop around in the water like a seal. Over the course of your adventure, you'll cover around a mile (up to 2 km) before climbing back up the cliffs, exhausted and perhaps a little bruised, but exhilarated in a way that could never be matched by a workout on a treadmill. Don't look for coasteering to be adopted as an Olympic sport anytime soon, but do consider it for a memorable outing.

The centre offers a selection of coasteering adventures based on your level of experience – and nerve. **Blue Line** sessions are for beginners and involve relatively-easy routes year-round. **White Line** sessions are reserved for strong swimmers confident in rough seas. Although they sound deceptively easy, Flat Line sessions cover longer routes – you need stamina, and it helps if you enjoy racing and triathlons. Finally, **Green Line** sessions explore the intertidal zone and offer a marine-life education along with your adventure. The centre provides wetsuits, helmets and buoyancy aids. You need to bring old trainers that can get wet, swimwear, old drawstring shorts to wear over your wetsuit and warm clothes to change into after the session.

If coasteering doesn't float your boat, you have several other outdoor adventures to fill your day. The centre, recognised as a Welsh Canoe Association Centre of Excellence, offers **sea-kayaking** courses using both single and tandem sit-on vessels in what are among the best kayaking waters in the UK. You get use of a wetsuit, helmet and sprayskirt, and the expertise of a guide. Half-day courses are geared towards beginners and include instruction before heading towards open waters. On calm days you can explore caves and may encounter curious porpoises and seals as you paddle around the coastline. Full-day outings are open to both beginners and more-experienced paddlers. Kayakers should bring towels, wetsuit boots, swimwear and warm clothes for after your trip. The centre also offers day trips to outlying islands several times a year.

If kayaking seems too tame, you can take to the waters on a board. While Pembrokeshire doesn't pretend to be Maui, the peninsula enjoys consistently-rideable waves throughout the year, including memorable winter swells. The half-day **surfing** classes will show you to handle and paddle a board and identify suitable waves. You'll also have a go at riding a wave both prone and standing, and learn to make simple turns. Full-day classes offer more time to work on your techniques as you develop confidence and ability. The centre provides a surfboard with leash and a wetsuit. You'll have to bring wetsuit boots, swimwear and warm clothes for after your trip. You also need a towel, and if you're the least bit modest, bring a large one because you'll be changing on the beach with minimal male–female separation, and you may want to cover up.

Finally, if you'd rather stay out of the water, you can always conquer the cliffs above it. The **rock-climbing** classes start with bouldering instruction and then move on to more-challenging routes, either on steep limestone or sandstone slabs. Half-day classes cover use of a climbing rope, belaying and actual climbs, while full-day courses allow for more-in-depth climbs. While scaling sea cliffs is not that different from climbing mountains, you'll probably find the dramatic setting makes it more physical and psychologically demanding – and rewarding.

TOURING TIPS Unlike in a theme park, these are not engineered activities. While some classes are geared towards beginners, you'll still be undertaking a physical activity. Have a change of clothes – when you're playing near water, you'll inevitably get wet. The centre also offers group and youth classes and corporate team-building sessions.

Welsh Mountain Zoo ★★★

APPEAL BY AGE	PRESCHOOL ★★★	PRIMARY SCHOOL ★★★	TEENS ★★	YOUNG ADULTS ★★★
		OVER 30 ★★★		SENIORS ★★★

Old Highway, Colwyn Bay, Clwyd LL28 5UY
☎ **01492 532 938; welshmountainzoo.org**

HOURS (April–October) 9.30 a.m–6 p.m. (November–March) 9.30 a.m–5 p.m. Last admission is 1 hour before closing. Closed Christmas Day.

COST £9.85 adults; £7.25 children aged 3–15 and students with NUS card; £8.60 senior citizens; £31.10 family ticket (2 adults, 2 children). Admission free for visitors who use wheelchairs. Tickets can also be bought through the Tesco Clubcard rewards scheme.

GETTING THERE *By car:* Located 3 minutes from the A55 Expressway. Exit at the Rhos-on-Sea interchange (Junction 20), and follow zoo signs. *By rail:* Colwyn Bay is the closest station, 1 mi (1.6 km) away (**nationalrail.co.uk**). *By bus:* Easter–mid-September the zoo operates a free minibus continually 10 a.m.–5 p.m. from the Colwyn Bay railway station (waiting times 20 minutes or less). (Route information: **transportdirect.info.**)

DESCRIPTION AND COMMENTS You'll find a zoo with a view at this small but thoughtful attraction on the North Wales coast. Humans and animals alike find spectacular vistas across Colwyn Bay, and even as far as Snowdonia. It's lovely land for the bears, chimps, leopards and tigers. But the scenery comes with a price. Although the zoo is on a hilltop, there's still a good deal of climbing – difficult with wheelchairs and pushchairs.

The 37-ac (15-ha) wooded attraction dates to 1963, when naturalist Robert Jackson, his wife and three sons moved to a former Victorian estate to open an animal-breeding and -display centre. The property had originally belonged to a Manchester doctor, and although he never built a home here, he did construct gardens designed by famous landscaper Thomas Mawson. After the doctor's death, the property was opened to the public as Flagstaff Gardens, and much of it still remains in its natural state as a wildlife preserve. But Jackson saw the potential for a zoo on the site. He was also a bit of a showman and developed then-innovative free-flight falconry demonstrations and sea-lion shows. Although the concepts have since spread far and wide, the shows remain a popular part of the Welsh Mountain Zoo experience. The zoo itself has more than 80 species and more than 270 specimens. While you won't see iconic animals such as elephants and giraffes, there is an impressive diversity, with snow leopards, red pandas and Andean condors.

It all makes for a pleasant day out. You'll drive up a steep hill and pay as you enter the property, which makes it easy to pop back to the car to grab a picnic basket or a fleece, as it can get quite windy here. As you enter through a main gate, you'll find nearly all the exhibits ahead and to the left. There is a cluster of buildings at the entrance, but we suggest that you save those until the end of your visit, when you're likely to be tired-out. Your first stop is an impressive one, **otters** and a pair of rare **red pandas,** named Ming Ming and Bron. Just behind are the deceptively-cuddly **European brown bears.** You'll pass **macaws** and **Azara's agoutis,** large South American rodents. Continuing up the path leads to one of the zoo's highlights, its huge **Andean condor aviary,** home to Sonya and Gus. The species has the widest wingspan of any land bird, reaching up to 10½ ft (3.2 m).

Near the top of the trail you'll find **Sumatran tigers,** which are extremely rare, with fewer than 500 in the wild. There's a café here if you fancy a snack, and then continuing anti-clockwise, any children in your group will sprint to **Jungle Adventureland,** an extensive hillside playground with swings and slides. It's by **Tarzan Trail,** a more challenging obstacle course for older kids, with nets and climbing equipment.

Just to the right, you'll find the **snow leopards,** beautiful animals that look a bit like tigers in sepia tone. And next door is the impressive **Chimp Encounter,** where you can catch a live performance at least twice daily. You take a seat in a tiered theatre-like space, where you watch a video about the animals' behaviour and then get to meet the zoo's dozen or so chimpanzees and observe them at play. It's next to **Chimpanzee World,** where the sometimes-naughty primates will be on display on sunny days and between shows. Up to the right, you'll encounter the ultimate odd couple, **Welsh mountain goats** and **wallabies.** Continue to the left to **ostriches,** and then take the path behind that enclosure to see the fascinating **Przewalski's horses.** This endangered, oddly-proportioned equine has always looked like a nuclear horse to us, so it's ironic that one of the few places you can find them in the wild is in the abandoned zone around the Chernobyl plant in the

Ukraine. Although the horses were at one time extinct in the wild, they have also been reintroduced in Mongolia.

Now heading back towards the centre of the park, stop to see the **Humboldt penguins.** April–October, there's a delightful **Penguin Parade** across an open field at midday and 3 p.m. and a **birds-of-prey free-flying display** in good weather. Cutting down towards the bottom left of the park brings you to **Sea Lion Rock,** where glass walls allow for underwater viewing, and a show is presented twice daily.

Continuing diagonally up towards the Trading Post gift shop, pass the **Macaw Walk,** and then cut down to the squirrel-sized **tamarins** and even smaller **marmosets,** monkeys just 8" (20 cm) long. Head over to the **polecats,** and then the distinctive two-humped **Bactrian camels.** The zoo has had luck with breeding, and if you're lucky, you may get to see a young one. Finally, it's time to cut back over towards the entrance, passing **emus** and the rare **margay,** a spotted feline from Central and South America.

Clustered around the entrance, you'll find buildings with **gibbons, spider monkeys, meerkats** and **porcupines,** which look cuddlier than they should, given their sharp quills. Before you exit, check out **Alligator Beach,** a place where – trust us – you don't want to go swimming. It's home to Mississippi alligators named Nancy and Albert, the only breeding pair in the UK. They keep warm under sunlamps in an open-topped enclosure, and for the most part they remain so still that they look like foam models – until, that is, they lunge at their meal.

To end your visit on a less-menacing note, head to the front of the zoo for the **Children's Farm,** where you'll find everything from African pygmy goats to rabbits, guinea pigs, ducks and chickens.

TOURING TIPS Study the zoo map carefully to minimise backtracking. Wheelchairs are available free of charge, but they can still be rough-going up hills. Bring a jacket, or at least have one in your car. When the sun is not out, it can get quite windy and chilly. Check the times of the shows; they really are a highlight and help make this small zoo a worthwhile outing.

FARM EXPERIENCES

BECAUSE THE VARIOUS FARM EXPERIENCES ARE SO SIMILAR (see page 13), we felt that it was unnecessary to provide individual profiles as we do with other types of attractions. Following is a selective list of farm experiences in Wales.

CANTREF ADVENTURE FARM
Cantref, Brecon
Powys LD3 8LR
☎ 01874 665 223
cantref.com
(Email via form at website)

CEFN MABLY FARM PARK
Began Road
Cefn Mably
Cardiff CF3 6XL
☎ 01633 680 312
cefnmablyfarmpark.com
mail@cefnmablyfarmpark.com

CLERKENHILL ADVENTURE PARK
(Irrespective of the name, it offers almost all the basic farm experience activities)
Slebech, Haverfordwest
Pembrokeshire SA62 4PE
☎ 01437 751 227
clerkenhill.co.uk
enquiries@clerkenhill.co.uk

FOLLY FARM ADVENTURE PARK
(Combination farm experience and small zoo with a few rides thrown in for good measure)
Folly Farm
Begelly, Kilgetty
Pembrokeshire SA68 0XA
☎ 01834 812 731
folly-farm.co.uk
info@folly-farm.co.uk

GREENMEADOW COMMUNITY FARM
Greenforge Way
Cwmbran, Torfaen NP44 5AJ
☎ 01633 647 662
**greenmeadowcommunityfarm
  .org.uk**
(Email via form at website)

PART SIXTEEN

In the FOOTSTEPS of HARRY POTTER

NEXT TO THE ROYAL FAMILY, no group has done more to define the UK's public image recently than Harry Potter and his classmates. You can thank J. K. Rowling not only for her incredible imagination but for sending scores of travellers tramping across the countryside seeking signs of Quidditch matches and mysterious soaring owls. Aside from London, her books are set in fictional locales. (Try as you might to find it, Hogsmeade isn't anywhere to be found on Google Earth.)

Instead, the Potter movies used locations across Great Britain. For example, the Hogwarts School of Witchcraft and Wizardry can't be found in one place: the institution was created by combining scenes from some of the most atmospheric historical buildings in the country. The film-makers took a cloister here, a crenellated tower there, and added a bit of digital touch-up work to create the beloved boarding school. Other scenes were filmed in side streets and alleys, even in government buildings. Some fans have built an entire holiday out of driving by places like the private home near Bracknell that stood in for the Dursley house.

We don't suggest that. But some Potter filming locations are worth seeing for their own sake – and if you can pick up a bit of wizarding lore while you're visiting, then that's as good as a fresh box of Bertie Botts Beans.

ATTRACTIONS

Alnwick Castle ★★★★

APPEAL BY AGE	PRESCHOOL ★★	PRIMARY SCHOOL ★★★★	TEENS ★★★★
YOUNG ADULTS ★★★★		OVER 30 ★★★★	SENIORS ★★★★

Alnwick, Northumberland NE66 1NQ
☎ 01665 510 777; alnwickcastle.com

HOURS (April–October) Grounds open 10 a.m.–6 p.m.; State Rooms open 11 a.m.–5 p.m. (last admission 4.15 p.m.); Knights Quest 10 a.m.–5 p.m.

COST £12.50 adults (£19.80 castle and gardens, valid for 2 days); £5.50 children (5–15) (£5.50 castle and gardens); £10.60 senior citizens, students (£16.80 castle and gardens); £32.50 family ticket (2 adults, up to 4 children).

GETTING THERE *By car:* Located 5 minutes off the A1; exit at Alnmouth and follow signs to the castle. Parking costs £2. *By rail:* The nearest station is Alnmouth, about 4 mi (6.4 km) from the castle (**nationalrail.co.uk**). *By bus:* The 519 service runs from Alnmouth Station to the castle. (Route information: **transportdirect.info**.)

DESCRIPTION AND COMMENTS Perhaps no site delights a Harry Potter fan more than this mediaeval castle, which served as the exterior of Hogwarts. But even if you couldn't tell a Nimbus 2000 from a nose-biting teacup, you'd probably enjoy it as well.

Alnwick, the second largest inhabited castle in England, has been called 'The Windsor of the North'. The castle dates to 1096, and the current building has been the home of the Percys, earls and dukes of Northumberland, since 1309. Although the castle looks like a relic, it has been modernised many times over the centuries. It fell into decay in the late 1600s but was rescued by Elizabeth Seymour and Hugh Smithson, who later became the first Duke and Duchess of Northumberland. They turned the fortress into a family residence with the help of architect Robert Adam and famed landscape designer Capability Brown, and their descendants still live on-site.

Over the centuries, the castle has been updated. In 1889, it became one of the first homes in the North East to have electricity when the owners added a hydro plant – a magical transformation at the time, worthy of Hogwarts.

Although you can't get a diploma from Hogwarts, you can still attend school here. Since the Second World War, part of the castle has housed educational institutions. It was formerly a high school for girls and a teacher-training college, and since 1981 it has served as a satellite campus for St Cloud State University in Minnesota, in the United States. Students live at the castle – without the help of elves cleaning up after them – and study humanities.

The castle can be an expensive day out. The grounds and home aren't well signed, but for Potter fans none of that matters. There's a clear effort here to make the castle family-friendly, with kid-themed tours and activities.

Parking is outside the castle grounds, and it can be quite a hike to the entrance. A castle outing includes visits to the lavish **State Rooms** and the **library,** with more than 16,000 books displayed in floor-to-ceiling bookshelves. The collection was started by the ninth Earl and later expanded by the fourth Duke. The **dining room,** renovated by the current Duchess, includes a carved Brunswick-pine ceiling and is decorated with the heraldry of the Percys. Look for the frieze honouring the fourth Duke and Duchess on the Italian-marble fireplace, and portraits of the first Duke and Duchess. Stare as you might, though, the figures don't appear to move. A priceless **porcelain collection** is displayed in the corridor. The tour also visits an **inner courtyard** where Harry first learned to fly on a broom and played in his first Quidditch match.

More elaborate is **Knight's Quest,** a child-themed programme that includes mediaeval costumes, sword-fighting and jousting, ending in a brief knightship ceremony. Then comes **Dragon's Quest**, a haunted house of sorts with ghouls, goblins and a mirror maze. You can also take in a **birds-of-prey demonstration** and **archery lessons,** which include a bit of instruction before you're given six arrows to shoot (extra cost of £2).

Outside, the terrace offers stirring views of the countryside, and you'll find small exhibits in the towers. The **Postern Tower** has archaeological items relating to ancient British history, while **Abbot's Tower** is home to the Fusiliers Museum of Northumberland, with an array of uniforms, medals, weapons and paintings. The **Coach House** contains the grand state coach, used in 1902 at the coronation of King Edward VII.

A more contemporary site is the nearby **Garden,** which has been recently restored. The highlight is the **Grand Cascade,** the largest water feature of its kind in England, and – designed for Potter fans, it would seem – a **poison garden.** It also has a **bamboo labyrinth** and a huge **tree house** with rope bridges, walkways and a treetop restaurant.

TOURING TIPS Before you visit, call ahead to see if the castle is offering its **Battleaxes to Broomsticks** tour – usually at 11.30 a.m. and 2 p.m. – as this is the easiest way to get your fill of Potter patter. These comprehensive tours cover the castle's history and are geared to young fans, who are urged to spot the owl and dragon in each room – a clever way, we think, to engage little visitors in studying an otherwise-tedious antiques-furnished parlour. Of course, plenty of attention is paid to the Potter movies, which were filmed on-site. During summers, you can also catch a magic show in the outer courtyard, performed by costumed actors who resemble Hagrid and Dumbledore.

Durham Cathedral ★★★½

APPEAL BY AGE	PRESCHOOL ★★	PRIMARY SCHOOL ★★	TEENS ★★★
YOUNG ADULTS ★★★		OVER 30 ★★★	SENIORS ★★★★

The Chapter Office, The College, Durham DH1 3EH
☎ **0191 386 4266; durhamcathedral.co.uk**

HOURS These vary for specific attractions, but the cathedral is generally open from 10 a.m. to 4 p.m. The Tower is open Monday–Saturday, 10 a.m.–4 p.m. (April–September; last entry 3.40 p.m.), and until 3 p.m. (last entry 2.40 p.m.) at other times of year.

COST During summer, a combined Cathedral Highlights ticket costs £5 adults; £2.50 children, students, senior citizens. It includes entry to The Treasures of St Cuthbert, the audio-visual display, the monks' dormitory and an exhibition on building the church. Admission to some sites is limited during the winter, when the tour ticket costs £3 adults, £1 children, students, senior citizens. Climbing the tower costs £5 adults; £2.50 children under 16.

GETTING THERE *By car:* Durham is about 90 mi (145 km) north of Leeds on the A1(M). The cathedral is in the city centre. Durham was one of the first cities in the UK with a congestion charge, which must be paid by coin if you exit the city between 10 a.m. and 4 p.m. Park at one of the several car parks in the city or three **Park & Ride** sites on the city outskirts. You can then reach the city on a **Park & Ride bus** for £1.70 per person, which is good for transportation all day. *By rail:* The closest station is Durham, a short walk from the city centre (**nationalrail.co.uk**). *By bus:* The train station is served by the **Cathedral Bus,** which operates every 20 minutes, 7 a.m.–5.40 p.m. An all-day ticket costs 50p (**durham.gov.uk/Pages/Service.aspx?ServiceId=6251**). (Route information: **transportdirect.info.**)

DESCRIPTION AND COMMENTS Some people have called this church the most beautiful building in Britain. Constructed more than 1,000 years ago and dedicated to the glory of God, its interior, with criss-crossing diamond patterns, is almost hypnotising. The cathedral is considered one of the finest examples of Norman architecture and has even been named a UNESCO World Heritage Site. But for a certain type of visitor who comes clutching a thick book (and we're not talking the Bible), the main attraction is that the building provided the setting for interior and exterior scenes of Hogwarts.

The cathedral's roots date to the seventh century and the tiny island of Lindisfarne, off the northeast coast of England. The monastery there produced a bishop who later became St Cuthbert. When the community was subjected to Viking raids, the residents gathered Cuthbert's relics and fled, eventually settling in Durham, where a cathedral was built. Construction of the existing building began in 1093, although it has changed much over the millennium. But if something looks out of place to Potter fans, it's because the film-makers had a spire digitally attached atop the famous towers, where Harry's owl, Hedwig, circled before heading off with a message. As you walk the grounds, you'll see where Harry and his cohorts had whispered conversations on the lawn; where Professor McGonagall's transfiguration lesson was taught in the cathedral's Chapter House; and where Quidditch practice was held.

TOURING TIPS The cathedral also has an excellent eatery, the **Undercroft Restaurant,** which is open 10 a.m.– 4.30 p.m. every day except Christmas Day, Boxing Day and Good Friday.

Gloucester Cathedral ★★★

| APPEAL BY AGE | PRESCHOOL ★★ | PRIMARY SCHOOL ★★ | TEENS ★★★ |
| YOUNG ADULTS ★★★ | | OVER 30 ★★★ | SENIORS ★★★★ |

12 College Green, Gloucester GL1 2LX
☎ **01452 528 095; gloucestercathedral.org.uk**

HOURS The cathedral is open daily. Tours are offered 10.45 a.m.–3.15 p.m. Monday–Saturday, and noon–2.30 p.m. Sundays.

COST Admission is free, although a £5 donation is requested. If you make the donation, photography is permitted.

GETTING THERE *By car:* Gloucester is on the M5, off Junction 12. The city is congested, and you may find it more convenient to use the **Park & Ride** car park on the city edge. *By rail:* The closest station is Gloucester, a 10-minute walk to the cathedral (**nationalrail.co.uk**). *By bus:* The city is a hub for buses mainly operated by **National Express** (**nationalexpress.com**). **Megabus** (**uk.megabus.com**) also serves the city to and from London. (Route information: **transportdirect.info**.)

DESCRIPTION AND COMMENTS For years visitors have been coming to this historic cathedral due to its connection with a children's book – but we're not talking about you-know-who. A century before Harry Potter, Beatrix Potter set *The Tailor of Gloucester* here. But it's fair to say that visitation picked up when the church was used in the set of the Harry Potter films. The fan-vaulted **cloisters** played Hogwarts' corridors, where, most dramatically, mysterious graffiti written in blood warned that the Chamber of Secrets had been opened. Moaning Myrtle's toilet flooded here, and Harry and Ron hid from a troll in the cathedral's **lavatorium,** where the monks once washed.

The cathedral, of course, has more to offer than its association with children's literature. The first religious building dates to the seventh century, and construction of a Benedictine abbey began in 1089. It was converted into a cathedral by Henry VIII, who abolished England's monasteries. The **cathedral crypt** holds the tombs of Edward II and William the Conqueror's son Robert. The church also has the extraordinary **Great East Window,** which shows Christ, saints and bishops. When it was constructed in 1350, it was the largest window in the world. Another window is one of the first to depict the sport of **golf** (which is practically a religion to some).

When you visit, you can take a tour offered by well-trained volunteer guides who focus on the building's extensive history and also touch on the Potter connection. They'll show you how film-makers carefully disguised elements that would identify the cathedral as a religious building in the movies. For example, images of Adam and Eve in the stained glass had to be clothed, and their foreheads were given a lightning-shaped scar like Harry's. And tombs on the crypt floor were covered with roofing-felt and stained to match the stonework.

TOURING TIPS You can also climb the 269 steps of the cathedral tower on a guided tour, offered Mondays and Tuesdays at 2.30 p.m. (school holidays only); Wednesday–Friday at 2.30 p.m.; Saturdays at 1.30 p.m. and 2.30 p.m., and bank holidays at 11.30 a.m., 1.30 p.m. and 2.30 p.m. Price: £3 adults, £1 children aged 6 and older.

Lacock Abbey ★★★★

APPEAL BY AGE	PRESCHOOL ★★	PRIMARY SCHOOL ★★★	TEENS ★★★★
YOUNG ADULTS ★★★★		OVER 30 ★★★★★	SENIORS ★★★★★

Lacock, Wiltshire SN15 2LG
☎ **01249 730 459; nationaltrust.org.uk/main/w-lacockabbeyvillage**

HOURS Opens at 11 a.m., with closing times varying from 4 to 5.30 p.m. The Abbey, grounds and museum are open daily mid-February–October, and on most weekends during the winter. Access to the Abbey is limited to cloisters only on Tuesdays and winter weekends.

COST Abbey, grounds, museum and exhibition: £11 adults, including Gift Aid (£10 without donation); £5.50 children (5–13) (£5 without donation); £28 family ticket (£25.40 without donation). Abbey (cloisters only), grounds, museum and exhibition: £8 adults (£7.20 without donation); £4 children (5–13) (£3.60 without donation); £20.40 family ticket (£18.50 without donation).

GETTING THERE *By car:* Located 3 mi (4.8 km) south of Chippenham. Take the M4 Junction 17, signposted to Chippenham on the A350. Follow the A350 (signposted Poole/Warminster) until you reach Lacock, and follow signs to the main car park. *By rail:* The nearest station is Melksham, 3 mi (4.8 km) away (**nationalrail.co.uk**). *By bus:* From Melksham station, take the **Faresaver X34** or the **First 234 Chippenham–Frome route** (**firstgroup.com** for information on both routes).

DESCRIPTION AND COMMENTS The site of a thirteenth-century nunnery, Lacock Abbey is now known for things the sisters could never have imagined: cloaks that make you invisible and a magical mirror that shows your deepest desires. And that's just for starters.

This beautiful building and adjacent village, about 15 mi (24 km) east of Bath on the River Avon, is worth a visit for its historical significance alone. But when you add some magic to the mix, it can cast a powerful spell on visitors. Along with Harry Potter sites, you'll find a peaceful, meditative atmosphere here that transcends any hubbub surrounding Daniel Radcliffe and his fellow actors.

It's just a warm-up for the sights awaiting in the abbey.

The institution was founded in 1229 for Augustinian nuns by Lady Ela, the Countess of Salisbury, who was married to an illegitimate but influential son of King Henry II. Its hallways and cloisters are marked by honey-coloured fan vaulting that you're sure to recognise from the films. The stone was obtained from a nearby quarry, and the timbers came from the Royal Forest. The convent prospered for several centuries, until Henry VIII separated England from the Catholic Church – the abbey was the last religious house to be dissolved by the King. The property was sold off and became a private mansion. Over the years it was modified by architects, becoming one of the loveliest homes in Britain. It eventually came into the hands of the Talbot family, who performed a bit of magic on the site. This is where William Henry Fox Talbot invented the photographic negative in the 1830s.

'Yeah, yeah,' we can hear you saying, as you impatiently tap your wand. 'What about Harry and Hogwarts?'

The building has played several roles in various films. Harry was selected for Gryffindor's high-flying Quidditch team in the hallways. And Professor Snape's potions classroom can be found here in the **Sacristy**. Also look in the **Warming Room** (it too was a Hogwarts classroom), where a large three-legged black cauldron has sat since the 1500s. In the **Chapter House,** where the nuns once listened to chapters from the Rule of Saint Benedict, Harry discovered the Mirror of Erised, the mystical object that lets you watch your desires come to life. As Dumbledore warned Harry, one can fritter away one's life peering at the images, consumed by wishes and dreams. Which, come to think of it, is a warning that might actually be in the spirit of a former religious institution.

Elsewhere, Harry wandered the hallways in his invisibility cloak. Trust us, you won't be the first visitor hoping to catch a glimpse of The Boy Who Lived slinking down the corridor. The building's upper floors were where the Talbots and generations of previous owners lived. Here you'll see a parlour, hand-printed wallpaper, antique furnishings, chandeliers and books.

TOURING TIPS The abbey is in Lacock village, which itself is worth touring. It lacks television aerials, yellow street markings and power lines, and with its lime-washed, half-timbered and stone houses, some dating to the thirteenth century, it provided a suitably-historic atmosphere for other Potter scenes. Look for the wooden gate that Voldemort opened as he approached a home on a mission to kill Harry's mother and father.

While there's no Potter history here, do take a look at the abbey's central oriel window, which was the subject of the first photographic negative. Without Talbot's invention, we never would have had Harry Potter films to enjoy.

University of Oxford ★★★★

APPEAL BY AGE	PRESCHOOL ★★	PRIMARY SCHOOL ★★★	TEENS ★★★★
YOUNG ADULTS ★★★★★		OVER 30 ★★★★★	SENIORS ★★★★★

☎ 01865 270 000; ox.ac.uk

GETTING THERE *By car:* Oxford is about 60 mi (96 km) northwest of London, easily reached by the M40 motorway. Parking can be difficult. Follow signs to short-stay car parks, which are about a 10-minute walk from the city centre. *By rail:* The city centre is less than a 10-minute walk from the Oxford train station (**nationalrail.co.uk**). *By bus:* The station is on Gloucester Green. (Route information: **transportdirect.info**.)

DESCRIPTION AND COMMENTS Perhaps it's fitting that Britain's most famous university should have such a direct connection to the wizarding world's most famous school. A collection of 38 independent colleges spread over 70 ac (30 ha), Oxford has played many roles in the Potter films. Although tourists have been coming for centuries – long before J. K. Rowling ever thought of a magic spell – the Potter movie connection has brought a new wave of visitors, and the august institution seems to enjoy the attention, offering tours that at least mention Potter, along with other real-life luminaries with connections to the university, like Sir Walter Raleigh, Adam Smith and Stephen Hawking.

You may want to head straight to **Christ Church College's dining hall,** which served as the Great Hall at Hogwarts, where the Sorting Hat decided that Harry was to be a Gryffindor. The hall is still used for dining but can be visited by the public most days of the year. Tours cost £6 and are available Monday–Saturday 9 a.m.–4.30 p.m., Sundays 1–4.30 p.m. Location: St Aldate's, Oxford OX1 1DP (☎ 01865 276 492; **chch.ox.ac.uk**).

The Divinity School at the Bodleian Library not only has a ceiling with images of beasts and biblical scenes that has been described as a 'masterpiece of English Gothic architecture', but it also was used in several films as the Hogwarts hospital. It can be visited weekdays between 9 a.m. and 5 p.m., Saturdays until 4.30 p.m. and Sundays 11 a.m.–5 p.m. Cost: £1. Ticket office: Great Gate to the Bodleian Library, Catte St (☎ 01865 277 224; **bodleian.ox.ac.uk/bodley/about/visitors/individual/divinityschool**).

Duke Humfrey's Library made an easy transition to Hogwarts Library. The library has more than 80 mi (129 km) of shelves, with many old, mysterious volumes that are sure to contain a magic spell or two. It can be seen only on a guided tour, open to visitors aged 11 and over. You'll have to book an extended **Explore the Reading Rooms Tour,** which costs £13 and is held most Wednesday, Saturday and Sunday mornings. Location: Broad St, Oxford OX1 3BG (☎ 01865 277 224; **bodleian.ox.ac.uk/bodley/about/visitors/individual/extended**).

TOURING TIPS While you can wander the campus and find many of the sites, the easiest way to get your magical fix is on a **Harry Potter tour** sponsored by the local city tourism office (☎ 01865 252 200; **visit oxfordandoxfordshire.com/official-tours**). Tours are offered only about a dozen times a year, though, so you'll need to plan and book ahead (£11.75 adults; £7.50 children). They depart from outside the Tourist Information Centre, 15–16 Broad St, OX1 3AS.

West Coast Railway Jacobite Steam Train ★★★★

APPEAL BY AGE	PRESCHOOL ★★★	PRIMARY SCHOOL ★★★	TEENS ★★★★
YOUNG ADULTS ★★★★		OVER 30 ★★★★	SENIORS ★★★★

Fort William Railway Station, Booking Office, Fort William, Inverness-Shire PH33 6EW; ☎ **01524 732 100; westcoastrailways.co.uk/jacobite/Jacobite_Details.html**

HOURS (Mid-May–October) The train leaves Fort William at 10.20 a.m.

and returns at 4 p.m. Monday–Friday. During July and August, the train also runs Saturdays and Sundays.

COST £31 adults, standard return fare (£23.50 one-way); £17.50 children, return (£13.50 one-way). First-class return tickets are £23 more for adults and £12.50 more for children. Book ahead, as trains often sell out and ticket availability is limited on the day of travel (all fares subject to a minimum £2.75 booking fee).

GETTING THERE *By car:* Fort William is about 110 mi (177 km) northwest of Glasgow, and easily reached on the A82. Parking is plentiful near Fort William's railway station and costs £1.50. (Do not park in the supermarket car park.) Allow at least 20 minutes for parking and ticket purchase. *By rail:* If you're travelling by train, you'll need to arrive in Fort William the day before your trip on the Jacobite, because your service arrives after the steam engine's 10.20 a.m. departure. However, the Jacobite returns to Fort William in time for you to catch a train to Glasgow or back to Mallaig (**nationalrail.co.uk**). *By bus:* **Scottish Citylink** provides service to Fort William from Glasgow and Edinburgh (**citylink.co.uk**). (Route information: **transportdirect.info.**)

DESCRIPTION AND COMMENTS While you can't actually catch the Hogwarts Express steam train from London's Kings Cross Station, Platform 9¾, you can take a ride on the famous train. The Jacobite's summer service runs between Fort William and Mallaig in northwest Scotland. Not only is the route shown in the movie, but the carriages were selected from the railway's rolling stock, so you'll be travelling in coaches similar to the ones that carried Harry and his classmates.

The route, known as The Iron Road to the Isles, started in 1901 to open the Atlantic coast of Scotland, and was taken over by the Jacobite tourist steam train in 1984. Its 84-mi (135-km) return trip leaves from **Fort William,** the largest town in the Highlands, at the southern end of the Great Glen and in the shadow of Ben Nevis, Britain's highest mountain. It's a memorable trip, with gradients and tight curves. For Potter fans, the highlight is crossing the 21-arched single-track **Glenfinnan viaduct.** If the train isn't pushed for time, the conductor may stop on the bridge to let you admire the view. But don't worry – you won't encounter Dementors, as Harry did. Shortly after the viaduct, the train makes a brief stop at **Glenfinnan Station,** where you'll find railway-history exhibits and can buy a drink and a snack.

The locomotive pulling your train is unlikely to be the 5972 Olton Hall, which starred as the Hogwarts Castle engine, but it will be a similar steam engine. On-board, first-class **Carriage A** serves tea and scones during the ride. The second-class carriages, **B** and **C,** have open seating and the option to buy refreshments during the journey. Seats in **Carriage D** have separate compartments, as in the films, and you may have to scramble to get these. The carriages have been painted red to match those in the movie as well.

Along the route, look carefully when you pass Scotland's deepest lake, **Loch Morar,** home to Morag, a mysterious serpent said to be related to the Loch Ness Monster. The scenery also includes glens and miles of open space devoid of human habitation. If you were going to establish a school for wizards, this wouldn't be a bad spot in which to do it.

TOURING TIPS The trip makes a stop at **Mallaig,** a fishing port and ferry terminal on the Atlantic coast. You'll have about 90 minutes to explore the town's shops, bars, restaurants and famous chip shops before heading back. You also have the option of staying in Mallaig, where ferries serve Scotland's coastal islands (**calmac.co.uk**).

ZSL London Zoo *See Greater London, page 109.*

INDEX

Note: Page numbers in *italics* indicate illustrative material.

accessibility issues, 49. *see also under* pushchairs; wheelchairs
accommodation, 42
    'alternative,' 52
    categories of, 51–52
    offsite, 49–50
    online research and booking, tips on, 52–53
    onsite, 42, 49
    ratings scheme, 50–51
    self-catering, 52
admission schemes, 42–45, 355
adults, touring plans for. *see* teens and adults, touring plans for
adventure activity centre, 448–450
Adventure Island Sunken Gardens, 219, 222–224
Adventure Land (Alton Towers), 289–291
Adventure Land (Legoland Windsor), 167–168
Aero Nomad (Legoland Windsor), 171
Africa Alive, 224–226
Air (Alton Towers), *26*, 26–27, 280
Alice ride (Pleasure Beach Blackpool), 394
Alnwick Castle, 455–457
'alternative' self-catering accommodation, 52
Alton Towers, 4, 6, 261, 264–272, *266–267*
    accommodation at, 42, 49
    rides and attractions at, 272–293
        best time to visit, 296–297
        Fastrack, 269–270
        not to be missed, 268
        single-rider queues, 270–271
        switching off technique, 271
    touring plans for
        one-day, 293–294, 298
        two-day, 298–299
amusement parks. *see* theme parks
animal gardens
    Birdland Park and Gardens, 300
    at Cornwall's Crealy Great Adventure Park, 197
    at Devon's Crealy Great Adventure Park, 200
    Dinosaur Adventure, 229–231
    Lorikeet Lagoon (Chessington World of Adventures), 96–97
anticipatory behaviour, in children, 65
anxiety in children, 74–76
aquariums, 10–12. *see also* marine-life attractions
    at Alton Towers, 275
    best time of day to visit, 41
    Blue Planet Aquarium, 365–367
    Blue Reef properties. *see* Blue Reef Aquariums
    The Deep, 333, 336–338
    Deep Sea World, 428–430
    Lakes Aquarium, 417–418
    National Marine Aquarium, 207–209
    National Sea Life Centre Birmingham, 312–313
    Oceanarium, 209–210
    Sea Life properties. *see* Sea Life properties
    SeaQuarium properties. *see* SeaQuariums
    St. Andrews Aquarium, 436–437
archeological attraction, 342–344
Arthurian legends, theme park dedicated to, 369–371
attractions. *see also* individually named attractions
    arrival time at. *see under* timing your visit
    British aristocracy and, 3–4
    defined, 2–3
    industrial, 13
    museums. *see* museums
    run by charitable organizations, ticket pricing and, 44
    variety of, 6
    zoological, 8–10. *see also* aquariums; marine-life attractions; safari parks; wild animal parks/gardens; zoos

INDEX

Avalanche (Pleasure Beach Blackpool), 27, 27, 390–391
aviation museum, 239–242

Balloon School (Legoland Windsor), 164
Banham Zoo, 226–229
Battle Galleons (Alton Towers), 272
B&B, defined, 51
The Beastie (Alton Towers), 290
The Beatles Story, 357, 360–362
Beaver Creek Children's Theme Park, at Pleasure Beach Blackpool, 401–404
Beaver Creek Log Flume (Pleasure Beach Blackpool), 402
The Beginning (Legoland Windsor), 158
behaviour, of child
    anticipatory, 65
    maintaining discipline/order while travelling, 65–66
    problematic
        avoiding, 66–68
        handling, 68–70
        suitable time-out places, 70
Berry Bish Bash (Alton Towers), 291–292
Berry Bouncers (Chessington World of Adventures), 91–92
Big Apple (M&D's, Scotland's Theme Park), 21
Big Blue Hotel (Pleasure Beach Blackpool), 49, 385
The Big Dipper (Pleasure Beach Blackpool), 391
Big Pit: National Coal Museum in Wales, 13, 439, 442–444
Birdland Park and Gardens, 300
birds-of-prey demonstrations/exhibits, 13, 226, 345, 383, 427. *see also* falconry demonstrations/exhibits
Black Buccaneer (Chessington World of Adventures), 88
Blackpool Zoo, 362–365
The Blade (Alton Towers), 278–279
Blair Drummond House, 4
Blair Drummond Safari and Adventure Park, 10, 423, 426–429
Bling (Pleasure Beach Blackpool), 390–391
Blue Planet Aquarium, 11, 365–367
Blue Reef Aquariums, 10–11
    at Bristol, 192–193
    at Hastings, 113, 116
    at Southsea/Portsmouth, 147, 150
    at Tynemouth, 411, 413
Boating School (Legoland Windsor), 164
bob sled coasters, 27, 27
Bomber Mark 2 (M&D's, Scotland's Theme Park), 21
bottlenecks, avoiding, 55. *see also* touring plans
Bourton Model Railway Exhibition, 301–302
Bourton-on-the-Water, Gloucestershire, 299–302
British Lawnmower Museum, 12, 367–369
Brunel's *SS Great Britain*, 194–196
Bubbleworks (Chessington World of Adventures), 22, 89

bumper cars. *see individually named rides*

Camelot Theme Park, 7, 369–371
Canada Creek Railway (Thorpe Park), 135
Canopy Capers (Chessington World of Adventures), 93
capacity, of rides, 31–32, 34–35
car parks/parking, 8, 48
Carousel (Chessington World of Adventures), 92
carousels, 17–18, 19. *see also individually named rides*
charitable donations, included in ticket price, 44
Charlie and the Chocolate Factory: The Ride (Alton Towers), 22, 284–285
Chessington World of Adventures, 49, 82–87, 84–85
    one-day touring plans for, 101, 103–104
    rides and attractions at, 87–100
        best time to visit, 102
        not to be missed, 86
Chessington Zoo, 100
Chester Zoo, 371–376
Chief Ranger's Carousel (Thorpe Park), 134–135
child swap. *see* switching off/child swap technique
children
    age of, one-day touring plans by.
        see older children; younger children
    anticipatory behaviour in, 65
    anxiety in, 74–76
    behavioural problems in, avoiding/handling, 66–70
    focusing on fun for, tips for parents, 63–70
    height of, one-day touring plans by.
        see small children
    hyperactive, 72
    likes and dislikes of, 65
    lost, 72–74
        potential causes, 73–74, 258, 316
    preparing for rides, 76
    visiting with, tips on, 64–66, 71, 76–77
children's playgrounds, 5
Chinese Puzzle Maze (Pleasure Beach Blackpool), 395
Chopper Squadron (Legoland Windsor), 161–162
closed rides/shows/exhibits, 47–48
clothing, suitable, 47, 71
Cloud Cuckoo Land (Alton Towers), 282–286
Cloud Cuckoo Land Theatre (Alton Towers), 286–287
coasteering, 448–449
Colossus (Thorpe Park), 25, 137
Congo River Rapids (Alton Towers), 32, 275
continuous loaders, 34
Cornwall's Crealy Great Adventure Park, 196–198
Cotswold Motoring Museum, 302
Cotswold Wildlife Park & Gardens, 150–151
country house hotel, defined, 51
coupons, how to find, 43, 44
credit cards, 47
Cumbria and the Lake District, 415, 416
    attractions in, 417–421
    farm experiences in, 421, 437

cycle ('stop and go') rides, 34
cycle time, 34

Dark Forest (Alton Towers), 281–282
dark rides, 22–23
The Deep, 11, 333, 336–338
Deep Sea World, 11, 428–430
Depth Charge (Thorpe Park), 129
Derby Racer (Pleasure Beach Blackpool), 395–396
Desert Chase (Legoland Windsor), 170–171
Detonator (Thorpe Park), 133
Devon's Crealy Great Adventure Park, 198–200
Digger Challenge (Legoland Windsor), 166
Dino Dipper (Legoland Windsor), 168
Dino Safari (Legoland Windsor), 168
Dinosaur Adventure, 229–231
directions
  to park, map vs. satnav device, 46
  within park, souvenir books vs. maps, 8
disabilities, visitors with, 49. *see also* wheelchairs
discipline, during visit with children, 65–66
discount tickets/coupons, where to find, 43–45
displays. *see* exhibits/displays
disposable rain outfits, 23
diving machines (coasters), 27
dodgems. *see individually named rides*
Dodgems (Pleasure Beach Blackpool), 396
Doodle Doo Derby (Alton Towers), 292
The Dragon (Legoland Windsor), 174–175
Dragon Falls (Chessington World of Adventures), 97
Dragon's Apprentice (Legoland Windsor), 175
Dragon's Fury (Chessington World of Adventures), 92–93
Dragon's Playhouse (Chessington World of Adventures), 93
Drayton Manor theme park, 303–307
Driving School (Legoland Windsor), 5, 163
driving to attraction, tips on, 46
'driving-school' attraction (L-Riders), 5
Duel (Alton Towers), 23
Duel–The Haunted House Strikes Back (Alton Towers), 277–278
Duplo Land (Legoland Windsor), 160–163
Duplo Playtown (Legoland Windsor), 160
Duplo Theatre (Legoland Windsor), 161
Duplo Train (Legoland Windsor), 160–161
Durham Cathedral, 457–458
duvets, 50
Duxford, Imperial War Museum at, 239–242

East and West Midlands, 261, *262–263*
  farm experiences in, 331–332
  theme parks and attractions in, 261, 264–330
East of England, 219, *220–221*
  farm experiences in, 258–260
  theme parks and attractions in, 219, 222–258
Eddie Stobart Convoy (Pleasure Beach Blackpool), 396
Eden Project, 200–204

The Edinburgh Dungeon, 430–432
educational attractions, 12, 41
  British Lawnmower Museum, 12, 367–369
  Eden Project, 200–204
  Gulliver's Dinosaur and Farm Park, 235–236
  Jorvik Viking Centre, 342–344
  National Coal Mining Museum, 348–350
  National Space Centre, 313–317
  There's Something in the Dung Heap (Alton Towers), 291
electric hand driers, how to use, 47
Enterprise (Alton Towers), 288–289
environmental parks/projects
  Amazonia (M&D's, Scotland's Theme Park), 200–204
  Eden Project, 200–204
  Gulliver's Dinosaur and Farm Park, 235–236
  Paignton Zoo Environmental Park, 210–212
exhibits/displays. *see also* birds-of-prey demonstrations/exhibits; falconry demonstrations/exhibits; sea-lion shows
  at Chester Zoo, 375
  closed, previsit checks for, 47–48
  Impossible (Pleasure Beach Blackpool), 398
  miniature. *see* miniature villages/exhibits
  Miniland (Legoland Windsor), 160
  optical illusions, at Pleasure Beach Blackpool, 398
Extreme Team Challenge (Legoland Windsor), 160–161

factory attractions. *see* industrial attractions
Fairy Tale Brook (Legoland Windsor), 162–163
falconry demonstrations/exhibits, 8, 13, 217, 322, 347, 381, 451. *see also* birds-of-prey demonstrations/exhibits
family tickets, 44
fan websites, 39
Fantasy Island, 231–235
farm experiences, 13–14
  best time of day for visiting, 14, 41
  in Cumbria and the Lake District, 421
  in East and West Midlands, 331–332
  in East of England, 256–258
  locating farm accurately, 14
  in North East England, 413
  in North West England, 408–409
  in Scotland, 437
  in South East England, 144–145
  in South England, 187
  in South West England, 217–218
  in Wales, 453
  in Yorkshire, 356
farmhouse accommodation, defined, 51
Fastrack scheme, 125, 128
  at Alton Towers, 269–270
  at Thorpe Park, 129
fear. *see* anxiety in children
Ferris wheels, 19–20, *20*.
  see also individually named rides

Fire Academy (Legoland Windsor), 164–165
first aid centres, 71–72
Flamingo Land, 338–342
floorless coasters, 27
The Flume (Alton Towers), 273–274
flume rides, 23
flying carousels, 18
flying coasters, 26, 26–27
Flying Fish (Thorpe Park), 130
Flying Jumbos (Chessington World of Adventures), 90–91
Flying Machines (Pleasure Beach Blackpool), 396–397
food, quality of, 7
Forbidden Kingdom (Chessington World of Adventures), 98–99
Forbidden Valley (Alton Towers), 278–280
Frisbees (pendulum rides), 21
Frog Hopper (Alton Towers), 284
Fruit Shoot the Ride (Pleasure Beach Blackpool), 402
fun, how to focus on having, 64–70

Gallopers (Pleasure Beach Blackpool), 397
Galloper's Carousel (Alton Towers), 285
games, while waiting in queue, 76
The Gardens (Alton Towers), 280–281
gardens/grounds
  animal. *see* animal gardens; wild animal parks/gardens
  as theme park backdrops, 5
getting there. *see* navigation; transportation
ghost rides, 22–23
Ghost Train (Pleasure Beach Blackpool), 22, 397–398
ghoulish attractions
  The Edinburgh Dungeon, 430–432
  The London Dungeon, 104–106
  The York Dungeon, 354–355
Gloomy Wood (Alton Towers), 277–278
Gloucester Cathedral, 459–460
Google Maps, 46
Grand National (Pleasure Beach Blackpool), 392
Grand Prix (Pleasure Beach Blackpool), 398
Greater London, 79, 80–81
  theme parks and attractions in, 82–112
Griffin's Galleon (Chessington World of Adventures), 94
guest house, defined, 51
guest relations/services, 8
  car problems and, 49
  ticketing and, 40
Gulliver's Dinosaur and Farm Park, 235–236
Gulliver's Kingdom, 307–310
Gulliver's Land, 236–239
Gulliver's World, 377–380

hand drying, tips on, 47
Harry Potter movie locations, 455–464
  Alnwick Castle, 455–457
  Durham Cathedral, 457–458
  Gloucester Cathedral, 459–460
  Lacock Abbey, 460–461
  London Zoo, 109–112
  University of Oxford, 461–462
  West Coast Railway Jacobite Steam Train, 462–464
Heave Ho! (Alton Towers), 273
height requirements, for rides, 76
  one-day touring plans and.
    see under small children
Helicopters (Pleasure Beach Blackpool), 402
Hex–The Legend of the Towers (Alton Towers), 287
high-mount horizontal-axle rides, 19–20
Hill Train (Legoland Windsor), 158
historical attractions
  The Beatles Story, 357, 360–362
  Jorvik Viking Centre, 342–344
  Warwick Castle, 320–323
HMS *Victory*, 12, 184–185, 186
HMS *Warrior*, 185
Hocus Pocus Hall (Chessington World of Adventures), 87
horror maze, at Thorpe Park, 138–139
hotel, defined, 51
Howletts Wild Animal Park, 116–119
hydraulic-lift-arm rides, 19
hyperactive children, 72

Ice Blast (Pleasure Beach Blackpool), 392–393
Imagination Centre (Legoland Windsor), 158–159
Imagination Theatre (Legoland Windsor), 159
Imperial War Museum Duxford, 12, 239–242
Impossible (Pleasure Beach Blackpool), 398
indoor coasters, 26
industrial attractions, 13, 41
  Big Pit: National Coal Museum in Wales, 439, 442–444
  Morgan Motor Company Factory Tour, 310–312
  National Coal Mining Museum, 348–350
infant care, 72
Infusion (Pleasure Beach Blackpool), 393
inn, defined, 51
Internet searches
  for accommodation, 52–53
  for discount coupons/tickets, 43, 44
  for information, tips on, 37–39
interval loaders, 34
inverted coasters, 26
Irn Bru Revolution (Pleasure Beach Blackpool), 393

Jolly Rocker (Legoland Windsor), 173–174
Jorvik Viking Centre, 342–344
Jungle Bus (Chessington World of Adventures), 95

Katanga Canyon (Alton Towers), 275–277
King Arthur's legends, theme park dedicated to, 369–371

INDEX

Kingdom of the Pharaohs (Legoland Windsor), 169–171
Knights Kingdom (Legoland Windsor), 174–175
Knowsley Safari Park, 380–384
Kobra (Chessington World of Adventures), 94–95

Lacock Abbey, 460–461
Lakes Aquarium, 12, 417–418
Land of the Dragons attraction (Chessington World of Adventures), 92–94
Land of the Vikings (Legoland Windsor), 171–172
Laser Raiders (Legoland Windsor), 22, 169
launched (accelerator) coasters, 27
lawnmowers, museum dedicated to, 12, 367–369
L-Drivers (Legoland Windsor), 163–164
learning experience, museums and, 12. *see also* educational attractions
Lego City (Legoland Windsor), 165–167
Legoland Windsor, 5, 152–158, *154–155*
  rides and attractions at, 158–174
    best time to visit, 178–179
    not to be missed, 153
    with Q-Bot queuing system, 157
    switching off technique, 157
  touring plans for, 175–180
leisure attractions. *see* attractions
leisure parks. *see* theme parks
Lightwater Valley, *20*, 344–348
load time, 34
loading/unloading methods, 34
log rides, 23
Logger's Leap (Thorpe Park), 135–136
Loki's Labyrinth (Legoland Windsor), 172
London. *see* Greater London
The London Dungeon, 104–106
London Zoo, 109–112
Longboat Invader (Legoland Windsor), 172
Longleat House and Safari Park, 204–27
Lorikeet Lagoon (Chessington World of Adventures), 96–97
lost children, 72–74
  potential causes, 73–74, 258, 316
lost property, preventing, 29
L-Riders (Legoland Windsor), 5, 163
Lunar Carousel (Pleasure Beach Blackpool), 403–404

Magic Mountain (Pleasure Beach Blackpool), 401
Magnus Mini Dodgems (Pleasure Beach Blackpool), 398–399
maize mazes, 6, 13
M&D's, Scotland's Theme Park, 432–434
maps
  of park, souvenir books vs., 8
  for road directions, vs. satnav device, 46
Marauder's Mayhem (Alton Towers), 273
marine museums, 12
  Brunel's SS Great Britain, 194–196
  HMS Victory, 12
  Mary Rose Museum, 184, 185
  National Museum of the Royal Navy, 184
marine-life attractions, 10–12. *see also* aquariums; Sea Life properties; SeaQuariums
Market Square (Chessington World of Adventures), 86–87
Mary Rose Museum, 184, 185
Matterhorn (roller coaster), history of, 24–25
mazes, 6, 13, 138–139, 172, 346, 378, 395
Merlin Annual Pass, 44, 82, 107, 124, 264, 265
merry-go-rounds (carousels), 17–18, *19*. *see also individually named rides*
metro hotel, defined, 51
Mexicana attraction (Chessington World of Adventures), 99–100
Midlands of England. *see* East and West Midlands
military museums
  Imperial War Museum Duxford, 239–242
  National Museum of the Royal Navy, 184
  The Tank Museum, 213–215
mine train coasters, 28, *28*
miniature villages/exhibits
  Bourton Model Railway Exhibition, 301–302
  The Model Village, 301
  at National Railway Museum, 351
Miniland (Legoland Windsor), 160
mining museums
  Big Pit: National Coal Museum in Wales, 439, 442–444
  National Coal Mining Museum, 348–350
model attractions. *see* miniature villages/exhibits
The Model Village, 301
Monkey Swinger (Chessington World of Adventures), 95–96
Monorail (Pleasure Beach Blackpool), 399
Morgan Motor Company Factory Tour, 13, 310–312
motion sickness, mitigating, 29
movie locations. *see* Harry Potter movie locations
Mr. Monkey's Banana Ride (Thorpe Park), 134
museums
  The Beatles Story, 357, 360–362
  Big Pit: National Coal Museum in Wales, 439, 442–444
  British Lawnmower Museum, 367–369
  Cotswold Motoring Museum, 302
  Imperial War Museum Duxford, 239–242
  at Jorvik Viking Centre, 342–344
  National Coal Mining Museum, 348–350
  National Museum of the Royal Navy, 184
  National Railway Museum, 350–353
  The Tank Museum, 213–215
  touring tips for, 12–13, 41
Mutiny Bay (Alton Towers), 272–275
Mystic East attraction (Chessington World of Adventures), 97–98

National Coal Mining Museum, 348–350
National Marine Aquarium, 11, 207–209

INDEX

National Museum of the Royal Navy, 184
National Railway Museum, 12, 350–353
National Sea Life Centre Birmingham, 312–313
National Space Centre, 12, 313–317
nausea from rides, mitigating, 29
navigation
    to park, satnav vs. maps, 46
    within park, souvenir books vs. maps, 8
Nemesis (Alton Towers), 279
Nemesis Inferno (Thorpe Park), 133–134
North East England, 411, *412*
    Blue Reef Aquarium–Tynemouth in, 411, 413
    farm experiences in, 413
North West England, 357, *358–359*
    farm experiences in, 408–409
    theme parks and attractions in, 357, 360–407

Oakfield Manor, at Chester Zoo, 376
Oakwood Theme Park, 444–447
Oblivion (Alton Towers), 27, 289
Oceanarium, 12, 209–210
off-season tickets, 44
Old MacDonald's Farmyard (Alton Towers), 291–293
Old MacDonald's Singing Barn (Alton Towers), 293
Old MacDonald's Tractor Ride (Alton Towers), 292–293
older children, one-day touring plans for
    Chessington World of Adventures, 101, 103
    Legoland Windsor, 176–177
    Pleasure Beach Blackpool, 405
online coupons, how to find, 43, 44
online searches. *see* Internet searches
opening schedules, 39–40
optical illusions, display at Pleasure Beach Blackpool, 398
organising your trip
    accommodation, 49–53
    admission schemes, 42–45
    car parks/problems, 48–49
    cardinal rules for touring, 53–55
    closed rides/shows/exhibits, checking for, 47–48
    computerized plans for touring, 55–61
    credit card acceptance, 49
    Internet searches for, 37–39
    preventing exhaustion, 41
    public loos, 47
    rain on day, how to handle, 23, 46, 47
    same-day re-entry, 48
    setting priorities for, 54
    smoking policies, 49
    special needs requirements, 49
    ticketing strategies, 40
    timing and. *see* timing your visit; visiting times, optimal
Orient Expedition (Legoland Windsor), 166–167
outdoor adventure centre, 448–450

Paignton Zoo Environmental Park, 210–212
paper coupons, where to find, 43, 44

Parent Queue Share pass, at Alton Towers, 271
parent swap. *see* switching off
parking, 8, 48
parks. *see* theme parks
Parques Reunidos properties, 12
    Lakes Aquarium, 417–418
    Oceanarium, 209–210
partner ticket deals, 44
Paultons Park, 180–183
Peeking Heights (Chessington World of Adventures), 97–98
pendulum rides, 19, 20–21, *21*
Pepsi Max Big One (Pleasure Beach Blackpool), 389–390
Peugeot Driving School (Alton Towers), 283
picnic areas, 5
Pirate Falls Dynamite Drench (Legoland Windsor), 173
Pirate Training Camp (Legoland Windsor), 173
Pirates Cove attraction (Chessington World of Adventures), 88–89
Pirates Landing (Legoland Windsor), 172–174
Pirates Ship (pendulum ride), 20
platform rides, 19
playgrounds, 5
Pleasure Beach Blackpool, 384–389, *386–387*
    accommodation at, 42, 49
    one-day touring plans for, 404–407
    rides and attractions at, 389–404
        best time to visit, 406–407
        family rides, 394–401
        not to be missed, 388
        'white-knuckle' rides, 389–394
Pleasure Beach Express (Pleasure Beach Blackpool), 399–400
Pleasure Island Theme Park, 242–245
Pleasurewood Hills, 245–248
Port Lympne Wild Animal Park, 120–123
Portsmouth Historic Dockyard, 12, 183–187
Potter, Harry. *see* Harry Potter movie locations
prams. *see* pushchairs
preschoolers. *see* small children
public loos, hand drying machines in, 47
public transport options, 39, 45–46
pushchairs, 72
    attraction accessibility and, 121, 158, 193, 225, 229, 250, 308, 323, 376, 450
    car park conditions and, 48
    for hire at park, 8, 86, 118, 120, 125, 156, 237, 256, 269, 307, 329, 373, 376, 388
    limitations on use of, 71

Q-Bot queuing system, 157–158
Q-Busters (jump-the-queue) scheme, 342
Quantum (Thorpe Park), 20, 140
queue/queuing
    length of, factors influencing, 31
    single-rider, 128
    strategies for parents with young children, 76–77

queuing areas, 8
queuing systems
  Fastrack scheme
    at Alton Towers, 269–270
    at Thorpe Park, 129
  Q-Busters, at Flamingo Land, 342
  virtual (Q-Bot), at Legoland Windsor, 157–158
queuing time, cutting
  for rides, 32–35
  schemes for. *see* queuing systems
  for shows, 36

raft rides, 23
railway excursions, 41
rain, how to handle, 23, 46, 47
Rameses Revenge (Chessington World of Adventures), 21, 98–99
Raptor Attack (Lightwater Valley), 26
Rattlesnake (Chessington World of Adventures), 99–100
re-entry, to park/attraction, 48
rest and relaxation, building into trip, 41
restaurant with rooms, defined, 51
restrooms, hand drying machines in, 47
Rhyl SeaQuarium, 447
ride operators, 5, 35
ride time, 34
ride vehicles, 18, 35
rides
  age-specific, 63
  capacity of, 31–32, 34–35
  closed, previsit checks for, 47–48
  cutting queuing time for, 32–35
  delayed opening schedules for, 40
  flexible duration of, 5
  height requirements for, 76
  last-minute cold feet, 77
  last-minute entry strategy, 77
  loading and unloading methods, 34
  location of, 31
  magnitude hierarchy, 54
  popularity of, 31, 33
  preparing children for, 76
  YouTube videos featuring, 38, 76
Ripsaw (Alton Towers), 21, *21*, 278
Rita (Alton Towers), 281
River Caves (Pleasure Beach Blackpool), 400
Riverbank Eye Spy (Alton Towers), 292
road map, vs. satnav device, 46
rock climbing, 448–450
Rocky Express (Thorpe Park), 135
roller coasters. *see also* individually named rides
  history of, 24–25
  physical problems and, 29
  preventing losing stuff while on, 29
  types of, 25–29
  world rankings, 30
rooms-only accommodation, defined, 51–52
Rumba Rapids (Thorpe Park), 132–133

Runaway Mine Train (Alton Towers), 276–277
Runaway Train (Chessington World of Adventures), 28, 99
Rush (Thorpe Park), 139–140

safari parks, 9–10
  best time of day to visit, 10, 40–41
  Blair Drummond Safari and Adventure Park, 423, 426–429
  Knowsley Safari Park, 380–384
  Longleat House and Safari Park, 204–27
  West Midland Safari & Leisure Park, 323–327
  Woburn Safari Park, 252–255
Safari Skyway (Chessington World of Adventures), 87
same-day re-entry, to park/attraction, 48
Samurai (Thorpe Park), 136–137
satnav devices, 46
Saw Alive (Thorpe Park), 138–139
Saw–The Ride (Thorpe Park), 7, 26, 138
Scarab-Bouncers (Legoland Windsor), 169–170
scenic railways, 22–23
school-age children. *see* older children; younger children
Scotland, 423, *424–425*
  farm experiences in, 437
  theme parks and attractions in, 423, 426–437
Sea Dragons (Chessington World of Adventures), 93
Sea Life properties, 10
  at Blackpool, 408
  at Brighton, 123
  at Great Yarmouth, 248–249
  at Loch Lomond, 434–435
  London Aquarium, 107–109
  at Scarborough, 353–354
  at Weymouth, 213
sea-kayaking, 448–449
sea-lion shows, 245, 246, 258, 325, 341, 363, 364, 381, 383, 427, 447, 451
SeaQuariums, 12
  at Rhyl, 447
  at Weston-Super-Mare, 216
Seastorm (Chessington World of Adventures), 88–89
self-catering accommodation, 52
setting limits, prior to visit with children, 64–65
setting priorities, for one-day tour, 54
Sharkbait Reef Aquarium (Alton Towers), 275
ships
  Brunel's *SS Great Britain*, 12, 194–196
  at Portsmouth Historic Dockyard, 183–187
    HMS *Victory*, 184–185, 186
    HMS *Warrior*, 185
    Mary Rose Museum, 184, 185
Shockwave (Drayton Park), 305
shows, 35. *see also* sea-lion shows
  at Alton Towers, 274, 286–287
  at The Beatles Story, 362
  at Chessington World of Adventures, 94

shows (*continued*)
  closed, previsit checks for, 47–48
  at Cornwall's Crealy Great Adventure Park, 197
  cutting queuing time for, 36
  at Drayton Manor theme park, 306
  at Flamingo Land, 341
  at IMAX (Blue Reef Aquarium–Bristol), 193–194
  last-minute entry strategy to, 77
  at Legoland Windsor, 159, 161, 165–166
  at National Marine Aquarium, 208
  at National Space Centre, 315
shuttle services, 46
single-rider queues
  at Alton Towers, 270–271
  at Thorpe Park, 128
Sky Rider (Legoland Windsor), 159
Skyride (Alton Towers), 274–275
Slammer (Thorpe Park), 136
small children
  under 3' tall, one-day touring plans with
    Alton Towers, 293–295
    Chessington World of Adventures, 101, 176–177
    Legoland Windsor, 175–176
    Pleasure Beach Blackpool, 404
    Thorpe Park, 142–143
  over 3' or at least 2'11" tall, one-day touring plans with
    Alton Towers, 294–295, 298
    Legoland Windsor, 177–180
    Thorpe Park, 142
  theme parks/park areas catering specifically to
    Cornwall's Crealy Great Adventure Park, 196–198
    Devon's Crealy Great Adventure Park, 198–200
    at Drayton Park, 303, 304
    Gulliver's Kingdom, 307–310
    Gulliver's Land, 236–239
    Gulliver's World, 377–380
    Legoland. *see* Legoland Windsor
    at Pleasure Beach Blackpool, 401–404
small hotel, defined, 51
smoking policies, 49
Sonic Spinball (Alton Towers), 290
sore feet, dealing with, 71
South East England, 113, *114–115*
  farm experiences in, 144–145
  theme parks and attractions in, 113, 116–144
South England, 147, *148–149*
  farm experiences in, 187
  theme parks and attractions in, 147, 150–187
South Lakes Wild Animal Park, 418–421
South West England, 189, *190–191*
  farm experiences in, 217–218
  theme parks and attractions in, 192–216
souvenir books, 8
space exploration, 313–317
Space Tower (Legoland Windsor), 22, 158–159
special needs visitors, 49. *see also* wheelchairs
Spinning Spider (Legoland Windsor), 172
Squirrel Nutty Ride (Alton Towers), 290–291
Stealth (Thorpe Park), 132

steel coasters, world rankings, 30
Steeplechase (Pleasure Beach Blackpool), 49, 400
Storm in a Teacup (Thorpe Park), 131
Storm Surge (Thorpe Park), 130–131
strollers. *see* pushchairs
Submission (Alton Towers), 288
Suffolk Wildlife Park. *see* Africa Alive
sunglasses, 72
surfing, 449–450
switching off/child swap technique, 77
  at Alton Towers, 271
  at Legoland Windsor, 157
  at Thorpe Park, 128
system capacity, 34–35

The Tank Museum, 213–215
tantrums in child, handling, 69–70
teacup rides, 18, 19
teens and adults, touring plans for
  one-day
    Alton Towers, 295, 298
    Chessington World of Adventures, 103–104
    Pleasure Beach Blackpool, 405–407
    Thorpe Park, 143–144
  two-day, at Alton Towers, 298–299
Temple of Mayhem (Chessington World of Adventures), 96
Tesco Clubcard, 44–45
Tetley Tea Cup Ride (Pleasure Beach Blackpool), 402–403
theatre presentations. *see* shows
theme parks. *see also individually named theme parks and/or geographic area*
  alternative names for, 2–3
  areas/parks for children in.
    see under small children
  authors' research methodology, 2, 7
  differences/similarities between, 5, 42
  as local vs. travel destination, 42
  nature of, 4–5
  touring tips for, 54–55
  websites for
    discount tickets/coupons on, 43, 44
    fan-based, 39
    official, 38
There's Something in the Dung Heap (Alton Towers), 291
Thomas Land (Drayton Manor theme park), 303, 304
Thorpe Park, 7, 124–129, *126–127*
  one-day touring plans for, 142–144
  rides and attractions at, 129–140
    best time to visit, 141
    Fastrack, 129
    not to be missed, 128
    single-rider queues, 128
    switching off technique, 128
Thor's Turnpike (Pleasure Beach Blackpool), 400
Thrigby Hall, 4
Thrigby Hall Wildlife Gardens, 249–251

thrill rides, 7–8, 19. *see also* roller coasters
  evolution of, 17–19
  types of, 19–23
TH13TEEN (Alton Towers), 281
Thunder Blazer (Legoland Windsor), 170
ticketing strategies
  discount tickets/coupons, where to find, 43–45
  inclusive charitable donation and, 44
  Merlin Annual Pass, 44
  prepaid vs. onsite, 40
  Tesco Clubcard, 44–45
Tidal Wave (Thorpe Park), 130
Tilt-A-Whirl, 18, 19
Time Voyagers (Thorpe Park), 131–132
time-outs, for children, 70
time-specific tickets, 44
timing your visit, 53–55
  arrival time at theme park, 54–55
  avoiding bottlenecks, 55. *see also* touring plans
  best time of day. *see* visiting times, optimal
  opening schedules and, 39–41
  ticket deals and, 44
Tiny Truckers (Chessington World of Adventures), 91
tipping in restaurants, 47
Toadie's Crazy Cars (Chessington World of Adventures), 91
toddler care, 72
toilet facilities, hand drying machines in, 47
Tomb Blaster (Chessington World of Adventures), 23, 98
Tornado (M&D's, Scotland's Theme Park), 433
touring plans, 58
  computer programme generating, 56–58
  credibility of, 55
  crisscrossing of park, 60
  current use of, 60
  flexibility in, 59
  interruption to, recovering from, 59–60
  one-day
    Alton Towers, 293–295, 298
    Chessington World of Adventures, 101, 103–104
    Legoland Windsor, 175–180
    Pleasure Beach Blackpool, 404–407
    Thorpe Park, 142–144
  rejecting, consequences of, 61
  spontaneity vs., 60–61
  success of, variables affecting, 59
  theory underlying, 54
  tracking progress through, 60
  two-day, at Alton Towers, 298–299
  using with children, expectations for, 66, 71
tourist attractions. *see* attractions
tourist websites, official, 38
tower rides, 21–22, 22
The Towers (Alton Towers), 286–287
town house hotel, defined, 51
Toytown attraction (Chessington World of Adventures), 89–92
Traffic (Legoland Windsor), 163–165

transport attractions
  Cotswold Motoring Museum, 302
  Imperial War Museum Duxford, 12, 239–242
  Morgan Motor Company Factory Tour, 310–312
  National Railway Museum, 350–353
transportation
  by car, tips on, 46
  public transport options, 39, 45–46
  shuttle services, 46
Transylvania attraction (Chessington World of Adventures), 89–90
travel directions, map vs. satnav device, 46
'travelling-salesman problem,' 57
Tsunami (M&D's, Scotland's Theme Park), 433
Tuk Tuk Turmoil Dodgems (Chessington World of Adventures), 96
Twirling Toadstool (Alton Towers), 283–284
Twr-y-Felin Outdoor Centre, 448–450
Twycross Zoo, 317–319

University of Oxford, 461–462
unloading/loading methods, 34
Unofficial Guide Touring Plan programme, 56–58

Valhalla (Pleasure Beach Blackpool), 22, 394
Vampire (Chessington World of Adventures), 89
vertical-hub rides, 19
Veteran Carousel (Pleasure Beach Blackpool), 403
Viking's River Splash (Legoland Windsor), 171–172
virtual (Q-Bot) queuing system, 157–158
virtual tours, 38
visiting times, optimal
  for specific theme park rides
    at Alton Towers, 296–297
    at Chessington World of Adventures, 102
    at Legoland Windsor, 178–179
    at Pleasure Beach Blackpool, 406–407
    at Thorpe Park, 141
  for other attractions
    aquariums, 41
    farms, 14, 41
    museums, 41
    safari parks, 10, 40–41, 205
    zoos, 40
visitors with special needs, 49. *see also* wheelchairs
Vortex (Thorpe Park), 140

Wales, 439, *440–441*
  farm experiences in, 453
  theme parks and attractions in, 439, 442–452
walking
  crisscrossing park, 60
  foot comfort and, 71
war museum, 239–242
Warwick Castle, 4, 6, 320–323
Waterworks (Legoland Windsor), 162
Wave Surfer (Legoland Windsor), 167–168
Wave Swinger (M&D's, Scotland's Theme Park), 433
Welsh Mountain Zoo, 450–452

INDEX

West Coast Railway Jacobite Steam Train, 462–464
West Midland Safari & Leisure Park, 323–327
Weston-Super-Mare SeaQuarium, 216
wet rides, tip on handling, 23
Wet Wet Wet (Thorpe Park), 129
wheel rides, 19–20, 20
wheelchairs
  attraction accessibility and, 49, 121, 158, 193, 225, 250, 256, 323, 349, 442, 450
  entrance fee waiver and, 210, 328, 450
  for hire at park, 8, 86, 118, 120, 121, 125, 157, 237, 256, 269, 307, 329, 373, 376, 388
whiplash, mitigating, 29
Whipsnade Zoo, 255–258
Whirlwind (Lightwater Valley), 33, 371
Wicksteed Park, 328–330
wild animal parks/gardens. see also animal gardens; safari parks; zoos
  Cotswold Wildlife Park & Gardens, 150–151
  Howletts Wild Animal Park, 116–119
  Paignton Zoo Environmental Park, 210–212
  Port Lympne Wild Animal Park, 120–123
  South Lakes Wild Animal Park, 418–421
  Thrigby Hall Wildlife Gardens, 249–251
Wild Asia attraction (Chessington World of Adventures), 94–97
Wild Mouse (Pleasure Beach Blackpool), 27, 394
Wobble World (Alton Towers), 285–286
Woburn Safari Park, 252–255
wooden coasters, world rankings, 30

X:\No Way Out (Thorpe Park), 26, 136
X-Sector (Alton Towers), 287–289

York Archeological Trust, attractions run by, 344
The York Dungeon, 6, 354–355
Yorkshire, 333, 334–335
  farm experiences in, 356
  theme parks and attractions in, 333, 336–338
younger children
  checking feet comfort of, 71
  one-day touring plans with
    Chessington World of Adventures, 101, 103
    Legoland Windsor, 176–177
    Pleasure Beach Blackpool, 405
  queue strategies for parents with, 76–77
YouTube videos, 38, 76

Zipper Dipper (Pleasure Beach Blackpool), 403
Zodiac (Thorpe Park), 139
zoological attractions, 8–10. see also animal gardens; aquariums; marine-life attractions; safari parks; wild animal parks/gardens; zoos
zoos
  Africa Alive, 224–226
  Banham Zoo, 226–229
  Blackpool Zoo, 362–365
  at Chessington World of Adventures, 100
  Chester Zoo, 371–376
  at Flamingo Land, 338–342
  London Zoo, 109–112
  Paignton Zoo Environmental Park, 210–212
  touring tips for, 39, 40, 44
  Twycross Zoo, 317–319
  Welsh Mountain Zoo, 450–452
  Whipsnade Zoo, 255–258
ZSL (Zoological Society of London)
  London Zoo, 109–112
  Whipsnade Zoo, 255–258

Unofficial Guide Reader Survey

If you would like to express your opinion in writing about days out in Britain or this guidebook, complete the following survey and mail it to:

Unofficial Guide Reader Survey
P.O. Box 43673
Birmingham, AL 35243, USA
unofficialguides@menasharidge.com

1. Where do you live? _____

2. What are the ages and genders of the persons in your family or travelling group?

	Person 1	Person 2	Person 3	Person 4	Person 5
Gender:	M F	M F	M F	M F	M F
Age:	[ ]	[ ]	[ ]	[ ]	[ ]

3. Who assumes responsibility for most of the planning for days out or a holiday?
   Mother____   Grandparent____
   Father____   Single adult male____
   Mother and father equally____   Single adult female____
   Whole family____   Couple equally____

4. In an average year, how many each of the following outings do you take?
   One-day outings____
   Two-day outings____
   Outing lasting more than two days but less than a week____
   Outings lasting more than a week____
   Outings or holidays outside the UK, including Ireland____

4. How far do you travel on average
   For a one-day outing?____
   For a weekend outing?____
   For a longer holiday in the UK?____

5. On what percentage of outings do you
   Use public transport?____
   Drive your own or a hired car?____
   Drive your own or a hired caravan?____

Continued on next page

Unofficial Guide Reader Survey

6. On your last multi-day outing, what is the name of the hotel at which you stayed? _____
   On a scale of 0–100, how would you rate this hotel? _____

7. On what percentage of outings do you
   Eat a picnic meal brought from home?____
   Eat at a full-service restaurant?____
   Eat at a counter-service restaurant?____
   Buy your meals from vendors?____

8. How many times in the past year have you visited
   A theme park?____   An historic home, manor or castle?____
   A zoo?____
   A safari park?____   A beach?____
   A farm experience?____   A swimming theme park?____
   A museum?____   An industrial site?____
   An aquarium?____

9. Did you use any of the touring plans? If so on a 0–100 scale with 100 being best, how would you rate the touring plans you used?
   for Alton Towers____
   for Chessington World of Adventures____
   for Leoland Windsor____
   for Pleasure Beach Blackpool____
   for Thorpe Park____

10. On a scale of 0–100, how would you rate this guide?____

11. Additional comments about your days out/holidays and/or this guide:

   _____
   _____
   _____
   _____
   _____
   _____
   _____